D1533449

This Book Comes With a Website

Nolo's award-winning website has a page dedicated just to this book, where you can:

KEEP UP TO DATE – When there are important changes to the information in this book, we'll post updates

READ BLOGS – Get the latest info from Nolo authors' blogs

LISTEN TO PODCASTS – Listen to authors discuss timely issues on topics that interest you

WATCH VIDEOS – Get a quick introduction to a legal topic with our short videos

You'll find the link in the introduction.

And that's not all. Nolo.com contains thousands of articles on everyday legal and business issues, plus a plain-English law dictionary, all written by Nolo experts and available for free. You'll also find more useful **books, software, online services,** and **downloadable forms.**

Get updates and more at
www.nolo.com

⚖️ NOLO The Trusted Name
(but don't take our word for it)

"In Nolo you can trust."
THE NEW YORK TIMES

"Nolo is always there in a jam as the nation's premier publisher of do-it-yourself legal books."
NEWSWEEK

"Nolo publications…guide people simply through the how, when, where and why of the law."
THE WASHINGTON POST

"[Nolo's]…material is developed by experienced attorneys who have a knack for making complicated material accessible."
LIBRARY JOURNAL

"When it comes to self-help legal stuff, nobody does a better job than Nolo…"
USA TODAY

"The most prominent U.S. publisher of self-help legal aids."
TIME MAGAZINE

"Nolo is a pioneer in both consumer and business self-help books and software."
LOS ANGELES TIMES

7th edition

Fiancé & Marriage Visas

A Couple's Guide to U.S. Immigration

Ilona M. Bray, J.D,
updated by Attorney Robert L. Herreria

Seventh Edition	AUGUST 2012
Cover Design	SUSAN PUTNEY
Book Design	TERRI HEARSH
Proofreading	ROBERT WELLS
Index	THÉRÈSE SHERE
Printing	BANG PRINTING

International Standard Serial Number (ISSN): 2168-6025
ISBN: 978-1-4133-1737-4 (pbk)
ISBN: 978-1-4133-1738-1 (epub ebook)

Copyright © 2001, 2004, 2005, 2006, 2008, 2010, and 2012 by Nolo.
All rights reserved. The NOLO trademark is registered in the U.S. Patent and Trademark
Office. Printed in the U.S.A.

No part of this publication may be reproduced, stored in a retrieval system, or
transmitted in any form or by any means, electronic, mechanical, photocopying,
recording, or otherwise without prior written permission. Reproduction prohibitions do
not apply to the forms contained in this product when reproduced for personal use. For
information on bulk purchases or corporate premium sales, please contact the Special
Sales Department. Call 800-955-4775 or write to Nolo, 950 Parker Street, Berkeley,
California 94710.

Please note

We believe accurate, plain-English legal information should help you solve many
of your own legal problems. But this text is not a substitute for personalized
advice from a knowledgeable lawyer. If you want the help of a trained
professional—and we'll always point out situations in which we think that's a
good idea—consult an attorney licensed to practice in your state.

Acknowledgments

Special thanks go to Judge Miriam Hayward, who taught me how to do these visas in the first place.

I'd also like to thank the many people who contributed their knowledge and experience to this book, including attorneys Angela Bean, Camille Kim-Cook, Carl Falstrom, Barbara Horn, Jacqueline Newman, Lynette Parker, and Carmen Reyes-Yossiff; the staff at the International Institute of the East Bay; and Mark Demming and Djamila Gonzalez.

Particular thanks go to Robert L. Herreria, an attorney in San Diego, who lent his expertise and careful eye to the task of ensuring that this seventh edition contains the latest information on immigration practices and policies.

Finally, a huge round of applause to my colleagues at Nolo, for the energy they put into this project and for making the process fun: Jake Warner, Spencer Sherman, Janet Portman, Catherine Caputo, Jaleh Doane, André Zivkovich, Terri Hearsh, and Toni Ihara.

About the Author

Ilona Bray, J.D., came to the practice of immigration law through her interest in international human rights issues. Before joining Nolo as legal editor in charge of immigration, she ran a solo law practice and worked for nonprofit immigration agencies including the International Institute of the East Bay (Oakland) and the Northwest Immigrant Rights Project (Seattle). Ms. Bray was also an intern in the legal office at Amnesty International's International Secretariat in London. She received her bachelor's degree in philosophy from Bryn Mawr College, and her law degree and a Master's degree in East Asian (Chinese) Studies from the University of Washington. Ms. Bray is a member of the American Immigration Lawyer's Association (AILA). She has authored other books for Nolo, including *Becoming a U.S. Citizen: A Guide to the Law, Exam & Interview*, and *Effective Fundraising for Nonprofits: Real-World Strategies That Work.*

Robert L. Herreria is an Associate Attorney with Luna & Associates, an immigration law firm in San Diego, California. He specializes in immigration law, including nonimmigrant and employment-based visas, work authorization, family-based immigration, permanent residence, and deportation/removal defense. Robert has over six years of experience in immigration matters, including practical experience as a Case Manager with a prominent employment-based immigration law firm in Boston, Massachusetts, as well as immigration litigation experience in legal internships with Immigration and Customs Enforcement, the Executive Office for Immigration Review, and the University of San Diego Immigration Law Clinic.

Robert received his J.D. from the University of San Diego School of Law and holds a B.A. in Ethnic Studies from Brown University. He is licensed to practice law in the state of California.

Robert is active with a number of bar associations based in San Diego, including Filipino American Lawyers of San Diego and Pan Asian Lawyers of San Diego. His hobbies include graphic and Web design, basketball, baseball, skiing, poker, and the occasional computer game.

You can contact Robert at Robert@luna-law.com, and learn more about him on his Google+ Profile.

Table of Contents

Glossary

Appendixes

Checklists for Overseas Fiancés of U.S. Citizens

Checklists for Overseas Spouses of U.S. Citizens

Checklists for Overseas Spouses of Lawful Permanent Residents

Checklist for Spouses of U.S. Citizens, Living in the U.S.

Checklist for Spouses of Permanent Residents, In the U.S.

Checklists for Applying for a Green Card at a USCIS Office

Checklist for After You Get Your Green Card

Index

Your Immigration Companion

"The marvel of all history is the patience with which men and women submit to burdens unnecessarily laid upon them by their governments."

—William E. Borah, former U.S. Senator from Idaho

You'll notice I haven't started this book with a quote about love or marriage. It's not that I'm a cynic—it's just that falling in love is the easy part. Obtaining the right to live happily ever after in the United States is more complicated than even the most difficult courtship. That's because it involves more than just you, your beloved, your families, and friends. You will also be inviting the U.S. immigration authorities into your lives for as long as it takes to convince them that you are in love, want to be married, and are eligible to enter and live in the United States. And believe me, this is a lot more complicated than simply saying, "I do."

The popular perception is that U.S. citizenship comes along with an American spouse. The reality is quite different. There are dozens of forms, months and possibly years of legal and bureaucratic delays, and countless ways to make the process move faster or end with a resounding "no entry" from an immigration officer. Even after you convince the U.S. government to let you in, most often you'll get only temporary permission to marry or live in the United States. You'll have to wait a couple of years before you can get permanent residence—and even longer before you can apply to become a U.S. citizen.

I have had many clients arrive at my office after they started the application process with no preparation other than picking up the forms from the U.S. Citizenship and Immigration Services (USCIS, formerly called the INS). They fled to a lawyer when the mountain of paperwork threatened to bury them. And there were the clients who didn't look before they leaped into the application process and found themselves denied or, worse, facing deportation or removal.

None of these people had the benefit of materials that tell you, in plain English, the laws you need to understand and the way to apply for a visa or green card based on marriage. The goal of this book is to fill that gap and to be your companion through the process. "Why a whole book?" you might ask. The answer is simple: Because I'm trying to make it possible for you to get through this complicated process without getting yourself into trouble. It would be a much shorter book if I told you to fill in the forms blindly, without explaining the legal implications or the "inside scoop" on how the USCIS or consular officer will view your case.

If there had been clear information available to them, many of my clients could have done without a lawyer and obtained a visa or green card on their own. I'm not antilawyer in the least, but I know that many would-be applicants cannot afford one or simply prefer not to use one. Having a lawyer is certainly not a required part of the immigration process. But the immigration bureaucracy has created an absurdly tangled system, in which reliable information is about as available as state secrets—and lawyers are, at the moment, the only people with some access to, or experience with, those secrets.

One of the ultimate ironies is that even if you get wrong advice from a member of the USCIS, you're still stuck with the consequences of having followed that advice. And the confusion accelerates every time Congress tacks amendments onto the immigration laws—which it does lately with every shift in the electorate's anti- and pro-immigrant sentiment. As a result, many immigrants end up having to hire lawyers for cases that, with information like the kind in this book, they could have handled on their own. That said, I haven't covered every possible complication here—there are times when people really do need a lawyer's help, and I try to alert readers to these times. And if you can afford a lawyer, hiring one is a worthwhile use of your money.

To write this book, I have drawn on my experience with hundreds of immigrant clients, and gathered stories from other lawyers. I've tried to anticipate a variety of complications that readers may encounter, so that their application process will go as smoothly as possible. When all is said and done, this process is just a lot of forms and paperwork, all used to show that two decent people are in love and deserve to live together in the United States.

Get Updates and More Online

When there are important changes to the information in this book, we'll post updates online, on a page dedicated to this book: **www.nolo.com/ back-of-book/IMAR.html**. You'll find other useful information there, too, including author blogs, podcasts, and videos.

First Things First

Every year, hundreds of thousands of foreign-born people become engaged or married to U.S. citizens and permanent residents. Just as no two romances are alike, none of these couples will have exactly the same immigration needs. Some will meet and marry overseas, then wish to move to the United States; some will meet in the United States and wish to marry and stay; and some will meet overseas and wish to come to the United States for the wedding. Each of these situations, and others, will require slightly different planning and procedures.

No matter what your situation, you have one thing in common with all the other fiancés and newlyweds (or even longtime spouses). Before you obtain the right to come to the United States, whether just to get married or to stay permanently, you will have to go through a lengthy process of submitting application forms and paperwork and meeting with government officials to prove your eligibility. The processes are not simple, but they are standard—meaning they can be done without a lawyer's help, if your case is straightforward and your marriage, or planned marriage, is for real.

CAUTION

If you are or have ever been in removal (deportation) proceedings, you must see a lawyer. If the proceedings aren't yet over or are on appeal, your entire immigration situation is in the hands of the courts and you are not allowed to use the procedures described in this book. Even if the proceedings are over, you should ask a lawyer whether the outcome affects your current application.

This book will show you how to:
- decide whether you are eligible
- choose the proper visa and submit the correct paperwork
- gather all necessary documents and prepare for interviews with U.S. government officials
- create and maintain documentary proof that your marriage is real
- deal with difficult bureaucrats and delays

- get a work permit in the United States
- make it through your two-year "testing period" to get your green card
- keep and enjoy your permanent residence status, and
- know when you need professional legal help.

"Visa" and "Green Card" Can Mean More Than One Thing

We're about to start using the words "visa" and "green card" a great deal. In a few situations, their meanings are distinct and narrow, but often they overlap or are the same.

Let's start with the narrow meanings. A visa gives you the right to seek entry to the United States. Physically, it usually appears as a stamp in your passport. When this book advises you to go to the consulate to pick up your visa, it means that you'll be getting this stamp or an equivalent document that allows you to seek entry to the United States.

"Green card" is a slang term. In the narrowest usage, it is the plastic photo identification card that you receive when you become a U.S. lawful permanent resident.

Now for the broader meanings. The word visa may also be used in situations involving immigrants who are already in the United States and won't need an entry visa. That's partly because someone in the deep dark offices of the State Department may have to allocate a visa number to these immigrants, though the immigrants may never even know it. When this book talks about your "visa eligibility" or "visa availability," it's not referring to the actual visa that you pick up overseas, but about the broader, theoretical visa that the State Department will allocate to you.

The term green card also takes on broader meanings at times. It's often used, in this book and elsewhere, to refer to lawful permanent residence or lawful conditional residence. When this book talks about a "green card application" it is actually referring to one of the several application processes (adjustment of status or consular processing) that could lead to obtaining U.S. residence.

CAUTION

Here comes the jargon. We try to keep the technical vocabulary to a minimum in this book, but there are times when no other word but the technical one will do. To check on the meaning of terms like "citizen," "permanent resident," or "green card," please see the Glossary at the end of the book.

Green Cards Don't Work Like Tourist Visas

Don't expect a green card to work as a frequent travel pass. A common misconception about green cards is that they allow you unlimited travel in and out of the United States without the hassle of reapplying for visas. The result of this confusion is the practice of overseas family members of U.S. citizens or residents who want to be able to pop in for impromptu visits—they sometimes apply for green cards. But if your plan is to maintain your primary home in another country, the U.S. government may eventually figure this out and cancel your green card. The legal term for this is that you abandoned your residency. You would have to start over and apply for another one.

If, for example, you're married to a U.S. citizen or resident but plan to live in your home country for much of your early marriage, or to shuttle back and forth, you may want to wait until you're really ready to settle in the United States to apply for your permanent resident status.

A. Who Should Use This Book

You probably picked up this book because you are the fiancé or spouse of a U.S. citizen or permanent resident and you want to marry and/or live in the United States. But a wedding plan or marriage certificate does not automatically grant you the right to be in the United States. How you apply for permission to come to or live in the United States depends on several factors. These include where you live now, whether you are married yet, whom you will be marrying (a U.S. citizen or lawful permanent resident), and (if you are in the country already) whether you entered the United States legally or illegally.

Upcoming chapters of this book will address various combinations of these factors separately, so that you'll understand whether and how to go forward with your application.

How We Talk to "You"

Throughout this book, we refer to the immigrant as "you," and the U.S. citizen or permanent resident as "your spouse" or "fiancé," as appropriate. That's to avoid using the corresponding legal terms "beneficiary" (the immigrant who will be getting the visa or green card) and "petitioner" (the U.S. citizen or lawful permanent resident who is sponsoring the immigrant) as much as possible. At times, however, we have no choice.

This doesn't mean that applying for your fiancé visa and/or green card won't be a joint process. You—the beneficiary—and your U.S. spouse or fiancé—the petitioner—will each have a role to play in successfully getting you the right to marry and/or live in the United States.

Also note that we spell fiancé with only one e, which technically refers only to male fiancés. This avoids using the awkward-looking "fiancé(e)." But unless we say otherwise, fiancé in this book refers to both men and women.

Both you and your spouse or fiancé should review and understand all of the paperwork and documents you submit. In fact, many couples find that it's easiest if the U.S. citizen or resident half of the couple prepares most of the paperwork, even the forms that are sent to and signed by the immigrant. This is because most of the written material must be in English and must conform to the requirements of U.S. bureaucracy.

B. Is a Fiancé or Marriage Visa the Best One for You?

Before we get too deep into the subject of this book, let's pause. You might be curious about whether there are alternate ways of getting a visa or green card—especially if you have read our early warnings about how complicated it is to get a visa or green card through marriage!

1. How Does Your Visa Option Compare to Others?

There are dozens of categories of visas and other immigration benefits for people wanting to visit or live in the United States. But none of them will get you a green card overnight or without significant effort. In fact, most experts would agree that if you are already engaged or married to a U.S. citizen or permanent resident, immigrating based on this marriage is likely to be your best bet. The eligibility criteria are reasonably straightforward and the waiting periods are generally better, or at least no worse, than for most other types of visas.

If you are married to a U.S. citizen, there is no waiting period or quota to delay your entry into the United States. You will be subject to the usual time period it takes to process your paperwork and for the government to make sure you are not excludable for any reason, such as criminal past or health problems. (See Chapter 2, Section A, for more on inadmissibility.)

Unfortunately, marriages to U.S. permanent residents don't result in such smooth sailing, immigration-wise. Spouses of permanent residents will probably have to spend a few years on a waiting list before their visa or green card becomes available to them. (See Chapter 2, Section A, for more on waiting periods.) However, spouses of permanent residents face shorter waits than many other family immigrant categories. For example, in early 2008, the waiting period for the spouse of a permanent resident was approximately four years. If the spouse also had a brother who was a U.S. citizen,

he or she could also apply for a visa based on that sibling relationship, but the waiting period for that category is typically ten years or longer.

The only categories of people who avoid the visa waiting list are those defined as immediate relatives, which include the spouses of U.S. citizens, the unmarried children of U.S. citizens, and the parents of an adult U.S. citizen (over 21). If you don't happen to be an immediate relative, then your potential green card through marriage to a lawful permanent resident is a fine option to have.

The spouse of a permanent resident might obtain a visa more quickly than waiting for a marriage-based visa if, for example, they:

- have a potential employer in the United States
- have parents or adult children who are U.S. citizens
- would be willing to invest $500,000 or more in a U.S. business
- have lived in the United States continuously since January 1, 1972
- come from a country from which they can apply for the Diversity Visa (known as the visa lottery), or
- fear political persecution in their home country.

Any of these categories might get a person permission to enter or stay in the United States more quickly than they could as the spouse of a permanent resident. But none of them is an instant answer.

 SEE AN EXPERT

If you fit into any of the categories above, you should consult an attorney. Chapter 17 contains tips on finding a good lawyer.

2. Why Can't You Just Use a Tourist Visa?

Many fiancés and spouses immigrating from overseas wonder why they cannot simply use a tourist visa to enter the United States. They know they will spend a long time outside the United

States waiting for their proper visa, while their fiancé or spouse is living inside the United States. But they also know that a tourist visa can be gotten in a few days. So why, they wonder, can't they just pick up a tourist visa, come to the United States, and then worry about the rest of the green card application process once they're together here?

There are two problems with this idea. First, if you pose as a tourist with the secret intention of staying in the United States for an indefinite time, you will have committed visa fraud. Visitor visas, or indeed any temporary visas, are for people who intend to stay temporarily—and then leave. They are not for people who plan to marry and live happily ever after in the United States. If U.S. Citizenship and Immigration Services (USCIS, formerly called "INS") chooses to make an issue of it, your misuse of a tourist visa could lead to your losing the right to obtain a marriage-based green card and most other types of visas.

USCIS will be especially suspicious if you get married within two months of entering the United States. Sometimes USCIS will turn a blind eye, or you may be able to convince them that when you entered the U.S. on a temporary visa you really planned a short stay (and only decided to marry after you arrived). If USCIS remains unconvinced, you can ask them to forgive your error, but obtaining such forgiveness (in legalese, a "waiver") is not easy and not covered in this book.

EXAMPLE 1: Detlef enters the United States as a tourist, marries Sally (a U.S. citizen) a week later, and they apply for his green card in San Francisco. At their green card interview, the officer asks, "When did you decide to get married?" Detlef answers, "Oh, I asked Sally to marry me during a phone call last month, and when she said yes, I was so happy that I got a tourist visa, got on the next plane, and we were married in the Elvis Chapel in Las Vegas the following Monday." This is an unfortunate answer, because it practically forces the immigration officer to notice that Detlef committed visa fraud.

EXAMPLE 2: Nigel enters the United States as a tourist, marries Ellen (a U.S. citizen) three months later and they apply for his green card in New York. At the green card interview the officer asks, "What was your intention when you entered the United States?" Nigel says, "Our relationship was going very well long-distance, so I decided to travel to the United States to see Ellen in person. Frankly, it was also time for a vacation. A few weeks after I arrived, we realized we were really and truly in love. And when that feeling didn't wear off, we decided to marry." This answer has promise. Even if this couple was contemplating marriage before Nigel arrived, Nigel's candid answer, plus the fact that they waited over two months to get married, makes clear that Nigel didn't just use the tourist visa to get around the U.S. immigration laws.

The second problem is that if your U.S. fiancé or spouse is a permanent resident (not a citizen), you will, as mentioned above, have to wait for years until you are eligible for permanent residence or a green card. That means that if you come to the United States as a tourist and your visa runs out, you will be here illegally for all of those years of waiting. Living here illegally will cause many problems described in detail later on. For now, just keep in mind that it could ultimately make getting a green card extremely difficult.

RESOURCE

Still curious about other visas? There are many types of visas and immigration benefits for temporary and permanent U.S. residence. Though in many cases they apply only to narrow categories of people, you might want to scan the summary provided in Appendix A. If you see any likely prospects, you can check out their advantages and disadvantages before continuing with the application covered by this book. You will find more detailed information on these visa categories in *U.S. Immigration Made Easy*, by Ilona Bray (Nolo).

C. Using a Fake Marriage to Come to the U.S.

It is illegal for anyone to get married solely for the purpose of getting, or helping someone to get, permanent residence in the United States. There are stiff fines and possible jail terms for people who are convicted of this crime. But we would be foolish not to address the fact that many people attempt to fake a marriage to obtain a green card.

SKIP AHEAD

If you are getting married for legitimate reasons, you can skip this section and continue reading at Section D.

If you are considering a fake, or sham, marriage, you probably already know that what you are planning is illegal. You should also know that this book is written with the assumption that you are marrying for love, not for a green card. We are not going to give you tips on making a fraudulent marriage look real. However, we will outline the risks for you.

1. What Is a Sham Marriage?

A sham marriage is one that is entered into in order to get around the U.S. immigration laws. For a marriage to be valid under the law, it is not enough that the couple had a real marriage ceremony and got all the right governmental stamps on their marriage certificate. They have to intend to live in a real marital relationship following the marriage ceremony—and prove their intention through their actions. If the couple doesn't intend to establish a life together, their marriage is a sham. (For more on what USCIS considers to be a real or bona fide marital relationship for purposes of green card eligibility, see Chapter 2, Section B.)

2. Will You Get Caught?

Detecting marriage frauds is a top priority for USCIS. USCIS officers still quote a survey from the 1980s which found that up to 30% of marriages between aliens and U.S. citizens are suspect. That survey has since been shown to be deeply flawed, but its legacy lives on.

In order to detect frauds, the immigration authorities require a lot of proof that a marriage is real, including more documentation than for other family-based immigration applicants. They subject marriage-based immigrants to a longer and more detailed personal interview and a two-year testing period for couples who have been married less than two years.

The government will not normally follow you around or investigate your life beyond the required paperwork and the interviews it always conducts. But it has the power to look deeply into your life if the authorities get suspicious. Government inspectors can visit your home, talk to your friends, interview your employers, and more. By requiring more of married couples than others, the government has already set up a system that gives it a lot of information about whether your marriage is real.

What is the U.S. government's view of a typical marriage? The statutes and regulations don't go into detail on this, so the following comes from a combination of court cases and attorneys' experiences.

According to USCIS, the typical couple has a fair amount in common. They share a language and religion. They live together and do things together, like take vacations, celebrate important events or holidays, and have sex and children. Typical couples also combine financial and other aspects of their lives after marriage. They demonstrate their trust in one another by sharing bank and credit card accounts and ownership of property, such as cars and houses.

The government usually expects applicants to prove that they share their lives in a way similar to what is described above. Applicants do this by providing copies of documents like rental agreements, bank account statements, and children's birth certificates. The government further tests the validity of the marriage by talking to the applicant and usually to his or her spouse. Every marriage-based applicant for a visa or green card (including fiancés), whether they are applying in the United States or overseas, will have to attend a personal interview with a U.S. government official.

U.S. government officials have developed amazing talents for discovering fraud by examining what look like insignificant details of people's lives. To ferret out lies, they have learned to cross-check dates and facts within the application forms and between the application forms and people's testimony.

> **EXAMPLE:** Rasputin has married Alice, a U.S. citizen, in the hopes of obtaining a green card. They submit an application for a green card in the United States. At Rasputin's green card interview, the officer asks for his full name, his address, and how he entered the United States. Rasputin can't believe how easy this all is. The officer goes on to ask for the dates of all of Rasputin's visits to the United States, the date of his divorce from his previous wife and the dates of all of his children's births. Rasputin is getting bored. Then the officer notices something funny. The date of birth of Rasputin's last child by his former wife is a full year after the date of their supposed divorce. The officer becomes suspicious, and Rasputin and Alice are taken to separate rooms for fraud interviews. They are examined in minute detail about their married lives. When neither of them can remember what the other one eats for breakfast or what they did for their last birthdays, the case is denied and referred to the local Immigration Court for proceedings to deport Rasputin.

If a couple has been married for less than two years when the immigrant first receives residency, USCIS gets a second chance at testing the validity of the marriage. The immigrants in such couples don't get a permanent green card right away. Instead, the law requires that their first green card

expire after another two years. (The technical term is that the immigrant has "conditional residency.")

When the two years are up, both members of the couple must file an application for the immigrant's permanent residency. They must include copies of documents showing that they are still married and sharing the important elements of their lives. This form is mailed to a USCIS office. As USCIS knows, it is extremely difficult for members of sham marriages to keep things together for a full two years, even on paper. If the marriage appears to be a real one when the two years is up, the conversion from conditional to permanent residency won't involve an intensive investigation—the application process doesn't even include an interview if the written application looks legit.

> **EXAMPLE:** Maria married Fred, a U.S. citizen, in order to get a green card. Fred was a friend of Maria's, who simply wanted to help her out. Maria manages to get approved by the consulate at her immigrant visa interview, and enters the United States. Because their marriage is new, Maria is given two years as a conditional resident. During those two years, Maria overdraws their joint checking account three times. Fred gets angry and closes the account. Maria has an accident with their jointly owned car and it goes to the junk yard. Fred buys another car in his own name and won't let Maria drive it. Fred gets fed up and wonders why he got into this in the first place. He falls in love with someone else and insists that Maria move out. At the end of her two years of conditional residency, Maria can't get Fred to answer her phone calls. In desperation, she fills out the application form on her own, fakes Fred's signature and lists his address as her own. However, the only documents she can attach are the same bank account statements and car registration she submitted to the consulate two years ago. USCIS checks the files and notices this. They call her and Fred in for an interview. It's not long

before the truth comes out and enforcement proceedings are begun.

As you see from the examples above, people who enter into sham marriages most often trip themselves up just trying to get through the standard process. It's not that USCIS can read people's minds or that it spends all its time peeking into applicants' bedrooms. They simply catch a lot of people who thought that a fake marriage was going to be easier than it really is.

References to the Immigration Laws in This Book

Throughout this book are references to the federal immigration laws that govern immigration through marriage and to the regulations that describe how USCIS will apply those laws to you. (They look like this: "I.N.A. § 319(a); 8 U.S.C. § 1430(a)," or "8 C.F.R. § 316.5.") We include these references where we feel it is important to indicate our sources for information and to help you research the immigration laws on your own. See Chapter 17, Section H, for more detail on what these references mean and how you can look them up.

---

3. What Happens If You Are Caught

The law pretty much speaks for itself on what happens to immigrants who commit marriage fraud. You can face prison, a fine, or both:

> *Any individual who knowingly enters into a marriage for the purpose of evading any provision of the immigration laws shall be imprisoned for not more than 5 years, or fined not more than $250,000, or both (I.N.A. § 275(c); 8 U.S.C. § 1325(c)).*

The U.S. citizen or resident could also face criminal prosecution, including fines or imprisonment, depending on the facts of the case. They are most likely to be prosecuted for either

criminal conspiracy (conspiring with the immigrant is enough; see *U.S. v. Vickerage*, 921 F.2d 143 (8th Cir. 1990)), or for establishing a "commercial enterprise" to get people green cards (see I.N.A. § 275(d); 8 U.S.C. § 1325(d)).

The extent to which these penalties are applied depends on the specifics of each case. The government tends to reserve the highest penalties for U.S. citizens or residents engaged in major conspiracy operations, such as systematically arranging fraudulent marriages. But that doesn't mean that small-time participants in marriage fraud can count on a soft punishment—though most immigrants will probably simply be deported and never allowed to return.

D. How to Use This Book

This book is a unique combination of legal analysis and form preparation instructions. If you're like most people, you'll be tempted to go straight to the form preparation portions of the book. After all, how many of us read the directions before we plug in a new appliance? But consider this a great big warning label: If you just "plug in" to the visa application process, it could blow up. The U.S. government may give the lucky ones a second chance, but many careless applicants have found themselves deported or prevented from coming to the United States for many years. You won't need to read every section of this book, but please figure out which ones apply to you, and read them.

First, however, a word of reassurance. Most applicants do get a second chance at bringing their application up to the government's standards. A number of people are going through the immigration process on their own, and the U.S. government is accustomed to seeing badly prepared applications. You don't need to worry that one little mistake will lead to an instant denial of your visa or green card. If there is a problem in your application that can be corrected, you'll usually be given time to correct it.

The trouble is, you could make a mistake that's irreversible—like unnecessarily revealing something that makes it look like you're ineligible. So you may as well use the advice in this book to get your application right the first time around.

1. Chapters Everyone Should Read

There are a few chapters that everyone needs to read. These include Chapters 1 and 2, which explain whether this book can help you; and whether the immigration laws might exclude you automatically for health, security, or other reasons. We also highly recommend that everyone read Chapter 3, dealing with the income levels necessary to support a new immigrant. Lack of financial support is now one of the most common reasons for green card denials.

If your visa or green card prospects still look promising, move on to Chapter 4, which contains important tips on handling all the necessary paperwork. This is a vital chapter—the first impression that you create with your paperwork often determines how much scrutiny the government will give your application.

> ⚠ **CAUTION**
>
> **Always watch for changes in the law.**
> The U.S. Congress, USCIS, and the State Department are constantly fixing, adjusting, and updating the immigration laws, procedures, fees, and forms. We can't track you down to tell you if anything in this book is affected—you'll need to watch the news and check the Updates to this book at www.nolo.com.

2. Chapters for Your Situation

After you read Chapters 1 through 4, skip to the chapter that best describes your situation. For example, as shown in "Which Chapter Is for You?" below, if you're living overseas and engaged to a U.S. citizen, you'd turn to Chapter 5. But if you're living in the United States and married to a lawful permanent resident, you'd read Chapter 12.

Each of Chapters 5 through 12 will help you analyze your immigration situation, discuss what options are available to you, and take you through any necessary preliminary procedures. If you qualify for and want to obtain a green card, you will also be coached to decide whether to apply in the United States, through a procedure called adjustment of status, or at a U.S. embassy or consulate abroad, through a procedure called consular processing, and directed to a chapter or section which explains these procedures.

You will be guided through each part of the process, using checklists designed for your immigration status. The checklists will summarize all the forms and documents that you need, and direct you to the proper forms, line-by-line discussions of how to fill out the forms, and other necessary information. Chapter 13 will instruct you on preparing for your visa or green card interview (the required final step for every applicant).

Which Chapter Is for You?			
Where is the immigrant?	Who is the immigrant?	Who is the fiancé or spouse?	Go to Chapter
Overseas	Fiancé	U.S. citizen	5
Overseas	Fiancé	Permanent resident	6
Overseas	Spouse	U.S. citizen	7
Overseas	Spouse	Permanent resident	8
In the U.S.	Fiancé	U.S. citizen	9
In the U.S.	Fiancé	Permanent resident	10
In the U.S.	Spouse	U.S. citizen	11
In the U.S.	Spouse	Permanent resident	12

3. Chapters for Unique or Problem Situations

Hopefully, the chapters described above will be all you need to get your visa or green card. However, things don't always happen as they should when dealing with the U.S. immigration bureaucracy. Therefore, we've included chapters to cover special situations or problems.

If you're lucky, you'll never have to read Chapter 15, Dealing With Bureaucrats, Delays, and Denials. But most people find their application takes longer than they think it should. In that case, you'll be glad to have this chapter, as well as the sample reminder and inquiry letters that accompany it. Chapter 15 also deals with what to do if your application is denied.

Finally, if your case is turning out to be much more complicated than you'd expected, you'll need to consider getting a lawyer or doing some legal research of your own. In that case, review Chapter 17.

4. Chapters to Save for Later

Even after you win a visa or new immigration status, you will still be required to follow some immigration rules. Chapter 16, After You Get Your Green Card, covers the rights and responsibilities of visa and green card holders, including you and members of your family. After all this hard work, you wouldn't want to lose your residency.

Chapter 16 also covers certain people with young marriages, whose green cards expire after a two-year testing period called "conditional residency." This chapter gives them all the instructions they need to go from conditional residency to a normal green card—that is, permanent residency.

Chapter 16 also gives you instructions on how to renew or replace the green card itself.

5. Appendixes

The appendixes to this book include a great deal of useful information, including a summary of the types of green cards and visas available to people and tear-out versions of the various handy checklists provided throughout this book.

 TIP

Remember to use the checklists. No matter which immigration status you plan to pursue, it will involve lots of paperwork and documents. If you rely on the proper checklist, you should avoid missing any steps.

E. Getting the Latest Forms and Fees

This book doesn't provide immigration application forms, for good reason. The U.S. immigration authorities revise these forms so often that by the time you're using this book, chances are the form will have gone out of date—and the government could refuse to accept it.

All the application forms you'll need—and we'll tell you exactly which ones they are—are either readily available or will be mailed to you by the immigration authorities when the time is right. Some can even be filled out online. This book also includes filled-in samples of the most important forms.

The main sources for immigration application forms are:

- U.S. Citizenship and Immigration Services, by visiting one of its local offices (though you will probably have to make an appointment first); through its website, www.uscis.gov (click the "Immigration Forms" tab, then scroll down until you find the form you need); or by calling 800-870-3676, and
- the U.S. State Department, through its website, www.state.gov (enter the search term "forms").

 CAUTION

It's getting harder and harder to visit your local USCIS office. There are a few times when you might wish to visit a USCIS office in person, for example, to pick up local forms or ask about delays. However, to reduce the long lines, the agency has begun a program called "InfoPass," requiring visitors to make appointments before they arrive. Check the USCIS website (www.uscis. gov; click "Schedule a FREE Appointment" on the left side of the page) before you go, to see whether InfoPass is in effect at your local USCIS district office. If it is, you have little choice but to make an appointment (some offices will allow walk-ins if there's space, but don't count on this). Appointments can be made only through the Internet. You'll need a computer with a printer, so that you'll have the required printout of your appointment notice when you visit. (Also, be sure to bring photo identification and any paperwork associated with your immigration case to your appointment.)

Immigration application fees, like the forms, change regularly. And most USCIS and consular applications require fees to accompany them. For up-to-date fees for U.S. filings (even USCIS forms sometimes print out-of-date fees) check the USCIS website at www.uscis.gov. Click on "Forms," and you'll find a complete fee table. Alternately, you could call the USCIS information line at 800-375-5283.

For up-to-date fees for consular filings, check the State Department's website, www.travel.state. gov. Under "Visas for Foreign Citizens," click "more," then choose "Fees and Reciprocity Tables" from the drop-down menu next to the "Frequently Requested Visa Information" box. This information may also be accessed through the U.S. State Department's Visa Services office, at 202-663-1225. The fee can be paid in dollars or in the local currency, at the current exchange rate.

CAUTION
There will be other expenses. If you're trying to figure out how much to budget for this process, don't forget the costs of required items other than the fees, such as photos, the medical exam, and having documents translated or notarized.

Are You Eligible for a Visa or Green Card?

You can think of your path toward a visa or green card as requiring you to pass through two main doors—theoretical doors, that is, though they can be harder than the wooden kind. The first door is the inadmissibility door: it can be closed on anyone whom the U.S. has decided is unfit to cross its borders. The second door is the eligibility door. It can be closed on you if you don't meet the criteria for the particular type of visa or green card for which you apply. This chapter covers these two doors.

A. Can You Enter the U.S. at All?

Whether you're coming to the United States for a short visit or to stay forever, the U.S. government has the power to tell you "no." Many people are shocked to learn that their engagement or marriage to a U.S. citizen or permanent resident is no guarantee of entry into the United States. The U.S. government has decided that certain types of people will not be allowed into the United States at all. These people are called inadmissible.

Much of your application process will involve proving that you don't fit into one of the categories of inadmissible people, primarily through answering questions and undergoing a security check and a medical exam. If you will be entering the United States on a fiancé visa, you may have to prove that you are not inadmissible twice: first, for the fiancé visa, and again if you are asking for permanent residence, as part of the green card application.

A list of the main grounds of inadmissibility is provided in "What Makes You Inadmissible?" below. As you'll see, the reasons concern health, criminal, security, and more specialized issues or problems. Some of the grounds make obvious sense (few would quibble about letting an international terrorist into the country); others are the topic of more controversy, such as the exclusion of people who have committed certain immigration violations.

TIP

You can read the law concerning inadmissibility yourself. The grounds for inadmissibility are in the Immigration and Nationality Act (the primary federal law covering immigrants) at I.N.A. § 212(a); 8 U.S.C. § 1182. You can read this Act at your local law library; at Nolo's website at www.nolo.com/statute; or at USCIS's website at www.uscis.gov (click "Laws & Regulations"). For more information on inadmissibility in plain English, including information on exceptions or waivers, see *U.S. Immigration Made Easy*, by Ilona Bray (Nolo).

The grounds of inadmissibility most likely to cause trouble for engaged or married couples are those concerning previous immigration violations, the immigrant's ability to support him or herself (those who can't support themselves become "public charges" in immigration law lingo), and health problems. Specific situations that might cause you difficulty under these categories include:

- You have lived or are living unlawfully in the United States, having stayed past the expiration date of your visa or entered the country illegally. (See Section A2, "Dealing With Unlawful Time in the United States," below.)

- In the past, you have committed marriage or other immigration fraud. Even if you haven't yet been found out, filing a new visa or green card application will give the immigration authorities an opportunity to snoop around a bit more.

- Your spouse is unable to support you financially, you don't have the means to support yourself in the United States, and the rest of the family won't pitch in. (An extensive discussion of the financial requirements to obtain a green card and further strategies for meeting these are set forth in Chapter 3, Meeting Income Requirements.)

- You have a communicable illness. You may request a waiver, but it involves an application and paperwork that we do not cover in this book. If you'll be applying for a K-1 fiancé visa, you'll have to apply for the waiver twice—once to the U.S. consulate when you get your fiancé visa, and again after you've gotten married and apply to adjust status. If, however, you are already married and will apply for a K-3 (a variation of the fiancé visa) to enter the U.S. in order to adjust status, you need to apply for the waiver only once, by filing Form I-601 with the consulate (which will forward it to the Department of Homeland Security) before you obtain your K-3 visa.

- If you've been convicted of a crime involving alcohol, you've got double trouble. Even if the crime itself doesn't make you inadmissible, USCIS can, and often does, argue that it's a sign that you have a physical or mental disorder associated with harmful behavior—in other words, that you're inadmissible on health, rather than criminal, grounds. This is most often a problem for people with convictions for "DUI" or "DWI" (Driving Under the Influence, or Driving While Intoxicated). Other crimes such as assaults or domestic violence where alcohol or drugs were contributing factors can lead to the same result.

SEE AN EXPERT

For any of the above situations, or if another item on the inadmissibility list seems to apply to you, you may need to see a lawyer. For information on finding an attorney see Chapter 17.

What Makes You Inadmissible?

The United States will not allow you to enter if you:

- have a communicable disease, such as tuberculosis
- have a physical or mental disorder that makes you harmful to others
- are likely to become a public charge (dependent on welfare)
- are a drug abuser ("tried it more than once" in the last three years is enough for USCIS)
- have committed or been convicted of a crime of "moral turpitude" (a criminal act that's considered morally wrong or done with a bad intention)
- have been convicted of multiple crimes with a combined sentence of five years or more
- have been convicted of certain specified crimes, such as prostitution or drug trafficking
- are the immediate family member of a drug trafficker and have knowingly benefited from their illicit money within the last five years
- have committed espionage or sabotage
- are a member of a totalitarian party (Communist in particular)
- are a Nazi or have participated in genocide
- have violated the immigration laws or committed immigration fraud
- falsely pretended to be a U.S. citizen
- are unlawfully present in the United States or haven't obtained proper documentation to enter the United States
- were previously removed or deported from the United States
- are a polygamist (have married more than one person at the same time)
- have committed international child abduction
- are on a J-1 or J-2 exchange visitor visa and are subject to the two-year foreign residence requirement.

Immigrants From Overseas May Not Be Able to Bring Certain Items or Goods

When you come to the United States, you'll not only have to think about whether you'll be admitted, but whether the contents of your luggage will be allowed in with you. U.S. Customs and Border Protection (CBP) regulates not only people, but also the goods and currency that all travelers bring to the United States. A CBP officer will question you and may search your luggage. Certain items are completely prohibited (such as drugs and weapons); others can be brought in only in limited amounts (such as alcohol and tobacco) and others are subject to more specific restrictions or taxes. For more information, see the CBP's website at www.customs.gov, and click "Travel," then "Clearing CBP," or ask your local U.S. consulate for more information.

1. You Must Pass a Medical Exam

As a test of whether you fall into a health-related ground of inadmissibility, your application for a fiancé or marriage-based visa will include a medical exam by a doctor approved by the U.S. consulate or USCIS. Your own doctor cannot do the exam unless he or she happens to be on the government's list of approved doctors.

The purpose of the exam is to make sure that you don't have any serious or communicable diseases, mental disorders, or drug problems that would make you inadmissible, and that you have had all the required vaccinations.

There is no official list of diseases or disorders that will make you inadmissible. The examining doctor will decide whether your condition and behavior has "posed or is likely to pose a threat to the property, safety, or welfare of the alien or others." The Centers for Disease Control and Prevention's "top suspect" diseases include infectious tuberculosis, untreated venereal and other sexually transmitted diseases, and untreated

Hansen's disease (leprosy). HIV was removed from the list in January of 2010.

If you have an illness that causes you trouble but won't infect or injure others, such as heart disease, cancer, or certain mental illnesses, you won't be inadmissible on medical grounds. However, watch out for inadmissibility as a public charge if you won't be able to work and don't have medical insurance. (Chapter 3 covers inadmissibility on the grounds of lack of support.)

In order to get a green card, you must demonstrate that you have had certain vaccinations. The list of those vaccinations is below. If you are entering the U.S. on a fiancé visa, however, you have the choice of either getting these vaccines as part of the medical exam you get for your fiancé visa, or as part of the medical exam you get when you later apply for your green card.

Vaccinations You Must Have

The required vaccinations presently include the ones listed below. Some of these are required only in certain age groups. If other diseases later become preventable by vaccines, they may be added to this list.

- mumps
- rubella
- measles
- polio
- tetanus and diphtheria toxoids
- pertussis
- influenza (including type B)
- hepatitis A and B
- varicella
- meningococcal bacteria
- pneumococcal bacteria
- rotavirus.

2. Dealing With Unlawful Time in the United States

In the late 1990s, Congress decided to punish people who spend time in the United States unlawfully, without permission from the immigration authorities. It created a penalty that prevents people from coming or returning to the United States for three years or ten years, depending on how long they stayed illegally in the country. These are usually referred to as the "time bars," or the "three- and ten-year bars."

In addition, people who lived in the United States illegally for a total, aggregate of more than a year and then left or were deported, but who returned to the United States illegally (or were caught trying to), can never get a green card. This is usually referred to as the "permanent bar," which we'll discuss in Subsection c, "The Permanent Bar," below. But first, let's look at the time bars that have some hope of being waived.

If you spent time in the United States unlawfully at any time after April 1997, this section could be one of the most important parts of this book for you to read and understand, no matter where you're living now.

SEE AN EXPERT

"Unlawful" is a difficult legal term. If you know that you were here without USCIS permission, it's safe to say that your stay was unlawful. But the boundaries are less clear if, for example, you were waiting for USCIS to approve or deny an application you'd filed, were in removal (Immigration Court) proceedings, or had a visa but violated its rules. For issues such as these, you'll need to consult a lawyer.

a. The Three- and Ten-Year Time Bars

The first thing to understand about the time bars is that (with rare exceptions) they are imposed only on people who are overseas and trying to return to the United States, not people who are already here and have the right to apply for their green card here. Unfortunately, a number of people have no choice but to leave the U.S. and apply for their immigrant visa and green card through an overseas U.S. consulate, either because they are already overseas, or because they are in the United States but ineligible to use the U.S. green card application

procedure called adjustment of status. If you are one of these people, the time bars could delay your immigrating to the United States as follows:

- **Three Years.** If you've spent more than 180 continuous days (approximately six months) in the United States unlawfully, you could be barred from coming back for three years.
- **Ten Years.** If you've spent more than one continuous year in the United States unlawfully, you could be barred from coming back for ten years.

Applicants who leave the United States to attend their immigrant visa interview at an overseas consulate probably won't be officially warned about the time bars before they leave. This means that you could get all the way through receiving approval of your initial visa petition (Form I-130), submitting your follow-up paperwork, and getting an interview appointment—only to leave the United States, attend your visa interview, and have the consular official inform you that although they would love to give you a visa, the time bars prevent you from actually reentering the United States for another three or ten years. By planning ahead, however, you can avoid this trap.

i. Loopholes in the Time Bar Law

Not everyone who has ever lived in the United States unlawfully will have a time bar problem. The law contains a few loopholes, as follows:

- Since the law didn't go into effect until April 1, 1997, no unlawful time before that date counts.
- None of your unlawful time when you were under the age of 18 counts against you for purposes of the three- and ten-year bars.
- The law imposes time bars only after certain lengths of "continuous" unlawful time; the time bars do not apply if no single stay lasted 180 days or more. So, generally, a few months here and there don't count, although they do add up toward the permanent bar.

Using these loopholes and some basic math, you might find that people who look like they have a time bar problem are safe after all. Here are some examples:

- Rosalie was a student in the United States from 1990 to 1995. She continued to live here unlawfully until April 1, 1997. She is not subject to the time bars because unlawful time doesn't start to count until April 1, 1997.
- Rosalie just checked her calendar and realized she stayed until July 1, 1997. But she still isn't subject to the time bars because her stay was for less than 180 continuous days after April 1, 1997.
- Juan crossed the Mexican border illegally six times in 2010, and stayed in the United States for time periods of two months each, for a total of 12 months. Now Juan wants to enter legally. The three- and ten-year time bars will not apply to him because he did not stay for more than 180 continuous days, and the permanent bar will not apply to him because his total stays did not exceed one year.
- Soraya entered the United States as a visitor on June 1, 2011 and her status expired three months later. She stayed in the United States until June 6, 2012. Soraya turned 18 on February 1, 2012. The time bars will not apply to her because only about four months of her unlawful time—less than 180 days—was while she was over the age of 18.

ii. Waivers of the Time Bar Law

If you have a time bar problem, don't just give up. If you're already married to a U.S. citizen or permanent resident, you are one of the lucky few who can ask for forgiveness, known in legal jargon as a waiver (in this case, using Form I-601). But you'll need a lawyer for this—these waivers are not easy to get.

To be eligible, you'll have to show that if you don't get the visa, your U.S. spouse will suffer extreme hardship. And when the immigration laws say "extreme" hardship, they mean it—the sadness that your spouse will feel at your living thousands of miles away won't even begin to get your waiver application granted. An example of a case where the government would recognize extreme hardship is

one where your spouse has a severe medical problem and requires your constant attention. Financial hardship will also be taken into consideration.

How Could a Lawyer Possibly Help?

Because the time bars are a fairly new area of the law, USCIS policy and legal interpretations are changing constantly. For that reason, anyone living in the United States with a time bar problem will want to get the latest information from a lawyer before making any decisions.

The lawyer could advise you, for example, whether there is any new legislation pending that would expand the right to use the adjustment of status procedure; when and if your spouse might be eligible for U.S. citizenship if your spouse is now a permanent resident (which would help you if you entered with a visa); and the current odds of being granted a waiver if you do decide to risk leaving and applying for your immigrant visa and green card through an overseas consulate. But be sure to find a lawyer who's an expert in this highly complex area.

If you happen to have U.S. citizen or lawful permanent resident parents living in the United States, the hardship that they would suffer upon your departure can also be counted toward a waiver. However, hardship that your U.S. citizen or permanent resident children would suffer doesn't count (although you could argue that their suffering affects your U.S. citizen or permanent resident spouse, emotionally, financially, or otherwise).

These time bars put visa applicants who must apply for their visas overseas at a huge disadvantage. Up to now, these applicants have had to leave the U.S. and apply for this waiver at a U.S. consulate in order to apply for permanent residence. This carried the huge risk that their waiver would be denied, blocking their return to the United States for several years.

Fortunately, USCIS recently announced a change to the I-601 rules, which allows immediate relatives of U.S. citizens to apply for a "provisional" I-601 waiver while still in the United States. That way, if the provisional waiver is approved, they can feel relatively safe leaving the U.S. for their green card interview. If the waiver is denied, they can at least remain with their family in the U.S. while they pursue any possible legal remedies—though subject to some risk that USCIS will place them in removal proceedings.

As of the publication of this book, the new provisional-waiver rules had not yet been finalized. But the proposals contained some important elements, including a requirement that the applicant not be inadmissible on any grounds other than unlawful presence in the U.S. of 180 days or more, be age 17 or older, and be (assuming the waiver is granted) otherwise eligible to receive an immigrant visa. The proposals also discuss requiring a brand new application form for this specific waiver, instead of Form I-601.

Until these rules are finalized, watch out. Scam artists calling themselves "immigration advisers" or "notarios" had already begun pretending this new procedure was available when this book went to print, and charging people to fill out the old, and incorrect, Form I-601. You should absolutely seek the help of a licensed attorney if you face time bar issues and need a waiver. See Chapter 17 for assistance on finding a licensed immigration attorney.

Another important point is that the time bars are not imposed on applicants who are within the United States, are eligible to adjust their status here, and who don't leave. So if you are eligible to file your green card application (adjust status) in the United States, you'd be wise to do so and stay put until it's granted. (See Subsection b below to find out whether you are eligible.) And if you are living in the United States unlawfully but are not eligible to adjust status here, see a lawyer.

EXAMPLE: Panos came to the United States on a temporary work visa. He fell in love with Debbie, a U.S. citizen. They got married and took a long honeymoon driving around the United States. The only trouble was, Panos's employer didn't authorize that vacation and it fired him—which meant that his work visa was no longer valid. While Panos tried to figure out what to do next, time ticked by. After he had been here unlawfully for six months, he heard about the time bars and panicked. But he didn't need to panic—the combination of his legal entry to the United States and his marriage to a U.S. citizen made him one of the lucky few immigrants who can apply to adjust their status at a USCIS office. Since Panos won't have to leave the United States, he won't be penalized for his unlawful stay.

b. Getting Around the Time Bars by Adjusting Status

One of the strangest features of the time bars is that they apply only to people who are outside the United States trying to get in, not to people who are submitting applications while they are in the United States. If you have stayed in the United States unlawfully and you are still in the United States now, it's essential that you stay here in order to avoid the time bars. Unfortunately, only certain types of people are eligible to adjust (change) their immigration status to get a green card in the United States. The rest will have to leave the country and apply from abroad—and face the potential roadblock of the time bars.

Under current law, only three categories of marriage-based visa applicants are allowed to adjust status and receive their green card in the United States. They include people who:

- entered the United States legally and are married to a U.S. citizen, in most cases, no matter how long they have overstayed their visa (I.N.A. §§ 245(a), 245(c)(2); 8 U.S.C. §§ 1255(a), 1255(c)(2))
- entered the U.S. legally, have not overstayed their visa, have never violated any visa terms or worked here illegally, and have a current Priority Date making a visa immediately

available to them (Priority Dates are discussed in Chapters 8 and 12; you'll later read whichever chapter is appropriate to your situation). See I.N.A. §§ 245(a), 245(c)(2), 245(c)(8); 8 U.S.C. §§ 1255(a); 1255(c)(2); 1255(c)(8). This section includes people who are marrying U.S. permanent residents.

- had initial labor certification or visa petitions filed for them long enough ago that their cases must be decided under old laws, which allowed applicants access to the adjustment of status procedure by paying a penalty fee.

Let's look at each of these categories in more detail.

Married to a U.S. citizen. In order to fall under the first category of people who can adjust status without leaving the United States, the applicant will have to prove that he or she entered the United States legally. Legal entries include those with a visa, under the Visa Waiver program, with a border-crossing card, or by some other means so long as the applicant was met and allowed to enter by an official of the U.S. government. The applicant's spouse must be a U.S. citizen, not just a permanent resident.

It does not matter when the spouse became a U.S. citizen—the minute they become one, an applicant who entered with a visa becomes eligible to use the adjustment of status procedure. This is true even if the person has overstayed the visa and been staying in the United States illegally.

CAUTION

Visa waiver entrants should check in with an attorney. Up until recently, USCIS (and the old INS) were inconsistent when dealing with adjustment of status (green card) applications from Visa Waiver Program (VWP) entrants. Some offices required a "compelling reason" to even consider processing them. However, under a new USCIS policy, all field offices are (or should be) accepting adjustment applications from immediate-relative applicants who came into the U.S. on a visa waiver, whether or not they apply within their 90-day period of legal status. Nevertheless, if a VWP

overstay is picked up and put into removal proceedings before having had a chance to submit the adjustment application, that person cannot adjust status at all, and has no ability to fight removal. It's as yet unclear what would happen if USCIS denied an adjustment application from a VWP entrant and placed that person into removal proceedings.

Married to a U.S. permanent resident. It is rare for spouses of permanent residents to be able to use the adjustment of status procedure. To do so, you would have to prove that:

- your most recent entry into the United States was legal
- you have not violated the terms of your recent entry visa or any other past visa
- you never worked illegally in the United States, and
- you are immediately eligible to apply for permanent residence, meaning you've already spent the years required on the government's waiting list, there is a visa number available to you, and the government is ready to let you take the final steps toward applying for your green card.

It would be highly unusual for anyone with a time bar problem to fit into this category. Even for people with no time bar problem, this combination of circumstances almost never occurs, but it could.

EXAMPLE: Megumi enters the United States as a student to enroll at UCLA. She falls in love with Shigeru, a U.S. permanent resident, and they marry six months later. He immediately files an initial petition with USCIS and Megumi is put on the waiting list. Five years later, while she's still working toward her degree, she reaches the top of the list and is allowed to apply for a green card. Since she has been legally in the United States, has not violated her student visa, and now has a visa number currently available to her, she can adjust her status to permanent resident in the United States.

Who Can Adjust Status in the United States		
	Applicant is married to a U.S. citizen	**Applicant is married to a lawful U.S. permanent resident**
Applicant entered the United States illegally	Cannot adjust status unless grandfathered in	Cannot adjust status unless grandfathered in
Applicant entered the United States legally and is within the expiration date of the visa or status	Okay to adjust status	Can adjust status only if an immigrant visa is immediately available (via a current Priority Date, discussed in Chapters 8 and 12); the person has not violated the terms of any visa; and the person has never worked illegally in the United States; or if and when spouse becomes a U.S. citizen or the person is grandfathered in
Applicant entered the United States legally but stayed past the expiration date of visa or status	Okay to adjust status	Cannot adjust status until and unless spouse becomes a U.S. citizen, or the person is grandfathered in

Visa petitions filed long ago and before certain deadlines. To fall into the third category, a family member or employer must have started the immigration process for you during a specific period of time. In the mid-1990s, Congress passed a piece of legislation called "Section 245(i)" of the immigration law. Section 245(i) said that anyone who was eligible for a green card, even if they entered illegally or were only married to a lawful permanent resident, could use the adjustment of status procedure so long as they paid a large penalty fee. It didn't matter how they entered the United States or who they married. Section 245(i) allowed many people to avoid the hassle of leaving the United States to do consular processing—and if it had remained on the law books, would have allowed a number of people to avoid the time bars.

But in 1998 Congress decided not to renew Section 245(i). The only people who can still use it are those for whom an employer or family member began their immigration process (such as by filing a labor certification or Form I-130) before certain dates. We will cover Form I-130 later, but briefly, it is the first filing that any couple submits, and your U.S. citizen or permanent resident wife or husband would probably be the one who submitted

it for you. You would probably know if one had been submitted for you. Ideally, you would have an approved I-130. But if your petition was mistakenly denied for some reason, you may still be able to use the petition to adjust your status to permanent resident (though you would likely need a lawyer's help for this).

You can be grandfathered in and allowed to use the old Section 245(i) if your I-130 (or a labor certification by employer) was submitted to the INS (as USCIS was then called) either:

- Before January 14, 1998 (the day § 245(i) was originally allowed to expire), or
- Between January 14, 1998 and April 30, 2001, if you can prove that you were physically present in the United States on December 21, 2000 (the day the legislation temporarily renewing § 245(i) was signed).

If your husband or wife did not submit an I-130 for you by one of these two dates, you may not be out of luck yet. In a wonderful policy move, USCIS has said that it will allow you to use an I-130 or labor certification filed by anyone on your behalf. If you had a prospective employer or a close family member (such as a parent, child, or brother) who tried to start the immigration process for you by filing a case before one of the dates listed above, that filing is transferable. It can become your ticket to using the adjustment of status procedure to apply for a green card in the United States based on your current marriage.

 TIP

Watch for Congress to extend Section 245(i) again. Before making any final determinations about whether you are eligible to adjust your status without leaving the United States, see if Congress has extended the dates described above, grandfathering you in; or better yet, has brought back Section 245(i).

To make use of the option of being grandfathered in under Section 245(i), you'll still have to pay a hefty penalty fee, currently $1,000 (I.N.A. § 245(i); 8 U.S.C. § 1255(i)).

If you are eligible to adjust status—that is, apply for your green card in the United States—you would be wise to take advantage of this procedure, especially if you have a time bar problem. Do not leave the United States until your adjustment of status application is pending and you have received what's called "Advance Parole" (explained in Chapter 14).

c. The Permanent Bar

The permanent bar applies to people who spend a total of one year's unlawful time in the United States or are ordered deported (even after spending less than one year there). If such a person then leaves and returns or attempts to return to the United States illegally (without a visa or other permission) he or she is permanently inadmissible to the United States. Known as the permanent bar, this law is one of the harshest aspects of the immigration laws. It even makes immigration lawyers shudder to think about. It is found at I.N.A. § 212(a)(9)(C); 8 U.S.C. § 1182(a)(9)(C).

Unlike the three- and ten-year time bars, the permanent bar applies only to people who have entered the United States illegally, or are trying to. If the total of all their previous stays is one year or more, then that person will never be allowed back into the United States or given a green card when they apply for one here.

The law took effect on April 1, 1997, so no illegal time before that date counts. Otherwise, however, there is almost no way to wiggle out of a permanent bar. An applicant can request a waiver (official forgiveness), but only after a full ten years have passed since leaving the United States. And you cannot avoid the penalty by staying in the United States to adjust status.

EXAMPLE 1: Cosimo came to the United States in 2008 on a three-month tourist visa. He stayed past the visa's expiration date and didn't leave until 2010; so he accrued over one year of illegal time after April 1, 1997. Then he went to Canada and lived there for a while. But he missed his U.S. citizen girlfriend, so he came back with a friend, who hid him in the back of his truck. Cosimo and his girlfriend married and he applied for a green card. However, the combination of his previous stay and his subsequent illegal entry is poison. He is subject to the permanent bar and cannot get a green card through his wife unless he spends the next ten years outside of the United States, remains married, and the U.S. government forgives him.

EXAMPLE 2: Jorge lives in Mexico, near the El Paso border. He is a pro at crossing illegally and picking up odd jobs on both sides of the border. Between April 1, 1997 and July 2007 he crossed the border illegally at least 17 times and stayed between two weeks and three months each time. The combination of all his stays, however, adds up to more than a year. When he marries his U.S. citizen girlfriend in July 2008 and tries to apply for a green card, he is hit with the permanent bar. Only if he can stay out and stay married for ten years can he apply for a waiver to return and claim permanent residency.

Here on an Employment Visa? The Risks of Applying for a Green Card

Are you already in the U.S. on an employment-based visa, and now want to apply for a green card through marriage? Be careful: Becoming a permanent resident can be trickier than you might expect.

Most employment-based visas are "nonimmigrant" visas. This means that the visa was granted on the understanding that, after you have finished working in the U.S. for a predefined period, you would return to your home country. When you applied for your employment-based visa, you likely assured the consular officer that you intended to leave the U.S. once your work was done.

Starting the immigrant visa process and applying for a green card is a bit like setting off fireworks around you. Not only does the process draw a lot of attention, it also signals your intention to stay in the U.S. permanently. You probably already recognize the problem: Although you promised the consulate, under oath, that you would eventually leave the U.S., your green card application is a break in that promise. This can have serious consequences. Not only could immigration authorities (depending on the facts of your situation) charge you with lying to a consular officer, they can also revoke your employment-based

visa and remove your ability to work in the United States.

Thankfully, the U.S. government recognized that disallowing all nonimmigrant workers from seeking permanent residence in the U.S. through marriage could be incredibly burdensome. Certain nonimmigrant visas benefit from a concept called "dual intent." This allows nonimmigrant workers to intend to eventually leave the U.S.—while seeking a green card and permanent residence all at the same time. This is perhaps one of the strangest legal concepts in all of U.S. immigration law. Regardless, the benefit to you is obvious: If you're in the U.S. on an employment-based visa that allows dual intent, you can pursue permanent residence and not worry.

Only certain types of employment-based visas benefit from dual intent. They include the H-1B, L-1, E-1, E-2, and O-1 visas. If you are in the U.S. on an employment-based visa that does not allow dual intent, try speaking with your employer about possible sponsorship under one of the other visa types. For more specific questions, consult an immigration attorney.

SEE AN EXPERT

If you think you might be subject to the permanent bar, see a lawyer immediately. Chapter 17 has tips on finding a good attorney.

d. Proving You Didn't Stay Unlawfully

The first question anyone asks when they hear about the time bars is, "How will anyone know? The United States is a huge country, and even with space-age technology, its government can't possibly trace who was living there and when."

But the real question to ask is, "What happens if they suspect that I was here illegally?" Because as soon as there is a hint that you might have lived in the United States illegally, it becomes your

problem. You have to prove to the U.S. government that you didn't live there illegally, not the other way around. People in this situation must come up with copies of their plane tickets, rent receipts, credit card statements, pay stubs, medical records, school transcripts, and more, all to prove that they were in the United States until a certain date and then left.

> **EXAMPLE:** Siri came to the United States from Norway on a six-month tourist visa in March 2006, but didn't leave until January of 2007—a four-month overstay. Her U.S. citizen boyfriend then petitioned for her as his fiancé. Everything was going fine until she went to the U.S. consulate in Norway for the final interview to get her fiancé visa. Siri explained

the four-month overstay, knowing that this wasn't long enough to subject her to any penalty, not even the three-year bar. But the consulate demanded proof that she wasn't in the United States longer than four months. Siri had lived with her parents after she got home and had thrown out her plane tickets. She had no paperwork with her to prove when she had returned to Norway. Luckily, the consulate gave her more time and she eventually came up with a copy of her frequent flier statement showing the date of her travel, as well as a prescription that she got in February 2007 in Oslo. The visa was granted.

TIP

If you have spent any time in the United States since 1997, make sure you are prepared to prove that you returned home on time. Begin gathering all relevant documents now, such as rent receipts, plane tickets, credit card statements, and more.

B. Are You Eligible for a Fiancé or Marriage-Based Visa or Green Card?

Section A above should have helped you determine whether you can get through the first door, which screens who is admissible to the United States. Now we're moving to the second door: Are you eligible for the particular type of visa or green card that you are seeking? This book covers two basic choices: the fiancé visa and the marriage-based visa or green card.

Remember, we're still not talking about the procedures to get these visas and green cards—this will come later. Of course, since we haven't gotten to the procedures yet, you might feel uncertain about which visa you'll be using. For now, it is safe to assume that you will be applying for a fiancé visa only if you are presently living overseas and are engaged to a U.S. citizen (but not a permanent

resident, since there are no fiancé visas for people engaged to permanent residents). Everyone else should apply for a marriage-based visa or green card. (In the unlikely event that you later decide that you want or need the other visa, don't worry—the eligibility criteria are so similar that you won't have wasted your time.)

SKIP AHEAD

Everyone applying for a marriage-based visa or green card, not a fiancé visa, skip ahead to Section 3.

1. The Legal Requirements for a K-1 Fiancé Visa

A fiancé visa will get you into the United States to get married. To be eligible for a fiancé visa, you do not have to intend to live permanently in the United States after your marriage. Whether you decide to stay in the United States and apply for a green card is up to you. (If you know in advance that you won't be staying in the United States, however, you could apply for a tourist visa instead—but see Chapter 5 for more on the risks and benefits of using that visa.)

In order to be eligible for a fiancé visa, the law requires that you:

- intend to marry a U.S. citizen (see Subsections a and b, below)
- have met your intended spouse in person within the last two years (though this can be waived based on cultural customs or extreme hardship; see Subsection c), and
- are legally able to marry (see Subsection d).

a. You Must Intend to Marry

The requirement that you intend to marry might seem obvious—you wouldn't be applying for a fiancé visa if you didn't plan to get married in the United States. But keep in mind that the U.S. government wants more than your assurance that a marriage is somewhere on your horizon. They will want proof that you've made actual plans, such as a place, a type of ceremony or proceedings (even if the proceedings are only in front of a judge), and more. We'll talk more about how to provide this evidence in the chapter matching your individual situation, below.

TIP

Make your wedding plans flexible. You can't know exactly how long it will take to get the fiancé visa, but you'll have to hold your wedding within 90 days of entering the United States. Before you sign any contracts for catering, photographic, or other services, discuss the situation with them and build some flexibility into your contracts or agreements in case the date needs to change.

b. Your Intended Spouse Must Be a U.S. Citizen

To be eligible for a fiancé visa, the person that you plan to marry must be a citizen, not a permanent resident, of the United States. A U.S. citizen is someone who either was:

- born in the United States or its territories
- became a citizen through application and testing (called naturalization), or
- acquired or derived citizenship through a family member. (Acquisition and derivation of citizenship are complex areas of the law. In general, however, people may acquire citizenship by being born abroad to one or two U.S. citizen parents; they may derive citizenship if they are lawful permanent residents first and one of their parents is or becomes a U.S. citizen.)

RESOURCE

 To learn more about acquired and derived citizenship: See the free article "U.S. Citizenship by Birth or Through Parents," on Nolo's website at www.nolo.com. Or see *U.S. Immigration Made Easy*, by Ilona Bray (Nolo).

Unlike some other countries, the United States does not require that its citizens carry any sort of national identity card. People who are U.S. citizens may have different types of documents that prove their status, such as a birth certificate, a U.S. passport, or a naturalization certificate. We'll talk more in later chapters about how your spouse can obtain documentary proof of his or her citizenship that will satisfy the immigration authorities.

CAUTION

Permanent residents of the United States— also known as green card holders—are not U.S. citizens. If your spouse is only a permanent resident, he or she can petition to obtain permanent residency for you, but your marriage must already have taken place— there are <u>no fiancé visas</u> available to you.

c. You Must Have Met in Person Within the Last Two Years

To protect against sham marriages, the law also requires that you and your intended have met in person within the last two years in order to be eligible for a fiancé visa. These days, a surprising number of couples fall in love over the Internet, or even through old-fashioned letter writing. Such couples will need to make sure they schedule at least one in-person meeting in the two years before applying for the fiancé visa. Even a brief meeting may be sufficient.

In some countries, prospective husbands and wives customarily do not meet before their wedding. If one or both of you come from a country where such a meeting would not be acceptable, you may find the meeting requirement a bit of a hurdle. Fortunately, if you provide documentation of the prevailing customs in your country, USCIS may overlook this requirement.

EXAMPLE: Dimple, a 21-year-old native and resident of India, is engaged to Athar, a naturalized U.S. citizen. Athar is 29 years old and lives and works in California. Athar remembers seeing Dimple playing in a nearby courtyard when they were both children in

India. They have exchanged recent photos and their parents, who are very traditional, have approved a marriage. Athar and Dimple will have no problem with two of the three eligibility criteria: they intend to marry (they can show evidence of wedding arrangements in California) and they are legally able to marry (for example, neither is underage, and neither is already married to someone else). But they don't meet the third eligibility criterion, since they haven't personally met within the last two years. To overcome this obstacle, in their application they include a letter from their religious leader, sworn statements by their parents, and other documents showing that they come from families and a culture where arranged marriage without a face-to-face meeting is an important and accepted practice. USCIS may waive the in-person meeting requirement.

The meeting requirement may also be waived if the U.S. citizen spouse can show that arranging a physical meeting would result in extreme hardship to him or her. This exception is usually granted only in cases where the U.S. citizen suffers from severe medical problems that would make an overseas visit difficult. Financial concerns are not usually considered sufficient to prove extreme hardship.

> **EXAMPLE:** Tom is a U.S. citizen confined to a wheelchair. He has severe environmental and food allergies. It is unsafe for him to leave the controlled environment of his home. He is also an Internet junkie and has been corresponding with Kathy, a native of Australia, for the last three years. They have exchanged not only emails, but photos and even videos, and have decided to marry. By providing copies of their communications with one another, as well as a letter from Tom's doctor and copies of his medical records, the couple may be able to obtain a waiver of the meeting requirement so that Kathy can enter the United States as a fiancé.

d. You Must Be Legally Able to Marry

Last but not least, to be eligible for a fiancé visa there must not be any legal barrier to your getting married. You may not have to provide anything at all to satisfy this requirement if you're an adult who's never been previously married and you're not a blood relative of your fiancé. This requirement is primarily directed at couples in which:

- one person is underage
- one person has been previously married and needs to prove that that marriage was legally ended, or
- the two members of the couple are related by blood.

If one of you is under the age of 18, you may be considered underage. Your legal ability to marry will depend on the laws of the state where you plan to get married. Each of the 50 U.S. states sets its own rules, and you will need to research them. For example, you may find that in one state you must be 18 years of age to marry, while in another you can marry younger if you can show the consent of your parents.

If you or your fiancé have been previously married, you will not be given a fiancé visa until you prove that that marriage was legally ended, for example by death, divorce, or annulment. This is usually easily proven, by obtaining copies of records from the court or local civic records office. If your divorce or annulment occurred overseas, the U.S. government will recognize it as long as it is recognized in the country where it took place, and as long as at least one of the divorcing parties had a residence in the place where the divorce took place.

If you and your fiancé are blood relations, your legal ability to marry will depend on the laws of the state where you plan to get married. You will need to research these rules. You'll find that all states prohibit marrying your sister or brother (sibling), half sibling, parent, grandparent, great grandparent, child, grandchild, great grandchild, aunt, uncle, niece, or nephew. But some states have additional prohibitions, such as marrying your first cousin.

RESOURCE

Need help researching marriage laws in the United States? See the "Marriage Requirements, Procedures, and Ceremonies FAQ" article on Nolo's website at www.nolo.com.

CAUTION

U.S. immigration law does not recognize homosexual marriages. USCIS persists in limiting its definition of marriage to heterosexual unions, even if the couple gets married in one of the few U.S. states that allow same-sex marriage or in one of the approximately 21 countries, such as Canada, Denmark, France, Italy, Norway, Greenland, South Africa, Spain, Sweden, and The Netherlands, that legally recognize some form of same-sex partnerships. If you are a lesbian or gay couple, the non-U.S. citizen partner will have to look for ways other than your marriage to get a green card or other right to live in the United States. If, however, your marriage includes a partner who has undergone surgery to change genders, you may have better luck. As of January 2009, USCIS recognizes a marriage between two persons of the same birth sex, provided that: (1) one partner has undergone sex reassignment surgery; (2) that person has taken legal steps to have the sex change recognized; and (3) the marriage is recognized as a legally valid heterosexual marriage under the law of the place where it was performed.

2. Your Children's Eligibility for a K-2 Visa

Your unmarried children under the age of 21, whether or not they are the biological children of your U.S. citizen fiancé, may be eligible to accompany you to the United States on your fiancé visa (they'll get "K-2" visas) and apply for green cards. Children include not only your natural children, but your adopted children and children born out of wedlock, if your home country legally recognizes them as yours.

Don't be confused by the fact that already-married applicants need to prove that their children fit the definition of "stepchildren," by showing that the parents' marriage took place before the children turned 18. You, as a fiancé visa applicant, don't need to fit those criteria. The only reason we even mention it is that immigration officials themselves sometimes get confused about it and try to deny K-2 fiancé visas to children who are over 18 but still under age 21. If this happens to you, understand that the official has gotten the laws mixed up, and suggest reading 8 C.F.R. § 214.2(k)(6)(ii).

Your children will have to go through the same (or a very similar) application process as you. They'll have to prove that they are not inadmissible and that they will be financially supported along with you. This book will give you an overview of the application procedures that your children will have to follow, but will not cover them in great detail.

For your planning purposes, however, note that the children must remain unmarried and under age 21 right up to the day they enter the United States on their K-2 visas. Fortunately, if you alert the immigration authorities to an upcoming 21st birthday, they can usually speed up the application process for you. (Unfortunately, a relatively new law you may have heard of called the Child Status Protection Act does not protect children on fiancé visas from the loss of visa rights caused by turning 21.)

CAUTION

Check your own country's law on taking your children if their other parent is staying behind. If you are planning to bring children to the United States who are not the biological children of your fiancé, it will be up to you to comply with any custody requirements. Even if the children are legally in your custody, you may need to get written consent from the other parent for you to take the children out of your country.

3. The Legal Requirements for a Marriage-Based Visa or Green Card

If you are already married to a U.S. citizen or permanent resident, you will apply for a marriage-based visa or green card. To be legally eligible, you and your spouse must show that you are:

- legally married (see Subsection a, below)
- in a bona fide marriage (see Subsection b, below)
- married to a U.S. citizen or lawful permanent resident (see Subsection c, below), and
- that neither you nor your spouse are married to anyone else (see Subsection d, below).

a. You Are Legally Married

To qualify for a marriage-based visa or green card, you must be legally married. A legal marriage is one that is officially recognized by the government in the country or state where you were married. This doesn't mean that the president has to give you a personal seal of approval, but it usually means that an official record of your marriage has been made or can be obtained from some public office.

For this reason, domestic partnerships, in which a couple lives together but have not formalized their relationship, are not normally recognized for immigration purposes. However, if you have lived together in a place that recognizes common law marriages, you may be able to show that you met the requirements for your marriage to be legally recognized in that state or country. We do not cover common law situations in this book. If you are in this circumstance, you may want to consult an attorney.

You do not need to have been married in the United States for your marriage to be legal. It is perfectly acceptable if you marry in your home country or in the luxurious or adventurous travel destination of your choice. A variety of marriage procedures are also recognized, from church weddings to customary tribal practices. But note that both you and your spouse must have actually attended your wedding ceremony—so-called "proxy" marriages, where another person stands in for the bride or groom, are not recognized by the U.S. government unless the couple later consummates the marriage, meaning they have sexual relations.

If you have not yet married, make sure you are eligible to do so. The state or federal government

where you intend to marry may have legal restrictions on who can marry. In the United States, each of the 50 states establishes its own marriage rules. For example, in some states you must be 18 years of age to marry, while in others you can marry younger if you can have the consent of your parents. If you and your spouse are related by blood, you'll also need to do some research. You'll find that all states prohibit marrying your sister or brother (sibling), half sibling, parent, grandparent, great grandparent, child, grandchild, great grandchild, aunt, uncle, niece, or nephew. But some states have additional prohibitions, such as marrying your first cousin.

 RESOURCE
Need more on marriage requirements in the United States? See "Marriage Requirements, Procedures, and Ceremonies FAQ" on Nolo's website at www.nolo.com.

Finally, you will need to provide a document to show you were legally married—most commonly, a marriage certificate issued by a legitimate governmental agency. A warning is in order here—a piece of paper from a church or a ship's captain won't, on its own, be enough to establish that you really are married. How you'll go about providing the appropriate documentation will be covered in later chapters.

b. Your Marriage Is "Bona Fide"

A bona fide marriage is one in which the two people intend, from the start, to establish a life together as husband and wife. Although this can mean different things to different people, one thing is clear: A marriage entered into for the sole purpose of getting the immigrant a green card is not bona fide. (It's called a "sham" or "fraudulent" marriage, and uncovering these relationships is a top USCIS priority.) When it comes to deciding whether a marriage is bona fide, USCIS is pretty strict.

EXAMPLE 1: Yoko has been studying in the United States for four years. She would like to stay permanently, but can't find an employer to sponsor her. A classmate tells her that for $5,000, he'll marry her and take care of sponsoring her as an immigrant. If Yoko agrees, this will be a classic case of marriage fraud.

EXAMPLE 2: Ermelinda and Joe are very close friends, who have occasionally had sexual relations, but are not now romantically involved. Ermelinda came to the United States on a student visa. However, because she dropped out of school, she no longer has any legal status or right to remain in the United States. When Ermelinda is threatened with deportation, Joe, a U.S. citizen, would like to help her. He figures he can live with her for a few years and then move on. Joe and Ermelinda get married. In the eyes of USCIS, this is marriage fraud.

EXAMPLE 3: Viktor and Beth have been living together in the United States since not long after Viktor came here on a student visa, two years ago. They are in love and have talked about marriage, but were nagged by doubts as to whether their marriage would work out. But when Viktor's student status ran out, he realized he'd either have to marry Beth or leave her and return to Russia. They marry and apply for his green card. This case is basically bona fide, since the relationship is real—but they will need to be careful in presenting it at the eventual green card interview. Viktor and Beth shouldn't offer up information about their doubts about the marriage. If this subject does arise, they'll emphasize their intention to make their marriage last.

c. You Married a Citizen or Permanent Resident of the United States

There are only two classes of people living in the United States who can obtain permanent residency or green cards for their spouses through the process described in this book: U.S. citizens and U.S. lawful permanent residents (green card holders). People with temporary rights to live in the United States (such as visas or work permits) cannot petition for their spouse to become a permanent resident.

i. Determining Whether Your Spouse Is a U.S. Citizen

Your spouse may have become a U.S. citizen in a variety of ways, including the following:

- being born in the United States or its territories
- becoming a citizen through application and testing (called naturalization), or
- acquiring or deriving citizenship through a family member. (Acquisition and derivation of citizenship are complex areas of the law. In general, however, people may acquire citizenship by being born abroad to one or two U.S. citizen parents; they may derive citizenship if they become lawful permanent residents first and then their parents are or become U.S. citizens.)

RESOURCE

Want to learn more about acquired and derived citizenship? Visit Nolo's website at www.nolo.com, see *U.S. Immigration Made Easy*, by Ilona Bray (Nolo), or ask your local nonprofit organization serving immigrants for more information.

Unlike some other countries, the United States does not require that its citizens carry any sort of national identity card. People who are U.S. citizens may have different types of documents that prove their status, such as a birth certificate, a U.S. passport, or a naturalization certificate. We'll talk more in later chapters about how your spouse can obtain documentary proof of his or her citizenship that will satisfy the immigration authorities.

ii. Determining Whether Your Spouse Is a U.S. Lawful Permanent Resident

A lawful permanent resident is someone with a legally obtained green card. This means that the person has a right to live in the United States permanently and may eventually become a U.S. citizen. The spouses of permanent residents are eligible for a green card.

You should know, however, that the fact that your spouse has a green card now doesn't guarantee that he or she will have it forever. Permanent residence can be lost, for example, if the person makes his or her home outside the United States or commits certain crimes or other acts that cause USCIS to begin removal proceedings and order them deported. If your spouse lost his or her permanent residence, you would also lose your right to immigrate through your marriage.

> ⓘ **CAUTION**
>
> **A green card is not the same thing as an Employment Authorization Document, border crossing card, or SENTRI card.** If your spouse carries a card with any of these titles, he or she is not a permanent resident. These cards grant the temporary right either to work in or gain entry to the United States. You can't get a green card through someone who only has one of these cards.

Sample U.S. Passport

d. This Is Your and Your Spouse's Only Marriage

Most people would love to leave their previous marriages far behind them. However, the U.S. government doesn't make it that easy if you want to enter this country via a new marriage. Any previous marriages must have ended by legal means—such as death, divorce, or annulment—and you'll have to present the official documents to prove it. Otherwise, USCIS will wonder whether your first marriage is still your active and real one—making your new marriage just a sham to get a green card. We'll talk more in later chapters about how to obtain the appropriate documents to prove a prior marriage has ended.

4. Your Children's Eligibility

Your foreign-born children, whether or not they are the biological children of your petitioning spouse, may be eligible to obtain green cards along with you. It won't happen automatically, however. They will have to go through the same or a very similar application process as you do. They'll have to prove that they are not inadmissible and that they will be financially supported along with you.

If your children are unmarried and under age 21, they will (with very few exceptions, as you'll see below) be placed in the same category of applicant as you. The result will be that they get a visa or green card at the same time as you do.

If your children are married or over age 21, they may or may not be able to get a visa, and any visa they might get will take years longer than

Sample U.S. Green Card

What If Your Spouse Dies Before You Get Your Green Card?

The last thing you probably need—or want—to worry about right now is whether your U.S. petitioner will pass away unexpectedly while you're in middle of the green card application process. For anyone affected by the untimely passing of a U.S. citizen spouse, however, at least know that in 2009, Congress changed the law to allow the surviving spouse of a U.S. citizen to petition for him- or herself, regardless of the length of the marriage prior to the spouse's death. This changed the old law, which had required the couple to have been married for at least two years at the time the U.S. citizen died in order for the surviving spouse to self-petition.

If you find yourself in this position, make sure you file your self-petition within two years of your U.S. citizen spouse's death (unless your spouse died before the passage of this new law—October 28, 2009—in which case, your petition must have been filed within two years of the new law, that is, by October 28, 2011).

You may include your children who are under 21 years old on the petition. You will still have to show that you and your spouse had a bona fide marriage, and that you have not remarried.

If you are the spouse of a deceased lawful permanent resident, you cannot self-petition the way the spouse of a deceased U.S. citizen can, but there are some other "survivor benefits" in the new law that might help you. If your deceased spouse filed a petition for you, you (and your children) may be able to adjust status once your Priority Date becomes current, despite the death of your spouse. If you are outside the country, under certain conditions USCIS may grant "humanitarian reinstatement" of the visa petition and may allow you to get your immigrant visa through consular processing.

This is a new area of the law. In December of 2009, DHS announced that the changes instituted by Congress had been fully implemented. However, this does not mean that all the potential issues have been worked out. Consult an immigration attorney for help and the latest information.

---

yours to obtain. Their eligibility will depend in part on whether your spouse is a U.S. citizen or a permanent resident, as discussed in Subsections b and c, below.

a. Who Counts as a Child

Some of the visa possibilities for your children will depend on a biological parent-child relationship between your new citizen or permanent resident spouse and your child. Luckily, immigration law also recognizes certain nonbiological parent-child relationships, and includes the following as "children."

- Your children who have become the step-children of your petitioning spouse, as long as your marriage took place before the child turned 18. Children who were born out of wedlock or legally adopted by you will qualify.
- Children born to unmarried parents. This provision might come in handy if you and

your spouse had a child before you were married, but the child doesn't qualify as your spouse's stepchild because the marriage took place after the child's 18th birthday. If your petitioning spouse is the child's mother, the case is handled just like any other. If the petitioner is the child's father, however, he will have to prove that he was the biological father, and either had a bona fide (real) relationship with the child before the child turned 21 (such as living together or financial support), or took legal steps to formally "legitimate" the child before its 18th birthday. At the time of legitimation, the child must have been in the legal custody of the father.

b. Children's Visa Eligibility If Your Spouse Is a U.S. Citizen

If your spouse is a U.S. citizen and your unmarried children under 21 are his or her biological children or legal stepchildren (you married when they were under age 18), they qualify for green cards as his or her immediate relatives. Immediate relatives are given high legal priority, with no quotas or waiting periods to slow their receipt of a green card. Their green card should be approved at the same time as yours (provided they remain unmarried).

If any of your children marry before they receive their visa or green card, they will automatically drop into category 3 of the Visa Preference System, which is subject to even longer waiting periods than category 1. (For more details, see Chapter 6 and Chapter 16, Section D, "Sponsoring Other Family Members.")

What if one of your children turns 21 before receiving a visa or green card? Formerly, they would have dropped into category 1 of the Visa Preference System, but that was changed with the Child Status Protection Act of 2002. As long as a child was under 21 when the visa petition was filed, the child will still be considered an immediate relative even after turning 21.

c. Children's Visa Eligibility If Your Spouse Is a Permanent Resident

If your spouse has a U.S. green card, your children who are unmarried and under age 21 are considered derivative beneficiaries. As a practical matter, this means that your children won't need a separate initial visa petition in order to be included in your immigration process. Unlike many other applicants, they also won't need to prove that your spouse is their parent or even stepparent, because they are riding on your application. (Eventually, however, they will have to fill out some forms of their own.) They will share your place on the visa/green card waiting list, and most likely get a visa at the same time as you (provided they remain unmarried).

Your children who have gotten married will not be able to immigrate to the United States at the same time as you. They will have no visa options until your spouse becomes a U.S. citizen and files a visa petition for them in category 3 of the Visa Preference System (which has a very long waiting period). Of course, to do this, your spouse would have to prove that he or she is the child's legal stepparent or biological parent.

Another issue to be aware of is how turning 21 will affect your child's eligibility for a visa or green card. If your child turns 21 before his or her Priority Date has become current (that is, before visas are being allotted to people who applied at the same time as you), the child could, in theory, "age out," or drop into a lower Visa Preference category (2B), with a longer waiting period. Thanks to a new law called the Child Status Protection Act (CSPA) however, a child can actually turn 21 without turning 21 in the eyes of the law! That's because the law allows you to subtract from the child's age the amount of time that it took USCIS to approve your family's immigrant visa petition.

For children who turn 21 after their Priority Date becomes current, the news is better—they can keep their 2A status—but there's a catch. The child who has turned 21 must submit his or her green card application within a year of when the Priority Date became current—just another good reason to keep a close watch on the *Visa Bulletin*.

For more details on how your children could move between visa categories, see Chapter 8 or 12, below, depending on which chapter matches your situation. Also see Chapter 16, Section D, "Sponsoring Other Family Members," for help with children who aren't eligible to immigrate at the same time as you.

> **CAUTION**
> **If your spouse becomes a U.S. citizen, the picture changes.** You will need to review Section 4b, above, to determine your children's visa eligibility.

> **NEXT STEP**
> **At this point you should know whether you are eligible to apply for a marriage or a fiancé visa.** If you are, read Chapters 3 and 4 before turning to the chapter that explains your application process in detail.

Meeting Income Requirements

Not everyone marries a millionaire, unfortunately (or not). Before any fiancé or spouse can immigrate, the U.S. citizen or permanent resident half of the couple must reveal their financial situation to the immigration authorities. The purpose is to show enough money to support the immigrant and to prevent him or her from becoming a public charge (the fancy term for going on welfare). Any immigrant who appears likely to rely on welfare or other publicly funded programs that support poor people is inadmissible. Requiring this showing of financial support is a way of testing the immigrant's admissibility.

Every U.S. fiancé or spouse petitioning for an immigrant must fill out a government form called an Affidavit of Support. By filling out this form, your fiancé or spouse becomes what is known as your sponsor. As you'll see, however, additional people can also serve as your financial sponsors.

A number of fiancé and green card applications are held up over the issue of whether the U.S. half of the couple can financially support the immigrant. The government has a very specific idea of how much money it takes to support someone. But even if your fiancé or spouse fills out the Affidavit of Support in a manner that shows that his or her income and assets meet this government-established minimum, the consulates and USCIS have the power to look at the bigger picture and decide that you are likely to become a public charge anyway. For example, your application could be denied if you have chronic health problems, are elderly, or your fiancé or spouse's income barely meets the minimum and you appear to be unemployable.

TIP

Married U.S. citizens with long work histories and long marriages may be able to avoid filling out an Affidavit of Support (Form I-864). The reason is that their obligations to act as sponsors end after the immigrant has worked 40 quarters (about ten years)—but, in an interesting twist, immigrants can be credited with work done by their U.S. citizen spouses while they were married. So, if your U.S. citizen spouse has worked 40 quarters in the U.S. during your marriage, he or she need not fill out Form I-864. Though it's the rare married couple who will have gone this many years without applying for a green card, this exception is highly useful for those to whom it applies. Use Form I-864W (available at www.uscis.gov) to help determine whether you are able to avoid the Form I-864 requirement and to show the immigration authorities if you are in fact exempt.

A. Meeting the Minimum Requirements

The minimum financial requirements for Affidavits of Support are determined according to the U.S. government's *Poverty Guidelines* chart, reproduced below and found on immigration Form I-864P.

Green card applicants must show that their sponsor is able to support them at 125% of the *Poverty Guidelines*. According to the Department of State, fiancé applicants need only to show that their sponsor is able to support them at 100% of the *Poverty Guidelines*. However, because the Affidavit of Support stays in the fiancé applicant's file, it is to the fiancés' advantage if the sponsor can already show an income level at or above the 125% guideline. That way, when (and if) the fiancé later applies for a green card, the financial requirement will have already been met. In addition, some consular officers are particularly strict in dealing with fiancé visas, and consider the 125% level that will be required when you apply for your green card. Other officers may simply apply the "eyeball" test for fiancés—if you look young and healthy, you're in.

CAUTION

The *Poverty Guidelines* chart changes regularly. The federal government usually updates it in February or March of each year, and the immigration authorities start to follow it two months later. When you attend your visa or green card interview, you will have to meet the most current guidelines.

OMB No. 1615-0116; Expires 10/31/2012

Department of Homeland Security
U.S.Citizenship and Immigration Services

I-864P, 2012 HHS Poverty Guidelines for Affidavit of Support

2012 HHS Poverty Guidelines*
Minimum Income Requirements for Use in Completing Form I-864

For the 48 Contiguous States, the District of Columbia, Puerto Rico, the U.S. Virgin Islands, Guam, and the Commonwealth of the Northern Mariana Islands:

Sponsor's Household Size	100% of HHS Poverty Guidelines*	125% of HHS Poverty Guidelines*
	For sponsors on active duty in the U.S. Armed Forces who are petitioning for their spouse or child	For all other sponsors
2	$15,130	$18,912
3	$19,090	$23,862
4	$23,050	$28,812
5	$27,010	$33,762
6	$30,970	$38,712
7	$34,930	$43,662
8	$38,890	$48,612
	Add $3,960 for each additional person.	Add $4,950 for each additional person.

For Alaska:

Sponsor's Household Size	100% of HHS Poverty Guidelines*	125% of HHS Poverty Guidelines*
	For sponsors on active duty in the U.S. Armed Forces who are petitioning for their spouse or child	For all other sponsors
2	$18,920	$23,650
3	$23,870	$29,837
4	$28,820	$36,025
5	$33,770	$42,212
6	$38,720	$48,400
7	$43,670	$54,587
8	$48,620	$60,775
	Add $4,950 for each additional person.	Add $6,187 for each additional person.

For Hawaii:

Sponsor's Household Size	100% of HHS Poverty Guidelines*	125% of HHS Poverty Guidelines*
	For sponsors on active duty in the U.S. Armed Forces who are petitioning for their spouse or child	For all other sponsors
2	$17,410	$21,762
3	$21,960	$27,450
4	$26,510	$33,137
5	$31,060	$38,825
6	$35,610	$44,512
7	$40,160	$50,200
8	$44,710	$55,887
	Add $4,550 for each additional person.	Add $5,687 for each additional person.

Means - Tested Public Benefits

Federal Means-Tested Public Benefits. To date, Federal agencies administering benefit programs have determined that Federal means-tested public benefits include Food Stamps, Medicaid, Supplemental Security Income (SSI), Temporary Assistance for Needy Families (TANF), and the State Child Health Insurance Program (SCHIP).

State Means-Tested Public Benefits. Each State will determine which, if any, of its public benefits are means-tested. If a State determines that it has programs which meet this definition, it is encouraged to provide notice to the public on which programs are included. Check with the State public assistance office to determine which, if any, State assistance programs have been determined to be State means-tested public benefits.

Programs Not Included: The following Federal and State programs are **not** included as means-tested benefits: emergency Medicaid; short-term, non-cash emergency relief; services provided under the National School Lunch and Child Nutrition Acts; immunizations and testing and treatment for communicable diseases; student assistance under the Higher Education Act and the Public Health Service Act; certain forms of foster-care or adoption assistance under the Social Security Act; Head Start Programs; means-tested programs under the Elementary and Secondary Education Act; and Job Training Partnership Act programs.

* These poverty guidelines remain in effect for use with Form I-864, Affidavit of Support, from March 1, 2012 until new guidelines go into effect in 2013.

Form I-864P 03/01/12 N

1. How to Read the *Poverty Guidelines* Chart

For green card and immigrant visa applications, the sponsor's income and assets must be enough to support the people who depend financially on the sponsor (also called household members or dependents), at 125% of the income level that the government believes puts a person into poverty. (Again, that number turns to 100% for fiancé visa applicants.) An exception is made for members of the U.S. Armed Forces, who need only reach 100% of the *Poverty Guidelines* levels when sponsoring someone for a green card.

To count the dependents who must be covered, add up the following:

- the sponsor
- the currently entering immigrant or immigrants (if children are also applying)
- any other immigrants for whom the sponsor has signed an I-864, and
- all family members listed as dependents on the sponsor's tax return.

Once you have calculated the number of household members and dependents, refer to the *Poverty Guidelines* chart. In the far left column, locate the line showing the number of people for whom the sponsor is responsible. Then look to the appropriate column to find how much the sponsor must show in income and assets.

Assets (such as savings, houses, or cars) are only counted at one fifth of their current market value, or one third if you're immigrating as the spouse or child of a U.S. citizen, after subtraction of debt liabilities, mortgages, and liens. Assets must also be readily convertible into cash (within one year). For example, if the sponsor owns a luxury house with major structural damage, there may not be a market for the house because no one wants to buy it. USCIS may decide that, even though the sponsor paid a million dollars for the house, this asset doesn't count—because it cannot be converted into cash within one year.

 CAUTION
Job offers with anticipated salaries don't count. If you are applying for your fiancé or immigrant visa from overseas, a job offer with a set salary in the United States might help a little, but it won't make up for a shortfall in your sponsor's ability to meet the *Poverty Guidelines* minimum.

USCIS also says that income you (the immigrant) earn overseas can't be counted, since you probably won't be able to keep such a job once you come to the United States. Finally, any income that you gained through unauthorized employment in the U.S. (when you didn't have a legal right or USCIS permission to work) can't be counted either.

2. Special Advice for Fiancé Visa Applicants

Because fiancé visas are, technically, only temporary, your U.S. citizen spouse's financial situation isn't seen as such a big deal. The Department of State says that the U.S. citizen sponsor needs only to demonstrate an income equal to, or greater than, 100% of the federal *Poverty Guidelines*. In contrast, when you eventually apply for your green card, your U.S. citizen petitioner will have to show an income equal to or greater than 125% of the *Poverty Guidelines*. Each consulate has a lot of discretion, however, in evaluating the income needed for a fiancé visa to be approved.

If you're having trouble meeting the consulate's standards for getting your fiancé visa, one option is to have another family member or friend in the United States agree to serve as a joint sponsor. A joint sponsor is someone who agrees to share responsibility for your financial support with your primary sponsor, up to the full amount of your support. In other words, if your sponsor can't support you, the joint sponsor can be held 100% responsible for your support—the joint sponsor is not allowed to choose a percentage or limit on how much he or she will support you. Joint sponsors can indicate their willingness to help support you by signing an Affidavit of Support on Form I-134 (different from the Form I-864 used by green card applicants).

Both the advantage and the disadvantage of the Form I-134 Affidavit of Support is that it is not considered to have much legal weight. In other words, although the government could take a sponsor to court to enforce it, they never seem to do so—probably because they realize they wouldn't win. That's an advantage because it allows you to easily persuade someone to sign the form, without endangering his or her financial future. It's also a disadvantage—since the consular officials know that the affidavit is hardly worth the paper it's written on, they may disregard the joint sponsor. For this reason, if you go the joint sponsor route, you might want to supplement the person's affidavit with a letter or a sworn statement expressing his or her heartfelt commitment to supporting you.

3. Special Advice for Green Card Applicants

Before exploring your options for meeting the *Poverty Guidelines* support levels or any higher level required by USCIS or a consulate, you need to understand more about the legal implications of the Form I-864 Affidavit of Support. If you can bear it, you should also try reading all the instructions that come with the form.

Some lucky sponsors now get to use a new, considerably simpler Form I-864EZ rather than the Form I-864. If your sponsor is sponsoring only you, and if your sponsor's income alone is enough to satisfy the *Poverty Guidelines*, read the rest of this chapter regarding your sponsor's general obligations, but be sure to use this easier form!

a. The Sponsor's Obligations

The Form I-864 Affidavit of Support is a legally enforceable contract, meaning that either the government or you, the sponsored immigrant, can take the sponsor to court if the sponsor fails to provide adequate support for you. When the government sues the sponsor, it collects enough money to reimburse any public agencies that have given public benefits to you, the immigrant. When the immigrant sues, he or she collects cash support up to 125% of the amount listed in the U.S. government's *Poverty Guidelines* (as shown in the chart in Form I-864P).

The sponsor's responsibility begins when the sponsored immigrant becomes a permanent resident and lasts until the immigrant becomes a U.S. citizen, has earned 40 work quarters credited toward Social Security (a work quarter is about three months, so this means about ten years of work), dies, or permanently leaves the United States. If you've been living in the U.S. and earned work credits before applying for your green card, those count toward the 40.

In fact, work done by your U.S. spouse during your marriage can be counted toward these 40 quarters.

CAUTION
A sponsor remains legally obligated even after a divorce. Yes, a divorced immigrant spouse could decide to sit on a couch all day and sue their former spouse for support. The sponsor may wish to have the immigrant sign a separate contract agreeing not to do this, but it's unclear whether courts will enforce such a contract.

b. Who Can Be a Sponsor

Your spouse and/or additional sponsor(s) must meet three requirements to be a sponsor. Each sponsor must be:

- a U.S. citizen, national, or permanent resident
- at least 18 years of age, and
- live in the United States or a U.S. territory or possession.

As a practical matter, of course, the sponsor will have to be in good shape financially to get you into the country. Even if your spouse's income and assets are lower than the *Poverty Guidelines* demand, however, he or she must sign an Affidavit of Support—but will have to look for additional sponsors to help you immigrate.

Take particular note of the third requirement if the two of you are presently living overseas. If your U.S. citizen spouse is not currently living in the U.S., the I-864 will be approved only if he or she can show that this is a temporary absence, that he or she has maintained ties to the U.S., and that he or she intends to reestablish domicile there no later than the date that you are admitted as a permanent resident. Some of the ways the U.S. citizen can show having maintained ties to the U.S. include having paid state or local taxes, kept U.S. bank accounts, kept a permanent U.S. mailing address, or voted in U.S. elections. Some of the ways the U.S. citizen can show intent to reestablish a domicile in the U.S. with you include leasing or buying a place to live together, opening a joint bank account with you, looking for a job, and the like. Different consulates are more and less strict about this, however, so your spouse should talk to someone at the consulate before making any major decisions.

 CAUTION

Sponsors who try to run away will face fines. The government has anticipated that some sponsors might try to escape their financial obligation by simply moving and leaving no forwarding address. That's why the law says that the sponsor must report a new address to USCIS on Form I-865 within 30 days of moving. If that does not happen, the sponsor will face fines of between $250 and $2,000; or $5,000 if the sponsor knows the immigrant has collected benefits.

If your sponsoring spouse can't meet the required income level alone, there are other possibilities. You may be able to enlist the help of members of your sponsor's household, as explained below in Subsection c. Or, you may find someone independent of the sponsor's household, as explained in Subsection d.

c. How Household Members Can Help Out

If your spouse cannot meet the financial minimum on his or her own, the first step is to see if another member of his or her household is willing to contribute income and assets to the mix. A household member is someone who:

- was listed as a dependent or joint filer on the sponsor's latest tax return, or
- is related to and shares a residence (home) with the sponsor.

The household member agrees to support the immigrant by signing a supplemental Form I-864A. One nice thing about using a household member's income is that it has to be only enough to make up the shortfall in the main sponsor's income (see examples below). However, the potential household joint sponsors should realize that if for any reason the main sponsor doesn't support the immigrant, the joint sponsors can be called upon for the full support amount. (The form itself supposedly warns the signer with the following legal jargon: "I, the Household Member, … Agree to be jointly and severally liable for payment of any and all obligations owed by the sponsor ….") This is where the immigrant really does need a fairy godmother—it's a lot to ask someone to sign onto such a long-term, substantial legal obligation.

> **EXAMPLE:** Lara is a U.S. citizen, sponsoring her husband, Dr. Z, who will be immigrating from Russia. Lara lives with her elderly mother and two adopted children. That means that Lara has to prove she can support a total of five people. For five people, the 2012 *Poverty Guidelines* chart mandates that she show $33,762 in income and assets. Lara earns $23,762 a year as a translator and has no assets, so she's $10,000 short. Will she and Dr. Z be parted forever? Not if:
>
> - Lara's mother (who is a household member) has an emerald ring that she could sell within a year for $50,000 (five times the shortfall of $10,000) or more, and Mom is willing to sign an I-864A; or
> - One of Lara's adopted children works, he happens to earn $10,000 (or more) a year, and he is willing to sign a Form I-864A.

Notice that if Lara were using her own assets to make up the difference between the *Poverty Guidelines* and her income, she would need only assets equal to three times the missing amount, because she is a U.S. citizen sponsoring her spouse. The other household members, however, must show that they have assets equal to five times the missing amount.

Immigrating spouses who live in the United States and are eligible to apply for adjustment of status have an advantage over those coming from overseas. Their income can be counted along with their spouse/sponsors' if they are living in the same household and their income came from authorized employment and is expected to continue from the same source after they become a permanent resident. It's as if they were another household joint sponsor. (They also won't need to sign Form I-864A unless they are agreeing to support children who are immigrating with them.)

Even if the immigrant hasn't been living in the sponsor's household, the immigrant's assets (but not income) can be added to the pot as well (again, minus debts, mortgages, and liens and at one-fifth the assets' value).

> **EXAMPLE:** Now assume that Dr. Z from the earlier example has a country house outside of St. Petersburg on which he owes 800,000 rubles (or $50,000 in U.S. dollars). He could sell it within a year for the U.S. equivalent of $100,000. Subtracting the $50,000 debt, this gives him $50,000, which conveniently enough, is five times the shortfall of $10,000. Dr. Z's contribution of assets would serve to make Lara's Affidavit of Support sufficient under the current *Poverty Guidelines* requirements.

d. How an Independent Joint Sponsor Can Help Out

If no one in the sponsor's household can help boost the sponsor's income and assets, you can look for a joint sponsor outside the household. Each sponsor needs to meet the basic sponsorship requirements as explained above in Subsection a. An independent joint sponsor must also be pretty well off financially.

Unlike household joint sponsors, joint sponsors who live outside the household will need to earn enough to cover the entire *Poverty Guidelines* minimum requirement for their own household *and* for the incoming immigrant or immigrants (if children will also be coming). The joint sponsor cannot simply make up the main sponsor's shortfall. It's as if they were the only sponsor. In fact, they must sign a separate Form I-864 Affidavit of Support. Like the household joint sponsor, an independent sponsor can be held 100% responsible for supporting the immigrant.

If there is more than one incoming immigrant, there can be up to two joint sponsors. This can be helpful, for example, where the incoming immigrants include an adult and two children, and neither of the joint sponsors earn enough to meet the minimum *Poverty Guidelines* for all three immigrants. As long as one of these joint sponsors earns enough to meet the *Poverty Guidelines* minimum for one immigrant, and the other joint sponsor earns enough to meet the *Poverty Guidelines* minimum for the other two immigrants, the I-864 requirements are met.

Although independent joint sponsors must meet the entire *Poverty Guidelines* minimum on their own, they at least will not be responsible for supporting people in the immigrant's household other than the immigrant(s). To meet the *Poverty Guidelines* requirements as a joint sponsor, don't just add up the number of people in the two households. Instead, add only the number of people in the joint sponsor's household plus the number of new immigrants.

> **EXAMPLE:** Imagine now that Dr. Z has a long-lost cousin, Leonid, who's an unmarried U.S. citizen, age 32, living in Seattle, who claims his parents as dependents. The cousin earns $34,000 a year from his espresso cart.

The cousin is willing to sign a separate Form I-864 as a joint sponsor on Dr. Z's behalf. The minimum Leonid would have to earn to be a joint sponsor according to the 2012 *Poverty Guidelines* would be $28,812, to cover himself, Dr. Z, and his (Leonid's) two parents. Leonid qualifies as a joint sponsor.

If the immigrant is also bringing in children to the United States, a last resort might have to be to leave some or all of the children behind for the moment. Once the immigrant arrives and begins earning an income, he or she (or potentially the U.S. spouse) can petition to bring the children over—and will be able to use his or her new income to meet the minimum requirements.

> **EXAMPLE:** Imagine that Dr. Z has two children from a previous marriage. They raise the minimum amount Lara must earn (in 2012) to $43,622 (for seven people in total). If she cannot reach that level or find someone to sign on for joint sponsorship, Dr. Z may have to leave his children behind for now. Once he gets established in the United States and begins earning income, Lara can petition for the children separately (as stepchildren, so long as her marriage took place before the children turned 18), using Dr. Z's new U.S. income to meet the shortfall. (They'll need to make sure the children aren't about to turn age 21 and fall into another visa category; see Chapter 8 or 12 for details.)

e. Should You Ask Family Members to Help?

The reaction of many applicants with inadequate financial resources is to ask another family member to pitch in and sign an additional Affidavit of Support (Form I-864). Think long and hard before doing this—and advise your family member to consult a lawyer before signing.

The Affidavit of Support is a binding, long-term contract, with ramifications the signer might not immediately realize. For example, the cosponsor will be obligated to continue supporting the immigrant spouse even if the couple divorces, or to support the immigrant in the event that the immigrant has a disabling accident. Even if these U.S. family members love and want to support the incoming immigrant, having to either support the immigrant directly or reimburse the U.S. government for large sums of welfare or public assistance money probably won't be a satisfying way of expressing that love. Try to keep your family members off the hook as much as possible.

 TIP
This book does not discuss the availability of public benefits to immigrants. Immigration law is federal, and doesn't prevent individual states from setting up special assistance programs that help immigrants. Indeed, some states make limited medical care, pregnancy care, or supplemental food available to low-income immigrants. If you're facing severe economic problems, the best thing to do is contact a nonprofit that serves immigrants to see what help is out there and how you can make use of it without jeopardizing your immigration status.

B. Applicants Who Must Meet More Than the Minimum

It's rare for a consulate or USCIS to ask you to show that your sponsor earns or owns *more* than the government's minimum requirements as announced in the *Poverty Guidelines*.

However, certain immigrants may have to produce sponsors who can exceed the minimum income requirement. Elderly applicants and those with severe health problems that might prevent them from working or result in large medical bills fall into this group. Finding additional sponsors as described in Subsections a and b, above, might be enough to help you overcome these added requirements. But if they're not, keep reading.

Have a Backup Plan

You won't know whether the government will ask you for an unusually high level of proven income and assets until you're in the visa or green card interview. If you're caught by surprise, don't worry—they'll always give you more time to provide new or further evidence that you'll be supported. But there are a couple of advantages to advance planning if you know that your case is a marginal one.

One advantage, of course, is that having extra documents or affidavits on hand may shorten the time before your case is approved. Another is that cases that aren't approved at the interview tend to get greater scrutiny when they're evaluated later by the interviewers and their supervisors. If you're understandably reluctant to turn in an extra Affidavit of Support from a joint sponsor, you can always keep it in your back pocket and give it to the interviewer only if he or she tells you she'll need it to approve your case.

---

1. Medical Expenses of Ill or Elderly Immigrants

Though you may have heard news stories about the United States considering a system of national health insurance, such a system has never been adopted—which can create huge challenges for immigrant couples. Without insurance, medical care can be hideously expensive—a single hospital stay could turn anyone into an instant "public charge."

The consulate or USCIS will learn of any significant health problems through the medical exam that is a required part of your application. Let's say that your medical exam shows that you have a kidney ailment and require regular dialysis. As you know from reading Chapter 2, Section A, applicants with communicable diseases (diseases that might infect others) may be excluded—but since a kidney ailment is not communicable, it does not make you inadmissible by itself. (Someone with

tuberculosis might be inadmissible because their illness could infect others.) Still, the consulate or USCIS may ask to see proof of your spouse's health insurance coverage, such as a copy of the insurance policy itself, to assure them that you will not need publicly funded medical care for your kidney disease after you arrive in the United States.

If your spouse is employed, he or she stands a decent chance of having coverage (although even that cannot be counted on—more and more companies use temporary or contract workers, to whom they don't give health benefits). But even if your spouse is covered, that coverage may not include you; or it may not cover your existing health condition for a period of months; or it may require large "co-payments" (money contributions by you, the patient). With all of your best intentions of being self-supporting, you might indeed find yourself in need of government help.

2. Sources of Medical Coverage

If you are elderly or do have a serious health problem and your spouse doesn't have health insurance that will cover you, your spouse has a major research project ahead. He or she will have to locate a source of health insurance coverage within the United States that will not refuse you on account of your age or refuse to cover your preexisting medical conditions. Such coverage is hard to find, and the premiums will be high.

For help, talk to a licensed, local health insurance broker, or see online price-quote services like eHealthInsurance.com, Insure.com, or DigitalInsurance.com. Also check your state insurance department's website, which may list companies selling individual coverage in your state and describe any special programs for people having trouble getting medical insurance.

Also, be careful: Even a partial state government contribution to a plan that covers preexisting conditions will lead USCIS or the consulate to deny your application on the grounds that you are receiving government support.

Applicants Who Have Already Received Government-Supported Medical Care in the U.S.

Past receipt of government-supported medical care in the United States will not automatically be used to conclude that you are likely to be a public charge in the future. In particular, USCIS is sympathetic if you needed emergency medical treatment. USCIS will look at your whole situation and the likelihood of your needing further such care before it approves or denies your green card. However, you should consult an attorney for help in showing that you won't need similar medical assistance in the future.

C. Increasing Your Sponsor's Income to Meet the Minimum

What if all of the above advice still isn't enough to get your spouse and cosponsors past the income requirement? Some couples don't have assets, household members, family, or friends that they can look to for financial support. To make up for financial shortfalls, the U.S. citizen spouse, or the immigrant if living in the United States, may have to find an additional job or a job with better pay and benefits.

Improving your financial situation may not be easy. It may mean moving to another city, dropping out of school for a while, or giving up enjoyable work or time with the children.

Luckily, after you are approved for your green card there is no obligation that you or your spouse stay with the new job. USCIS will not send inspectors to your or your spouse's workplace or check up on you.

If you and your family can survive on less than the U.S. government thinks possible, that's your choice—so long as you do not go on welfare for the first five years after your green card approval. The way the law works, you wouldn't face any repercussions for postapproval reductions in your family's income until and unless you tried to apply for welfare. You would probably be denied the welfare benefits—or forced to pay them back later.

If you don't find out until your visa or green card interview that you can't be approved without showing more financial support, you will usually be given a time limit to send in new evidence. The time limit may approach all too quickly while your spouse looks for a better job, health insurance, or other source of family support. If the deadline is about to pass and you have nothing new to show, at least send a letter saying that you are still interested in pursuing your application. Ask for more time to provide the requested documents (you usually will not be reinterviewed).

If you are in the United States, it is especially important to send such a letter, because once USCIS denies your application, it will transfer your case to the Immigration Court for removal proceedings. The consulates and USCIS will generally give you a total of six months to a year after your interview before they declare your application dead.

The Right Way to Prepare, Collect, and Manage the Paperwork

As you've probably figured out by now, you're going to have to collect and keep track of a lot of paperwork. This chapter will give you instructions on how to keep the paperwork organized, and how to make sure that all documents are of a type and quality that USCIS and the consulates will accept (Sections A and B). We also tell you how to locate and translate some of the documents that you'll need to support your application (Section C). And finally, Section D explains how to protect your application before you mail it from being lost by the U.S. government.

For where to get the latest forms, see Chapter 1.

A. Getting Organized

Start by setting up a good system to keep track of all the forms and documents that you'll need during this application process. There is no feeling worse than being in front of an impatient government official while you desperately go through piles of stuff looking for that one vital slip of paper. Take our word for it, you'll need a lot more than one jumbo folder.

We suggest using manila file folders and putting them in a box or drawer (or use a series of large envelopes or an accordion file). Label one folder or envelope Original Documents, for things like your birth certificate, marriage certificate, and USCIS or consular approval notices. Keep this file in a very safe place (such as a safe deposit box at your local bank). Be sure to remember to retrieve your originals in time to take them to your interview.

Label the other files or envelopes according to which packets, forms, or documents they contain. If you're applying for a green card within the United States, you might label one folder Visa Petition; another Adjustment of Status Packet; another Interview Materials (containing copies of the documents you'll want to take to your interview); and another Old Drafts/Copies. Similarly, if you're applying from overseas, one folder might be labeled Visa Petition, another Mailed to Consulate, another Affidavit of Support and Financial Documents,

How Nightmarish Can It Get?

Maybe you'll turn in your application and everything will go like clockwork: USCIS and consular files all in order, approval received on time. Educating yourself about the process and preparing everything carefully certainly improves your chances. But we wouldn't be doing our job if we didn't warn you about how the government bureaucracy can chew up and spit out even the best-prepared application.

Every immigration lawyer has his or her favorite horror stories. For instance, there was the client whose visa petitions were lost by USCIS—so after many months, the lawyer filed new petitions and cancelled the checks that went with the lost ones. But USCIS then found the old petitions, tried to cash the "lost" checks and to collect from the client for the bank charges when the checks bounced.

Then there was the woman who waited over six months for USCIS to approve her work permit— only to have them finally send her a work permit with someone else's name and photo. By the time that finally got straightened out, the work permit had expired and USCIS forced her to apply, and pay again, for a new one.

And let's not forget the woman who nearly got stuck outside the United States because USCIS refused to renew her Refugee Travel Document on the nonsensical grounds that she hadn't provided a valid address in the application. (She had, and it was the same address that USCIS had been using to correspond with her for years.)

What can you do about such absurd and Orwellian horrors? Mostly just know in advance that they may happen to you, leave time to deal with them, and keep copies of everything.

another Interview Materials, and the rest as described above.

You should also keep a separate file for correspondence from USCIS or the consulate. Include in this file your handwritten notes on any phone conversations you've had with USCIS or consular personnel. Don't forget to write the date on your notes, so you can refer to them later in further correspondence.

As you're preparing your forms and documents, attach our checklists on the outside of each folder or envelope and check the boxes off as the items have been completed and put inside. When you've finished filling a folder or envelope, take out some of the old drafts or items you've decided not to use and move them to the Old Drafts/Copies folder, so as not to clutter up the materials you'll take to your interview. Carefully write "final copy, mailed xx/xx/20xx" (you fill in the date) on the top of the copy of the application or petition you've mailed to USCIS or the consulate.

B. How to Prepare USCIS and Consular Forms

Now, let's make sure the government doesn't return your forms for technical reasons. Follow these instructions for printing and filling out the forms.

1. How the Forms Print Out

When downloading forms from government websites, here are some things to keep in mind.

You'll see that some forms print out many copies of the same page. This isn't a mistake. You're getting multiple copies of the same page because you're supposed to submit the page in triplicate, quadruplicate, or whatever (in other words, USCIS wants to receive multiple but identical copies). It may be easier for you to complete only one set, then make the required number of copies and attach them to the original.

If this seems like too much trouble and you want to get USCIS forms directly from them, the

telephone order number is 800-870-3676. It usually takes a few weeks for the forms to arrive by mail. To download USCIS forms from their website, go to www.uscis.gov.

Many consular forms can be obtained directly from the particular consulate only. Check the consulate's website by visiting www.usembassy. gov. In the last few years, the State Department has been promoting standardized visa application forms by moving them online.

2. Form Names, Numbers, and Dates

The government refers to its forms not by their name or title, but by the tiny numbers in the lower left or right corner. For example, if you look at the sample form in Chapter 7 entitled Petition for Alien Relative, you'll see I-130 there at the bottom. And because USCIS uses these numbers, we usually do, too.

Another thing you'll find in the corner is the date the form was issued. That's an important date, because once USCIS issues a later version (which they're doing a lot of these days), you'll usually need to use the later one. That means that for every form you plan to submit, you should check the USCIS website just before actually mailing it. (Go to www. uscis.gov, click "Immigration Forms" and you will find a list you can scroll down by form number.)

After you have submitted the form, you can stop worrying—you won't need to redo it even if USCIS issues a new form before your application has been decided.

3. Instructions That Come With the Forms

USCIS provides instructions with each form. Save yourself a little postage and don't send the instruction pages back to them when the time comes to submit your application. USCIS wants only the part of the form you fill in. Sadly, the instructions are often hard to understand (that's why we wrote this book) and at times they even contain information that is wrong or misleading (which we point out whenever possible).

4. Filing Fees

Many of the immigration forms require you to pay a fee in order to file them. (No, you can't get your money back if your case is not approved.) Don't go by the fees listed on the USCIS form instructions; they may be out of date. Definitely double-check the fees at the USCIS website at www.uscis.gov, or call their information line at 800-375-5283.

You must pay the fees by personal check or money order, made out to the Department of Homeland Security. Don't send cash! To make sure they see your check, paperclip or staple it to the upper left-hand corner of your main application form.

Although you can combine all the amounts owed for one person into one check (for example, adding up the application fee and the biometrics fee) it's better not to combine fees for the whole family when applying together. That's because if one person's application has a mistake, USCIS will send the entire package back to you if you've sent in only one check, delaying the process. With separate checks, they're more likely to start the process rolling and send a letter regarding the mistake or missing item.

5. Typing or Ink?

This isn't the time to express your individuality with purple ink. Fill in all immigration forms using a typewriter or, if you must prepare them by hand, use black ink.

Of course, some forms can now be filled out on the computer—but this can be inconvenient because they may not save—you have to do the whole form in one sitting.

6. Questions That Don't Apply to You

If a question just doesn't fit your situation, write "N/A" (not applicable) rather than leaving the space blank. Or, if the answer is "none," as in "number of children," answer "none."

Try not to mix these two up—it irritates the government officials reading your application. But if you're not sure how or whether to answer a question, seek skilled legal help (Chapter 17 gives you information on finding a good lawyer).

7. Tell the Truth

There will be many temptations to lie in this process—to hide a ground of inadmissibility, ignore a previous marriage, or avoid questions about previous visits to the United States, for example. But lying to the government or even omitting information can get you in bigger trouble than the problem you are lying about. And you've never seen anyone angrier than a USCIS or State Department official who discovers that you've lied to them.

If you feel you just can't complete the form without hiding a certain piece of information—or you really don't know how to answer or explain a key question—see a lawyer. The lawyer may be able to show you how to be truthful in a way that doesn't risk having your application denied.

8. What's Your Name?

The easiest thing on a form should be filling out your name, right? Not in this bureaucratic morass. USCIS will want not only your current name, but on certain of its forms, "other names used." Here are some important things to get straight before you start writing your name(s) in the forms to follow:

- **Married name.** If you've just married and changed your last name as part of your marriage, use your married name. But women shouldn't feel pressured into taking on a married name for the sake of the green card application. By now USCIS is well aware that not all women change their name when they marry. They will not look upon keeping your name as a sign that your marriage is a sham. Nor does having different last names seem to cause any confusion in the processing of your application (after all, USCIS thinks of you as a number, not a name).

- **Current name.** When your current name is requested, it is best to insert the name you currently use for legal purposes. This will normally be the name on your bank account, driver's license, and passport. If you've always gone by a nickname (for example, your name is Richard but you always use the common nickname "Dick"), it's okay to fill in the application as "Dick," as long as you list "Richard" where the form asks for other names used. This will avoid confusion when USCIS compares your application form with the accompanying documents (your employer, for example, will probably write a letter saying "Dick worked here ....."). But there's no way to avoid a little confusion, since your birth certificate will still say Richard.

- **Legal name changes.** If you've actually done a court-ordered legal name change, include a copy of the court order, to help dispel some of the inevitable confusion. If you have changed your name without a court order (by simply beginning to use a different name and using it consistently, which is legal in many states) and you use your changed name for all legal purposes, list it as your current name.

- **Other names.** The category for "other names used" could include nicknames. USCIS will want to know about nicknames that might have made their way onto your various legal documents (or criminal record). You should also include names by which you have been commonly known, especially as an adult. However, "pet" names such as "sweetie-pie" need not be included. Nor should unwanted childhood nicknames. For example, if your name is Roberto Malfi but your oh-so-clever high school buddies called you "Mafia," best forget about it.

- **Previous married names.** If you have been married previously, don't forget to list your name from that marriage in the boxes requesting other names used.

9. Be Consistent

As you might have guessed from the previous section, it's important not to cause confusion when filling out the forms. At worst, not getting your facts straight can cause the person reviewing your application to think you cannot be believed. For example, you might live with a group of friends but use your parents' address to get mail. Notice the places on the forms that ask for your actual residence, and the places on the forms that ask for your mailing address. Be careful to answer correctly and consistently in response.

C. How to Obtain Needed Documents

You would be lucky if forms were the only paperwork you had to worry about—but no, there are documents, too. At a minimum, you are going to need your long-form, government issued birth certificate to complete your visa or green card application. You will also need your marriage certificate, if you're past the fiancé stage. You may also need other documents, such as death or divorce certificates and your spouse's birth certificate or U.S. passport.

When it's time for your visa or green card approval, you will need a passport from your own country (either to travel to the United States or to hold a stamp showing your residence status). If you get married in your home country and you change your name, make sure your passport is either updated or is still considered valid with your maiden name in it.

Within the United States, official copies of birth, death, marriage, and divorce certificates can usually be obtained from the Vital Records office (called the Registrar's or Recorder's office in some areas) of the appropriate county or locality. Even if you already have your own copy of these items, it's a good idea to request a certified copy from the Vital Records office. That's because your copy may not have been given all the official governmental stamps necessary for USCIS to accept it as authentic.

You can find more details on the National Center for Health Statistics website at www.cdc.gov/nchs. (Click "Need a birth, death or marriage certificate?" in the box on the right. Or, check the blue pages of a U.S. phone book.) There are also services that will order your vital records for a fee, such as www. Vitalchek.com.

U.S. passports are available to U.S. citizens through the State Department; see www.state.gov (click "Passports for U.S. Citizens") or the federal government pages of a U.S. phone book.

Outside of the United States, records should be obtained from official, government sources wherever possible. The sources that USCIS and the State Department consider acceptable are listed in the State Department's *Foreign Affairs Manual* (FAM). It's accessible at www.state.gov. (Under "Travel" click "Visas," then select "Fees and Reciprocity Tables" from the sidebar on the left side of the page. Once you have opened that page, click on "Visa Issuance Fee - Reciprocity Tables," then select the country about which you want information.) You'll access information about the country you're interested in using an alphabetical index. U.S. law libraries may also be able to locate copies of the FAM for you.

In the FAM, you can discover such fun (and relevant) facts as that Ascension Island doesn't grant divorce certificates because of the lack of a supreme court, and that the place to obtain vital documents in Lithuania is called the Marriage Palace.

If you are overseas and do not have Web access, talk to your local U.S. consulate about what form of record will be acceptable, particularly if you need to document an event for which your government does not issue certificates.

1. Translate Non-English Documents

If the documents you are submitting are in a language other than English, you will need to submit both:

- a copy of the original document and
- a certified, word-for-word translation (summaries are not acceptable).

This is particularly true if you're submitting the document to a USCIS office; consulates can often deal with documents that are in the language of that country (their instructions will usually tell you if they can't).

There is no need to hire a certified translator. Any trustworthy friend who is fluent in English and the language of the document and is not your close relative can do the job. That person should simply type out the translated text, then add at the bottom:

I certify that I am competent to translate from [*the language of the document*] to English and that the above [*identify the document and to whom it pertains; for example, "Birth Certificate of Maritza Malakoff"*] is a correct and true translation to the best of my knowledge and belief.

Signed: _____ [*translator's full name*] _____

Address: _____

Telephone: _____

Date: _____

If you prefer, you can hire a professional translator, who should also add the same certification at the bottom of the translation.

2. Substitute for Unavailable Documents

If you cannot obtain a needed document, USCIS may, under some circumstances, accept another type of evidence. For example, if your birth certificate was destroyed in a fire, USCIS may accept in its place school records or sworn statements by people who knew you to prove your date of birth.

USCIS instructions included with Forms I-129F (for the fiancé visa petition) and I-130 (the immigrant visa petition) outline the other types of evidence that USCIS accepts. If you substitute a new type of evidence for a missing document, you should also include a statement from the local civil authorities explaining why the original document is unavailable.

3. Homemade Documents

One form of substitute document that you may need to use is a sworn declaration. For example, you might need to ask a friend or family member to prepare one affirming your date and place of birth. If so, emphasize to the person that fancy legal language is not as important as detailed facts when it comes to convincing an immigration official to accept this person's word in place of an official document.

Someone could write, for example, "I swear that Francois was born in Paris in 1962 to Mr. and Mrs. Marti." But it would be much more compelling for them to write, "I swear that I am Francois' older brother. I remember the morning that my mother brought him home from the hospital in 1962 (I was then five years old), and we grew up together in our parent's home (Mr. and Mrs. Xavier Marti) in Paris."

The full declaration should be longer and contain more details than this example. The more details that are offered, the more likely USCIS or the consulate is to accept the declaration as the truth.

To start the declaration, the person should state his or her complete name and address, as well as country of citizenship. At the bottom of the declaration, the person should write:

I swear, under penalty of perjury, that the foregoing is true and correct to the best of my knowledge.

Signed: _____

Date: _____

If preparing sworn declarations seems like too much to accomplish, you could hire a lawyer for this task only. Below is a sample of a full sworn declaration, written to prove that an immigrant who is applying through marriage is no longer married to his first wife, due to her death. (Remember, when writing your own declaration, tailor it to your situation—don't follow the wording of the sample too closely.)

Declaration in Support of Application of Guofeng Zheng

I, Shaoling Liu, hereby say and declare as follows:

1. I am a U.S. permanent resident, residing at 222 Rhododendron Drive, Seattle, WA 98111. My telephone number is 206-555-1212. I have been living in the United States since January 2, 1999.

2. I am originally from Mainland China, where I grew up in the same town (called Dahuo, in Suzhou province) as Guofeng Zheng.

3. I knew Guofeng's first wife, Meihua. I attended their wedding, and had dinner at their home several times. I also remember when Meihua fell ill with cancer. She was sick for many months before passing away on October 31, 1998.

4. I received the news of Meihua's death a few days later, in early November of 1998. I knew the doctor who had treated her, and he was very sad that his treatments had failed. I also attended Meihua's funeral on November 7th. Her ashes are buried in the local cemetery.

5. I am also aware that the municipal records office, where all deaths are recorded, burnt down in the year 2002. I myself had difficulty with this, when I tried to get a copy of my mother's birth certificate last year.

I swear, under penalty of perjury, that the foregoing is true and correct to the best of my knowledge.

Signed: *Shaoling Liu*

Date: *August 4, 2012*

Don't confuse a declaration with an affidavit. An affidavit is very similar—a written statement that the author dates and signs—but it has one additional feature. Affidavits are notarized, which means that they are signed in front of someone who is authorized by the government to attest to, or certify, the authenticity of signatures. When you bring a declaration to a notary, that person will ask for identification, such as your passport or driver's license, to make sure that you are the person whose signature is called for on the declaration. You sign the declaration in the presence of the notary, who makes a note of this in his or her notary book. The notary also places a stamp, or seal, on your document.

As you can see, affidavits are more formal and more trouble than simple declarations. An affidavit is not required for substitute documents such as we're describing now—but if you want to make the document look more official, and know where to find a notary, you might want to take the extra trouble. If an immigration process described in this book requires an affidavit, we'll alert you.

D. Before You Mail an Application

There are three rules to remember before you mail anything to USCIS, consulate, or other government office:

1. Make copies.
2. Mail your applications by a traceable method.
3. Don't mail anything that you can't replace.

We'll explain the reasons for these maxims—and how to follow them.

1. Make Complete Copies

When you've at last finished filling out a packet of required immigration forms, your first instinct will be to seal them in an envelope, pop them in the mail, and forget about them for awhile. That could waste all of your hard work.

Find a photocopy machine and make copies of every page of every application, as well as any photos, documents, checks, and money orders. Carefully keep these in your records. This will help you recreate these pages and items if they're lost in the mail or in the overstuffed files of some government office. It may also help convince USCIS or the consulate to take another look for the lost items.

2. Mail by a Traceable Method

In any government agency, things get lost. The sorting of newly arrived applications seems to be a common time for them to disappear. If this happens to your application, it can become important to prove that you mailed it in the first place.

In the United States, it's best to go to the Post Office and use certified mail with a return receipt for all your applications or correspondence with USCIS or the consulates. When you request a return receipt, you will prepare a little postcard that is attached to your envelope and will be signed by the person at USCIS or the consulate who physically receives your envelope. The postcard will be mailed to you, which will be your proof that the envelope was received. You can use this postcard to convince USCIS or the consulate to look for the application if it gets misplaced.

If you're mailing something from overseas, you'll have to find out the most reliable method. Unfortunately, courier services often don't work because they can't deliver to a post office box, and many USCIS addresses (in particular those of the Service Centers) are at post office boxes. You'll have to use regular mail if mailing to a P.O. box. Some Service Centers provide alternate addresses for delivery by courier.

3. If You Want It Back, Don't Send It

Many immigration applications require that certain documents be attached (paper-clipping them to the form is fine). Some documents must be included in packets of forms you must file and others brought to interviews. Whatever you do, *don't send originals* to USCIS.

We used to give the same advice about not sending originals to the consulate, but now the National Visa Center explicitly asks for the originals of certain documents, and will not forward your case to the consulate until it receives them. (Whenever you send an original, be sure to make a copy for yourself first.)

Whenever USCIS or the National Visa Center (or consulate) does not explicitly request an original document, simply photocopy any document (as long as the original is the official version), and send the copy. The USCIS or consular officer will have a chance to view the originals when you bring them to your interview. It's best to write the word "COPY" in red letters at the top, and to add the following text, right on the front of the copy, if there's room:

Copies of documents submitted are exact photocopies of unaltered original documents and I understand that I may be required to submit original documents to an immigration or consular official at a later date.

Signature: _____

Typed or printed name: _____

Date: _____

Always make photocopies for USCIS on one-sided, 8½" × 11" paper. Some applicants have been known to try to create exact copies of things by cutting the image out of the full page of paper—creating, for example, a tiny photocopied green card. The government doesn't appreciate these minicopies.

By the same token, 8½" × 14" paper (or larger) doesn't fit well into the government's files—use a photocopy machine that will reduce your document image to 8½" × 11", if possible.

Overseas Fiancés of U.S. Citizens

If you are not yet married, your intended spouse is a U.S. citizen, and you are living overseas, you will have a choice among visa options. Depending on your own preference or the length of time each will take to obtain, you can choose to pursue:

- a fiancé visa (for readers who won't marry until they come to the U.S.), explained in Section A
- a marriage-based visa (for readers who decide to marry overseas and then apply to come to the U.S.), explained in Section B, or
- a tourist visa (if you just want to marry in the U.S. and return home), explained in Section C.

This chapter explains these options in detail. In Section D, we'll help you decide which is best for you. If you decide to get married overseas, we'll send you on to Chapter 7, where the application process for a spouse of a U.S. citizen is explained. Or, if you decide that a quick trip to the U.S. for the wedding, followed by a return to your home country, is all that you need, we'll discuss the tourist visa process, though not in great detail (Section E). And for those of you who are engaged to be married and want to come to the U.S. for the wedding, Sections F, G, and H give you the information you need to prepare the applications and obtain your fiancé visa.

A. The Fiancé Visa Option

Since you are presently a fiancé, the most obvious option is the fiancé visa. If you need to review whether you would be eligible for a fiancé visa, see Chapter 2, Section B. A fiancé visa allows you to enter the United States, marry within 90 days, and apply for your green card in the United States. Your unmarried children under age 21 are eligible to accompany you.

There are no quotas or limits on the number of people who can obtain fiancé visas and subsequent green cards through marriage to a U.S. citizen. A fiancé visa can take anywhere from six months to a year or more to obtain—depending on how backed up the various offices dealing with your file are.

1. You Must Marry in the U.S.

A fiancé visa gives you no choice but to hold your marriage ceremony in the United States. In fact, you'll have to get married fairly quickly if you plan to go on to apply for a U.S. green card. Although technically you have 90 days to get married, waiting until the latter part of that time period is risky, because even after you're married, it may take weeks to get the all-important marriage certificate that you'll need to apply for your green card.

Couples often ask whether their overseas marriage really counts, or wonder why they can't just get married for a second time after entering on a fiancé visa.

Unfortunately, once you're legally married, no matter where the marriage took place, you no longer qualify for a traditional, K-1 fiancé visa.

Married couples do have other options, however, assuming you're planning to apply for U.S. permanent residency. See Section B, below.

 TIP
Wedding ceremonies that don't result in legally binding marriages won't stand in your way. If you don't feel right leaving home unmarried, see if you can arrange for a religious or other ceremony that won't be recorded or recognized by your country's civil authorities. USCIS does not recognize these as valid marriages. You will need to have a legal marriage in the United States once you get there.

2. The Green Card Application Will Be Separate

Fiancés wishing to live in the United States will need to apply for their green card within the 90 days that they're allowed in the United States on the fiancé visa, and then file the application for a green card using a procedure called adjustment of status. Although you are not required to file for adjustment of status within the 90-day period that you are allowed to stay in the U.S., it is wise to do so, as your marriage alone does not extend your period of authorized stay past the original 90 days. Once you file your application for adjustment of status, however, you are legally authorized to stay in the U.S. while the government makes a decision on the application. This application procedure involves even more paperwork than the fiancé visa.

At the time this book went to press, most USCIS offices were scheduling adjustment of status interviews within five months of when the application was filed. For the most up-to-date information on how long you can expect to wait for an interview, go to www.uscis.gov, and in the box on the left-hand side, under "Find," click "Processing Times." You will have to click "Processing Times" on the next pages, too. That will take you to the page that allows you to select your local USCIS office and click on the "Field Office Processing Dates" button to get updated information on how long your local office is taking to interview people on the applications listed.

B. The Marriage-Based Visa Option

The second option is for you to get married outside of the United States, before applying for any visa. In that case you would be eligible to apply for either an immigrant visa or a nonimmigrant, K-3 visa (a hybrid version of the fiancé visa adapted for use by married couples) as the immediate relative of your U.S. citizen spouse. If you need to review whether you would be eligible for a marriage-based immigrant visa, see Chapter 2, Section B.

You would use your immigrant visa to enter the United States and become a U.S. resident immediately. Alternately, you would use your nonimmigrant, K-3 visa to enter the United States, but you wouldn't be a permanent resident yet— you would be expected to complete the process by applying for adjustment of status in the United States. (The point of the K-3 was supposed to be to get applicants into the U.S. faster than with an immigrant visa, but lately it hasn't been working this way, because USCIS has been taking so long to approve the fiancé visa petition that starts off the process.)

There are no quotas or limits on the number of people who can obtain visas or green cards through marriage to a U.S. citizen. A marriage-based immigrant visa usually takes around one year to obtain. Although the procedural steps are very similar to those for obtaining a traditional, K-1 fiancé visa, the application itself is somewhat more demanding.

A nonimmigrant, K-3 visa can also take up to a year to obtain. However, finishing up the process in the United States (getting approved for a green card) adds another several months to the process.

C. The Tourist Visa Option

A third option is available to fiancés who want to hold their marriage ceremony in the United States, but do not wish to live there after the ceremony. They can apply for a tourist visa at a local U.S. consulate. A tourist visa usually takes between a few days and ten weeks to obtain. However, using a tourist visa carries certain risks, primarily the possibility of being denied entry at the U.S. border. These risks are explained more fully in Section E, below.

D. Choosing Among the Visa Options

Your choice of visa may be based simply on where you wish to hold your wedding.

- If your heart is set on marrying in the United States and remaining there, a fiancé visa is probably the most appropriate.
- If you would like to marry in the United States and return to your home country to live, either a fiancé visa or a tourist visa would be appropriate.
- If you would like to be married in your own country, or at least get the wedding out of the way before you embark on your immigration

process, the marriage-based nonimmigrant K-3 visa option might be the one for you.

- If you want to get married in your home country, and want to enter the U.S. as a permanent resident, then a marriage-based immigrant visa should suit you well.

1. Immigrant Visas Can Take the Longest to Get

Of all your visa options permitting you U.S. entry, you'll probably wait longest for a marriage-based immigrant visa, because it represents the completion of your quest for permanent residence. Accordingly, the consular officers who decide your immigrant visa will have to review more than one set of paperwork, and you will have to go through various procedural hoops, before the visa can be approved.

By contrast, both of your nonimmigrant visa possibilities—the K-1 fiancé visa and the K-3 adapted fiancé visa for married couples—are considered short-term visas. That means that they have fewer requirements than the marriage-based immigrant visa. Accordingly, there are fewer opportunities for a consular officer to delay your application for more information.

Short-term visas also have fewer consequences for the U.S. government—the K-1 visa has a 90-day limit, the K-3 visa has a ten-year limit, and neither visa guarantees that you'll be approved for a green card. USCIS and the consulates know that they'll get a second look at you if and when you apply for the actual green card.

This doesn't mean that K-1 or K-3 fiancé visas are given out like free candy—in fact, the internal rules tell consular officers to give both types of fiancé visa applications almost as hard a look as marriage-based immigrant visa applications. Nevertheless, most attorneys find that USCIS and the consulates make smoother and quicker decisions on K-1 and K-3 fiancé, as opposed to marriage-based immigrant, visa applications.

At the time this book went to print, the initial visa petitions that start the process on all of these types of cases—the Form I-130 for people who will enter the U.S. as permanent residents, and the Form 1-129F for people who will enter on either the K-1 or the K-3 visa—were all being processed by USCIS within approximately five months. Once USCIS has forwarded the petition to the consulate, however, people with nonimmigrant petitions—K-1s and K-2s—are often interviewed more quickly and are able to enter the U.S. sooner than those who will be entering as permanent residents.

In sum, if you plan to remain in the United States permanently and your main consideration is which visa will get you into the United States the fastest, the traditional K-1 fiancé visa may be your best bet.

> **CAUTION**
>
> **If you have children between the ages of 18 and 21 who are not the natural children or stepchildren of your U.S. spouse-to-be, choose a fiancé visa (K-1 or K-3).** Due to a strange twist in the immigration laws, children under 21 can accompany a fiancé on their visa, but only children whose parents married while they were under 18 can qualify as stepchildren for purposes of getting an immigrant visa.

2. Fiancé Visa Applications Require Less Financial Support Information

The biggest difference between the nonimmigrant fiancé and immigrant marriage visa applications concerns your fiancé's ability to support you financially. Although fiancé applicants as well as marriage visa applicants must both prove that they'll be supported in the United States, fiancés usually do so using the Form I-134 Affidavit of Support. Form I-134 is fairly simple to prepare and is not considered legally binding—even if the government took you (the sponsor) to court to enforce it, it would probably lose.

By contrast, if you were applying for a marriage-based immigrant visa, your spouse would definitely have to submit an Affidavit of Support on Form

I-864. This form is several pages long, demands detailed financial information, and is legally binding. The U.S. government takes it seriously and scrutinizes it carefully. Problems with Form I-864 are a frequent cause of delays in approving immigrant visas. If you apply for a fiancé visa, you can probably (depending on the consulate where you live) avoid submitting the Form I-864 until you are already in the United States (where it will be a required part of your green card application). Chapter 3 contains detailed explanations of the workings of Form I-864.

3. Fiancé Visas Involve More Paperwork and Expense

If your primary concern is how much paperwork you'll have to deal with, you should know that getting a K-1 or K-3 fiancé visa adds an extra step to the green card application process compared to a marriage-based immigrant visa application. Even after you've gotten the fiancé visa and entered the United States, you'll have to prepare and submit another heavy round of paperwork for a green card, as much as if you'd just gotten married in the first place and applied for an immigrant visa through the U.S. consulate. And the green card application in the United States will probably take another four or five months to be approved.

Another concern is money. With both K-1 and K-3 visas, you'll finish the process by adjusting status in the United States—where the fees are much higher than if you were doing everything overseas. The difference is currently greater than $500 per person.

4. Problems Are Easier to Resolve With Fiancé Visas

Once an application gets postponed overseas, things get difficult—neither your fiancé nor any lawyer whom you hire is going to have an easy time reaching the consular officials. The officials can get away with some fairly arbitrary behavior because of their isolation. This could, of course, also happen with your fiancé visa application, but because the process is shorter and easier, the chances are less.

Next Step	
You want to get a K-1 fiancé visa and marry in the U.S.:	Continue on to Section F, below.
You want a tourist visa to hold a wedding in the United States and then return home:	Read Section E, below.
You want to get married overseas and apply for an immigrant visa or a K-3 nonimmigrant "fiancé" visa:	See Chapter 7.

E. How to Use a Tourist Visa

If you want only to get married in the United States—but not live there—you can apply for a visitor or tourist visa, known as a B-2 visa. The application process is probably the easiest and fastest in the immigration law world. However, it carries certain risks.

First, there is the risk that you may unwittingly get the visa under false pretenses. You must make sure to tell the consular officer that you intend to use the visa in order to get married to a U.S. citizen. Otherwise, USCIS may later claim that you obtained the visa through fraud (pretending to be "only" a tourist), which can prevent you from getting a green card if you want one later.

Second, you could face problems at the U.S. border when you enter. Even after you've convinced the consular officer that your intention after marrying is to return to your home country, you'll still have to convince the U.S. border official. If you get a reasonable official, this should be no problem—your use of a tourist visa is perfectly legal. If you get an official who is inclined to be suspicious, however, it's another matter. The border officials can keep you out if they think you've used fraud to obtain the visa, such as having lied about your intentions to return home after the wedding. Once you've been removed this way, you may be prevented from reentering the United States for five years. The border officials have reason to be suspicious, since many people have used tourist visas as a way to enter the United States precisely for the purpose of applying for a green card there.

To prepare for the possibility of meeting a skeptical border official, you can bring along some of the following to demonstrate your plan to return home (these are the same things you would have shown the consular officer in order to get the visitor visa):

- a copy of your lease or rental agreement
- a letter from your employer stating that you are expected back by a certain date, and
- copies of birth certificates from close family members remaining behind.

Also make sure there is nothing in your luggage to contradict this evidence. If your luggage is searched and the official realizes you are carrying enough prescription medication for a three-year stay and a letter from your fiancé saying, "Can't wait until you are here and we can settle down in our new house," you will find yourself on the next return plane.

We can't decide for you whether it's better to use a tourist or a fiancé visa if you're only coming to the United States to hold your wedding and then leave. If you don't like risk, and the cost of your plane ticket is high or will wipe out your savings, the fiancé visa might be more appropriate for you. With a fiancé visa, the border officer doesn't have to worry about whether your secret intention is to remain in the United States and apply for a green card, because you would have every right, under the fiancé visa, to do just that. On the other hand, the fiancé visa takes much longer to get, and there is no way to remove every element of risk. Even with a fiancé visa, your entry to the United States depends on the perception and decision of a single border patrol official. It's as simple as that.

F. The K-1 Fiancé Visa Application Process

If you are reading this section, it means that you are not married yet and have decided that you want, and are eligible for, a fiancé visa. Let's get to the nuts and bolts of the fiancé visa application process—and what nuts and bolts they are. The amount of paperwork and the number of forms and appointments that you'll have to deal with can be daunting, bewildering, and frustrating. But countless other immigrants have made it through, and so can you.

 TIP

Don't be discouraged by mounds of paperwork—but do get it right. Read Chapter 4 on how to organize yourself to make sure you keep good track of the paperwork involved in the visa process. This chapter also gives detailed instructions on how to enter the requested information.

Obtaining a K-1 fiancé visa involves three major steps:

Step 1: Your U.S. citizen fiancé submits a fiancé visa petition to USCIS.

Step 2: Your approval is sent to the National Visa Center (NVC) which advises you which consulate it's forwarding your case to, and

Step 3: You fill out forms and present them to a U.S. consulate in your home country, where you attend an interview and receive your visa.

In rare instances, some couples have to attend a fraud interview if the government has doubts about their intended marriage being the real thing. This could happen either as part of Step One or after Step Three.

Below we describe, in detail, what happens at each of these steps.

Stay Put During the Application Process

Once this process has started, you're better off if you don't change addresses or take any long trips. USCIS or the consulate could send you a request for more information or call you in for your interview at any time. Missing such a notification could result in long delays in getting your visa application back on track.

If you do change addresses, be sure to notify the last USCIS or consular office you heard from. But don't assume they'll pay attention. USCIS and the consulates are notorious for losing change-of-address notifications. So, as a backup plan, have your mail forwarded or check in regularly with the new people living in your former home.

Many couples wish that they could take a quick trip to the United States while waiting for the fiancé visa to be granted. Unfortunately, once you've submitted any part of your fiancé visa application, you're unlikely to be granted a tourist visa. This is because the consulate will likely believe that your real intention in using the tourist visa is to get married and then apply for your green card in the United States, which is an inappropriate use of the tourist visa and could be considered visa fraud.

1. Step One: The Initial Fiancé Visa Petition

The first person that the U.S. government wants to hear from in this process is your U.S. citizen fiancé. He or she will be responsible for preparing what's called a fiancé visa petition. The purpose of this petition is to alert the immigration authorities that your fiancé is planning to marry you and that he or she is willing to participate in your visa application. You play a minor role at this step, but you should help your fiancé gather certain information and documents.

We'll go through how to prepare and assemble the various forms and documents, one by one. To keep track of them all, refer to the Fiancé Visa Petition Checklist, below. A few items on this checklist are self-explanatory, so they aren't discussed in the following text.

a. Line-by-Line Instructions for K-1 Fiancé Visa Petition Forms

This section will give you precise instructions for filling out the forms that are listed on the Fiancé Visa Petition Checklist in Section 2. Your U.S. citizen fiancé should be handling the original forms and paperwork, but should send you copies of the drafts to review and discuss. Whoever reads these instructions should also have a copy of the appropriate form in hand. Refer to Chapter 4 if you need to refresh your understanding of how to print and manually fill out an immigration form.

 CAUTION

Don't confuse your forms. Form I-129F is the proper one to use for a fiancé visa petition. There is another USCIS form called simply I-129, without the letter F. It is completely different (and much longer), so don't confuse the two or you'll be sorry!

i. Form I-129F

 WEB RESOURCE

This form is available on the USCIS website at www.uscis.gov. A sample filled-in version of this form is shown below.

The first thing to notice about Form I-129F is that it runs in two columns. The left column, or Section A, asks for information about the U.S. citizen fiancé. The right column asks for information about you, the immigrating fiancé.

Part A

Question 1: The U.S. citizen fiancé must enter his/her last name (surname) in all capital letters, but the other name(s) in small letters. For example, if your fiancé's name is Sam Lawrence Cole, he would enter "COLE" in the first box, "Sam" in the second box, and "Lawrence" in the third box. Always spell out the entire middle name.

Sample Form I-129F, Petition for Alien Fiancé(e)—Page 1

OMB No. 1615-0001; Expires 02/29/2012

Department of Homeland Security
U.S. Citizenship and Immigration Services

**I-129F, Petition
for Alien Fiancé(e)**

Do not write in these blocks.   **For USCIS Use Only**

Case ID #	Action Block	Fee Stamp
A #		
G-28 #		

The petition is approved for status under Section 101(a)(5)(k). It is valid for four months from the date of action. _____

AMCON: _____

☐ Personal Interview   ☐ Previously Forwarded

☐ Document Check   ☐ Field Investigation

Remarks:

Part A. Start Here. Information about you.

1. Name *(Family name in CAPS)* *(First)* *(Middle)*

BEACH   Sandra   Leah

2. Address *(Number and Street)*   **Apt. #**

114 Fulton St.   6E

(Town or City) *(State or Country)* *(Zip/Postal Code)*

New York   New York   10038

3. Place of Birth *(Town or City)*   *(State/Country)*

Horseheads   New York

4. Date of Birth *(mm/dd/yyyy)*   **5. Gender**

12/20/1986   ☐ Male ☒ Female

6. Marital Status

☐ Married ☒ Single ☐ Widowed ☐ Divorced

7. Other Names Used *(including maiden name)*

None

8a. U.S. Social Security Number   **8b. A# *(if any)***

123-45-6789

9. Names of Prior Spouses   **Date(s) Marriage(s) Ended**

None   n/a

10. My citizenship was acquired through *(check one)*

☒ Birth in the U.S.   ☐ Naturalization

Give number of certificate, date and place it was issued.

☐ Parents

Have you obtained a certificate of citizenship in your name?

☐ Yes   ☐ No

If "Yes," give certificate number, date and place it was issued.

11. Have you ever filed for this or any other alien fiancé(e) or husband/wife before?

☐ Yes   ☒ No

If "Yes," give name of all aliens, place and date of filing, A# and result. *(Attached additional sheets as necessary.)*

Part B. Information about your alien fiancé(e).

1. Name *(Family name in CAPS)* *(First)* *(Middle)*

Hollis   Nigel   Ian

2. Address *(Number and Street)*   **Apt. #**

123 Limestone Way   7

(Town or City) *(State or Country)* *(Zip/Postal Code)*

Penzance   U.K.   TR197NL

3a. Place of Birth *(Town or City)*   *(State/Country)*

Port Navas   U.K.

3b. Country of Citizenship

U.K.

4. Date of Birth *(mm/dd/yyyy)*   **5. Gender**

8/17/1984   ☒ Male ☐ Female

6. Marital Status

☐ Married ☐ Single ☐ Widowed ☒ Divorced

7. Other Names Used *(including maiden name)*

None

8. U.S. Social Security #   **9. A# *(if any)***

n/a

10. Names of Prior Spouses   **Date(s) Marriage(s) Ended**

Jane Simpson   5/20/2010

11. Has your fiancé(e) ever been in the U.S.?

☒ Yes   ☐ No

12. If your fiancé(e) is currently in the U.S., complete the following:

He or she last arrived as a: *(visitor, student, exchange alien, crewman, stowaway, temporary worker, without inspection, etc.)*

Arrival/Departure Record (I-94) Number

☐☐☐ — ☐☐☐☐☐☐☐☐

Date of Arrival *(mm/dd/yy)*

Date authorized stay expired, or will expire as shown on I-94 or I-95

INITIAL RECEIPT	RESUBMITTED	RELOCATED: Rec'd.	Sent	COMPLETED: Appv'd.	Denied	Ret'd.

Form I-129F (Rev. 11/23/10) Y

Sample Form I-129F, Petition for Alien Fiancé(e)—Page 2

Part B. Information about your alien fiancé(e). *(Continued.)*

13. List all children of your alien fiancé(e) *(if any)*

Name *(First/Middle/Last)*	Date of Birth *(mm/dd/yyyy)*	Country of Birth	Present Address
None			

14. Address in the United States where your fiancé(e) intends to live.

(Number and Street)	(Town or City)	(State)
114 Fulton St.	New York	NY

15. Your fiancé(e)'s address abroad.

(Number and Street)	(Town or City)	(State or Province)
123 Limestone Way	Penzance	Cornwall

(Country)	(Phone Number; Include Country, City and Area Codes)
U.K.	1234 123456

16. If your fiancé(e)'s native alphabet uses other than Roman letters, write his or her name and address abroad in the native alphabet.

(Name)	(Number and Street)
n/a	

(Town or City)	(State or Province)	(Country)

17. Is your fiancé(e) related to you? ☐ Yes ☒ No

If you are related, state the nature and degree of relationship, e.g., third cousin or maternal uncle, etc.

18. Has your fiancé(e) met and seen you within the two-year period immediately preceding the filing of this petition?

☒ Yes ☐ No

Describe the circumstances under which you met. If you have not personally met each other, explain how the relationship was established. If you met your fiancé(e) or spouse though an international marriage broker, please explain those circumstances in Question 19 below. Explain also in detail any reasons you may have for requesting that the requirement that you and your fiancé(e) must have met should not apply to you.

See attached statement.

19. Did you meet your fiancé(e) or spouse through the services of an international marriage broker?

☐ Yes ☒ No

If you answered yes, please provide the name and any contact information you may have (including internet or street address) of the international marriage broker and where the international marriage broker is located. Attach additional sheets of paper if necessary.

20. Your fiancé(e) will apply for a visa abroad at the American embassy or consulate at:

(City)	(Country)
London	England

NOTE: (Designation of a U.S. embassy or consulate outside the country of your fiancé(e)'s last residence does not guarantee acceptance for processing by that foreign post. Acceptance is at the discretion of the designated embassy or consulate.)

Sample Form I-129F, Petition for Alien Fiancé(e)—Page 3

Part C. Other information.

1. If you are serving overseas in the Armed Forces of the United States, please answer the following:

I presently reside or am stationed overseas and my current mailing address is:

2. Have you ever been convicted by a court of law (civil or criminal) or court martialed by a military tribunal for any of the following crimes:

- Domestic violence, sexual assault, child abuse and neglect, dating violence, elder abuse or stalking. (Please refer to page 3 of the instructions for the full definition of the term "domestic violence.)

- Homicide, murder, manslaughter, rape, abusive sexual contact, sexual exploitation, incest, torture, trafficking, peonage, holding hostage, involuntary servitude, slave trade, kidnapping, abduction, unlawful criminal restraint, false imprisonment or an attempt to commit any of these crimes, or

- Three or more convictions for crimes relating to a controlled substance or alcohol not arising from a single act.

☐ Yes   ☐ No

Answering this question is required even if your records were sealed or otherwise cleared or if anyone, including a judge, law enforcement officer, or attorney, told you that you no longer have a record. Using a separate sheet(s) of paper, attach information relating to the conviction(s), such as crime involved, date of conviction and sentence.

3. If you have provided information about a conviction for a crime listed above and you were being battered or subjected to extreme cruelty by your spouse, parent, or adult child at the time of your conviction, check all of the following that apply to you:

☐ I was acting in self-defense.

☐ I violated a protection order issued for my own protection.

☐ I committed, was arrested for, was convicted of, or plead guilty to committing a crime that did not result in serious bodily injury, and there was a connection between the crime committed and my having been battered or subjected to extreme cruelty.

Part D. Penalties, certification and petitioner's signature.

PENALTIES: You may by law be imprisoned for not more than five years, or fined $250,000, or both, for entering into a marriage contract for the purpose of evading any provision of the immigration laws, and you may be fined up to $10,000 or imprisoned up to five years, or both, for knowingly and willfully falsifying or concealing a material fact or using any false document in submitting this petition.

YOUR CERTIFICATION: I am legally able to and intend to marry my alien fiancé(e) within 90 days of his or her arrival in the United States. I certify, under penalty of perjury under the laws of the United States of America, that the foregoing is true and correct. Furthermore, I authorize the release of any information from my records that U.S. Citizenship and Immigration Services needs to determine eligibility for the benefit that I am seeking.

Moreover, I understand that this petition, including any criminal conviction information that I am required to provide with this petition, as well as any related criminal background information pertaining to me that U.S. Citizenship and Immigration Services may discover independently in adjudicating this petition will be disclosed to the beneficiary of this petition.

Signature	Date *(mm/dd/yyyy)*	Daytime Telephone Number *(with area code)*
Sandra Leah Beach	8/2/2012	212-555-1212

E-Mail Address (if any)

Part E. Signature of person preparing form, if other than above. *(Sign below.)*

I declare that I prepared this application at the request of the petitioner and it is based on all information of which I have knowledge.

Signature	Print or Type Your Name	G-28 ID Number	Date *(mm/dd/yyyy)*

Firm Name and Address	Daytime Telephone Number *(with area code)*
	E-Mail Address (if any)

Sample Fiancé Meeting Statement—Attachment to Form I-129F

FILED BY SANDRA BEACH ON BEHALF OF NIGEL HOLLIS

QUESTION 18

I met my fiancé 18 months ago, while visiting a college friend who has settled in England. My friend Carrie had been telling me for months that she wanted to introduce me to Nigel, because of our offbeat senses of humor and shared interest in long-distance swimming. I've had bad experiences with friends trying to set me up before, so I didn't take it very seriously. But when vacation plans took me to England, I let her arrange for me and Nigel to meet over lunch at a pub.

To my amazement, we clicked right away. We had a lot to talk about—he had completed an English Channel swim a few months before, and I'm hoping to swim the Channel next year. Both of us have built our lives around swimming, which sometimes leaves little time for other things, including relationships. We compared notes on training techniques, equipment, dealing with cold water, rip tides, and more.

Our lunch lasted all afternoon and into the evening. By the end of that evening, I considered Nigel a friend, and someone I could very easily fall in love with.

Nigel and I spent almost all my remaining week's vacation together. Poor Carrie joked that her plan had backfired, because I spent embarrassingly little time at her house. By the end of the week, we both knew this was headed toward a serious relationship.

Since then, Nigel and I have corresponded almost constantly by email, and call each other twice a week. During one long phone call, we decided to get married.

It was difficult deciding where we would live after marrying—Nigel has a beautiful cottage in Cornwall, and I could happily live in England. However, my mother is in poor health, and ever since my father passed away last year, she has relied on my help, so we agreed to make our home in New York.

As proof that Nigel and I are in love and plan to marry, I am attaching copies of his plane tickets to New York; photos of the two of us together; copies of our telephone bills and some of our emails; copies of catering and other contracts showing that the two of us plan to marry in July; and copies of our travel itinerary for New Zealand, where we will honeymoon.

Signed: *Sandra Leah Beach*
Sandra Beach

Date: 8/2/2012

Questions 2-5: Self-explanatory.

Question 6: Check only one box, and make sure it is not the one that says "married." At the moment, you can't be already married and use a K-1 fiancé visa.

Question 7: Don't let the phrase "including maiden name" throw you. (A maiden name is the woman's name before marriage; in many cultures, she takes the husband's name upon marrying.) You shouldn't yet be married to one another. (If you are married, you don't qualify for a K-1 fiancé visa and should instead be applying for a K-3 visa or an immigrant visa as an immediate relative (spouse). See Chapter 7.) But if the U.S. citizen fiancé has had other names by previous marriages, include these here.

Question 8: Self-explanatory.

Question 9: There's a reason for these questions: The U.S. citizen fiancé's prior marriages must have ended before he/she is eligible to sponsor you. Make sure that under **Date(s) Marriage(s) Ended** he or she gives the date the divorce became final, not the date they split up housekeeping. USCIS will only accept a final divorce as proof that the marriage ended.

Question 10: If the U.S. citizen fiancé's citizenship was obtained through naturalization, the number can be found at the top right-hand side of the naturalization certificate. The date and place issued are also shown on the certificate.

Question 11: If the U.S. citizen has tried to or succeeded in sponsoring other fiancés, USCIS will surely take a look at those files to make sure there was no fraud involved. There's nothing automatic about their decision—after all, it's possible for a U.S. citizen to fall in love with more than one foreign-born person, and for the first marriage to end. But there are U.S. citizens who charge money to marry and sponsor noncitizens, and USCIS is on the lookout for them.

Part B:

Now we're back to you, the fiancé.

Questions 1-5: Self-explanatory.

Question 6: Check only one box, and make sure it is not the one that says "married."

Question 7: See explanation, Part A, Question 7.

Question 8: You won't have a Social Security number unless you have lived in the United States; insert "N/A" if you don't have one.

Question 9: The Alien Registration Number or A-Number is an eight- or nine-digit number following the letter "A" (for "Alien") that USCIS (or the former INS) assigns to you. You won't have one yet unless you've previously applied for permanent or in some cases temporary residency, or have been in deportation/removal proceedings. If you have a number, you must enter it here.

SEE AN EXPERT

If your previous application was denied because you were inadmissible, or if you lied on that application, call a lawyer before going any further. See Chapter 17 for tips on finding a good attorney.

Questions 10 and 11: These questions relate to the eligibility requirement that previous marriages must have ended through valid means such as divorce or death. See explanation of eligibility in Chapter 2, Section B.

Question 12: You can enter "N/A" here, since you are not in the United States.

Question 13: This refers to all your children, whether born of this relationship or a previous one.

Question 14: Hopefully your intended address in the United States is the same as that of your U.S. citizen fiancé, or USCIS will raise questions. Even if you will spend some time away from your married home, such as for school or work, you should consider your married home to be your permanent address. If there is a compelling reason that you will have a completely separate residence, attach documents to explain why, or consult with a lawyer.

Question 15: Self-explanatory.

Question 16: If your native language uses a non-Roman script (for example, Russian, Chinese, or Arabic) you'll need to write your name and address in that script.

Question 17: If you and your fiancé are related by blood, you'll need to make sure that a marriage between you is allowed in the state (geographical) where you plan to marry. (See Chapter 2, Section B1, "The Legal Requirements for a K-1 Fiancé Visa.")

Question 18: You'll need to attach a page to fully answer this question; see our sample Fiancé Meeting Statement, above. Note that this is also where you'd need to explain any reason why you need a waiver of the personal meeting requirement. Although the main purpose is to show that you've fulfilled the personal meeting requirement, it's a fine opportunity to include extra detail about your life with your fiancé to show USCIS that this is a real relationship. You don't need to sound like a lawyer, but should provide enough personal detail that USCIS sees that you didn't just get a sample statement out of a book!

Question 19: This is a new question, a result of recent concern by Congress that so-called "mail-order" spouses (who meet through the services of an international matchmaking agency) are especially susceptible to domestic violence and abuse. In response, Congress passed the International Marriage Brokers Regulation Act of 2005 (IMBRA). IMBRA requires you to state here whether you met your fiancé or spouse through an international marriage broker, and if so, to give information about the broker.

Question 20: Enter the name of the U.S. consulate with a visa processing office in your country; or if none exists, the one with power to handle visa requests from your country. (Don't worry too much about getting it wrong; the USCIS Service Center will redirect your application for you when it approves the petition.) Also write "Please Cable" in this section, as an effort to speed up the Service Center's notification of the consulate after your petition is approved.

Part C:

Now the questions once again refer to the U.S. citizen petitioner.

Question 1: Self-explanatory.

Questions 2-3: If the U.S. citizen petitioner has a history of violent crime, crime relating to alcohol, or controlled substance abuse, he or she may be

required to reveal this to USCIS. The petitioner should see an attorney if there is any question about whether this section applies. You will also be told of any relevant history.

Part D:

The U.S. citizen needs to sign and date the forms under the paragraph that starts **Your Certification**.

Part E:

Signature of person preparing form if other than above: This need not be filled in if you just got a little help from a friend. This line is mainly for lawyers or agencies who fill out these forms on others' behalf.

ii.   Form G-325A

The government can use the information you supply on this form to check your background (although it's unclear whether they consistently do so). This form is single-sided.

You and your fiancé each need to fill out a Form G-325A. Your fiancé must submit a single copy, but you must submit four exact copies.

Most of the form is self-explanatory. If you really can't remember or don't know an exact date, enter whatever you can remember, such as the year. Alternately, you can simply say "unknown," but if you overuse the "unknowns," USCIS may return your entire application for another try. Since the questions aren't numbered, we refer to them by the approximate line.

    WEB RESOURCE
This form is available on the USCIS website at www.uscis.gov. Below is a sample filled-in version of this form.

Lines 1, 2 (Family Name, etc.): Self-explanatory.
Line 3 (Father/Mother): Self-explanatory.
Line 4 (Husband or Wife): Self-explanatory.
Line 5 (Former Husbands or Wives): Make sure to fill this in. The date of "termination" could be either the date of divorce, annulment, or death.
Line 6 (Applicant's residence last five years): Be careful here—these need to be in reverse

Sample Form G-325-A, Biographic Information

OMB No. 1615-0008; Expires 08/31/2012

Department of Homeland Security
U.S. Citizenship and Immigration Services

G-325A, Biographic Information

(Family Name)	(First Name)	(Middle Name)	☒ Male ☐ Female	Date of Birth (mm/dd/yyyy)	Citizenship/Nationality	File Number
Hollis	Nigel	Ian		8/17/1984	U.K.	A

All Other Names Used (include names by previous marriages)	City and Country of Birth	U.S. Social Security # (if any)
None	Penzance, U.K.	N/A

	Family Name	First Name	Date of Birth (mm/dd/yyyy)	City, and Country of Birth (if known)	City and Country of Residence
Father	Hollis	Kevin	1/12/1957	York, U.K.	York, U.K.
Mother (Maiden Name)	Chumley	Sarah	4/7/1961	York, U.K.	York, U.K.

Current Husband or Wife (If none, so state) Family Name (For wife, give maiden name)	First Name	Date of Birth (mm/dd/yyyy)	City and Country of Birth	Date of Marriage	Place of Marriage
None					

Former Husbands or Wives (If none, so state) Family Name (For wife, give maiden name)	First Name	Date of Birth (mm/dd/yyyy)	Date and Place of Marriage	Date and Place of Termination of Marriage
Simpson	Jane	10/31/1985	6/10/2006 London	5/20/2010 Penzance

Applicant's residence last five years. List present address first.

Street and Number	City	Province or State	Country	From Month	From Year	To Month	To Year
123 Limestone #7	Penzance	Cornwall	U.K.	7	2001	Present Time	

Applicant's last address outside the United States of more than 1 year.

Street and Number	City	Province or State	Country	From Month	From Year	To Month	To Year
N/A							

Applicant's employment last five years. (If none, so state.) List present employment first.

Full Name and Address of Employer	Occupation (Specify)	From Month	From Year	To Month	To Year
Outbound Design, Inc., 222 Heather Lane, Penzance, U.K. TR198NL	Sportswear Designer	8	2004	Present Time	
Fish & Chips Shop, 3 Bolford Street, Cambridge, U.K. CB4 2JQ	Fryer	9	2003	6	2004

Last occupation abroad if not shown above. (Include all information requested above.)

N/A			

This form is submitted in connection with an application for:	Signature of Applicant	Date
☐ Naturalization ☒ Other (Specify): Fiancé Visa ☐ Status as Permanent Resident	*Nigel I. Hollis*	08/03/2012

If your native alphabet is in other than Roman letters, write your name in your native alphabet below:

Penalties: Severe penalties are provided by law for knowingly and willfully falsifying or concealing a material fact.

Applicant: Print your name and Alien Registration Number in the box outlined by heavy border below.

Complete This Box (Family Name)	(Given Name)	(Middle Name)	(Alien Registration Number)
HOLLIS	Nigel	Ian	A

Form G-325A (Rev. 08/08/11) Y

chronological order, starting with your most recent address and working your way down the last five years. For example, if you live in Beijing now but lived in Xian before, your Beijing address would go on the top line. Practice this on another sheet of paper before you enter the information here.

Line 7 (Applicant's last address outside the United States of more than one year): This may overlap with one of the addresses in Line 6—that's okay.

Line 8 (Applicant's employment last five years): Again, be careful to put this in reverse chronological order. If you've been unemployed, self-employed, or were a housewife or house-husband, say so here—in other words, try to account for all of the five years. If you have worked illegally in the United States, you will need to identify your employers. In our experience, this doesn't cause USCIS to go after the employers.

 SEE AN EXPERT
Use of false documents is a ground of inadmissibility. If you used false documents, such as a fake green card or Social Security card, to work illegally in the United States or to receive any other kind of benefit, see a lawyer.

Line 9 (Show below last occupation abroad if not shown above): People tend to overlook this line—you shouldn't.

Line 10 (This form is submitted in connection with application for): The U.S. citizen should check "other," and write "in support of spouse's I-129F"; you should also check "other" and write "Fiancé Visa Application."

Line 11 (If your native alphabet uses non-Roman letters): Self-explanatory.

Line 12 (The large box): Self-explanatory.

b. Documents That Must Accompany Your Fiancé Visa Petition

You need to do more than just fill in the blanks for your fiancé visa petition. The government wants additional written proof of two issues—that the two of you have met in person within the last two years, and that you really intend to marry. This section contains detailed instructions about how you can satisfy these requirements. It also describes some of the miscellaneous requirements, such as photos and fees.

i. Proof That You Have Met in Person or Qualify for an Exception

If you and your fiancé have met in person, look for documents that will illustrate your meetings. Documents from a neutral, outside source such as an airline or landlord are best. Some possibilities are:

- dated photos of you together (if your camera doesn't put an electronic date on the photo, write it on the back, and also write where you were)
- copies of plane tickets (including boarding passes) that you used to meet each other
- copies of your passports showing the stamps from when you traveled to see each other, and
- credit card receipts showing that you spent money at the same place and same time.

If you and your fiancé have not met in person, include documentation that will prove that this was for religious or medical reasons, such as

- a letter from your parents
- a letter from your religious guide
- a detailed letter from a medical professional, and
- copies of relevant medical records.

ii. Additional Proof That You Intend to Marry

Now that you've found a way to prove that you and your fiancé have met, you need to go one step further and show that you plan to marry. Some possible documents to gather are:
- copies of cards and letters between you discussing your marriage plans (it's okay to block out the most intimate sections)
- copies of phone bills showing that you called each other
- wedding announcements, and
- evidence of other wedding arrangements (such as a letter from the religious leader or justice

of the peace who will perform the ceremony, contracts for catering, photography, rented chairs, dishes, or other equipment, flowers, and musical entertainment).

iii. Proof That You're Legally Able to Marry

If you're an adult who's never been previously married and you're not a blood relative of your fiancé, and your fiancé hasn't been previously married, you may not have to attach any documents under this category. See Chapter 2, Section B, for details. In many couples, however, one of the two people has been previously married, in which case you will need to prove that that marriage was legally ended. To do so, attach copies of such documents as:

- divorce decree
- annulment decree, or
- death certificate.

iv. Additional Items to Accompany Fiancé Visa Petition

In addition, your Fiancé Visa Petition will need to include the following:

- **Proof of the U.S. citizenship status of your petitioning spouse.** Depending on how your spouse became a citizen, this might include a copy of a birth certificate, passport, certificate of naturalization, certificate of citizenship, or Form FS-20 (Report of Birth Abroad of a U.S. Citizen).
- **Photos.** You must submit one passport-style color photograph of yourself and one passport-style color photograph of your fiancé, two by two inches in size, showing your current appearance. Both photos must have been taken within 30 days of the date of filing the petition. The photos must have a white background, be glossy, unretouched, and not mounted. Passport style means that the photo shows your full face from the front, with a plain white or off-white background—and your face must measure between one inch and 1⅜ inches from the bottom of your chin to the top of your head. For more information,

see the State Department website at http://travel.state.gov (under "Visas for Foreign Citizens," click "more," then in the box on the left side of the page, click on "A–Z Subject Index," then go to "Photo Requirements" under letter "P" and scroll down to "Nonimmigrant Visas"). However, USCIS regulations permit you to submit a photo that doesn't completely follow the instructions if you live in a country where such photographs are unavailable or are cost prohibitive.

- **Fee.** The 2012 fee for an I-129F visa petition for a K-1 visa is $340. However, USCIS fees go up fairly regularly, so double-check them at www.uscis.gov or by calling 800-375-5283. Make checks or money orders payable to U.S. Department of Homeland Security (don't send cash).

v. Document Requirements If U.S. Citizen Has a Criminal Record

If the U.S. citizen petitioner has ever been convicted of any violent crime, sexual assault, or a crime involving domestic violence or substance abuse (a more complete list of crimes is provided in the instructions to Form I-129F), he or she must submit certified copies of all police and court records showing the outcome. This is required even if the records were sealed or otherwise cleared. All of this information (except for victim's names) will be passed on to the immigrant during the consular interview. Get a lawyer's help in this instance.

vi. Waiver Request If U.S. Citizen Has Filed Previous I-129fs

To prevent abuse of immigrants, the law limits the number of times a U.S. citizen can petition for a K-1 (but not a K-3) fiancé. If the U.S. citizen has filed two or more K-1 visa petitions for other immigrants in the past (no matter how long ago), or had a K-1 visa petition approved for another immigrant within the two years before filing your petition, the U.S. citizen must request a waiver (official forgiveness) from USCIS.

To succeed with the waiver request, your best bet is to show unusual circumstances, such as the death (by natural causes, of course) of the prior immigrant. If the U.S. citizen has a history of violent crime, the waiver will be denied.

The procedure for requesting a waiver is to attach a signed and dated letter to Form I-129F, along with any supporting evidence. However, we strongly recommend getting a lawyer's help with your waiver request.

c. Where to Send the Fiancé Visa Petition

When your U.S. citizen fiancé has finished the Fiancé Visa Petition, the next step is to send it to the USCIS Dallas Lockbox Facility. The address will be the same whether your U.S. citizen fiancé resides in the United States or abroad.

If sending the petition by the U.S. Postal Service, the address is:

USCIS
Attn: I-129F
P.O. Box 660151
Dallas, TX 75266

If sending the petition by express mail or a courier service, the address is:

USCIS
Attn: I-129F
2501 South State Highway 121 Business
Suite 400
Lewisville, TX 75067

Appendix B also contains a handy chart with these addresses.

Your U.S. citizen fiancé should also photocopy and send a copy of the Fiancé Visa Petition to you. File it carefully with your other records and familiarize yourself with the answers so you'll be prepared to explain anything on it during your upcoming visa interview.

d. What Will Happen After Sending in the Fiancé Visa Petition

A few weeks after sending in the Fiancé Visa Petition, the USCIS Service Center should mail your U.S. citizen fiancé a notice titled Notice of Action and numbered I-797C (see sample below). This notice will tell you to check the USCIS website for information on how long the visa petition is likely to remain in processing (usually at least two to six months). Until that date, the Service Center will ignore any letters asking what is going on.

These Service Centers seem like walled fortresses. You can't visit them and it's impossible to speak with the person working on your case. If the petition is delayed past the processing time predicted (and delays are fairly normal), you can contact USCIS to try to get the petition back on track by calling 800-375-5283, where a live person will take your question from 8 a.m. until 8 p.m. local time. Although the person you speak with will most likely not be able to tell you anything useful during that phone call, he or she will start an inquiry for you and will tell you when you can expect a response.

Another approach is to make an appointment at your local USCIS office by using the online INFOPASS system. At your appointment, ask the officer what can be done to get your petition back on track. Officers sometimes have more information than the people at the 800 number, although usually they also will just start an inquiry for you and tell you when you can expect a response. Unfortunately, if you write a letter to USCIS you are not likely to get a response, other than a boilerplate letter telling you to call the 800 number or to make an INFOPASS appointment.

If USCIS needs additional documentation to complete the Fiancé Visa Petition, they will send the U.S. citizen a letter asking for it. You should strictly follow any deadlines given by USCIS if you receive such a letter.

Once the petition is approved (see the sample Approval Notice below), the Service Center will notify your U.S. citizen fiancé and transfer your case to the National Visa Center (NVC). The NVC will take care of some processing matters, then transfer your file to the U.S. consulate in your home country. The NVC will notify you when the case has been transferred (see sample below).

Sample Receipt Notice Form for I-129F

Department of Homeland Security
U.S. Citizenship and Immigration Services

I-797C, Notice of Action

THE UNITED STATES OF AMERICA

RECEIPT NUMBER		CASE TYPE I129F
WAC-12-041-00000		PETITION FOR FIANCE(E)
RECEIVED DATE	**PRIORITY DATE**	**PETITIONER**
August 5, 2012		BEACH, SANDRA
NOTICE DATE	**PAGE**	**BENEFICIARY**
August 10, 2012	1 of 1	HOLLIS, NIGEL

ILONA BRAY
RE: NIGEL IAN HOLLIS
950 PARKER ST.
BERKELEY, CA 94710

Notice Type: Receipt Notice

Amount received: $ 340.00

Receipt notice - If any of the above information is incorrect, call customer service immediately.

Processing time - Processing times vary by kind of case.
- You can check our current processing time for this kind of case on our website at **uscis.gov**.
- On our website you can also sign up to get free e-mail updates as we complete key processing steps on this case.
- Most of the time your case is pending the processing status will not change because we will be working on others filed earlier.
- We will notify you by mail when we make a decision on this case, or if we need something from you. If you move while this case is pending, call customer service when you move.
- Processing times can change. If you don't get a decision or update from us within our current processing time, check our website or call for an update.

If you have questions, check our website or call customer service. Please save this notice, and have it with you if you contact us about this case.

Notice to all customers with a pending I-130 petition - USCIS is now processing Form I-130, Petition for Alien Relative, as a visa number becomes available. Filing and approval of an I-130 relative petition is only the first step in helping a relative immigrate to the United States. Eligible family members must wait until there is a visa number available before they can apply for an immigrant visa or adjustment of status to a lawful permanent resident. This process will allow USCIS to concentrate resources first on cases where visas are actually available. This process should not delay the ability of one's relative to apply for an immigrant visa or adjustment of status. Refer to **www.state.gov/travel** <http://www.state.gov/travel> to determine current visa availability dates. For more information, please visit our website at www.uscis.gov or contact us at 1-800-375-5283.

Always remember to call customer service if you move while your case is pending. If you have a pending I-130 relative petition, also call customer service if you should decide to withdraw your petition or if you become a U.S. citizen.

Please see the additional information on the back. You will be notified separately about any other cases you filed.
U.S. CITIZENSHIP & IMMIGRATION SVC
CALIFORNIA SERVICE CENTER
P.O. BOX 30111
LAGUNA NIGUEL CA 92607-0111
Customer Service Telephone: (800) 375-5283

Form I-797C (Rev. 08/31/04) N

Sample Approval Notice Form for I-129F

Department of Homeland Security
U.S. Citizenship and Immigration Services

I-797, Notice of Action

THE UNITED STATES OF AMERICA

RECEIPT NUMBER		CASE TYPE I129F
WAC-12-041-00000		PETITION FOR FIANCE(E)

RECEIPT DATE	PRIORITY DATE	PETITIONER
August 5, 2012		BEACH, SANDRA

NOTICE DATE	PAGE	BENEFICIARY
February 10, 2013	1 of 1	HOLLIS, NIGEL

ILONA BRAY
RE: NIGEL IAN HOLLIS
950 PARKER ST.
BERKELEY, CA 94710

Notice Type: Approval Notice

Valid from 02/10/2013 to 06/10/2013

The above petition has been approved. We have sent the original visa petition to the Department of State National Visa Center (NVC), 32 Rochester Avenue, Portsmouth, NH 03801-2909. The INS has completed all action; further inquiries should be directed to the NVC.

The NVC now processes all approved fiance(e) petitions. The NVC processing should be complete within two to four weeks after receiving the petition from INS. The NVC will create a case record with your petition information. NVC will then send the petition to the U.S. Embassy or Consulate where your fiance(e) will be interviewed for his or her visa.

You will receive notification by mail when NVC has sent your petition to the U.S. Embassy or Consulate. The notification letter will provide you with a unique number for your case and the name and address of the U.S. Embassy or Consulate where your petition has been sent.

If it has been more than four weeks since you received this approval notice and you have not received notification from NVC that your petition has been forwarded overseas, please call NVC at (603) 334-0700. Please call between 8:00am-6:45pm Eastern Standard Time. You will need to enter the INS receipt number from this approval notice into the automated response system to receive information on your petition.

THIS FORM IS NOT A VISA NOR MAY IT BE USED IN PLACE OF A VISA.

Please see the additional information on the back. You will be notified separately about any other cases you filed.
U.S. CITIZENSHIP & IMMIGRATION SVC
CALIFORNIA SERVICE CENTER
P. O. BOX 30111
LAGUNA NIGUEL CA 92607-0111
Customer Service Telephone: (800) 375-5283

Form I-797 (Rev. 01/31/05) N

Sample NVC Notice Transferring Fiancé Visa Case to Consulate

August 16, 2009

Dear Petitioner:

The State Department's National Visa Center has recently received an approved I-129F petition filed on behalf of your spouse. This letter is to let you know that within a week the petition will be forwarded to the visa-issuing post overseas that is responsible for processing visa cases originating in the country where you were married.

Our records show that you filed the I-129F petition for:

Name of Spouse:

INS Receipt Number: MSC09

Case Number: SAA2009
The case must be processed at:

   Post: *SANAA*
     EMBASSY OF THE UNITED STATES
     P.O. BOX 22347, DHAHR HIMYAR ZONE
     SHERATON HOTEL DIST, SANAA
     REPUBLIC OF YEMEN

Your spouse will soon receive a packet with instructions from the consular section at this post on how to apply for the K3 visa at that post and what documents will be required. For further information on the K3 visa process, please consult our Website at: http://travel.state.gov.

         Sincerely,

         Bureau of Consular Affairs

Fianceé Visa Application Process

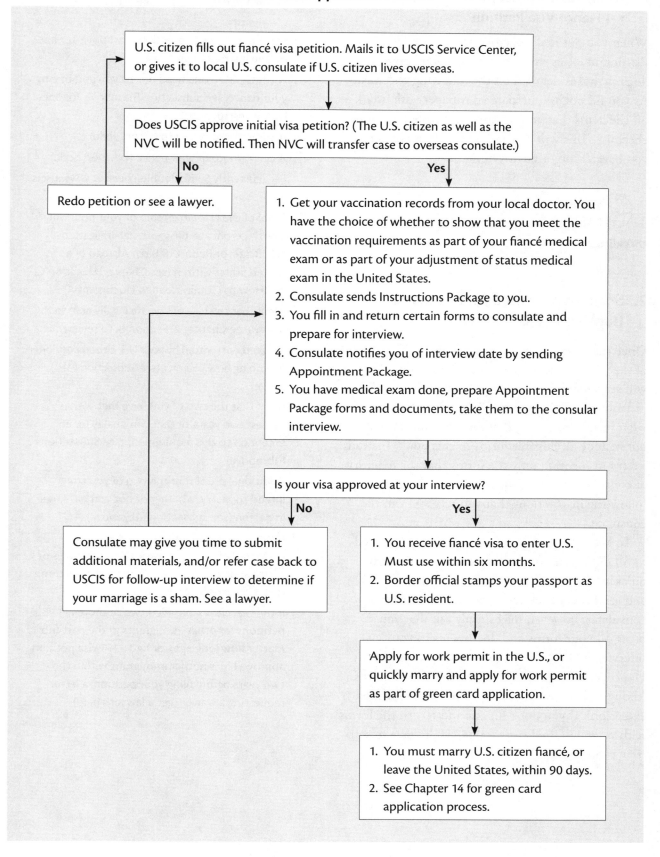

e. Using the Checklist for the K-1 Fiancé Visa Petition

When you put it all together, the Fiancé Visa Petition involves three forms and some supporting documents, as detailed on the following checklist. As you fill out and prepare your paperwork, mark off the items that you've found or finished on your checklist. This will be the best way to make sure you haven't forgotten anything.

 CHECKLIST
Appendix C includes a tear-out copy of this checklist.

2. Step Two: Fiancé Mails Forms Back to the Consulate

Once the U.S. consulate receives the NVC notice of the approval of your Fiancé Visa Petition, it will send you a follow-up application and further instructions. Which forms they send, and with what instructions, varies among consulates. We do not include all possible forms in this book. Instead, we try to mention only the forms that the majority of consulates ask for. The important thing is to follow the instructions that you receive from the consulate.

To keep the process moving, you may be asked to fill out certain of the forms you receive fairly quickly (the consulate will tell you which forms) and send them back to the consulate. (Other consulates, however, may simply ask that you bring all your forms and documents to your visa interview.) Don't delay, since the approval of your Fiancé Visa Petition is good for only four months (though the consulate can give you one four-month extension). If you don't fill out and return the forms within the required time frame, you'll have to start over at Step One.

Checklist for K-1 Fiancé Visa Petition

☐ Form I-129F (see Subsection F1a, above, for line-by-line instructions)

☐ Form G-325A (one filled out by you and one by your fiancé; see Subsection F1a, above, for line-by-line instructions)

☐ A color photo of you (passport style)

☐ A color photo of your fiancé (passport style)

☐ Fee (currently $340; double-check at www.uscis.gov)

☐ Proof of the U.S. citizenship of your petitioner: a birth certificate, passport, naturalization certificate, or Report of Birth Abroad of a United States Citizen (see Chapter 4, Section C, on "How to Obtain Needed Documents")

☐ Proof that the two of you are legally able to marry (see Chapter 2, Section B, to review)

☐ A statement written by your U.S. citizen petitioner describing how you met (see Subsection F1b, above)

☐ Proof that the two of you have met within the last two years, or that you qualify for an exception to this requirement (see Subsection F1b, above)

☐ Additional proof that the two of you truly intend to marry, whether or not you have met in person (see Subsection F1b, above)

☐ If the U.S. citizen petitioner has ever been convicted of certain crimes, certified copies of police and court records showing the outcome (get a lawyer's help)

☐ If the U.S. citizen has filed two or more K-1 visa petitions for other immigrants in the past (no matter how long ago), or had a K-1 visa petition approved for another immigrant within the two years before filing your petition, a letter requesting a waiver (get a lawyer's help)

Sample Form DS-156, Nonimmigrant Visa Application, Page 1

U.S. Department of State
NONIMMIGRANT VISA APPLICATION

Approved OMB 1405-0018
Expires 06/30/2014
Estimated Burden 1 hour
See Page 2

PLEASE TYPE OR PRINT YOUR ANSWERS IN THE SPACE PROVIDED BELOW EACH ITEM

1. Passport Number	2. Place of Issuance:			DO NOT WRITE IN THIS SPACE
22431	City: London	Country: Great Britain	State/Province:	B-1/B-2 MAX B-1 MAX B-2 MAX

Other _____ MAX

3. Issuing Country	4. Issuance Date (dd-mmm-yyyy)	5. Expiration Date (dd-mmm-yyyy)
Great Britain	18-Jan-2011	18-Jan-2016

Visa Classification

Mult or _____

Number of Applications

Months _____

6. Surnames (As in Passport)

Hollis

Issued/Refused   Validity

On _____ By _____

7. First and Middle Names (As in Passport)

Nigel Ian

Under SEC.   214(b)   221(g)

8. Other Surnames Used (Maiden, Religious, Professional, Aliases)

Other _____ INA

Reviewed By _____

9. Other First and Middle Names Used	10. Date of Birth (dd-mmm-yyyy)
none	17-Aug-1984

11. Place of Birth			12. Nationality
City: Penzance	Country: Great Britain	State/Province: Cornwall	Great Britain

13. Sex	14. National Identification Number (If Applicable)	15. Home Address (Include Apartment Number, Street, City, State or Province, Postal Zone and Country)
✕ Male ☐ Female	none	123 Limestone Way, Apt 7

16. Home Telephone Number	Business Phone Number	Mobile/Cell Number
1234 123456	1234 654321	1234 567891
Fax Number	Business Fax Number	Pager Number
none	1234 654444	none

17. Marital Status	18. Spouse's Full Name (Even if divorced or separated, include maiden name.)	19. Spouse's DOB (dd-mmm-yyyy)
☐ Married ☐ Single (Never Married) ☐ Widowed ✕ Divorced ☐ Separated	Jane Simpson	31-Oct-1986

20. Name and Address of Present Employer or School

Name: Outbound Design Incorporated   Address: 222 Heather Lane, Penance, U.K. TR198NL

21. Present Occupation (If retired, write "retired". If student, write "student".)	22. When do you intend to arrive in the U.S.? (Provide specific date if known) (dd-mmm-yyyy)	23. E-Mail Address
Sportswear Designer	08-Apr-2013	nihollis@outbanddesign.com

24. At what address will you stay in the U.S.?

114 Fulton St., 6E
New York, New York 10038

BARCODE

25. Name and telephone numbers of person in U.S. who you will be staying with or visiting for tourism or business:

Name	Home Phone
Sandra Lee Beach	215-555-1212
Business Phone	Cell Phone

DO NOT WRITE IN THIS SPACE

26. How long do you intend to stay in the U.S.?	27. What is the purpose of your trip?
Permanently, after application for adjustment status	Get married, apply for adjustment of status

50 mm x 50 mm

PHOTO

staple or glue photo here

28. Who will pay for your trip?	29. Have you ever been in the U.S.? ✕ Yes ☐ No
I will.	When? 12 August 2005 For how long? 3 weeks

Sample Form DS-156, Nonimmigrant Visa Application, Page 2

30. Have you ever been issued a U.S. visa? ☒ Yes ☐ No	31. Have you ever been refused a U.S. visa? ☐ Yes ☒ No
When? _____15 July 2005_____	When? _____
Where? _____London, England_____	Where? _____
What type of visa? _____B1/B2-Visa for business and pleasure_____	What type of visa? _____

32. Do you intend to work in the U.S.? ☒ Yes ☐ No	33. Do you intend to study in the U.S.? ☐ Yes ☒ No
(If YES, give the name and complete address of U.S. employer.) Will apply for U.S. work permit when I apply for adjustment of status, then seek work.	(If YES, give the name and complete address of the school.)

34. Names and relationships of persons traveling with you

35. Has your U.S. visa ever been cancelled or revoked? ☐ Yes ☒ No	36. Has anyone ever filed an immigrant visa petition on your behalf? ☐ Yes ☒ No If Yes, who?

37. Are any of the following persons in the U.S., or do they have U.S. legal permanent residence or U.S. citizenship?
Mark YES or NO and indicate that person's status in the U.S. (i.e., U.S. legal permanent resident, U.S. citizen, visiting, studying, working, etc.).

☐ Yes ☒ No Husband/ Wife _____ ☐ Yes ☒ No Fiance/ Fiancee _____U.S. citizen_____ ☐ Yes ☒ No Brother/ Sister _____

☐ Yes ☒ No Father/ Mother _____ ☐ Yes ☒ No Son/ Daughter _____

38. IMPORTANT: ALL APPLICANTS MUST READ AND CHECK THE APPROPRIATE BOX FOR EACH ITEM.
A visa may not be issued to persons who are within specific categories defined by law as inadmissible to the United States (except when a waiver is obtained in advance). Is any of the following applicable to you?

- Have you ever been arrested or convicted for any offense or crime, even though subject of a pardon, amnesty or other similar legal action? Have you ever unlawfully distributed or sold a controlled substance (drug), or been a prostitute or procurer for prostitutes?   ☐ Yes ☒ No

- Have you ever been refused admission to the U.S., or been the subject of a deportation hearing, or sought to obtain or assist others to obtain a visa, entry into the U.S., or any other U.S. immigration benefit by fraud or willful misrepresentation or other unlawful means? Have you attended a U.S. public elementary school on student (F) status or a public secondary school after November 30, 1996 without reimbursing the school?   ☐ Yes ☒ No

- Do you seek to enter the United States to engage in export control violations, subversive or terrorist activities, or any other unlawful purpose? Are you a member or representative of a terrorist organization as currently designated by the U.S. Secretary of State? Have you ever participated in persecutions directed by the Nazi government of Germany; or have you ever participated in genocide? Have you ever participated in, ordered, or engaged in genocide, torture, or extrajudicial killings? Have you ever engaged in the recruitment of or the use of child soldiers?   ☐ Yes ☒ No

- Have you ever violated the terms of a U.S. visa, or been unlawfully present in, or deported from, the United States?   ☐ Yes ☒ No
- Have you ever withheld custody of a U.S. citizen child outside the United States from a person granted legal custody by a U.S. court, voted in the United States in violation of any law or regulation, or renounced U.S. citizenship for the purpose of avoiding taxation?   ☐ Yes ☒ No

- Have you ever been afflicted with a communicable disease of public health significance or a dangerous physical or mental disorder, or ever been a drug abuser or addict?   ☐ Yes ☒ No

While a YES answer does not automatically signify ineligibility for a visa, if you answered YES you may be required to personally appear before a consular officer.

39. Was this application prepared by another person on your behalf? (If answer is YES, then have that person complete item 40.) ☐ Yes ☒ No

40. Application Prepared By

Name _____ Relationship to Applicant _____

Address _____

Signature of Person Preparing Form _____ Date (dd-mmm-yyyy) _____

41. I certify that I have read and understood all the questions set forth in this application and the answers I have furnished on this form are true and correct to the best of my knowledge and belief. I understand that any false or misleading statement may result in the permanent refusal of a visa or denial of entry into the United States. I understand that possession of a visa does not automatically entitle the bearer to enter the United States of America upon arrival at a port of entry if he or she is found inadmissible.

Applicant's Signature _____*Nigel I Hollis*_____ Date (dd-mmm-yyyy) _____25 April 2013_____

Privacy Act and Paperwork Reduction Act Statements

INA Section 222(f) provides that visa issuance and refusal records shall be considered confidential and shall be used only for the formulation, amendment, administration, or enforcement of the immigration, nationality, and other laws of the United States. Certified copies of visa records may be made available to a court which certifies that the information contained in such records is needed in a case pending before the court.

Public reporting burden for this collection of information is estimated to average 1 hour per response, including time required for searching existing data sources, gathering the necessary data, providing the information required, and reviewing the final collection. You do not have to provide the information unless this collection displays a currently valid OMB number. Send comments on the accuracy of this estimate of the burden and recommendations for reducing it to: U.S. Department of State, A/GIS/DIR, Washington, DC 20520.

Sample Form DS-156, Nonimmigrant Visa Application, Page 3

U.S. Department of State
SUPPLEMENT TO
NONIMMIGRANT VISA APPLICATION

PLEASE BE SURE TO SUBMIT THIS PAGE WITH THE REST OF YOUR APPLICATION

DO NOT MARK OR WRITE IN THIS SPACE

Nigel Ian Hollis

Barcode Number: Q20B3T5KUP

29. Additional Visits to the U.S.:

30. Additional Visa Issuances:

31. Additional Visa Refusals:

FILTERED NAMES
When 'None' or 'NA' are entered into any of the following the fields: 'Other Surnames Used', 'Other First and Middle Names Used', and 'National Identification Number', the text will be removed by the EVAF software from the data in the 2D barcode. If the applicant's name actually is None or NA the post must enter the name manually into NIV or RDS. The following fields have been removed:

- 'none' was removed from the 2D barcode for Item 8 (Other Surnames Used)
- 'none' was removed from the 2D barcode for Item 9 (Other First and Middle Names Used)

EVAF 02.02.12

a. Line-by-Line Instructions for Fiancé Forms for Mailing

This section will give you instructions for filling out the forms that you may be asked to mail in. Remember, you may not receive all of them—and you may get others not listed here. Be sure to have a copy of the appropriate form in hand as you go through these instructions.

Many consulates are modernizing the process by moving these forms online. The instructions you will receive should indicate if you will have to use the online forms instead. In most cases, the online forms are extremely similar to, if not exactly the same as, the sample forms provided here.

i. Form DS-156

Form DS-156 is a basic form used to test the eligibility of immigrants coming for temporary stays, including not only fiancés, but tourists and students. Don't be confused by the sections that don't seem to apply to you—tourists and students must promise that they don't plan to stay in the United States permanently, whereas you are permitted to intend to stay permanently.

 WEB RESOURCE
This form is available on the State Department website at www.state.gov. However, use the form that you get from the consulate if it's different, or complete it online if instructed. Above is a sample filled-in version of this form.

Questions 1-16: Self-explanatory.

Question 17: Check any appropriate box except "married" or "separated." You're only supposed to be a fiancé at this point, not a married person. If you are separated from a previous spouse, the divorce needs to be finalized before you continue with this application.

Questions 18 and 19: If you have never married before, write "None" in both boxes. If you have been married previously, remember that you cannot be currently married to be eligible for the fiancé visa. If your previous marriage ended

in divorce or annulment, fill in your previous spouse's information here. Include a separate sheet containing a short explanation of your divorce or annulment, along with copies of the court or government-issued documents confirming that your prior marriage ended. (See Form DS-156K in the next section.) If the marriage ended in death, check "widowed" and enter the former spouse's name, and include the marriage and death certificate.

Question 22: It's okay to approximate an arrival date if you haven't yet purchased tickets. After all, you might want to wait to buy a ticket until the consulate has approved your visa.

Question 23: If you don't have an email address, write "None."

Questions 24 and 25: The name of whom you'll be staying with and their address will hopefully be your fiancé's. If you will be staying with someone else temporarily until the wedding, you might want to attach their address as a separate page, with an explanation.

Question 26: If you plan to apply for your green card in the United States, write "permanently; will apply for permanent residence following marriage." If you are going to return after your marriage, write "90 days," or a lower number, if you don't need a whole 90 days.

Question 27: The purpose of your trip is to "Marry U.S. citizen fiancé" (if it's a man) or "fiancée" (if it's a woman).

Question 28: To avoid raising questions, the person named here as paying for your trip should either be your fiancé and/or you, or the person who signed an additional Affidavit of Support for you as a joint sponsor. (See Chapter 3 for further explanation of Affidavits of Support.)

Question 29: Self-explanatory. Again, they'll be looking for past visa fraud or unlawful time spent in the United States.

Question 30: This question calls for any immigrant (permanent) or nonimmigrant (temporary) visas that you might have applied for in the past. (See the Glossary for definition of nonimmigrant—it includes visas like tourist and student.) If you applied for an immigrant visa in the past, then the question of what happened to it will arise—if you were denied, why, and if you were approved, why do you now need to apply for another immigrant visa?

Almost none of the nonimmigrant visas would create problems for returning to the United States unless you had overstayed the visa expiration date and spent time there unlawfully. (See Chapter 2, Section A.) The exception is if you were in the United States on a J-1 (exchange student) visa and haven't yet completed your two-year "home country" residency requirement. If you had a J-1 or J-2 visa within the last two years, consult a lawyer.

Question 31: This question asks whether you have ever been refused a visa. Many people have been refused visas to the United States, particularly in the tourist visa category. Therefore, admitting that you have been denied a visa is not necessarily a strike against you. However, if you have ever been denied a visa because of attempted fraud, this may lead USCIS to deny your current application.

Question 32: If you plan to work in the United States, it's fine to say so here, since as a fiancé you have the right to work (as long as you have gotten the proper authorization stamp or document; see Section H, below for further explanation). To answer this question, you should say "Fiancé applicant; will seek work authorization."

Question 33: This question is primarily for student visa applicants. You're best off inserting "N/A."

Question 34: Enter the names of any of your children who will be accompanying you to the United States. As the form mentions, a separate Form DS-156 will have to be submitted for each child.

Question 35: If you have ever had a visa cancelled or revoked, consult a lawyer before continuing.

Question 36: This question asks about any immigrant (permanent, green card) petitions that you filed for, perhaps by a family member who is a U.S. citizen or resident, or an employer.

If these petitions are still pending, no problem —as a fiancé, you're allowed to have more than

one petition going on at the same time, so long as they don't reveal contradictory intentions on your part. (For example, if one petition was filed by a different fiancé, that's a problem.) If the petitions have already been decided, and were denied, then problems could also arise if the denials were for reasons that reflect badly on you, such as fraud.

Question 37: Self-explanatory. This question—about family members in the United States—has more to do with tourist visa applicants than you. They want to make sure that tourists and other temporary visitors don't plan to join their families and stay permanently.

Question 38: These questions are designed to see if you are inadmissible (see Chapter 2 for more on the grounds of inadmissibility). If your answer to any of the questions is "yes," see a lawyer before continuing.

Questions 39 and 40: These questions concern whether lawyers, paralegals, or other agencies may have filled in this form for you—it's okay if they did, assuming they didn't just tell you what to say or counsel you to lie.

Question 41: Sign and date the application.

ii. Form DS-156K

This is a very short form designed to collect some information concerning fiancé applicants that Form DS-156 neglected to ask for.

 WEB RESOURCE
This form is available on the State Department website at www.state.gov, and you may be instructed to complete it online. However, use the form that you get from the consulate if it's different. Below is a sample filled-in version of this form.

Questions 1-3: Self-explanatory.

Question 4: Self-explanatory, but don't make the mistake of listing your current fiancé as a spouse. This question only asks about previous marriages, or marriages that you should have ended by now.

Question 5: List all of your children, whether or not they are immigrating. Then check the boxes at the right to tell the consulate whether they are

Sample DS-156K, Supplement to Form DS-156

U.S. Department of State

NONIMMIGRANT FIANCÉ(E) VISA APPLICATION

USE WITH FORM DS-156

OMB APPROVAL NO.1405-0096
EXPIRES: 11/30/2013
ESTIMATED BURDEN: 1 HOUR*

The following questions must be answered by all applicants for visas to enter the United States as the fiancée or fiancé of a U.S. citizen in order that a determination may be made as to visa eligibility.

This form, together with Form DS-156, Nonimmigrant Visa Application, completed in duplicate, constitutes the complete application for a "K" Fiancé(e) Nonimmigrant Visa authorized under Section 222(c) of the Immigration and Nationality Act.

1. Family Name	First Name	Middle Name
Hollis	Nigel	Ian

2. Date of Birth (mm-dd-yyyy)	3. Place of Birth (City, Province, Country)
08/17/1984	Penzance, Cornwall, England, U.K.

4. Marital Status

If you are now married or were previously married, answer the following:

a. Name of Spouse   Jane Simpson

b. Date (mm-dd-yyyy) and Place of Marriage   6/10/2006   London

c. How and When was Marriage Terminated   5/20/2010   Divorce

d. If presently married, how will you marry your U.S. citizen fiancé(e)? Explain*

* NOTE If presently married to anyone, you are not eligible for a fiancé(e) visa.

5. List name, date and place of birth of all unmarried children under 21 years of age.

Name	Birth Date (mm-dd-yyyy)	Birth Place	Will Accompany You Yes	No	Will Follow You Yes	No
None			☐	☐	☐	☐
			☐	☐	☐	☐
			☐	☐	☐	☐
			☐	☐	☐	☐
			☐	☐	☐	☐

THE FOLLOWING DOCUMENTS MUST BE ATTACHED IN ORDER TO APPLY FOR A FIANCE(E) NONIMMIGRANT VISA.

• Your Birth Certificate   • Marriage Certificate (if any)   • Evidence of Engagement to Your Fiancé(e)   • Evidence of Financial Support

• Divorce Decree (if any)   • Death Certificate of Spouse (if any)   • Birth Certificates of All Children Listed in Number Five   • Police Certificates

NOTE All of the above documents will also be required by U.S. Citizenship and Immigration Services (USCIS) when you apply for adjustment of status to lawful permanent resident. The USCIS will accept these documents for that purpose.

DO NOT WRITE BELOW THIS LINE
The consular officer will assist you in answering this part.

I understand that I am required to submit my visa to the United States Immigration Officer at the place where I apply to enter the United States, and that the possession of a visa does not entitle me to enter the United States if at that time I am found to be inadmissible under the immigration laws. I further understand that my adjustment of status to permanent resident alien is dependent upon marriage to a U.S. citizen and upon meeting all of the requirements of the U.S. Department of Homeland Security.

I understand that any willfully false or misleading statement or willful concealment of a material fact made by me herein may subject me to permanent exclusion from the United States and, if I am admitted to the United States, may subject me to criminal prosecution and/or deportation.

I hereby certify that I am legally free to marry and intend to marry _____ , a U.S. citizen, within 90 days of my admission into the United States.

I do solemnly swear or affirm that all statements which appear in this application have been made by me and are true and complete to the best of my knowledge and belief.

_____
Signature of Applicant

Subscribed and sworn to before me this _____ day of _____ , _____ at: _____

_____
United States Consular Officer

Confidentiality Statement - INA Section 222(f) provides that visa issuance and refusal records shall be considered confidential and shall be used only for the formulation, amendment, administration, or enforcement of the immigration, nationality, and other laws of the United States. Certified copies of visa records may be made available to a court which certifies that the information contained in such records is needed in a case pending before the court.

Paperwork Reduction Act Statement - *Public reporting burden for this collection of information is estimated to average 1 hour per response, including time required for searching existing data sources, gathering the necessary documentation, providing the information and/or documents required, and reviewing the final collection. You do not have to supply this information unless this collection displays a currently valid OMB control number. If you have comments on the accuracy of this burden estimate and/or recommendations for reducing it, please send them to: A/GIS/DIR, Room 2400 SA-22, U.S. Department of State, Washington, DC 20522-2202.

DS-156K
06-2011

PREVIOUS EDITIONS OBSOLETE

immigrating. If they'll be coming at the same time as you, check the "yes" box on the left. If they'll follow you some months later, check the "yes" box at the right.

Don't write anything else on this form—you won't sign it until your interview.

iii. Form DS-230, Application for Immigrant Visa and Alien Registration, Part I— Biographic Information

The purpose of this form is to gather some additional identifying information about you. It is somewhat repetitive—just make sure you're consistent with the other forms.

 WEB RESOURCE
This form is available on the State Depart-ment website at www.state.gov. However, use the form that you get from the U.S. consulate if it's different. Below is a filled-in sample of the first page of this form.

Questions 1-8: Self-explanatory.

Question 9: Again, make sure not to say that you're married or separated.

Questions 10-28: Self-explanatory.

Question 29: List all your children. You'll have a chance to identify which ones are traveling with you in a later question.

Question 30: This list of addresses is collected for security reasons—for your interview, you'll be asked to provide police certificates from places you've lived.

Question 31a: List only those children who will be immigrating with you at the same time.

Question 31b: List only those children who will join you after you arrive in the United States.

Question 32: Try not to leave any gaps in your employment history. For example, mention periods when you are unemployed or a homemaker.

Questions 33-34: Self-explanatory.

Question 35: If you've spent more than 180 days in the United States without a valid visa or other right to be in the United States after April 1, 1997, you need to see a lawyer before going any further. (See Chapter 2, Section A.)

b. Where to Send Your Packet

Unless you're instructed otherwise, the normal procedure is to send your completed packet of forms back to the consulate that sent them to you. Its address (which may be just a post office box) will be in the materials that you received. This consulate will probably be the one nearest to you in your home country. But if your country doesn't have diplomatic relations with the United States, or the nearest consulate doesn't offer this type of visa service, a consulate in a more distant city or country may be designated.

If you are filling out this packet on your own, we also recommend photocopying it and sending a copy to your fiancé both before and after you send the final version to the consulate. That way your fiancé can review it and make sure that it is consistent with the other materials that the two of you are submitting.

c. What Will Happen After You Mail in the Packet of Forms

Once you've sent the consulate the required packet of forms, it will request a security clearance from every place you've lived since the age of 16. (They'll get this information from your forms.) Usually, the consulate simply asks a government office to check its records to see if you have a police record; and to send the consulate a copy of that record or a statement that you have no record. Assuming your records come back clean, the consulate will move to the third step.

 CAUTION
If you know or are advised by the U.S. consulate that you have a criminal record, consult a lawyer right away, no matter how minor the crime.

d. Using the Checklist for Fiancé Mailing to Consulate

These forms shouldn't take you very long to prepare. Using the checklist, check off the forms as you finish them and get your packet in the mail.

Sample DS-230 Part I, Application for Immigrant Visa and Alien Registration—Page 1

U.S. Department of State

APPLICATION FOR IMMIGRANT VISA AND ALIEN REGISTRATION

OMB APPROVAL NO. 1405-0015
EXPIRES: 03/31/2012
ESTIMATED BURDEN: 1 HOUR*
(See Page 2)

PART I - BIOGRAPHIC DATA

Instructions: Complete one copy of this form for yourself and each member of your family, regardless of age, who will immigrate with you. Please print or type your answers to all questions. Mark questions that are Not Applicable with "N/A". If there is insufficient room on the form, answer on a separate sheet using the same numbers that appear on the form. Attach any additional sheets to this form.

Warning: Any false statement or concealment of a material fact may result in your permanent exclusion from the United States.
This form (DS-230 Part I) is the first of two parts. This part, together with Form DS-230 Part II, constitutes the complete Application for Immigrant Visa and Alien Registration.

1. Family Name: Hollis — First Name: Nigel — Middle Name: Ian

2. Other Names Used or Aliases (If married woman, give maiden name): None

3. Full Name in Native Alphabet (If Roman letters not used):

4. Date of Birth (mm-dd-yyyy): 8/17/1984 — 5. Age: 29 — 6. Place of Birth (City or Town): Penzance — (Province): Cornwall — (Country): England

7. Nationality (If dual national, give both.): U.K. — 8. Gender: [X] Male, [ ] Female — 9. Marital Status: [ ] Single (Never Married) [ ] Married [ ] Widowed [X] Divorced [ ] Separated. Including my present marriage, I have been married ___1___ times.

10. Permanent address in the United States where you intend to live, if known (street address including ZIP code). Include the name of a person who currently lives there.
Sandra Beach
114 Fulton Street #6E
New York, NY 10038
Telephone number: 212-555-1212

11. Address in the United States where you want your Permanent Resident Card (Green Card) mailed, if different from address in item #10 (include the name of a person who currently lives there).
Telephone number:

12. Present Occupation: Sportswear Designer

13. Present Address (Street Address) (City or Town) (Province) (Country): 123 Limestone Way, Cornwall, Penzance, U.K. TR197NL
Telephone Number (Home): 1234 123456 — Telephone Number (Office): 1234 654321 — Email Address:

14. Spouse's Maiden or Family Name: None — First Name: — Middle Name:

15. Date (mm-dd-yyyy) and Place of Birth of Spouse:

16. Address of Spouse (If different from your own): — 17. Spouse's Occupation:

18. Date of Marriage (mm-dd-yyyy):

19. Father's Family Name: Hollis — First Name: Kevin — Middle Name: Andrew

20. Father's Date of Birth (mm-dd-yyyy): 1/12/1957 — 21. Place of Birth: York, England — 22. Current Address: 83 Herriott Rd., York — 23. If Deceased, Give Year of Death:

24. Mother's Family Name at Birth: Chumley — First Name: Sarah — Middle Name: Elizabeth

25. Mother's Date of Birth (mm-dd-yyyy): 4/7/1961 — 26. Place of Birth: York, England — 27. Current Address: 83 Herriott Rd., York — 28. If Deceased, Give Year of Death:

DS-230 Part I
03-2012

This Form May be Obtained Free at Consular Offices of the United States of America
Previous Editions Obsolete

Page 1 of 4

Sample DS-230 Part I, Application for Immigrant Visa and Alien Registration—Page 2

29. List Names, Dates and Places of Birth, and Addresses of ALL Children.

Name	Date (mm-dd-yyyy)	Place of Birth	Address (If different from your own)
None			

30. List below all places you have lived for at least six months since reaching the age of 16, including places in your country of nationality. Begin with your present residence.

City or Town	Province	Country	From/To (mm-yyyy) or "Present"	
Penzance	Cornwall	U.K.	7/2001	present
Cambridge	9/2000-7/2001	U.K.	9/2000	7/2001
York	8/1984-9/2000	U.K.	8/1984	9/2000

31a. Person(s) named in 14 and 29 who will accompany you to the United States now.

n/a

31b. Person(s) named in 14 and 29 who will follow you to the United States at a later date.

32. List below all employment for the last ten years.

Employer	Location	Job Title	From/To (mm-yyyy) or "Present"	
Outbound Design	Penzance	Sportswear Designer	8/2004	present
Fish & Chips Shop	Cambridge	Fryer	9/2001	6/2004

In what occupation do you intend to work in the United States? _____

33. List below all educational institutions attended.

School and Location	From/To (mm-yyyy)	Course of Study	Degree or Diploma
Cambridge Technical College	9/1996-6/2004	design	B.A.

Languages spoken or read — English, French

Professional associations to which you belong — International Design Group

34. Previous Military Service ☐ Yes ☒ No

Branch _____ Dates of Service (mm-dd-yyyy) _____

Rank/Position _____ Military Speciality/Occupation _____

35. List dates of all previous visits to or residence in the United States. (If never, write "never") Give type of visa status, if known. Give DHS "A" number if any.

From/To (mm-yyyy)	Location	Type of Visa	"A" Number (If known)
8/2005-8/2005	New York, San Francisco	B-2	None

Signature of Applicant

Nigel I. Hollis

Date (mm-dd-yyyy)

04/25/2013

Privacy Act and Paperwork Reduction Act Statements

The information asked for on this form is requested pursuant to Section 222 of the Immigration and Nationality Act. The U.S. Department of State uses the facts you provide on this form primarily to determine your classification and eligibility for a U.S. immigrant visa. Individuals who fail to submit this form or who do not provide all the requested information may be denied a U.S. immigrant visa. If you are issued an immigrant visa and are subsequently admitted to the United States as an immigrant, the Department of Homeland Security will use the information on this form to issue you a Permanent Resident Card, and, if you so indicate, the Social Security Administration will use the information to issue you a social security number and card.

*Public reporting burden for this collection of information is estimated to average 1 hour per response, including time required for searching existing data sources, gathering the necessary documentation, providing the information and/or documents required, and reviewing the final collection. You do not have to supply this information unless this collection displays a currently valid OMB control number. If you have comments on the accuracy of this burden estimate and/or recommendations for reducing it, please send them to: A/GIS/DIR, Room 2400 SA-22, U.S. Department of State, Washington, DC 20522-2202

Checklist for Fiancé Mailing to Consulate

- ☐ Form DS-156 (prepared in duplicate; see Subsection F2a, above, for line-by-line instructions)
- ☐ Form DS-156K (filled in but unsigned; see Subsection F2a, above, for line-by-line instructions)
- ☐ Form DS-230, Part I (see Subsection F2a, above, for line-by-line instructions).

 CHECKLIST
Appendix C includes a tear-out copy of this checklist.

3. Step Three: Final Forms and the Visa Interview

For the third and final step in the fiancé visa application process, the consulate will send you an interview notice and some additional forms and instructions (including one for the medical exam). You'll get two to four weeks notice of your upcoming interview.

Your Appointment Package may contain forms and instructions specially prepared by your local consulate and therefore not covered in this book. Always use the forms provided by the consulate if they are different from the ones in this book.

a. Line-by-Line Form Instructions for Fiancé Interview Forms

This section will give you precise instructions for filling out the forms that you'll receive in your Appointment Package. They are listed on the Checklist for Fiancé Appointment Package, below.

i. Form DS-230, Application for Immigrant Visa and Alien Registration, Part II—Sworn Statement

Most of this form is self-explanatory, and not all consulates require it. Because of variations between consulates, we can't give you exact instructions for every question.

 WEB RESOURCE
Form DS-230 Part II is available on the State Department website at www.state.gov, and you may be instructed to complete it online. However, use the form you receive from the U.S. consulate, if you receive one, because it may be a bit different. Below is a sample filled-in version of this form.

The **"yes or no"** questions (with boxes to check) refer to the grounds of inadmissibility described in Chapter 2. If you check "yes" on any of them, consult a lawyer immediately and do not file the form until after this consultation.

Signature line: Do not sign this form until you are at your interview.

ii. Form I-134

Form I-134 is filled out by the U.S. citizen to show the U.S. government that the citizen can and will support you financially. Not all consulates require the use of Form I-134 as part of the fiancé visa application, though all will require some evidence that you won't need to go on welfare or receive other government assistance. If you have children immigrating with you, the children won't need separate Forms I-134; listing them in Question 3 is sufficient.

 WEB RESOURCE
This form is available on the USCIS website at www.uscis.gov. Below is a sample filled-in version of this form.

What this form doesn't tell you is that the government can be very strict in its opinion of how much income it takes to support someone. Read Chapter 3 for further discussion of how to satisfy the government's requirements. After your U.S. citizen fiancé is done filling in the blanks on this form, refer to the instructions at the bottom of this section to find out if the amount is sufficient. If it isn't, go back to Chapter 3 for suggestions.

Sample DS-230 Part II, Application for Immigrant Visa and Alien Registration—Page 3

U.S. Department of State

APPLICATION FOR IMMIGRANT VISA AND ALIEN REGISTRATION

OMB APPROVAL NO. 1405-0015
EXPIRES: 02/29/2012
ESTIMATED BURDEN: 1 HOUR*

PART II - SWORN STATEMENT

Instructions: Complete one copy of this form for yourself and each member of your family, regardless of age, who will immigrate with you. Please print or type your answers to all questions. Mark questions that are Not Applicable with "N/A". If there is insufficient room on the form, answer on a separate sheet using the same numbers that appear on the form. Attach any additional sheets to this form. The fee should be paid in United States dollars or local currency equivalent, or by bank draft.

Warning: Any false statement or concealment of a material fact may result in your permanent exclusion from the United States. Even if you are issued an immigrant visa and are subsequently admitted to the United States, providing false information on this form could be grounds for your prosecution and/or deportation.

This form (DS-230 Part II), together with Form DS-230 Part I, constitutes the complete Application for Immigrant Visa and Alien Registration.

36. Family Name	First Name	Middle Name
Hollis	Nigel	Ian

37. Other Names Used or Aliases (If married woman, give maiden name)
None

38. Full Name in Native Alphabet (If Roman letters not used)
NA

39. Name and Address of Petitioner
SANDRA LEAH BEACH
114 FULTON STREET, #6E
NEW YORK, NY 10038

Telephone number

Email Address

40. United States laws governing the issuance of visas require each applicant to state whether or not he or she is a member of any class of individuals excluded from admission into the United States. The excludable classes are described below in general terms. You should read carefully the following list and answer Yes or No to each category. The answers you give will assist the consular officer to reach a decision on your eligibility to receive a visa.

Except as Otherwise Provided by Law, Aliens Within the Following Classifications are Ineligible to Receive a Visa. Do Any of the Following Classes Apply to You?

a. An alien who has a communicable disease of public health significance; who has failed to present documentation of having received vaccinations in accordance with U.S. law; who has or has had a physical or mental disorder that poses or is likely to pose a threat to the safety or welfare of the alien or others; or who is a drug abuser or addict. ☐ Yes ☒ No

b. An alien convicted of, or who admits having committed, a crime involving moral turpitude or violation of any law relating to a controlled substance or who is the spouse, son or daughter of such a trafficker who knowingly has benefited from the trafficking activities in the past five years; who has been convicted of 2 or more offenses for which the aggregate sentences were 5 years or more; who is coming to the United States to engage in prostitution or commercialized vice or who has engaged in prostitution or procuring within the past 10 years; who is or has been an illicit trafficker in any controlled substance; who has committed a serious criminal offense in the United States and who has asserted immunity from prosecution; who, while serving as a foreign government official, was responsible for or directly carried out particularly severe violations of religious freedom; or whom the President has identified as a person who plays a significant role in a severe form of trafficking in persons, who otherwise has knowingly aided, abetted, assisted or colluded with such a trafficker in severe forms of trafficking in persons, or who is the spouse, son or daughter of such a trafficker who knowingly has benefited from the trafficking activities within the past five years. ☐ Yes ☒ No

c. An alien who seeks to enter the United States to engage in espionage, sabotage, export control violations, terrorist activities, the overthrow of the Government of the United States or other unlawful activity; who is a member of or affiliated with the Communist or other totalitarian party; who participated, engaged or ordered genocide, torture, or extrajudicial killings; or who is a member or representative of a terrorist organization as currently designated by the U.S. Secretary of State. ☐ Yes ☒ No

d. An alien who is likely to become a public charge. ☐ Yes ☒ No

e. An alien who seeks to enter for the purpose of performing skilled or unskilled labor who has not been certified by the Secretary of Labor; who is a graduate of a foreign medical school seeking to perform medical services who has not passed the NBME exam or its equivalent; or who is a health care worker seeking to perform such work without a certificate from the CGFNS or from an equivalent approved independent credentialing organization. ☐ Yes ☒ No

f. An alien who failed to attend a hearing on deportation or inadmissibility within the last 5 years; who seeks or has sought a visa, entry into the United States, or any immigration benefit by fraud or misrepresentation; who knowingly assisted any other alien to enter or try to enter the United States in violation of law; who, after November 30, 1996, attended in student (F) visa status a U.S. public elementary school or who attended a U.S. public secondary school without reimbursing the school; or who is subject to a civil penalty under INA 274C. ☐ Yes ☒ No

Privacy Act and Paperwork Reduction Act Statements

The information asked for on this form is requested pursuant to Section 222 of the Immigration and Nationality Act. The U.S. Department of State uses the facts you provide on this form primarily to determine your classification and eligibility for a U.S. immigrant visa. Individuals who fail to submit this form or who do not provide all the requested information may be denied a U.S. immigrant visa. If you are issued an immigrant visa and are subsequently admitted to the United States as an immigrant, the Department of Homeland Security will use the information on this form to issue you a Permanent Resident Card, and, if you so indicate, the Social Security Administration will use the information to issue you a social security number and card.

*Public reporting burden for this collection of information is estimated to average 1 hour per response, including time required for searching existing data sources, gathering the necessary documentation, providing the information and/or documents required, and reviewing the final collection. You do not have to supply this information unless this collection displays a currently valid OMB control number. If you have comments on the accuracy of this burden estimate and/or recommendations for reducing it, please send them to: A/GIS/DIR, Room 2400 SA-22, U.S. Department of State, Washington, DC 20522-2202

Sample DS-230 Part II, Application for Immigrant Visa and Alien Registration—Page 4

g. An alien who is permanently ineligible for U.S. citizenship; or who departed the United States to evade military service in time of war. ☐ Yes ☒ No

h. An alien who was previously ordered removed within the last 5 years or ordered removed a second time within the last 20 years; who was previously unlawfully present and ordered removed within the last 10 years or ordered removed a second time within the last 20 years; who was convicted of an aggravated felony and ordered removed; who was previously unlawfully present in the United States for more than 180 days but less than one year who voluntarily departed within the last 3 years; or who was unlawfully present for more than one year or an aggregate of one year within the last 10 years. ☐ Yes ☒ No

i. An alien who is coming to the United States to practice polygamy; who withholds custody of a U.S. citizen child outside the United States from a person granted legal custody by a U.S. court or intentionally assists another person to do so; who has voted in the United States in violation of any law or regulation; or who renounced U.S. citizenship to avoid taxation. ☐ Yes ☒ No

j. An alien who is a former exchange visitor who has not fulfilled the 2-year foreign residence requirement. ☐ Yes ☒ No

k. An alien determined by the Attorney General to have knowingly made a frivolous application for asylum. ☐ Yes ☒ No

l. An alien who has ordered, carried out or materially assisted in extrajudicial and political killings and other acts of violence against the Haitian people; who has directly or indirectly assisted or supported any of the groups in Colombia known as FARC, ELN, or AUC; who through abuse of a governmental or political position has converted for personal gain, confiscated or expropriated property in Cuba, a claim to which is owned by a national of the United States, has trafficked in such property or has been complicit in such conversion, has committed similar acts in another country, or is the spouse, minor child or agent of an alien who has committed such acts; who has been directly involved in the establishment or enforcement of population controls forcing a woman to undergo an abortion against her free choice or a man or a woman to undergo sterilization against his or her free choice; or who has disclosed or trafficked in confidential U.S. business information obtained in connection with U.S. participation in the Chemical Weapons Convention or is the spouse, minor child or agent of such a person; or who has ever engaged in the recruitment of or the use of child solders. ☐ Yes ☒ No

41. Have you ever been charged, arrested or convicted of any offense or crime? (If answer is Yes, please explain) ☐ Yes ☒ No

42. Have you ever been refused admission to the United States at a port-of-entry? (If answer is Yes, please explain) ☐ Yes ☒ No

43a. Have you ever applied for a Social Security Number (SSN)?

☐ Yes

Give the number _____
Would you like to receive a replacement card? (You must answer YES to question 43b. to receive a card.)

☐ Yes ☐ No

☒ No
Do you want the Social Security Administration to assign you a SSN and issue a card? (You must answer YES to question 43b. to receive a number and a card.)

☒ Yes ☐ No

43b. Consent to Disclosure: I authorize disclosure of information from this form to the Department of Homeland Security (DHS), the Social Security Administration (SSA), such other U.S. Government agencies as may be required for the purpose of assigning me an SSN and issuing me a Social Security card, and I authorize the SSA to share my SSN with the INS.

☒ Yes ☐ No

The applicant's response does not limit or restrict the Government's ability to obtain his or her SSN, or other information on this form, for enforcement or other purposes as authorized by law.

44. Were you assisted in completing this application? ☐ Yes ☒ No
(If answer is Yes, give name and address of person assisting you, indicating whether relative, friend, travel agent, attorney, or other)

DO NOT WRITE BELOW THE FOLLOWING LINE
The consular officer will assist you in answering item 45.
DO NOT SIGN this form until instructed to do so by the consular officer

45. I claim to be:

☐ A Family-Sponsored Immigrant
☐ An Employment-Based Immigrant
☐ A Diversity Immigrant
☐ A Special Category (Specify) _____
(Returning resident, Hong Kong, Tibetan, Private Legislation, etc.)

☐ I derive foreign state chargeability under Sec. 202(b) through my _____

☐ Preference _____

☐ Numerical limitation _____
(foreign state)

I understand that I am required to surrender my visa to the United States Immigration Officer at the place where I apply to enter the United States, and that the possession of a visa does not entitle me to enter the United States if at that time I am found to be inadmissible under the immigration laws.
I understand that any willfully false or misleading statement or willful concealment of a material fact made by me herein may subject me to permanent exclusion from the United States and, if I am admitted to the United States, may subject me to criminal prosecution and/or deportation.
I, the undersigned applicant for a United States immigrant visa, do solemnly swear (or affirm) that all statements which appear in this application, consisting of Form DS-230 Part I and Part II combined, have been made by me, including the answers to items 1 through 45 inclusive, and that they are true and complete to the best of my knowledge and belief. I do further swear (or affirm) that, if admitted into the United States, I will not engage in activities which would be prejudicial to the public interest, or endanger the welfare, safety, or security of the United States; in activities which would be prohibited by the laws of the United States relating to espionage, sabotage, public disorder, or in other activities subversive to the national security; in any activity a purpose of which is the opposition to or the control, or overthrow of, the Government of the United States, by force, violence, or other unconstitutional means.
I understand that completion of this form by persons required by law to register with the Selective Service System (males 18 through 25 years of age) constitutes such registration in accordance with the Military Selective Service Act.

_____
Signature of Applicant

Subscribed and sworn to before me this _____ day of _____ at: _____

_____
Consular Officer

One very important difference between the Affidavit of Support for a fiancé (Form I-134) and the Affidavit of Support that eventually needs to be used at time of adjustment of status (Form I-864) is that the income requirements are different. For the Form I-134, the petitioner needs to show that his or her income is at least 100% of amounts listed per family size in the federal *Poverty Guidelines*. For the Form I-864, the petitioner needs to show an income of at least 125% of amounts listed in the *Poverty Guidelines*.

The Form I-134 becomes part of your permanent record, however, and consular officers are aware that you will have to meet the 125% requirement just a few months later when you adjust your status to permanent resident. Therefore, we recommend that, if possible, you show that your spouse meets the 125% requirement even at this point.

Paragraph 1: Self-explanatory, calling for the U.S. citizen to fill in his or her name and address.

Question 1: Self-explanatory.

Question 2: Self-explanatory.

Question 3: This is for information about you, the intending immigrant. "Marital Status" should, of course, be "single," "divorced," "widowed," or anything other than "married," since you are coming to the United States for the specific purpose of getting married. "Relationship to Sponsor" asks what relation you are to the U.S. citizen. Enter "fiancé" if you are a man and "fiancée" if you are a woman. The "spouse" line should be left blank, but if any children will be immigrating with you, enter their information on the following lines.

Question 7: Back to the U.S. citizen, who must enter information about his or her place of employment. For "type of business" one may enter one's position (such as "secretary" or "accountant") or a more generic description, such as "medicine" or "sales."

On the next set of lines, the U.S. citizen enters his or her income and assets. If the U.S. citizen's income is sufficient for the Form I-134, the Department of State will not care about the citizen's assets, so the U.S. citizen won't really need to list each and every asset. The questions about assets become more

Is the Total Support Amount Sufficient?

Technically, Form I-134 only covers your first 90 days in the United States, so the consulate may not require your U.S. citizen fiancé to show a certain income level—despite the fact that they've asked him or her to fill out this form. However, it's wise to look at the *Poverty Guidelines* chart to see what income level is required for fiancés (100% of the *Poverty Guidelines*) and even what income level you will have to show at the time of your adjustment of status (125%).

Go back to the form you've filled out and follow these steps.

1. Remember, it is the U.S. citizen's income that is most important. Compare that income to the *Poverty Guidelines* chart located in Chapter 3, Section A (after checking for a more recent version at uscis.gov, on Form I-864P). In the left column, find the line corresponding to the number of people that the U.S. citizen is responsible for supporting. Now look to the right column. That's the total amount of income that the U.S. government will want to see when you apply for your green card. If your U.S. citizen fiancé's income comfortably reaches that level, you are fine, and the U.S. citizen should not have to also list assets.

2. If your U.S. citizen fiancé's income does not reach the level required by the *Poverty Guidelines*, total up additional assets.

3. Subtract the mortgages and other debts from the assets' worth and divide that total by three.

4. Add the figure to the amount of income. How does this figure compare to the total amount of income that the U.S. government will want to see when you apply for your green card? Check this, and if it still does not reach that level, reread Chapter 3.

Fortunately, by the time you've reached your U.S. green card interview, you will have had a work permit for several months, and can contribute to the household income.

Sample Form I-134, Affidavit of Support—Page 1

Department of Homeland Security
U.S. Citizenship and Immigration Services

OMB No. 1615-0014

Form I-134, Affidavit of Support

(Answer all items. Type or print in black ink.)

I, Sandra Leah Beach residing at 114 Fulton St., Apt. 6E
　　(Name)　　　　　　　　　　　　　　　　　　　　(Street Number and Name)

New York　　　　　　　　　NY　　　　　10038　　　　　U.S.A.
　(City)　　　　　　　　　(State)　　(Zip Code if in U.S.)　(Country)

certify under penalty of perjury under U.S. law, that:

1. I was born on 12/20/1986 in Horseheads New York U.S.A.
　　　　　　　(Date-*mm/dd/yyyy*)　　　(City)　　(State)　　(Country)

If you are not a U.S. citizen based on your birth in the United States, or a non-citizen U.S. national based on your birth in American Samoa (including Swains Island), answer the following as appropriate:

    a. If a U.S.citizen through naturalization, give Certificate of Naturalization number _____

    b. If a U.S. citizen through parent(s) or marriage, give Certificate of Citizenship number _____

    c. If U.S. citizenship was derived by some other method, attach a statement of explanation.

    d. If a Lawful Permanent Resident of the United States, give A-Number _____

    e. If a lawfully admitted nonimmigrant, give Form I-94, Arrival-Departure Record, number _____

2. I am 27 years of age and have resided in the United States since birth
　　　　　　　　　　　　　　　　　　　　　　　　　　　　　　　(Date-*mm/dd/yyyy*)

3. This affidavit is executed on behalf of the following person:

Name (Family Name)	(First Name)	(Middle Name)	Gender	Age
Hollis	Nigel	Ian	M	29

Citizen of (Country)	Marital Status	Relationship to Sponsor
United Kingdom	Divorced	Fiancé

Presently resides at (Street Number and Name)	(City)	(State)	(Country)
123 Limestone Way #7	Penzance	Cornwall	U.K.

Name of spouse and children accompanying or following to join person:

Spouse	Gender	Age	Child		Gender	Age
Child	Gender	Age	Child		Gender	Age
Child	Gender	Age	Child		Gender	Age

4. This affidavit is made by me for the purpose of assuring the U.S. Government that the person(s) named in **item (3)** will not become a public charge in the United States.

5. I am willing and able to receive, maintain, and support the person(s) named in **item 3**. I am ready and willing to deposit a bond, if necessary, to guarantee that such person(s) will not become a public charge during his or her stay in the United States, or to guarantee that the above named person(s) will maintain his or her nonimmigrant status, if admitted temporarily, and will depart prior to the expiration of his or her authorized stay in the United States.

6. I understand that:

    a. Form I-134 is an "undertaking" under section 213 of the Immigration and Nationality Act, and I may be sued if the person(s) named in **item 3** becomes a public charge after admission to the United States;

    b. Form I-134 may be made available to any Federal, State, or local agency that may receive an application from the person(s) named in **item 3** for Food Stamps, Supplemental Security Income, or Temporary Assistance to Needy Families; and

    c. If the person(s) named in **item 3** does apply for Food Stamps, Supplemental Security Income, or Temporary Assistance for Needy Families, my own income and assets may be considered in deciding the person's application. How long my income and assets may be attributed to the person(s) named in **item 3** is determined under the statutes and rules governing each specific program.

Form I-134 (Rev. 05/25/11) Y

Sample Form I-134, Affidavit of Support—Page 2

7. I am employed as or engaged in the business of _____Executive Assistant_____ with _____Helport Foundation_____
   (Type of Business)   (Name of Concern)

at _____87 W. 57th St._____ _____New York_____ _____NY_____ _____10039_____
   (Street Number and Name)   (City)   (State)   (Zip Code)

I derive an annual income of: *(If self-employed, I have attached a copy of my last income tax return or report of commercial rating concern which I certify to be true and correct to the best of my knowledge and belief. See instructions for nature of evidence of net worth to be submitted.)* $ _____45,000_____

I have on deposit in savings banks in the United States: $ _____8,200_____

I have other personal property, the reasonable value of which is: $ _____7,500_____

I have stocks and bonds with the following market value, as indicated on the attached list, which I certify to be true and correct to the best of my knowledge and belief: $ _____0_____

I have life insurance in the sum of: $ _____0_____

With a cash surrender value of: $ _____

I own real estate valued at: $ _____0_____

     With mortgage(s) or other encumbrance(s) thereon amounting to: $ _____

     Which is located at: _____
                (Street Number and Name)   (City)   (State)   (Zip Code)

8. The following persons are dependent upon me for support: *(Check the box in the appropriate column to indicate whether the person named is **wholly** or **partially** dependent upon you for support.)*

Name of Person	Wholly Dependent	Partially Dependent	Age	Relationship to Me
None	☐	☐		
	☐	☐		
	☐	☐		

9. I have previously submitted affidavit(s) of support for the following person(s). If none, state "None".

Name of Person	Date submitted
None	

10. I have submitted a visa petition(s) to U.S. Citizenship and Immigration Services on behalf of the following person(s). If none, state "None".

Name of Person	Relationship	Date submitted
Nigel Ian Hollis	Fiancé	04/30/2013

11. I ☐ intend   ☒ do not intend to make specific contributions to the support of the person(s) named in **item 3**.

     (If you check "intend," indicate the exact nature and duration of the contributions. For example, if you intend to furnish room and board, state for how long and, if money, state the amount in U.S. dollars and whether it is to be given in a lump sum, weekly or monthly, and for how long.)

_____

_____

_____

Oath or Affirmation of Sponsor

I acknowledge that I have read "Sponsor and Alien Liability" on Page 2 of the instructions for this form, and am aware of my responsibilities as a sponsor under the Social Security Act, as amended, and the Food Stamp Act, as amended. _____
I certify under penalty of perjury under United States law that I know the contents of this affidavit signed by me and that the statements are true and correct.

Signature of Sponsor _____   **Date** _____

Form I-134 (Rev. 05/25/11) Y Page 2

important when the U.S. citizen's income does not meet the *Poverty Guidelines* levels. The question about the amount **"on deposit in savings banks in the United States"** is a little misleading, because it's okay to also include amounts in checking accounts. For **"personal property,"** the U.S. citizen doesn't need to consider the value of every item he or she owns. An approximate total value of his or her cars, jewelry, appliances (stereo, television, refrigerator), automobiles, cameras, and other equipment will do. Nor does he or she have to supply proof of their ownership—yet. But when it comes time for the green card application in the United States, the U.S. citizen sponsor will have to provide proof of ownership of any assets that he or she uses to show financial capacity—so it's best not to exaggerate on Form I-134.

Question 8: Anyone whom the sponsor has listed on his/her tax returns should be entered here.

Question 9: This question attempts to find out whether the U.S. citizen is overextending him or herself financially. If he or she has filled out this form or Form I-864 (the Affidavit of Support used in green card applications) on behalf of any other immigrant, these lines should be filled in.

Question 10: For the reasons that underlie Question 9, the U.S. government wants to know whether the U.S. citizen is planning to sponsor anyone else, having filed a visa petition on their behalf. Even if you are the only person being sponsored, the U.S. citizen should fill in your name here, with a notation by your name saying "subject of this affidavit."

Question 11: Enter "N/A" (not applicable). This is only for visitors that are truly temporary, such as tourists.

Oath or Affirmation of Sponsor. Here is a lovely example of excruciating legalese. Don't try to puzzle this out. The U.S. citizen should just be sure, before signing the form, that to the best of his or her knowledge, the answers provided are correct.

iii. Form DS-1858

This form is not included in this book. Use the form that you receive from the U.S. consulate (if the consulate requires it).

There isn't much to fill in on this form. As you'll see, it mostly asks you to read information regarding the responsibilities of the person who signs the Affidavit of Support. The U.S. citizen sponsor simply needs to enter his or her name and certain other vital information and sign at the bottom. Check the consulate's instructions carefully; they may require the sponsor to notarize the form as well.

b. Document Instructions for Appointment Package

This section contains detailed instructions about some of the documents on the Checklist for Fiancé Appointment Package in Subsection f, below.

i. Copy of U.S. Citizen's Most Recent Federal Tax Return

As part of proving that your fiancé can support you financially, he or she will probably be asked to provide a complete copy of his or her federal tax return, including the W-2 slips—at least one year's worth, and maybe three. There is no need to include the state tax form.

The consulate prefers to see the tax return in the form of IRS transcripts (an IRS-generated summary of the return that your U.S. citizen fiancé filed), which your fiancé can request using IRS Form 4506T, available through the IRS website at www.irs.gov or by calling 800-829-1040. However, it is usually a wait of several weeks to get the transcript. Don't let this hold up the immigration process. If the transcript hasn't come by the time of your interview, simply use your U.S. citizen petitioner's own copies of the tax returns.

 TIP

We're advising you to prepare more than the minimum financial documents. Technically, you're supposed to be asked for only one year's tax returns, and that's it. But because so many consulates ask for more, it makes sense to be ready with additional years' tax returns plus a bank and employer letter.

ii. Letter From U.S. Citizen's Bank(s) Confirming the Account(s)

The U.S. citizen should ask all of his or her banks reported on page one of Form I-134 to draft simple letters confirming the accounts. The letters can be addressed "To Whom It May Concern," and should state the date the account was opened, the total amount deposited over the last year, and the present balance.

Banks will often (without your asking) also state an average balance. Be aware that if this is much lower than the present amount, the consulate will wonder whether the U.S. citizen got a quick loan from a friend to make the financial situation look more impressive.

Some consulates prefer a recent bank statement instead.

iii. Employer Letter

Here is a sample of a letter from the sponsor's employer. This letter should accompany Form I-134.

Sample Letter From Employer

Hitting the Road Trucking
222 Plaza Place
Outthereville, MA 90000

May 22, 20xx

To Whom It May Concern:

Ron Goodley has been an employee of Hitting the Road Trucking since September 4, 20xx, a total of over five years. He has a full-time position as a driver. His salary is $45,000 per year. This position is permanent, and Ron's prospects for performance-based advancement and salary increases are excellent.

Very truly yours,

Bob Bossman

Bob Bossman
Personnel Manager
Hitting the Road Trucking

iv. The Medical Exam

To prove that you are not inadmissible for medical reasons, you will have to present the results of a medical exam done by a doctor approved by the U.S. consulate. Your Appointment Package will give you complete instructions on where and when to visit the appropriate clinic or doctor. It's best to go around a week before your interview, so as to allow time for the test results to come in. And allow several hours for the appointment. There will be a base fee of about $150, plus additional fees for X-rays and tests.

When you go for your medical exam, make sure to bring the following:

- a form you fill out describing your medical history, if requested
- your visa appointment letter
- the doctor's fee
- your vaccination records, and
- photo identification—the doctor must make sure you don't send a healthier person in your place. You may also be requested to bring a passport-style photo.

The doctor will examine you, ask you questions about your medical and psychiatric history and drug use, and test you (including blood tests and chest X-rays). Pregnant women can (if they bring proof of pregnancy) refuse the chest X-ray until after the baby is born if they have no symptoms of tuberculosis.

As a fiancé, you are not required to fulfill the vaccination requirements at the time of your medical examination for a fiancé(e) visa. These vaccinations are required when you adjust status following your marriage, however, so you might decide to get them out of the way at this time.

When the laboratory results are in, the doctor will fill out the appropriate form and may return it to you in a sealed envelope. DO NOT open the envelope—this will invalidate the results. In some countries, the doctor will send your results straight to the consulate. The doctor should supply you with a separate copy of your results, or tell you whether any illnesses showed up.

TIP

Want to plow through the government's technical guidance on the medical exam? It's published by the Centers for Disease Control and Prevention (CDC). Call 800-311-3435 and ask for a copy of *Technical Instructions for Medical Examination of Aliens*, or go to www.cdc.gov/immigrantrefugeehealth/exams/ti/civil/technical-instructions-civil-surgeons.html.

c. Where You'll Take Your Appointment Package

On the day of your interview, you will be expected to arrive at the consulate with forms and documents in hand, according to the consulate's instructions. After you've attended your interview and been approved, the consulate will give you a visa to enter the United States. Ideally you'll receive the visa within a few days of your interview, but recent delays for FBI and CIA security checks have been adding weeks to the process, especially for people with common names.

Actually, your visa will be a thick, sealed envelope, stuffed full of most of the forms and documents that you've submitted over the course of this process.

CAUTION

Do not open the envelope! Your visa envelope must be presented to a U.S. border official before it is opened. If you open it, the immigration officials will probably assume that you've tampered with it. At best, the border official might send you back to the consulate for another try; at worst, he or she might accuse you of visa fraud and use summary exclusion powers to prohibit you from entering the United States for the next five years.

To prepare for your interview, you'll not only want to read the sections on filling out the forms and gathering documents below, but also read Chapter 13, Interviews With USCIS or Consular Officials.

Also prepare to go through a security checkpoint before entry to the U.S. consulate, as most now require (similar to most busy airports). Portable electronics, like portable music players, mobile phones, or digital cameras, are usually not allowed at the consulate; leave them at home. Carry all of your visa and application documents—and there will be a lot of them—in a clear, plastic folder or something similar, so that consulate security can easily identify your materials as safe.

d. After You Receive Your Fiancé Visa

Once you receive your fiancé visa, you'll have six months to enter the United States. At the U.S. port of entry, the border officer will examine the contents of your visa envelope and ask you a few questions.

Though this part shouldn't be a problem, don't treat it lightly. If the official spots a reason that you shouldn't have been given the fiancé visa, he or she has the power—called expedited removal—to deny your entry right there. You would have no right to a lawyer or a hearing, but would simply have to turn around and find a flight or other means of transport home. And you wouldn't be allowed back for five years (unless the border officials allowed you to withdraw the application before they officially denied it, which is entirely at their discretion).

After advice like this, the hardest thing to hear is "just stay calm." It may be impossible to control your beating heart—but whatever you do, don't start speaking more than is necessary. The worst thing someone could do at this stage is to make a nervous little joke like, "Yeah, I'll see if I still like him, and maybe I'll marry him." Border officials are not known for their sense of humor, and a statement like this could be used as a reason to deny your entry.

Assuming all goes well, the border official will stamp your passport with your K-1 fiancé status, and give you a small white I-94 card showing the 90-day duration of your visa.

e. When to Marry and Apply for Your Green Card

You should start working on your green card application as soon as you arrive in the United States. Once your 90 days expires, you will not be authorized to remain in the U.S. until such time as you file the green card application. (For complete instructions, see Chapter 14.)

In fact, it's a good idea to get married fairly soon after your arrival. Doing so will give you the maximum amount of time after your marriage to prepare the green card application (which is even longer than the fiancé visa application). Also assume that the local government authorities may take a while (up to three months) to produce their final version of your marriage certificate, which you'll need for the green card application.

Contact your local (usually county) Registrar, Recorder, or Vital Records office before you get married to find out their time estimate. Ask whether there is any way to speed up the process. In some areas, couples have found that by hand-carrying the certificate that they receive at the wedding ceremony to the county office, they can shave weeks off the processing time.

f. Using the Checklist for Your Fiancé Appointment Package

Which forms you are required to prepare for your fiancé visa Appointment Package may vary among consulates. The ones listed on the checklist below are those most commonly required. You can strike off any that you don't receive from the consulate, and proceed to use the checklist as usual.

Checklist for Fiancé Appointment Package

☐ Original USCIS Notice of Action approving your K-1, or fiancé, visa petition

☐ A complete copy of your Fiancé Visa Petition (the items in the checklist in Section F2, above) in case USCIS did not forward it to the consulate

☐ Originals of documents submitted in connection with the visa petition, such as your fiancé's U.S. birth certificate and proof that any previous marriages were legally ended

☐ Form DS-230, Part II (see line-by-line instructions in Subsection F3a, above)

☐ Form I-134, Affidavit of Support, if the consulate requested it (see line-by-line instructions in Subsection F3a, above)

   ☐ Documents to accompany Form I-134, including:

   ☐ Proof of U.S. citizen's employment (see sample letter in Subsection F3b, above)

   ☐ Copy of U.S. citizen's most recent federal tax return(s) (see further discussion in Subsection F3b, above)

☐ Letter from U.S. citizen's bank(s) confirming the account(s) (see further discussion in Subsection F3b, above)

☐ Form DS-1858, Sponsor's Financial Responsibility Under the Social Security Act (if the consulate requests it; see instructions in Subsection F3a, above)

☐ A valid passport from your home country, good for at least six months

☐ Your original birth certificate

☐ An original police clearance certificate, if this is available in your country (the instructions from the consulate will tell you)

☐ Three additional photographs of you, the immigrating fiancé (according to the consulate's photo instructions)

☐ Fingerprints (you'll receive instructions from the consulate)

☐ Results of your medical examination, in an unopened envelope, unless the doctor sent the results directly to the consulate (see Chapter 2, Section A, for more on the medical exam)

☐ Additional documents proving your relationship (to cover the time period since submitting the fiancé visa petition), such as copies of:

   ☐ phone bills showing calls to one another

   ☐ correspondence between you

   ☐ photos taken together while one fiancé visited the other

☐ Any other items or forms requested by the consulate

☐ Visa Application fee (currently $240). In some countries, you may also be charged an issuance fee if your visa is approved.

CHECKLIST
Appendix C includes a tear-out copy of this checklist.

G. How to Have Your Children and Pets Accompany You

Although your whole family cannot immigrate right now, U.S. laws and regulations do recognize the need for certain of your loved ones to accompany you to the United States and live there with you, including your children and certain pets.

1. Your Children

If you have unmarried children under age 21 who are interested in accompanying you to the United States and applying for green cards, review Chapter 2 to make sure they fit the basic eligibility requirements. This book does not cover in detail the application process for children. However, it is very similar to your own visa application process. Once you've become familiar with the process, handling your children's applications should not be difficult. We'll give you some tips here to get you started.

All you have to do at the beginning of the fiancé visa application process is to include your children's names on Question 13 of the Fiancé Visa Petition (Form I-129F). The consular officials should then send you extra sets of the required forms for the children to fill out. If you don't receive these extra forms, contact the consulate. For young children, it's okay for you to fill out the form, and even sign it, on their behalf. (Just sign your name, then write *Parent of [name of your child]*.)

Your children will probably be asked to attend your consular interview with you (although some consulates permit younger children to stay at home). The children will receive their visas on the same day you do. The technical name for their visa will be K-2 (if you're on a K-1) or K-4 (if you're married and on a K-3). The materials that children are normally asked to bring to the visa interview include:

- consular forms (not all provided in this book; follow the consulate's instructions)
- child's long-form birth certificate
- child's police record (if the child is over age 16)
- child's passport (unless your country permits the children to be included on your passport)
- four photos of child passport-style, and
- medical exam results.

Even if your children don't accompany you when you first enter as a fiancé, they can join you under the same visa for a year after yours was approved. (Just make sure they remain unmarried and are still under the age of 21.) If they decide to follow you, they will need to contact the U.S. consulate. The consulate will verify your initial visa approval, ask your children to fill in the same forms that you did, interview them regarding their admissibility, and hopefully grant them a visa.

The children will need to submit their green card applications in the United States before their visa expires. (For further information on the children's green card ("adjustment of status") applications, see Chapter 14.)

If you have children who would just like to come for your wedding ceremony, they may be able to obtain a tourist visa. Talk to your local U.S. consulate about the application procedure.

2. Your Pets

Good news for your dog and cat, who may not have learned to sign their names yet—they won't need a visa. Bringing pets into the United States is not an immigration law matter. But before bringing any pets to the United States, you will need to check into U.S. customs restrictions. In general, pets will be allowed in if they are in good health and have had all the proper vaccinations. Certain more specific restrictions apply, however. For example, monkeys aren't allowed into the United States at all, and some states don't allow certain animals. Check with your local U.S. consulate for details, or read more at www.cbg.gov (enter "pets" into the search box, which will bring up a publication called "Pets and Wildlife: Licensing and Health Requirements").

H. Your 90 Days on a K-1 Fiancé Visa

If you're reading this after getting your K-1 fiancé visa, congratulations! But don't stop reading. It's important to understand how to protect and enjoy your visa and how to continue the process toward obtaining a green card, if you plan to make your home in the United States.

1. Are You Permitted to Work?

In theory, fiancés have the right to work in the United States during the 90-day duration of their visa. In practice, taking advantage of this right is more complicated than it sounds.

a. Whether You Should Apply for a Work Permit

You can work in the United States only if, after entering, you apply for and receive a work permit. This is known by USCIS as an Employment Authorization Document, and it's a small plastic card with your photo on it. For application procedures, see Subsection b, below; but first, keep reading for the reasons you might not want to apply.

The problem with applying for a work permit is that USCIS Service Centers routinely take from 45 to 90 days to issue them. This means that your chances of receiving your work permit while you're still eligible for it, as the holder of a fiancé visa, are slim.

You might be better off just getting to work on your adjustment of status application and submitting it as soon as possible after you are married. Once you submit your adjustment of status application, you will still probably wait anywhere from 60 to 90 days for your work permit. You can check the USCIS website to find out the current processing times at the time that you file. Go to www.uscis.gov and, in the box on the left-hand side, under "Find," click "Processing Times." At the bottom of the next page, click "NBC Processing Dates." (Although you will be interviewed for your adjustment of status application at a local office, your work permit application is processed at the National Benefits Center.)

b. How to Apply for a Work Permit

If you still want to apply for a work permit, use Form I-765, Application for Employment Authorization.

 WEB RESOURCE
This form is available on the USCIS website at www.uscis.gov. Below is a sample filled-in version of this form.

Go straight to the last page of the form. This is the only page that you'll have to submit.

Assuming this is your first work permit, under **"I am applying for,"** check "Permission to Accept Employment."

Questions 1-14: Self-explanatory.

Question 15: You are a "K-1 Visa-holder."

Question 16: Your eligibility category is (a)(6) as a fiancé. Sign your name in the section titled "Certification." The following section is only for use by lawyers, paralegals, or anyone else who filled out the form for you.

When you're finished, mail the form, the fee (currently $380), two passport-style photos, and proof of your fiancé visa status (such as a copy of your approval notice, the stamp in your passport, and your I-94 card) to the appropriate USCIS Service Center. The addresses of the Service Centers are in Appendix B.

Alternatively, you can file your Form I-765 electronically, through the USCIS website. However, you will still need to mail your supporting documentation to USCIS (using the address that you'll get in your confirmation receipt). Complete

Sample Form I-765, Application for Employment Authorization

OMB No. 1615-004(

I-765, Application For
Employment Authorization

Department of Homeland Security
U.S. Citizenship and Immigration Services

Do not write in this block.

Remarks	Action Block	Fee Stamp
A#		

Applicant is filing under §274a.12 _____

☐ Application Approved. Employment Authorized / Extended *(Circle One)*   until _____ (Date).
_____ (Date).

Subject to the following conditions: _____
Application Denied.
  ☐ Failed to establish eligibility under 8 CFR 274a.12 (a) or (c).
  ☐ Failed to establish economic necessity as required in 8 CFR 274a.12(c)(14), (18) and 8 CFR 214.2(f)

I am applying for:
☒ Permission to accept employment.
☐ Replacement *(of lost employment authorization document).*
☐ Renewal of my permission to accept employment *(attach previous employment authorization document).*

1. Name (Family Name in CAPS) (First) (Middle) HOLLIS Nigel Ian	Which USCIS Office? Date(s)
2. Other Names Used (include Maiden Name) None	Results (Granted or Denied - attach all documentation)
3. Address in the United States (Street Number and Name) (Apt. Number) 114 Fulton Street 6E	**12.** Date of Last Entry into the U.S. (mm/dd/yyyy) 12/02/2012
(Town or City) (State/Country) (ZIP Code) New York NY 10038	**13.** Place of Last Entry into the U.S. New York
4. Country of Citizenship/Nationality U.K./English	**14.** Manner of Last Entry (Visitor, Student, etc.) K-1 fiance visa
5. Place of Birth (Town or City) (State/Province) (Country) Penzance Cornwall U.K.	**15.** Current Immigration Status (Visitor, Student, etc.) K-1 visa holder
6. Date of Birth (mm/dd/yyyy) **7.** Gender 8/17/84 ☒ Male ☐ Female	**16.** Go to **Part 2** of the Instructions, Eligibility Categories. In the space below, place the letter and number of the category you selected from the instructions (For example, (a)(8), (c)(17)(iii), etc.).
8. Marital Status ☐ Married ☐ Single ☐ Widowed ☒ Divorced	Eligibility under 8 CFR 274a.12 ( ) (a) (6)
9. Social Security Number (include all numbers you have ever used) (if any) N/A	**17.** If you entered the Eligibility Category, (c)(3)(C), in item 16 above, list your degree, your employer's name as listed in E-Verfy, and your employer's E-Verify Company Identification Number or a valid E-Verify Client Company Identification Number in the space below.
10. Alien Registration Number (A-Number) or I-94 Number (if any) N/A	Degree: _____
11. Have you ever before applied for employment authorization from USCIS? ☐ Yes (If "Yes," complete below) ☒ No	Employer's Name as listed in E-Verify: _____ Employer's E-Verify Company Identification Number or a valid E-Verify Client Company Identification Number

Certification

Your Certification: I certify, under penalty of perjury under the laws of the United States of America, that the foregoing is true and correct. Furthermore, I authorize the release of any information that U.S. Citizenship and Immigration Services needs to determine eligibility for the benefit I am seeking. I have read the Instructions in **Part 2** and have identified the appropriate eligibility category in **Block 16**.

Signature *Nigel I. Hollis*	Telephone Number 1234 123456	Date 12/01/2011

Signature of Person Preparing Form, If Other Than Above: I declare that this document was prepared by me at the request of the applicant and is based on all information of which I have any knowledge.

Print Name	Address	Signature	Date

Remarks	Initial Receipt	Resubmitted	Relocated		Completed		
			Rec'd	Sent	Approved	Denied	Returned

Form I-765 (Rev. 01/19/11)Y

instructions for "E-Filing" can be found on the USCIS website (when you go to the page to download the form, click "Electronic Filing" under "Related Links").

c.   How to Get a Social Security Number

With the employment stamp in your passport or your new work permit in your wallet, you can visit your local Social Security office to get a Social Security number. You'll need this number before you start work—your employer will ask for it in order to file taxes on your behalf. To find your local Social Security office, check your phone book in the federal government pages or look on the Social Security Administration's website at www. socialsecurity.gov. You'll need to show them either your K-1 fiancé visa or your work permit.

2.   Are You Permitted to Leave the United States?

If you are planning to make your home in the United States, don't count on leaving for the five months or more that it will take to get your U.S. residency.

a.   You Can Use Your K-1 Visa Only Once

A fiancé visa is good for only one entry, so you can't go out and come back on it. If an emergency comes up before your marriage and you have to leave, try to make time to apply for a travel document ("Advance Parole") at your local USCIS office, using Form I-131 (available on the USCIS website). If you leave without a travel document, the consulate may be able to revalidate your visa back in your home country, but they'll take a hard look at your situation first. You could end up having to start over with a new fiancé visa petition.

b.   Leaving After You've Applied for a Green Card: Advance Parole

In theory, once you've turned in your green card application, any departure from the United States automatically cancels that application. However,

if you obtain special permission—called Advance Parole—the application won't be cancelled while you're away. Obtaining Advance Parole is usually fairly easy, though not guaranteed. Instructions for this application are included in Chapter 14, Section D.

Advance Parole only keeps your application alive while you're gone, it doesn't guarantee your reentry to the United States. Any time you ask to enter the United States, the border officer has a chance to keep you out if he or she determines you are inadmissible. Consult a lawyer before leaving if this is a possible concern.

3.   What Rights Do Family Members Have?

Your children who accompanied you on your fiancé visa have basically the same immigration-related rights as you. They must either leave within the 90 days on their K-2 visas or, after you've married, file applications for green cards along with you.

In order to obtain green cards, each child must submit a separate application. At no point in the process can they be included automatically within your application. However, if you and your children submit your green card applications at the same time, you'll normally be scheduled to attend your green card interview together. (For guidance on preparing green card applications for your children, see Chapter 14.)

4.   Can You Renew or Extend Your K-1 Fiancé Visa Status?

A K-1 fiancé visa cannot be renewed. You are expected to get married within 90 days or leave the United States.

But if something happens and you weren't able to marry within the 90 days, go ahead and marry (if the marriage is still what you want). As long as USCIS hasn't caught up with you before you're ready to submit the application, you should be able to apply for your green card through normal procedures, as explained below.

a. Filing Late for Your Green Card

If you marry after the 90 days permitted by your fiancé visa, your spouse will have to submit an I-130 visa petition on your behalf. (It's similar to Form I-129F, but for married couples.) Because you're already legally in the U.S., however, the I-130 can be submitted with the rest of your green card application to USCIS. Form I-130 shows your eligibility to immigrate (this time as the immediate relative (spouse) of a U.S. citizen, rather than as a fiancé) and your spouse's willingness to support your application. (Instructions for preparing the I-130 as the spouse of a U.S. citizen living in the United States are included in Chapter 11.)

Another consequence of marrying after the 90-day expiration of your visa is that you will be living in the United States unlawfully. Although this is a serious concern, it is unlikely that the immigration enforcement authorities will search you out anytime soon. They have higher enforcement priorities than going after people who will ultimately have the right to a green card, but are simply late in applying for it.

> **CAUTION**
>
> **Don't even think of leaving the United States if you've stayed six or more months past the expiration date on your fiancé visa.** If your 90 days is up and you still haven't filed your green card or adjustment

of status application, you are in the United States unlawfully. However, leaving the U.S. and starting the process over could be the worst thing to do at this point. If you have stayed in the United States more than six months beyond your visa expiration date, leaving would subject you to laws preventing your return for three or ten years. (See Chapter 2, Section A.)

b. Filing in Immigration Court for Your Green Card

If you're late in getting married and turning in your green card application, and the immigration authorities do catch up with you and place you in removal proceedings, it's not a complete disaster. You can apply for your green card in Immigration Court. The application paperwork is mostly the same. However, the law requires the judges to look even harder at your case than a USCIS officer would. That means you will have to do extra work to convince the judge that despite your late marriage, this marriage is bona fide, not a sham.

> **SEE AN EXPERT**
>
> **If you're called into Immigration Court, you'll need a lawyer's help.** Going to court requires some knowledge of official court procedures, and the lawyer can help you prepare extra evidence that your marriage is bona fide.

Overseas Fiancés of U.S. Permanent Residents

If you are the fiancé of a U.S. lawful permanent resident (someone who is not a citizen) and you currently live outside the United States, your options are limited, whether you want to stay in the United States for a short time or permanently. There are no fiancé visas available for foreign nationals wishing to marry U.S. permanent residents. Fiancé visas are only available to people coming to the United States to marry U.S. citizens.

Don't lose hope, however. There are three ways to get yourself into the United States if you are the fiancé of a permanent resident. You can:

- Marry your fiancé first, then begin the entry process as a spouse of a permanent resident. This method is described in Section A.
- Wait until your fiancé becomes a U.S. citizen, and begin your entry process as a fiancé of a citizen. Section B covers this approach, or
- Come to the United States on a tourist visa and get married here (with the idea of returning home afterward). This strategy is described in Section C.

Each of these options has drawbacks, unfortunately. It may not be feasible to have your fiancé travel to you so that you can get married—and if you feel strongly about having your wedding in the U.S., this may not be what you want. And even after you're married, it will take a while before you can move to the United States. Waiting for your fiancé to become a citizen may take a similarly long time. And entering as a tourist will get you in—but you'll have to leave within six months. But these methods are the best we can offer, so take a look and see what's best for you.

> **CAUTION**
> **If the U.S. petitioner has a criminal record, see an attorney.** Under the Adam Walsh Child Protection and Safety Act of 2006, U.S. citizens and lawful permanent residents who have been convicted of any "specified offense against a minor" are prohibited from filing a family-based immigrant petition on behalf of any beneficiary (whether a child or not). USCIS will run security checks on all petitions and may call the petitioner in for fingerprinting. If the petitioner has a conviction for one of the specified offenses against a minor, then the petition will not be approved unless USCIS determines that the U.S. petitioner poses no risk to the beneficiary.

A. The Marriage Visa Option

If you plan to live in the United States permanently, the first thing you should do is to get married. It doesn't matter where you get married. You can have the ceremony in your home country, a third country, or in the United States, if you can get a tourist visa to come here (see Section C below for more on tourist visas).

After you are married, you will be eligible to immigrate to the United States as the spouse of a permanent resident. But first you will have to wait—and wait. Only a limited number of visas are given to spouses of U.S. permanent residents each year, and the demand for these visas is far greater than the supply. (For more on the waiting periods and other aspects of the process of applying as the spouse of a permanent resident see Chapter 8.) It can take three to five years or more to secure a visa this way.

You can't get on the waiting list for a marriage-based visa until you are married. But as soon as your spouse has your marriage certificate in hand, he or she can submit a visa petition that puts you in line. Unfortunately, you will not be allowed to live in the United States while you wait. You should marry as soon as possible in order to secure your place on the list.

B. If Your Fiancé or Spouse Becomes a U.S. Citizen

If your permanent resident fiancé or spouse becomes a U.S. citizen, your ability to obtain a fiancé or marriage-based visa improves tremendously. The process of obtaining a visa itself takes time, but there are no waiting periods for beginning the process if you are the foreign-born fiancé or spouse of a U.S. citizen.

The quicker your fiancé or spouse becomes a citizen, the quicker you can enter the United States. Unless your fiancé faces some serious impediment to citizenship—like not knowing English or having a criminal record—he or she can help your immigration application by applying for citizenship as soon as possible. A permanent resident can apply for U.S. citizenship five years after getting a green card (unless he or she qualifies for one of various exceptions). In fact, USCIS currently permits people to submit the application three months before the end of the required years (but no more than three months before, or they'll reject the application as premature).

There are other requirements to become a U.S. citizen, such as being of good moral character, having lived in the United States for at least half of the previous five years, being able to speak English, and passing a test covering U.S. history and government.

RESOURCE
Need more information on the process and requirements of applying for U.S. citizenship? See the USCIS website at www.uscis.gov and *Becoming a U.S. Citizen: A Guide to the Law, Exam & Interview*, by Ilona Bray (Nolo).

The decision whether to apply for U.S. citizenship is a personal one. Your fiancé may not be interested in U.S. citizenship, perhaps out of a sense of allegiance to his or her home country. Having a green card does allow your fiancé to live in the United States permanently (though a permanent resident can lose his or her right to a green card, by living outside the United States for too long, committing crimes, or otherwise becoming deportable). Your fiancé should know, however, that dual citizenship may be a possibility—if his or her home country allows it, so will the United States.

1. If You're Still Unmarried When Your Fiancé Becomes a Citizen

As the fiancé of a U.S. citizen, you will be eligible to apply for a fiancé visa. This will permit you to enter the United States, marry within 90 days, and apply for your green card in the United States. By applying as a fiancé, you'll avoid the waiting list for foreign spouses married to U.S. permanent residents (see Chapter 8 for more on the waiting lists).

However, unless you are extremely certain that your fiancé is about to become a citizen, it might be wiser to marry now and apply as the spouse of a permanent resident (see Section A, above). Your spouse's citizenship could be delayed or denied—leaving you nowhere. You would then have to marry and join the waiting list later than you otherwise could have.

2. If You're Already Married When Your Spouse Becomes a Citizen

The moment your spouse obtains citizenship, you become what is called an immediate relative. That means that you are immediately eligible for a marriage-based visa to enter the United States and obtain permanent residence, although the application process itself often takes about a year. Alternately, you can use a special variant of the fiancé visa called a K-3 visa, which allows married people to enter on temporary (nonimmigrant) visas, then do the remaining green card paperwork in the United States, just as fiancés do.

You can apply for entry as an immediate relative no matter where you are in the immigration process. So, for example, if your spouse filed the application to put you on the visa waiting list when he or she was a permanent resident (Form I-130), all you'll have to do is tell USCIS about the grant of citizenship for you to jump off the waiting list and move forward in your progress toward a green card. Or, if you want to use the K-3 visa, your spouse would need to separately file a Form I-129F, but wouldn't have to file Form I-130 (which is normally part of the K-3 application procedure) a second time.

C. Fiancés Coming as Tourists

Fiancés who only want to hold their marriage ceremony in the United States, knowing that they will not be permitted to remain here to apply for a green card, may be able to obtain a tourist visa (also called a visitor or B-2 visa). This is done at your local U.S. consulate. The application for a tourist visa is not terribly complicated, and usually takes between one day and six weeks to obtain. You will be given up to a six months' permitted stay.

1. Problems Getting a Tourist Visa

Obtaining and using a tourist visa isn't a sure thing. First, you must convince the consular officer that you really plan to leave your new spouse and return home when your visa expires. You may be tempted to lie and say you are coming only as a tourist, not to get married. This is a bad idea. If the consular official or immigration officer at the border catches you in this lie, it will reinforce his suspicion that your true intention is to live in the United States permanently. You could be denied the tourist visa and accused of visa fraud—which would make it difficult, if not impossible, to eventually obtain your green card.

To convince a skeptical consular official that you intend to return to your home country, bring along documents like:

- a copy of your lease or rental agreement
- a letter from your employer stating that you are expected back by a certain date, or
- copies of birth certificates from close family members remaining behind.

2. Problems at the U.S. Border With a Tourist Visa

Even after obtaining your tourist visa, you could face problems at the U.S. border. Even if the consular officer in your home country believed your plan to return home, the border official might not. If you meet with a reasonable official, this should be no problem—your use of a tourist visa is perfectly legal.

If you get an official who is inclined to be suspicious, however, it's another matter. The border officials have what are called expedited removal powers. This means that they can keep you out if they think you've used fraud, such as lying about your intentions to return home after the wedding. The border official has reason to be suspicious, since many people have used tourist visas as a way to enter the United States precisely for the purpose of living here illegally while they wait to apply for their green card. Once you've been kept out of the United States this way, you may be prevented from returning for five years.

To prepare for the possibility of meeting a wary border official, bring along the same things you showed the consular officer in order to get the visitor visa, explained above in Section 1. Also make sure there is nothing in your luggage to contradict this evidence. If your luggage is searched and the official realizes you are carrying enough prescription medication for a three-year stay and a letter from your fiancé saying, "Can't wait until you are here and we can settle down in our new house," you will find yourself on the next return plane.

Unfortunately, there is no way to remove every element of risk—your entry to the United States depends on the perception and decision of a single border patrol official. It's as simple as that.

3. Staying in the U.S. on a Tourist Visa

No matter how you entered the United States, it will be natural for you to want to stay there with your new spouse after your marriage. You may even know people who have entered on tourist visas and ultimately been able to apply for a green card. However, because of recent changes in the immigration laws, this is no longer a workable plan, particularly for the spouses of lawful permanent residents as opposed to U.S. citizens.

As you may know, spouses of U.S. permanent residents are normally not eligible to stay in the United States during the years they are on the waiting list for a green card. And even if they do stay, they must leave the United States in most circumstances to perform the final step of the process, visiting a U.S. consulate to obtain an immigrant visa leading to permanent resident status. So even if you managed to stay in the United States illegally, you would, as the spouse of a permanent resident, have to return to a U.S. consulate eventually.

"No problem," you might think, "I'll take my chances on living in the United States illegally until then." But the U.S. Congress thought of this possibility too, and created a law to make you think twice. Once you leave to pick up your marriage-based visa at the U.S. consulate in your home country, the law will prevent you from coming back to the United States for a long time. (See Chapter 2, Section A.) If your illegal stay lasts six months or more, you won't be allowed back into the United States for three years. If your stay extends for one year or more, you will be kept out for ten years. That's a strong incentive to comply with the laws and wait for your immigrant visa outside the United States.

On the other hand, if your spouse becomes a U.S. citizen, and you've stayed in the United States as a tourist without getting caught, the law does allow you to file your green card (adjustment of status) application in the United States, without leaving. Since you wouldn't have to leave, you wouldn't face the time bars described above, which are only handed down once you're outside the United States. But you could have another problem. You could be denied your green card (or at least have to apply for a waiver first) for having misused your tourist visa, pretending to be a mere tourist when your intention was to stay in the United States permanently. You would need a lawyer's help to apply for a waiver of your visa fraud.

Next Step	
If you decide to get a tourist visa:	Learn the procedures from your local U.S. consulate. The application form is fairly simple. You will need to convince the consulate that you will return home after the wedding.
If you marry (abroad or in the U.S.) and file for permanent resident status:	See Chapter 8 covering overseas spouses of lawful permanent residents.
If you marry (abroad or in the U.S.) and your spouse becomes a U.S. citizen:	See Chapter 7 for overseas spouses of U.S. citizens.

Overseas Spouses of U.S. Citizens

I f you are married to a U.S. citizen and are living overseas, you are called an "immediate relative" in immigration law terminology. Your road to a green card should be fairly smooth. There are no waiting periods or quotas for people in your category. Your U.S. entry visa and green card are available to you as soon as you can get through the application procedures, which usually takes ten to 12 months.

However, one of your first tasks is to decide which set of application procedures to use. You have two choices: the old-fashioned "immigrant visa," meaning that you'd complete all of your paperwork overseas and enter the U.S. with full rights as a permanent resident (see Section B, below); or the newer, "K-3" nonimmigrant visa, which is an adaptation of the fiancé visa (see Section C, below). The K-3 visa would allow you to enter the United States on a temporary basis, then leave it up to you to submit the paperwork for "adjustment of status," or a green card after arriving.

A. Choosing Among Marriage-Based Visa Options

A marriage-based visa or green card is available to anyone whose marriage to a U.S. citizen is real and legally valid, and who is not inadmissible for any other reason. (See Chapter 2, Section B, if you need to review the complete eligibility criteria.)

If you'll be applying for a K-3 visa, however, there's one limitation to consider—you may apply for your visa only at a consulate in the same country where you held your wedding (or, if you got married in the United States, at a consulate in the country where you (the immigrating spouse) now live). That means if you held your wedding in Italy, but now live in Thailand, using a K-3 visa could be rather inconvenient, since you would have to travel to Italy for the visa interview.

1. Comparing Immigrant Visa and K-3 Visa

Whether you apply for an immigrant visa or a K-3, your initial application to come from overseas will be reviewed by a USCIS office in the United States. It will then be transferred to a U.S. consulate in your home country. The final decision will be made by the consulate, after interviewing you personally.

For immigrant visas, it usually takes ten to 12 months from the initial filing with USCIS until the consulate's final decision. However, your application could go faster or slower, depending on a variety of factors including the complexities of your case and the efficiency and workload of your spouse's nearest USCIS Service Center and the U.S. consulate in your country. (The slow end of things is discussed in more detail in Chapter 15, Dealing With Bureaucrats, Delays, and Denials.)

For K-3 visas, the time period between the initial filing with USCIS and the consulate's decision to give you a visa to the United States is supposed to go faster—but often doesn't.

As always, however, times may vary, depending mostly on the workloads of the offices handling your file. Remember also that with a K-3 visa you'll likely spend four to six months dealing with the U.S. government after you arrive in the United States and apply for your green card.

CAUTION
The urgency you feel to get settled into your new home is not shared by the government officials who'll be dealing with your application. They've long since gotten used to the fact that they have thousands of applications to get through. Once in a while, a miracle will happen; but usually your green card application will take longer than you want.

Applying for Immigrant Visa (Overseas Spouses of U.S. Citizens)

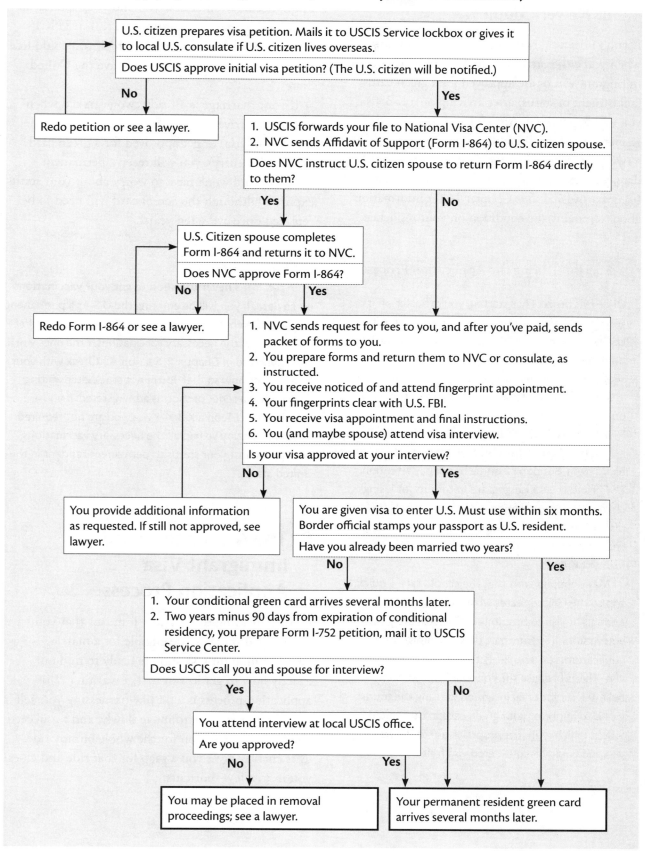

2. Conditional Residence for Newer Couples

If you've been married for less than two years when you either arrive in the United States on an immigrant visa or are approved for a green card (adjustment of status) after arriving on a K-3 visa, you will begin life in America as a conditional resident. Your conditional residency will expire after a two-year "testing" period. Just before the expiration date, you will have to apply for permanent status by filing Form I-751. See Chapter 16 for information about removing the condition on your residence.

Stay Put During the Application Process

Once this process has started, you're better off if you don't change addresses or take any long trips. USCIS or the consulate could send you a request for more information or call you in for your interview at any time. Missing such a notification could result in long delays in getting your visa application back on track.

If you do change addresses, be sure to send notification to the last USCIS or consular office you heard from. But don't assume they'll pay attention. USCIS and the consulates are notorious for losing change-of-address notifications. So, as a backup plan, make sure to have your mail forwarded or check in regularly with the new people living in your former home.

Many couples wish that they could take a quick trip to the United States while waiting for their immigrant visa to be granted. Unfortunately, once you've submitted any part of your immigrant visa application, you're unlikely to be granted a tourist visa. This is because the consulate will probably believe that your real intention in using the tourist visa is to apply for your green card in the United States, which is an inappropriate use of the tourist visa and could be considered visa fraud.

USCIS will review your file at that time and might decide to interview you and your spouse, to find out whether your marriage is real. If USCIS determines your marriage is not real, you could lose your status entirely and have to leave the United States.

If your marriage is already two years old when you either arrive at the U.S. border (with an immigrant visa) or get approved for a green card (after a K-3 entry), you will receive permanent residency and won't have to worry about your status expiring (although the actual card will need to be replaced once every ten years).

TIP

It's never too soon to get your vaccinations up to date. If you will be entering the U.S. as a permanent resident, then before you enter, you'll have to prove that you've had all the necessary vaccinations. (The ones you'll need are listed in Chapter 2, Section A.) Check with your local doctor now so that you're not stuck later waiting weeks while a series of shots is administered. If you are entering the U.S. on a K-3/K-4 visa, you are not required to prove that you've had all the necessary vaccinations until you adjust your status to permanent resident in the United States.

B. The Marriage-Based Immigrant Visa Application Process

If you're reading this section, it means that you have determined that you are eligible for a marriage-based immigrant visa and are ready to find out exactly how to get it. But first, a warning: This application process is a bit like harnessing yourself to a turtle. It's going to move slowly, and to succeed you'll have to hang on for the whole bumpy ride. This chapter gives you a map for that ride and clues you in to a few shortcuts.

1. The Four Steps to an Immigrant Visa

Obtaining a marriage-based visa and green card involves four major steps:

1. Your U.S. citizen spouse submits a visa petition on Form I-130 to USCIS in the United States.

2. You and your spouse pay fees, gather documents, and fill out forms based on instructions sent to you by the National Visa Center (NVC) and return the forms, most likely to the NVC.

3. The NVC transfers your case to a U.S. consulate, where you attend an interview (in your home country) and receive your immigrant visa (then or soon after), and

4. You present your visa at a U.S. border where it is examined. Assuming you are approved, your passport will be stamped for U.S. residency (in other words, you get your green card status).

In rare instances, USCIS will ask your spouse to attend a "fraud interview" if they or the consulate have doubts about your marriage being the real thing. This could happen as part of Step One or after Step Three.

This entire process usually takes approximately ten to 12 months. First you wait for USCIS to approve your initial visa petition, which currently is taking about five months. Then you'll normally have to wait another two months to receive the follow-up paperwork (Step Two) from the NVC, and another three months until the consulate in your home country calls you for your interview (Step Three).

CAUTION

If the U.S. petitioner has a criminal record, see an attorney. Under the Adam Walsh Child Protection and Safety Act of 2006, U.S. citizens who have been convicted of any "specified offense against a minor" are prohibited from filing a family-based immigrant petition on behalf of any beneficiary (whether a child or not). USCIS will run security checks on all petitions and may call the petitioner in for fingerprinting. If the petitioner has a conviction for one of the specified offenses against a minor, then the petition will not be approved unless USCIS determines that the U.S. petitioner poses no risk to the beneficiary.

2. Step One: The I-130 Visa Petition

Your U.S. citizen spouse will initiate the green card application process by filing a visa petition—Form I-130, Petition for Alien Relative and attached documents—with a USCIS "lockbox," which will forward it to a USCIS Service Center in the United States.

We'll go through how to prepare and assemble the various forms and documents, one by one. To keep track of them all, use the "Checklist for Marriage-Based Immigrant Visa Petition" in Subsection d, below. A few items on this checklist are self-explanatory, so they aren't discussed in the following text.

a. Line-by-Line Instructions for Form I-130 Visa Petition

This section will give you precise instructions for filling out the three forms that are required in Step One. Before proceeding, take a look at the general instructions for printing and filling in USCIS immigration forms in Chapter 4. Also, whoever reads these instructions should have a copy of the appropriate form in hand.

i. Form I-130

Form I-130 is one of the most important ones in your immigration process. It will be your spouse's first opportunity to explain who each of you are, where you live, and why you qualify for a visa.

The first thing to notice about Form I-130 is that it runs in two columns (except for the tiny Part A near the top). The left column, or Part B, asks for information about the petitioner—that's your U.S. citizen spouse. Don't be thrown off by the fact that the form addresses your spouse as "you"—after all, it's your spouse who fills out this form. The right column asks for information about you, the immigrant, referred to as the relative.

WEB RESOURCE
Form I-130 is available on the USCIS
website, at www.uscis.gov. Below is a sample filled-in version of this form.

Part A

Question 1: Check the first box, Husband/Wife.

Question 2: This question, about whether you're related by adoption, is meant for people who use this form to petition for an adopted child. We're assuming you can answer this question "No."

Question 3: If your petitioning spouse gained permanent residence through adoption (if he or she immigrated to the United States before becoming a citizen), check **Yes.** But no matter which box you check, it won't affect the application, since this question is mainly directed at people immigrating through parent/child relationships—something not covered in this book.

Part B

Question 1: The petitioning spouse must enter his/her last name (surname) in capital letters, but the first and middle name in small letters. For example, Sam L. Cole would write COLE, Sam L. Your spouse should use his/her current married name if it was changed at the time of your marriage. (If you have questions about how to list your name, see "What's Your Name?" in Chapter 4, Section B).

Questions 2-5: Self-explanatory.

Question 6: This refers only to the petitioning spouse's most recent marital status, so he or she should only check married, even if there was a previous divorce.

Question 7: See "What's Your Name?" in Chapter 4, Section B.

Question 8: Self-explanatory.

Question 9: Self-explanatory.

Question 10: A U.S. citizen can put N/A here, even if he or she was once a lawful permanent resident and had an Alien Registration Number (known as an A-Number).

Question 11: Self-explanatory.

Question 12: This question of when your spouse's prior marriage ended is intended to make sure your current marriage is valid. If your petitioning spouse's prior marriage(s) ended after your present marriage began, yours is not a lawful marriage. If your petitioning spouse has just discovered that the divorce wasn't final when your marriage took place, it may not be necessary to run to a lawyer. Assuming that the divorce has since become final, you can simply correct the problem by remarrying. (If there was fraud involved in your hasty marriage, consult a lawyer before proceeding.)

Question 13: If your petitioning spouse is a naturalized U.S. citizen (meaning he or she wasn't born a citizen, but became one after an application and exam), his or her number can be found at the top right-hand side of the naturalization certificate. The date and place issued are also shown on the certificate.

Question 14a: U.S. citizens can write N/A here.

Question 14b: If your petitioning spouse checks "yes" here, indicating that he or she received U.S. permanent residence through marriage, calculate how long it has been since your spouse's approval for permanent residence. A petitioning spouse who immigrated through marriage cannot petition a new spouse for five years, unless the first spouse died or your spouse can prove by "clear and convincing evidence" that the previous marriage was bona fide (real). USCIS is concerned that the first marriage was just a sham, with the long-term goal of getting both of you into the United States by piggybacking on a sham marriage. To prove that the first marriage was bona fide, your spouse should enclose documentary evidence showing that he or she and the former spouse shared a life, such as shared rent receipts or a mortgage, club memberships, children's birth certificates, utility bills, and insurance agreements. As for what makes for "clear and convincing" evidence, this is one of those legal standards that is easy to state but hard to pin down. The bottom line is, a spouse in this situation will have a hard time persuading a suspicious government official that his or her previous marriage was bona fide.

Sample Form I-130, Petition for Alien Relative—Page 1

Department of Homeland Security
U.S. Citizenship and Immigration Services

OMB No. 1615-0012; Expires 01/31/2012

I-130, Petition for Alien Relative

DO NOT WRITE IN THIS BLOCK - FOR USCIS OFFICE ONLY

A#	Action Stamp	Fee Stamp

Section of Law/Visa Category
- [ ] 201(b) Spouse - IR-1/CR-1
- [ ] 201(b) Child - IR-2/CR-2
- [ ] 201(b) Parent - IR-5
- [ ] 203(a)(1) Unm. S or D - F1-1
- [ ] 203(a)(2)(A)Spouse - F2-1
- [ ] 203(a)(2)(A) Child - F2-2
- [ ] 203(a)(2)(B) Unm. S or D - F2-4
- [ ] 203(a)(3) Married S or D - F3-1
- [ ] 203(a)(4) Brother/Sister - F4-1

Petition was filed on: _____ (priority date)
- [ ] Personal Interview   [ ] Previously Forwarded
- [ ] Pet. [ ] Ben. " A" File Reviewed   [ ] I-485 Filed Simultaneously
- [ ] Field Investigation   [ ] 204(g) Resolved
- [ ] 203(a)(2)(A) Resolved   [ ] 203(g) Resolved

Remarks:

A. Relationship You are the petitioner. Your relative is the beneficiary.

1. I am filing this petition for my:
[X] Husband/Wife [ ] Parent [ ] Brother/Sister [ ] Child

2. Are you related by adoption?
[ ] Yes [X] No

3. Did you gain permanent residence through adoption?
[ ] Yes [X] No

B. Information about you

1. Name (Family name in CAPS) (First) (Middle)
Mancini   Alberto   Ilario

2. Address (Number and Street) (Apt. No.)
800 Broadway

(Town or City) (State/Country) (Zip/Postal Code)
Lindenhurst   NY   11757

3. Place of Birth (Town or City) (State/Country)
Los Angeles   U.S.

4. Date of Birth **5. Gender** **6. Marital Status**
03/30/1974   [X] Male [X] Married [ ] Single
              [ ] Female [ ] Widowed [ ] Divorced

7. Other Names Used (including maiden name)
None

8. Date and Place of Present Marriage (if married)
01/01/2011 Venice, Italy

9. U.S. Social Security Number (If any) **10. Alien Registration Number**
222-22-2222   None

11. Name(s) of Prior Husband(s)/Wive(s) **12. Date(s) Marriage(s) Ended**
Stella Mancini   03/07/88

13. If you are a U.S. citizen, complete the following:
My citizenship was acquired through (check one):
[X] Birth in the U.S.
[ ] Naturalization. Give certificate number and date and place of issuance.

[ ] Parents. Have you obtained a certificate of citizenship in your own name?
  [ ] Yes. Give certificate number, date and place of issuance. [ ] No

14. If you are a lawful permanent resident alien, complete the following:
Date and place of admission for or adjustment to lawful permanent residence and class of admission.

14b. Did you gain permanent resident status through marriage to a U.S. citizen or lawful permanent resident?
[ ] Yes [X] No

C. Information about your relative

1. Name (Family name in CAPS) (First) (Middle)
Mancini   Terese   Maria

2. Address (Number and Street) (Apt. No.)
108 Piazza D'Azeglio

(Town or City) (State/Country) (Zip/Postal Code)
Venice   Italy   99999

3. Place of Birth (Town or City) (State/Country)
Venice   Italy

4. Date of Birth **5. Gender** **6. Marital Status**
02/15/1978   [ ] Male [X] Married [ ] Single
              [X] Female [ ] Widowed [ ] Divorced

7. Other Names Used (including maiden name)
Terese Brabantio, Terese Moreno

8. Date and Place of Present Marriage (if married)
01/01/2011 Venice, Italy

9. U.S. Social Security Number (If any) **10. Alien Registration Number**
None   None

11. Name(s) of Prior Husband(s)/Wive(s) **12. Date(s) Marriage(s) Ended**
Giovanni Moreno   07/10/2004

13. Has your relative ever been in the U.S.? [ ] Yes [X] No

14. If your relative is currently in the U.S., complete the following:
He or she arrived as a:
(visitor, student, stowaway, without inspection, etc.) N/A

Arrival/Departure Record (I-94) Date arrived

Date authorized stay expired, or will expire, as shown on Form I-94 or I-95

15. Name and address of present employer (if any)
self-employed

Date this employment began
08/06/2001

16. Has your relative ever been under immigration proceedings?
[X] No [ ] Yes Where _____ When _____
[ ] Removal [ ] Exclusion/Deportation [ ] Rescission [ ] Judicial Proceedings

INITIAL RECEIPT	RESUBMITTED	RELOCATED: Rec'd	Sent	COMPLETED: Appv'd	Denied	Ret'd

Form I-130 (01/08/12) Y

Sample Form I-130, Petition for Alien Relative—Page 2

C. Information about your alien relative (continued)

17. List husband/wife and all children of your relative.

(Name)	(Relationship)	(Date of Birth)	(Country of Birth)
Alberto Ilario Mancini	husband	03/30/72	U.S.A.
Giovanna Moreno	daughter	06/01/00	Italy

18. Address in the United States where your relative intends to live.

(Street Address)	(Town or City)	(State)
800 Broadway	Lindenhurst	NY

19. Your relative's address abroad. (Include street, city, province and country)

108 Piazza D'Azeglio, Venice, Italy

Phone Number (if any)
764 290-7645

20. If your relative's native alphabet is other than Roman letters, write his or her name and foreign address in the native alphabet.

(Name)   Address (Include street, city, province and country):

N/A

21. If filing for your husband/wife, give last address at which you lived together. (Include street, city, province, if any, and country):

N/A

From: To:

22. Complete the information below if your relative is in the United States and will apply for adjustment of status. N/A

Your relative is in the United States and will apply for adjustment of status to that of a lawful permanent resident at the USCIS office in:

If your relative is not eligible for adjustment of status, he or she will apply for a visa abroad at the American consular post in:

(City)	(State)	(City)	(Country)

NOTE: Designation of a U.S. embassy or consulate outside the country of your relative's last residence does not guarantee acceptance for processing by that post. Acceptance is at the discretion of the designated embassy or consulate.

D. Other information

1. If separate petitions are also being submitted for other relatives, give names of each and relationship.

Giovanna Moreno, stepdaughter

2. Have you ever before filed a petition for this or any other alien? ☐ Yes ☒ No

If "Yes," give name, place and date of filing and result.

WARNING: USCIS investigates claimed relationships and verifies the validity of documents. USCIS seeks criminal prosecutions when family relationships are falsified to obtain visas.

PENALTIES: By law, you may be imprisoned for not more than five years or fined $250,000, or both, for entering into a marriage contract for the purpose of evading any provision of the immigration laws. In addition, you may be fined up to $10,000 and imprisoned for up to five years, or both, for knowingly and willfully falsifying or concealing a material fact or using any false document in submitting this petition.

YOUR CERTIFICATION: I certify, under penalty of perjury under the laws of the United States of America, that the foregoing is true and correct. Furthermore, I authorize the release of any information from my records that U.S. Citizenship and Immigration Services needs to determine eligiblity for the benefit that I am seeking.

E. Signature of petitioner

Alberto Ilario Mancini   Date 7/6/2012   Phone Number (212) 222-9822

F. Signature of person preparing this form, if other than the petitioner

I declare that I prepared this document at the request of the person above and that it is based on all information of which I have any knowledge.

Print Name _____   Signature _____   Date _____

Address _____   G-28 ID or VOLAG Number, if any. _____

Form I-130 (01/08/12) Y Page 2

Part C: (Now referring to you, the immigrant beneficiary)

Question 1: Your current name, with your last name (surname) in capital letters. (If you have any doubt about what name to use, see "What's Your Name?" in Chapter 4, Section B.)

Questions 2-5: Self-explanatory.

Question 6: Your current marital status only, that is, "married."

Question 7: See "What's Your Name?" in Chapter 4, Section B.

Question 8: Self-explanatory.

Question 9: You won't have a Social Security number until you have lived in the United States and have had a work permit, a visa allowing you to work, or U.S. residence. If you don't have a Social Security number, just write N/A.

Question 10: The Alien Registration Number is an eight- or nine-digit number following a letter A that USCIS (or the formerly named INS) would have assigned to you if you'd previously applied for permanent (or, in some cases, temporary) residence or been in deportation/removal proceedings. Of course, if that previous application was denied because you were inadmissible or you lied on that application, you should call a lawyer before going any further.

Question 11: Self-explanatory.

Question 12: See advice to Question 12 on Part B, above.

Question 13: Self-explanatory.

Question 14: Enter N/A here, since you are living outside the United States.

Question 15: State your employer's name and address.

Question 16: If you've been placed in Immigration Court proceedings, see a lawyer, particularly if you lost.

Question 17: This is the continuation of Part C, so all questions still refer to you, the immigrant beneficiary. Since your spouse is already covered in this application, just list your children, if any. This means all your children, including any by previous relationships.

Question 18: Self-explanatory. Hopefully, you intend to live at your spouse's address, or USCIS will raise questions.

Question 19: Self-explanatory.

Question 20: If your native language uses a non-Roman script (for example, Russian, Chinese, or Arabic), you will need to write your name and address in that script.

Question 21: If you've ever lived together, put the last address here. If not, write "N/A."

Question 22: You don't need to answer this question, since you'll be arriving from overseas on an immigrant visa. USCIS will figure out which consulate your case will be sent to, based on where you live. If your country doesn't have diplomatic relations with the United States, USCIS will locate a consulate in a nearby country to handle your case. (**Note:** You'd handle this question differently if you were applying for a K-3 visa, instead; K-3 applicants should refer back to the special instructions in their own section of this chapter.)

Part D: Other Information

Now we're back to questions to be answered by the petitioning spouse.

Question 1: This refers to other petitions being submitted simultaneously, (for example, for your children from this or other marriages), so that USCIS can process the petitions together.

Question 2: This question is meant to uncover the U.S. spouse's history (if any) of petitioning other immigrants to come to the United States. As you can probably imagine, if the petitioning spouse has a history of short marriages to people whom he/she then helped to obtain green cards, you can expect a major marriage fraud investigation. Consult a lawyer before proceeding.

Signature Line: The U.S. citizen, petitioning spouse signs here.

Signature of person preparing form if other than the petitioner. If you or your spouse is filling out your own application, write N/A here. A little typing assistance or advice from a friend doesn't count—the only people who need to complete this line are lawyers or agencies who fill out these forms on others' behalf.

ii.   Form G-325A

You and your spouse must each fill out this form. The information will allow the U.S. government to check your background. Most of the form is self-explanatory. If you really can't remember or are unable to find out an exact date, enter whatever you can remember, such as the year. Alternately, you can simply say "unknown," but if you overuse the "unknowns," USCIS may return your entire application for another try. Since the questions aren't numbered, we refer to them by the approximate line.

 WEB RESOURCE

Form G-325A is available on the USCIS website at www.uscis.gov. Below is a sample filled-in version of this form.

Lines 1 and 2 (Family Name, etc.): Self-explanatory.

Line 3 (Father/Mother): Self-explanatory.

Line 4 (Husband or Wife): Self-explanatory.

Lines 5 and 6 (Former Husbands or Wives): Self-explanatory.

Lines 7–12 (Applicant's residence last five years): Be careful here. These need to be in reverse chronological order, starting with your most recent address and working your way down the last five years. Practice making this list on another sheet of paper before you enter the information here. For example, if you live in Munich now but lived in Bonn before, your Munich address would go on the top line.

Lines 13 and 14 (Applicant's last address outside the United States of more than one year): This may overlap with one of the addresses in Line 6—that's okay.

Lines 15–20 (Applicant's employment last five years): Again, be careful to put this in reverse chronological order. If you've been unemployed, self-employed, or were a housewife or house-husband, say so here—in other words, try to account for all five years.

Line 21 (Show below last occupation abroad if not listed above): This question asks you to list your last overseas job—but only if you didn't already list it on Line 8. People tend to overlook this line, because it's so small—make sure you don't accidentally skip over it.

Line 22 (This form is submitted in connection with application for): Your U.S. citizen spouse should check "other" and write "in support of spouse's I-130." You should check "status as permanent resident."

Line 23 (If your native alphabet uses non-Roman letters): Enter the native spelling of your name here.

Line 24 (The dark box): Self-explanatory.

b.   Documents to Have on Hand for Visa Petition

The I-130 visa petition asks you to submit supporting documents and payment along with the form. You're not done with this form until you have gathered together the following:

- **Proof of the U.S. citizen status of your petitioning spouse.** Depending on how your spouse became a citizen, he or she should copy a birth certificate, passport, certificate of naturalization, or Form FS-20 (Report of Birth Abroad of a United States Citizen).

- **Proof that you're legally married.** This should include at a minimum a copy of your marriage certificate, most likely from a government source (see Chapter 4, Section C, for details). In addition, if either you or your spouse have been previously married, you must include proof that these marriages were terminated, such as a copy of a death, divorce, or annulment certificate.

- **Photos.** Attach one passport photo of yourself to your G-325A, and one passport photo of your spouse to your spouse's G-325A. The photos should be in color, 2 x 2 inches in size, taken within the past six months, showing your current appearance. "Passport style" means that the photo shows your full face from the front, with a plain white or off-white background—

Sample Form G-325A, Biographic Information

Department of Homeland Security
U.S. Citizenship and Immigration Services

OMB No. 1615-0008; Expires 08/31/2012

G-325A, Biographic Information

(Family Name)	(First Name)	(Middle Name)	☐ Male ☒ Female	Date of Birth (mm/dd/yyyy)	Citizenship/Nationality	File Number
Mancini	Terese	Maria		02-15-1978	Italy	A None

All Other Names Used (include names by previous marriages)	City and Country of Birth	U.S. Social Security # (if any)
Terese Brabantio	Venice Italy	

	Family Name	First Name	Date of Birth (mm/dd/yyyy)	City, and Country of Birth (if known)	City and Country of Residence
Father	Brabantio	Francisco	08/02/1957	Venice, Italy	deceased
Mother (Maiden Name)	Gallo	Magdalena	04/24/1964	Venice, Italy	Venice, Italy

Current Husband or Wife (If none, so state) Family Name (For wife, give maiden name)	First Name	Date of Birth (mm/dd/yyyy)	City and Country of Birth	Date of Marriage	Place of Marriage
Mancini	Alberto	03/30/74	Los Angeles, U.S.A.	01/01/2011	Venice, Italy

Former Husbands or Wives (If none, so state) Family Name (For wife, give maiden name)	First Name	Date of Birth (mm/dd/yyyy)	Date and Place of Marriage	Date and Place of Termination of Marriage
Moreno	Giovanni	11/16/1972	08/05/1995 Venice	07/10/2004 Venice

Applicant's residence last five years. List present address first.

Street and Number	City	Province or State	Country	From Month	From Year	To Month	To Year
108 Piazza d'Azeglio	Venice		Italy	08	2001	Present Time	
90 Piazza d'Azeglio	Venice		Italy	02	1978	08	2001

Applicant's last address outside the United States of more than 1 year.

Street and Number	City	Province or State	Country	From Month	From Year	To Month	To Year
N/A							

Applicant's employment last five years. (If none, so state.) List present employment first.

Full Name and Address of Employer	Occupation (Specify)	From Month	From Year	To Month	To Year
Terese Maria Mancini, 108 Piazza d'Azeglio, Venice	freelance writer	08	2001	Present Time	
Venice High School, Italy	student	09	1998	06	2001

Last occupation abroad if not shown above. (Include all information requested above.)

N/A

This form is submitted in connection with an application for:	Signature of Applicant	Date
☐ Naturalization ☐ Other (Specify): ☒ Status as Permanent Resident	Terese Mancini	7/30/2012

If your native alphabet is in other than Roman letters, write your name in your native alphabet below:

Penalties: Severe penalties are provided by law for knowingly and willfully falsifying or concealing a material fact.

Applicant: Print your name and Alien Registration Number in the box outlined by heavy border below.

Complete This Box (Family Name)	(Given Name)	(Middle Name)	(Alien Registration Number)
MANCINI	Terese	Maria	A

Form G-325A (Rev. 08/08/11) Y

Sample I-130 Receipt Notice

Department of Homeland Security
U.S. Citizenship and Immigration Services

I-797C, Notice of Action

THE UNITED STATES OF AMERICA

RECEIPT NUMBER		CASE TYPE 1130	IMMIGRANT PETITION FOR RELATIVE, FIANCE(E), OR ORPHAN
MSC-12-047-00000			
RECEIVED DATE	PRIORITY DATE	PETITIONER	
August 1, 2010		MANCINI, ALBERTO	
NOTICE DATE	PAGE	BENEFICIARY	
AUGUST 10, 2012	1 of 1	MANCINI, TERESE	

ILONA BRAY
RE: TERESE MARIA MANCINI
950 PARKER STREET
BERKELEY, CA 94710

Notice Type: Receipt Notice

Amount received: $ 420.00

Receipt notice - If any of the above information is incorrect, call customer service immediately.

Processing time - Processing times vary by kind of case.
- You can check our current processing time for this kind of case on our website at **uscis.gov**.
- On our website you can also sign up to get free e-mail updates as we complete key processing steps on this case.
- Most of the time your case is pending the processing status will not change because we will be working on others filed earlier.
- We will notify you by mail when we make a decision on this case, or if we need something from you. If you move while this case is pending, call customer service when you move.
- Processing times can change. If you don't get a decision or update from us within our current processing time, check our website or call for an update.

If you have questions, check our website or call customer service. Please save this notice, and have it with you if you contact us about this case.

Notice to all customers with a pending I-130 petition - USCIS is now processing Form I-130, Petition for Alien Relative, as a visa number becomes available. Filing and approval of an I-130 relative petition is only the first step in helping a relative immigrate to the United States. Eligible family members must wait until there is a visa number available before they can apply for an immigrant visa or adjustment of status to a lawful permanent resident. This process will allow USCIS to concentrate resources first on cases where visas are actually available. This process should not delay the ability of one's relative to apply for an immigrant visa or adjustment of status. Refer to **www.state.gov/travel** <http://www.state.gov/travel> to determine current visa availability dates. For more information, please visit our website at www.uscis.gov or contact us at 1-800-375-5283.

Always remember to call customer service if you move while your case is pending. If you have a pending I-130 relative petition, also call customer service if you should decide to withdraw your petition or if you become a U.S. citizen.

Please see the additional information on the back. You will be notified separately about any other cases you filed.
U.S. CITIZENSHIP & IMMIGRATION SERVICES
P.O. BOX 68005
LEE'S SUMMIT, MO 68005
Customer Service Telephone: (800) 375-5283

Form I-797C (Rev. 08/31/04) N

Sample I-130 Approval Notice

Department of Homeland Security
U.S. Citizenship and Immigration Services

I-797, Notice of Action

THE UNITED STATES OF AMERICA

RECEIPT NUMBER		CASE TYPE I130 IMMIGRANT PETITION FOR
MSC-12-047-00000		RELATIVE, FIANCE(E), OR ORPHAN

RECEIPT DATE	PRIORITY DATE	PETITIONER
August 1, 2012		MANCINI, ALBERTO

NOTICE DATE	PAGE	BENEFICIARY
April 11, 2013	1 of 1	MANCINI, TERESE

ILONA BRAY
RE: TERESE MARIA MANCINI
950 PARKER STREET
BERKELEY, CA 94710

Notice Type: Approval Notice

Section: Husband or wife of U.S. citizen, 201(b)(2)(A)(i) INA

The above petition has been approved. We have sent the original visa petition to the **Department of State National Visa Center (NVC), 32 Rochester Avenue, Portsmouth, NH 03801-2909.** NVC processes all approved immigrant visa petitions that need consular action. It also determines which consular post is the appropriate consulate to complete visa processing. NVC will then forward the approved petition to that consulate.

The NVC will contact the person for whom you are petitioning(beneficiary) concerning further immigrant visa processing steps.

If you have any questions about visa issuance, please contact the NVC directly. However, please allow at least 90 days before calling the NVC if your beneficiary has not received correspondence from the NVC. The telephone number of the NVC is **(603) 334-0700**.

THIS FORM IS NOT A VISA NOR MAY IT BE USED IN PLACE OF A VISA.

Please see the additional information on the back. You will be notified separately about any other cases you filed.

U.S. CITIZENSHIP & IMMIGRATION SERVICES
P.O. BOX 68005
LEE'S SUMMIT, MO 68005
Customer Service Telephone: (800) 375-5283

Form I-797 (Rev. 01/31/05) N

and your face must measure between one inch and 1⅜ inches from the bottom of your chin to the top of your head. For more information, see the State Department website at http://travel.state.gov (under "Visas for Foreign Citizens," click "more," then "A–Z Subject Index," then go to "Photo Requirements" under letter "P"). However, USCIS regulations permit you to submit a photo that doesn't completely follow the instructions if you live in a country where such photographs are unavailable or are cost prohibitive.

- **Fees.** The current fee for an I-130 visa petition is $420. However, these fees go up fairly regularly, so double-check this on the USCIS website at www.uscis.gov, or by calling USCIS at 800-375-5283.

c. Using the Checklist for Step One, Visa Petition

When you put it all together, the visa petition that your spouse files for Step One will include three forms and some supporting documents, photos, and a fee, as explained above and detailed on the following checklist. As you fill out and prepare your paperwork, mark off the items that you've found or finished on your checklist. This will be the best way to make sure you haven't forgotten anything.

 CHECKLIST
Appendix C includes a tear-out copy of this checklist.

d. Where to Send Form I-130 Visa Petition

After your spouse has—with your help—prepared and assembled all the forms and other items from the checklist below, make photocopies for your records. Your spouse should send the whole visa petition to a USCIS office called a "lockbox" for the region where he or she lives. (The lockbox will process your fee payment then forward the petition to a USCIS Service Center.)

> ## Checklist for Marriage-Based Immigrant Visa Petition
>
> This checklist shows every form, document, and other item needed for the initial visa petition that your spouse, with your help, will assemble and submit to USCIS.
>
> ☐ Form I-130 (see line-by-line instructions in Subsection B2a, above)
>
> ☐ Documents to accompany Form I-130:
>
>   ☐ Your marriage certificate (see Chapter 4, Section C, on obtaining such documents)
>
>   ☐ Proof of the U.S. citizen status of your petitioning spouse (see Subsection B2b, above)
>
>   ☐ Proof of termination of all previous marriages, such as a copy of a death, divorce, or annulment certificate (see Chapter 4, Section C, on how to obtain vital documents)
>
> ☐ One color photo of you (see Subsection B2b, above)
>
> ☐ One color photo of your spouse
>
> ☐ Fee: currently $420 but double-check this at www.uscis.gov (see Subsection B2b, above)
>
> ☐ Form G-325A, Biographic Information, filled out by you (see Subsection B2a, above, for line-by-line instructions)
>
> ☐ Form G-325A, Biographic Information, filled out by your spouse

If your spouse is mailing this in the United States, certified mail with a return receipt is the safest way to send it. The return receipt will prove that USCIS received the petition and help convince them to track it down if it's misplaced. The lockbox address is below (and in Appendix B). You can double-check this information on the USCIS website.

If your spouse lives overseas, he or she should ask the local U.S. consulate where to send the I-130 visa petition. In most cases, an overseas U.S. citizen spouse will send the I-130 to the USCIS Chicago Lockbox.

e. What Happens After Sending in the Form I-130 Visa Petition

A few weeks after your spouse sends in your visa petition, he or she should get a receipt notice from a different USCIS processing center (see sample above). The receipt notice will tell you to check the USCIS website for information on how long the application is likely to remain in processing—currently about five months, but processing times can change, so checking the USCIS website is a good idea. Do so by going to www.uscis.gov, and in the box on the left side, under "Find," clicking "Processing Times." At the bottom of the following page, from the drop-down menu, select the Service Center listed on the I-130 receipt notice and click "Service Center Processing Dates." The Service Center with jurisdiction over your case is based on where you live.

Where to Send the Form I-130 Visa Petition			
If the U.S. petitioner lives in:			**Send Form I-130 to:**

Alaska
American Samoa
Arizona
California
Colorado
Florida
Guam
Hawaii
Idaho
	Kansas
	Montana
	Nebraska
	Nevada
	New Mexico
	North Dakota
	Northern Mariana Islands
	Oklahoma
		Oregon
		Puerto Rico
		South Dakota
		Texas
		Utah
		Virgin Islands
		Washington
		Wyoming
			USCIS Phoenix Lockbox
			
			For U.S. Postal Service (USPS) deliveries:
			    USCIS ATTN: I-130
			    P.O. Box 21700
			    Phoenix, AZ 85036
			
			For Express Mail and courier deliveries:
			    USCIS
			    Attn: I-130
			    1820 E. Skyharbor Circle S
			    Suite 100
			    Phoenix, AZ 85034

Alabama
Arkansas
Connecticut
Delaware
District of Columbia
Georgia
Illinois
Indiana
Iowa
Kentucky
Louisiana
	Maine
	Maryland
	Massachusetts
	Michigan
	Minnesota
	Mississippi
	Missouri
	New Hampshire
	New Jersey
	New York
		North Carolina
		Ohio
		Pennsylvania
		Rhode Island
		South Carolina
		Tennessee
		Vermont
		Virginia
		West Virginia
		Wisconsin
			USCIS Chicago Lockbox
			
			For U.S. Postal Service:
			    USCIS
			    P.O. Box 804625
			    Chicago, IL 60680-4107
			
			For Express Mail and courier deliveries:
			    USCIS
			    Attn: I-130
			    131 South Dearborn–3rd Floor
			    Chicago, IL 60603-5517

If the U.S. petitioner prefers to send the I-130 by private courier (non-U.S. Postal Service), then regardless of where the petitioner lives, send Form I-130 to:			**USCIS Lockbox**
			    Attn: SAI-130
			    131 South Dearborn–3rd Floor
			    Chicago, IL 60603-5517

TIP

Look for your receipt number. When you get your USCIS receipt, you will see this number in the upper left-hand corner. You can use this number to check the status of your case online by going to www.uscis.gov, and in the box on the left-hand side of the page, clicking "Sign-up for Case Updates." When you do this, you will also be able to sign up for automatic email updates about your case from USCIS. There is also a pilot program that lets you sign up to receive a text message on your mobile phone when a case status update occurs. If you sign up for either the email updates or the text messaging, you will still receive information about your case by regular mail.

Until the completion time predicted by the USCIS website, USCIS will ignore any inquiries from you or your spouse asking what is going on. These processing centers seem like walled fortresses. You can't visit them, nor talk to a live person there. (See Chapter 15 for what to do if you don't get a timely answer from USCIS.) If USCIS needs additional documentation to complete your application, they will send your spouse a letter asking for it.

Eventually your spouse will either receive an approval or a denial of the visa petition.

i. If the Visa Petition Is Denied

If the visa petition is denied, USCIS will tell you the reason for the denial. The fastest thing to do is to fix the problem and try again. For example, if the denial came because your petitioning spouse did not appear to be actually divorced from his or her previous spouse, your spouse would need to see a lawyer and obtain new and better documentation showing that there was a final divorce. Then he or she can file a new visa petition.

ii. If the Visa Petition Is Approved

When your visa petition is approved, your spouse will receive a notice from the USCIS processing center. An example of a visa petition approval notice is shown above. As you can see, it's nothing fancy. But it is an important document. Make a few photocopies of it and store these and the original in safe places.

At the same time that USCIS notifies your spouse of the approval of your visa petition, it will forward your case to the National Visa Center (NVC) in New Hampshire. This office will take over and guide you through Step Two.

3. Step Two: Pay Fees, Prepare Forms and Documents

Next, you, the immigrant, will receive what's called a Choice of Address and Agent form (DS-3032) from the NVC. This is a fairly simple form—but don't let its simplicity fool you. By choosing an "agent," as the form asks for, you're essentially deciding where all the important mail from the U.S. government regarding your immigration should go—to you at your overseas address, or to someone else, most likely your petitioner in the U.S. (if you're not using an attorney). If mail service from the U.S. has been at all unreliable where you live, or if you might be moving before your visa interview, it's safest to choose your petitioner as agent, and write in the U.S. address.

WEB RESOURCE

This form is available on the State Department website at www.state.gov. A sample filled-in version of this form is shown below.

At the same time, the NVC will send a bill for processing the Affidavit of Support (Form I-864—the fee is currently $88) to your petitioner. After the petitioner pays the fee, the NVC will send further instructions on preparing and submitting Form I-864.

Then, once the NVC receives your Form DS-3032, it will mail you a bill for the immigrant visa processing fee (currently $330). Once the visa fee is paid, the NVC will send you further instructions.

Those instructions will probably tell you to fill out various forms (either sent to you by the NVC or that you'll be told where to download online) and

Sample DS-3032, Choice of Address and Agent

Make sure the address is complete and correct. We will use this address for future mailings.

OMB No. 1405-0126
EXPIRATION DATE: 01/31/2013
ESTIMATED BURDEN: 10 minutes*

Place Case Barcode Strip Here Before Mailing to the National Visa Center

U.S. Department of State
CHOICE OF ADDRESS AND AGENT
For Immigrant Visa Applicants
Print or Type your Full Name

Mancini   Terese   M

(Last Name)   (First Name)   (MI.)

Check one box only to the left of the statement that is your choice.

☐ I Appoint _____ _____

Telephone Number

as my agent or attorney to receive mail about my application. Mail from the U.S. Department of State concerning my immigrant visa application should be sent to:

_____ _____

Name of the person who will act as your agent or attorney for receipt of mail   Telephone Number

_____ _____

Street Address (where my agent or attorney will receive mail about my application)   *Email Address

_____ _____ _____ _____

City   State/Province   Postal Code   Country

☒ I do not appoint an agent or an attorney to receive mail about my application. Mail from the U.S. Department of State concerning my immigrant visa application should be sent to me at:

108 Piazza d'Azeglio   terese123@email.com

Street Address (Include "in care of" if Needed)   *Email Address

Venice   _____   _____   Italy

City   State/Province   Postal Code   Country

☐ I have already legally immigrated to the U.S. and do not need to apply for an immigrant visa. I received my Green Card through the _____ (City) USCIS office. My A# is

_____ .

☐ I no longer wish to apply for an immigrant visa.

As proof of your choice, sign and date this document:

Terese Mancini   04/20/2013

Signature of Applicant   Date of Signature (mm-dd-yyyy)

*The Department is currently testing an electronic application system for nonimmigrant visa application that will allow electronic submission and eliminate paper forms. Once testing on this application system is completed the Department is examining whether or not the system can be used for the immigrant visa system.

Paperwork Reduction Act Statement

*Public reporting burden for this collection of information is estimated to average 10 minutes per response, including time required for searching existing data sources, gathering the necessary documentation, providing the information and/or documents required, and reviewing the final collection. You do not have to supply this information unless this collection displays a currently valid OMB control number. If you have comments on the accuracy of this burden estimate and/or recommendations for reducing it, please send them to: A/GIS/DIR, Room 2400 SA-22, U.S. Department of State, Washington, DC 20522-2202.

Confidentiality Statement

INA Section 222(f) provides that visa issuance and refusal records shall be considered confidential and shall be used only for the formulation, amendment, administration, or enforcement of the immigration, nationality, and other laws of the United States. Certified copies of visa records may be made available to a court which certifies that the information contained in such records is needed in a case pending before the court.

DS-3032
06-2011

return them to the NVC. The NVC will review all of your documents before finally sending you an appointment notice for your interview at a U.S. consulate in your home country.

However, this whole system is still in transition—some applicants will still have their files transferred to a U.S. consulate early in the process (the old system), and will receive instructions and an appointment notice directly from the consulate.

In either case, the important thing will be for you to follow the instructions carefully. If you make a mistake—for example you forget to send in a form or document, forget to sign one of the forms, or you enter inconsistent information on different forms—you'll normally get a second chance. The NVC will send you what's called a "checklist," setting out what you need to do and giving you a barcode sheet to include with your response. Again, read the instructions carefully and try to get it exactly right—every mistake you make delays your case and could eventually lead to the visa being denied.

TIP

When sending original documents, always include a copy. The NVC will request various original documents, like your original birth and marriage certificate. You may feel understandably nervous about sending in these original documents. So long as you remember to also include a copy of the document, you'll get the original back when you go to your visa interview.

a. Line-by-Line Instructions for Step Two Forms

You will receive all the forms you need (or instructions on downloading them) from the NVC or the relevant consulate after your I-130 visa petition has been approved and your fees paid. Certain forms vary among consulates (for example, some include translations into the language of that country), so they may not look exactly like the samples in this book.

i. Form DS-230 Part I

This form is used to collect basic biographic information about you, such as your address and the names of your children.

WEB RESOURCE

Form DS-230 Part I is available on the State Department website at www.state.gov. You may be asked to complete it online. However, use the form that you get from the U.S. consulate if it's different. Below is a sample filled-in version of this form.

Questions 1-28: Self-explanatory (similar to the questions on Form I-130; see Subsection 2a, above).

Question 29: List all your children. You'll have a chance to identify which ones are immigrating with you later.

Question 30: Self-explanatory.

Question 31a: List only those children of yours who also have an approved I-130 visa petition and will be immigrating with you at the same time.

Question 31b: List only those children who have an approved I-130 visa petition and will be following to join you.

Questions 32-34: Self-explanatory.

Question 35: If you've spent more than 180 days in the United States without a valid visa or other right to live in the United States after April 1, 1997 you need to see a lawyer before going any further. (See Chapter 2, Section A, for more information on this issue.)

Don't forget to sign this form at the bottom.

ii. Form DS-230 Part II

Form DS-230 Part II is fairly short—it's intended to give final confirmation of who you are and where you're going. Most of this form is self-explanatory. Because consulates use different versions of this form, we can't give you the number that a question will appear under.

Sample Form DS-230 Part I, Application for Immigration Visa and Alien Registration—Page 1

U.S. Department of State

APPLICATION FOR IMMIGRANT VISA AND ALIEN REGISTRATION

OMB APPROVAL NO. 1405-0015
EXPIRES: 03/31/2012
ESTIMATED BURDEN: 1 HOUR*
(See Page 2)

PART I - BIOGRAPHIC DATA

Instructions: Complete one copy of this form for yourself and each member of your family, regardless of age, who will immigrate with you. Please print or type your answers to all questions. Mark questions that are Not Applicable with "N/A". If there is insufficient room on the form, answer on a separate sheet using the same numbers that appear on the form. Attach any additional sheets to this form.

Warning: Any false statement or concealment of a material fact may result in your permanent exclusion from the United States. This form (DS-230 Part I) is the first of two parts. This part, together with Form DS-230 Part II, constitutes the complete Application for Immigrant Visa and Alien Registration.

1. Family Name: Mancini | First Name: Terese | Middle Name: Maria

2. Other Names Used or Aliases (If married woman, give maiden name): Terese Brabantio

3. Full Name in Native Alphabet (If Roman letters not used): n/a

4. Date of Birth (mm-dd-yyyy): 02/15/1978 | 5. Age: 35 | 6. Place of Birth (City or Town): Venice | (Province) | (Country): Italy

7. Nationality (If dual national, give both.): Italian | 8. Gender: [X] Female [ ] Male | 9. Marital Status: [ ] Single (Never Married) [ ] Married [ ] Widowed [ ] Divorced [ ] Separated
Including my present marriage, I have been married _two_ times.

10. Permanent address in the United States where you intend to live, if known (street address including ZIP code). Include the name of a person who currently lives there.
Alberto Ilario Mancini
800 Broadway
Lindenhurst, NY 11757
Telephone number: 212 222-2121

11. Address in the United States where you want your Permanent Resident Card (Green Card) mailed, if different from address in item #10 (include the name of a person who currently lives there).
Telephone number

12. Present Occupation: Freelance writer

13. Present Address (Street Address) (City or Town) (Province) (Country): 108 Piazza d'Azeglio, Venice, Italy
Telephone Number (Home): 764-290-7645 | Telephone Number (Office): none | Email Address

14. Spouse's Maiden or Family Name: Mancini | First Name: Alberto | Middle Name: Ilario

15. Date (mm-dd-yyyy) and Place of Birth of Spouse: 3/30/1974, Los Angeles, CA

16. Address of Spouse (If different from your own): 800 Broadway Lindenhurst, NY 11757 | 17. Spouse's Occupation: cook | 18. Date of Marriage (mm-dd-yyyy): 01/01/2011

19. Father's Family Name: Brabantio | First Name: Francisco | Middle Name: Noffo

20. Father's Date of Birth (mm-dd-yyyy): 08/02/1957 | 21. Place of Birth: Venice, Italy | 22. Current Address: deceased | 23. If Deceased, Give Year of Death: 1995

24. Mother's Family Name at Birth: Gallo | First Name: Magdalena | Middle Name: Alcine

25. Mother's Date of Birth (mm-dd-yyyy): 04/24/1964 | 26. Place of Birth: Venice, Italy | 27. Current Address: 90 Piazza d'Azeglio, Venice, Italy | 28. If Deceased, Give Year of Death

DS-230 Part I 03-2012 | This Form May be Obtained Free at Consular Offices of the United States of America Previous Editions Obsolete | Page 1 of 4

Sample Form DS-230 Part I, Application for Immigration Visa and Alien Registration—Page 2

29. List Names, Dates and Places of Birth, and Addresses of ALL Children.

Name	Date (mm-dd-yyyy)	Place of Birth	Address (If different from your own)
Giovanna Moreno	6/01/1998	Florence, Italy	

30. List below all places you have lived for at least six months since reaching the age of 16, including places in your country of nationality. Begin with your present residence.

City or Town	Province	Country	From/To (mm-yyyy) or "Present"	
Venice		Italy	1978	present

31a. Person(s) named in 14 and 29 who will accompany you to the United States now.

Giovanna Moreno

31b. Person(s) named in 14 and 29 who will follow you to the United States at a later date.

32. List below all employment for the last ten years.

Employer	Location	Job Title	From/To (mm-yyyy) or "Present"	
Self-employed	108 Piazza d'Azeglio Venice, Italy	Writer	Aug. 2001	present

In what occupation do you intend to work in the United States? _Writer_

33. List below all educational institutions attended.

School and Location	From/To (mm-yyyy)		Course of Study	Degree or Diploma
Venice University, Italy	9/2002	6/2006	Linguistics	B.A.
Venice High School, Italy	9/1996	6/2000		Diploma
Venice Primary School	9/1984	6/1998		Certificate

Languages spoken or read— Italian, English

Professional associations to which you belong Italian Writer's Guild

34. Previous Military Service [ ] Yes [X] No

Branch _____ Dates of Service (mm-dd-yyyy) _____

Rank/Position _____ Military Speciality/Occupation _____

35. List dates of all previous visits to or residence in the United States. (If never, write "never") Give type of visa status, if known. Give DHS "A" number if any.

From/To (mm-yyyy)	Location	Type of Visa	"A" Number (If known)
Never			

Signature of Applicant	Date (mm-dd-yyyy)
Terese Mancini	06/20/2013

Privacy Act and Paperwork Reduction Act Statements

The information asked for on this form is requested pursuant to Section 222 of the Immigration and Nationality Act. The U.S. Department of State uses the facts you provide on this form primarily to determine your classification and eligibility for a U.S. immigrant visa. Individuals who fail to submit this form or who do not provide all the requested information may be denied a U.S. immigrant visa. If you are issued an immigrant visa and are subsequently admitted to the United States as an immigrant, the Department of Homeland Security will use the information on this form to issue you a Permanent Resident Card, and, if you so indicate, the Social Security Administration will use the information to issue you a social security number and card.

*Public reporting burden for this collection of information is estimated to average 1 hour per response, including time required for searching existing data sources, gathering the necessary documentation, providing the information and/or documents required, and reviewing the final collection. You do not have to supply this information unless this collection displays a currently valid OMB control number. If you have comments on the accuracy of this burden estimate and/or recommendations for reducing it, please send them to: A/GIS/DIR, Room 2400 SA-22, U.S. Department of State, Washington, DC 20522-2202

Sample Form DS-230 Part II, Application for Immigration Visa and Alien Registration—Page 1

U.S. Department of State

APPLICATION FOR IMMIGRANT VISA AND ALIEN REGISTRATION

OMB APPROVAL NO. 1405-0015
EXPIRES: 02/29/2012
ESTIMATED BURDEN: 1 HOUR*

PART II - SWORN STATEMENT

Instructions: Complete one copy of this form for yourself and each member of your family, regardless of age, who will immigrate with you. Please print or type your answers to all questions. Mark questions that are Not Applicable with "N/A". If there is insufficient room on the form, answer on a separate sheet using the same numbers that appear on the form. Attach any additional sheets to this form. The fee should be paid in United States dollars or local currency equivalent, or by bank draft.

Warning: Any false statement or concealment of a material fact may result in your permanent exclusion from the United States. Even if you are issued an immigrant visa and are subsequently admitted to the United States, providing false information on this form could be grounds for your prosecution and/or deportation.

This form (DS-230 Part II), together with Form DS-230 Part I, constitutes the complete Application for Immigrant Visa and Alien Registration.

36. Family Name	First Name	Middle Name
Mancini	Terese	Maria

37. Other Names Used or Aliases (If married woman, give maiden name)
Terese Brabantio

38. Full Name in Native Alphabet (If Roman letters not used)
n/a

39. Name and Address of Petitioner

Alberto Mancini
800 Broadway
Lindenhurst, NY 11757

Telephone number
(212) 222-2121

Email Address

40. United States laws governing the issuance of visas require each applicant to state whether or not he or she is a member of any class of individuals excluded from admission into the United States. The excludable classes are described below in general terms. You should read carefully the following list and answer Yes or No to each category. The answers you give will assist the consular officer to reach a decision on your eligibility to receive a visa.

Except as Otherwise Provided by Law, Aliens Within the Following Classifications are Ineligible to Receive a Visa.
Do Any of the Following Classes Apply to You?

a. An alien who has a communicable disease of public health significance; who has failed to present documentation of having received vaccinations in accordance with U.S. law; who has or has had a physical or mental disorder that poses or is likely to pose a threat to the safety or welfare of the alien or others; or who is a drug abuser or addict.   ☐ Yes ☒ No

b. An alien convicted of, or who admits having committed, a crime involving moral turpitude or violation of any law relating to a controlled substance or who is the spouse, son or daughter of such a trafficker who knowingly has benefited from the trafficking activities in the past five years; who has been convicted of 2 or more offenses for which the aggregate sentences were 5 years or more; who is coming to the United States to engage in prostitution or commercialized vice or who has engaged in prostitution or procuring within the past 10 years; who is or has been an illicit trafficker in any controlled substance; who has committed a serious criminal offense in the United States and who has asserted immunity from prosecution; who, while serving as a foreign government official, was responsible for or directly carried out particularly severe violations of religious freedom; or whom the President has identified as a person who plays a significant role in a severe form of trafficking in persons, who otherwise has knowingly aided, abetted, assisted or colluded with such a trafficker in severe forms of trafficking in persons, or who is the spouse, son or daughter of such a trafficker who knowingly has benefited from the trafficking activities within the past five years.   ☐ Yes ☒ No

c. An alien who seeks to enter the United States to engage in espionage, sabotage, export control violations, terrorist activities, the overthrow of the Government of the United States or other unlawful activity; who is a member of or affiliated with the Communist or other totalitarian party; who participated, engaged or ordered genocide, torture, or extrajudicial killings; or who is a member or representative of a terrorist organization as currently designated by the U.S. Secretary of State.   ☐ Yes ☒ No

d. An alien who is likely to become a public charge.   ☐ Yes ☒ No

e. An alien who seeks to enter for the purpose of performing skilled or unskilled labor who has not been certified by the Secretary of Labor; who is a graduate of a foreign medical school seeking to perform medical services who has not passed the NBME exam or its equivalent; or who is a health care worker seeking to perform such work without a certificate from the CGFNS or from an equivalent approved independent credentialing organization.   ☐ Yes ☒ No
   ☐ Yes ☒ No

f. An alien who failed to attend a hearing on deportation or inadmissibility within the last 5 years; who seeks or has sought a visa, entry into the United States, or any immigration benefit by fraud or misrepresentation; who knowingly assisted any other alien to enter or try to enter the United States in violation of law; who, after November 30, 1996, attended in student (F) visa status a U.S. public elementary school or who attended a U.S. public secondary school without reimbursing the school; or who is subject to a civil penalty under INA 274C.   ☐ Yes ☒ No

Privacy Act and Paperwork Reduction Act Statements

The information asked for on this form is requested pursuant to Section 222 of the Immigration and Nationality Act. The U.S. Department of State uses the facts you provide on this form primarily to determine your classification and eligibility for a U.S. immigrant visa. Individuals who fail to submit this form or who do not provide all the requested information may be denied a U.S. immigrant visa. If you are issued an immigrant visa and are subsequently admitted to the United States as an immigrant, the Department of Homeland Security will use the information on this form to issue you a Permanent Resident Card, and, if you so indicate, the Social Security Administration will use the information to issue you a social security number and card.

*Public reporting burden for this collection of information is estimated to average 1 hour per response, including time required for searching existing data sources, gathering the necessary documentation, providing the information and/or documents required, and reviewing the final collection. You do not have to supply this information unless this collection displays a currently valid OMB control number. If you have comments on the accuracy of this burden estimate and/or recommendations for reducing it, please send them to: A/GIS/DIR, Room 2400 SA-22, U.S. Department of State, Washington, DC 20522-2202

DS-230 Part II   Previous Editions Obsolete   Page 3 of 4

Sample Form DS-230 Part II, Application for Immigration Visa and Alien Registration—Page 2

g. An alien who is permanently ineligible for U.S. citizenship; or who departed the United States to evade military service in time of war. ☐ Yes ☒ No

h. An alien who was previously ordered removed within the last 5 years or ordered removed a second time within the last 20 years; who was previously unlawfully present and ordered removed within the last 10 years or ordered removed a second time within the last 20 years; who was convicted of an aggravated felony and ordered removed; who was previously unlawfully present in the United States for more than 180 days but less than one year who voluntarily departed within the last 3 years; or who was unlawfully present for more than one year or an aggregate of one year within the last 10 years. ☐ Yes ☒ No

i. An alien who is coming to the United States to practice polygamy; who withholds custody of a U.S. citizen child outside the United States from a person granted legal custody by a U.S. court or intentionally assists another person to do so; who has voted in the United States in violation of any law or regulation; or who renounced U.S. citizenship to avoid taxation. ☐ Yes ☒ No

j. An alien who is a former exchange visitor who has not fulfilled the 2-year foreign residence requirement. ☐ Yes ☒ No

k. An alien determined by the Attorney General to have knowingly made a frivolous application for asylum. ☐ Yes ☒ No

l. An alien who has ordered, carried out or materially assisted in extrajudicial and political killings and other acts of violence against the Haitian people; who has directly or indirectly assisted or supported any of the groups in Colombia known as FARC, ELN, or AUC; who through abuse of a governmental or political position has converted for personal gain, confiscated or expropriated property in Cuba, a claim to which is owned by a national of the United States, has trafficked in such property or has been complicit in such conversion, has committed similar acts in another country, or is the spouse, minor child or agent of an alien who has committed such acts; who has been directly involved in the establishment or enforcement of population controls forcing a woman to undergo an abortion against her free choice or a man or a woman to undergo sterilization against his or her free choice; or who has disclosed or trafficked in confidential U.S. business information obtained in connection with U.S. participation in the Chemical Weapons Convention or is the spouse, minor child or agent of such a person; or who has ever engaged in the recruitment of or the use of child soldiers. ☐ Yes ☒ No

41. Have you ever been charged, arrested or convicted of any offense or crime? (If answer is Yes, please explain) ☐ Yes ☒ No

42. Have you ever been refused admission to the United States at a port-of-entry? (If answer is Yes, please explain) ☐ Yes ☒ No

43a. Have you ever applied for a Social Security Number (SSN)?

☐ Yes ☒ No

Give the number _____
Would you like to receive a replacement card? (You must answer YES to question 43b. to receive a card.)

Do you want the Social Security Administration to assign you a SSN and issue a card? (You must answer YES to question 43b. to receive a number and a card.)

☐ Yes ☐ No

☒ Yes ☐ No

43b. Consent to Disclosure: I authorize disclosure of information from this form to the Department of Homeland Security (DHS), the Social Security Administration (SSA), such other U.S. Government agencies as may be required for the purpose of assigning me an SSN and issuing me a Social Security card, and I authorize the SSA to share my SSN with the INS.

☒ Yes ☐ No

The applicant's response does not limit or restrict the Government's ability to obtain his or her SSN, or other information on this form, for enforcement or other purposes as authorized by law.

44. Were you assisted in completing this application? ☐ Yes ☒ No
(If answer is Yes, give name and address of person assisting you, indicating whether relative, friend, travel agent, attorney, or other)

DO NOT WRITE BELOW THE FOLLOWING LINE
The consular officer will assist you in answering item 45.
DO NOT SIGN this form until instructed to do so by the consular officer

45. I claim to be:

☐ A Family-Sponsored Immigrant
☐ An Employment-Based Immigrant
☐ A Diversity Immigrant
☐ A Special Category (Specify)

☐ I derive foreign state chargeability under Sec. 202(b) through my _____

☐ Preference _____

☐ Numerical limitation _____ (foreign state)

(Returning resident, Hong Kong, Tibetan, Private Legislation, etc.)

I understand that I am required to surrender my visa to the United States Immigration Officer at the place where I apply to enter the United States, and that the possession of a visa does not entitle me to enter the United States if at that time I am found to be inadmissible under the immigration laws.

I understand that any willfully false or misleading statement or willful concealment of a material fact made by me herein may subject me to permanent exclusion from the United States and, if I am admitted to the United States, may subject me to criminal prosecution and/or deportation.

I, the undersigned applicant for a United States immigrant visa, do solemnly swear (or affirm) that all statements which appear in this application, consisting of Form DS-230 Part I and Part II combined, have been made by me, including the answers to items 1 through 45 inclusive, and that they are true and complete to the best of my knowledge and belief. I do further swear (or affirm) that, if admitted into the United States, I will not engage in activities which would be prejudicial to the public interest, or endanger the welfare, safety, or security of the United States; in activities which would be prohibited by the laws of the United States relating to espionage, sabotage, public disorder, or in other activities subversive to the national security; in any activity a purpose of which is the opposition to or the control, or overthrow of, the Government of the United States, by force, violence, or other unconstitutional means.

I understand that completion of this form by persons required by law to register with the Selective Service System (males 18 through 25 years of age) constitutes such registration in accordance with the Military Selective Service Act.

_____
Signature of Applicant

Subscribed and sworn to before me this _____ day of _____ at: _____

_____
Consular Officer

WEB RESOURCE

Form DS-230 Part II is available on the State Department website at www.state.gov. However, it's best to use the form you receive from the NVC or U.S. consulate because it may be slightly different. Above is a sample filled-in version of this form.

If the form asks, the **"person you intend to join"** and the **"sponsoring person"** are both your spouse, and you'll need to enter his or her name, perhaps twice.

A few versions of the form still ask about your **"purpose in going to the United States"**; the answer is to "immigrate." And, if the form asks, your **"length of intended stay"** is "permanent."

The **"yes or no"** questions (with boxes to check) refer to the grounds of inadmissibility described in Chapter 2. If you check "yes" on any of them, consult a lawyer immediately, before sending in the form.

Signature line: Don't sign until the interview!

iii. Form I-864

Form I-864, the Affidavit of Support, is the primary form that your spouse and any joint sponsor will use to prove that he, she, or they are willing and able to support you. (You might need a joint sponsor to assist in supporting you if your spouse's income and assets aren't high enough to reach the government's guidelines, as covered in Chapter 3.)

TIP

Some sponsors can use a simpler version of Form I-864. If the sponsor has enough income so that he or she doesn't need to resort to assets or other help to sponsor the immigrant(s), it's okay to use Form I-864EZ, available at www.uscis.gov.

Before you fill out this form, look again at Chapter 3, Meeting Income Requirements, which explains how USCIS will evaluate your finances and those of your spouse. This chapter gives you strategies on meeting the minimum requirements if your own resources are too low. The following

subsection, "Financial Documents to Have on Hand," gives you information on how to create, assemble, or prepare the supporting documentation that you may need to attach to the forms discussed below.

TIP

U.S. citizens with long work histories and long marriages may be able to avoid filling out an Affidavit of Support (Form I-864). The reason is that their obligations to act as sponsors end after the immigrant has worked 40 quarters (about ten years, depending on earnings amounts)—but, in an interesting twist, the immigrants can be credited with work done by their U.S. citizen spouses while they were married. So, if your U.S. citizen spouse has worked 40 quarters in the U.S. during your marriage, he or she need not fill out Form I-864. Though it's the rare married couple who will have gone this many years without applying for a green card, the exception is highly useful for those to whom it applies. You will need to submit Form I-864W (available from www.uscis.gov) in order to claim this exception (and attach a Social Security Statement as proof).

WEB RESOURCE

Form I-864 is available on the USCIS website at www.uscis.gov. Below is a sample filled-in version of this form.

Because this form may be filled out either by your spouse or by a joint sponsor, the instructions below usually refer to the "sponsor," which refers to either of them.

Parts 1-4

These sections are self-explanatory, with the following notes:

- **In Part 1,** spouses check box a; long-lost cousins, fairy godmothers, and other nice friends who agreed to fill in this form as joint sponsors check either box d or box e.
- **In Part 3,** note that there's a place to list children. You don't need to name children who were born in the United States, because

the sponsor has no obligation to support them (at least not under the immigration laws, though they will be counted elsewhere within this form to test the sponsor's overall financial capacity). Similarly, you shouldn't name children who are immigrating with you. Because each of them had their own visa petition (Form I-130), each is considered a "principal immigrant" and needs a separate Form I-864 prepared for him or her.

- **In Part 4,** note that the sponsor's place of residence must be in the United States in order for him or her to be eligible as a financial sponsor. In theory, if your petitioner lives outside the U.S., he or she can meet this requirement by showing the steps taken to return to the U.S. and make the U.S. his or her residence as soon as you enter. Such steps might include finding U.S. employment, locating a place to live, and registering children in U.S. schools. The Affidavit of Support should also show that the petitioner has made arrangements to give up residence outside the United States.

Part 5, Sponsor's household size

This section is self-explanatory. Remember not to count anyone twice! In other words, there's no need to put a "1" in line "c," because you've already counted your spouse.

Part 6, Sponsor's income and employment

Question 22: The sponsor needs to fill in information about his or her employment here. Self-employment is fine. Be aware that if a self-employed sponsor has underreported income in the past, the earnings shown may not be sufficient to support you. In that case, the sponsor will need to file an amended tax return and pay a penalty before the newly reported income is accepted as meeting the guidelines for sponsorship.

Question 23: Here, the sponsor is supposed to enter the income shown on his or her most recent tax return. But what if the sponsor's income has risen since filing those taxes? In that case, the sponsor should enter the more recent income figure, but put an asterisk (an *) next to it. Then find some white space somewhere on the page and write "this figure reflects present earnings, not earnings shown on tax return; see supporting documentation." The documentation the sponsor is already providing, such as an employer's letter, should be enough to show current income.

Question 24: This question is important for sponsors whose income is not enough by itself, but who will be using the income of members of their household to help meet the *Poverty Guidelines* minimum requirements. First, every sponsor must state his or her own income. Then, if the sponsor wants other people's income counted, they must be mentioned in Question 24b and the sponsor must check box 24d. Unless any one of these household members is the actual immigrant, they must plan to complete a separate agreement with the sponsor, using Form I-864A. The total income from the sponsor and household members goes in Question 24c.

Question 25: Self-explanatory.

Part 7, Use of assets to supplement income

The sponsor needs to complete this section only if his or her income wasn't enough by itself to meet the *Poverty Guidelines* requirements. If the sponsor needs to add assets, he or she may include such items as a house, car, or boat, but should remember to subtract debts, mortgages, and liens before writing down their value in Question 26. And remember that the value of these assets will later be divided by three before being used to meet the *Poverty Guidelines* minimum. (Or divided by five if someone other than your spouse is filling out the form.)

If some of the assets being used to meet the minimum belong to a household member, enter the household member's name in Question 27, along with the total amount the assets are worth.

If some of the assets being used to meet the minimum belong to the immigrant, state their value in Question 28.

Sample Form I-864 Affidavit of Support—Page 1

OMB No. 1615-0075; Expires 09/30/2012

Department of Homeland Security
U.S. Citizenship and Immigration Services

**I-864, Affidavit of Support
Under Section 213A of the Act**

Part 1.   Basis for filing Affidavit of Support.

1. I, Alberto Ilario Mancini   ,
am the sponsor submitting this affidavit of support because (Check only one box):

a. [X] **I am the petitioner. I filed or am filing for the immigration of my relative.**

b. [ ] **I filed an alien worker petition on behalf of the intending immigrant, who is related to me as my** _____

c. [ ] **I have an ownership interest of at least 5 percent in** _____ , **which filed an alien worker petition on behalf of the intending immigrant, who is related to me as my** _____

d. [ ] **I am the only joint sponsor.**

e. [ ] **I am the** [ ] **first** [ ] **second of two joint sponsors.** *(Check appropriate box.)*

f. [ ] **The original petitioner is deceased. I am the substitute sponsor. I am the intending immigrant's** _____ .

For Government Use Only

This I-864 is from:

[ ] the Petitioner

[ ] a Joint Sponsor #

_____

[ ] the Substitute Sponsor

[ ] 5% Owner

This I-864:

[ ] does not meet the requirements of section 213A.

[ ] meets the requirements of section 213A.

Reviewer

Location

Date *(mm/dd/yyyy)*

Number of Affidavits of Support in file:

[ ] 1   [ ] 2

Part 2. Information on the principal immigrant.

2. Last Name Mancini

First Name	Middle Name
Terese	Maria

3. Mailing Address Street Number and Name *(Include Apartment Number)*
108 Piazza d'Azeglio

City	State/Province	Zip/Postal Code	Country
Venice		99999	Italy

4. Country of Citizenship	**5. Date of Birth** *(mm/dd/yyyy)*
Italy	02/15/1978

6. Alien Registration Number *(if any)*	**7. U.S. Social Security Number** *(if any)*
A- none	none

Part 3. Information on the immigrant(s) you are sponsoring.

8. [X] I am sponsoring the principal immigrant named in Part 2 above.

[X] Yes   [ ] No (Applicable only in cases with two joint sponsors)

9. [X] I am sponsoring the following family members immigrating at the same time or within six months of the principal immigrant named in **Part 2** above. Do not include any relative listed on a separate visa petition.

Name	Relationship to Sponsored Immigrant	Date of Birth *(mm/dd/yyyy)*	A-Number *(if any)*	U.S.Social Security Number *(if any)*
a.				
b.				
c.				
d.				
e.				

10. Enter the total number of immigrants you are sponsoring on this form from **Part 3**, Items **8** and **9**.   [2] [   ]

Form I-864 (09/19/11) Y

Sample Form I-864 Affidavit of Support—Page 2

Part 4. Information on the Sponsor.

			For Government Use Only
11. Name	Last Name Mancini		
	First Name Albert	Middle Name Ilario	

12. Mailing Address

Street Number and Name *(Include Apartment Number)* 800 Broadway	
City Lindenhurst	State or Province New York
Country USA	Zip/Postal Code 11757

13. Place of Residence *(if different from mailing address)*

Street Number and Name *(Include Apartment Number)* same as above	
City	State or Province
Country	Zip/Postal Code

14. Telephone Number *(Include Area Code or Country and City Codes)*

212-222-2121

15. Country of Domicile

USA

16. Date of Birth *(mm/dd/yyyy)*

03/30/1974

17. Place of Birth *(City)*

Los Angeles	State or Province California	Country USA

18. U.S. Social Security Number *(Required)*

222-22-2222

19. Citizenship/Residency

[X] I am a U.S. citizen.

[ ] I am a U.S. national (for joint sponsors only).

[ ] I am a lawful permanent resident. My alien registration number is A-_____

If you checked box (b), (c), (d), (e) or (f) in line 1 on Page 1, you must include proof of your citizen, national, or permanent resident status.

20. Military Service (To be completed by petitioner sponsors only.)

I am currently on active duty in the U.S. armed services.   [ ] Yes   [X] No

Sample Form I-864 Affidavit of Support—Page 3

Part 5. Sponsor's household size.

21. Your Household Size - <u>DO NOT COUNT ANYONE TWICE</u>

Persons you are sponsoring in this affidavit:

a. Enter the number you entered on line 10. `2`

Persons NOT sponsored in this affidavit:

b. Yourself. `1`

c. If you are currently married, enter "1" for your spouse.

d. If you have dependent children, enter the number here.

e. If you have any other dependents, enter the number here.

f. If you have sponsored any other persons on an I-864 or I-864 EZ who are now lawful permanent residents, enter the number here.

g. OPTIONAL: If you have <u>siblings, parents, or adult children</u> with the same principal residence who are combining their income with yours by submitting Form I-864A, enter the number here. `1`

h. Add together lines and enter the number here. **Household Size:** `4`

For Government Use Only

Part 6. Sponsor's income and employment.

22. I am currently:

a. ☒ Employed as a/an _Shift manager_ .

Name of Employer #1 *(if applicable)* _Bob's Diner_ .

Name of Employer #2 *(if applicable)* _____ .

b. ☐ Self-employed as a/an _____ .

c. ☐ Retired from _____ since _____ .
    (Company Name)   *(Date)*

d. ☐ Unemployed since _____ .
    (Date)

23. My current individual annual income is: $ _20,000_
    (See Step-by-Step Instructions)

Sample Form I-864 Affidavit of Support—Page 4

24. My current annual household income:

a. List your income from line 23 of this form. $ ___20,000___

b. **Income you are using from any other person who was counted in your household size,** including, in certain conditions, the intending immigrant. (See step-by-step instructions.) Please indicate name, relationship and income.

Name	Relationship	Current Income
Stella Mancini	Daughter	$ ___18,000___
_____	_____	$ _____
_____	_____	$ _____
_____	_____	$ _____

c. **Total Household Income:** $ ___38,000___

(Total all lines from 24a and 24b. Will be Compared to Poverty Guidelines -- See Form I-864P.)

d. ☒ The persons listed above have completed Form I-864A. I am filing along with this form all necessary Forms I-864A completed by these persons.

e. ☐ The person listed above, _____ does not need to
    (Name)
    complete Form I-864A because he/she is the intending immigrant and has no accompanying dependents.

For Government Use Only

Household Size =

_____

Poverty line for year

_____ is:

$ _____

25. Federal income tax return information.

☒ I have filed a Federal tax return for each of the three most recent tax years. I have attached the required photocopy or transcript of my Federal tax return for only the most recent tax year.

My total income (adjusted gross income on IRS Form 1040EZ) as reported on my Federal tax returns for the most recent three years was:

Tax Year		Total Income
2011	*(most recent)*	$ 20,000
2010	*(2nd most recent)*	$ 19,000
2009	*(3rd most recent)*	$ 19,000

☒ *(Optional)* I have attached photocopies or transcripts of my Federal tax returns for my second and third most recent tax years.

Sample Form I-864 Affidavit of Support—Page 5

	For Government Use Only
Part 7. Use of assets to supplement income. *(Optional)*	

If your income, or the total income for you and your household, from line 24c exceeds the Federal Poverty Guidelines for your household size, YOU ARE NOT REQUIRED to complete this Part. Skip to Part 8.

26. Your assets *(Optional)*

   a. Enter the balance of all savings and checking accounts. $ _____

   b. Enter the net cash value of real-estate holdings. (Net means current assessed value minus mortgage debt.) $ _____

   c. Enter the net cash value of all stocks, bonds, certificates of deposit, and any other assets not already included in lines 26 (a) or (b). $ _____

   d. **Add together lines 26 a, b and c and enter the number here.**   **TOTAL:** $ _____

27. Your household member's assets from Form I-864A. *(Optional)*

   Assets from Form I-864A, line 12d for

   $ _____

   _____
   (Name of Relative)

28. Assets of the principal sponsored immigrant. *(Optional)*

   The principal sponsored immigrant is the person listed in line 2.

   a. Enter the balance of the sponsored immigrant's savings and checking accounts. $ _____

   b. Enter the net cash value of all the sponsored immigrant's real estate holdings. (Net means investment value minus mortgage debt.) $ _____

   c. Enter the current cash value of the sponsored immigrant's stocks, bonds, certificates of deposit, and other assets not included on line a or b. $ _____

   d. **Add together lines 28a, b, and c, and enter the number here.** $ _____

29. Total value of assets.

   Add together lines 26d, 27 and 28d and enter the number here.   **TOTAL:** $ _____

For Government Use Only

Household Size =

_____

Poverty line for year

_____ is:

$ _____

The total value of all assests, line 29, must equal 5 times (3 times for spouses and children of USCs, or 1 time for orphans to be formally adopted in the U.S.) the difference between the poverty guidelines and the sponsor's household income, line 24c.

Sample Form I-864 Affidavit of Support—Page 6

Part 8. Sponsor's Contract.

Please note that, by signing this Form I-864, you agree to assume certain specific obligations under the Immigration and Nationality Act and other Federal laws. The following paragraphs describe those obligations. Please read the following information carefully before you sign the Form I-864. If you do not understand the obligations, you may wish to consult an attorney or accredited representative.

What is the Legal Effect of My Signing a Form I-864?

If you sign a Form I-864 on behalf of any person (called the "intending immigrant") who is applying for an immigrant visa or for adjustment of status to a permanent resident, and that intending immigrant submits the Form I-864 to the U.S. Government with his or her application for an immigrant visa or adjustment of status, under section 213A of the Immigration and Nationality Act these actions create a contract between you and the U. S. Government. The intending immigrant's becoming a permanent resident is the "consideration" for the contract.

Under this contract, you agree that, in deciding whether the intending immigrant can establish that he or she is not inadmissible to the United States as an alien likely to become a public charge, the U.S. Government can consider your income and assets to be available for the support of the intending immigrant.

What If I choose Not to Sign a Form I-864?

You cannot be made to sign a Form I-864 if you do not want to do so. But if you do not sign the Form I-864, the intending immigrant may not be able to become a permanent resident in the United States.

What Does Signing the Form I-864 Require Me to do?

If an intending immigrant becomes a permanent resident in the United States based on a Form I-864 that you have signed, then, until your obligations under the Form I-864 terminate, you must:

-- Provide the intending immigrant any support necessary to maintain him or her at an income that is at least 125 percent of the Federal Poverty Guidelines for his or her household size (100 percent if you are the petitioning sponsor and are on active duty in the U.S. Armed Forces and the person is your husband, wife, unmarried child under 21 years old.)

-- Notify USCIS of any change in your address, within 30 days of the change, by filing Form I-865.

What Other Consequences Are There?

If an intending immigrant becomes a permanent resident in the United States based on a Form I-864 that you have signed, then until your obligations under the Form I-864 terminate, your income and assets may be considered ("deemed") to be available to that person, in determining whether he or she is eligible for certain Federal means-tested public benefits and also for State or local means-tested public benefits, if the State or local government's rules provide for consideration ("deeming") of your income and assets as available to the person.

This provision does **not** apply to public benefits specified in section 403(c) of the Welfare Reform Act such as, but not limited to, emergency Medicaid, short-term, non-cash emergency relief; services provided under the National School Lunch and Child Nutrition Acts; immunizations and testing and treatment for communicable diseases; and means-tested programs under the Elementary and Secondary Education Act.

Contract continued on following page.

Sample Form I-864 Affidavit of Support—Page 7

What If I Do Not Fulfill My Obligations?

If you do not provide sufficient support to the person who becomes a permanent resident based on the Form I-864 that you signed, that person may sue you for this support.

If a Federal, State or local agency, or a private agency provides any covered means-tested public benefit to the person who becomes a permanent resident based on the Form I-864 that you signed, the agency may ask you to reimburse them for the amount of the benefits they provided. If you do not make the reimbursement, the agency may sue you for the amount that the agency believes you owe.

If you are sued, and the court enters a judgment against you, the person or agency that sued you may use any legally permitted procedures for enforcing or collecting the judgment. You may also be required to pay the costs of collection, including attorney fees.

If you do not file a properly completed Form I-865 within 30 days of any change of address, USCIS may impose a civil fine for your failing to do so.

When Will These Obligations End?

Your obligations under a Form I-864 will end if the person who becomes a permanent resident based on a Form I-864 that you signed:

- Becomes a U.S. citizen;

- Has worked, or can be credited with, 40 quarters of coverage under the Social Security Act;

- No longer has lawful permanent resident status, and has departed the United States;

- Becomes subject to removal, but applies for and obtains in removal proceedings a new grant of adjustment of status, based on a new affidavit of support, if one is required; or

- Dies.

Note that divorce **does not** terminate your obligations under this Form I-864.

Your obligations under a Form I-864 also end if you die. Therefore, if you die, your Estate will not be required to take responsibility for the person's support after your death. Your Estate may, however, be responsible for any support that you owed before you died.

30. I, ___Alberto Ilario Mancini_____ ,

(Print Sponsor's Name)

certify under penalty of perjury under the laws of the United States that:

a. I know the contents of this affidavit of support that I signed.

b. All the factual statements in this affidavit of support are true and correct.

c. I have read and I understand each of the obligations described in Part 8, and I agree, freely and without any mental reservation or purpose of evasion, to accept each of those obligations in order to make it possible for the immigrants indicated in Part 3 to become permanent residents of the United States;

d. I agree to submit to the personal jurisdiction of any Federal or State court that has subject matter jurisdiction of a lawsuit against me to enforce my obligations under this Form I-864;

e. Each of the Federal income tax returns submitted in support of this affidavit are true copies, or are unaltered tax transcripts, of the tax returns I filed with the U.S. Internal Revenue Service; and

Sign on following page.

Sample Form I-864 Affidavit of Support—Page 8

f. I authorize the Social Security Administration to release information about me in its records to the Department of State and U.S. Citizenship and Immigration Services.

g. Any and all other evidence submitted is true and correct.

31. _Alberto I. Mancini_   02/20/2013
     (Sponsor's Signature)   *(Date-- mm/dd/yyyy)*

Part 9. Information on Preparer, if prepared by someone other than the sponsor.

I certify under penalty of perjury under the laws of the United States that I prepared this affidavit of support at the sponsor's request and that this affidavit of support is based on all information of which I have knowledge.

Signature: _____   **Date:** _____
                                                  (mm/dd/yyyy)

Printed Name: _____

Firm Name: _____

Address: _____

Telephone Number: _____

E-Mail Address : _____

Business State ID # *(if any)* _____

Be sure to attach documents to prove the ownership, location, and value of any assets claimed.

If the combination of the sponsor's available income and one third of the sponsor's and/or the immigrant's assets don't yet meet the *Poverty Guidelines* minimum, you'll still need to hand in this Affidavit. But you'll definitely want to look for a joint sponsor or a participating household member.

Part 8, Sponsor's Contract

Unlike past versions of this form, the sponsor's signature no longer needs to be witnessed by a notary public.

TIP

Need to prepare Affidavits for several family members at once? If the sponsor is bringing in more than one person (you and your children) in the same process, he or she can simply copy Form I-864 (with supporting documents) the appropriate number of times after signing it.

iv. Form I-864A

Not every immigrant needs to submit this form. It is only required if, on the main Form I-864, the sponsor had to use the income of members of the sponsor's household to meet the *Poverty Guidelines*. In that case, these household member(s) will need to fill out portions of Form I-864A. The sponsor must attach the Form I-864A to the main Form I-864.

WEB RESOURCE

Form I-864A is available on the USCIS website at www.uscis.gov. Below is a sample filled-in version of this form.

Part I: Self-explanatory; to be filled out by the household member.

Part 2: This part is filled out and signed by the main sponsor (the U.S. citizen spouse). Just fill in the names of the immigrants being sponsored and don't worry about the legal language.

Part 3: This is where the household member will fill in and sign the form.

v. Form I-864W

Only a few lucky people will be able to use this form, namely those who are exempt from the Affidavit of Support requirement because the immigrant has either:

- worked lawfully for 40 Social Security quarters (approximately ten years) in the U.S.
- been married while the U.S. spouse worked for 40 Social Security quarters, or
- a combination of the above.

The deal is that a financial sponsor's responsibility lasts until the immigrant has (among other possibilities) earned 40 work quarters credited toward Social Security. A work quarter is approximately three months, but it depends partly on how much you earn. So if you've already reached that amount of work on your own, through lawful employment—perhaps while in the U.S. as a student or H-1B worker—there's no point in the sponsor filling out an Affidavit of Support for you. And, in an interesting twist, you can be credited for work done by your U.S. spouse if it was during your marriage.

You'll need to prove to USCIS how many quarters of work your spouse or you has done. Contact Social Security about getting a certified statement with this information.

Because Form I-864W is fairly easy to fill out, we won't include a sample here. The form is available at www.uscis.gov. In Part 2, you would check the first box.

b. Financial Documents to Have on Hand

To prove that your spouse or additional sponsors are able and willing to support you, the consulate will require detailed, up-to-date information from trustworthy sources. The types of documents they look for are described below.

Sample Form I-864A, Contract Between Sponsor and Household Member—Page 1

OMB No. 1615-0075; Expires 09/30/2012

Department of Homeland Security
U.S. Citizenship and Immigration Services

I-864A, Contract Between Sponsor and Household Member

Part 1. Information on the Household Member. (You.)			For Government Use Only
1. Name	Last Name Mancini		This I-864A relates to a household member who:
	First Name Beatrice	Middle Name Stella	☐ is the intending immigrant.
2. Mailing Address	Street Number and Name *(include apartment number)* 800 Broadway		☐ is not the intending immigrant.
	City Lindenhurst	State or Province New York	
	Country USA	Zip/Postal Code 11757	
3. Place of Residence *(if different from mailing address)*	Street Number and Name *(include apartment number)* same as above		
	City	State or Province	Reviewer
	Country	Zip/Postal Code	Location
4. Telephone Number	*(Include area code or country and city codes)* 212-222-9822		
5. Date of Birth	*(mm/dd/yyyy)* 03/06/1988		Date *(mm/dd/yyyy)*
6. Place of Birth	City State/Province Country Syracuse New York USA		
7. U.S. Social Security Number *(if any)*	206-45-9872		

8. Relationship to Sponsor (Check either a, b or c.)

a. ☐ I am the intending immigrant and also the sponsor's spouse.

b. ☐ I am the intending immigrant and also a member of the sponsor's household.

c. ☒ I am not the intending immigrant. I am the sponsor's household member. I am related to the sponsor as his/her.

☐ Spouse

☒ Son or daughter *(at least 18 years old)*

☐ Parent

☐ Brother or sister

☐ Other dependent (specify)

Form I-864A (09/19/11) Y

Sample Form I-864A, Contract Between Sponsor and Household Member—Page 2

9. I am currently:

a. ☐ Employed as a/an _____ .

   Name of Employer # 1 *(if applicable)* _____ .

   Name of Employer #2 *(if applicable)* _____ .

b. ☒ Self-employed as a/an ___Freelance graphics designer_____ .

c. ☐ Retired from_____ since _____ .
   (Company Name)   *(mm/dd/yyyy)*

d. ☐ Unemployed since _____
   (mm/dd/yyyy)

For Government Use Only

10. My current individual annual income is: $ _18,000_____ .

11. Federal income tax information.

☒ I have filed a Federal tax return for each of the three most recent tax years. I have attached the required photocopy or transcript of my Federal tax return for only the most recent tax year.

My total income (adjusted gross income on IRS Form 1040EZ) as reported on my Federal tax returns for the most recent three years was:

Tax Year		Total Income
2011 *(most recent)*	$	18,000
2010 *(2nd most recent)*	$	21,000
2009 *(3rd most recent)*	$	19,500

☐ *(Optional)* I have attached photocopies or transcripts of my Federal tax returns for my second and third most recent tax years.

12. My assets (complete only if necessary).

a. Enter the balance of all cash, savings, and checking accounts. $_____ .

b. Enter the net cash value of real-estate holdings. (Net means assessed value minus mortgage debt.) $_____ .

c. Enter the cash value of all stocks, bonds, certificates of deposit, and other assets not listed on line a or b. $_____ .

d. **Add together Lines a, b, and c and enter the number here.** $_____ .

Sample Form I-864A, Contract Between Sponsor and Household Member—Page 3

	For Government Use Only

Part 2. Sponsor's Promise.

13. I, THE SPONSOR, ___Alberto Ilario Mancini___
(Print Name)

in consideration of the household member's promise to support the following intending immigrant(s) and to be jointly and severally liable for any obligations I incur under the affidavit of support, promise to complete and file an affidavit of support on behalf of the following ___2___ named intending *(Indicate Number)* immigrant(s) (see Step-by-Step instructions).

Name	Date of Birth *(mm/dd/yyyy)*	A-number *(if any)*	U.S. Social Security Number *(if any)*
a. Terese M. Mancini	02/15/1978	None	None
b. Giovanna Moreno	06/01/2000	None	None
c.			
d.			
e.			

14. ___Alberto I. Mancini___   ___02/20/2013___
(Sponsor's Signature)   *(Date--mm/dd/yyyy)*

Part 3. Household Member's Promise.

15. I, THE HOUSEHOLD MEMBER, ___Beatrice Stella Mancini___
(Print Name)

in consideration of the sponsor's promise to complete and file an affidavit of support on behalf of the above ___2___ named intending immigrant(s):
(Number from line 13)

a. Promise to provide any and all financial support necessary to assist the sponsor in maintaining the sponsored immigrant(s) at or above the minimum income provided for in section 213A(a)(1)(A) of the Act (not less than 125 percent of the Federal Poverty Guidelines) during the period in which the affidavit of support is enforceable;

b. Agree to be jointly and severally liable for payment of any and all obligations owed by the sponsor under the affidavit of support to the sponsored immigrant(s), to any agency of the Federal Government, to any agency of a State or local government, or to any other private entity that provides means-tested public benefit;

c. Certify under penalty under the laws of the United States that all the information provided on this form is true and correct to the best of my knowledge and belief and that the Federal income tax returns submitted in support of the contract are true copies or unaltered tax transcripts filed with the Internal Revenue Service.

d. **Consideration where the household member is also the sponsored immigrant:** I understand that if I am the sponsored immigrant and a member of the sponsor's household that this promise relates only to my promise to be jointly and severally liable for any obligation owed by the sponsor under the affidavit of support to any of my dependents, to any agency of the Federal Government, to any agency of a State or local government, and to provide any and all financial support necessary to assist the sponsor in maintaining any of my dependents at or above the minimum income provided for in section 213A(s)(1)(A) of the Act (not less than 125 percent of the Federal poverty line) during the period which the affidavit of support is enforceable.

e. I authorize the Social Security Administration to release information about me in its records to the Department of State and U.S. Citizenship and Immigration Services.

16. ___Beatrice S. Mancini___   ___02/20/2013___
(Household Member's Signature)   *(Date--mm/dd/yyyy)*

i. Documents to Accompany Form I-864

Form I-864 asks for several supporting documents. If your spouse is relying on a joint sponsor (outside the household), that person should also be told to assemble a set of these documents:

- **A copy of your spouse/sponsor's federal income tax returns for the last three years, with W-2s.** Don't include state tax forms. The immigration authorities prefer to see federal tax returns in the form of Internal Revenue Service (IRS) transcripts (an IRS-generated summary of the return that was filed). Transcripts can be requested using IRS Form 4506T (available from www.irs.gov or by calling 800-829-1040). However, it usually takes several weeks to receive the transcript. Don't let this hold up the immigration process—if the transcript hasn't come by the time you need to submit the Form I-864, simply use your sponsor's personal photocopies of his or her tax returns. And if the sponsor wasn't legally required to submit a tax return, perhaps because his or her income was too low, submit a written explanation of this.

> **TIP**
> **We're advising you to prepare more than the minimum financial documents.** Technically, you're supposed to be asked for only one year's tax returns, and that's it. But because so many consulates ask for more, it makes sense to be ready with additional years' tax returns plus a bank and employer letter.

- **Proof of your sponsor's current employment.** Start with a letter from the sponsor's employer describing the dates of employment, nature of the job, wages/salary, time worked per week, and prospects for advancement. (See the sample employer letter below.) Also include copies of pay stubs covering the last six months, or the most recent stub if it shows cumulative pay. If the sponsor is self-employed, a tax return is acceptable, but it's a good idea to add a business license, copies of current receipts, or other supporting documents.

- **A list of assets (the sponsor's and/or the immigrant's), if they must be used to meet the** *Poverty Guidelines'* **minimum.** There is no form to use for creating this list. Simply prepare (on a typewriter or word processor) a list or table with the following information:
  - a brief description of the item
  - current value
  - remaining debt (if any)
  - a brief description of the document you've attached to prove ownership.

- **Proof of ownership of assets (the sponsor's and/or the immigrant's), if any were listed.** Form I-864 itself does a good job of detailing which documents will be accepted as proof of ownership of assets, as explained in Part 7 of the instructions, Use of Assets to Supplement Income. The value must be the likely sale price, not how much the sponsor paid for the property. For real estate, you can use a tax assessment to show the value. If the assessment seems too low, or for property other than real estate, the sponsor can hire a professional appraiser to prepare an estimate and report. For cars, the value listed in the *Kelley Blue Book* is acceptable. Look for the *Kelley Blue Book* at a library or bookstore, or online at www.kbb.com. The sponsor must also document the amount of any debt remaining on the property. If no debt remains, submit proof of final payment.

> **CAUTION**
> **You may need to update your information later.** By the time you get to your visa interview, circumstances may have changed for your sponsor, joint sponsor, or household joint sponsor. For example, if the sponsor or joint sponsor have new or different employment, bring a job letter and copies of recent pay stubs; and if a new tax year has begun, bring copies of the sponsor(s)' most recent tax returns.

Sample Letter Showing Sponsor's Employment

Hitting the Road Trucking
222 Plaza Place
Outthereville, MA 90000
May 22, 20xx

To Whom It May Concern:

Ron Goodley has been an employee of Hitting the Road Trucking since September 4, 20xx, a total of over five years. He has a full-time position as a driver. His salary is $45,000 per year. This position is permanent, and Ron's prospects for performance-based advancement and salary increases are excellent.

Very truly yours,
Bob Bossman
Bob Bossman
Personnel Manager
Hitting the Road Trucking

---

ii. Documents to Accompany Form I-864A

You will submit Form I-864A only if your spouse needs to rely on the financial contributions of members of his or her household. Form I-864A also requires several supporting documents. These include not only proof of the joint sponsors' financial capacity, but proof that they live with and are related to the main sponsor.

- **Proof that the household joint sponsors live with the primary sponsor.** Such proof can include a copy of the rental agreement showing the household member's name, and copies of items that show the same address as the sponsor (such as a driver's license, copies of school records, copies of utility bills, or personal correspondence).
- **Proof that the household joint sponsors are related to the primary sponsor (if they're not already listed as relations on the sponsor's tax return).** The best way to prove this family relationship is through birth certificates. If,

for example, the sponsor and household joint sponsor are parent and child, the child's birth certificate will do. If they are brother and sister, providing both birth certificates will work (as long as the certificates show that they share the same parent or parents). If the birth certificates don't make the family relationships clear, look for other official documents such as court or school records to confirm the parent-child links.

- **Copies of the household joint sponsors' tax returns for the last three years.** As with the primary sponsor, the government prefers to see IRS-generated tax transcripts.
- **Proof of the household joint sponsors' employment.** This can include a letter from their employer confirming employment, as in the sample above, and recent pay stubs.
- **A list of the household joint sponsors' assets if they must be used to meet the *Poverty Guidelines'* minimum.** There is no form for creating this list. Using a typewriter or word processor, the household joint sponsors should prepare a list or table with the following information:
  - brief description of item
  - current value
  - remaining debt (if any)
  - brief description of the document attached to prove ownership.
- **Proof of ownership of household joint sponsors' assets, if any were listed.**
- **A list of the benefits programs and dates of receipt if the household joint sponsors or their dependents have used financial need-based public benefits in the last three years.**

c. Other Documents to Prepare

You'll be asked to prepare various other documents, such as your birth certificate, marriage certificate, passport, and police certificates from countries where you've lived. These will be well explained in the instructions you receive, so we won't review them further here.

You'll need to obtain a police certificate (hopefully showing your clean record) only if such certificates are available in your country. You can find information on whether and how to obtain police certificates in your country on the State Department's visa reciprocity tables at http://travel.state.gov (under "Visa for Foreign Citizens," click "more," then in the box on the left-hand side of the page click on "Fees and Reciprocity Tables," then click "Visa Issuance Fee–Reciprocity Tables," enter your country in the box, and scroll down for information).

If you don't have a clean record, see a lawyer.

d. Documenting That Your Marriage Is Bona Fide

You may be asked for evidence that your marriage is a real one, not a sham. Gather and photocopy as many of the following items as possible:

- rental agreements, leases, or mortgages showing that you have lived together and/or have leased or bought property in both spouses' names
- hotel and airplane receipts showing trips that you have taken together or to visit one another
- phone bills showing your conversations
- copies of letters and emails between you
- your mutual child's birth certificate or a doctor's report saying that you are pregnant
- joint bank statements
- joint credit card statements
- evidence that one spouse has made the other a beneficiary on his/her life or health insurance or retirement account
- auto registrations showing joint ownership and/or addresses
- joint club memberships
- receipts for gifts that you purchased for one another (these should be items that are normally considered gifts, such as flowers, candy, jewelry, and art)
- letters from friends and family to each or both of you, mailed to an address where you were living together

- photos of you and your spouse taken before and during your marriage, including at your wedding (the government knows wedding pictures can be faked, but some officers enjoy seeing them anyway). The photos should, if possible, include parents and other relatives from both families. Write the date the picture was taken and a brief description of what the photo shows on the back (or underneath, if you're photocopying them). Don't bother with the wedding or other videos; there won't be time or a space to view them.

e. Using the Checklist for Forms and Documents

Although you must fill out only a few forms, you and your spouse will be responsible for pulling together a great deal of supporting documents, financial and otherwise. It will be particularly important to use the checklist to keep track of everything.

All the checklist items concerning Form I-864 apply whether it's your spouse filling it out or a joint sponsor who is willing to assist in supporting you; see Chapter 3 for more on joint sponsorship.

 CHECKLIST

Appendix C includes a tear-out copy of this checklist.

4. Step Three: Attend Your Visa Interview

On the appointed day, you and your petitioning spouse (if he or she can possibly make it—it's optional) will go to a U.S. consulate for an interview. See a detailed description of the interview and how to prepare for it in Chapter 13.

Which consulate you go to depends on where you're from and where you live now. If you've been living (legally) in a country that is not your country of citizenship, you'll probably be told to work with the consulate in the country where you now live.

Checklist for Immigrant Visa Forms and Documents

This checklist lists the forms, documents, and other items that your spouse, with your help, will need to assemble.

☐ Form DS 230, Parts I and II (see Subsection B3a, above for line-by-line instructions)

☐ Form I-864, Affidavit of Support (see Subsection B3a, above, for line-by-line instructions)

☐ Documents to accompany Form I-864 (see Subsection B3b, above):

　☐ A copy of your spouse/sponsor's federal income tax returns for the last one to three years, with W-2s

　☐ Proof of your sponsor's current employment

　☐ A list of assets, (the sponsor's and/or the immigrant's) if they must be used to meet the *Poverty Guidelines'* minimum

　☐ Proof of ownership of assets (the sponsor's and/or the immigrant's), if any were listed

　☐ If sponsor or sponsor's dependents have used financial need-based public benefits in the last three years, a list of the programs and dates of receipt

☐ Form I-864A, Contract Between Sponsor and Household Member (only needed if sponsor's income is insufficient; see line-by- instructions to Form I-864A in Subsection B3a, above)

☐ Documents to accompany Form I-864A (see Subsection B3b, above):

　☐ Proof that the household joint sponsors live with the primary sponsor

　☐ Proof that the household joint sponsors are related to the primary sponsor (if they're not already listed as dependents on the sponsor's tax return)

　☐ Copies of the household joint sponsors' tax returns for the last one to three years

　☐ Proof of the household joint sponsors' employment

　☐ Proof of ownership of household joint sponsors' assets, if any were listed

　☐ If the household joint sponsors or their dependents have used financial need-based public benefits in the last three years, a list of the benefits programs and dates of receipt

☐ If you're exempt from the Affidavit of Support requirement, Form I-864W, together with a certified statement of your Social Security earnings history

☐ Other documents:

　☐ Original and one photocopy of your birth certificate (see Chapter 4, Section C, for how to obtain vital documents)

　☐ Original and one photocopy of your marriage certificate (see Chapter 4, Section C, for how to obtain vital documents)

　☐ If applicable, original and one photocopy of proof of termination of all previous marriages, such as a death, divorce, or annulment certificate

　☐ Original INS or USCIS notice of approved I-130 (Form I-797)

　☐ Two color photographs of you (passport style)

　☐ Police Certificate, if available in your country

　☐ Military records, if applicable

　☐ Court and prison records, if applicable

☐ Fees (currently $330, plus a $74 security surcharge)

If your country of residence doesn't have diplomatic relations with the United States, the NVC will name another consulate to handle your case. And of course, if you'll be getting a K-3 visa, you'll need to go to the consulate in the country where you were married.

At a minimum, you'll need to bring to your interview:

- the results of your medical exam (described below)
- evidence that your marriage is bona fide (as described in Subsection 3d, above)
- financial documents to bring the Affidavit of Support up to date if it was prepared many months ago, and
- your passport, valid for at least six months.

a. The Medical Exam

To prove that you are not inadmissible for medical reasons, you will have to present the results of a medical exam done by a doctor approved by the U.S. consulate. Your appointment notice will give you complete instructions on where and when to visit the appropriate clinic or doctor. There will be a fee of about $150, plus other fees for tests and any needed vaccinations.

When you go for your medical exam, make sure to bring the following:

- your visa appointment letter
- the doctor's fee
- a form you fill out describing your medical history, if requested
- your vaccination records, and
- photo identification—the doctor must make sure you don't send a healthier person in your place. You may also be requested to bring a passport-style photo.

The doctor will examine you, ask you questions about your medical and psychiatric history and drug use, and test you (including blood tests and chest X-rays). Pregnant women can (with proof of pregnancy) refuse the chest X-ray until after the baby is born if they have no symptoms of tuberculosis. When the laboratory results are in, the doctor will fill out the appropriate form and return it to you in a sealed envelope or forward it directly to the consulate. DO NOT open the envelope— this will invalidate the results. The doctor should supply you with a separate copy of your results, or tell you whether any illnesses showed up.

 RESOURCE

Want to plow through the government's technical guidance on the medical exam? It's published by the Centers for Disease Control and Prevention (CDC). Call 800-311-3435 and ask for a copy of *Technical Instructions for Medical Examination of Aliens,* or go to www.cdc.gov/immigrantrefugeehealth/exams/ti/civil/ technical-instructions-civil-surgeons.html.

b. Fingerprinting

Before your interview, you'll also need to have your fingerprints taken. The consulate will send you a date and location. After your appointment, you'll have to wait until your prints have cleared with the U.S. FBI and other security agencies. After that, assuming you have no criminal record, your case can continue forward. (See Chapter 2 regarding how a criminal record can make you inadmissible to the U.S.)

5. Step Four: At the Border

Assuming all goes well at the visa interview, you will be given an immigrant visa. But wait—you're not a U.S. resident yet. You'll have six months to use the visa to enter the United States.

TIP

If you're about to reach your two-year wedding anniversary, don't rush to enter the United States. An immigrating spouse whose marriage is less than two years old when he or she becomes a U.S. resident receives conditional, not permanent residency. USCIS will reexamine the marriage after another two years. So if your marriage is nearly two years old when you get your visa to enter the United States, make the most of that six-month entry window and wait to enter until your two-year wedding anniversary has passed. That way, you'll enter as a permanent resident. Point out your anniversary date to the border official, to be sure that he or she stamps your passport for permanent, not conditional, residence.

At the border, airport, or other port of entry, a U.S. border officer will open the sealed envelope containing your visa documents and do a last check to make sure you haven't used fraud. The border officer has expedited removal powers, which means he or she can turn you right around and send you home if he or she sees anything wrong in your packet or with your answers to his or her questions. When the officer is satisfied that everything is in order, he or she will stamp your passport to show that you're now a U.S. resident (see reproduction of this stamp below—the CR-1 means that this person entered as a conditional resident).

If your marriage is less than two years old on that day, the border officer will make you a conditional resident; if your marriage is older than two years, you'll be made a permanent resident. Your actual green card will arrive several months later. If you receive conditional residence, you'll want to read Chapter 16, Section G. In about 21 months, you'll have to file an application with USCIS asking to convert this into permanent residency.

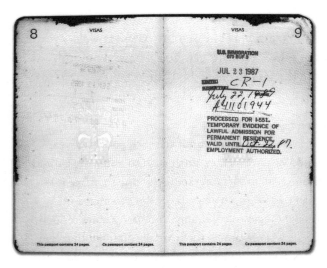

Sample Conditional Residence Stamp

 SKIP AHEAD
We haven't forgotten your children and pets. For information on bringing them along, see Section D, below.

C. The K-3 Visa Application Process

If you're reading this section, it means that you have decided not to go through the whole immigrant visa application process while you're overseas, but will instead use an alternate way of entering the United States—a K-3 visa for entry, to be followed by a green card application in the United States. This section will explain how to get the K-3 visa, and refer you to a later chapter for the green card (adjustment of status) application instructions.

1. The Five Steps to a K-3 Visa

Obtaining a K-3 nonimmigrant visa involves five major steps, four of which are your job to handle:

1. Your U.S. citizen spouse submits a visa petition (Form I-130) to a USCIS "lockbox" office in the United States. That office will forward the petition to a USCIS Service Center. If you have children immigrating with you, your U.S. citizen spouse should also submit separate visa petitions on their behalf as well (to do so, your spouse must qualify as the child's parent or stepparent, and can be their stepparent only if your marriage took place before the child's 18th birthday). Separate visa petitions will be required for each child when it comes time to adjust status (apply for a green card), and the sooner you get them in, the better, particularly if the child is likely to turn 21 before the process ends.

2. After the U.S. citizen receives an I-797 receipt notice for the I-130, he or she submits a separate, "fiancé" visa petition (Form I-129F) to whichever USCIS Service Center has the file.

3. After USCIS approves Form I-129F, it sends word to the National Visa Center (NVC), which conducts some preprocessing procedures, and then transfers your case to the U.S. consulate that will be handling your case.

4. After receiving your files, the consulate sends you instructions about forms to fill out and documents to prepare, and ultimately schedules you for an interview appointment. Soon after your interview, you'll be approved for your K-3 visa. (Your children, if any, will get K-4 visas.)

5. You present your K-3 (and K-4) visa(s) at a U.S. border, where they are examined. Assuming everything is in order, you will be admitted to the United States in K-3 (and K-4) status. After your arrival, you'll be able to apply for adjustment of status in the United States. (Formerly, you had to wait until the I-130 visa petition was approved before submitting your adjustment of status application, but that is no longer true. USCIS will now transfer your pending I-130 file internally, so long as you submit a copy of the I-130 receipt notice with your adjustment of status application.)

In rare instances, USCIS will also ask your spouse to attend a "fraud interview" if USCIS or the consulate has doubts about whether your marriage is the real thing. This could happen as part of Step One or after Step Four.

How long this entire process of getting you into the U.S. takes depends mostly on how long it takes for the I-129F visa petition to be approved. This can be many months by itself. After that, expect another six weeks or so to get your consular instructions, and, assuming you send your forms back in right away, another six weeks or so for you to get your appointment.

What if the I-130 petition is approved before your interview and the paperwork gets forwarded to the consulate? In that case, you're no longer eligible for a K-3 visa, and will have to go through the entire immigrant visa application process. (The concept behind the K-3 visa is to compensate

for the delays experienced by married couples as they wait for approval of their Form I-130.) That can be a good thing—you won't have to submit a whole separate application to adjust status and get a green card after you're in the U.S., but can obtain an immigrant visa at the consulate that lets you become a permanent resident the minute you enter the United States.

TIP

Check current processing times for I-130s and I-129Fs before proceeding to use the K-3 visa. If I-130s and I-129Fs are being processed in the same average amount of time (as they were when this book went to press), then the consulate will insist on having you go through the entire immigrant visa application process, and will not allow you to use the K-3 visa. To check processing times, go to www.uscis.gov, and in the box on the left-hand side, under "Find" click "Processing Times," and at the bottom of the following page next to "Service Center," select the service center closest to the U.S. spouse's residence. Click "Service Center Processing Dates" and a table will appear. Look for the times listed next to "I-130" and "I-129F."

2. Step One: The I-130 Visa Petition

The I-130 visa petition is used by every U.S. petitioner bringing in a family member from overseas. Accordingly, your U.S. citizen spouse can follow the instructions earlier in this chapter on how to fill in this petition, and prepare the other forms and documents (such as Form G-325A, proof of citizenship, photos, and fees) that must accompany it. Complete instructions are found in Section B2, above, including Subsections a, b, and c. There's only one change to these instructions, based on your plans to apply for a K-3 visa: On Form I-130, Question 22, your U.S. spouse should write: "Applicant plans to obtain a K-3 visa abroad and adjust status in the United States," then fill in the lines regarding which city you plan to adjust status (apply for your green card) in, and which consulate you'd return to, if necessary, as a backup.

Expect the decision on this petition to take a long time. See Chapter 15 for what to do if the answer seems to be taking even longer than expected.

3. Step Two: The I-129F Fiancé Visa Petition

Your U.S. citizen spouse indicates that you're interested in a K-3 visa by filing a fiancé visa petition—Form I-129F, Petition for Alien Fiancé(e)—with whichever USCIS Service Center in the United States sends you a receipt notice saying it got your Form I-130.

We'll go through how to prepare and assemble the various forms and documents that go into this petition, one by one. To keep track of them all, use the "Checklist for K-3 Fiancé Visa Petition," in Subsection e, below.

a. Line-by-Line Instructions for Form I-129F Visa Petition

This section will give you precise instructions for filling in the forms required for your K-3 visa petition. Whoever reads these instructions should have a copy of the appropriate forms in hand.

i. Form I-129F

Form I-129F is also used by unmarried fiancés, so don't be worried if some questions don't apply to you.

 WEB RESOURCE
This form is available on the USCIS website at www.uscis.gov. A sample filled-in version of this form is shown below.

The first thing to notice about Form I-129F is that it runs in two columns. The left column, or Section A, asks for information about your U.S. citizen fiancé. (Don't be confused by the fact that the form calls your fiancé "you.") The right column asks for information about you, the immigrating ("alien") spouse (although it says fiancé—someday, they'll revise this form!).

Part A

Question 1: The U.S. citizen spouse must enter his/her last name (surname) in all capital letters, but the other names in small letters. For example, if your spouse's name were Samuel Lawrence Cole, he would enter, "COLE" in the first box, "Samuel" in the second box, and "Lawrence" in the third. (Always spell out the entire middle name.)

Questions 2-5: Self-explanatory.

Question 6: Check the box that says "Married." Only check one box (so that, for example, if your spouse had been previously married, he or she wouldn't also check "Divorced.")

Question 7: Self-explanatory. (A maiden name is the woman's name before marriage.)

Question 8: Self-explanatory.

Question 9: There's a reason for these questions: If your U.S. citizen spouse's earlier marriages weren't already over by the time he or she married you, your marriage may not be valid, and you'll be ineligible to immigrate. (Make sure that under "Date(s) Marriages" the U.S. citizen gives both the date the marriage started and the date the divorce became final, as opposed to the date the two split up housekeeping.) See a lawyer if there's a problem.

Question 10: If the U.S. citizen spouse's citizenship was obtained through naturalization, the number can be found on the top right-hand side of the naturalization certificate. The date and place issued are also shown on the certificate. If your spouse's citizenship was obtained through parents, he or she may have a certificate of citizenship, which would clearly show a number that can be entered on this form. (It's possible, however, that your spouse has only a U.S. passport, which is also an acceptable form of proof of citizenship.)

Question 11: If the U.S. citizen has ever submitted other Forms I-129F, USCIS may take a look at those files to make sure there was no fraud involved. There's nothing automatic about its decision—after all, it is perfectly possible for a U.S. citizen to fall in love with more than one foreign-born person, and for the first marriage to end. But there are U.S. citizens who charge money to marry and sponsor noncitizens, and USCIS is on the lookout for them.

Sample Form I-129F, Petition for Alien Fiancé(e)—Page 1

OMB No. 1615-0001; Expires 02/29/2012

Department of Homeland Security
U.S. Citizenship and Immigration Services

**I-129F, Petition
for Alien Fiancé(e)**

Do not write in these blocks. **For USCIS Use Only**

Case ID #	Action Block	Fee Stamp
A #		
G-28 #		
The petition is approved for status under Section 101(a)(5)(k). It is valid for four months from the date of action. _____		AMCON: _____ ☐ Personal Interview ☐ Previously Forwarded ☐ Document Check ☐ Field Investigation
Remarks:		

Part A.   Start Here. Information about you.

1. Name *(Family name in CAPS) (First)   (Middle)*

ANDERSON	Christa	Lee

2. Address *(Number and Street)*   Apt. #

123 4th Street	2

(Town or City)   (State or Country)   (Zip/Postal Code)

San Diego	CA	92120

3. Place of Birth *(Town or City)*   *(State/Country)*

Portland	OR

4. Date of Birth *(mm/dd/yyyy)*   **5. Gender**

4/18/1984	☐ Male ☒ Female

6. Marital Status
☒ Married ☐ Single ☐ Widowed ☐ Divorced

7. Other Names Used *(including maiden name)*

None

8a. U.S. Social Security Number   **8b. A#** *(if any)*

122-33-4444	

9. Names of Prior Spouses   **Date(s) Marriage(s) Ended**

None	

10. My citizenship was acquired through *(check one)*

☒ Birth in the U.S.   ☐ Naturalization
Give number of certificate, date and place it was issued.

☐ Parents
Have you obtained a certificate of citizenship in your name?
☐ Yes   ☐ No
If "Yes," give certificate number, date and place it was issued.

11. Have you ever filed for this or any other alien fiancé(e) or husband/wife before?

☐ Yes   ☒ No
If "Yes," give name of all aliens, place and date of filing, A# and result. *(Attached additional sheets as necessary.)*

Part B.   Information about your alien fiancé(e).

1. Name *(Family name in CAPS) (First)   (Middle)*

CUEVAS	Bernardo	Cristobal

2. Address *(Number and Street)*   Apt. #

123 Calle Centro	42

(Town or City)   (State or Country)   (Zip/Postal Code)

Bogota	Colombia	

3a. Place of Birth *(Town or City)*   *(State/Country)*

Bucaramanga	Colombia

3b. Country of Citizenship

Colombia

4. Date of Birth *(mm/dd/yyyy)*   **5. Gender**

7/24/1984	☒ Male ☐ Female

6. Marital Status
☒ Married ☐ Single ☐ Widowed ☐ Divorced

7. Other Names Used *(including maiden name)*

None

8. U.S. Social Security #   **9. A#** *(if any)*

None	None

10. Names of Prior Spouses   **Date(s) Marriage(s) Ended**

Sonya Carcamo	11/2/2007

11. Has your fiancé(e) ever been in the U.S.?

☒ Yes   ☐ No

12. If your fiancé(e) is currently in the U.S., complete the following:

He or she last arrived as a: *(visitor, student, exchange alien, crewman, stowaway, temporary worker, without inspection, etc.)*

Arrival/Departure Record (I-94) Number

☐☐☐☐ — ☐☐☐☐☐☐☐☐☐

Date of Arrival *(mm/dd/yy)*   **Date authorized stay expired, or will expire as shown on I-94 or I-95**

INITIAL RECEIPT _____ RESUBMITTED _____ RELOCATED: Rec'd _____ Sent _____ COMPLETED: Appv'd _____ Denied _____ Ret'd _____

Form I-129F (Rev. 11/23/10) Y

Sample Form I-129F, Petition for Alien Fiancé(e)—Page 2

Part B. Information about your alien fiancé(e). *(Continued.)*

13. List all children of your alien fiancé(e) *(if any)*

Name *(First/Middle/Last)*	Date of Birth *(mm/dd/yyyy)*	Country of Birth	Present Address
Jorge Cuevas Carcamo	2/21/2006	Colombia	1100 Calle de Las Montañas, Bogota

14. Address in the United States where your fiancé(e) intends to live.

(Number and Street)	(Town or City)	(State)
123 4th Street	San Diego	CA

15. Your fiancé(e)'s address abroad.

(Number and Street)	(Town or City)	(State or Province)
123 Calle Centro #42	Bogota	

(Country)	(Phone Number; Include Country, City and Area Codes)
Colombia	57 1 2223333

16. If your fiancé(e)'s native alphabet uses other than Roman letters, write his or her name and address abroad in the native alphabet.

(Name)	(Number and Street)
N/A	

(Town or City)	(State or Province)	(Country)

17. Is your fiancé(e) related to you? ☐ Yes ☐ No N/A

If you are related, state the nature and degree of relationship, e.g., third cousin or maternal uncle, etc.

18. Has your fiancé(e) met and seen you within the two-year period immediately preceding the filing of this petition?

☐ Yes ☐ No N/A

Describe the circumstances under which you met. If you have not personally met each other, explain how the relationship was established. If you met your fiancé(e) or spouse though an international marriage broker, please explain those circumstances in Question 19 below. Explain also in detail any reasons you may have for requesting that the requirement that you and your fiancé(e) must have met should not apply to you.

19. Did you meet your fiancé(e) or spouse through the services of an international marriage broker?

☐ Yes ☒ No

If you answered yes, please provide the name and any contact information you may have (including internet or street address) of the international marriage broker and where the international marriage broker is located. Attach additional sheets of paper if necessary.

20. Your fiancé(e) will apply for a visa abroad at the American embassy or consulate at:

(City)	(Country)
Bogota	Colombia

NOTE: (Designation of a U.S. embassy or consulate outside the country of your fiancé(e)'s last residence does not guarantee acceptance for processing by that foreign post. Acceptance is at the discretion of the designated embassy or consulate.)

Sample Form I-129F, Petition for Alien Fiancé(e)—Page 3

Part C. Other information.

1. If you are serving overseas in the Armed Forces of the United States, please answer the following:

I presently reside or am stationed overseas and my current mailing address is:

N/A

2. Have you ever been convicted by a court of law (civil or criminal) or court martialed by a military tribunal for any of the following crimes:

- Domestic violence, sexual assault, child abuse and neglect, dating violence, elder abuse or stalking. (Please refer to page 3 of the instructions for the full definition of the term "domestic violence.)

- Homicide, murder, manslaughter, rape, abusive sexual contact, sexual exploitation, incest, torture, trafficking, peonage, holding hostage, involuntary servitude, slave trade, kidnapping, abduction, unlawful criminal restraint, false imprisonment or an attempt to commit any of these crimes, or

- Three or more convictions for crimes relating to a controlled substance or alcohol not arising from a single act.

☐ Yes ☐ No

Answering this question is required even if your records were sealed or otherwise cleared or if anyone, including a judge, law enforcement officer, or attorney, told you that you no longer have a record. Using a separate sheet(s) of paper, attach information relating to the conviction(s), such as crime involved, date of conviction and sentence.

3. If you have provided information about a conviction for a crime listed above and you were being battered or subjected to extreme cruelty by your spouse, parent, or adult child at the time of your conviction, check all of the following that apply to you:

☐ I was acting in self-defense.

☐ I violated a protection order issued for my own protection.

☐ I committed, was arrested for, was convicted of, or plead guilty to committing a crime that did not result in serious bodily injury, and there was a connection between the crime committed and my having been battered or subjected to extreme cruelty.

Part D. Penalties, certification and petitioner's signature.

PENALTIES: You may by law be imprisoned for not more than five years, or fined $250,000, or both, for entering into a marriage contract for the purpose of evading any provision of the immigration laws, and you may be fined up to $10,000 or imprisoned up to five years, or both, for knowingly and willfully falsifying or concealing a material fact or using any false document in submitting this petition.

YOUR CERTIFICATION: I am legally able to and intend to marry my alien fiancé(e) within 90 days of his or her arrival in the United States. I certify, under penalty of perjury under the laws of the United States of America, that the foregoing is true and correct. Furthermore, I authorize the release of any information from my records that U.S. Citizenship and Immigration Services needs to determine eligibility for the benefit that I am seeking.

Moreover, I understand that this petition, including any criminal conviction information that I am required to provide with this petition, as well as any related criminal background information pertaining to me that U.S. Citizenship and Immigration Services may discover independently in adjudicating this petition will be disclosed to the beneficiary of this petition.

Signature	Date *(mm/dd/yyyy)*	Daytime Telephone Number *(with area code)*
Christa Anderson	02/28/2012	858-555-1214

E-Mail Address (if any)

Part E. Signature of person preparing form, if other than above. *(Sign below.)*

I declare that I prepared this application at the request of the petitioner and it is based on all information of which I have knowledge.

Signature	Print or Type Your Name	G-28 ID Number	Date *(mm/dd/yyyy)*

Firm Name and Address

Daytime Telephone Number *(with area code)*

E-Mail Address (if any)

Part B

Now we're back to you, the foreign-born spouse.

Questions 1-5: Self-explanatory.

Question 6: Check only the "Married" box.

Question 7: Self-explanatory (maiden name is your name before you were married, if you changed it afterward).

Question 8: You won't have a Social Security number unless you have lived in the United States; insert "N/A" if you don't have one.

Question 9: The Alien Registration Number or A-Number is an eight- or nine-digit number following the letter "A" (for Alien) that USCIS or the former INS will have assigned to you if you previously applied for permanent or in some cases temporary residency, or have been in deportation or removal proceedings. If you have an A-Number, you must enter it here.

SEE AN EXPERT

If your previous application was denied because you were inadmissible, or if you lied on that application, call a lawyer before going any further. See Chapter 17 for tips on finding a good attorney.

Question 10: These questions relate to the eligibility requirement that this be your only marriage. See explanation of eligibility in Chapter 2, Section B.

Question 11: Self-explanatory.

Question 12: You can enter "N/A" here, since you are not in the United States.

Question 13: This refers to all your (the immigrant's) children, whether born of this relationship or a previous one.

Question 14: Hopefully your intended address in the United States is the same as that of your U.S. citizen spouse, or USCIS will raise questions. Even if you will spend some time away from your married home, such as for school or work, you should consider your married home to be your permanent address. If there is a compelling reason that you will have a completely separate residence, attach documents to explain why, or consult a lawyer.

Question 15: Self-explanatory.

Question 16: If your native language uses a non-Roman script (for example, Russian, Chinese, or Arabic), you'll need to write your name and address in that script.

Questions 17 and 18: These questions are meant for fiancés. You can simply answer "N/A" here.

Question 19: This is a new question, a result of recent concern by Congress that so-called "mail-order" spouses (who meet through the services of an international matchmaking agency) are especially susceptible to domestic violence and abuse. In response, Congress passed the International Marriage Brokers Regulation Act of 2005 (IMBRA). IMBRA requires you to state here whether you met your fiancé or spouse through an international marriage broker, and if so, to give information about the broker.

Question 20: Enter the name of the U.S. consulate where you plan to attend your visa interview. This must be in the same country where you got married—or, if you married in the United States, in the country where the immigrating spouse now lives.

Part C

Now the questions once again refer to the petitioning U.S. citizen spouse.

Question 1: Self-explanatory.

Questions 2-3: If the petitioner has a history of violent crime, crime relating to alcohol, or controlled substance abuse, he or she may be required to reveal this to USCIS. The petitioner should see an attorney if there is any question about whether this section applies. You, the immigrant, will also be told of any of your U.S. spouse's relevant history.

Part D

The U.S. citizen needs to sign and date the forms under the paragraph that starts **Your Certification.**

Part E

This section need not be filled in if you just got a little help from a friend. This line is mainly for lawyers or agencies that fill out these forms on clients' behalf.

ii. Form G-325A

Along with your K-3 visa petition package, you'll need to submit two Forms G-325A, one for you and one for your spouse. Because this is the exact same form as was submitted with Form I-130, we won't repeat the instructions here. However, it's best to submit forms with original signatures to USCIS, instead of photocopying the ones you submitted with Form I-130.

b. Documents That Must Accompany Your K-3 Visa Petition

In addition to filling in forms, you must also provide various documents and other items in support of your K-3 visa petition. This section contains detailed instructions on how to satisfy these requirements, which are also summarized on the checklist at the end of this section.

- **Proof of the U.S. citizenship status of your petitioning spouse.** Depending on how your spouse became a citizen, this might include a copy of a birth certificate, passport, certificate of naturalization, certificate of citizenship, or Form FS-20 (Report of Birth Abroad of a U.S. Citizen).
- **Proof that your spouse filed Form I-130 with USCIS.** You need to wait until the USCIS Service Center sends a Form I-797C receipt notice, then photocopy this and send the copy.
- **Photos of the immigrant and spouse.** These must be taken in U.S. passport style. They must be identical photos, 2 x 2 inches in size, taken within the past six months, showing your current appearance. Passport style means that the photo shows your full face from the front, with a plain white or off-white background—and your face must measure between one inch and 1⅜ inches from the bottom of your chin to the top of your head. For more information, see the State Department website at http://travel.state. gov. (under "Visas for Foreign Citizens," click

"more," then "A–Z Subject Index," and go to "Photo Requirements" under letter "P"). However, USCIS regulations permit you to submit a photo that doesn't completely follow the instructions if you live in a country where such photographs are unavailable or are cost prohibitive.
- **No fee.** You don't need to pay the usual fee for an I-129F visa petition when submitting it as part of a K-3 visa application.

c. Where to Send the K-3 Visa Petition

When your U.S. citizen spouse has finished filling out and assembling everything for the K-3 visa petition, he or she must send it to the USCIS Service Center that sent you a receipt for the I-130 visa petition.

Your spouse should also photocopy and send a copy of the K-3 visa petition packet to you. File it carefully with your other records and familiarize yourself with the materials and answers so you'll be prepared to explain anything contained in that packet during your upcoming visa interview.

d. What Will Happen After Sending in the K-3 Visa Petition

A few weeks after sending in the K-3 Fiancé Visa Petition, the USCIS office will send your spouse a receipt notice titled Notice of Action, and numbered I-797C. (See the sample below.) This notice will tell you to check the USCIS website for information on how long the petition is likely to remain in processing (usually around three months). Until that predicted decision date, USCIS will ignore any letters from you asking what is going on. If there are any delays, the most reliable way to communicate with USCIS is by letter (see Chapter 15).

If USCIS needs additional documentation to complete the Fiancé Visa Petition, it will send the U.S. citizen a letter asking for it. It's best to respond to these requests as soon as possible, though taking care, as always, to keep copies of whatever you send for your records (and to prove it was sent).

Sample Form I-129F Receipt Notice

Department of Homeland Security U.S. Citizenship and Immigration Services				I-797C, Notice of Action

THE UNITED STATES OF AMERICA

RECEIPT NUMBER MSC-12-041-00000	CASE TYPE I129F	PETITION FOR FIANCE(E)
RECEIVED DATE March 30, 2012	PRIORITY DATE	PETITIONER ANDERSON, CHRISTA
NOTICE DATE April 1, 2012	PAGE 1 of 1	BENEFICIARY CUEVAS, BERNARDO

ILONA BRAY
RE: BERNARDO CUEVAS
950 PARKER STREET
BERKELEY, CA 94710

Notice Type: Receipt Notice

Receipt notice - If any of the above information is incorrect, call customer service immediately.

Processing time - Processing times vary by kind of case.
- You can check our current processing time for this kind of case on our website at **uscis.gov**.
- On our website you can also sign up to get free e-mail updates as we complete key processing steps on this case.
- Most of the time your case is pending the processing status will not change because we will be working on others filed earlier.
- We will notify you by mail when we make a decision on this case, or if we need something from you. If you move while this case is pending, call customer service when you move.
- Processing times can change. If you don't get a decision or update from us within our current processing time, check our website or call for an update.

If you have questions, check our website or call customer service. Please save this notice, and have it with you if you contact us about this case.

Notice to all customers with a pending I-130 petition - USCIS is now processing Form I-130, Petition for Alien Relative, as a visa number becomes available. Filing and approval of an I-130 relative petition is only the first step in helping a relative immigrate to the United States. Eligible family members must wait until there is a visa number available before they can apply for an immigrant visa or adjustment of status to a lawful permanent resident. This process will allow USCIS to concentrate resources first on cases where visas are actually available. This process should not delay the ability of one's relative to apply for an immigrant visa or adjustment of status. Refer to **www.state.gov/travel** <http://www.state.gov/travel> to determine current visa availability dates. For more information, please visit our website at www.uscis.gov or contact us at 1-800-375-5283.

Always remember to call customer service if you move while your case is pending. If you have a pending I-130 relative petition, also call customer service if you should decide to withdraw your petition or if you become a U.S. citizen.

Please see the additional information on the back. You will be notified separately about any other cases you filed.
U.S. CITIZENSHIP & IMMIGRATION SVC
CALIFORNIA SERVICE CENTER
P.O. BOX 30111
LAGUNA NIGUEL CA 92607-0111
Customer Service Telephone: (800) 375-5283

Form I-797C (Rev. 08/31/04) N

Sample Form I-129F Approval Notice

Department of Homeland Security
U.S. Citizenship and Immigration Services

I-797, Notice of Action

THE UNITED STATES OF AMERICA

RECEIPT NUMBER		CASE TYPE	I129F PETITION FOR FIANCE(E)
MSC-12-041-00000			

RECEIPT DATE	PRIORITY DATE	PETITIONER	
March 30, 2012		ANDERSON, CHRISTA	

NOTICE DATE	PAGE	BENEFICIARY	
June 29, 2012	1 of 1	12345678 CUEVAS, BERNARDO	

ILONA BRAY
RE: BERNARDO CUEVAS
950 PARKER STREET
BERKELEY, CA 94710

Notice Type: Approval Notice

Valid from 06/30/2010 to 12/30/2010

The above petition has been approved. We have sent the original visa petition to the Department of State National Visa Center (NVC), 32 Rochester Avenue, Portsmouth, NH 03801-2909. The INS has completed all action; further inquiries should be directed to the NVC.

The NVC now processes all approved fiance(e) petitions. The NVC processing should be complete within two to four weeks after receiving the petition from INS. The NVC will create a case record with your petition information. NVC will then send the petition to the U.S. Embassy or Consulate where your fiance(e) will be interviewed for his or her visa.

You will receive notification by mail when NVC has sent your petition to the U.S. Embassy or Consulate. The notification letter will provide you with a unique number for your case and the name and address of the U.S. Embassy or Consulate where your petition has been sent.

If it has been more than four weeks since you received this approval notice and you have not received notification from NVC that your petition has been forwarded overseas, please call NVC at (603) 334-0700. Please call between 8:00am-6:45pm Eastern Standard Time. You will need to enter the INS receipt number from this approval notice into the automated response system to receive information on your petition.

THIS FORM IS NOT A VISA NOR MAY IT BE USED IN PLACE OF A VISA.

Please see the additional information on the back. You will be notified separately about any other cases you filed.
U.S. CITIZENSHIP & IMMIGRATION SVC
CALIFORNIA SERVICE CENTER
P. O. BOX 30111
LAGUNA NIGUEL CA 92607-0111
Customer Service Telephone: (800) 375-5283

Form I-797 (Rev. 01/31/05) N

Once the petition is approved, USCIS will notify the U.S. citizen spouse by sending an approval notice on Form I-797 (see sample above). It will also notify the NVC, which will transfer the case to the consulate where the interview is to take place (in your country of marriage or, if you were married in the U.S., in the country where the immigrating spouse lives). This stage can take some weeks.

e. Using the Checklist for K-3 Visa Petition

When you put it all together, the K-3 Visa Petition involves three forms and some supporting documents, as detailed on the following checklist. As you fill out and prepare your paperwork, mark off the items that you've found or finished on this checklist. This will be the best way to make sure you haven't forgotten anything.

Checklist for K-3 Visa Petition

☐ Form I-129F (see Subsection C3a, above, for line-by-line instructions)

☐ Form G-325A (one filled out by you and one by your spouse, identical to the G-325As you already filled out to accompany the Form I-130 visa petition)

☐ Proof that U.S. citizen already filed Form I-130 Visa Petition with USCIS (a copy of I-797 receipt notice is best)

☐ A color photo of you (passport style)

☐ A color photo of your spouse (passport style)

☐ Proof of U.S. citizenship of U.S. citizen spouse

CHECKLIST
Appendix C includes a tear-out copy of the K-3 Visa Petition checklist.

4. Step Three: Immigrant Mails in Forms

After the Form I-129F has been approved, USCIS will forward your file to a central processing facility called the National Visa Center (NVC). The NVC will transfer your case file to the U.S. consulate in the country where you were married. The consulate will then send you, the immigrant, an Appointment Package containing forms and instructions. You may be asked to fill out certain of these forms and return them to the consulate in preparation for your interview.

We'll go through these forms step by step.

a. Line-by-Line Instructions for Forms That K-3 Applicant Mails to Consulate

This section will give you instructions for filling in the forms that you receive. Be sure to have a copy of the appropriate form in hand as you go through these instructions. However, be aware that some of the forms may vary from the samples in this book, since they've been adapted for use by particular consulates.

i. Form DS-156, Nonimmigrant Visa Application

Form DS-156 is a basic form consulates use to test the eligibility of immigrants coming for temporary stays, including not only truly unmarried fiancés, but tourists, students, and others. Don't be confused by the sections that don't apply to you—in particular, those demanding that the applicant prove that he or she doesn't intend to stay in the United States permanently. You're permitted to stay in the United States permanently (assuming all goes well with your green card application), and you don't need to hide that fact.

 WEB RESOURCE
This form is available on the State Department website at www.state.gov. You may be asked to complete it online. However, use the form that you get from the consulate if it's different. Below is a sample filled-in version of this form. The first two pages are as you would see them online *before* clicking "continue."

Questions 1-16: Self-explanatory.
Question 17: Check the "Married" box, and no other box.

Sample Form DS-156, Nonimmigrant Visa Application—Page 1

U.S. Department of State
NONIMMIGRANT VISA APPLICATION

Approved OMB 1405-0018
Expires 06/30/2014
Estimated Burden 1 hour
See Page 2

PLEASE TYPE OR PRINT YOUR ANSWERS IN THE SPACE PROVIDED BELOW EACH ITEM

				DO NOT WRITE IN THIS SPACE

1. Passport Number

1234567

2. Place of Issuance:

City: Bogota
Country: Colombia
State/Province: Santander

DO NOT WRITE IN THIS SPACE

B-1/B-2 MAX   B-1 MAX   B-2 MAX

Other _____ MAX

Visa Classification

3. Issuing Country

Colombia

4. Issuance Date (dd-mmm-yyyy)

20-Jul-1994

5. Expiration Date (dd-mmm-yyyy)

29-Jul-2014

Mult or _____

Number of Applications

6. Surnames (As in Passport)

Cuevas

Months _____

Validity

Issued/Refused

7. First and Middle Names (As in Passport)

Bernardo Cristobal

On _____ By _____

8. Other Surnames Used (Maiden, Religious, Professional, Aliases)

Under SEC.   214(b)   221(g)

Other _____ INA

9. Other First and Middle Names Used

10. Date of Birth (dd-mmm-yyyy)

24-Jul-1984

Reviewed By _____

11. Place of Birth

City: Bucaramanga
Country: Colombia
State/Province: Santander

12. Nationality

Colombia

13. Sex

[X] Male
[ ] Female

14. National Identification Number (If Applicable)

24071982123

15. Home Address (Include Apartment Number, Street, City, State or Province, Postal Zone and Country)

123 Calle Centro, Apt. 42, Bogota, Santander, COLOMBIA

16. Home Telephone Number

571-222-4444

Business Phone Number

571-210-9990

Mobile/Cell Number

571-123-4567

Fax Number

Business Fax Number

571-210-9999

Pager Number

17. Marital Status

[X] Married   [ ] Single (Never Married)
[ ] Widowed   [ ] Divorced   [ ] Separated

18. Spouse's Full Name (Even if divorced or separated, include maiden name.)

Christa Lee Anderson

19. Spouse's DOB (dd-mmm-yyyy)

18-Apr-1985

20. Name and Address of Present Employer or School

Name: BC Grupo

Address: 321 Calle Internacional, Bogota, Colombia

21. Present Occupation (If retired, write "retired". If student, write "student".)

Engineer

22. When do you intend to arrive in the U.S.? (Provide specific date if known) (dd-mmm-yyyy)

20-May-2013

23. E-Mail Address

bcc2cla@freemail.net

24. At what address will you stay in the U.S.?

123 4th Street, Apt. 2
San Diego, California 92120

BARCODE

25. Name and telephone numbers of person in U.S. who you will be staying with or visiting for tourism or business:

Name: Christa Lee Anderson

Home Phone: 858-444-3210

DO NOT WRITE IN THIS SPACE

Business Phone: 858-555-1214

Cell Phone: 858-555-1212

26. How long do you intend to stay in the U.S.?

Will apply for permanent residence after arrival with K-3 visa

27. What is the purpose of your trip?

Join U.S. citizen spouse, complete application for U.S. permanent residence.

50 mm x 50 mm

PHOTO

staple or glue photo here

28. Who will pay for your trip?

29. Have you ever been in the U.S.? [X] Yes [ ] No

When? 01 July 2004

For how long? 3 weeks

DS-156
06-2011

PREVIOUS EDITIONS OBSOLETE

Page 1 of 2

Sample Form DS-156, Nonimmigrant Visa Application—Page 2

30. Have you ever been issued a U.S. visa? ☒ Yes ☐ No
When? 02 June 2004
Where? Bogota, Colombia
What type of visa? B2 - Visitor for pleasure

31. Have you ever been refused a U.S. visa? ☐ Yes ☒ No
When?
Where?
What type of visa?

32. Do you intend to work in the U.S.? ☒ Yes ☐ No
(If YES, give the name and complete address of U.S. employer.)

Will seek employment after applying for adjustment of status

33. Do you intend to study in the U.S.? ☐ Yes ☒ No
(If YES, give the name and complete address of the school.)

34. Names and relationships of persons traveling with you

Jorge Cuevas Carcamo, son

35. Has your U.S. visa ever been cancelled or revoked? ☐ Yes ☒ No

36. Has anyone ever filed an immigrant visa petition on your behalf? ☐ Yes ☒ No   If Yes, who?

37. Are any of the following persons in the U.S., or do they have U.S. legal permanent residence or U.S. citizenship?
Mark YES or NO and indicate that person's status in the U.S. (i.e., U.S. legal permanent resident, U.S. citizen, visiting, studying, working, etc.).

☒ Yes ☐ No Husband/Wife U.S. Citizen
☐ Yes ☒ No Fiance/Fiancee
☐ Yes ☐ No
☐ Yes ☒ No Father/Mother
☐ Yes ☒ No Son/Daughter
Brother/Sister

38. IMPORTANT: ALL APPLICANTS MUST READ AND CHECK THE APPROPRIATE BOX FOR EACH ITEM.
A visa may not be issued to persons who are within specific categories defined by law as inadmissible to the United States (except when a waiver is obtained in advance). Is any of the following applicable to you?

● Have you ever been arrested or convicted for any offense or crime, even though subject of a pardon, amnesty or other similar legal action? Have you ever unlawfully distributed or sold a controlled substance (drug), or been a prostitute or procurer for prostitutes? ☐ Yes ☒ No

● Have you ever been refused admission to the U.S., or been the subject of a deportation hearing, or sought to obtain or assist others to obtain a visa, entry into the U.S., or any other U.S. immigration benefit by fraud or willful misrepresentation or other unlawful means? Have you attended a U.S. public elementary school on student (F) status or a public secondary school after November 30, 1996 without reimbursing the school? ☐ Yes ☒ No

● Do you seek to enter the United States to engage in export control violations, subversive or terrorist activities, or any other unlawful purpose? Are you a member or representative of a terrorist organization as currently designated by the U.S. Secretary of State? Have you ever participated in persecutions directed by the Nazi government of Germany; or have you ever participated in genocide? Have you ever participated in, ordered, or engaged in genocide, torture, or extrajudicial killings? Have you ever engaged in the recruitment of or the use of child soldiers? ☐ Yes ☒ No

● Have you ever violated the terms of a U.S. visa, or been unlawfully present in, or deported from, the United States? ☐ Yes ☒ No

● Have you ever withheld custody of a U.S. citizen child outside the United States from a person granted legal custody by a U.S. court, voted in the United States in violation of any law or regulation, or renounced U.S. citizenship for the purpose of avoiding taxation? ☐ Yes ☒ No

● Have you ever been afflicted with a communicable disease of public health significance or a dangerous physical or mental disorder, or ever been a drug abuser or addict? ☐ Yes ☒ No

While a YES answer does not automatically signify ineligibility for a visa, if you answered YES you may be required to personally appear before a consular officer.

39. Was this application prepared by another person on your behalf? ☐ Yes ☒ No
(If answer is YES, then have that person complete item 40.)

40. Application Prepared By
Name _____   Relationship to Applicant _____
Address _____
Signature of Person Preparing Form _   Date (dd-mmm-yyyy) _____

41. I certify that I have read and understood all the questions set forth in this application and the answers I have furnished on this form are true and correct to the best of my knowledge and belief. I understand that any false or misleading statement may result in the permanent refusal of a visa or denial of entry into the United States. I understand that possession of a visa does not automatically entitle the bearer to enter the United States of America upon arrival at a port of entry if he or she is found inadmissible.

Applicant's Signature _____   Date (dd-mmm-yyyy) _____

Privacy Act and Paperwork Reduction Act Statements

INA Section 222(f) provides that visa issuance and refusal records shall be considered confidential and shall be used only for the formulation, amendment, administration, or enforcement of the immigration, nationality, and other laws of the United States. Certified copies of visa records may be made available to a court which certifies that the information contained in such records is needed in a case pending before the court.
Public reporting burden for this collection of information is estimated to average 1 hour per response, including time required for searching existing data sources, gathering the necessary data, providing the information required, and reviewing the final collection. You do not have to provide the information unless this collection displays a currently valid OMB number. Send comments on the accuracy of this estimate of the burden and recommendations for reducing it to: U.S. Department of State, A/GIS/DIR, Washington, DC 20520.

Sample Form DS-156, Nonimmigrant Visa Application—Page 3

U.S. Department of State
SUPPLEMENT TO
NONIMMIGRANT VISA APPLICATION

PLEASE BE SURE TO SUBMIT THIS PAGE WITH THE REST OF YOUR APPLICATION

DO NOT MARK OR WRITE IN THIS SPACE

Bernardo Cristobal Cuevas

Barcode Number: M20J3NDA3J

29. Additional Visits to the U.S.: none
30. Additional Visa Issuances:
31. Additional Visa Refusals:

FILTERED NAMES
When 'None' or 'NA' are entered into any of the following the fields: 'Other Surnames Used', 'Other First and Middle Names Used', and 'National Identification Number', the text will be removed by the EVAF software from the data in the 2D barcode. If the applicant's name actually is None or NA the post must enter the name manually into NIV or RDS. The following fields have been removed:

- 'none' was removed from the 2D barcode for Item 8 (Other Surnames Used)
- 'none' was removed from the 2D barcode for Item 9 (Other First and Middle Names Used)

EVAF 02.02.12

Questions 18-21: Self-explanatory.

Question 22: It's okay to approximate an arrival date if you haven't yet purchased tickets. After all, you might want to wait to buy your ticket until the consulate has approved your K-3 visa.

Question 23: If you don't have an email address, write "None."

Questions 24 and 25: The name and address of where you will stay in the United States will hopefully be your spouse's.

Question 26: Write "permanently; will apply for permanent residence upon arriving in U.S. with K-3 visa."

Question 27: The purpose of your trip is "join U.S. citizen spouse and complete application for permanent residence."

Question 28: The person named here as paying for your trip should either be you, your spouse, or the person who signed an Affidavit of Support on your behalf, to avoid confusion about whether you'll be adequately supported in the United States.

Question 29: Self-explanatory—they'll be looking for past visa fraud or time spent unlawfully in the United States.

Question 30: This question calls for you to mention any visas that you might have applied for in the past, whether immigrant (permanent) or nonimmigrant (temporary, such as student or visitor) visas. If you applied for an immigrant visa in the past, then the question of what happened to it will arise—if you were denied, why, and if you were approved, why do you now need to apply for another immigrant visa? If you applied for a nonimmigrant visa, this shouldn't create any problems unless you used fraud, or after arriving in the United States, you stayed past the date when you were supposed to leave. Another problem might arise if you were in the United States on a J-1 (exchange student) visa and you haven't yet completed your two-year "home country" residency requirement. If you had a J-1 or J-2 visa in the last two years, consult a lawyer.

Question 31: This asks whether you have ever been refused a visa. Many people have been refused

visas to the United States, particularly in the tourist visa category. Therefore admitting that you're one of the many is not necessarily a strike against you. However, if the reason for the denial was fraud or something similar, it may lead USCIS to deny your current, K-3 visa application.

Question 32: If you plan to work in the United States, it's fine to say so here—this question is mostly meant for tourists and others who aren't allowed to work.

Question 33: This question is primarily for student visa applicants. You're best off inserting "N/A."

Question 34: Enter the names of any of your children who will be accompanying you to the United States. As the form mentions, a separate Form DS-156 will have to be submitted for each of them.

Question 35: If you have ever had a visa cancelled or revoked, consult a lawyer before continuing.

Question 36: This question asks about any immigrant (permanent) petitions filed for you, perhaps by a family member who is a U.S. citizen or resident, or an employer. If these petitions are still pending, no problem—you're allowed to have more than one petition going on at the same time, so long as they don't reveal contradictory intentions on your part. (For example, if one of the petitions was filed by a different spouse, that's a problem.) If the petitions have already been decided, and were denied, then problems could also arise if the denials were for reasons that reflect badly on you, such as fraud.

Question 37: Self-explanatory. This question is mainly directed at tourist visa applicants—the government wants to make sure that tourists and other temporary visitors don't plan to join their family and stay permanently.

Question 38: These questions are designed to see if you are inadmissible to the United States (see Chapter 2 for more on the grounds of inadmissibility). If your answer to any of these questions is "yes," see a lawyer before continuing.

Questions 39 and 40: These questions concern whether lawyers, paralegals, or other agencies may have filled in this form for you—it's okay if they did, assuming they didn't just tell you what to say or counsel you to lie.

Question 41: Sign and date the application.

ii. Form DS-156K

This is a very short form designed to collect some information that Form DS-156 neglected to ask for.

 WEB RESOURCE
This form is available on the State Department website at www.state.gov. You may be required to complete it online. However, use the form that you get from the consulate if it's different. Below is a sample filled-in version of the form.

Questions 1-4: Self-explanatory.

Question 5: List all of your children, whether or not they are immigrating to the United States. Then check the boxes at the right to tell the consulate whether they are, indeed, immigrating. If they'll be coming at the same time as you, check the "yes" box on the left. If they'll follow you some months later, check the "yes" box on the right.

Don't write anything else on this form—you won't sign it until your consular interview.

b. Where to Send Your Completed Forms

After you've filled in these forms mailed to you by the NVC, you'll mail them to the consulate, whose address will be in the materials that you received. If the consulate is in your home country, it will probably be the one located nearest to you. But if you were married in a different country, then it will be at a consulate there. Also, if your country doesn't have diplomatic relations with the United States, it will be at a consulate in a different country.

If the NVC instructs you to submit the forms online, follow the NVC's instructions carefully. Print out copies of any online forms you complete, for your records. If you are filling these forms in on your own, we recommend photocopying them and sending a copy to your U.S. citizen spouse both before and after you mail them. That way your spouse can make sure the forms are consistent with everything else that you two are submitting.

c. What Happens After You Mail in Packet of Forms

Once you've sent the required forms, the people handling your case will request a security clearance from every place you've lived since age 16. Usually, they simply ask a government office to check its records to see whether you have a police record, and to send notification of what it finds. They will also send your name to be checked against the records of the U.S. FBI and CIA. Assuming your records come back clean, the consulate will move to the next step.

d. Using the Checklist of Forms K-3 Applicant Mails to the Consulate

These forms shouldn't take you very long to prepare. Check them off the list below as you finish them, make copies, and get your packet in the mail. Also be sure to follow any additional instructions your local consulate may add.

 CHECKLIST
Appendix C includes a tear-out copy of this checklist.

Checklist of Forms K-3 Applicant Mails In

☐ Form DS-156 Part I (see Subsection C4a(i), above, for line-by-line instructions)
☐ Form DS-156K (see Subsection C4a(ii), above, for line-by-line instructions).

---

5. Step Four: Final Forms and K-3 Visa Interview

For the fourth step in the K-3 visa application process, you will receive an Appointment Package, containing an appointment date and additional instructions and possibly forms (depending on the consulate). These will include instructions for getting your medical exam. There will be a fee for this exam, usually around $150, but it varies between doctors and countries.

Sample Form DS-156K, Supplement to Form DS-156

U.S. Department of State

NONIMMIGRANT FIANCÉ(E) VISA APPLICATION

USE WITH FORM DS-156

OMB APPROVAL NO.1405-0096
EXPIRES: 11/30/2013
ESTIMATED BURDEN: 1 HOUR*

The following questions must be answered by all applicants for visas to enter the United States as the fiancée or fiancé of a U.S. citizen in order that a determination may be made as to visa eligibility.

This form, together with Form DS-156, Nonimmigrant Visa Application, completed in duplicate, constitutes the complete application for a "K" Fiancé(e) Nonimmigrant Visa authorized under Section 222(c) of the Immigration and Nationality Act.

1. Family Name	First Name	Middle Name
Cuevas	Bernardo	Cristobal

2. Date of Birth (mm-dd-yyyy)	3. Place of Birth (City, Province, Country)
07-24-1984	Bucaramanga Colombia

4. Marital Status

If you are now married or were previously married, answer the following:

a. Name of Spouse   Christa Lee Anderson; former spouse: Sonya Carcamo

b. Date (mm-dd-yyyy) and Place of Marriage   12-22-2010   Bogota, Colombia; former marriage 01-01-2002 Bogota

c. How and When was Marriage Terminated   former marriage: divorced 11-02-2006

d. If presently married, how will you marry your U.S. citizen fiancé(e)? Explain*

(Not applicable — applying for K-3 visa based on marriage.)

* NOTE If presently married to anyone, you are not eligible for a fiancé(e) visa.

5. List name, date and place of birth of all unmarried children under 21 years of age.

Name	Birth Date (mm-dd-yyyy)	Birth Place	Will Accompany You Yes	Will Accompany You No	Will Follow You Yes	Will Follow You No
Jorge Cuevas Carcamo	02-21-2006	Colombia	[X]	[ ]	[ ]	[X]
			[ ]	[ ]	[ ]	[ ]
			[ ]	[ ]	[ ]	[ ]
			[ ]	[ ]	[ ]	[ ]
			[ ]	[ ]	[ ]	[ ]

THE FOLLOWING DOCUMENTS MUST BE ATTACHED IN ORDER TO APPLY FOR A FIANCE(E) NONIMMIGRANT VISA.

• Your Birth Certificate   • Marriage Certificate (if any)   • Evidence of Engagement to Your Fiancé(e)   • Evidence of Financial Support

• Divorce Decree (if any) • Death Certificate of Spouse (if any) • Birth Certificates of All Children Listed in Number Five • Police Certificates

NOTE All of the above documents will also be required by U.S. Citizenship and Immigration Services (USCIS) when you apply for adjustment of status to lawful permanent resident. The USCIS will accept these documents for that purpose.

DO NOT WRITE BELOW THIS LINE
The consular officer will assist you in answering this part.

I understand that I am required to submit my visa to the United States Immigration Officer at the place where I apply to enter the United States, and that the possession of a visa does not entitle me to enter the United States if at that time I am found to be inadmissible under the immigration laws. I further understand that my adjustment of status to permanent resident alien is dependent upon marriage to a U.S. citizen and upon meeting all of the requirements of the U.S. Department of Homeland Security.

I understand that any willfully false or misleading statement or willful concealment of a material fact made by me herein may subject me to permanent exclusion from the United States and, if I am admitted to the United States, may subject me to criminal prosecution and/or deportation.

I hereby certify that I am legally free to marry and intend to marry _____ , a U.S. citizen, within 90 days of my admission into the United States.

I do solemnly swear or affirm that all statements which appear in this application have been made by me and are true and complete to the best of my knowledge and belief.

_____
Signature of Applicant

Subscribed and sworn to before me this —— day of _____, ———— at: _____

_____
United States Consular Officer

Confidentiality Statement - INA Section 222(f) provides that visa issuance and refusal records shall be considered confidential and shall be used only for the formulation, amendment, administration, or enforcement of the immigration, nationality, and other laws of the United States. Certified copies of visa records may be made available to a court which certifies that the information contained in such records is needed in a case pending before the court.

Paperwork Reduction Act Statement - *Public reporting burden for this collection of information is estimated to average 1 hour per response, including time required for searching existing data sources, gathering the necessary documentation, providing the information and/or documents required, and reviewing the final collection. You do not have to supply this information unless this collection displays a currently valid OMB control number. If you have comments on the accuracy of this burden estimate and/or recommendations for reducing it, please send them to: A/GIS/DIR, Room 2400 SA-22, U.S. Department of State, Washington, DC 20522-2202.

DS-156K
06-2011

PREVIOUS EDITIONS OBSOLETE

The consulate may also require Form I-134, an Affidavit of Support that your U.S. citizen spouse must fill out to show that you'll be supported financially (see line-by-line instructions below).

You'll get two to four weeks notice of your upcoming visa interview.

a. Line-by-Line Instructions for Form I-134

Not all consulates require Form I-134 as part of the K-3 visa application, though all will require some evidence that you won't need to go on welfare or receive other government assistance. If you have children immigrating with you, the children won't need separate Forms I-134—listing their names in Question 3 is sufficient.

 WEB RESOURCE
This form is available on the USCIS website at www.uscis.gov. Below is a sample filled-in version of this form.

What this form doesn't tell you is that the U.S. government can be very strict in its opinion of how much it takes to support someone. Read Chapter 3 for further discussion of how to satisfy the government's requirements. After your U.S. citizen spouse is done filling in the blanks on the form, refer to the instructions at the bottom of this section to find out if the amount is sufficient. Because you are using the Form I-134 rather than the I-864, the petitioner needs to show an income of at least 100% of the federal *Poverty Guidelines*. (For the Form I-864 used by people getting immigrant visas, the petitioner needs to show an income of at least 125% of the *Poverty Guidelines*.) If your petitioner's income is not sufficient, go back to Chapter 3 for suggestions.

Paragraph 1: Self-explanatory.

Questions 1 and 2: Self-explanatory.

Question 3: This is for information about you, the intending immigrant.

Question 7: Back to the U.S. citizen, who must enter information about his or her employment. For "type of business" it's fine to state one's position,

Is the Total Support Amount Sufficient?

Technically, Form I-134 only covers your temporary stay in the United States, until you get your green card, so the consulate may not require your U.S. citizen spouse to show a specific income level— despite the fact that they have asked him or her to fill out this form. Anyone using this form, however, is supposed to show a combination of income and assets that reaches at least 100% of the *Poverty Guidelines*. In addition, because your petitioner will have to show income/assets of at least 125% of the *Poverty Guidelines* when you apply for permanent residence, it may be helpful to look at that higher level now.

If your petitioner's income level is not sufficient by itself to meet the *Poverty Guidelines*, here is how to tell whether your support amount is sufficient when assets are also considered.

Go back to the form you filled out and follow these steps:

1. Total up all the assets listed (everything except income).
2. Subtract the mortgages and encumbrances, and divide that total by three.
3. Add this figure to the amount of income.
4. Total up the number of people the U.S. citizen will have to support. This should include: the citizen, the immigrant, any children immigrating at the same time, and any additional persons listed in questions 8 and 9.
5. Check the *Poverty Guidelines* chart located in Chapter 3, Section A. In the left column, find the line corresponding to the number of people that the U.S. citizen is responsible for supporting. Now look at the right column. That's the total amount of income plus assets that the U.S. government will want to see when you apply for your green card. If your U.S. citizen spouse's income and assets (the sum you calculated earlier) don't reach that level, reread Chapter 3.

The good news is that by the time you have reached your U.S. green card interview, you will probably have had a work permit for several months, and can contribute to the household income.

Sample Form I-134, Affidavit of Support—Page 1

Department of Homeland Security
U.S. Citizenship and Immigration Services

OMB No. 1615-0014

Form I-134, Affidavit of Support

(Answer all items. Type or print in black ink.)

I, _____Christa Lee Anderson_____ residing at _____123 4th Street, Apt #2_____
(Name)   (Street Number and Name)

_____San Diego_____ _____CA_____ _____92120_____ _____U.S._____
(City)   (State)   (Zip Code if in U.S.)   (Country)

certify under penalty of perjury under U.S. law, that:

1. I was born on _____04/18/1984_____ in _____Portland_____ _____U.S._____
   (Date-*mm/dd/yyyy*)   (City)   (State)   (Country)

If you are not a U.S. citizen based on your birth in the United States, or a non-citizen U.S. national based on your birth in American Samoa (including Swains Island), answer the following as appropriate:

    a. If a U.S. citizen through naturalization, give Certificate of Naturalization number _____

    b. If a U.S. citizen through parent(s) or marriage, give Certificate of Citizenship number _____

    c. If U.S. citizenship was derived by some other method, attach a statement of explanation.

    d. If a Lawful Permanent Resident of the United States, give A-Number _____

    e. If a lawfully admitted nonimmigrant, give Form I-94, Arrival-Departure Record, number _____

2. I am _____28_____ years of age and have resided in the United States since _____04/18/1984_____
                                                                                     (Date-*mm/dd/yyyy*)

3. This affidavit is executed on behalf of the following person:

Name (Family Name)	(First Name)	(Middle Name)	Gender	Age
Cuevas	Bernardo	Cristobal	M	28

Citizen of (Country)	Marital Status	Relationship to Sponsor
Colombia	married	spouse

Presently resides at (Street Number and Name)	(City)	(State)	(Country)
123 Calle Centro, Apt. #42	Bogota		Colombia

Name of spouse and children accompanying or following to join person:

Spouse	Gender	Age	Child		Gender	Age
Child Jorge Cuevas Carcamo	M	5	Child		Gender	Age
Child	Gender	Age	Child		Gender	Age

4. This affidavit is made by me for the purpose of assuring the U.S. Government that the person(s) named in **item (3)** will not become a public charge in the United States.

5. I am willing and able to receive, maintain, and support the person(s) named in **item 3**. I am ready and willing to deposit a bond, if necessary, to guarantee that such person(s) will not become a public charge during his or her stay in the United States, or to guarantee that the above named person(s) will maintain his or her nonimmigrant status, if admitted temporarily, and will depart prior to the expiration of his or her authorized stay in the United States.

6. I understand that:

    a. Form I-134 is an "undertaking" under section 213 of the Immigration and Nationality Act, and I may be sued if the person(s) named in **item 3** becomes a public charge after admission to the United States;

    b. Form I-134 may be made available to any Federal, State, or local agency that may receive an application from the person(s) named in **item 3** for Food Stamps, Supplemental Security Income, or Temporary Assistance to Needy Families; and

    c. If the person(s) named in **item 3** does apply for Food Stamps, Supplemental Security Income, or Temporary Assistance for Needy Families, my own income and assets may be considered in deciding the person's application. How long my income and assets may be attributed to the person(s) named in **item 3** is determined under the statutes and rules governing each specific program.

Form I-134 (Rev. 05/25/11) Y

Sample Form I-134, Affidavit of Support—Page 2

7. I am employed as or engaged in the business of _structural engineer_ with _View Development_
(Type of Business)   (Name of Concern)

at _43 Sunset Drive_ _San Diego_ _CA_ _92128_
(Street Number and Name)   (City)   (State)   (Zip Code)

I derive an annual income of: *(If self-employed, I have attached a copy of my last income tax return or report of commercial rating concern which I certify to be true and correct to the best of my knowledge and belief. See instructions for nature of evidence of net worth to be submitted.)* $ _$45,000_

I have on deposit in savings banks in the United States: $ _____

I have other personal property, the reasonable value of which is: $ _____

I have stocks and bonds with the following market value, as indicated on the attached list, which I certify to be true and correct to the best of my knowledge and belief: $ _$11,000_

I have life insurance in the sum of: $ _____

With a cash surrender value of: $ _____

I own real estate valued at: $ _____

    With mortgage(s) or other encumbrance(s) thereon amounting to: $ _____

    Which is located at: _____
    (Street Number and Name) (City) (State) (Zip Code)

8. The following persons are dependent upon me for support: *(Check the box in the appropriate column to indicate whether the person named is **wholly** or **partially** dependent upon you for support.)*

Name of Person	Wholly Dependent	Partially Dependent	Age	Relationship to Me
Jorge Cuevas Carcamo	☐	☒	5	stepson
	☐	☐		
	☐	☐		

9. I have previously submitted affidavit(s) of support for the following person(s). If none, state "None".

Name of Person	Date submitted
None	

10. I have submitted a visa petition(s) to U.S. Citizenship and Immigration Services on behalf of the following person(s). If none, state "None".

Name of Person	Relationship	Date submitted
None		

11. I ☐ intend ☒ do not intend to make specific contributions to the support of the person(s) named in **item 3**.

(If you check "intend," indicate the exact nature and duration of the contributions. For example, if you intend to furnish room and board, state for how long and, if money, state the amount in U.S. dollars and whether it is to be given in a lump sum, weekly or monthly, and for how long.)

_____

_____

_____

Oath or Affirmation of Sponsor

I acknowledge that I have read "Sponsor and Alien Liability" on Page 2 of the instructions for this form, and am aware of my responsibilities as a sponsor under the Social Security Act, as amended, and the Food Stamp Act, as amended. _____
I certify under penalty of perjury under United States law that I know the contents of this affidavit signed by me and that the statements are true and correct.

Signature of Sponsor _Christa Anderson_ Date _04/03/2013_

Form I-134 (Rev. 05/25/11) Y Page 2

such as "accountant," or a more generic description, such as "sales."

On the next set of lines, the U.S. citizen enters his or her income and assets. If the U.S. citizen's income is sufficient to meet the *Poverty Guidelines*, the Department of State will not care about the citizen's assets, so the U.S. citizen need not list each and every asset. The questions about assets become more important when the income of the U.S. citizen is close to or does not meet the *Poverty Guidelines*.

Some of the questions about assets need explanation. The question about the amount **"on deposit in savings banks in the United States"** is a little misleading—amounts in checking accounts count, too. For **"personal property,"** the U.S. citizen doesn't need to consider the value of every item he or she owns. An approximate total value on his or her cars, jewelry, appliances (stereo, television, refrigerator), cameras, and other equipment will do. But when it comes time for the green card application in the United States, the U.S. citizen sponsor will have to provide proof of ownership of any assets claimed here.

Question 8: Anyone whom the sponsor has listed on his or her tax returns should be entered here.

Question 9: This question attempts to find out whether the U.S. citizen is overextending him or herself financially. If he or she has filled in this form or Form I-864 (the Affidavit of Support used in green card applications) on behalf of any other immigrant, these lines should be filled in.

Question 10: For the reasons that underlie Question 9, the U.S. government wants to know whether the U.S. citizen is planning to sponsor anyone else, having filed a visa petition on their behalf. Even if you are the only person being sponsored, the U.S. citizen should fill in your name here, with a notation by your name saying "subject of this Affidavit."

Question 11: Enter "N/A" (Not Applicable). This is only for visitors who are truly temporary, such as tourists.

Oath or Affirmation of Sponsor: Here is a lovely example of excruciating legalese. What is most important in this section is that prior to signing this form, the signer verify that the information submitted is correct according to the best of his or her knowledge.

Although prior versions of this form had to be notarized, that is no longer a requirement.

b. Document Instructions for K-3 Application Process

This section contains detailed instructions about some of the documents on the Checklist for K-3 Appointment Package listed below.

i. Copy of U.S. Citizen's Most Recent Federal Tax Return

As part of proving that your spouse can support you financially, he or she will probably be asked to provide a complete copy of his or her federal tax return—from one to three years' worth—including the W-2 slips. There is no need to include the state tax form.

The consulate prefers to see the tax return in the form of IRS transcripts (an IRS-generated summary of the return that your U.S. citizen spouse filed), which your spouse can request using IRS Form 4506T, available through the IRS website at www.irs.gov or by calling 800-829-1040. However, it is usually a wait of several weeks to get the transcript. Don't let this hold up the immigration process. If the transcript hasn't come by the time of your interview, simply use your U.S. citizen petitioner's own copies of the tax return.

 TIP

We're advising you to prepare more than the minimum financial documents. Technically, you're supposed to be asked for only one year's tax returns, and that's it. But because so many consulates ask for more, it makes sense to be ready with additional years' tax returns plus a bank and employer letter.

ii. Letter From U.S. Citizen's Bank(s) Confirming the Account(s)

The U.S. citizen should ask all of his/her banks reported on page 1 of Form I-134 to draft simple letters confirming the accounts. The letters can be addressed to "To Whom It May Concern," and should state the date the account was opened, the total amount deposited in the last year, and the present balance.

Banks will often (without your asking) also state an average balance. Be aware that if this is much lower than the present amount, the consulate will wonder whether the U.S. citizen got a quick loan from a friend to make the financial situation look more impressive.

Some consulates prefer to see a monthly bank statement.

iii. Employer Letter

With Form I-134, your U.S. citizen spouse will also need to enclose a letter from his or her employer confirming the employment and salary. For a sample letter, see Section B3b of this chapter.

Some consulates also want to see paycheck stubs.

iv. Medical Exam

To prove that you are not inadmissible for medical reasons, you will have to present the results of a medical exam done by a doctor approved by the U.S. consulate. This is the same type of medical exam you would have to have if you were applying for a marriage-based immigrant visa, except that you won't be required to complete all your vaccinations until you're in the United States and applying for your green card. For more details on this exam, see Section B4a of this chapter.

v. Birth Certificates

You, as well as any of your children who will be accompanying you on K-4 visas, will be asked to provide copies of birth certificates, and to show the originals as well. If these documents are not in English, you'll also need to provide a word-for-word translation, created and signed by someone competent in both languages. See Chapter 4,

Section C, for more on appropriately formatting document translations.

vi. Proof of Bona Fide Marriage

Some consulates also want to see proof that you and your spouse are truly a married couple—in other words, that you did not get married merely in order to get a green card. Such proof might include copies of your personal letters, emails, phone bills, wedding photos, joint credit card bills, and the like.

c. Where You Will Take Your K-3 Appointment Package

On the day of your interview, you will be expected to arrive at the U.S. consulate with forms and documents in hand, according to the instructions. To prepare for your interview, you will not only want to read the section in this chapter on filling out the forms and gathering documents, but also read Chapter 13, Interviews With USCIS or Consular Officials.

Soon after you have attended your interview and been approved, the consulate will give you a visa to enter the United States. Ideally you will receive the visa within a few days of your interview, but recent delays for FBI and CIA security checks have been adding weeks to the process, especially for people with common names.

Your "visa" will actually be a thick sealed envelope, stuffed full of most of the forms and documents that you have submitted over the course of this process. Do not open the envelope! You must present this sealed envelope to immigration officials when you enter the United States. Once you receive your K-3 visa, you will have six months to enter the United States. The visa will be good for multiple entries to the United States for up to ten years, or in the case of children, for up to the child's 21st birthday.

d. When to Apply for Your Green Card

You should start working on your green card application as soon as you arrive in the United States. For complete instructions on the remainder of the green card application package, see Chapter 14, Applying for a Green Card at a USCIS Office.

e. Using the Checklist for K-3 Appointment Package

Which forms you are required to prepare for your K-3 Appointment Package may depend on your consulate. The ones listed on the checklist below are those most commonly required. However, if the consulate adds any to this list, you will of course need to provide those as well.

 CHECKLIST

Appendix C includes a tear-out copy of this checklist.

6. Step Five: At the Border

Assuming all goes well at the visa interview you will be given a K-3 visa, and your children, if any, will be given K-4 visas. You will have six months to use the visa(s) to enter the United States.

At the border, airport, or other port of entry, a U.S. border officer will open the sealed envelope containing your visa documents, and do a last check to make sure that you have not used fraud. Though this part of the process should not be a problem, don't treat it lightly. If the officer spots a reason why you should not have been given the K-3 visa, he or she has the power (called expedited removal) to deny your entry right there. You would

---

Checklist for K-3 Appointment Package

☐ Original INS or USCIS Notice of Action approving your I-129F visa petition

☐ A complete copy of your I-129F visa petition (the items in the checklist earlier) in case USCIS did not forward it to the consulate

☐ Originals of documents submitted in connection with the I-129F visa petition, such as your spouse's U.S. birth certificate and proof that any previous marriages were legally ended, and photocopies of each original

☐ Two copies of Form DS-156, nonimmigrant visa application

☐ One copy of Form DS-156K, nonimmigrant fiancé visa application form

☐ Form I-134, Affidavit of Support, if the consulate requested it (see line-by-line instructions in Section C5a, above)

☐ Documents to accompany Form I-134, including:

    ☐ Proof of U.S. citizen's employment

    ☐ Copy of U.S. citizen's federal tax return(s)

    ☐ Letter from U.S. citizen's bank confirming the account

☐ A valid passport from your home country, good for at least six months after the interview

☐ Your original birth certificate plus a copy, and birth certificates for any children who will be accompanying you

☐ An original police clearance certificate, if this is available in your country (the instructions from the consulate will tell you)

☐ Your original marriage certificate

☐ Two color photos of you, the immigrating fiancé, passport style

☐ Your medical examination, in an unopened envelope (see Chapter 2, Section A, for more on the medical exam)

☐ Fingerprints (you will receive instructions from the consulate)

☐ Proof that your marriage is the real thing

☐ Any other items or forms requested by the consulate

☐ Nonimmigrant visa application fee (currently $240)

K-3 Visa Application Process

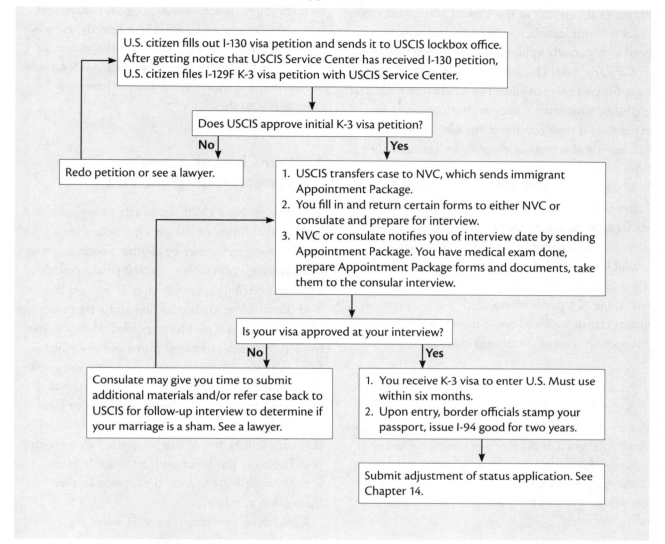

have no right to a lawyer or a hearing but would simply have to turn around and find a flight or other means of transport home. And you wouldn't be allowed back within five years unless the border officials asked you to withdraw the application before they officially denied it, which is entirely at their discretion.

After advice like this, the hardest thing to hear is "just stay calm." It may be impossible to control your beating heart, but whatever you do, don't start speaking more than is necessary. The worst thing someone could do at this stage is to make a nervous joke. Border officials are not known for their sense

of humor, and some statements could be used as a reason to question you further or to deny you entry.

When the officer is satisfied that everything is in order, he or she will give you a small white card called an I-94 to put into your passport, allowing you to stay in the United States for two years. You are allowed to go in and out of the United States during that time.

You may notice that the K-3 visa that the consulate stamped in your passport was good for multiple entries over ten years. Indeed, if you leave the United States and your green card application has not yet been resolved, you can continue to use the K-3 visa stamp to reenter for up to ten years. However if you stay in the United States past two years without leaving and coming in again, you will need to separately apply for an extension of status.

Similarly, your children will be admitted on K-4 visas for two years or until the day before their 21st birthday, whichever is shorter, but can apply for extensions if they remain in the United States, or can leave and return on their K-4 visas until they expire.

If you plan to work while you are in the United States before submitting your adjustment of status application, you will need to apply for work authorization, using Form I-765. This form is available on the USCIS website at www.uscis.gov. The I-765 should be filed at the same Service Center where the K-3 petition was filed. But it's probably just as fast to wait and apply for a work permit with your adjustment of status application.

SKIP AHEAD

For how to obtain your green card after you are in the United States, see Chapter 14. Also note that if your local USCIS office is extremely backed up, it is possible for you to return to an overseas consulate for completion of your immigrant visa processing. However, you will need to wait for approval of Form I-130 before taking this step.

D. How to Have Your Children and Pets Accompany You

Although your whole family cannot immigrate right now, U.S. laws and regulations do recognize the need for certain of your loved ones to accompany you to the United States and live there with you, including your children and certain pets.

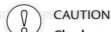

CAUTION

Check your own country's law on taking your children if their other parent is staying behind. If you will be bringing children to the United States who are not the biological children of your U.S. spouse, or who

became the adopted children of another person, it will be up to you to comply with any custody requirements. Even if the children are legally in your custody, you may need to get written consent from the other parent for you to take the children out of the country. U.S. consular officials may also require proof that you have legal custody of your children.

1. Your Children If You're Using an Immigrant Visa

Your foreign-born children, whether they are the biological children or the stepchildren of your petitioning spouse, may be eligible to obtain green cards through him or her. For the fundamentals of children's eligibility, see Chapter 2, Section B.

If the children are unmarried and were under age 21 when their visa petition was filed, they will have to go through the identical four steps described in Section B, above. As part of these steps, you must prove that the children are not only yours, but are also your spouse's biological children or legal stepchildren, that they are not inadmissible, and that they will be financially supported along with you. For more guidance on how to apply Steps One through Four to a child's application, see Subsection a, below.

Children who were over age 21 when their visa petition was filed, or who don't qualify as stepchildren or are married, will not be able to immigrate to the United States at the same time as you. As a U.S. citizen, your spouse may file visa petitions for them if they are his or her biological children or legal stepchildren, but they will be subject to quotas and waiting periods. This book does not cover how to file these visa petitions.

a. Immigrant Visa Application Procedures for Children

This section contains a brief overview of the procedures for immigrating children, but complete details (especially line-by-line instructions on filling out the forms) are outside the scope of this book. Once you've filled in all the paperwork described in this book, you will have a good basis of knowledge with which to fill in these forms for your children; or you might be more comfortable using a lawyer.

To start the process, your U.S. citizen spouse will need to fill in a separate visa petition (Form I-130) for each child. However, the children do not need to fill in Form G-325A, nor do they need to have their photos included in the visa petition. Include copies of your and your spouse's marriage certificate, but also include copies of the children's birth certificates to show the family relationships.

At the Step Two (NVC mailing) stage, you will have to send a Form DS-230 Part I for each of your children (the same form you filled in for yourself). The National Visa Center should send you separate forms for each child. If they don't, either ask for separate packets or simply make photocopies of the forms sent to you.

When it's time for your interview, the children will have to submit all the same types of forms and documents as you, including separately filled out versions of the Affidavit of Support (Form I-864). Of course, you'll want to make sure that the income and assets shown are sufficient to cover them. If your child is under the age of 16, he or she will not need to submit a police certificate.

You can expect to attend your interviews together. The children probably won't have to answer more than one or two questions.

2. Your Children If You're Using a K-3 Visa

Your foreign-born children, whether they are the biological children or the stepchildren of your petitioning spouse, may be eligible to obtain what are called K-4 visas to accompany you to the United States, and then to obtain green cards once you are all in the United States. For the fundamentals of children's eligibility, see Chapter 2, Section B.

If the children are unmarried and under age 21, they will have to go through nearly the identical five steps you did in applying for the entry visa. (See Subsection b, below.)

As part of the application process in getting your children a K-4 visa, you will need to prove that the children are yours, using a birth certificate or other proof. In addition, you will need to prove that they are not inadmissible, and that they will be financially supported along with you. For more guidance on the application process, see Subsection a, below.

Children who are over age 21, or are married, will not be able to immigrate to the United States at the same time as you. As a U.S. citizen, your spouse may file visa petitions for them if they are his or her biological children or legal stepchildren, but they will be subject to quotas and waiting periods. This book does not cover how to file these visa petitions.

a. K-4 Visa Application Procedures for Children

This section contains a brief overview of the procedures for immigrating children, but complete details (especially line-by-line instructions on filling in the forms) are outside the scope of this book. Once you have filled in all the paperwork described in this book, you will have a good basis of knowledge with which to fill in the forms for your children, or you may be more comfortable getting a lawyer.

To start the process, your U.S. citizen spouse will need to name the children on the I-129F filed in the United States. (They don't need separate Forms I-129F.) Your spouse should, however, also fill in a separate Form I-130 for each child—not as a prerequisite to getting the K-4 visa, but in order to make the children eligible for green cards after they have entered the United States. Although these Forms I-130 do not need to be submitted at the same time as yours, it's a good idea to do so, particularly because the waiting periods for these approvals can be years in length. And, having I-130 receipt notices is necessary before you file your children's applications for green cards in the United States. (Like you, they will each need to apply for a green card, through a process called adjustment of status. They cannot be included in your application at the adjustment stage.)

When filling in Forms I-130 for your children, note that they do not need to fill in form G-325A (as you do), nor do they need to have their photos included in the visa petition. Include copies of your and your spouse's marriage certificates plus the children's birth certificates to show the family relationships.

At the Step Two stage of mailing forms back to the consulate, you will have to send separate DS forms for each child. The consulate should send you a package of forms for each child. If it doesn't, either ask for these forms or simply make photocopies of the forms sent to you.

When it is time for your consular interview, the children will have to submit all the same types of forms and documents as you, except they can simply submit photocopies of the Affidavit of Support (Form I-134). Of course, you will want to make sure that their names are listed on your Form I-134, and that the income and assets shown are sufficient to cover each child. If your child is under the age of 16, he or she will not need to submit a police certificate.

You can expect to attend your K-3/K-4 visa interview together. The children will probably not have to answer more than one or two questions.

b. Children About to Turn 21 Could Lose Out

If there is a chance that your child will turn 21 before actually claiming a K-4 visa, watch out! The minute a child hits age 21, the child will no longer be eligible for the K-4 visa. This problem is known as "aging out."

Here is how to avoid having your child miss his/her chance to get a K-4 visa at the same time as you get your K-3. Write, "PLEASE EXPEDITE, AGE-OUT MM/DD/YY" (the exact date your child will turn 21) in red ink on the top of any cover letters and primary applications. If you have any personal contact with a consular officer during the application process, be sure to bring up the age-out issue.

The consulate should be able to schedule your K-3 visa earlier when they learn of the age-out issue.

If you don't hear from them within eight weeks of submitting your materials to the NVC or consulate, start writing reminder letters or visit the consulate in person.

Don't make the mistake of thinking that you have solved the problem by simply getting your child's K-4 visa before your child's 21st birthday. Your child has to use that visa to enter the United States before he or she turns 21. Until your child shows up at the border, the process is not complete, and the border guard can keep your child out because, having turned 21, your child no longer qualifies for the visa he or she was given.

After your child is in the United States and ready to adjust status, the Child Status Protection Act will protect him or her from the consequences of turning 21, so long as a Form I-130 was filed on his or her behalf before the child's 21st birthday.

3. Your Pets

Good news for your dog and cat, who may not have learned to sign their names yet—they won't need a visa. Bringing pets into the United States is not an immigration law matter. But before bringing any pets to the United States, you will need to check into U.S. customs restrictions. In general, pets will be admitted if they are in good health and have had all the proper vaccinations. There are some restrictions, however. For example, certain states don't allow specific animals, and monkeys aren't allowed into the United States at all. Check with your local U.S. consulate for details, or read more on the Web at www.cbp.gov (enter "pets" into the search box, which will bring up a publication called "Pets and Wildlife: Licensing and Health Requirements").

SKIP AHEAD
For what to do after you have obtained your visa and entered the United States, see Chapter 16.

Overseas Spouses of Lawful Permanent Residents

A marriage-based visa or green card is available to anyone who is living overseas, married to a U.S. permanent resident, and whose marriage is real and legally valid. In addition, they must not be inadmissible to the United States for any of the reasons covered in Chapter 2, Section A. To confirm that you are eligible for a marriage-based green card, review Chapter 2, Section B.

Unfortunately, there are many people like you—known as a preference relative—but few available visas year by year. After your spouse files an application to start the process, you will become one of many prospective immigrants on a long and somewhat mysterious waiting list. This wait will add, on average, three to five years to the one-year (or more) application process. You will most likely have to wait outside the United States. (Read Section A2, later in this chapter, for how to estimate your wait.)

The only good thing about this long wait is that, when you ultimately are allowed to enter the United States, your residence status will be permanent. Here's why: Immigrants who enter the United States before completing two years of marriage are given only conditional residence. USCIS puts their marriage through a two-year testing period to make sure the marriage is not a sham, and makes a final decision on the green card (granting permanent residency) only after those two years are up. Since it is very unlikely that you, as the spouse of a permanent resident, will get through the application and waiting within two years of your marriage, you won't have to go through this two-year testing period.

Your immigration application will be handled initially by USCIS offices in the United States and will be transferred to a U.S. consulate in your home country. We'll explain the various steps involved in this application process in this chapter.

CAUTION

If your permanent resident spouse has made his or her home outside the United States, his or her permanent residence may now be lost. Permanent residents are expected to make their primary home in the United States. Any absence longer than six months will raise questions. Before you rely on your permanent resident spouse to petition for you, make sure this isn't a problem. See Chapter 16 for more on how permanent residents can lose their residency this way.

A. The Immigrant Visa Application Process

If you are reading this section, it means that you have determined that you are eligible for a marriage-based visa and are ready to find out exactly how to get it. But first, a warning: This application process is a bit like harnessing yourself to a turtle. It's going to move slowly, and to succeed you'll have to hang on for the whole bumpy ride. This chapter gives you a map for that ride and offers a few shortcuts.

Obtaining an immigrant visa and green card through a permanent resident spouse involves five major steps:

Step 1: Your spouse submits a visa petition to USCIS.

Step 2: Your petition is approved, and your file is transferred to the National Visa Center (NVC) in the United States and you wait for a visa to become available to you.

Step 3: When a visa is about to become available, the NVC sends you forms to fill out and instructions.

Step 4: You attend an interview at a U.S. consulate in your home country, which later gives you your immigrant visa.

Step 5: You present your visa at a U.S. border, where it is examined and you are approved and stamped for U.S. residency.

In addition to the steps above, a few couples (or more likely the U.S.-based spouse) are required to attend a "fraud interview" if the government has doubts about their marriage being the real thing.

This could happen either as part of Step One or after Step Four, above.

Now you may have a clearer picture of why your application process will take so long. The total time often (but not always) includes:

- between one and three years for approval of the initial visa petition (Step One) (they're not in a hurry, because they know you'll need to wait even longer until a visa is available to you, as described next)
- another one to three years before a visa is available to you (Step Two)
- another month at least—or possibly many months—to receive the follow-up paperwork (Step Three) from the National Visa Center (NVC) (after which how long it takes you to collect documents and fill out forms is largely up to you)
- another four months or so after receiving all the paperwork you sent in until you're scheduled for an interview at the consulate in your home country (Step Four), and
- no more than six months before you take your immigrant visa in hand, to take Step Five and enter the United States.

These time periods are mere educated guesses, based on averages over the last few years. Your application could go faster or slower, depending on a variety of factors including the current demand for visas, the complexities of your own case, and the efficiency and workload of the U.S. consulate in your country. (These issues and hassles are discussed in more detail in Chapter 15, Dealing With Bureaucrats, Delays, and Denials.)

CAUTION
The urgency you feel to get settled into your new home is not shared by the government officials who'll be dealing with your application. They've long since gotten used to the fact that they have thousands of applications to get through. Once in a while, a miracle will happen; but usually your green card application will take longer than you ever imagined.

1. Step One: The I-130 Visa Petition

Your U.S. permanent resident spouse will initiate the green card application process by sending a visa petition—Form I-130, Petition for Alien Relative and attached documents—to a USCIS office. This petition asks USCIS to acknowledge your marriage and allow you to go forward with green card processing.

Approval of the visa petition does not mean you're guaranteed approval of your green card, however. Like every immigrant, you will eventually have to file your own, extensive portion of the immigrant visa and green card application. At that time, the consulate will take a hard look at your financial situation and other factors that might disqualify you from entering the United States.

CAUTION
If the U.S. petitioner has a criminal record, see an attorney. Under the Adam Walsh Child Protection and Safety Act of 2006, U.S. citizens and lawful permanent residents who have been convicted of any "specified offense against a minor" are prohibited from filing a family-based immigrant petition on behalf of any beneficiary (whether a child or not). USCIS will run security checks on all petitions and may call the petitioner in for fingerprinting. If the petitioner has a conviction for one of the specified offenses against a minor, then the petition will not be approved unless USCIS determines that the U.S. petitioner poses no risk to the beneficiary.

a. Line-by-Line Instructions for Visa Petition Forms

This section will give you precise instructions for filling out the forms that are listed on the visa petition checklist in Subsection e, below. Before proceeding, take a look at the general instructions on printing and filling in USCIS forms in Chapter 4. Also, as you read these instructions, you should have a copy of the appropriate form in hand. In Subsection b, below, we advise you on how to gather the supporting documentary proof and other items required for Form I-130, such as photos and filing fees.

i. Form I-130

The first thing to notice about Form I-130 is that it runs in two columns (except for the tiny Part A near the top). The left column, or Part B, asks for information about the petitioner—that's your U.S. permanent resident spouse. Don't be thrown off by the fact that the form addresses your spouse as "you"—after all, it's your spouse who fills out and signs this form. The right column, Part C, asks for information about you, referred to as the relative. Now for the questions.

 WEB RESOURCE

Form I-130 is available on the USCIS website at www.uscis.gov. Below is a sample filled-in version of this form.

Part A

Question 1: Check the first box, Husband/Wife.

Question 2: This question, about whether you're related by adoption, is meant for people who use this form to apply for an adopted child. We're assuming you can answer this question "No."

Question 3: If the petitioning spouse gained permanent residence through adoption, check **Yes.** But no matter which box you check, it won't affect the application, since this question is mainly directed at people immigrating through parent/child relationships—something not covered in this book.

Part B

Question 1: The petitioning spouse must enter his/her last name (surname) in capital letters, but the first and middle name in small letters. For example, Samuel Lawrence Cole would write COLE, Samuel Lawrence. Your spouse should use his/her current married name if it was changed at the time of your marriage. If you are unclear on which name to use, see "What's Your Name?" in Chapter 4, Section B.

Questions 2-5: Self-explanatory.

Question 6: This refers only to the petitioning spouse's most recent marital status. He or she should check "Married," even if there was a previous divorce.

Question 7: See "What's Your Name?" in Chapter 4 Section B.

Question 8: Self-explanatory.

Question 9: Self-explanatory.

Question 10: Enter the eight- or nine-digit A-number found on the U.S. permanent resident's green card.

Question 11: Self-explanatory.

Question 12: There's a reason for this question: If the petitioning spouse's prior marriage(s) ended after your present marriage began, yours is not a lawful marriage. If your petitioning spouse has just discovered that the divorce wasn't final when your marriage took place, it may not be necessary to run to a lawyer. Assuming that the divorce has since become final, you can simply correct the problem by remarrying. (If there was fraud involved in your hasty marriage, consult a lawyer.)

Question 13: Leave blank, since your spouse is not yet a citizen.

Question 14a: Some of the information requested here is on the petitioner's green card. (See the illustration below.) The date of admission shown on the older cards usually starts with the year, so that Dec. 3, 1998 would be 981203. The city is in code on the old cards: for example, SFR is San Francisco, BUF is Buffalo, and LIN is the Service Center in Lincoln, Nebraska. Why a Service Center? The applicant became a conditional resident first, then two years later received permanent residence from the Lincoln, Nebraska, Service Center. If you have a new card, you'll have to figure out where you entered the U.S. with your immigrant visa or were approved for a green card. Class of Admission asks for the type of visa or remedy through which the person got permanent residence, such as a Fourth Preference visa or political asylum.

Sample Form I-130, Petition for Alien Relative—Page 1

Department of Homeland Security
U.S. Citizenship and Immigration Services

OMB No. 1615-0012; Expires 01/31/2012

I-130, Petition for Alien Relative

DO NOT WRITE IN THIS BLOCK - FOR USCIS OFFICE ONLY

A#	Action Stamp	Fee Stamp

Section of Law/Visa Category
- [ ] 201(b) Spouse - IR-1/CR-1
- [ ] 201(b) Child - IR-2/CR-2
- [ ] 201(b) Parent - IR-5
- [ ] 203(a)(1) Unm. S or D - F1-1
- [ ] 203(a)(2)(A)Spouse - F2-1
- [ ] 203(a)(2)(A) Child - F2-2
- [ ] 203(a)(2)(B) Unm. S or D - F2-4
- [ ] 203(a)(3) Married S or D - F3-1
- [ ] 203(a)(4) Brother/Sister - F4-1

Petition was filed on: _____ (priority date)
- [ ] Personal Interview
- [ ] Pet. [ ] Ben. " A" File Reviewed
- [ ] Field Investigation
- [ ] 203(a)(2)(A) Resolved
- [ ] Previously Forwarded
- [ ] I-485 Filed Simultaneously
- [ ] 204(g) Resolved
- [ ] 203(g) Resolved

Remarks:

A. Relationship   You are the petitioner.   Your relative is the beneficiary.

1. I am filing this petition for my:
[X] Husband/Wife [ ] Parent [ ] Brother/Sister [ ] Child

2. Are you related by adoption?
[ ] Yes [X] No

3. Did you gain permanent residence through adoption?
[ ] Yes [X] No

B. Information about you

1. Name (Family name in CAPS) (First) (Middle)
DEBDEN   Alice   Anne

2. Address (Number and Street) (Apt. No.)
432 Fairfax Street   A

(Town or City) (State/Country) (Zip/Postal Code)
Alexandria   VA   22314

3. Place of Birth (Town or City) (State/Country)
Dublin   Ireland

4. Date of Birth
03/03/1974

5. Gender
[ ] Male [X] Female

6. Marital Status
[X] Married [ ] Single [ ] Widowed [ ] Divorced

7. Other Names Used (including maiden name)
Madison

8. Date and Place of Present Marriage (if married)
03/05/2006   London U.K.

9. U.S. Social Security Number (If any)
123-12-1234

10. Alien Registration Number
A22334455

11. Name(s) of Prior Husband(s)/Wive(s)
David Madison

12. Date(s) Marriage(s) Ended
09/22/1997

13. If you are a U.S. citizen, complete the following:

My citizenship was acquired through (check one):
- [ ] Birth in the U.S.
- [ ] Naturalization. Give certificate number and date and place of issuance.

_____

- [ ] Parents. Have you obtained a certificate of citizenship in your own name?
- [ ] Yes. Give certificate number, date and place of issuance. [ ] No

14. If you are a lawful permanent resident alien, complete the following:

Date and place of admission for or adjustment to lawful permanent residence and class of admission.

01/2008   SFR,   IR1

14b. Did you gain permanent resident status through marriage to a U.S. citizen or lawful permanent resident?
[ ] Yes [X] No

C. Information about your relative

1. Name (Family name in CAPS) (First) (Middle)
LINDSEY   Edmund   Alexander

2. Address (Number and Street) (Apt. No.)
10 Walden Road

(Town or City) (State/Country) (Zip/Postal Code)
London   U.K.   SW1H OBD

3. Place of Birth (Town or City) (State/Country)
Thaxted   U.K.

4. Date of Birth
11/21/1973

5. Gender
[X] Male [ ] Female

6. Marital Status
[X] Married [ ] Single [ ] Widowed [ ] Divorced

7. Other Names Used (including maiden name)
none

8. Date and Place of Present Marriage (if married)
03/05/2006   London U.K.

9. U.S. Social Security Number (If any)
None

10. Alien Registration Number
None

11. Name(s) of Prior Husband(s)/Wive(s)
none

12. Date(s) Marriage(s) Ended

13. Has your relative ever been in the U.S.? [ ] Yes [X] No

14. If your relative is currently in the U.S., complete the following:
He or she arrived as a:
(visitor, student, stowaway, without inspection, etc.)

Arrival/Departure Record (I-94)   Date arrived
| | | | ▬ | | | | | |

Date authorized stay expired, or will expire, as shown on Form I-94 or I-95

15. Name and address of present employer (if any)
London Underground, 55 Broadway, London U.K. SW1H OBD

Date this employment began   07/14/2004

16. Has your relative ever been under immigration proceedings?
[X] No [ ] Yes Where _____ When _____
[ ] Removal [ ] Exclusion/Deportation [ ] Rescission [ ] Judicial Proceedings

INITIAL RECEIPT	RESUBMITTED	RELOCATED: Rec'd	Sent	COMPLETED: Appv'd	Denied	Ret'd

Form I-130 (01/08/12) Y

Sample Form I-130, Petition for Alien Relative—Page 2

C. Information about your alien relative (continued)

17. List husband/wife and all children of your relative.

(Name)	(Relationship)	(Date of Birth)	(Country of Birth)
Alice Debden	wife	03/03/1974	Ireland

18. Address in the United States where your relative intends to live.

(Street Address)	(Town or City)	(State)
432 Fairfax Street #A	Alexandria	VA

19. Your relative's address abroad. (Include street, city, province and country)   Phone Number (if any)

10 Walden Road, London U.K.   44 20 7363 1323

20. If your relative's native alphabet is other than Roman letters, write his or her name and foreign address in the native alphabet.

(Name)   Address (Include street, city, province and country):

21. If filing for your husband/wife, give last address at which you lived together. (Include street, city, province, if any, and country):

	From:	To:
10 Walden Road, London U.K.	08/2005	04/2006

22. Complete the information below if your relative is in the United States and will apply for adjustment of status.

Your relative is in the United States and will apply for adjustment of status to that of a lawful permanent resident at the USCIS office in: If your relative is not eligible for adjustment of status, he or she will apply for a visa abroad at the American consular post in:

(City)	(State)	(City)	(Country

NOTE: Designation of a U.S. embassy or consulate outside the country of your relative's last residence does not guarantee acceptance for processing by that post. Acceptance is at the discretion of the designated embassy or consulate.

D. Other information

1. If separate petitions are also being submitted for other relatives, give names of each and relationship.

2. Have you ever before filed a petition for this or any other alien? ☐ Yes ☒ No

If "Yes," give name, place and date of filing and result.

WARNING: USCIS investigates claimed relationships and verifies the validity of documents. USCIS seeks criminal prosecutions when family relationships are falsified to obtain visas.

PENALTIES: By law, you may be imprisoned for not more than five years or fined $250,000, or both, for entering into a marriage contract for the purpose of evading any provision of the immigration laws. In addition, you may be fined up to $10,000 and imprisoned for up to five years, or both, for knowingly and willfully falsifying or concealing a material fact or using any false document in submitting this petition.

YOUR CERTIFICATION: I certify, under penalty of perjury under the laws of the United States of America, that the foregoing is true and correct. Furthermore, I authorize the release of any information from my records that U.S. Citizenship and Immigration Services needs to determine eligiblity for the benefit that I am seeking.

E. Signature of petitioner

Alice Debden   Date 3/15/2006   Phone Number (703) 555-1212

F. Signature of person preparing this form, if other than the petitioner

I declare that I prepared this document at the request of the person above and that it is based on all information of which I have any knowledge.

Print Name _____   Signature _____   Date _____

Address _____   G-28 ID or VOLAG Number, if any. _____

Form I-130 (01/08/12) Y Page 2

New-Style Green Card (Front)

Date of Admission

Question 14b: A petitioning spouse who immigrated through marriage cannot petition for a new spouse for five years, unless the first spouse died or your spouse can prove by "clear and convincing evidence" that the previous marriage was bona fide (real). USCIS is concerned that the first marriage was just a sham, with the long-term goal of getting both of you into the United States by piggybacking on a sham marriage. To prove that the first marriage was bona fide, your spouse should enclose documentary evidence showing that he or she and the former spouse shared a life, such as shared rent receipts, club memberships, children's birth certificates, utility bills, and insurance agreements. Will USCIS find this evidence to be "clear and convincing"? Unfortunately, this legal standard is easy to state but hard to pin down or apply. The bottom line is that your spouse has a lot of proving to do to persuade a suspicious government official that the previous marriage was bona fide.

Part C: (Now referring to you, the immigrant beneficiary)

Question 1: Your current name, with your last name (surname) in capital letters. If you have any doubt about what name to use, see "What's Your Name?" in Chapter 4, Section B.

Question 2: Self-explanatory.

Questions 3-5: Self-explanatory.

Question 6: Your current marital status only.

Question 7: See "What's Your Name?" in Chapter 4, Section B.

Question 8: Self-explanatory.

Question 9: If you don't have a Social Security number, just write "None." You probably wouldn't have a Social Security number unless you have lived in the United States and had a work permit, a visa allowing you to work, or U.S. residence.

Question 10: The Alien Registration Number is an eight- or nine-digit number following a letter A that USCIS will assign to you. You won't have one yet unless you've previously applied for permanent or, in some cases, temporary residence; or been in deportation/removal proceedings. (Of course, if your previous application was denied because you were inadmissible or you lied on that application, you should call a lawyer before going any further.) If you've never been assigned an A number, write "None."

Questions 11 and 12: See advice to Questions 11 and 12 in Part B, above.

Question 13: Self-explanatory.

Question 14: Enter N/A here, since you're living outside the United States.

Question 15: State your employer's name and address.

Question 16: If you've been placed in Immigration Court proceedings, see a lawyer, particularly if you lost.

Question 17: This is the continuation of Part C, so all questions still refer to you, the immigrant beneficiary. Since your spouse is already covered in this application, just list your children, if any. This means all your children, including any by previous relationships.

Question 18: Self-explanatory. Hopefully, your address will be the same as that of your spouse, or USCIS may raise questions.

Question 19: Enter N/A if you're living in the United States. This is self-explanatory if you're living overseas.

Question 20: If your native language uses a non-Roman script (for example, Russian, Chinese, or

Arabic), you'll need to write your name and address in that script.

Question 21: Self-explanatory.

Question 22: You need not fill out Question 22 if you are overseas.

Part D: Other Information.

Now we're back to questions to be answered by the petitioning spouse.

Question 1: This refers to other petitions being submitted simultaneously (for example, for your children from this or other marriages), so that USCIS can process the petitions together. Enter the children's names here.

Question 2: This refers to previous filed petitions—which may include petitions for other spouses. As you might imagine, if the petitioning spouse has a history of short marriages to people whom he/she then helped get green cards, USCIS may initiate a marriage fraud investigation, and you should see a lawyer.

Signature Line: The petitioning spouse signs here.

Signature of person preparing this form if other than above. If you or your spouse is preparing your own application, you can leave this blank. A little typing assistance or advice from a friend doesn't count—the only people who need to complete this line are lawyers or agencies that fill out these forms on others' behalf.

ii. Form G-325A

The information you and your spouse supply on this form will allow the U.S. government to check your background. Most of the form is self-explanatory. If you really can't remember or are unable to find out an exact date, enter whatever you can remember, such as the year. Alternately, you can simply say "unknown," but if you overuse the "unknowns" USCIS may return your entire application for another try. Since the questions aren't numbered, we refer to them by the approximate line.

 WEB RESOURCE

Form G-325A is available on the USCIS website at www.uscis.gov. Below is a sample filled-in version of this form (done by the immigrating half of the couple).

You and your spouse each fill one out.

Lines 1 and 2 (Family Name, etc.): Self-explanatory.

Line 3 (Father/Mother): Self-explanatory.

Line 4 (Husband or Wife): Self-explanatory.

Line 5 (Former Husbands or Wives): Self-explanatory.

Line 7 (Applicant's residence last five years): Be careful here. These need to be in reverse chronological order, starting with your most recent address and working your way down the last five years. For example, if you now live in Beijing but lived in Xian before, your Beijing address would go on the top line. Practice making this list on another sheet of paper before you enter the information here.

Line 12 (Applicant's last address outside the United States of more than one year): This may overlap with one of the addresses in Line 6—that's okay.

Line 13 (Applicant's employment last five years): Again, be careful to put this in reverse chronological order. If you've been unemployed, self-employed, or were a housewife or house-husband, say so here—in other words, try to account for all five years.

Line 18 (Show below last occupation abroad if not listed above): This question asks you to list your last overseas job—but only if you didn't already list it on Line 8. People tend to overlook this line, because it's so small—make sure you don't accidentally jump over it.

Line 19 (This form is submitted in connection with application for): On your spouse's form, he or she should check "other" and write "in support of spouse's I-130." On your form, you should check "status as permanent resident."

Line 20 (If your native alphabet uses non-Roman letters): Self-explanatory.

Line 21 (The dark box): Self-explanatory.

Sample Form G-325A, Biographic Information

Department of Homeland Security
U.S. Citizenship and Immigration Services

OMB No. 1615-0008; Expires 08/31/2012

G-325A, Biographic Information

(Family Name)	(First Name)	(Middle Name)	[X] Male [ ] Female	Date of Birth (mm/dd/yyyy)	Citizenship/Nationality	File Number
Lindsey	Edmund	Alexander		11-21-1973	English	A

All Other Names Used (include names by previous marriages)	City and Country of Birth	U.S. Social Security # *(if any)*
none	Thaxted U.K.	

	Family Name	First Name	Date of Birth (mm/dd/yyyy)	City, and Country of Birth (if known)	City and Country of Residence
Father	Lindsey	Thomas	10-22-1951	London U.K.	London U.K.
Mother (Maiden Name)	Herries	Janice	8-17-1955	Haddington U.K.	London U.K.

Current Husband or Wife (If none, so state) Family Name (For wife, give maiden name)	First Name	Date of Birth (mm/dd/yyyy)	City and Country of Birth	Date of Marriage	Place of Marriage
wife Debden	Alice	03-03-1974	Dublin, Ireland	03/05/2006	London, U.K.

Former Husbands or Wives (If none, so state) Family Name (For wife, give maiden name)	First Name	Date of Birth (mm/dd/yyyy)	Date and Place of Marriage	Date and Place of Termination of Marriage
none				

Applicant's residence last five years. List present address first.

Street and Number	City	Province or State	Country	From Month	From Year	To Month	To Year
10 Walden Road	London	U.K.		09	2001	Present Time	

Applicant's last address outside the United States of more than 1 year.

Street and Number	City	Province or State	Country	From Month	From Year	To Month	To Year
10 Walden Road	London	U.K.		09	2004	present	time

Applicant's employment last five years. (If none, so state.) List present employment first.

Full Name and Address of Employer	Occupation (Specify)	From Month	From Year	To Month	To Year
London Underground, 55 Broadway, London SW1H 0BD U.K.	Asst. Processing & Fleets Manager	07	2004	Present Time	

Last occupation abroad if not shown above. (Include all information requested above.)

This form is submitted in connection with an application for:	Signature of Applicant	Date
[ ] Naturalization [ ] Other (Specify): [X] Status as Permanent Resident	Edmund A. Lindsey	3/15/2006

If your native alphabet is in other than Roman letters, write your name in your native alphabet below:

Penalties: Severe penalties are provided by law for knowingly and willfully falsifying or concealing a material fact.

Applicant: Print your name and Alien Registration Number in the box outlined by heavy border below.

Complete This Box (Family Name)	(Given Name)	(Middle Name)	(Alien Registration Number)
			A

Form G-325A (Rev. 08/08/11) Y

b. Documents to Have on Hand for Visa Petition

The I-130 visa petition asks you to submit supporting documents along with the form. Among these are the following, which are listed on the Checklist in Subsection e:

- **Proof of the U.S. Permanent Resident Status of Your Petitioning Spouse.** To prove permanent residency, your spouse should make a copy of his or her green card (front and back). If your spouse hasn't yet been issued a green card, a copy of the stamp placed in his or her passport indicating permanent residence will be sufficient. Or, your spouse can submit a copy of the Form I-797 notice approving his or her permanent resident status, if issued one.
- **Photos.** You and your spouse must each submit a color passport-style photo, 2 x 2 inches in size, taken within the past six months, showing your current appearances. Passport style means that the photo shows your full face from the front, with a plain white or off-white background—and your face must measure between one inch and 1⅜ inches from the bottom of your chin to the top of your head. For more information, see the State Department website at http://travel.state.gov (under "Visas for Foreign Citizens," click "more," then "A–Z Subject Index," and go to "Photo Requirements" under letter "P"). However, USCIS regulations permit you to submit a photo that doesn't completely follow the instructions if you live in a country where such photographs are unavailable or are cost prohibitive.
- **Fees.** The current fee for an I-130 visa petition is $420. However, these fees go up fairly regularly, so double-check this on the USCIS website at www.uscis.gov, or by calling USCIS at 800-375-5283.

c. Where to Send Visa Petition

After your spouse has prepared and assembled all the forms and other items from the checklist below, (including the G-325A and photos that you'll have to send him or her) your spouse should make photocopies for your records. Then your spouse must send the packet to the USCIS "lockbox" office for the region where he or she lives. Certified mail with a return receipt is the safest way to send anything to USCIS.

The address is below and in Appendix B. You can double-check this information on the USCIS website.

If your spouse lives outside the United States or its territories, he or she should contact the nearest U.S. consulate about where to send the visa petition.

d. What Happens After Sending in the Form I-130 Visa Petition

A few weeks after your spouse sends in your visa petition, he or she should get a receipt notice from a USCIS Service Center (a different office from the lockbox the I-130 was sent to—the lockbox will have forwarded the file to a USCIS Service Center). The receipt notice will tell you to check the USCIS website for information on how long the application is likely to remain in processing. A sample receipt notice is included below.

In a way, how long your I-130 petition spends in processing doesn't matter. As soon as the petition is received by USCIS, you've established your place in line (known as your Priority Date, which we'll discuss in Section 2, below). And no matter when the petition is approved, you'll have to wait anywhere from three to five years from that Priority Date until a visa becomes available to you. For that reason, USCIS takes its time making a decision on these petitions—almost three years when this book went to press.

You can check current processing times when your spouse files by going to the USCIS website at www.uscis.gov, clicking "Processing Times" in the bar on the left side of the page, scrolling to the bottom of the next page, selecting the Service Center with jurisdiction over your petition, and clicking "Service Center Processing Dates." Be sure

Where to Send the Form I-130 Visa Petition			
If the U.S. petitioner lives in:			**Send Form I-130 to:**
Alaska American Samoa Arizona California Colorado Florida Guam Hawaii Idaho	Kansas Montana Nebraska Nevada New Mexico North Dakota Northern Mariana Islands Oklahoma	Oregon Puerto Rico South Dakota Texas Utah Virgin Islands Washington Wyoming	**USCIS Phoenix Lockbox** For U.S. Postal Service (USPS) deliveries: USCIS ATTN: I-130 P.O. Box 21700 Phoenix, AZ 85036 For Express Mail and courier deliveries: USCIS Attn: I-130 1820 E. Skyharbor Circle S Suite 100 Phoenix, AZ 85034
Alabama Arkansas Connecticut Delaware District of Columbia Georgia Illinois Indiana Iowa Kentucky Louisiana	Maine Maryland Massachusetts Michigan Minnesota Mississippi Missouri New Hampshire New Jersey New York	North Carolina Ohio Pennsylvania Rhode Island South Carolina Tennessee Vermont Virginia West Virginia Wisconsin	**USCIS Chicago Lockbox** For U.S. Postal Service: USCIS P.O. Box 804625 Chicago, IL 60680-4107 For Express Mail and courier deliveries: USCIS Attn: I-130 131 South Dearborn–3rd Floor Chicago, IL 60603-5517
If the U.S. petitioner prefers to send the I-130 by private courier (non-U.S. Postal Service), then regardless of where the petitioner lives, send Form I-130 to:			**USCIS Lockbox** Attn: SAI-130 131 South Dearborn–3rd Floor Chicago, IL 60603-5517

to look in the column for I-130s filed by permanent residents for spouses. That tells you that USCIS is currently working on visa petitions that were filed on that date.

If your visa petition was filed *later than* that date, USCIS considers your petition to be within normal processing time and will ignore any inquiry from you or your spouse asking about the progress of your visa petition. These Service Centers seem like walled fortresses—you can't visit them, and it's impossible to speak with the person who's actually working on your case. If you still don't have a decision on your case after USCIS's normal

processing time has passed, then call 800-375-5283, where a live person will take your questions from 8 a.m. to 8 p.m. local time.

Although the person you speak with will most likely not be able to tell you anything useful during that phone call, he or she will start an inquiry for you and tell you when you can expect a response. (See Chapter 15 for more on what to do if you don't get a timely answer from the USCIS Service Center.) If USCIS needs additional documentation to complete your application, they will send your spouse a letter asking for it.

Sample I-130 Receipt Notice

Department of Homeland Security
U.S. Citizenship and Immigration Services

I-797C, Notice of Action

THE UNITED STATES OF AMERICA

RECEIPT NUMBER		CASE TYPE	I130 IMMIGRANT PETITION FOR RELATIVE, FIANCE(E), OR ORPHAN
WAC-06-054-00000			
RECEIVED DATE	PRIORITY DATE	PETITIONER	
December 15, 2006		LINDSAY, EDMUND	
NOTICE DATE	PAGE	BENEFICIARY	
December 20, 2006	1 of 1	DEBDEN, ALICE	

ILONA BRAY
RE: EDMUND ALEXANDER LINDSEY
950 PARKER STREET
BERKELEY, CA 94710

Notice Type: Receipt Notice
Amount received: $ 420.00

Section: Husband or wife of permanent resident, 203(a)(2)(A)INA

Receipt notice - If any of the above information is incorrect, call customer service immediately.

Processing time - Processing times vary by kind of case.
- You can check our current processing time for this kind of case on our website at **uscis.gov**.
- On our website you can also sign up to get free e-mail updates as we complete key processing steps on this case.
- Most of the time your case is pending the processing status will not change because we will be working on others filed earlier.
- We will notify you by mail when we make a decision on this case, or if we need something from you. If you move while this case is pending, call customer service when you move.
- Processing times can change. If you don't get a decision or update from us within our current processing time, check our website or call for an update.

If you have questions, check our website or call customer service. Please save this notice, and have it with you if you contact us about this case.

Notice to all customers with a pending I-130 petition - USCIS is now processing Form I-130, Petition for Alien Relative, as a visa number becomes available. Filing and approval of an I-130 relative petition is only the first step in helping a relative immigrate to the United States. Eligible family members must wait until there is a visa number available before they can apply for an immigrant visa or adjustment of status to a lawful permanent resident. This process will allow USCIS to concentrate resources first on cases where visas are actually available. This process should not delay the ability of one's relative to apply for an immigrant visa or adjustment of status. Refer to **www.state.gov/travel** <http://www.state.gov/travel> to determine current visa availability dates. For more information, please visit our website at www.uscis.gov or contact us at 1-800-375-5283.

Always remember to call customer service if you move while your case is pending. If you have a pending I-130 relative petition, also call customer service if you should decide to withdraw your petition or if you become a U.S. citizen.

Please see the additional information on the back. You will be notified separately about any other cases you filed.
U.S. CITIZENSHIP & IMMIGRATION SVC
CALIFORNIA SERVICE CENTER
P.O. BOX 30111
LAGUNA NIGUEL CA 92607-0111
Customer Service Telephone: (800) 375-5283

Form I-797C (Rev. 08/31/04) N

Sample I-130 Approval Notice

Department of Homeland Security U.S. Citizenship and Immigration Services	I-797, Notice of Action

THE UNITED STATES OF AMERICA

RECEIPT NUMBER WAC-04-054-00000	CASE TYPE I130 IMMIGRANT PETITION FOR RELATIVE, FIANCE(E), OR ORPHAN
RECEIPT DATE December 15, 2006	PRIORITY DATE December 14, 2006	PETITIONER LINDSAY, EDMUND
NOTICE DATE APRIL 11, 2012	PAGE 1 of 1	BENEFICIARY DEBDEN, ALICE

ILONA BRAY RE: EDMUND ALEXANDER LINDSEY 950 PARKER STREET BERKELEY, CA 94710	Notice Type: Approval Notice Section: Husband or wife of U.S. permanent resident, 201(b)(2)(A)(i) INA

The above petition has been approved. We have sent the original visa petition to the Department of State National Visa Center (NVC), 32 Rochester Avenue, Portsmouth, NH 03801-2909. The INS has completed all action; further inquiries should be directed to the NVC.

The NVC now processes all approved fiance(e) petitions. The NVC processing should be complete within two to four weeks after receiving the petition from INS. The NVC will create a case record with your petition information. NVC will then send the petition to the U.S. Embassy or Consulate where your fiance(e) will be interviewed for his or her visa.

You will receive notification by mail when NVC has sent your petition to the U.S. Embassy or Consulate. The notification letter will provide you with a unique number for your case and the name and address of the U.S. Embassy or Consulate where your petition has been sent.

If it has been more than four weeks since you received this approval notice and you have not received notification from NVC that your petition has been forwarded overseas, please call NVC at (603) 334-0700. Please call between 8:00am-6:45pm Eastern Standard Time. You will need to enter the INS receipt number from this approval notice into the automated response system to receive information on your petition.

THIS FORM IS NOT A VISA NOR MAY IT BE USED IN PLACE OF A VISA.

Please see the additional information on the back. You will be notified separately about any other cases you filed.
U.S. CITIZENSHIP & IMMIGRATION SVC
CALIFORNIA SERVICE CENTER
P. O. BOX 30111
LAGUNA NIGUEL CA 92607-0111
Customer Service Telephone: (800) 375-5283

Form I-797 (Rev. 01/31/05) N

Eventually, your spouse will receive an approval or a denial of the visa petition.

i. If the Visa Petition Is Denied

If the visa petition is denied, the fastest thing to do is to fix the problem and try again. For example, if the denial was because your petitioning spouse did not appear to be actually divorced from a previous spouse, your spouse will need to see a lawyer and obtain new and better documentation showing that there had been a final divorce. Then your spouse can file a new visa petition.

ii. If the Visa Petition Is Approved

When your visa petition is approved, your spouse will receive a notice from the USCIS Service Center. An example of a visa petition approval notice is shown above. As you can see, it's nothing fancy. But it is an important document. Make a few photocopies of it and store these and the original in safe places. Note the "Priority Date" listed in the box of that name—that is the date that USCIS received the I-130 visa petition your spouse filed for you, and that date will become very important in determining your place on the waiting list, as discussed in Section 2, below.

At the same time that the USCIS Service Center notifies your spouse of the approval of your visa petition, it will forward your case to the National Visa Center (NVC) in New Hampshire. This office will then take over and maintain your file through Step Two.

e. Using the Checklist for Step One, Visa Petition

When you put it all together, the visa petition that your spouse files will include three forms and some supporting documents, photos, and a fee, as detailed on the checklist below. As you fill out and prepare your paperwork, mark off the items that you've found or finished with on your checklist. This will be the best way to make sure you haven't forgotten anything.

> ## Checklist for Visa Petition by Lawful Permanent Resident
>
> ☐ Form I-130 (see line-by-line instructions in Subsection A1a, above)
>
> ☐ Documents to accompany Form I-130:
>
> > ☐ Proof of the U.S. permanent resident status of your petitioning spouse (see Subsection A1b, above)
> >
> > ☐ Your marriage certificate (see Chapter 4, Section C, for how to obtain such documents)
> >
> > ☐ Proof of termination of all previous marriages, yours or your spouse's, such as certificates of death, divorce, or annulment
> >
> > ☐ One color photo of you (passport style)
> >
> > ☐ One color photo of your spouse (passport style)
> >
> > ☐ Fee: currently $420 (see Subsection 1b, above)
>
> ☐ Form G-325A, Biographic Information, filled out by you (see line-by-line instructions in Subsection A1a, above)
>
> ☐ Form G-325A, Biographic Information, filled out by your spouse (see line-by-line instructions in Subsection A1a, above)

 CHECKLIST
Appendix C includes a tear-out copy of this checklist.

2. Step Two: The Waiting Period (Your "Priority Date")

Visa waiting periods are not set periods of time. Some attorneys tell their clients, "It will probably be two years"—then when two years go by and the visa hasn't come through, the clients worry that something has gone wrong. The truth is that waiting periods are only partly predictable. They depend on visa supply and demand, combined with monthly decisions by the U.S. government.

You won't know for sure how long you'll have to wait until your wait is almost over. This section will help you to understand the mechanics of this wait and how to deal with it.

a. Preference Categories

As the spouse of a lawful permanent resident, you're known as a "preference relative." The U.S. government ranks preference relatives, usually giving visas quicker to those at the top. As you'll see, you are in the second category down ("2A" or "F2A"). This means that the U.S. government has allotted a higher priority to your visa than to those of the people in categories 3 and 4. That may be small comfort as the months and years go by, however. Here is how the preferences are arranged:

- **First Preference:** The unmarried sons or daughters of a U.S. citizen who are over 21 and are therefore no longer considered children. (If they were still children, they could qualify as immediate relatives, who are immediately eligible for visas.)
- **Second Preference:** The second preference category, which is where you fit, is actually made up of two subcategories, each with different waiting periods. In subcategory 2A are spouses or unmarried sons or daughters under age 21 of a permanent resident (green card holder). In subcategory 2B are the unmarried sons and daughters *over* age 21 of a permanent resident (they usually wait longer than 2As).
- **Third Preference:** The married sons or daughters, any age, of a U.S. citizen.
- **Fourth Preference:** The brothers or sisters of a U.S. citizen. The citizen must be age 21 or older.

b. How Visas Are Allotted Year by Year

Each year, the U.S. government allots a certain number of immigrant visas in each preference category. For purposes of visa allocation, the government follows its fiscal year, which starts and ends in October. This might affect you if the government runs out of visas for your category before October. You'll know at that point that you have no chance of advancing on the waiting list until the "new year" begins October 1.

Currently, the total worldwide numbers are:
- **First Preference:** 23,400, plus any visas not used for fourth preference
- **Second Preference:** 114,200, with 77% of these going to category 2A, 23% to category 2B
- **Third Preference:** 23,400, plus any not used for first and second preference
- **Fourth Preference:** 65,000 plus any not used for the first three preferences.

This may sound like a lot of visas, but far more people want immigrant visas than can get them every year. The government gives out visas month by month, making sure never to go over the annual limit.

There are also limits on the number of visas allowed for any one country. No more than 7% of the total visas each year can go to any one country, and often the percentage turns out to be less.

There are more complexities to the allocation and numbers of these visas, but a full understanding of these numbers won't help you speed up your waiting time. The important thing to know is how to chart your own place on the visa waiting list.

c. How to Chart Your Place on the Waiting List

It would be nice if you could just call the government and ask how long you have to wait for your green card. No such luck. Instead, the State Department publishes a monthly *Visa Bulletin*, the one source of information on visa waiting periods. The *Visa Bulletin* is accessible online at http://travel.state.gov (under "Visas for Foreign Citizens," click "more," then from the left-hand side of the page click on "Visa Bulletin" and then choose "this month's visa bulletin"). The same information is available by phone at 202-663-1541, but you have to be quick with your pencil and paper, because they talk fast.

The *Visa Bulletin* comes out monthly, around the middle of the month, but not on any particular day.

Below is a sample of what a family-based chart in the *Visa Bulletin* looks like.

Although it's confusing at first glance, you will be able to make your way through this chart. Here's how:

1. Locate your preference category (2A or F2A) in the left column.
2. Locate your country across the top. China, India, Mexico, and the Philippines often have their own columns because of the large number of applicants—as a result, people from these countries wait longer than others. All other countries are included in the second column called "All Chargeability Areas Except Those Listed."
3. Draw a line across from your preference category (2A or F2A) and down from your country of origin. Where the two lines cross is what is called the Visa Cutoff Date—the key date that you will compare with your own Priority Date to chart your progress.

Every prospective immigrant has his or her own Priority Date—the date that USCIS first received their I-130. Your Priority Date is on the approval notice you received after the initial approval of your Form I-130 visa petition. Prospective immigrants whose Priority Dates are at or earlier than the Cutoff Date listed in that month's bulletin will become eligible for visas or green cards.

The earlier your Priority Date, the better off you are, because it means you are in line ahead of other applicants. But as you can see, the current Cutoff Date doesn't tell you how long it will be before your own visa or green card is issued.

Look again at the example of the approval notice in Subsection 1d, above. The Priority Date is in the middle of the second line, and says December 14, 2006. The following examples will help you understand how to read the *Visa Bulletin* chart.

EXAMPLE 1: Toshiko is a citizen of Japan, married to a U.S. permanent resident.

Toshiko's husband submitted an I-130 for her several years ago and she received a Priority Date of September 12, 2009. What does Toshiko learn by looking at the *Visa Bulletin* chart below? After locating the box for Japan (under All Chargeability Areas) in category 2A, she sees that the Priority Date that is now current is October 8, 2009.

That means that Toshiko, with her Priority Date of September 12, 2009, is now eligible for a visa. If you're confused by the fact that Toshiko's Priority Date isn't an exact match with the *Visa Bulletin* Cutoff Date, look at it this way. Earlier is always better. Toshiko's husband actually submitted her I-130 a few weeks before some other people who also became current under this month's *Visa Bulletin*. If this process were like taking a number at the bakery counter, she would have become eligible for her visa (or get to choose her doughnut) a little before the people with October 8 Priority Dates. But the *Visa Bulletin*

Cutoff Dates for April 2012					
Family	All Chargeability Areas Except Those Listed	China— mainland born	India	Mexico	Philippines
F1	01APR05	01APR05	01APR05	08MAY93	22JUN97
F2A	08OCT09	08OCT09	08OCT09	01SEP09	08OCT09
F2B	15JAN04	15JAN04	15JAN04	01DEC92	08DEC01
F3	15FEB02	15FEB02	15FEB02	15JAN93	22JUL92
F4	08NOV00	08NOV00	08NOV00	01JUN96	08JAN89

jumps by days and weeks worth of Priority Dates every month, so people get lumped into larger groups. Anyone with a Priority Date of October 8, 2009 or earlier is therefore considered to have become visa eligible, or "current."

EXAMPLE 2: Yumiko is also a citizen of Japan, who got married to a U.S. permanent resident more recently than Toshiko in the example above. Yumiko's husband submitted her I-130 on August 1, 2010, so that is now her Priority Date.

What does Yumiko learn by looking at the *Visa Bulletin* chart? She must look at the same box as Toshiko did, to see that the current Cutoff Date is October 8, 2009. But with Yumiko's Priority Date of August 1, 2010 she is certainly not current, and not yet eligible for a visa. It's safe to say there are a number of people in line ahead of her, and thus a long wait ahead.

If you follow the *Visa Bulletin* chart month by month, you might notice a couple of odd things. Sometimes the government gets backed up with visa applications and the Cutoff Dates just don't change. In the example above, it could be that Toshiko's Priority Date actually became current a month earlier—but she forgot to check it then, and the number didn't change. Sometimes the Cutoff Dates get stuck for months at a time, while the government deals with a backlog of visa applications. If the government hits a huge logjam, you may even see the Cutoff Dates go backwards.

Another odd thing you might see is a box that contains the letter C or U, instead of a date. The letter C (for "current") means there are plenty of visas in that category and no one has to wait. It's as if everyone's Priority Date suddenly were current. The letter U (for "unavailable") is the opposite; it means that all the visas have been used up for that year. If, for example, this were February 2012, and Yumiko saw a U in her category 2A box, she'd

know she could forget about getting closer to a visa until October 2012 (when the new year starts in the visa allocation process).

d. Figuring How Long You Will Wait

To roughly determine how long you will have to wait for a visa, you can subtract the Cutoff Date on the current month's *Visa Bulletin* chart from today's date. That will tell you the approximate length of time that other applicants are now waiting for a visa—though this method is complicated by the fact that they applied during a different time period than you, and demand in your category may have risen or fallen during that time. There is no exact science to computing your probable wait.

e. How to Deal With the Long Wait

You will probably feel like nothing at all is happening during the years that you wait for your visa to become available. But in fact, the Priority Dates will be inching forward, and there are steps that you should be taking to make sure that you can claim your visa as soon as it becomes available.

i. Organizing Your Papers and Checking the *Visa Bulletin*

After your U.S. permanent resident spouse files a visa petition for you, you will get your own approval notice; looking much like the one shown in Subsection 1d, above. The approval notice will show your Priority Date. Take careful note of the date and keep the notice in a safe place. Look in the current *Visa Bulletin* to get an idea of how long your wait will be. If your wait looks to be three years, for example, for the first year and a half you probably don't need to check the *Visa Bulletin* more than every six months. Then start checking the bulletin every three months after that. As your Priority Date gets close to being current, check it monthly, so you can find out as soon as you are current and can make sure that the U.S. government realizes that you are current and still alive and interested, as explained below.

TIP

You can ask to have the *Visa Bulletin* sent to you monthly, by email. This is a great way to make sure you don't forget to check how your Priority Date is advancing. Complete instructions for how to subscribe to this service can be found toward the bottom of any *Visa Bulletin*.

ii. If You Change Addresses

Don't rely on the U.S. government to tell you when your Priority Date is current—the National Visa Center makes an effort, but some files will get buried in the shuffle. However, you're guaranteed not to hear from them if they don't know where to find you. Also, under rare circumstances, such as a major change in the U.S. immigration laws, the government may send out mass mailings that you also wouldn't want to miss.

If either you or your petitioning spouse change addresses, the place to contact is the National Visa Center (NVC), which keeps your case file until your Priority Date is close to being current. You can advise the NVC of your new address by writing to them at The National Visa Center, 32 Rochester Avenue, Portsmouth, NH 03801-2909. You can also send them an email at NVCINQUIRY@state.gov. Be sure to include your case number from the USCIS approval notice.

iii. What to Do When Your Priority Date Is Current

One day, your Priority Date will become current— in other words, you'll finally see the exact date of your original application, or a later date, on the *Visa Bulletin* chart. Then you'll know that it's time for you to move forward in the process of getting your visa or green card.

When you see that your Priority Date is current, don't wait for the government to call you. If you don't hear from them within a few weeks, contact the National Visa Center (see Subsection ii directly above for contact information) and ask it to send you the appropriate paperwork.

iv. What Happens If No One Notices Your Current Priority Date

Some immigrants forget to check the *Visa Bulletin,* and their Priority Date becomes current without their noticing. Sometimes, the NVC has tried to notify them, but has only an old address. Or, the NVC may have failed to keep track of the person's file. These problems can delay or destroy a person's hopes of immigrating.

You have one year after your Priority Date becomes current to pursue your visa or green card. If you do not, the government assumes you have abandoned it—and will give your visa to the next person in line. You may have an argument for getting the visa back if the government completely failed to contact you, but it's better to avoid such situations altogether. Keep track of your own Priority Date and follow the procedures in Subsection iii, directly above, as soon as your date, or a later date, is listed in the *Visa Bulletin*.

f. How to Get Your Children Onto the Waiting List

Like other immigrants, you can bring certain family members along when you come to the United States. Your children who are unmarried and under age 21 qualify as what are called derivative beneficiaries. See Chapter 2, Section B, to review who counts as a child. As a practical matter, this means that your children won't need a separate visa petition to start off the process. Simply by being named on your Form I-130, they will share your Priority Date and place on the waiting list. (Eventually, however, they will have to fill out some forms of their own.)

As you'll see in Section B, below, children can lose their derivative beneficiary status. For example, if your spouse becomes a U.S. citizen, or if children turn 21 or get married, the children would no longer be considered derivative beneficiaries and would have to find another way to immigrate. Section B, below, tells you which of these situations can be cured and how to cure them.

g. If the Permanent Resident Petitioner Dies

Until recently, if you were the spouse of a permanent resident who died before you could immigrate, the visa petition was cancelled and you could no longer become a permanent resident.

However, in October of 2009, Congress changed the law so that under certain conditions, the visa petition that was filed by your now-deceased spouse may still be decided on. Assuming you are outside the United States, if the petition was approved prior to your spouse's death, "humanitarian reinstatement" provisions may allow the visa petition to remain valid, and you may be allowed to continue with the application through the U.S. consulate.

Unlike the spouse of a U.S. citizen, however, this new law does not allow you to petition for yourself if your spouse never filed the petition.

This is a new area of the law. As of the time we went to press, USCIS had implemented regulations allowing humanitarian reinstatement for alien beneficiaries of family-based petitions if they are already in the United States. However, the guidelines remain unclear regarding beneficiaries who are outside the United States. So, if you are in the unfortunate situation of dealing with the untimely death of the petitioner in your immigration case, consult an immigration attorney.

CAUTION

Grandchildren can't come along. If your derivative beneficiary children have children of their own, those children (your grandchildren) will not be considered your derivative beneficiaries. The law says that no one can be the derivative of someone who is already a derivative beneficiary. In this circumstance, the grandchildren would have to stay behind for at least a few years—a heartbreaking situation for some families. Unfortunately, there are no separate visas for grandchildren.

h. Changing Visa Preference Categories

It is possible for people to move into a different preference category, which will speed up or delay their waiting time. For example, you would get a visa quicker—by moving to the immediate relative category—if your spouse became a U.S. citizen.

Or, life changes could push you out of your visa category and into a lower one or out of the race altogether. This section explains the most typical situations affecting married couples and shows you how to keep or improve on your visa category. For situations affecting only your children, see Section B, below.

i. If a Permanent Resident Petitioner Becomes a Citizen

If your spouse becomes a citizen, it is good news for you. You go from category 2A straight to immediate relative. This means that you jump off the waiting list and immediately move forward with your visa processing.

If your permanent resident spouse already meets the legal requirements for U.S. citizenship, he or she would be wise to apply as soon as possible. Most permanent residents can apply within five years of receiving their residence (this changes to four years or less if your spouse received residency as a refugee or through political asylum). They must also be of good moral character, meet certain U.S. residency requirements, and be able to pass a test on the English language and U.S. history and government. (If you know that your spouse is going to become a U.S. citizen very soon, read Chapter 7 covering overseas spouses of U.S. citizens.)

If your petitioner becomes a citizen, advise the government and send them a copy of your spouse's citizenship certificate and your I-130 approval notice. The National Visa Center (NVC) will upgrade your status to immediate relative. The sample letter below shows how to explain this fortunate turn of events.

RESOURCE

Need more information on the eligibility and procedural requirements for obtaining U.S. citizenship? See the USCIS website at www.uscis.gov or *Becoming a U.S. Citizen: A Guide to the Law, Exam & Interview,* by Ilona Bray (Nolo).

Letter Requesting Upgrade to Immediate Relative

123 Salmon Way
Seattle, WA 98105
(206) 555-1212

April 20, 20xx

National Visa Center
32 Rochester Avenue
Portsmouth, NH 03801-2909
RE: Petitioner: Sam Washington
Beneficiary: Marta Moscow
Preference Category: 2A, Spouse of LPR
Case Number: [*Enter your number*]

Dear Sir/Madam:

I am the petitioner in the above case. I recently became a U.S. citizen. A copy of my citizenship certificate is enclosed. Please upgrade my wife, Marta Moscow, from category 2A to immediate relative, and proceed with consular processing.

Thank you.

Very truly yours,

Sam Washington

Sam Washington

Encl: Copy of U.S. citizenship certificate

SKIP AHEAD

If your spouse becomes a citizen and you have children who will be immigrating with you, be sure to read Section B, below. For certain children, immigrating may now become more difficult.

ii. If the Petitioner and Beneficiary Divorce

If you and your spouse get divorced before you apply for your immigrant visa or green card, you are out of luck. The visa petition is cancelled and you and your derivative beneficiaries lose your green card eligibility.

There is an exception for immigrants who are victims of emotional or physical abuse by their spouse. They can file a special self-petition (Form I-360) any time until the divorce becomes final or for two years afterward, if they can show that the divorce was related to the domestic violence. (These self-petitions are not covered in this book. Talk to a U.S. nonprofit organization or consult an attorney. See Chapter 17 for suggestions on how to locate nonprofits and good attorneys.)

iii. If a Beneficiary Dies

If you were to die, your children would lose their opportunity for a visa as well—unless your spouse has filed or can file a separate petition for them in category 2A or 2B.

If your family is in this situation, the U.S. permanent resident petitioner should ask USCIS to "recapture" the deceased parent's Priority Date when the permanent resident submits the new visa petitions. If USCIS assigns the deceased parent's date to the children, the children won't have to start the waiting game all over.

iv. If a U.S. Petitioner Loses Permanent Resident Status

If the permanent resident petitioner loses the right to live in the United States, the immigrant applicants lose the right to live there also. In theory, permanent residence or a green card gives a person the right to live in the United States permanently—but this right can be taken away. If, for example the petitioner spends many months overseas, USCIS may decide that he or she abandoned U.S. residency and refuse to let him or her reclaim it. Or, if the petitioner commits certain crimes, permanent residency could be taken away and he or she could be deported.

Even if a permanent resident has had a crime on record for a long time, it may not be safe. Recent laws have allowed USCIS to deport people for crimes that would not have made them deportable when the crime was committed. Since the goal of the law is to reunite families, it makes sense that the government would refuse to grant immigrant visas to the family members of former permanent residents.

i. Should You Wait Until Your Spouse Is a U.S. Citizen?

Applicants sometimes ask, "If I can avoid the Visa Preference System by waiting for my spouse to become a U.S. citizen, shouldn't I do so and avoid the quotas and waiting period?" The answer is no, you don't really gain anything by waiting, and you may actually lose time if your spouse's citizenship gets delayed.

You don't gain anything because your spouse will have to submit the visa petition sometime, even after she or he becomes a U.S. citizen. The form is the same, whether your spouse is a citizen or permanent resident. Your approval notice will remain good even after your spouse becomes a citizen. Besides this, the longer you wait, the higher the application fee is likely to go (it's already $420). Finally, you can't predict for sure when your spouse will actually become a citizen—and you will lose time until that happens.

Let's take an imaginary permanent resident spouse named Kari. Kari is only one year away from being eligible to apply for citizenship. Her immigrating spouse, Sven, might think it's better to wait until she's a citizen before she files the I-130 on his behalf. But after Kari turns in the citizenship application, she waits another year before her interview. Then the officer tells her, "I can't approve this until you show me proof of all your divorces, and you need to amend your last year's tax return and pay back the extra tax that you owe to show me that you have good moral character." This takes time to pull together, and Kari waits a few months more for the final approval.

You can see how things might drag on. Even after your spouse is approved for citizenship, it could be a few months more before he or she attends the ceremony making him or her a U.S. citizen. By waiting for your spouse to attain U.S. citizenship, you could end up waiting even longer than you would have as a Preference Relative.

3. Step Three: Pay Fees, Prepare Forms and Documents

Finally, after years of waiting, your Priority Date will become current. If the National Visa Center doesn't contact you within a matter of weeks, go back to Subsection 2e regarding how to contact it.

> **CAUTION**
> **If you used this book for Step One, you probably need a new edition now.** In the years that you waited for your Priority Date to become current, the immigration laws or procedures may have changed. Check with Nolo's customer service department regarding how to obtain a new edition. You will receive a discount on the new edition if you return the cover of the old one.

Once the NVC sees that your Priority Date is current, it will send you what's called a Choice of Address and Agent form (DS-3032). This is a very simple form—but don't let its simplicity fool you. By choosing an "agent," as the form asks for, you're essentially deciding where all the important mail from the U.S. government regarding your immigration should go—to you, at your overseas address, or to someone else, most likely your petitioner in the U.S. (if you're not using an attorney). If mail service from the U.S. has been at all unreliable where you live, or if you might be moving before your visa interview, it's safest to choose your U.S. petitioner as agent, and write in the U.S. address.

> **WEB RESOURCE**
> **This form is available on the State Department website at www.state.gov.** A sample filled-in version of this form is shown below.

At the same time, the NVC will send a bill for processing the Affidavit of Support (Form I-864—fee currently $88) to your petitioner. After the petitioner pays the fee, the NVC will send further instructions on preparing and submitting Form I-864. Then, once the NVC receives your Form

DS-3032, it will mail you a bill for the immigrant visa processing fee (currently $230). Once the visa fee is paid, the NVC will send you further instructions.

Those instructions will probably tell you to fill out various forms (either sent to you by the NVC or that you'll be told where to download online) and return them to the NVC. The NVC will review all of your documents before finally sending you an appointment notice for your interview at a U.S. consulate in your home country.

However, this whole system is still in transition—some applicants will still have their files transferred to a U.S. consulate early in the process (the old system), and will receive instructions and an appointment notice directly from the consulate.

In either case, the important thing will be for you to follow the instructions carefully. If you make a mistake—for example you forget to send in a form or document, forget to sign one of the forms, or you enter inconsistent information on different forms—you'll normally get a second chance. The NVC will send you what's called a "checklist," setting out what you need to do and giving you a barcode sheet to include with your response. Again, read the instructions carefully and try to get it exactly right—every mistake you make delays your case and could eventually lead to the visa being denied.

TIP

When sending original documents, always include a copy. The NVC will request various original documents, like your original birth and marriage certificate. You may feel understandably nervous about sending in these original documents. So long as you remember to also *include a copy* of the document, you'll get the original back when you go to your visa interview.

TIP

It's never too soon to get your vaccinations up to date. Before you're allowed to enter the United States, you'll have to prove that you've had all the necessary vaccinations, as listed in Chapter 2, Section

A. Check with your local doctor now so that you're not stuck later waiting weeks while a series of shots is administered.

a. Line-by-Line Instructions for Step Three Forms

Certain forms vary among consulates (for example, some include translations into the language of that country). Although versions of these forms are provided in this book, it's better to use the one that you receive from the NVC, in case it's different.

i. Form DS-230 Part I

Form DS-230 Part I is designed to collect basic identifying information about you, including your physical features and the names of your children.

WEB RESOURCE

Form DS-230 Part I is available on the State Department website at www.state.gov. You may be asked to prepare and submit the form online. However, if you receive a paper version from the consulate, use that one instead. (It may be different than the online version.) Below is a sample filled-in version of this form.

Questions 1-28: Self-explanatory (similar to the questions on Form I-130; see Subsection 1a, above).

Question 29: List all your children. You'll have a chance to identify which ones are immigrating with you later.

Question 30: Self-explanatory.

Question 31a: List only those children of yours who also have an approved I-130 visa petition and will be immigrating with you.

Question 31b: List only those children who have an approved I-130 visa petition and will be following to join you.

Questions 32-34: Self-explanatory.

Question 35: If you've spent more than 180 days in the United States without a valid visa or other right to live in the United States after April 1, 1997, you need to see a lawyer before going any further. (See Chapter 2, Section A2, "Dealing With Unlawful Time in the United States.")

Sample Form DS-3032, Choice of Address and Agent

Make sure the address is complete and correct. We will use this address for future mailings.

OMB No. 1405-0126
EXPIRATION DATE: 01/31/2013
ESTIMATED BURDEN: 10 minutes*

Place Case Barcode Strip Here Before Mailing to the National Visa Center

U.S. Department of State
CHOICE OF ADDRESS AND AGENT
For Immigrant Visa Applicants

Print or Type your Full Name

Lindsey
(Last Name)

Edmund
(First Name)

A.
(MI.)

Check one box only to the left of the statement that is your choice.

☐ I Appoint _____

Telephone Number _____

as my agent or attorney to receive mail about my application. Mail from the U.S. Department of State concerning my immigrant visa application should be sent to:

_____
Name of the person who will act as your agent or attorney for receipt of mail

_____
Telephone Number

_____
Street Address (where my agent or attorney will receive mail about my application)

_____
*Email Address

_____   _____   _____   _____
City   State/Province   Postal Code   Country

☒ I do not appoint an agent or an attorney to receive mail about my application. Mail from the U.S. Department of State concerning my immigrant visa application should be sent to me at:

10 Walden Road
Street Address (Include "in care of" if Needed)

_____
*Email Address

London
City

_____
State/Province

SW1H OBD
Postal Code

U.K.
Country

☐ I have already legally immigrated to the U.S. and do not need to apply for an immigrant visa. I received my Green Card through the _____ (City) USCIS office. My A# is

_____ .

☐ I no longer wish to apply for an immigrant visa.

As proof of your choice, sign and date this document:

Edmund A. Lindsey
Signature of Applicant

05/08/2012
Date of Signature (mm-dd-yyyy)

*The Department is currently testing an electronic application system for nonimmigrant visa application that will allow electronic submission and eliminate paper forms. Once testing on this application system is completed the Department is examining whether or not the system can be used for the immigrant visa system.

Paperwork Reduction Act Statement

*Public reporting burden for this collection of information is estimated to average 10 minutes per response, including time required for searching existing data sources, gathering the necessary documentation, providing the information and/or documents required, and reviewing the final collection. You do not have to supply this information unless this collection displays a currently valid OMB control number. If you have comments on the accuracy of this burden estimate and/or recommendations for reducing it, please send them to: A/GIS/DIR, Room 2400 SA-22, U.S. Department of State, Washington, DC 20522-2202.

Confidentiality Statement

INA Section 222(f) provides that visa issuance and refusal records shall be considered confidential and shall be used only for the formulation, amendment, administration, or enforcement of the immigration, nationality, and other laws of the United States. Certified copies of visa records may be made available to a court which certifies that the information contained in such records is needed in a case pending before the court.

DS-3032
06-2011

Sample Form DS-230 Part I—Page 1

U.S. Department of State

APPLICATION FOR IMMIGRANT VISA AND ALIEN REGISTRATION

OMB APPROVAL NO. 1405-0015
EXPIRES: 03/31/2012
ESTIMATED BURDEN: 1 HOUR*
(See Page 2)

PART I - BIOGRAPHIC DATA

Instructions: Complete one copy of this form for yourself and each member of your family, regardless of age, who will immigrate with you. Please print or type your answers to all questions. Mark questions that are Not Applicable with "N/A". If there is insufficient room on the form, answer on a separate sheet using the same numbers that appear on the form. Attach any additional sheets to this form.

Warning: Any false statement or concealment of a material fact may result in your permanent exclusion from the United States.
This form (DS-230 Part I) is the first of two parts. This part, together with Form DS-230 Part II, constitutes the complete Application for Immigrant Visa and Alien Registration.

1. Family Name: Lindsey — First Name: Edmund — Middle Name: Alexander

2. Other Names Used or Aliases (If married woman, give maiden name): N/A

3. Full Name in Native Alphabet (If Roman letters not used): N/A

4. Date of Birth (mm-dd-yyyy): 11-21-1973
5. Age: 38
6. Place of Birth (City or Town): Thaxted — (Province) — (Country): U.K.

7. Nationality (If dual national, give both.): English
8. Gender: ☐ Female ☒ Male
9. Marital Status: ☐ Single (Never Married) ☒ Married ☐ Widowed ☐ Divorced ☐ Separated
Including my present marriage, I have been married one times.

10. Permanent address in the United States where you intend to live, if known (street address including ZIP code). Include the name of a person who currently lives there.
Alice Debden
432 Fairfax Street #A
Alexandria, VA 22314
Telephone number: 703-555-1212

11. Address in the United States where you want your Permanent Resident Card (Green Card) mailed, if different from address in item #10 (include the name of a person who currently lives there).
Telephone number

12. Present Occupation: Assistant Processing and Fleets Manager

13. Present Address (Street Address) (City or Town) (Province) (Country): 10 Walden Road, London U.K.
Telephone Number (Home): 44 20 7363 1323
Telephone Number (Office): 44 20 7222 1234
Email Address

14. Spouse's Maiden or Family Name: Debden — First Name: Alice — Middle Name: Anne

15. Date (mm-dd-yyyy) and Place of Birth of Spouse: 03-03-1974, Dublin, Ireland

16. Address of Spouse (If different from your own): 432 Fairfax Street #A, Alexandria, VA 22314

17. Spouse's Occupation: ceramist
18. Date of Marriage (mm-dd-yyyy): 03-05-2006

19. Father's Family Name: Lindsey — First Name: Thomas — Middle Name: Alexander

20. Father's Date of Birth (mm-dd-yyyy): 10-22-1951
21. Place of Birth: London
22. Current Address: 195 Piccadilly, London W1J 9LL
23. If Deceased, Give Year of Death:

24. Mother's Family Name at Birth: Herries — First Name: Janice — Middle Name: Lynn

25. Mother's Date of Birth (mm-dd-yyyy): 08-17-1955
26. Place of Birth: Haddington
27. Current Address: 195 Piccadilly, London W1J 9LL
28. If Deceased, Give Year of Death:

DS-230 Part I
03-2012

This Form May be Obtained Free at Consular Offices of the United States of America
Previous Editions Obsolete

Page 1 of 4

Sample Form DS-230 Part I—Page 2

29. List Names, Dates and Places of Birth, and Addresses of ALL Children.

Name	Date (mm-dd-yyyy)	Place of Birth	Address (If different from your own)
none			

30. List below all places you have lived for at least six months since reaching the age of 16, including places in your country of nationality. Begin with your present residence.

City or Town	Province	Country	From/To (mm-yyyy) or "Present"
London		U.K.	09-2004 to present
Greenwich		U.K.	03-2002 to 09-2004
London		U.K.	11-1973 to 03-2002

31a. Person(s) named in 14 and 29 who will accompany you to the United States now.

N/A

31b. Person(s) named in 14 and 29 who will follow you to the United States at a later date.

N/A

32. List below all employment for the last ten years.

Employer	Location	Job Title	From/To (mm-yyyy) or "Present"	
London Underground	55 Broadway, London	Asst. Processing & Fleets Mgr.	07-2004	present time
Greater London Arts	30 White Chapel High St., London	gallery staff	02-2002	07-2004
Sainsbury's	101 Waterloo Road, London	grocery checker	10-1997	12-2001

In what occupation do you intend to work in the United States? _____

33. List below all educational institutions attended.

School and Location	From/To (mm-yyyy)		Course of Study	Degree or Diploma
London City University, London	09-2004	05-2008	project mgmnt	degree
Warren Street School, London	01-1984	12-1989	high school	diploma
Clerkenwell Grammar School, London	01-1979	12-1983	elementary	graduated

Languages spoken or read— English, French

Professional associations to which you belong _____

34. Previous Military Service ☐ Yes ☒ No

Branch _____ Dates of Service (mm-dd-yyyy) _____

Rank/Position _____ Military Speciality/Occupation _____

35. List dates of all previous visits to or residence in the United States. (If never, write "never") Give type of visa status, if known. Give DHS "A" number if any.

From/To (mm-yyyy)	Location	Type of Visa	"A" Number (If known)
never			

Signature of Applicant	Date (mm-dd-yyyy)
Edmund G. Lindsey	05/08/2012

Privacy Act and Paperwork Reduction Act Statements

The information asked for on this form is requested pursuant to Section 222 of the Immigration and Nationality Act. The U.S. Department of State uses the facts you provide on this form primarily to determine your classification and eligibility for a U.S. immigrant visa. Individuals who fail to submit this form or who do not provide all the requested information may be denied a U.S. immigrant visa. If you are issued an immigrant visa and are subsequently admitted to the United States as an immigrant, the Department of Homeland Security will use the information on this form to issue you a Permanent Resident Card, and, if you so indicate, the Social Security Administration will use the information to issue you a social security number and card.

*Public reporting burden for this collection of information is estimated to average 1 hour per response, including time required for searching existing data sources, gathering the necessary documentation, providing the information and/or documents required, and reviewing the final collection. You do not have to supply this information unless this collection displays a currently valid OMB control number. If you have comments on the accuracy of this burden estimate and/or recommendations for reducing it, please send them to: A/GIS/DIR, Room 2400 SA-22, U.S. Department of State, Washington, DC 20522-2202

Sample Form DS-230 Part II, Application for Immigrant Visa and Alien Registration—Page 1

U.S. Department of State

APPLICATION FOR IMMIGRANT VISA AND ALIEN REGISTRATION

OMB APPROVAL NO. 1405-0015
EXPIRES: 02/29/2012
ESTIMATED BURDEN: 1 HOUR*

PART II - SWORN STATEMENT

Instructions: Complete one copy of this form for yourself and each member of your family, regardless of age, who will immigrate with you. Please print or type your answers to all questions. Mark questions that are Not Applicable with "N/A". If there is insufficient room on the form, answer on a separate sheet using the same numbers that appear on the form. Attach any additional sheets to this form. The fee should be paid in United States dollars or local currency equivalent, or by bank draft.

Warning: Any false statement or concealment of a material fact may result in your permanent exclusion from the United States. Even if you are issued an immigrant visa and are subsequently admitted to the United States, providing false information on this form could be grounds for your prosecution and/or deportation.

This form (DS-230 Part II), together with Form DS-230 Part I, constitutes the complete Application for Immigrant Visa and Alien Registration.

36. Family Name	First Name	Middle Name
Lindsey	Edmund	Alexander

37. Other Names Used or Aliases (If married woman, give maiden name)
N/A

38. Full Name in Native Alphabet (If Roman letters not used)
N/A

39. Name and Address of Petitioner	Alice A. Debden 432 Fairfax Street #A Alexandria, VA 22314	Telephone number 703-555-1212
		Email Address

40. United States laws governing the issuance of visas require each applicant to state whether or not he or she is a member of any class of individuals excluded from admission into the United States. The excludable classes are described below in general terms. You should read carefully the following list and answer Yes or No to each category. The answers you give will assist the consular officer to reach a decision on your eligibility to receive a visa.

Except as Otherwise Provided by Law, Aliens Within the Following Classifications are Ineligible to Receive a Visa.
Do Any of the Following Classes Apply to You?

a. An alien who has a communicable disease of public health significance; who has failed to present documentation of having received vaccinations in accordance with U.S. law; who has or has had a physical or mental disorder that poses or is likely to pose a threat to the safety or welfare of the alien or others; or who is a drug abuser or addict. ☐ Yes ☒ No

b. An alien convicted of, or who admits having committed, a crime involving moral turpitude or violation of any law relating to a controlled substance or who is the spouse, son or daughter of such a trafficker who knowingly has benefited from the trafficking activities in the past five years; who has been convicted of 2 or more offenses for which the aggregate sentences were 5 years or more; who is coming to the United States to engage in prostitution or commercialized vice or who has engaged in prostitution or procuring within the past 10 years; who is or has been an illicit trafficker in any controlled substance; who has committed a serious criminal offense in the United States and who has asserted immunity from prosecution; who, while serving as a foreign government official, was responsible for or directly carried out particularly severe violations of religious freedom; or whom the President has identified as a person who plays a significant role in a severe form of trafficking in persons, who otherwise has knowingly aided, abetted, assisted or colluded with such a trafficker in severe forms of trafficking in persons, or who is the spouse, son or daughter of such a trafficker who knowingly has benefited from the trafficking activities within the past five years. ☐ Yes ☒ No

c. An alien who seeks to enter the United States to engage in espionage, sabotage, export control violations, terrorist activities, the overthrow of the Government of the United States or other unlawful activity; who is a member of or affiliated with the Communist or other totalitarian party; who participated, engaged or ordered genocide, torture, or extrajudicial killings; or who is a member or representative of a terrorist organization as currently designated by the U.S. Secretary of State. ☐ Yes ☒ No

d. An alien who is likely to become a public charge. ☐ Yes ☒ No

e. An alien who seeks to enter for the purpose of performing skilled or unskilled labor who has not been certified by the Secretary of Labor; who is a graduate of a foreign medical school seeking to perform medical services who has not passed the NBME exam or its equivalent; or who is a health care worker seeking to perform such work without a certificate from the CGFNS or from an equivalent approved independent credentialing organization. ☐ Yes ☒ No

f. An alien who failed to attend a hearing on deportation or inadmissibility within the last 5 years; who seeks or has sought a visa, entry into the United States, or any immigration benefit by fraud or misrepresentation; who knowingly assisted any other alien to enter or try to enter the United States in violation of law; who, after November 30, 1996, attended in student (F) visa status a U.S. public elementary school or who attended a U.S. public secondary school without reimbursing the school; or who is subject to a civil penalty under INA 274C. ☐ Yes ☒ No

Privacy Act and Paperwork Reduction Act Statements

The information asked for on this form is requested pursuant to Section 222 of the Immigration and Nationality Act. The U.S. Department of State uses the facts you provide on this form primarily to determine your classification and eligibility for a U.S. immigrant visa. Individuals who fail to submit this form or who do not provide all the requested information may be denied a U.S. immigrant visa. If you are issued an immigrant visa and are subsequently admitted to the United States as an immigrant, the Department of Homeland Security will use the information on this form to issue you a Permanent Resident Card, and, if you so indicate, the Social Security Administration will use the information to issue you a social security number and card.

*Public reporting burden for this collection of information is estimated to average 1 hour per response, including time required for searching existing data sources, gathering the necessary documentation, providing the information and/or documents required, and reviewing the final collection. You do not have to supply this information unless this collection displays a currently valid OMB control number. If you have comments on the accuracy of this burden estimate and/or recommendations for reducing it, please send them to: A/GIS/DIR, Room 2400 SA-22, U.S. Department of State, Washington, DC 20522-2202

DS-230 Part II	Previous Editions Obsolete	Page 3 of 4

Sample Form DS-230 Part II, Application for Immigrant Visa and Alien Registration—Page 2

g. An alien who is permanently ineligible for U.S. citizenship; or who departed the United States to evade military service in time of war.	☐ Yes ☒ No
h. An alien who was previously ordered removed within the last 5 years or ordered removed a second time within the last 20 years; who was previously unlawfully present and ordered removed within the last 10 years or ordered removed a second time within the last 20 years; who was convicted of an aggravated felony and ordered removed; who was previously unlawfully present in the United States for more than 180 days but less than one year who voluntarily departed within the last 3 years; or who was unlawfully present for more than one year or an aggregate of one year within the last 10 years.	☐ Yes ☒ No
i. An alien who is coming to the United States to practice polygamy; who withholds custody of a U.S. citizen child outside the United States from a person granted legal custody by a U.S. court or intentionally assists another person to do so; who has voted in the United States in violation of any law or regulation; or who renounced U.S. citizenship to avoid taxation.	☐ Yes ☒ No
j. An alien who is a former exchange visitor who has not fulfilled the 2-year foreign residence requirement.	☐ Yes ☒ No
k. An alien determined by the Attorney General to have knowingly made a frivolous application for asylum.	☐ Yes ☒ No
l. An alien who has ordered, carried out or materially assisted in extrajudicial and political killings and other acts of violence against the Haitian people; who has directly or indirectly assisted or supported any of the groups in Colombia known as FARC, ELN, or AUC; who through abuse of a governmental or political position has converted for personal gain, confiscated or expropriated property in Cuba, a claim to which is owned by a national of the United States, has trafficked in such property or has been complicit in such conversion, has committed similar acts in another country, or is the spouse, minor child or agent of an alien who has committed such acts; who has been directly involved in the establishment or enforcement of population controls forcing a woman to undergo an abortion against her free choice or a man or a woman to undergo sterilization against his or her free choice; or who has disclosed or trafficked in confidential U.S. business information obtained in connection with U.S. participation in the Chemical Weapons Convention or is the spouse, minor child or agent of such a person; or who has ever engaged in the recruitment of or the use of child soldiers.	☐ Yes ☒ No

41. Have you ever been charged, arrested or convicted of any offense or crime? (If answer is Yes, please explain)	☐ Yes ☒ No

42. Have you ever been refused admission to the United States at a port-of-entry? (If answer is Yes, please explain)	☐ Yes ☒ No

43a. Have you ever applied for a Social Security Number (SSN)? ☐ Yes Give the number _____ Would you like to receive a replacement card? (You must answer YES to question 43b. to receive a card.) ☐ Yes ☐ No ☒ No Do you want the Social Security Administration to assign you a SSN and issue a card? (You must answer YES to question 43b. to receive a number and a card.) ☒ Yes ☐ No	**43b.** Consent to Disclosure: I authorize disclosure of information from this form to the Department of Homeland Security (DHS), the Social Security Administration (SSA), such other U.S. Government agencies as may be required for the purpose of assigning me an SSN and issuing me a Social Security card, and I authorize the SSA to share my SSN with the INS. ☒ Yes ☐ No The applicant's response does not limit or restrict the Government's ability to obtain his or her SSN, or other information on this form, for enforcement or other purposes as authorized by law.

44. Were you assisted in completing this application? ☐ Yes ☒ No

(If answer is Yes, give name and address of person assisting you, indicating whether relative, friend, travel agent, attorney, or other)

DO NOT WRITE BELOW THE FOLLOWING LINE
The consular officer will assist you in answering item 45.
DO NOT SIGN this form until instructed to do so by the consular officer

45. I claim to be:

☐ A Family-Sponsored Immigrant   ☐ I derive foreign state chargeability   ☐ Preference _____
☐ An Employment-Based Immigrant   under Sec. 202(b) through my _____
☐ A Diversity Immigrant   ☐ Numerical limitation _____
☐ A Special Category (Specify) _____   (foreign state)
    (Returning resident, Hong Kong, Tibetan, Private Legislation, etc.)

I understand that I am required to surrender my visa to the United States Immigration Officer at the place where I apply to enter the United States, and that the possession of a visa does not entitle me to enter the United States if at that time I am found to be inadmissible under the immigration laws.

I understand that any willfully false or misleading statement or willful concealment of a material fact made by me herein may subject me to permanent exclusion from the United States and, if I am admitted to the United States, may subject me to criminal prosecution and/or deportation.

I, the undersigned applicant for a United States immigrant visa, do solemnly swear (or affirm) that all statements which appear in this application, consisting of Form DS-230 Part I and Part II combined, have been made by me, including the answers to items 1 through 45 inclusive, and that they are true and complete to the best of my knowledge and belief. I do further swear (or affirm) that, if admitted into the United States, I will not engage in activities which would be prejudicial to the public interest, or endanger the welfare, safety, or security of the United States; in activities which would be prohibited by the laws of the United States relating to espionage, sabotage, public disorder, or in other activities subversive to the national security; in any activity a purpose of which is the opposition to or the control, or overthrow of, the Government of the United States, by force, violence, or other unconstitutional means.

I understand that completion of this form by persons required by law to register with the Selective Service System (males 18 through 25 years of age) constitutes such registration in accordance with the Military Selective Service Act.

_____
Signature of Applicant

Subscribed and sworn to before me this _____ day of _____ at: _____

_____
Consular Officer

DS-230 Part II	This Form May be Obtained Free at Consular Offices of The United States of America	Page 4 of 4

Don't forget to sign this form at the bottom.

ii. Form DS-230 Part II

WEB RESOURCE
Form DS-230 Part II is available on the State Department website at www.state.gov. You may be asked to prepare and submit the form online. However, if you receive a paper version from the consulate, use that one instead. (It may be different than the online version.) Above is a sample filled-in version of this form.

Form DS-230 Part II is fairly short—it's intended to give final confirmation of who you are and where you're going. Most of this form is self-explanatory. Because consulates use slightly different versions of this form, we can't give you the number that a question will appear under. Consequently, we'll identify the questions by the language that they contain.

The **"person you intend to join"** and the **"sponsoring person"** both refer to your spouse. Enter his or her name, perhaps twice.

A few versions of the form still ask about your **"purpose in going to the United States."** The answer is to "immigrate." If the form asks for **"length of intended stay,"** your answer is "permanent."

The **"yes or no"** questions (with boxes to check) refer to the grounds of inadmissibility described in Chapter 2. If you check "yes" on any of them, consult a lawyer immediately, before sending in the form.

Signature line: Don't sign until the interview!

iii. Form I-864

Form I-864, the Affidavit of Support, is the primary form that your spouse and any joint sponsor will use to prove that he, she, or they are willing and able to support you. (You might need a joint sponsor to assist in supporting you if your spouse's income and assets aren't high enough to reach the government's guidelines, as covered in Chapter 3.)

TIP
Some sponsors can use a simpler version of Form I-864. If the sponsor has enough income so that he

or she doesn't need to resort to assets or other help to sponsor the immigrant(s), it's okay to use Form I-864EZ. And for those lucky couples who have been married long enough that the immigrant can be credited with 40 quarters of work through the U.S. citizen spouse, fill out Form I-864W to tell USCIS that you don't need to fill out an Affidavit of Support at all. Both forms are available at www.uscis.gov.

Be sure to read Chapter 3, Section A, before beginning to fill in this form. The chapter contains analysis of the legal implications of this form and your strategy in filling it out.

WEB RESOURCE
Form I-864 is available on the USCIS website at www.uscis.gov. Below is a sample filled-in version of this form. Note that our sample assumes that the sponsor has a child of her own, from a previous relationship, who agrees to contribute to the household income.

As explained in Section 3, above, some applicants will be asked to submit this form before sending in their forms from the NVC. If you are one of these applicants, make sure your spouse sends you a copy to review and have with you at your visa interview.

Because this form may be filled in either by your spouse or by a joint sponsor, the instructions below usually refer to the "sponsor," which refers to either of them.

These sections are self-explanatory, with the following notes:

- **In Part 1,** spouses check box a; long-lost cousins, fairy godmothers, and other nice friends who agreed to fill in this form as joint sponsors check either box d or box e.
- **In Part 3,** note that the list of children should include only those who will be immigrating with the immigrant spouse. If you mention any other children here, it will mean that the sponsor is agreeing to be sued if he or she fails to support them. In particular, it is unnecessary to name children who were born in the United States, because the sponsor has no obligation to support them (at least not

under the immigration laws, though they will be counted elsewhere within this form to test the sponsor's overall financial capacity).

- **In Part 4,** note that the sponsor's place of residence must be in the United States in order for him or her to be eligible as a financial sponsor. If the sponsor is not currently living in the U.S., the I-864 will be approved only with a showing that he or she is abroad temporarily, has maintained ties to the U.S., and intends to reestablish domicile in the U.S. no later than the date that you are admitted to the U.S. as a permanent resident.

Some of the ways your spouse can show having maintained ties to the U.S. include having paid state or local taxes, maintained bank accounts in the U.S., and maintained a permanent U.S. mailing address. (Of course, if a permanent resident has been outside the U.S. for more than a year at a time without first getting USCIS permission, or has made so many short trips outside the U.S. for the last few years that he or she appears to be living outside the U.S. and only visiting, that person may be in danger of having the U.S. government decide that he or she has abandoned the right to permanent residence. That would be a disaster and the visa petition for you would be revoked.)

Part 5, Sponsor's household size

This section is self-explanatory. Remember not to count anyone twice!

Part 6, Sponsor's income and employment

Question 22: The sponsor needs to fill in information about his or her employment here. Self-employment is fine. Be aware that if a self-employed sponsor has underreported income in the past, the earnings shown may not be sufficient to support you. In that case, the sponsor will need to file an amended tax return and pay a penalty before the newly reported income is accepted as meeting the guidelines for sponsorship.

Question 23: Here, the sponsor is supposed to enter the income shown on his or her most recent tax return. But what if the sponsor's income has risen since filing those taxes? In that case, the sponsor should enter the more recent income figure, but put an asterisk (an *) next to it. Then find some white space somewhere on the page and write "this figure reflects present earnings, not earnings shown on tax return; see supporting documentation." The documentation the sponsor is already providing, such as an employer's letter, should be enough to show current income.

Question 24: This question is important for sponsors whose income is not enough by itself, but who will be using the income of members of their household to help meet the *Poverty Guidelines* minimum requirements. First, every sponsor must state his or her own income. Then, if the sponsor wants other people's income counted, they must be mentioned in Question 24b and the sponsor must check box d. Unless any one of these household members is the actual immigrant, they must plan to complete a separate agreement with the sponsor, using Form I-864A. The total income from the sponsor and household members goes in Question 24c.

Question 25: Self-explanatory.

Part 7, Use of assets to supplement income

The sponsor needs to complete this section only if his or her income wasn't enough by itself to meet the *Poverty Guidelines* requirements. If the sponsor needs to add assets and he or she includes such items as a house, car, or boat, remember to subtract debts, mortgages, and liens before writing down their value in Question 26. And remember that the value of these assets will later be divided by five before being used to meet the *Poverty Guidelines* minimum.

If some of the assets being used to meet the minimum belong to a household member, enter the household member's name in Question 27, along with the total amount the assets are worth. If some of the assets being used to meet the minimum belong to the immigrant, attach a separate page

Sample Form I-864, Affidavit of Support—Page 1

OMB No. 1615-0075; Expires 09/30/2012

I-864, Affidavit of Support
Under Section 213A of the Act

Department of Homeland Security
U.S. Citizenship and Immigration Services

Part 1. Basis for filing Affidavit of Support.

1. I, _Alice Anne Debden_ ,

am the sponsor submitting this affidavit of support because **(Check only one box):**

a.	[X]	**I am the petitioner. I filed or am filing for the immigration of my relative.**
b.	[ ]	I filed an alien worker petition on behalf of the intending immigrant, who is related to me as my _____
c.	[ ]	I have an ownership interest of at least 5 percent in _____ , which filed an alien worker petition on behalf of the intending immigrant, who is related to me as my _____
d.	[ ]	I am the only joint sponsor.
e.	[ ]	I am the [ ] first [ ] second of two joint sponsors. *(Check appropriate box.)*
f.	[ ]	The original petitioner is deceased. I am the substitute sponsor. I am the intending immigrant's _____ .

For Government Use Only

This I-864 is from:

[ ] the Petitioner

[ ] a Joint Sponsor # _____

[ ] the Substitute Sponsor

[ ] 5% Owner

This I-864:

[ ] does not meet the requirements of section 213A.

[ ] meets the requirements of section 213A.

_____
Reviewer

_____
Location

_____
Date *(mm/dd/yyyy)*

Number of Affidavits of Support in file:

[ ] 1   [ ] 2

Part 2. Information on the principal immigrant.

2. Last Name _Lindsey_

First Name _Edmund_   Middle Name _Alexander_

3. Mailing Address Street Number and Name *(Include Apartment Number)*
10 Walden Road

City	State/Province	Zip/Postal Code	Country
London		SW1H OBD	U.K.

4. Country of Citizenship _U.K._ | **5.** Date of Birth *(mm/dd/yyyy)* _11/21/1973_

6. Alien Registration Number *(if any)* **A-** _none_ | **7.** U.S. Social Security Number *(if any)* _none_

Part 3. Information on the immigrant(s) you are sponsoring.

8. [X] I am sponsoring the principal immigrant named in Part 2 above.

[X] Yes   [ ] No (Applicable only in cases with two joint sponsors)

9. [ ] I am sponsoring the following family members immigrating at the same time or within six months of the principal immigrant named in **Part 2** above. Do not include any relative listed on a separate visa petition.

	Name	Relationship to Sponsored Immigrant	Date of Birth *(mm/dd/yyyy)*	A-Number *(if any)*	U.S.Social Security Number *(if any)*
a.					
b.					
c.					
d.					
e.					

10. Enter the total number of immigrants you are sponsoring on this form from **Part 3**, Items **8** and **9**. [ ] 1

Form I-864 (09/19/11) Y

Sample Form I-864, Affidavit of Support—Page 2

Part 4. Information on the Sponsor.

			For Government Use Only
11. Name	Last Name Debden		
	First Name Alice	Middle Name Anne	
12. Mailing Address	Street Number and Name *(Include Apartment Number)* 432 Fairfax Street #A		
	City Alexandria	State or Province Virginia	
	Country USA	Zip/Postal Code 22314	
13. Place of Residence *(if different from mailing address)*	Street Number and Name *(Include Apartment Number)* same as above		
	City	State or Province	
	Country	Zip/Postal Code	

14. Telephone Number *(Include Area Code or Country and City Codes)*
703-555-1212

15. Country of Domicile
USA

16. Date of Birth *(mm/dd/yyyy)*
03/03/1974

17. Place of Birth *(City)*	State or Province	Country
Dublin		Ireland

18. U.S. Social Security Number *(Required)*
123-12-1234

19. Citizenship/Residency

☐ I am a U.S. citizen.

☐ I am a U.S. national (for joint sponsors only).

☒ I am a lawful permanent resident. My alien registration number is A- 088-888-888

If you checked box (b), (c), (d), (e) or (f) in line 1 on Page 1, you must include proof of your citizen, national, or permanent resident status.

20. Military Service (To be completed by petitioner sponsors only.)

I am currently on active duty in the U.S. armed services.　　☐ Yes　　☒ No

Sample Form I-864, Affidavit of Support—Page 3

Part 5. Sponsor's household size.

	For Government Use Only

21. Your Household Size - <u>DO NOT COUNT ANYONE TWICE</u>

Persons you are sponsoring in this affidavit:

    a. Enter the number you entered on line 10.   ☐ `1`

Persons NOT sponsored in this affidavit:

    b. Yourself.   **1**

    c. If you are currently married, enter "1" for your spouse.   ☐

    d. If you have dependent children, enter the number here.   ☐ ☐

    e. If you have any other dependents, enter the number here.   ☐ ☐

    f. If you have sponsored any other persons on an I-864 or I-864 EZ who are now lawful permanent residents, enter the number here.   ☐ ☐

    g. OPTIONAL: If you have <u>siblings, parents, or adult children</u> with the same principal residence who are combining their income with yours by submitting Form I-864A, enter the number here.   ☐ `1`

    h. Add together lines and enter the number here. **Household Size:**   ☐ `3`

Part 6. Sponsor's income and employment.

22. I am currently:

    a. ☒ Employed as a/an   Potter   .

         Name of Employer #1 *(if applicable)*   Alexandria Quartet Potters   .

         Name of Employer #2 *(if applicable)*   .

    b. ☐ Self-employed as a/an   .

    c. ☐ Retired from   since   .
                 (Company Name)   *(Date)*

    d. ☐ Unemployed since   .
                         (Date)

23. My current individual annual income is: $ 18,500
                                             (See Step-by-Step Instructions)

Sample Form I-864, Affidavit of Support—Page 4

24. My current annual household income:

a. List your income from line 23 of this form. $ __18,500__

b. **Income you are using from any other person who was counted in your household size,** including, in certain conditions, the intending immigrant. (See step-by-step instructions.) Please indicate name, relationship and income.

Name	Relationship	Current Income
Louisa Jane Madison	Daughter	$ 38,000
		$
		$
		$

c. **Total Household Income:** $ __56,500__

(Total all lines from 24a and 24b. Will be Compared to Poverty Guidelines -- See Form I-864P.)

d. [X] The persons listed above have completed Form I-864A. I am filing along with this form all necessary Forms I-864A completed by these persons.

e. [ ] The person listed above, _____ does not need to
(Name)
complete Form I-864A because he/she is the intending immigrant and has no accompanying dependents.

For Government Use Only

Household Size =
_____

Poverty line for year
_____ is:

$ _____

25. Federal income tax return information.

[X] I have filed a Federal tax return for each of the three most recent tax years. I have attached the required photocopy or transcript of my Federal tax return for only the most recent tax year.

My total income (adjusted gross income on IRS Form 1040EZ) as reported on my Federal tax returns for the most recent three years was:

Tax Year		Total Income
2011	_(most recent)_	$ 18,500
2010	_(2nd most recent)_	$ 18,000
2009	_(3rd most recent)_	$ 15,000

[X] _(Optional)_ I have attached photocopies or transcripts of my Federal tax returns for my second and third most recent tax years.

Sample Form I-864, Affidavit of Support—Page 5

Part 7. Use of assets to supplement income. *(Optional)*	For Government Use Only

If your income, or the total income for you and your household, from line 24c exceeds the Federal Poverty Guidelines for your household size, YOU ARE NOT REQUIRED to complete this Part. Skip to Part 8.

Household Size =

26. Your assets *(Optional)*

_____

    a. Enter the balance of all savings and checking accounts. $ _____

Poverty line for year

    b. Enter the net cash value of real-estate holdings. (Net means current assessed value minus mortgage debt.) $ _____ *O* _____

_____ **is:**

$ _____

    c. Enter the net cash value of all stocks, bonds, certificates of deposit, and any other assets not already included in lines 26 (a) or (b). $ _____

    d. Add together lines 26 a, b and c and enter the number here.   **TOTAL:** $ _____

27. Your household member's assets from Form I-864A. *(Optional)*

    Assets from Form I-864A, line 12d for

    $ _____

_____
(Name of Relative)

28. Assets of the principal sponsored immigrant. *(Optional)*

    The principal sponsored immigrant is the person listed in line 2.

    a. Enter the balance of the sponsored immigrant's savings and checking accounts. $ _____

    b. Enter the net cash value of all the sponsored immigrant's real estate holdings. (Net means investment value minus mortgage debt.) $ _____

    c. Enter the current cash value of the sponsored immigrant's stocks, bonds, certificates of deposit, and other assets not included on line a or b. $ _____

    d. Add together lines 28a, b, and c, and enter the number here. $ _____

The total value of all assets, line 29, must equal 5 times (3 times for spouses and children of USCs, or 1 time for orphans to be formally adopted in the U.S.) the difference between the poverty guidelines and the sponsor's household income, line 24c.

29. Total value of assets.

    Add together lines 26d, 27 and 28d and enter the number here.   **TOTAL:** $ _____

Sample Form I-864, Affidavit of Support—Page 6

Part 8. Sponsor's Contract.

Please note that, by signing this Form I-864, you agree to assume certain specific obligations under the Immigration and Nationality Act and other Federal laws. The following paragraphs describe those obligations. Please read the following information carefully before you sign the Form I-864. If you do not understand the obligations, you may wish to consult an attorney or accredited representative.

What is the Legal Effect of My Signing a Form I-864?

If you sign a Form I-864 on behalf of any person (called the "intending immigrant") who is applying for an immigrant visa or for adjustment of status to a permanent resident, and that intending immigrant submits the Form I-864 to the U.S. Government with his or her application for an immigrant visa or adjustment of status, under section 213A of the Immigration and Nationality Act these actions create a contract between you and the U. S. Government. The intending immigrant's becoming a permanent resident is the "consideration" for the contract.

Under this contract, you agree that, in deciding whether the intending immigrant can establish that he or she is not inadmissible to the United States as an alien likely to become a public charge, the U.S. Government can consider your income and assets to be available for the support of the intending immigrant.

What If I choose Not to Sign a Form I-864?

You cannot be made to sign a Form 1-864 if you do not want to do so. But if you do not sign the Form I-864, the intending immigrant may not be able to become a permanent resident in the United States.

What Does Signing the Form I-864 Require Me to do?

If an intending immigrant becomes a permanent resident in the United States based on a Form I-864 that you have signed, then, until your obligations under the Form I-864 terminate, you must:

-- Provide the intending immigrant any support necessary to maintain him or her at an income that is at least 125 percent of the Federal Poverty Guidelines for his or her household size (100 percent if you are the petitioning sponsor and are on active duty in the U.S. Armed Forces and the person is your husband, wife, unmarried child under 21 years old.)

-- Notify USCIS of any change in your address, within 30 days of the change, by filing Form I-865.

What Other Consequences Are There?

If an intending immigrant becomes a permanent resident in the United States based on a Form I-864 that you have signed, then until your obligations under the Form I-864 terminate, your income and assets may be considered ("deemed") to be available to that person, in determining whether he or she is eligible for certain Federal means-tested public benefits and also for State or local means-tested public benefits, if the State or local government's rules provide for consideration ("deeming") of your income and assets as available to the person.

This provision does **not** apply to public benefits specified in section 403(c) of the Welfare Reform Act such as, but not limited to, emergency Medicaid, short-term, non-cash emergency relief; services provided under the National School Lunch and Child Nutrition Acts; immunizations and testing and treatment for communicable diseases; and means-tested programs under the Elementary and Secondary Education Act.

Contract continued on following page.

Sample Form I-864, Affidavit of Support—Page 7

What If I Do Not Fulfill My Obligations?

If you do not provide sufficient support to the person who becomes a permanent resident based on the Form I-864 that you signed, that person may sue you for this support.

If a Federal, State or local agency, or a private agency provides any covered means-tested public benefit to the person who becomes a permanent resident based on the Form I-864 that you signed, the agency may ask you to reimburse them for the amount of the benefits they provided. If you do not make the reimbursement, the agency may sue you for the amount that the agency believes you owe.

If you are sued, and the court enters a judgment against you, the person or agency that sued you may use any legally permitted procedures for enforcing or collecting the judgment. You may also be required to pay the costs of collection, including attorney fees.

If you do not file a properly completed Form I-865 within 30 days of any change of address, USCIS may impose a civil fine for your failing to do so.

When Will These Obligations End?

Your obligations under a Form I-864 will end if the person who becomes a permanent resident based on a Form I-864 that you signed:

- Becomes a U.S. citizen;
- Has worked, or can be credited with, 40 quarters of coverage under the Social Security Act;
- No longer has lawful permanent resident status, and has departed the United States;
- Becomes subject to removal, but applies for and obtains in removal proceedings a new grant of adjustment of status, based on a new affidavit of support, if one is required; or
- Dies.

Note that divorce **does not** terminate your obligations under this Form I-864.

Your obligations under a Form I-864 also end if you die. Therefore, if you die, your Estate will not be required to take responsibility for the person's support after your death. Your Estate may, however, be responsible for any support that you owed before you died.

30. I, _____ ,
(Print Sponsor's Name)

certify under penalty of perjury under the laws of the United States that:

a. I know the contents of this affidavit of support that I signed.

b. All the factual statements in this affidavit of support are true and correct.

c. I have read and I understand each of the obligations described in Part 8, and I agree, freely and without any mental reservation or purpose of evasion, to accept each of those obligations in order to make it possible for the immigrants indicated in Part 3 to become permanent residents of the United States;

d. I agree to submit to the personal jurisdiction of any Federal or State court that has subject matter jurisdiction of a lawsuit against me to enforce my obligations under this Form I-864;

e. Each of the Federal income tax returns submitted in support of this affidavit are true copies, or are unaltered tax transcripts, of the tax returns I filed with the U.S. Internal Revenue Service; and

Sign on following page.

Sample Form I-864, Affidavit of Support—Page 8

f. I authorize the Social Security Administration to release information about me in its records to the Department of State and U.S. Citizenship and Immigration Services.

g. Any and all other evidence submitted is true and correct.

31. *Alice Anne Debden*
_____
(Sponsor's Signature)

04/01/2013
_____
(Date-- mm/dd/yyyy)

Part 9. Information on Preparer, if prepared by someone other than the sponsor.

I certify under penalty of perjury under the laws of the United States that I prepared this affidavit of support at the sponsor's request and that this affidavit of support is based on all information of which I have knowledge.

Signature: _____   **Date:** _____
(mm/dd/yyyy)

Printed Name: _____

Firm Name: _____

Address: _____

Telephone Number: _____

E-Mail Address : _____

Business State ID # *(if any)* _____

describing these (and of course attach documents to prove the assets' ownership, location, and value).

If the combination of the sponsor's available income and one-fifth of the sponsor's and/or the immigrant's assets don't yet meet the *Poverty Guidelines* minimum, you'll still need to hand in this Affidavit. But you'll definitely want to look for a joint sponsor or a participating household member.

Part 8, Sponsor's Contract

Unlike past versions of this form, the sponsor's signature no longer needs to be witnessed by a notary public.

TIP

Need to prepare Affidavits for several family members at once? If the sponsor is bringing in more than one person (you and your children) in the same process, he or she can simply copy Form I-864 (with supporting documents) the appropriate number of times after signing it.

iv.   Form I-864A

Not every immigrant needs to submit Form I-864A. It is required only if, on the main Form I-864, the sponsor had to use the income of members of his or her own household to meet the *Poverty Guidelines*. In that case, the sponsor will have to ask these persons to fill in portions of Form I-864A. The sponsor must then attach the Form I-864A to the main Form I-864.

WEB RESOURCE

Form I-864A is available on the USCIS website at www.uscis.gov. Below is a sample filled-in version of this form.

Page 1 heading: Filled out by the household member. Self-explanatory.

Part 1: Self-explanatory; filled out by household member.

Part 2: This part is filled out and signed by the sponsor.

Part 3: Filled out and signed by the household member.

v. Form I-864W

Only a few lucky people will be able to use this form, namely those who are exempt from the Affidavit of Support requirement because the immigrant has either:

- worked lawfully for 40 Social Security quarters (approximately ten years) in the U.S.
- been married while the U.S. spouse worked for 40 Social Security quarters, or
- a combination of the above.

The deal is that a financial sponsor's responsibility lasts until the immigrant has (among other possibilities) earned 40 work quarters credited toward Social Security. A work quarter is approximately three months, but it depends partly on how much you earn. So if you've already reached the 40 quarters on your own, through lawful employment—perhaps while in the U.S. as a student or H-1B worker—there's no point in the sponsor filling out an Affidavit of Support for you. And, in an interesting twist, you can be credited for work done by your U.S. spouse if it was during your marriage.

You'll need to prove to USCIS how many quarters of work your spouse or you have done. Contact Social Security about getting a certified statement with this information.

Because Form I-864W is fairly easy to fill out, we won't include a sample here. The form is available at www.uscis.gov. In Part 2, you would check the first box.

b.   Financial Documents to Have on Hand

When it comes to proving your sponsor's capacity to support you financially, the consulate will require detailed, up-to-date information from trustworthy sources, as detailed below.

i.   Documents to Accompany Form I-864

Form I-864 asks for several supporting documents. If your spouse is relying on a joint sponsor (someone outside the household), that person should also be told to assemble a set of these documents:

- **A copy of your spouse/sponsor's federal income tax returns for the last three years, with W-2s.** Don't include state tax forms. The immigration authorities prefer to see federal tax returns in the form of Internal Revenue Service (IRS) transcripts (an IRS-generated summary of the return that was filed). Transcripts can be requested using IRS Form 4506T (available from www.irs.gov or by calling 800-829-1040). However, it usually takes several weeks to receive the transcript. Don't let this hold up the immigration process—if the transcript hasn't come by the time you need to submit the Form I-864, simply use your sponsor's personal photocopies of his or her tax returns.

- **Proof of your sponsor's current employment.** Start with a letter from the sponsor's employer describing the dates of employment, nature of the job, wages/salary, time worked per week, terms, and prospects for advancement. The sample letter below shows how one employer described a sponsor's job and compensation. Also include copies of pay stubs covering the last six months, or the most recent stub if it shows cumulative pay. If the sponsor is self-employed, a tax return is acceptable, but it's a good idea to add a business license, copies of current receipts, or other supporting documents.

- **A list of assets, (the sponsor's and/or the immigrant's) if they must be used to meet the** *Poverty Guidelines'* **minimum.**

TIP

We're advising you to prepare more than the minimum financial documents. Technically, you're supposed to be asked for only one year's tax returns, and that's it. But because so many consulates ask for more, it makes sense to be ready with additional years' tax returns plus a bank and employer letter.

There is no form to use for creating this list. Using a typewriter or word processor, prepare a list or table with the following information:

- a brief description of the item
- the item's current value
- remaining debt (if any), and
- a brief description of the document you've attached to prove ownership (see below).
- **Proof of ownership of assets (the sponsor's and/ or the immigrant's), if any were listed.** The Form I-864 itself does a good job of detailing which documents will be accepted as proof of ownership of assets, as explained on page 5, Use of Assets to Supplement Income. The value must be the likely sale price, not how much the sponsor paid for the property. For real estate, you can use a tax assessment to show the value. If the assessment seems too low, or for property other than real estate, the sponsor can hire a professional appraiser to prepare an estimate and report. For cars, the value listed in the *Kelley Blue Book* is acceptable. Look for the *Kelley Blue Book* at a library or bookstore, or online at www.kbb.com. The sponsor must also document the amount of any debt remaining on the property. If no debt remains, submit proof of final payment.

CAUTION

You may need to update your information later. By the time you get to your visa interview, circumstances may have changed for your sponsor, joint sponsor, or household joint sponsor. For example, if the sponsor or joint sponsor have new or different employment, bring a job letter and copies of recent pay stubs; and if a new tax year has begun, bring copies of the sponsor(s)' most recent tax returns.

Sample Form I-864A, Contract Between Sponsor and Household Member—Page 1

OMB No. 1615-0075; Expires 09/30/2012

Department of Homeland Security
U.S. Citizenship and Immigration Services

I-864A, Contract Between
Sponsor and Household Member

Part 1. Information on the Household Member. (You.)			For Government Use Only
1. Name	Last Name Madison		**This I-864A relates to a household member who:**
	First Name Louisa	Middle Name Jane	☐ is the intending immigrant.
2. Mailing Address	Street Number and Name *(include apartment number)* 432 Fairfax St. #A		
	City Alexandria	State or Province VA	☐ is not the intending immigrant.
	Country USA	Zip/Postal Code 22314	
3. Place of Residence *(if different from mailing address)*	Street Number and Name *(include apartment number)* same as above		
	City	State or Province	Reviewer
	Country	Zip/Postal Code	Location
4. Telephone Number	*(Include area code or country and city codes)* 705-555-1212		Date *(mm/dd/yyyy)*
5. Date of Birth	*(mm/dd/yyyy)* 10/18/1967		
6. Place of Birth	City State/Province Country Dublin Ireland		
7. U.S. Social Security Number *(if any)*	404-44-4004		

8. Relationship to Sponsor (Check either a, b or c.)

a. ☐ I am the intending immigrant and also the sponsor's spouse.

b. ☐ I am the intending immigrant and also a member of the sponsor's household.

c. ☒ I am not the intending immigrant. I am the sponsor's household member. I am related to the sponsor as his/her.

☐ Spouse

☐ Son or daughter *(at least 18 years old)*

☐ Parent

☒ Brother or sister

☐ Other dependent (specify)

Form I-864A (09/19/11) Y

Sample Form I-864A, Contract Between Sponsor and Household Member—Page 2

9. I am currently:

a. [X] Employed as a/an ___Bookkeeper___.

    Name of Employer # 1 *(if applicable)* ___Hutt Tax Service___.

    Name of Employer #2 *(if applicable)* _____.

b. [ ] Self-employed as a/an _____.

c. [ ] Retired from_____ since _____.
                (Company Name)   *(mm/dd/yyyy)*

d. [ ] Unemployed since _____.
                           (mm/dd/yyyy)

For Government Use Only

10. My current individual annual income is: $ ___38,000___.

11. Federal income tax information.

[X] I have filed a Federal tax return for each of the three most recent tax years. I have attached the required photocopy or transcript of my Federal tax return for only the most recent tax year.

My total income (adjusted gross income on IRS Form 1040EZ) as reported on my Federal tax returns for the most recent three years was:

Tax Year		Total Income
2011	*(most recent)*	$ 38,000
2010	*(2nd most recent)*	$ 36,000
2009	*(3rd most recent)*	$ 35,000

[ ] *(Optional)* I have attached photocopies or transcripts of my Federal tax returns for my second and third most recent tax years.

12. My assets (complete only if necessary).

a. Enter the balance of all cash, savings, and checking accounts. $_____.

b. Enter the net cash value of real-estate holdings. (Net means assessed value minus mortgage debt.) $_____.

c. Enter the cash value of all stocks, bonds, certificates of deposit, and other assets not listed on line a or b. $_____.

d. **Add together Lines a, b, and c and enter the number here.** $_____.

Sample Form I-864A, Contract Between Sponsor and Household Member—Page 3

Part 2. Sponsor's Promise.	For Government Use Only

13. I, THE SPONSOR, _____Alice Anne Debden_____
(Print Name)

in consideration of the household member's promise to support the following intending immigrant(s)

and to be jointly and severally liable for any obligations I incur under the affidavit of support, promise

to complete and file an affidavit of support on behalf of the following ____1____ named intending
(Indicate Number)

immigrant(s) (see Step-by-Step instructions).

Name	Date of Birth (mm/dd/yyyy)	A-number (if any)	U.S. Social Security Number (if any)
a. Edmund A. Lindsey	11/21/1973	None	None
b.			
c.			
d.			
e.			

14. _____Alice Anne Debden_____   04/01/2013
(Sponsor's Signature)   *(Date--mm/dd/yyyy)*

Part 3. Household Member's Promise.

15. I, THE HOUSEHOLD MEMBER, _____Louisa Jane Cartwright_____
(Print Name)

in consideration of the sponsor's promise to complete and file an affidavit of support on behalf of the

above ____1____ named intending immigrant(s):
(Number from line 13)

a. Promise to provide any and all financial support necessary to assist the sponsor in maintaining the sponsored immigrant(s) at or above the minimum income provided for in section 213A(a)(1)(A) of the Act (not less than 125 percent of the Federal Poverty Guidelines) during the period in which the affidavit of support is enforceable;

b. Agree to be jointly and severally liable for payment of any and all obligations owed by the sponsor under the affidavit of support to the sponsored immigrant(s), to any agency of the Federal Government, to any agency of a State or local government, or to any other private entity that provides means-tested public benefit;

c. Certify under penalty under the laws of the United States that all the information provided on this form is true and correct to the best of my knowledge and belief and that the Federal income tax returns submitted in support of the contract are true copies or unaltered tax transcripts filed with the Internal Revenue Service.

d. **Consideration where the household member is also the sponsored immigrant:** I understand that if I am the sponsored immigrant and a member of the sponsor's household that this promise relates only to my promise to be jointly and severally liable for any obligation owed by the sponsor under the affidavit of support to any of my dependents, to any agency of the Federal Government, to any agency of a State or local government, and to provide any and all financial support necessary to assist the sponsor in maintaining any of my dependents at or above the minimum income provided for in section 213A(s)(1)(A) of the Act (not less than 125 percent of the Federal poverty line) during the period which the affidavit of support is enforceable.

e. I authorize the Social Security Administration to release information about me in its records to the Department of State and U.S. Citizenship and Immigration Services.

16. _____Louisa Jane Madison_____   04/03/2013
(Household Member's Signature)   *(Date--mm/dd/yyyy)*

Sample Letter Showing Sponsor's Employment

Alexandria Quartet Potters
123 Fourth Street
Alexandria, VA 22315
May 22, 20xx

To Whom It May Concern:

Alice Debden has been an employee of Alexandria Quartet Potters since September 4, 20xx, a total of over five years. She has a full-time position as a ceramist. Her salary is $22,000 per year. This position is permanent, and Alice's prospects for performance-based advancement and salary increases are excellent.

Very truly yours,

Bob Bossman

Bob Bossman
Personnel Manager
Alexandria Quartet Potters

ii. Documents to Accompany Form I-864A

Form I-864A, the contract between your spouse and any household joint sponsors who are willing to contribute financially, also requires several supporting documents. These include not only proof of the joint sponsors' financial capacity, but proof that they live with and are related to the main sponsor.

- **Proof that the household joint sponsors live with the primary sponsor.** To satisfy this requirement, you can include a copy of the rental agreement showing the household member's name and copies of items that show the same address as the sponsor (such as a driver's license, copies of school records, copies of utility bills, or personal correspondence).

- **Proof that the household joint sponsors are related to the primary sponsor (if they're not already listed as relations on the sponsor's tax return).** The best way to prove this family relationship is through birth certificates. For example, if the sponsor and household joint sponsor are parent and child, the child's birth certificate will do. If they are brother and sister, providing both birth certificates will work (as long as the certificates show that they share the same parent or parents). If the birth certificates don't make the family relationships clear, look for other official documents such as court or school records to confirm the parent-child links.

- **Copies of the household joint sponsors' tax returns for the last one to three years, preferably IRS-generated tax transcripts.**

- **Proof of the household joint sponsors' employment, such as a letter from their employer confirming employment and recent pay stubs.**

- **A list of the household joint sponsors' assets if they must be used to meet the *Poverty Guidelines'* minimum.** There is no form to use for creating this list. The household joint sponsors should simply prepare (on a typewriter or word processor) a list or table with the following information:
  - a brief description of the item
  - its current value
  - remaining debt (if any), and
  - brief description of the document that has been attached to prove the sponsor owns the asset.

- **Proof of ownership of household joint sponsors' assets, if any were listed.**

- **A list of the benefit programs and dates of receipt if the household joint sponsor or their dependents have used financial need-based public benefits in the last three years.**

c. Other Documents to Prepare

You'll be asked to prepare various other documents, such as your birth certificate, marriage certificate, passport, and police certificates from countries where you've lived. These will be well explained in the instructions you receive, so we won't review them further here.

You need to obtain a police certificate (hopefully showing your clean record) only if such certificates are available in your country. You can find information on whether and how to obtain police certificates in your country on the State Department's visa reciprocity tables at http://travel.state.gov (under "Visa for Foreign Citizens," click "more," from the left-hand column click "Fees and Reciprocity Tables," then "Visa Issuance Fee–Reciprocity Tables," from the drop-down menu; click "Visa Issuance Fee–Reciprocity Tables," enter your country in the box, then scroll down for information).

If you don't have a clean record, see a lawyer.

d. Documents Proving Your Marriage Is Bona Fide

You must present evidence that your marriage is a real one, not a sham. Gather and photocopy as many of the following items as possible:

- rental agreements, leases, or mortgages showing that you have lived together and/or have leased or bought property in both spouses' names
- hotel and airplane receipts showing trips that you have taken together or to visit one another
- phone bills showing your conversations; copies of letters and emails
- your mutual child's birth certificate, or a doctor's report saying that you are pregnant
- joint bank statements
- joint credit card statements
- evidence that one spouse has made the other a beneficiary on his/her life or health insurance or retirement account
- auto registrations showing joint ownership and/or addresses
- joint club memberships
- receipts from gifts that you purchased for one another (these should be obvious gift-type purchases, like from a flower shop or candy store)
- letters from friends and family to each or both of you mailed at an address where you were living together

- photos of you and your spouse taken before and during your marriage, including at your wedding (the government knows wedding pictures can be faked, but some officers enjoy seeing them anyway). The photos should, if possible, include parents and other relatives from both families. Write the date taken and a brief description of what the photo shows on the back (or underneath, if you're photocopying them). Don't bother with the wedding or other videos—there won't be time or a space to view them.

e. Using the Checklist for Step Four Interview Packet

This checklist notes every form, document, and other item included in the final packet that you and your spouse will need to assemble in preparation for your immigrant visa interview.

 CHECKLIST
Appendix C includes a tear-out copy of this checklist.

4. Step Four: Attend Your Visa Interview

On the appointed day, you and your petitioning spouse (if he or she can possibly make it) will go to the consulate for an interview. See a detailed description of the interview and how to prepare for it in Chapter 13.

Which consulate you go to depends on where you're from and where you live now. If you've been living (legally) in a country that is not your country of citizenship, you'll probably be told to work with the consulate in the country where you now live. If your country of residence doesn't have diplomatic relations with the United States, the NVC will name another consulate to handle your case.

Checklist for Immigrant Visa Forms and Documents

- ☐ Form DS 230 Parts I and II (see Subsection A3a (i and ii), above, for line-by-line instructions)
- ☐ Form I-864, Affidavit of Support (see Subsection A3a(iii), above, for line-by-line instructions)
- ☐ Documents to accompany Form I-864 (see Subsection A3b(i), above):
  - ☐ A copy of your spouse/sponsor's federal income tax returns for the last one to three years, with W-2s
  - ☐ Proof of your sponsor's current employment
  - ☐ A list of assets, (the sponsor's and/or the immigrant's) if they're being used to meet the *Poverty Guidelines'* minimum
  - ☐ Proof of ownership of assets (the sponsor's and/or the immigrant's), if any were listed
  - ☐ If sponsor or sponsor's dependents have used financial need-based public benefits in the last three years, a list of the programs and dates of receipt
- ☐ Form I-864A, Contract Between Sponsor and Household Member (only needed if sponsor's income is insufficient; see line-by-line instructions in Subsection A3a(iv), above)
- ☐ Documents to accompany Form I-864A (see Subsection A3b(ii), above):
  - ☐ Proof that the household joint sponsors live with the primary sponsor
  - ☐ Proof that the household joint sponsors are related to the primary sponsor (if they're not already listed as dependents on the sponsor's tax return)
- ☐ Copies of the household joint sponsors' tax returns for the last one to three years
- ☐ Proof of the household joint sponsors' employment
- ☐ Proof of ownership of household joint sponsors' assets, if any were listed
- ☐ If the household joint sponsor or their dependents have used financial need-based public benefits in the last three years, a list of the benefits programs and dates of receipt
- ☐ If you're exempt from the Affidavit of Support requirement, Form I-864W, together with a certified statement of your Social Security earnings history
- ☐ Additional documents to accompany forms:
  - ☐ Original and one photocopy of your birth certificate (see Chapter 4, Section C, for how to obtain vital documents)
  - ☐ Original and one photocopy of your marriage certificate (see Chapter 4, Section C, for how to obtain vital documents)
  - ☐ If applicable, original and one photocopy of proof of termination of all previous marriages
  - ☐ Original INS or USCIS notice of approved I-130 (Form I-797)
  - ☐ Two color photographs of you (passport style)
  - ☐ Police Certificate, if available in your country
  - ☐ Military records, if applicable
  - ☐ Court and prison records, if applicable
  - ☐ Fees (currently $230 plus a $74 security surcharge)

At a minimum, you'll need to bring to your interview:

- ☐ the results of your medical exam (described below)
- ☐ evidence that your marriage is bona fide (as described in Subsection 3d, above)
- ☐ financial documents to bring the Affidavit of Support up to date if it was prepared many months ago, and
- ☐ your passport, valid for at least six months.

a. The Medical Exam

To prove that you are not inadmissible for medical reasons, you will have to present the results of a medical exam done by a doctor approved by the U.S. consulate. Your appointment notice will give you complete instructions on where and when to visit the appropriate clinic or doctor. There will be a fee of about $150 plus more for tests and any vaccinations.

When you go for your medical exam, make sure to bring the following:

- your visa appointment letter
- the doctor's fee
- a form you fill out describing your medical history, if requested
- your vaccination records, and
- photo identification—the doctor must make sure you don't send a healthier person in your place. You may also be requested to bring a passport-style photo.

The doctor will examine you, ask you questions about your medical and psychiatric history and drug use, and test you (including blood tests and chest X-rays). Pregnant women can refuse the chest X-ray until after the baby is born if they have no symptoms of tuberculosis. When the laboratory results are in, the doctor will fill out the appropriate form and either send it directly to the consulate or return it to you in a sealed envelope. DO NOT open the envelope—this will invalidate the results. The doctor should supply you with a separate copy of your results, or tell you whether any illnesses showed up.

RESOURCE

Want to plow through the government's technical guidance on the medical exam? It's published by the Centers for Disease Control and Prevention (CDC). Call 800-311-3435 and ask for a copy of *Technical Instructions for Medical Examination of Aliens,* or go to www.cdc.gov/immigrantrefugeehealth/exams/ti/civil/technical-instructions-civil-surgeons.html.

5. Step Five: At the Border

Assuming all goes well at the visa interview, you will be given an immigrant visa in a sealed envelope (which you must NOT open). But wait—you're not a U.S. resident yet. You'll have six months to use the visa to enter the United States.

At the border, airport, or other port of entry a U.S. border officer will open the sealed envelope containing your visa documents and do a last check to make sure you haven't used fraud. The border officer has expedited removal powers, which means he or she can turn you right around and send you home if he or she sees anything wrong in your packet or with your answers to his questions. When the officer is satisfied that everything is in order, he or she will stamp your passport to show that you're now a U.S. resident (see reproduction of this stamp below; yours will probably have slightly different codes written on it).

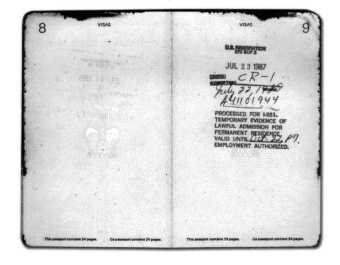

Applying for Immigrant Visa Overseas (Spouses of Permanent Residents)

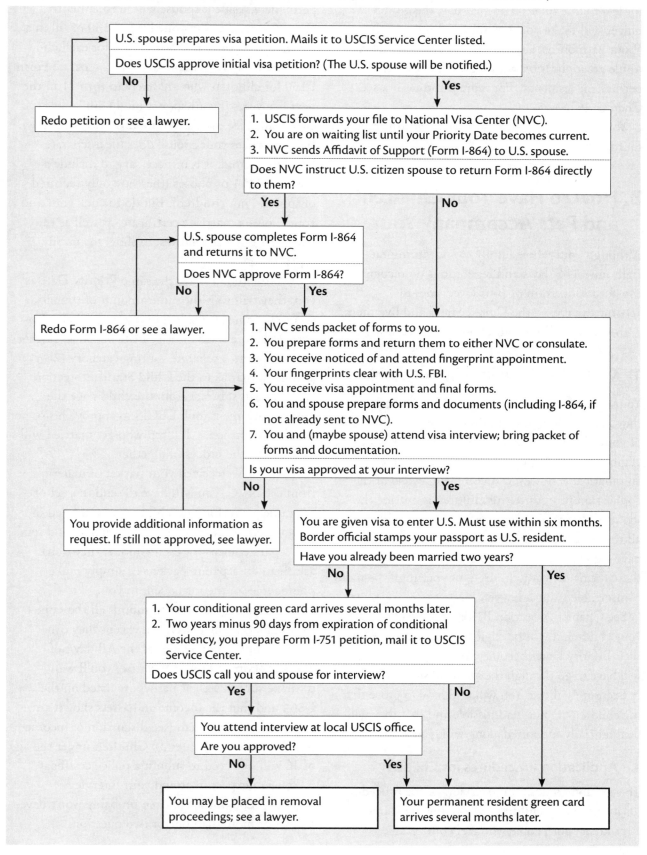

In the unlikely event that you have been married for less than two years on that day, the border officer will make you a conditional resident. In about 21 months, conditional residents will have to file an application with USCIS to convert to permanent residency. For more information, see Chapter 16, Section G.

Your actual green card will arrive within three to four weeks.

B. How to Have Your Children and Pets Accompany You

Although your whole family cannot immigrate right now, U.S. laws and regulations do recognize the need for certain of your loved ones to accompany you to the United States and live there with you, including your children and certain pets.

1. Children of the Immigrant Spouse

Your unmarried foreign-born children, whether they are the biological children or the stepchildren of your U.S. permanent resident spouse, may be eligible to obtain green cards. It won't happen automatically, however. A complete review of the application procedures for children is outside the scope of this book. However, once you've filled in all the paperwork described in this book, you will have a good basis of knowledge with which to fill in these forms for your children; or you might be more comfortable using a lawyer.

See Chapter 2, Section B, for a review of which of your children might be eligible to immigrate. After their Priority Dates become current, your children will have to go through the identical steps described in Section A, above. You will also have to prove that the children are not inadmissible and that they will be financially supported along with you.

a. Application Procedures for Children

This section contains an overview of the procedures for immigrating children. The following is intended as guidance for people who feel comfortable undertaking this process on their own.

To start the process (Step One), your U.S. permanent resident spouse will need either to name the children on your Form I-130 or fill in a separate visa petition (Form I-130) for each child. It is particularly advisable to fill in a separate Form I-130 for children who are likely to turn 21 in the next five years if your spouse might apply for U.S. citizenship (see discussion in Subsection d, below). In cases where your spouse does file a separate I-130 for a child, it is unnecessary to include a Form G-325A or photos (these are only required of spouses, not children). But do include your and your spouse's marriage certificate, as well as the children's birth certificates, to show the family relationships.

If your children have the same Priority Date as you, they will wait the same amount of time for a visa to become available. However, children who turn 21 before their Priority Date becomes current may drop into a separate waiting category (2B); although, thanks to the Child Status Protection Act, you can subtract from the child's age the amount of time it took USCIS to approve his or her I-130 visa petition. Children who get married will drop out of the process altogether.

After you've received your packet of materials from the NVC, you will have to send in a set of the same forms for your children as you filled in for yourself. The National Visa Center should send you separate forms for each child. If they don't, ask them for separate packets or simply make photocopies of the forms sent to you.

The children will have to submit all the same forms and documents as you, except they can simply submit photocopies of the Affidavit of Support (Form I-864). Of course, you'll want to make sure that their names are listed on the I-864 and that the income and assets shown are sufficient to cover them (see discussion of income requirements in Chapter 3). Children under the age of 16 will not need to submit a police certificate.

You can expect to attend your interviews together, though the children probably won't have to answer more than one or two questions.

CAUTION
Check your own country's law on taking your children if their other parent is staying behind. If you will be bringing children to the United States who are not the biological children of your U.S. spouse, or who became the adopted children of another person, it will be up to you to comply with any custody requirements. Even if the children are legally in your custody, you may need to get written consent from the other parent for you to take the children out of the country. U.S. consular officials may also require proof that you have legal custody of your children.

b. What Happens When a Child Beneficiary Turns 21

If there is a chance that your child might turn 21 *before* his or her Priority Date becomes current, watch out! The minute a child hits the 21st birthday, he will automatically drop into a different visa category, from 2A to 2B. The child can, however, subtract from his or her age the amount of time it took USCIS to approve the initial visa petition. This is a protection created in 2002 by the Child Status Protection Act (CSPA). Basically, you have to wait until two events have occurred: your family's visa petition has been approved, and the child's Priority Date has become current. At that time, you add up the number of days that the visa petition was pending with USCIS, and subtract it from the child's actual age. If the result of the calculation is a number less than 21, the child may continue with his or her green card application. (Act quickly, however; the child has only a year after becoming eligible to submit the green card application.)

EXAMPLE 1: Nengah's mother marries a U.S. permanent resident named Frank when Nengah is 17 years old. Immediately after, Frank files a visa petition for the mother that includes Nengah as a derivative. USCIS takes five years to approve the petition, which coincidentally happens right around the time their Priority Date becomes current. By now, Nengah is 22 years old—which, in theory, should drop her into category 2B. Fortunately, under the CSPA, she can subtract the five years that it took USCIS to approve the petition—which puts her age back under 21. As long as Nengah files for permanent residence within one year of becoming eligible, her case should be approved.

EXAMPLE 2: Kareem's father marries a U.S. permanent resident woman named Alyssa when Kareem is 17 years old. Immediately after, Alyssa files a visa petition for the father that includes Kareem as a derivative. It takes USCIS only one year to approve the visa petition. However, another five years pass before Kareem and his father's Priority Date becomes current. By this time, Kareem is 23 years old. Kareem can subtract only one year from his age of 23, which makes him legally 22 years old under the CSPA formula, and thus ineligible to adjust status under category 2A—he'll drop to category 2B and face a longer wait before immigrating.

If the CSPA doesn't help and your child does drop into category 2B, he or she will face a wait of up to a few years before being eligible for a visa. This problem is known as "aging out." (However, if your child turns 21 after your spouse has become a U.S. citizen, his or her prospects may be brighter, as discussed below in Subsection d and Chapter 2, Section B.)

It can be very stressful when a child beneficiary is close to getting his or her visa or green card and is about to turn 21. But until your family's Priority Date has become current, or your spouse becomes a U.S. citizen, there's nothing you can do.

c. What Happens When a Child Beneficiary Marries

In preference categories 2A (children of permanent residents, under age 21) and 2B (children of permanent residents, over age 21), the beneficiaries must be unmarried. If your children marry, their beneficiary status is revoked forever. Their only hope is for you or your spouse to become a U.S. citizen and file a new petition for them later.

If you plan to bring along your children in either the 2A or 2B categories, make sure to advise them not to marry until after they get their green card. (USCIS may not find out about the marriage now, but it often catches such cases when the immigrant applies for U.S. citizenship—and then it strips them of their green card.)

d. What Happens to Your Children When Your Spouse Becomes a U.S. Citizen

As you remember from Section A2, above, if your spouse becomes a U.S. citizen it will help you immigrate more quickly. The same is true for your children's immigration—but there's a twist. Children of U.S. citizens need to have their own visa petitions (Forms I-130) on file with USCIS in order to immigrate as children of a U.S. citizen. They can't enjoy the benefits of that parent's new citizenship if they are merely named on their immigrating parent's petition.

When this whole process began, your spouse may have simply entered your children's names on the I-130 visa petition for you—which would have been enough for them to immigrate if he or she had remained a permanent resident. To put this in more technical terms, your children were eligible to immigrate as your derivative beneficiaries when your spouse was a permanent resident, but once your spouse became a U.S. citizen, they lost their derivative beneficiary status. They now need to have visa petitions of their own.

Fortunately, it's not too late for your spouse to file separate visa petitions for your children even after becoming a citizen. So long as the children are still unmarried, under age 21, and are your spouse's natural children or legal stepchildren (that is, the marriage took place before they turned 18), they qualify as immediate relatives just like you. As immediate relatives, they will be able to immigrate at the same time as you. It may take several months for the new visa petitions to be approved, but for

most children, it should all work out in the end. However, there are three groups of children who are, to varying degrees, still left out in the cold: those who have married, those who are not your spouse's legal stepchildren, and those who have turned 21.

Children who have married. Your children who have married could not have immigrated with you when your spouse was a permanent resident, so your spouse's citizenship doesn't actually make their situation worse. In fact, it could improve their situation if your spouse is the children's natural father or legal stepfather, because your spouse can file a visa petition for them in the third preference category.

Children who are not your spouse's legal stepchildren. As part of filing new visa petitions for your children, your spouse will have to prove that he or she has a direct relationship with each child, either as natural parent or legal stepparent. To be their legal stepparent, your spouse will have to show that your marriage took place before the child turned 18. If it didn't, then that child cannot immigrate until you yourself become a permanent resident and file a second preference visa petition for your child.

Children who have turned 21. If your child has turned 21 and no separate visa petition was filed for him or her, you're in for some extra work. As with your other children, your U.S. citizen spouse can file a new, separate visa petition if he or she is the child's natural parent or legal stepparent— but if you don't alert them to the situation, your child won't become an immediate relative like you. Instead, the child will be put into the first preference visa category, which is subject to annual quotas. The child will get a Priority Date, but it will be at the very end of the first preference waiting list.

> **EXAMPLE:** Ricardo, a U.S. permanent resident, filed an I-130 visa petition for his Mexican wife Soledad and their four children on January 2, 2006. Soledad got an approval notice showing her January 2, 2006 Priority Date. Because the children were named

on the I-130 visa petition and Ricardo was a permanent resident, USCIS knew that the children were derivative beneficiaries and shared Soledad's Priority Date. But on February 3, 2010 Ricardo was sworn in as a U.S. citizen. No more derivative beneficiaries for this family; Ricardo must file a separate I-130 for each child. He does so, on February 10, 2010. That works fine for three of his children, who are under age 21—as minor, unmarried children of a U.S. citizen, they are still immediate relatives and immediately eligible for a visa, just like their mother. But the fourth child, Jorge, has since turned 21. Jorge's Priority Date is now February 10, 2010. If you look on the *Visa Bulletin* chart in Section A2, above, you'll see that in his category, Mexico first preference, the current Priority Date is October 15, 1992. Jorge is facing an approximate 18-year wait for a visa. If Ricardo had planned ahead and filed a separate I-130 for Jorge in 2006 when he filed for the rest of the family, he could have shaved at least four years off Jorge's wait.

But this isn't fair! True enough. Luckily, there is a remedy for children in this situation. When your U.S. citizen spouse files the new visa petition, he or she can ask the USCIS Service Center not to put the child at the bottom of the waiting list, but to give him or her the same Priority Date as the rest of the family, even in this new category. In other words, your spouse asks USCIS to pretend that a separate I-130 visa petition was submitted for the over-21-year-old at the same time that the visa petition for the whole family was submitted, perhaps years ago.

This is called "recapturing" a Priority Date. Below is a sample letter showing how to ask for a recapture. The petitioner also needs to include complete copies of the original I-130 visa petition, the original INS or USCIS approval notice showing the family's old Priority Date, and the petitioner's citizenship certificate.

Approval of recaptured dates is supposed to be automatic. Unfortunately, the USCIS Service Centers aren't used to this procedure and may pay no attention to your request—even if you write the most compelling letter and include complete documentation. You might get an approval notice showing a new Priority Date rather than your family's old one. Your only recourse would be to write many letters trying to get USCIS to correct the date.

> **TIP**
> **Plan ahead—submit separate I-130 visa petitions for any children who will soon turn 21.** If you are at the beginning of the immigration process, have children who may turn 21 before the process ends, and your spouse is likely to apply for U.S. citizenship, you can avoid the hassles involved in recapturing Priority Dates. Your spouse should simply file separate petitions for them from the outset.

2. Your Pets

Good news for your dog and cat, who may not have learned to sign their names yet—they won't need a visa. Bringing pets into the United States is not an immigration law matter. But before bringing any pets to the United States, check into U.S. customs restrictions. In general, pets will be allowed in if they are in good health and have had all the proper vaccinations. Some restrictions apply, however. For example, some states do not permit certain kinds of animals, and monkeys aren't allowed into the United States at all. Check with your local U.S. consulate for details, or read more at www.cbg.gov (enter "pets" into the search box, which will bring up a publication called "Pets and Wildlife: Licensing and Health Requirements").

> **SKIP AHEAD**
> **For what to do after you have obtained your visa and entered the United States, see Chapter 16.**

Letter Requesting Recaptured Priority Date

111 Seaside Lane
Orlando, FL 32801

June 1, 20xx

USCIS
P.O. Box XXX
[See Appendix B for the complete address of the USCIS office serving your geographic region.]

RE: Petitioner: Ricardo Torres
       Beneficiary: Jorge Torres
       I-130 Visa Petition with Priority Date Recapture Request

Dear Sir/Madam:

I am the Petitioner named above. Enclosed please find an I-130 visa petition for the above-named Beneficiary (my son) with supporting documents, including:

1. Copy of my son's birth certificate

2. Copy of his mother's and my marriage certificate

3. Copy of my citizenship certificate

4. Fee of $420 (money order).

In addition, please note that I am requesting a recapture of an earlier Priority Date for this application. My son was formerly a Derivative Beneficiary on an approved visa petition that I filed for his mother in 20xx, with Priority Date January 2, 20xx. I recently became a U.S. citizen, and so my son lost his derivative status. Please grant my son the earlier, January 2, 20xx, Priority Date on the approval of this I-130 petition. In support of this request, I also enclose the following:

1. Copy of original I-130, showing my son's name

2. Copy of USCIS notice approving this I-130, with January 2, 20xx, Priority Date.

Thank you for your attention to this matter.

Very truly yours,

Ricardo Torres

Ricardo Torres

Fiancés in the U.S. Engaged to U.S. Citizens

If you are in the United States—legally or illegally—and are engaged to marry a U.S. citizen, you are one step away from being, in immigration law lingo, an immediate relative. Of all the different classes of applicants for U.S. visas, immediate relatives will get them the quickest.

That one step, however, is to get married. Once you are married, a green card will be available to you as soon as you can get through the application procedures. There are no limits to the numbers of immediate relatives allowed to apply for permanent residence each year, and the only waiting period is the time it takes for your paperwork to be processed by the U.S. immigration authorities.

If you marry and apply as an immediate relative, the application process you'll use and where you'll live during the process—in the U.S. or abroad—depends on whether you entered the United States legally or illegally. For example, if you entered legally with a tourist visa but stayed beyond the expiration date, you have entered the country legally and may apply for your visa here. On the other hand, if you entered without permission, such as by crossing at an unguarded point on the U.S. border, you entered illegally and must apply from abroad. Start by reading Section A to see whether your entry is considered legal or illegal, then move on to the sections that match your current situation.

Because of the benefits of being an immediate relative, there is very little reason to delay your marriage. However, this chapter will discuss all your immigration options, including returning home and applying for either a fiancé visa or a marriage-based immigrant or nonimmigrant visa. Once you decide what procedure you want to use, you'll be directed to the appropriate chapter to begin the process.

A. Did You Enter Legally or Illegally?

If you entered the United States with permission of the U.S. authorities, you entered legally. Whether you got that permission in advance or were simply allowed in when you arrived, the important thing is that you were personally met and allowed to enter by an officer of the U.S. border control. This could occur either at the border itself or at some other port of entry such as an airport, seaport, or bus station. The usual ways people enter legally are:

- with a visa, such as a tourist, student, or temporary worker visa
- with a border crossing card (a special pass allowing regular entries), and
- under the Visa Waiver Program, where citizens of certain countries are allowed to enter the U.S. as tourists by showing their passport, without first obtaining an entry visa.

An illegal entry is, naturally, the opposite of a legal entry. People entering illegally have failed to obtain permission to enter. They may pay someone to sneak them across the U.S. border, wait until the dead of night and find an unguarded point on the U.S. border, or conceal themselves in the trunk of someone's car. USCIS says that they entered "without inspection," which means that they weren't personally met and approved for entry by a U.S. border control official. (USCIS refers to such people as "EWIs," pronounced "ee-wee," which stands for entry without inspection.) People who entered the United States without inspection, or illegally, will have a very difficult time obtaining a green card.

 SKIP AHEAD
If you entered the United States by crossing the border illegally, skip ahead to Section C.

B. Fiancés Who Entered the U.S. Legally

This section explains the entry options for foreign nationals who entered the United States legally and still live there. If this describes your situation, you have a choice among three immigration paths:

- Get married and immediately apply for your green card at a USCIS office (even if the expiration date of your visa has passed). This path is explained below in Section 1.

- Leave the United States before you have overstayed your visa by six months or more and apply at a U.S. consulate to return on a fiancé visa. This choice is explained below in Section 2.
- Leave the United States before you have overstayed your visa by six months or more, get married, and apply at a U.S. consulate to return on an immigrant visa (green card) or nonimmigrant visa (a special version of the fiancé visa for married couples). This option is explained below in Section 3.

> **CAUTION**
>
> **If you overstay your visa.** If you have stayed in the United States without permission for six months or more at any time since April 1, 1997, you shouldn't leave at all until you have a green card. That's because you could be barred from returning for three or ten years, depending how long you overstayed. See Chapter 2, Section A, for more on this issue.

1. Overview of the U.S. Marriage-Based Green Card Option

If you and your U.S. citizen fiancé get married, you will, as someone who entered legally, be one of few immigrants eligible to stay in the United States while you apply and wait for your green card. The fact that you entered the United States legally and that your spouse is a U.S. citizen is a magic combination. It allows you to get your green card through a procedure called adjustment of status. Using this procedure, you can apply for permanent residence without leaving the United States, even if you have stayed past the date when you were originally supposed to leave (which is most likely the expiration date of your visa).

EXAMPLE: Marbelita came to the United States in May, on a tourist visa. While enjoying the view from the Empire State Building, she struck up a conversation with Bill, a U.S. citizen. They fell in love, and Marbelita couldn't bear to leave when her tourist visa expired in July. She and Bill married in August. Although she is now in the United States illegally, the combination of her legal entry and Bill's status as a U.S. citizen allows her to apply for her green card (adjustment of status) at a local USCIS office. As soon as Marbelita submits that application, her stay will become legal and she and Bill can live together in the United States while awaiting approval of her green card. Of course, there are other hurdles they must cross, including convincing USCIS that their marriage is real and not simply a way for Marbelita to stay in the United States.

There are many benefits to staying in the United States during the application process. You will avoid being separated from your spouse and will receive a permit to work while you wait to attend the final green card interview at a local USCIS office. Although your spouse will be required to accompany you to that interview (which is not required of overseas applicants), this is actually an advantage, both for moral support and because a large part of the discussion will concern your spouse's ability to support you financially. And unlike overseas interviews, at a stateside interview you can bring an attorney with you if your case has become complicated during the application process. For instance, if you realize that you might fall into a ground of inadmissibility, you'll need a lawyer's help to argue that it doesn't apply.

a. Entering on a Temporary Visa Might Pose a Problem

If you used a temporary visa—such as a tourist visa—to enter the United States, planning all along to get married, you might find yourself facing accusations of visa fraud if you apply to adjust status in the United States. Particularly if you knew your spouse before arriving in the United States, and you used a temporary visa to enter, USCIS is likely to be suspicious. At the interview where your green card would normally be approved, USCIS might question you about whether your real intention when you arrived was to apply for permanent residence after your marriage. Unless you entered on a fiancé visa, the discovery that this was your real intention will lead USCIS to demand that you file an additional application requesting a waiver or forgiveness of your visa fraud. (See Chapter 1, Section B2, if you think you might be in this category.)

Of course, if you met your spouse after you arrived in the United States, this won't be a problem. And even for other couples, uncertainties about their marriage plans, as well as the length of time they waited to get married, often satisfy USCIS that they didn't misuse an entry visa.

b. Two-Year Testing Period for New Marriages

You must be married for two years to obtain a permanent green card. Since most people will apply for their adjustment of status soon after marrying, they will first be given a conditional green card, which is valid for only two years. You won't be kicked out of the country after the two years—provided you don't forget to file the next application. This is an application for a permanent green card, which sometimes involves an interview to allow USCIS to take a second look at whether your marriage is real. (See Chapter 16, Section G, for more on this issue.)

c. Your Children

Your unmarried children under age 21 may also be eligible to submit applications to adjust status along with you.

SKIP AHEAD

If you are certain that you wish to marry and adjust status in the United States, go straight to Chapter 11 for instructions on the first step, the visa petition to be filed by your spouse.

2. Overview of the Fiancé Visa Option

As long as you leave the United States before overstaying your visa by six months or more, your planned marriage to a U.S. citizen should qualify you for a fiancé ("K-1") visa in order to return. (See Chapter 2, Section B, for the eligibility requirements for a fiancé visa.) If you overstay by six months or more or have stayed in the United States illegally for six continuous months at any time after April 1997, however, this option disappears. You will need a waiver (official government forgiveness) of your illegal stay in order to return before three or ten years are up. You won't be eligible for a waiver unless you're married—these waivers are not available to mere fiancés of U.S. citizens.

If you decide to leave and apply for a fiancé visa, it will allow you to enter the United States, marry within 90 days, and apply for your green card in the United States. Your unmarried children under age 21 will be eligible to accompany you. There are no quotas or limits on the number of people who can obtain fiancé visas and subsequently green cards through marriage to a U.S. citizen. A fiancé visa usually takes at least six months to obtain.

a. For a U.S. Marriage Only

A fiancé visa gives you no choice but to hold your marriage ceremony in the United States. Couples often ask whether their overseas marriage really counts, or wonder why they can't just get married for a second time after entering on a fiancé visa.

Unfortunately, once you're legally married, no matter where the marriage occurred, you no longer qualify for a fiancé (K-1) visa. You must apply for U.S. entry as the spouse of a U.S. citizen.

However, married people can use a type of fiancé visa called a "K-3," which is intended to save them a little time (but doesn't always). To find out more about K-3 visas, see Section 3, below.

TIP

Wedding ceremonies that don't result in legally binding marriages won't stand in your way. If you don't feel right leaving home unmarried, see if you can arrange for a religious or other ceremony that will not be legally recognized or registered in your country. USCIS does not recognize these as valid marriages. You will need to have a legal marriage in the United States once you get here.

b. The Green Card Application Will Be Separate

Fiancés wishing to live in the United States will need to marry and apply for their green card within the 90 days they are allowed to stay in the United States on their fiancé visa, using a procedure called adjustment of status. This application procedure usually takes between five months and a year to complete and involves even more paperwork than the fiancé visa.

SKIP AHEAD

If you are certain that you wish to leave the United States and apply for a fiancé visa overseas, go straight to Chapter 5, Section F, for further instructions. This petition can be filed before or after you leave the United States.

3. Overview of the Marriage-Based Visa (Consular) Option

For most married applicants, adjustment of status in the United States is the preferred way to obtain permanent residence. However, a second option for people who haven't overstayed their visa by six months or more is to leave the United States and apply for a green card at a U.S. consulate overseas.

Although the procedural steps to apply for a green card are very similar to those for obtaining a fiancé visa, the application itself is somewhat more demanding. At the final interview, you can be accompanied by your spouse if you wish, but not by an attorney.

It makes sense to apply for your U.S. residency at a consulate only if doing so will significantly speed up the green card approval process. The adjustment of status process in the United States usually takes between five months and a year. The application process for a green card through a consulate may take a year, but some consulates are much more efficient and will approve an application within months.

By the way, another visa option for married couples at U.S. consulates is a K-3 nonimmigrant visa, but it doesn't get you a green card—it only gets you back into the United States, where you have to spend another four or five months applying for your green card. That means it's probably not a good option for you.

Contact the U.S. consulate in your home country (and ask other immigrants about their experience with that consulate) to find out how long the consulate takes for green card application and approval.

To find out how long it is taking your local USCIS office to process applications for adjustment of status, go www.uscis.gov and, in the bar on the left-hand side of the page, click "Processing Times," then click on the next page, choose your local field office from the "Field Office" drop-down menu, and click "Field Office Processing Dates." In the table that appears, you'll find the I-485 processing time frame.

CAUTION

Carry proof of when you depart the United States. If you decide to apply for your green card at a U.S. consulate, your history of U.S. visits will trigger a request that you prove you left on time. Collect and keep all evidence, such as your plane tickets, store receipts, medical records, credit card statements, and anything else relevant. (See Chapter 2, Section A, for the rules on and penalties for overstaying a U.S. visa by six months or more.)

a. Two-Year Testing Period for New Marriages

You must be married for two years to obtain a permanent green card. Since most people will apply for their immigrant visa and green card soon after marrying, they will be given only a conditional green card, which is valid for two years. You won't be kicked out of the country after the two years—provided you don't forget to file the next application. This is an application for a permanent green card, which sometimes involves an interview to allow USCIS to take a second look at whether your marriage is real. (See Chapter 16, Section G, for more on this issue.)

b. Your Children

Your unmarried children under age 21 may also be eligible to submit applications for immigrant visas along with you.

> **SKIP AHEAD**
>
> **If you are certain that you wish to leave the United States and apply overseas, go straight to Chapter 7 for instructions on the first step, the visa petition to be filed by your spouse.** This petition can be filed before or after you leave the United States.

4. If You Have Children 18–21

If you have children between the ages of 18 and 21 who are not the biological children or stepchildren of your spouse and you want to bring them to the United States, you should, if possible, leave and apply for a fiancé visa. Due to a nonsensical twist in the immigration laws, children under 21 can accompany a fiancé on his or her visa and then apply for a green card, but only children whose parents married when the child was under 18 can qualify as stepchildren and accompany a just-married spouse on an immigrant visa or apply for a green card.

Don't even think of leaving the United States if, after April 1, 1997, you or your children have overstayed your right to be there by six months or more, on this visa or any other visa. You could be barred from reentering the United States for up to ten years under these circumstances. (See the discussion of time bars in Chapter 2, Section A.)

C. Fiancés Who Entered the U.S. Illegally

This section explains the immigration choices for foreign nationals who entered the United States illegally and still live there. If you've come to the United States illegally more than once, spent a total of a year or more during your previous visits, and/or were deported at the end of a visit, see an attorney before going any further. You may be permanently barred from immigrating to the United States. (See Chapter 2, Section A, for further review of the permanent bar.)

Assuming these difficulties don't apply to you, there are three options for you to consider if you entered the United States illegally and are engaged to marry a U.S. citizen. You can:

- Marry, stay, and see if you will be allowed to adjust your status to permanent resident in the United States. This path is explained below in Section 1.
- Marry and leave, then apply for an immigrant visa to return. If you stayed illegally in the United States for more than six months, accompany your application with a request for a waiver (forgiveness) of your illegal stay. If the waiver is denied, you may be barred from returning for three or ten years. This choice is covered in Section 2, below.
- Leave the United States before you have been here illegally for six months and apply at a U.S. consulate to return on a fiancé visa. This option is described in Section 3, below.

1. Marry and Adjust Status in the United States

As the fiancé of a U.S. citizen, you are theoretically one step away from being an immediate relative—an immigrant who is immediately eligible for a green card. You will be an immediate relative as soon as you get married. Unfortunately, your eligibility may not get you a green card anytime soon. The trouble is that only certain categories of immigrants are allowed to apply for their green card in the United States (using the procedure called adjustment of status). People who entered the United States without being inspected and admitted by a U.S. official are not among them.

However, a very few people might be lucky enough to fall into an exception, based on having started the application process before the laws changed and made them ineligible. You may be eligible to adjust status in the United States if an employer or a family member of yours (whether it was your spouse or someone else) filed an immigrant visa petition (Form I-130 for family members) on your behalf either:

- before January 14, 1998, or
- between January 14, 1998 and April 30, 2001, if you can also prove that you were physically present in the United States on December 21, 2000.

If your visa petition was approved, or was denied only because of a mistake by USCIS, you may be allowed to adjust status in the United States. (For more details on this issue, see Chapter 2, Section A.) If you have the I-130 petition on file as described above, you have a ticket to adjust your status and get your green card without leaving, even though you entered the United States illegally.

If you fall into this exception, by all means get married and file for adjustment of status in the United States. This is especially true if you have stayed in the United States for more than six months. If you were to leave and try to apply for your green card at a U.S. consulate overseas, the consulate could punish your illegal stay by preventing your return to the United States for three or ten years.

SKIP AHEAD

If you are sure this option will work for you, proceed directly to Chapter 11, Section D, for instructions on how to begin the application process.

2. Marry, Leave, and Apply for an Immigrant Visa to Return

If you do not fall into one of the exceptional categories of immigrants who are allowed to stay in the United States to use the adjustment of status procedure, you must decide whether you can get a visa overseas at a U.S. consulate. This will depend on how long you have stayed illegally in the United States. If you have not stayed in the United States more than six months, proceed to Subsection a, below. If you have stayed in the United States illegally longer than six months, proceed to Subsection b below.

a. If You Have Stayed Illegally for Fewer Than Six Months

If you don't fit into the exceptions described in Section C1 above, but you haven't yet stayed in the United States illegally for more than six months, your safest bet is to get married and leave before that date rolls around. Leaving now will at least protect you from being found inadmissible based on your unlawful presence.

After leaving, you can get a marriage-based immigrant visa because of your immediate relative status (spouse of a U.S. citizen). This may mean many months of separation from your spouse while you wait overseas for your green card to be approved. But months of separation now might be better than being denied a green card later, if you stay too long illegally in the United States.

CAUTION

Carry proof of when you depart the United States. If you decide to apply for your green card at a U.S. consulate, your history of U.S. visits will trigger a request that you prove how much time you spent there. Collect and keep all evidence, such as your plane tickets, store receipts, medical records, credit card statements, and anything else relevant. (See Chapter 2, Section A, for the rules on and penalties for staying in the U.S. illegally for six months or more.)

SKIP AHEAD

If you are sure you will use this option, go to Chapter 7 for further instructions on your immigration process.

SKIP AHEAD

If you are ineligible to adjust status and definitely have a time bar problem, skip to Section 3 below.

b. If You Have Stayed Illegally for More Than Six Months

If you are not eligible to apply for a green card (adjust status) in the United States upon marrying, and you have stayed illegally in the United States for more than six months, you are in a tough situation. You can't get a green card by staying in the United States; but if you leave, you face being barred from reentering the United States—for three years if your stay was between six months and a year, and for ten years if your stay was more than one year.

You should see an attorney, and not just any immigration lawyer. Look for an attorney who has actual experience with this problem. The attorney can help you consider whether you can ask the U.S. government to forgive your illegal stay. Previously, applicants for this waiver (called an "I-601") would have to leave the U.S. and apply at a U.S. consulate along with their application for permanent residence. This carried the significant risk that their waiver might be denied, blocking their return to the United States for either three or ten years, depending on the length of their unlawful stay.

However, USCIS recently announced a proposed rules change, which would allow applicants to apply for the I-601 waiver while still in the United States. That way, they could wait for an approval of their waiver before leaving for their consular interview.

As of the publication of this book, these new rules had not yet been implemented, so you'll definitely need to see an attorney for the latest (and check for updates on Nolo's website).

In the meantime, watch out for so-called "immigration advisers" or "notarios," who pretend to help with immigration applications but are not licensed to practice law. They have already begun telling people they can help file an I-601 under the new procedures, and charging them for an application that may only get the applicant into trouble. See Chapter 17 for assistance on finding a licensed immigration attorney.

Unfortunately, there's no guarantee that you'll get a waiver. You'll have to prove that the denial of your visa would cause extreme hardship to your U.S. spouse or children—and when the law says extreme, it means much more than the sadness your spouse and children will feel at your being thousands of miles away. The classic case of extreme hardship is someone whose U.S. citizen spouse has severe medical problems that require the other spouse's constant attention.

There is another option, which we don't recommend. You could stay in the United States illegally, hoping that the immigration laws change in your favor and make you eligible for a green card. Many couples have done this, but it is a huge gamble. Recent changes in the immigration laws have made them harsher, not gentler, on immigrants; and there is no sign that this trend will change. But none of us have a crystal ball, and some families find it unthinkable to separate now, come what may later. If you take this option, however, you must be aware that you will likely never obtain legal residence in the United States and will face the ever-present possibility of being caught, deported, and prevented from reentering the United States for at least ten years.

3. Leave Before Six Months and Apply for a K-1 Fiancé Visa to Return

If you have been in the United States for less than six months and you have not married, you can consider leaving and applying for a K-1 fiancé visa to return. Stay over six months, however, and this option disappears. You will need a waiver (official government forgiveness) of your illegal stay in order to return before three or ten years are up. These waivers are not available to fiancés—as opposed to spouses—of U.S. citizens.

Assuming you haven't stayed six months illegally, your planned marriage to a U.S. citizen should qualify you for a fiancé visa. (See Chapter 2, Section B, for the eligibility requirements.) A fiancé visa will allow you to enter the United States, marry within 90 days, and apply for your green card in the United States. Your unmarried children under age 21 will be eligible to accompany you.

There are no quotas or limits on the number of people who can obtain fiancé visas and subsequent green cards through marriage to a U.S. citizen. A fiancé visa usually takes at least six months to obtain.

a. For U.S. Marriage Only

A K-1 fiancé visa gives you no choice but to hold your marriage ceremony in the United States. Couples often ask whether their overseas marriage really counts, or wonder why they can't just get married for a second time after entering on a fiancé visa. Unfortunately, once you're legally married, no matter where the marriage occurred, you no longer qualify for a K-1 fiancé visa and you must apply for U.S. residency as the spouse of a U.S. citizen.

You should also know about an alternative visa, call the K-3 visa, available to already-married couples. The K-3 visa is a special form of fiancé visa, which allows a married immigrant to enter the United States as a temporary nonimmigrant, and then complete a green card application process after arriving in the United States. For more information on K-3 fiancé visas, see Chapter 7.

TIP

Wedding ceremonies that don't result in legally binding marriages won't stand in your way. If you don't feel right leaving home unmarried, see if you can arrange for a religious or other ceremony that will not be legally recognized or registered in your country. USCIS does not recognize these as valid marriages. You will need to have a legal marriage in the United States once you get here.

b. The Green Card Application Will Be Separate

Fiancés wishing to live in the United States will need to marry and apply for their green card during the 90 days they are allowed to stay in the United States on their fiancé visa, using a procedure called adjustment of status. This application procedure usually takes between five months and a year to complete and involves even more paperwork than the fiancé visa.

4. If You Have Children 18–21

If you have children between the ages of 18 and 21 who are not the biological children or stepchildren of your spouse, and you want to bring them to the United States, you should, if possible, leave and apply for a fiancé visa. Due to a nonsensical twist in the immigration laws, children under 21 can accompany a fiancé on his or her visa, but only children whose parents married while the child was under 18 can qualify as stepchildren and accompany a just-married spouse on an immigrant visa or apply for a green card.

Don't even think of leaving the United States if you or your children have stayed there illegally for six months or more, at any time since April 1, 1997. You could be barred from reentering the United States for up to ten years under these circumstances. (See the discussion of time bars in Chapter 2, Section A.)

Next Step If You Entered The U.S. Legally

If you decide to get married and apply for your green card in the United States:	See Chapter 11 covering spouses of U.S. citizens living in the U.S. Go to Section D, which covers the first application.
If you decide to leave the United States unmarried before overstaying by six months or more, and apply for a K-1 fiancé visa:	See Chapter 5, Section F, for fiancé visa application procedures.
If you decide to marry (abroad or in the U.S.), leave the United States, and apply for an immigrant visa:	See Chapter 7 for marriage-based visa application procedures.
If none of the above options work:	See an attorney; Chapter 17 contains tips on finding a good one.

Next Step If You Entered The U.S. Ilegally

If you decide to get married and can adjust in the United States:	See Chapter 11 for spouses of U.S. citizens living in the United States. Go to Section D, which covers the first application.
If you have not stayed illegally for more than six months and decide to leave the United States and apply for a fiancé visa:	See Chapter 5, Section F, regarding fiancé visa application procedures.
If you have not stayed illegally for more than six months and decide to leave the United States and apply for a marriage-based immigrant visa:	See Chapter 7 regarding marriage visa application procedures for overseas spouses of U.S. citizens.
If none of the above options work:	See an attorney; Chapter 17 contains tips on finding a good one.

Fiancés in the U.S. Engaged to Permanent Residents

If you are in the United States—legally or illegally —and are engaged to marry a U.S. lawful permanent resident, you are not immediately eligible to obtain permanent residence (a green card) on this basis. Only foreign nationals married to *U.S. citizens* are immediately eligible for permanent residence.

No one will stop you from getting married in the United States—in fact, getting married will take you one step closer to a green card, by allowing you to get on the waiting list for one. But there are quotas for the number of spouses of permanent residents who are allowed green cards each year, which means there are long waiting lists. Many newlyweds will have to live outside the United States while their names sit on a waiting list for a marriage-based visa—a wait of three to five years.

The key to knowing how and where—in the U.S. or overseas—you'll get your green card is whether you entered the United States legally or illegally. For example, if you entered with permission, such as with a tourist visa, but stayed beyond the expiration date, you have entered the country legally and may be able to get your green card in the United States. On the other hand, if you entered illegally, for example by crossing secretly at an unguarded point, you lose certain important procedural rights—you may have to leave the United States right away if you want to get a green card later. Start by reading Section A to see whether your entry is considered legal or illegal, then move to the subsections that match your current situation.

A. Did You Enter Legally or Illegally?

If you entered the United States with permission of the U.S. authorities, you entered legally. Whether you got that permission in advance or were simply allowed in when you arrived, the important thing is that you were personally met and allowed to enter by an officer of the U.S. border control. This could occur either at the border itself or at some other port of entry such as an airport, seaport, or bus station. The usual ways people enter legally are:

- with a visa (a tourist, student, or temporary worker visa, for example)
- with a border crossing card (a special pass allowing regular entries)
- under the Visa Waiver Program (where citizens of certain countries are allowed to enter the U.S. as tourists by showing their passport, without first obtaining an entry visa).

An illegal entry is, naturally, the opposite of a legal entry. People entering illegally have failed to obtain permission to enter. They may pay someone to sneak them across the U.S. border, wait until the dead of night and find an unguarded point on the U.S. border, or conceal themselves in the trunk of someone else's car. USCIS says that they entered "without inspection," which means that they weren't personally met and approved for entry by a U.S. border control official. (USCIS refers to such people as "EWIs," pronounced "ee-wee," which stands for entry without inspection.) The immigration laws make getting a green card very difficult for people who entered the United States without inspection, or illegally.

SKIP AHEAD
If you entered the United States by crossing the border illegally, skip ahead to Section C.

B. Fiancés Who Entered the U.S. Legally

This section explains the immigration options for foreign nationals who entered the United States legally, as defined in Section A above, and still live there. Even if you are living in the U.S. illegally now, this section is for you.

Before we discuss your actual visa options, let's sweep away one myth. A fiancé visa is not an option for you. Fiancé visas are not given to fiancés of permanent residents, and they're not given to people already inside the United States. They are only available to the fiancés of U.S. citizens living overseas.

This said, you do have two options. You can:
- wait until your fiancé becomes a U.S. citizen, then apply for a fiancé or a marriage-based visa, as explained below in Section 1, or
- marry your fiancé and request a green card as the spouse of a lawful permanent resident, covered in Section 2.

CAUTION
Don't delay. If you are close to the end of your legal stay in the United States you must act quickly. Despite your planned marriage, it may be necessary to leave the United States very soon in order to get a green card later. See Chapter 2, Section A, for more on the consequences of visa overstays.

1. If Your Fiancé Becomes a U.S. Citizen

In order to become a U.S. citizen, your fiancé must have been a U.S. permanent resident for five years (with some exceptions), lived in the United States for at least half of those years, be of good moral character, and pass an exam covering the English language as well as U.S. history and government. To learn more about becoming a U.S. citizen, see the USCIS website at www.uscis.gov or *Becoming a U.S. Citizen: A Guide to the Law, Exam & Interview*, by Ilona Bray (Nolo).

To help speed your progress toward a green card, your fiancé should look into the requirements for U.S. citizenship, and apply as soon as he or she can. As soon as your fiancé obtains U.S. citizenship, you can:
- get married and immediately apply for your green card at a USCIS office (even if the expiration date of your visa has passed)
- leave the United States before overstaying your visa by six months or more and apply at a U.S. consulate to return on a fiancé visa, or

- leave the United States before overstaying your visa by six months or more and, once you're married, apply at a U.S. consulate to return on an immigrant visa (green card) or a K-3 nonimmigrant visa.

These options are discussed fully in Chapter 9, covering fiancés of U.S. citizens living in the United States.

CAUTION
Be careful about leaving the United States if you have an expired visa or status. If you have stayed six months or more past the expiration date of your visa, try to avoid the options that involve leaving the United States before obtaining your permanent resident status. You could be barred from returning to the United States for three or ten years, depending how long you overstayed. See Chapter 2, Section A, for more on this issue.

2. If You Marry Your Permanent Resident Fiancé

If you marry your permanent resident fiancé while in the United States or abroad, you become what the immigration law calls a preference relative. This means that you become eligible for permanent residence in the United States—but not right away. There are annual quotas and long waiting lists for people in this category. You will not be able to legally live in the United States with your spouse during the waiting period unless you have another type of visa that allows you to stay the entire time. Your options boil down to the following:
- stay in the United States legally (if your nonimmigrant visa lasts long enough to get you through the waiting period) and adjust your status to permanent resident in the United States
- stay in the United States illegally, hoping to adjust your status to green card holder in the United States
- leave the United States before you have overstayed your visa by six months or more,

wait overseas, then apply for a green card at a U.S. consulate

- leave the United States after you have overstayed your visa by more than six months but less than one year (thereby avoiding the more severe ten-year time bar), wait overseas, then apply for a green card at a U.S. consulate, or

- leave the United States after you have overstayed your visa by more than six months or a year, wait overseas, then apply for your green card and request a waiver (forgiveness) of your overstay at a U.S. consulate.

Learn more about each of the above options in Chapter 12 covering spouses of U.S. permanent residents.

C. Fiancés Who Entered the U.S. Illegally

The advice in this section is for foreign fiancés living in the United States after crossing the border illegally. If you are close to having stayed illegally for six months in the United States, you must act quickly. When you ultimately go to a U.S. consulate to apply for your green card, you could face severe penalties if you've passed the six-month mark. You may not be able to return to the United States for up to ten years. See Chapter 2, Section A, for more on the consequences of visa overstays.

⊘ **CAUTION**
If this is your second time (or more) in the United States and you spent a total of a year or more during your previous visits and/or were deported at the end of a visit, see an attorney before going any further. You may be permanently barred from immigrating to the United States. See Chapter 2, Section A, for further review of the permanent bar.

Before we discuss your actual visa options, let's sweep away one myth. A fiancé visa is not an option for you. Fiancé visas are not given to fiancés of permanent residents, and they're not given to people already inside the United States. They are

available only to the fiancés of U.S. citizens living overseas.

This said, you do have a choice of methods for immigrating to the United States:

- wait until your fiancé becomes a U.S. citizen, then apply for a fiancé or a marriage-based visa (either will probably involve leaving the United States first), as explained in Section 1

- marry your fiancé and request a green card application as the spouse of a lawful permanent resident (which will probably involve leaving the United States first), as explained in Section 2.

⊘ **CAUTION**
Be careful about leaving the United States if you have stayed illegally for six months or more. If you have, try to avoid the options that involve leaving before obtaining your permanent resident status. You could be barred from returning to the United States for three or ten years, depending how long you stayed illegally. See Chapter 2, Section A, for more on this issue.

1. If Your Fiancé Becomes a U.S. Citizen

In order to become a U.S. citizen, your fiancé must have been a U.S. permanent resident for five years (with some exceptions), lived in the United States for at least half of those years, be of good moral character, and pass an exam covering the English language as well as U.S. history and government. To learn more about becoming a U.S. citizen, see the USCIS website at www.uscis.gov or *Becoming a U.S. Citizen: A Guide to the Law, Exam & Interview*, by Ilona Bray (Nolo).

To help speed your progress toward a green card, your fiancé should look into the requirements for U.S. citizenship and apply as soon as he or she can. As soon as your fiancé obtains U.S. citizenship, you can:

- marry and leave, then apply for an immigrant visa to return. If you stayed illegally in the United States for more than six months, accompany your application with a request for a waiver (forgiveness) of your illegal stay. Get a lawyer's help with this—if the waiver is denied, you may be barred from returning for three or ten years.

- leave the United States before you have been here illegally for six months and apply at a U.S. consulate to return on a fiancé visa.

These options are discussed fully in Chapter 9, covering fiancés of U.S. citizens living in the United States.

2. If You Marry Your Permanent Resident Fiancé

If you marry your permanent resident fiancé while in the United States or abroad, you become a so-called preference relative. That means you will become eligible for permanent residence in the United States. But there are annual quotas and long waiting lists for people in this category. You also will not be able to legally live in the United States with your spouse during the waiting period (unless you were able to apply for another immigration program that allowed you to stay legally for a time, such as political asylum, but this is unlikely). Because of your illegal entry, you will probably not be allowed to apply for your green card inside the United States, even after your long wait. Your four options are to:

- stay in the United States illegally, hoping to adjust your status to permanent residence through USCIS, probably through an eventual change in the laws
- leave the United States before you have stayed illegally for six months or more, wait out your waiting period, and apply for your green card through a U.S. consulate overseas
- leave the United States after you have stayed illegally for more than six months but less than a year, wait out your waiting period as well as your three-year inadmissibility period,

and apply for your green card through a U.S. consulate overseas, or

- leave the United States after you have stayed illegally for more than a year, wait overseas, then apply for your green card along with a waiver of your illegal stay through a U.S. consulate overseas.

Learn more about these options in Chapter 12, covering spouses of U.S. permanent residents living in the United States.

Next Step If You Entered The U.S. Legally	
Your fiancé will become a U.S. citizen:	See Chapter 9 covering fiancés of U.S. citizens living in the United States.
You will marry soon:	See Chapter 12 covering spouses of U.S. permanent residents living in the United States.

Next Step If You Entered The U.S. Ilegally	
Your fiancé will become a U.S. citizen:	See Chapter 9 covering fiancés of U.S. citizens living in the United States.
You will marry soon:	See Chapter 12 covering spouses of lawful permanent residents living in the United States.

Spouses of U.S. Citizens, Living in the U.S.

If you are married to a U.S. citizen, you are what is called an "immediate relative" in USCIS terminology. There are no limits on the number of immediate relatives allowed to apply for permanent residence each year. The only waiting period is the time it takes for your paperwork to be processed by the U.S. government. A green card will be available to you just as soon as you can get through the application procedures—but watch out, this is where things can get complicated.

Even though you are in the United States now, you may have to leave and apply for your green card overseas. The key to knowing how and where you'll get your green card is whether you entered the United States legally or illegally. Here's how it works: If you entered with permission, such as with a student or tourist visa (and with the intent to be a tourist, not to misuse the visa by applying for a green card), you have entered the country legally. That's true even if you stayed beyond the visa expiration date. Your road to a green card should be fairly smooth—you should be able to stay in the United States for your entire application process, which will take about a year.

On the other hand, if you entered illegally, for example by crossing secretly at an unguarded border point, you lose certain important procedural rights—you may have to leave the United States and apply for your green card at a U.S. consulate abroad—which could be difficult, depending on how long you have lived in the United States after that illegal entry. Start by reading Section A to see whether your entry is considered legal or illegal, then move to the subsections that match your current situation.

CAUTION

Even if you are married to a U.S. citizen, there are reasons USCIS could reject your application and move to deport you. See Chapter 2, Section A, for a discussion of the grounds of inadmissibility and review Chapter 2, Section B, to make sure you meet the basic eligibility criteria for a green card.

A. Did You Enter Legally or Illegally?

If you entered the United States with permission of the U.S. authorities, you entered legally. Whether you got that permission in advance or were simply allowed in when you arrived, the important thing is that you were personally met and allowed to enter by an officer of the U.S. border control. This could occur either at the border itself or at some other port of entry such as an airport, seaport, or bus station. The usual ways people enter legally are:

- with a visa (a tourist, student, or temporary worker visa, for example)
- with a border crossing card (a special pass allowing regular entries)
- under the Visa Waiver Program (where citizens of certain countries are allowed to enter the U.S. as tourists by showing their passport, without first obtaining an entry visa).

An illegal entry is, naturally, the opposite of a legal entry. People entering illegally have failed to obtain permission to enter. They may pay someone to sneak them across the U.S. border, wait until the dead of night and find an unguarded point on the U.S. border, or conceal themselves in the trunk of someone else's car. USCIS says that they entered "without inspection," which means that they weren't personally met and approved for entry by a U.S. border control official. (USCIS refers to such people as "EWIs," pronounced "ee-wee," which stands for entry without inspection.) The immigration laws make getting a green card very difficult for people who entered the United States without inspection, or illegally.

SKIP AHEAD

If you entered the United States by crossing the border illegally, skip ahead to Section C.

B. Spouses Who Entered the U.S. Legally

This section is for foreign nationals married to U.S. citizens and living in the United States after entering legally. There are two ways to apply for your green card. You can:

- stay in the United States and submit your application to adjust status to permanent residence at a local USCIS office, as explained in Section 1, below, or
- leave the United States before you have over-stayed your visa by six months or more and apply for your immigrant visa/green card at an overseas U.S. consulate, as covered in Section 2.

1. Stay in the U.S. to Apply

The fact that you entered the United States legally and that your spouse is a U.S. citizen is a magic combination. It should allow you to get your green card through a procedure called adjustment of status (unless you tried to create your own magic by misusing an entry visa, as described in Subsection 1a, below). Using this procedure, you can apply for permanent residence without leaving the United States, even if you have stayed past the date when you were originally supposed to leave (which is most likely the expiration date shown on your I-94 card).

> **EXAMPLE:** Marbelita came to the United States in May 2007, on a tourist visa. While enjoying the view from the Empire State Building, she struck up a conversation with Bill, a U.S. citizen. They fell in love and Marbelita couldn't bear to leave when her tourist visa expired in July. She and Bill married in August. Although she is now in the United States illegally, the combination of her legal entry and Bill's status as a U.S. citizen allows her to apply for her green card (adjustment of status) through a local USCIS office. As soon as Marbelita submits that application, her stay will become legal and she and Bill can live together in the United States while awaiting approval of her green card. Of course, there are other hurdles they must cross, including convincing USCIS that their marriage is real and not simply a way for Marbelita to stay in the United States.

There are many benefits to staying in the United States during the application process. You won't be separated from your spouse, and will receive a permit to work while you wait to attend the final green card interview at a local USCIS office. Although your spouse will be required to accompany you to that interview (which is not required for interviews attended by immigrants coming from overseas), having your spouse present is an advantage, both for moral support and because a large part of the discussion will be your spouse's ability to support you financially. And, unlike an overseas interview, you can bring an attorney with you—which you might decide to do if your case has become complicated during the application process. You may want a lawyer, for example, if you realize that you might fall into a ground of inadmissibility (see Chapter 17 for more on how to find and use a lawyer).

a. Entering on a Temporary Visa Might Pose a Problem

If you used a temporary visa—such as a tourist visa—to enter the United States, planning all along to get married, you might find yourself facing accusations of visa fraud if you apply to adjust status in the United States. Particularly if you knew your spouse before arriving in the United States and used a temporary visa to enter, USCIS is likely to be suspicious. At the interview where your green card would normally be approved, USCIS might question you about whether your real intention when you arrived was to apply for permanent residence after your marriage. Unless you entered on a fiancé visa, the discovery that this was your real intention will lead USCIS to demand that you file an additional application requesting a waiver or forgiveness of your visa fraud. (See Chapter 1,

Section B2, if you think you might be in this category.) This really happens, so watch out!

Of course, if you met your spouse after you arrived in the United States, this won't be a problem. And even for other couples, uncertainties about their marriage plans as well as the length of time they waited to get married—at least 60 days after entry is best—often satisfy USCIS that they didn't misuse an entry visa.

> ⓘ **CAUTION**
>
> **Watch out if you're in the U.S. on an employment-based visa.** If you entered the U.S. on certain types of employment-based visas, applying for a green card through your U.S. citizen spouse puts you at risk of losing your visa status. See the discussion called, "Here on an Employment Visa? The Risks of Applying for a Green Card," in Chapter 2, Section A.

b. Two-Year Testing Period for New Marriages

You must be married for two years to obtain a permanent green card. If you apply before your marriage is two years old, you'll get a conditional card, good for only two years. Since most people apply for their green card soon after marrying, they get a conditional green card.

You won't be kicked out of the country after the two years—provided you don't forget to file the next application. This is an application for a permanent green card, which sometimes involves an interview to allow USCIS to take a second look at whether your marriage is real. (See Chapter 16, Section G, for more on this issue.)

c. Your Children

Your unmarried children under age 21 may also be eligible to apply for green cards along with you (see Chapter 2, Section B, if you have children).

2. Introduction to the Application Process in the U.S.

Getting your marriage-based green card is normally a two-step process. First, your spouse submits a petition (Form I-130) telling USCIS that he or she wants to help you immigrate. After USCIS approves this petition, you submit an application for permanent residence (a green card), showing that you are interested and are eligible to immigrate.

But for the spouse of a U.S. citizen who entered the country legally, the process usually gets condensed into one step. Your spouse's petition and your green card application can be filed together. Nevertheless, we cover the visa petition and your green card application in separate sections: Section D, below, covers the I-130 visa petition, and Chapter 14 covers the remainder of your green card application. You should have no trouble following the instructions in both sections and then combining the visa petition and green card application before submitting them.

> ⮕ **SKIP AHEAD**
>
> **If you're ready to get to work on the visa petition,** jump to Section D below for complete instructions.

3. Leave and Apply at an Overseas Consulate

For most married applicants, staying in the U.S. and adjusting status is the preferred way to obtain permanent residence. However, a second option for people who haven't overstayed their visa by six months or more is to leave the United States and apply for a green card at a U.S. consulate overseas.

At the time this book went to press, applications to adjust status in the U.S. were taking about five months. If the processing time were to lengthen— as it has in the past—applying at a consulate could be a quicker way to get your green card. Or you might prefer to apply at a consulate if you need to leave the U.S. right away and cannot wait for the processing of an adjustment of status application and a travel permit. Although the application process through an overseas consulate can take close to a year, some consulates are much more efficient and can approve you for a green card in a matter of months.

Contact the U.S. consulate in your home country to find out how long its application and approval process takes. Also, ask other immigrants about their experience with that consulate.

To compare that to how long your local USCIS office is taking to process applications for adjustment of status, go www.uscis.gov, and in the bar on the left side of the page, click "Processing Times," then on the next page, choose your local field office from the drop-down menu, and click "Field Office Processing Dates." In the table that appears, you'll find the I-485 processing time frame.

Keep in mind that if your application gets delayed or the consulate asks you to supplement your application before it will approve it, your overseas stay could last longer.

There are some immigrants who should not leave the U.S. to apply for their green card, no matter how efficient their consulate will be. These are the people who have stayed past the expiration date on their visa by six months or more. Such people could be found inadmissible and prevented from returning for three or ten years, as described in Chapter 2, Section A.

> **EXAMPLE:** Asma is in the United States on a student visa, and recently married Fred, a U.S. citizen. Asma's elderly mother lives alone in Ethiopia, under very difficult circumstances. Asma is her mother's only hope to leave Ethiopia. Once Asma becomes a U.S. citizen, she can file an immediate relative petition for her mother to immigrate. But Asma can't apply for U.S. citizenship until she has been a U.S. resident for three years—so she needs that green card approval as soon as possible. In her case, it may be worthwhile to compare processing times between her local USCIS office and the U.S. consulate in Ethiopia. Asma understands that if she stays past the expiration of her student visa by six months or more, she should not even consider leaving the United States to apply for her green card, since

she might face penalties of three or ten years, depending on how long she overstayed.

CAUTION

Carry proof of when you depart the United States. If you decide to apply for your green card at a U.S. consulate, your history of U.S. visits will trigger a request that you prove you left on time. Collect and keep all evidence, such as your plane tickets, store receipts, medical records, credit card statements, and anything else relevant. (See Chapter 2, Section A, for the rules on and penalties for overstaying a U.S. visa by six months or more.)

a. Two-Year Testing Period for New Marriages

You must be married for two years to obtain a permanent green card. If you use your immigrant visa to enter the U.S. before your marriage is two years old, you'll get a conditional card, good for only two years. Since most people will apply for their green card soon after marrying, they will get a conditional green card.

You won't be kicked out of the country after the two years—provided you don't forget to file the next application. This is an application for a permanent green card, which sometimes involves an interview to allow USCIS to take a second look at whether your marriage is real. (See Chapter 16, Section G, for more on this issue.)

b. Your Children

Your unmarried children under age 21 may also be eligible to submit applications for immigrant visas along with you (see Chapter 2, Section B, if you have children).

SKIP AHEAD

If you are certain that you wish to leave the United States and apply overseas, go straight to Section D below. This section contains instructions on the first step, the visa petition to be filed by your spouse. This petition can be filed before or after you leave the United States.

C. Spouses Who Entered the U.S. Illegally

This section is for foreign nationals living in the United States after entering illegally. Unfortunately, your path to a green card is a difficult one, involving unattractive choices. Before explaining them in detail, we need to warn readers to see an attorney if:

- you've entered the U.S. illegally two or more times and
- the total amount of illegal time in the U.S. totals one year or more; or
- you've been deported (removed).

These would-be immigrants may be permanently barred from immigrating to the United States. See Chapter 2, Section A, for further information about the permanent bar.

Now, for those of you who have entered illegally only once, or whose previous illegal entries and stays total less than one year, here are your choices. As the spouse of a U.S. citizen, you are known as an immediate relative. A visa or green card is theoretically available as soon as you can get through the application procedures. Unfortunately, the procedures themselves make it difficult or impossible to get a green card. Unless you fall into a rare exception, you will not be allowed to apply for your green card at a USCIS office in the United States. But if you leave after living here illegally for more than six months, you risk having the consulate punish you by refusing to let you return to the United States for three or ten years. (Chapter 2 has a full discussion of these time bars.)

To avoid being punished by the time bars, you need to act carefully and quickly. You have three options to consider:

- see if you fit into an exception and can apply to change your status to green card holder in the United States; this path is covered below in Section 1
- leave the United States before you have been here six months and apply to an overseas U.S. consulate to return immediately with an immigrant visa; this option is explained below in Section 2, or
- leave the United States after you have been here more than six months and apply to an overseas U.S. consulate for a waiver of your illegal stay along with an immigrant visa to return; this choice is explained in Section 3.

1. Can You Adjust Your Status in the U.S.?

Most married immigrants want to get their green card without leaving the United States. But in the late 1990s, the U.S. Congress made it more difficult for many immigrants to fulfill that hope. Only certain categories of immigrants are now allowed to apply for their green card in the United States using the adjustment of status procedure. People who entered the United States illegally are normally not among them.

However, a very few people will be lucky enough to fall into an exception to these laws if they started the application process before the laws changed. The key is whether a prospective employer or a close family member of yours, even if it wasn't your spouse, filed an immigrant visa petition (Form I-130 for family members) on your behalf either:

- before January 14, 1998, or
- between January 14, 1998 and April 30, 2001, if you can prove that you were physically present in the United States on December 21, 2000.

If the visa petition was approved (or denied only because of a mistake by USCIS), you may be allowed to adjust your status to permanent resident without leaving the United States. (See Chapter 2, Section A, for more details on who may take advantage of these time windows. Also don't forget to check the legal updates to this book on Nolo's website at www.nolo.com in case Congress extends the time frames of these windows.) In short, if your Form I-130 was on file as described above, you have a ticket to adjust your status in the United States, even though you entered the country illegally.

If you fall into this exception, by all means plan to change (adjust) your status to green card holder in the United States. This is especially true if you have stayed in the United States illegally for more than six months. If you were to leave and try to apply for your green card at a U.S. consulate, the officials could punish you for your illegal stay by preventing your return for three or ten years.

SKIP AHEAD

If you are sure you will be able to adjust status in the United States, go to Section D, below for the first step.

If you don't fall into this exception but are determined not to leave the United States at all, your only option (which we don't recommend) is to stay illegally, hoping that the immigration laws will change in your favor. Many couples have chosen this route, but it is a huge gamble. Recent changes in the immigration laws have made them harsher, not gentler on immigrants, and there is little hope that this trend will change. If you chose this option, you must be aware that you may never obtain legal residence in the United States and will face the ever-present possibility of being caught, deported, and prevented from returning to the United States for at least ten years.

2. Leave the U.S. Before Six Months Have Passed

If you don't fit into an exception as described in Section 1, above, but you haven't yet stayed in the United States illegally for more than six months, your safest bet is to leave the United States before that date rolls around. Leaving now would protect you from having a three-year bar assessed against you when you later visit the U.S. consulate overseas to apply for your green card (and from a ten-year bar if you stayed illegally for more than a year).

After leaving, other visa options will open up to you: As the overseas spouse of a U.S. citizen, you can get a marriage-based immigrant visa based on your immediate relative status. This may mean many months of separation from your spouse while you wait overseas for your green card to be approved. A second visa option is also available to you: to use a K-3 "fiancé visa" to enter the United States, after which you would complete the green card application process at a local USCIS office.

Months of separation now might be better than three or ten years of separation later. See Chapter 7 for instructions on how to apply overseas for immigrant or K-3 visas as the spouse of a U.S. citizen.

CAUTION

Make sure you can prove you stayed illegally for less than six months. When the time comes to apply for your green card, the consulate will want to see proof of how long you stayed illegally in the United States. Collect and keep all evidence, such as your plane tickets, store receipts, medical records, credit card statements, and anything else relevant.

SKIP AHEAD

If you are certain that you wish to leave the United States and apply overseas, go straight to Section D, below. This section contains instructions on the first step, the visa petition to be filed by your spouse. This petition can be filed before or after you leave the United States.

3. Leave the U.S. After Six or More Months and Apply for a Waiver

If you are not eligible to adjust status in the United States, but your unlawful stay was long enough that you would face a three- or ten-year bar on returning if you left, see an attorney. (See Chapter 2 for more on the three- and ten-year bars, and Chapter 17 for tips on finding a good attorney.) The attorney can help you decide whether you should risk leaving the United States and applying for a marriage-based visa along with a waiver of the time bars (in other words, forgiveness of your unlawful stay).

Unfortunately, you cannot submit your request for a waiver until you are at your interview. The government requires the interviewing officer to make an official determination that you are inadmissible—and therefore need a waiver—before it will take your waiver request or begin processing it. The additional amount of time that you will have to wait for your waiver request to be decided upon varies from consulate to consulate, ranging from several weeks to as many as 20 months. Check with the consulate to find out its average time.

It's not easy to get a waiver. You'll have to convince the immigration authorities that if your visa were denied, it would cause extreme hardship to your U.S. spouse or parents (if they happen to be U.S. citizens or permanent residents)—and when the law says extreme, it means much more than the sadness your spouse and parents will feel at your being thousands of miles away. The classic case of extreme hardship is someone whose U.S. citizen spouse has severe medical problems that require the other spouse's constant attention.

Assuming your waiver request is granted, you will then be able to return to the U.S. as a permanent resident, without having to wait the additional three to ten years that you would have waited without the waiver.

SEE AN EXPERT

Time bar waivers are relatively new. Look for an attorney who has had experience preparing and arguing for them.

D. The First Application: I-130 Visa Petition

Your U.S. citizen spouse initiates the green card application process by preparing a visa petition— Form I-130, Petition for Alien Relative, and attached documents. Your spouse can start and submit this any time, before or after you have left the United States.

With the visa petition, you're asking USCIS to acknowledge that you're married and to let you go forward with green card processing. Approval of the visa petition does not guarantee approval of your green card. This is only the first step in the process. Your portion of the application is still to come, and you will have to pass all the tests USCIS gives before allowing someone to live in the United States permanently.

We'll go through how to prepare and assemble the various forms and documents, one by one. To keep track of them all, refer to the checklist in Section 5, below. You'll find a few items on this checklist that are self-explanatory, so they aren't discussed in the following text.

Before proceeding, take a look at the general instructions for printing and filling in USCIS forms in Chapter 4. Also, as you read these instructions, you should have a copy of the appropriate form in hand.

CAUTION

If the U.S. petitioner has a criminal record, see an attorney. Under the Adam Walsh Child Protection and Safety Act of 2006, U.S. citizens and lawful permanent residents who have been convicted of any "specified offense against a minor" are prohibited from filing a family-based immigrant petition on behalf of any beneficiary (whether a child or not). USCIS will run security checks on all petitions and may call the petitioner in for fingerprinting. If the petitioner has a conviction for one of the specified offenses against a minor, then the petition will not be approved unless USCIS determines that the U.S. petitioner poses no risk to the beneficiary.

1. Form I-130

Form I-130 is one of the most important ones in your immigration process. It will be your spouse's first opportunity to explain who each of you are, where you live, and why you qualify for a visa.

The first thing to notice about Form I-130 is that it runs in two columns (except for the tiny Part A near the top). The left column, or Part B, asks for information about the petitioner—that's your U.S. citizen spouse. Don't be thrown off by the fact that the form addresses your spouse as "you"—after all, it's your spouse who fills out and signs this form. The right column asks for information about you, referred to as the relative.

 WEB RESOURCE
Form I-130 is available on the USCIS website at www.uscis.gov. Below is a sample filled-in version of this form.

Part A

Question 1: Check the first box, Husband/Wife.

Question 2: This question, about whether you're related by adoption, is meant for people who use this form to apply for an adopted child. We're assuming you can answer this question "No."

Question 3: If your petitioning spouse gained U.S. permanent residence through adoption before becoming a citizen, check Yes. But no matter which box you check, it won't affect the application, since this question is mainly directed at people immigrating through parent/child relationships—something not covered in this book.

Part B

Question 1: The petitioning spouse must enter his/her last name (surname) in capital letters, but the first and middle name in small letters. For example, Samuel Lawrence Cole would write COLE, Samuel Lawrence. Use his/her current married name if it was changed at the time of your marriage. (See "What's Your Name?" in Chapter 4, Section B.)

Questions 2-5: Self-explanatory.

Question 6: This question refers only to the petitioning spouse's most recent marital status. He or she should check only "married," even if there was a previous divorce.

Question 7: See "What's Your Name?" in Chapter 4, Section B.

Question 8: Your marriage date is self-explanatory.

Question 9: Your spouse's Social Security number is self-explanatory.

Question 10: A U.S. citizen can put N/A here, even if your spouse was once a lawful permanent resident and had an Alien Registration Number (known as an A-Number).

Question 11: Self-explanatory.

Question 12: This question of when your spouse's prior marriage ended is intended to make sure your current marriage is valid. If your petitioning spouse's prior marriage(s) ended after your present marriage began, yours is not a lawful marriage. If your petitioning spouse has just discovered that the divorce wasn't final when your marriage took place, it may not be necessary to run to a lawyer. Assuming that the divorce has since become final, you can simply correct the problem by remarrying. (If there was fraud involved in your hasty marriage, consult a lawyer before proceeding.)

Question 13: If your petitioning spouse is a naturalized U.S. citizen (meaning he or she wasn't born a citizen, but had to apply and take a citizenship exam), his or her number is on the top right-hand side of the naturalization certificate. The date and place issued are also shown on the certificate.

Question 14a: U.S. citizens can write N/A here.

Question 14b: If your petitioning spouse checks "yes" here, indicating that he or she received U.S. permanent residence through marriage, find out how long it has been since your spouse's approval for permanent residence. A petitioning spouse who him or herself immigrated through marriage cannot petition for a new spouse for five years after approval, unless the first spouse died or your spouse can prove by "clear and convincing evidence" that the previous marriage was bona fide (real). USCIS is concerned that the first marriage was just a sham, with the long-term goal of getting both of you into the United States by piggybacking on a sham marriage.

To prove that the first marriage was bona fide, your spouse should enclose documentary evidence, such as shared rent receipts, club memberships, children's birth certificates, utility bills, and insurance agreements showing that he or she and the former spouse shared a life together. As for what makes for "clear and convincing evidence," this is one of those legal standards that is easy to state but hard to pin down. The bottom line is, your spouse has a lot of proving to do to persuade a suspicious government official that the previous marriage was bona fide.

Part C: (Now referring to you, the immigrant beneficiary)

Question 1: Your current name, with your last name (surname) in capital letters, like this: SMITH. (If you have any doubts about what name to use, see "What's Your Name?" in Chapter 4, Section B.)

Questions 2-5: Self-explanatory.

Question 6: Your current marital status only.

Question 7: See "What's Your Name?" in Chapter 4 Section B.

Question 8: Your marriage date: self-explanatory.

Question 9: You shouldn't have a Social Security number until you have had a work permit, a visa allowing you to work, or U.S. residence. If you don't have a valid Social Security number, write "None."

Question 10: The Alien Registration Number is an eight- or nine-digit number following a letter A that USCIS or the former INS will have assigned to you. You won't have one yet unless you've previously applied for immigration benefits, or been in deportation/removal proceedings. (If your previous application was denied because you were inadmissible, or you lied on that application, you should call a lawyer before going any further.)

Question 11: Self-explanatory.

Question 12: See advice to Question 12 on Part B, above.

Question 13: Put an X in the "Yes" box. Since you have chosen to read this chapter, you have apparently been (and may still be) in the United States.

Question 14: Enter information about your most recent entry to the United States, even if this was only after a brief trip and you moved to the United States long ago.

 CAUTION

If you know that you must leave the United States to get your green card, be careful here. This question gives the government information on when you were living in the United States—perhaps unlawfully. It could lead to your being punished for your illegal stay with a three- or ten-year bar on reentry (see Chapter 2, which explains the time bars in detail). Ideally, if you will have already left the United States when your spouse sends this in, he or she won't have to answer the question at all.

If you entered legally. State the type of visa you used to enter the United States, such as F-1 student or Visa Waiver (if you came from a country from which you didn't have to get a formal U.S. visa). Your I-94 is the little white or green card that the consulate or the border official gave you when you arrived; the number is on the card. The date your stay expires or expired should be on the I-94 card (or in rare cases, in your passport). Note that this date is different than the expiration date on your original visa.

If you entered illegally. Write "without inspection."

Question 15: State your employer's name and address. USCIS appears not to use this information to go after employers who hired people illegally. However, if you not only worked illegally but used false documents to do it (such as a fake green card), consult with an attorney. (See Chapter 17 for information on finding a good lawyer.)

Question 16: If you've been placed in Immigration Court proceedings, see a lawyer, particularly if you lost.

Question 17: This is the continuation of Part C, so all questions still refer to you, the immigrant beneficiary. Since your spouse is already covered in this application, just list your children, if any. This means all your children, including any by previous relationships.

Question 18: Self-explanatory.

Question 19: Self-explanatory.

Question 20: If your native language uses a non-Roman script (for example, Russian, Chinese, or Arabic), you'll need to write your name and address in that script.

Sample Form I-130, Petition for Alien Relative—Page 1

Department of Homeland Security
U.S. Citizenship and Immigration Services

OMB No. 1615-0012; Expires 01/31/2012

I-130, Petition for Alien Relative

DO NOT WRITE IN THIS BLOCK - FOR USCIS OFFICE ONLY

A#	Action Stamp	Fee Stamp

Section of Law/Visa Category
- [ ] 201(b) Spouse - IR-1/CR-1
- [ ] 201(b) Child - IR-2/CR-2
- [ ] 201(b) Parent - IR-5
- [ ] 203(a)(1) Unm. S or D - F1-1
- [ ] 203(a)(2)(A)Spouse - F2-1
- [ ] 203(a)(2)(A) Child - F2-2
- [ ] 203(a)(2)(B) Unm. S or D - F2-4
- [ ] 203(a)(3) Married S or D - F3-1
- [ ] 203(a)(4) Brother/Sister - F4-1

Petition was filed on: _____ (priority date)
- [ ] Personal Interview
- [ ] Pet. [ ] Ben. " A" File Reviewed
- [ ] Field Investigation
- [ ] 203(a)(2)(A) Resolved
- [ ] Previously Forwarded
- [ ] I-485 Filed Simultaneously
- [ ] 204(g) Resolved
- [ ] 203(g) Resolved

Remarks:

A. Relationship   You are the petitioner.   Your relative is the beneficiary.

1. I am filing this petition for my:
[X] Husband/Wife [ ] Parent [ ] Brother/Sister [ ] Child

2. Are you related by adoption?
[ ] Yes [X] No

3. Did you gain permanent residence through adoption?
[ ] Yes [X] No

B. Information about you

1. Name (Family name in CAPS) (First) (Middle)
MICHELA   Grun   Branimir

2. Address (Number and Street) (Apt. No.)
68 Watertown Boulevard   #12

(Town or City) (State/Country) (Zip/Postal Code)
Erie   PA   19380

3. Place of Birth (Town or City) (State/Country)
Hershey   U.S.

4. Date of Birth
03/17/1985

5. Gender
[X] Male [ ] Female

6. Marital Status
[X] Married [ ] Single [ ] Widowed [ ] Divorced

7. Other Names Used (including maiden name)
None

8. Date and Place of Present Marriage (if married)
12/17/2010   Hershey, PA

9. U.S. Social Security Number (If any)
111-11-1111

10. Alien Registration Number
N/A

11. Name(s) of Prior Husband(s)/Wive(s)
None

12. Date(s) Marriage(s) Ended

13. If you are a U.S. citizen, complete the following:

My citizenship was acquired through (check one):
- [X] Birth in the U.S.
- [ ] Naturalization. Give certificate number and date and place of issuance.

- [ ] Parents. Have you obtained a certificate of citizenship in your own name?
  - [ ] Yes. Give certificate number, date and place of issuance. [ ] No

14. If you are a lawful permanent resident alien, complete the following:
Date and place of admission for or adjustment to lawful permanent residence and class of admission.
N/A

14b. Did you gain permanent resident status through marriage to a U.S. citizen or lawful permanent resident?
[ ] Yes [ ] No

C. Information about your relative

1. Name (Family name in CAPS) (First) (Middle)
MICHELSKI   Anda   M.

2. Address (Number and Street) (Apt. No.)
68 Watertown Boulevard   #12

(Town or City) (State/Country) (Zip/Postal Code)
Erie   PA   19380

3. Place of Birth (Town or City) (State/Country)
Sofia   Bulgaria

4. Date of Birth
06/28/1984

5. Gender
[ ] Male [X] Female

6. Marital Status
[X] Married [ ] Single [ ] Widowed [ ] Divorced

7. Other Names Used (including maiden name)
None

8. Date and Place of Present Marriage (if married)
12/17/2010   Hershey, PA

9. U.S. Social Security Number (If any)
387-33-8877

10. Alien Registration Number
12345677

11. Name(s) of Prior Husband(s)/Wive(s)
None

12. Date(s) Marriage(s) Ended

13. Has your relative ever been in the U.S.? [X] Yes [ ] No

14. If your relative is currently in the U.S., complete the following:
He or she arrived as a:
(visitor, student, stowaway, without inspection, etc.)   H-1B worker

Arrival/Departure Record (I-94)   Date arrived
| 1 | 2 | 3 | | 2 | 3 | 1 | 2 | 3 | | | | 11/04/2011

Date authorized stay expired, or will expire, as shown on Form I-94 or I-95   11/04/2013

15. Name and address of present employer (if any)
Berlitz Cultural Center, Penn Center, Ste. 800, Pittsburgh, PA 15276

Date this employment began
12/06/2011

16. Has your relative ever been under immigration proceedings?
[X] No [ ] Yes Where _____ When _____
[ ] Removal [ ] Exclusion/Deportation [ ] Rescission [ ] Judicial Proceedings

INITIAL RECEIPT	RESUBMITTED	RELOCATED: Rec'd	Sent	COMPLETED: Appv'd	Denied	Ret'd

Form I-130 (01/08/12) Y

Sample Form I-130, Petition for Alien Relative—Page 2

C. Information about your alien relative (continued)

17. List husband/wife and all children of your relative.

(Name)	(Relationship)	(Date of Birth)	(Country of Birth)
Grun Michela	spouse	03/17/1985	U.S.

18. Address in the United States where your relative intends to live.

(Street Address)	(Town or City)	(State)
68 Watertown Boulevard, #12	Erie	PA

19. Your relative's address abroad. (Include street, city, province and country)   Phone Number (if any)

20. If your relative's native alphabet is other than Roman letters, write his or her name and foreign address in the native alphabet.

(Name)   Address (Include street, city, province and country):

21. If filing for your husband/wife, give last address at which you lived together. (Include street, city, province, if any, and country):

	From:	To:
68 Watertown Blvd. #12, Erie, PA 19380	11/2008	present

22. Complete the information below if your relative is in the United States and will apply for adjustment of status.

Your relative is in the United States and will apply for adjustment of status to that of a lawful permanent resident at the USCIS office in:

If your relative is not eligible for adjustment of status, he or she will apply for a visa abroad at the American consular post in:

Philadelphia	PA	Sofia	Bulgaria
(City)	(State)	(City)	(Country)

NOTE: Designation of a U.S. embassy or consulate outside the country of your relative's last residence does not guarantee acceptance for processing by that post. Acceptance is at the discretion of the designated embassy or consulate.

D. Other information

1. If separate petitions are also being submitted for other relatives, give names of each and relationship.

2. Have you ever before filed a petition for this or any other alien? ☐ Yes ☒ No

If "Yes," give name, place and date of filing and result.

WARNING: USCIS investigates claimed relationships and verifies the validity of documents. USCIS seeks criminal prosecutions when family relationships are falsified to obtain visas.

PENALTIES: By law, you may be imprisoned for not more than five years or fined $250,000, or both, for entering into a marriage contract for the purpose of evading any provision of the immigration laws. In addition, you may be fined up to $10,000 and imprisoned for up to five years, or both, for knowingly and willfully falsifying or concealing a material fact or using any false document in submitting this petition.

YOUR CERTIFICATION: I certify, under penalty of perjury under the laws of the United States of America, that the foregoing is true and correct. Furthermore, I authorize the release of any information from my records that U.S. Citizenship and Immigration Services needs to determine eligiblity for the benefit that I am seeking.

E. Signature of petitioner

Grun Michela   Date 4/20/12   Phone Number (610) 555-1212

F. Signature of person preparing this form, if other than the petitioner

I declare that I prepared this document at the request of the person above and that it is based on all information of which I have any knowledge.

Print Name _____   Signature _____   Date _____

Address _____   G-28 ID or VOLAG Number, if any. _____

Question 21: Self-explanatory. But if you're going to be leaving the United States after living here unlawfully, this is another time to be careful—the information about how long you and your spouse lived at the same address could be used against you.

Question 22:

If you entered legally. If you plan to take advantage of the option to stay in the United States to adjust your status, enter the closest city and state with a U.S. immigration office. Add the name of the consulate from your last country of residence, as a backup—though if you've followed our instructions, you won't need to go there.

If you are choosing to return to your home country and apply through a U.S. consulate, you need not fill out this box.

If you entered illegally. Unless you fall into an exception and are therefore allowed to stay in the United States to apply for your green card, you'll have to complete your application at a U.S. consulate, and need not fill out this box.

Part D: Other Information.

Now we're back to questions to be answered by the U.S. petitioning spouse.

Question 1: If your spouse is also submitting petitions for your children, this is where he should enter their names and relationship to him or her (such as child or stepchild). This will result in USCIS processing all of your petitions together.

Question 2: As you can probably imagine, if your petitioning spouse has a history of short marriages to people whom he/she then helped get green cards, USCIS will conduct a major marriage fraud investigation. See a lawyer (Chapter 17 has more on how to find and use a lawyer).

Signature Line: The petitioning spouse signs here.

Signature of person preparing this form if other than the petitioner. If you or your spouse are filling out your own application, leave this blank. A little typing assistance or advice from a friend doesn't count—the only people who need to complete this line are lawyers or agencies who fill out these forms on others' behalf.

2. Form G-325A

The data collected on this form will give the U.S. government information with which to check your background. Most of the form is self-explanatory. If you really can't remember or are unable to find out an exact date, enter whatever you can remember, such as the year. Alternately, you can simply say "unknown"; but don't overuse the "unknowns," or USCIS may return your entire application for another try. Since the questions aren't numbered, we refer to them by the approximate line.

Remember, you and your spouse each fill one in.

WEB RESOURCE

Form G-325A is available on the USCIS website at www.uscis.gov. Below is a sample filled-in version of this form.

Lines 1 and 2 (Family Name, etc.): Self-explanatory.

Line 3 (Father/Mother): Self-explanatory.

Line 4 (Husband or Wife): Self-explanatory.

Line 5 (Former Husbands or Wives): Self-explanatory.

Line 7 (Applicant's residence last five years): Be careful here; these addresses need to be in reverse chronological order, starting with your most recent address and working your way down the last five years. For example, if you now live in Detroit but lived in Ann Arbor before, your Detroit address would go on the top line. Practice making this list on another sheet of paper before you enter the information here.

Line 12 (Applicant's last address outside the United States of more than one year): This may overlap with one of the addresses in Line 6—that's okay.

Line 13 (Applicant's employment last five years): Again, be careful to put this in reverse chronological order. If you've been unemployed, self-employed, or were a housewife or house-husband, say so here—in other words, try to account for the whole five years.

Line 14 (Show below last occupation abroad if not listed above): This line asks you to list your last overseas employment—if you didn't already

Sample Form G-325A, Biographic Information

Department of Homeland Security
U.S. Citizenship and Immigration Services

OMB No. 1615-0008; Expires 08/31/2012

G-325A, Biographic Information

(Family Name)	(First Name)	(Middle Name)	☐ Male ☒ Female	Date of Birth (mm/dd/yyyy)	Citizenship/Nationality	File Number
Michelski	Anda	Marina		06-28-1984	Bulgarian	A 12345677

All Other Names Used (include names by previous marriages)	City and Country of Birth	U.S. Social Security # (if any)
none	Sofia Bulgaria	

	Family Name	First Name	Date of Birth (mm/dd/yyyy)	City, and Country of Birth (if known)	City and Country of Residence
Father	Michelski	Liski	12/24/64,	Sofia, Bulgaria	Sofia, Bulgaria
Mother (Maiden Name)	Borisova	Anastasia	3/10/65,	Sofia, Bulgaria	Sofia, Bulgaria

Current Husband or Wife (If none, so state) Family Name (For wife, give maiden name)	First Name	Date of Birth (mm/dd/yyyy)	City and Country of Birth	Date of Marriage	Place of Marriage
Michela	Grun	03-17-1985	Hershey U.S.	12-17-2010	Hershey, PA

Former Husbands or Wives (If none, so state) Family Name (For wife, give maiden name)	First Name	Date of Birth (mm/dd/yyyy)	Date and Place of Marriage	Date and Place of Termination of Marriage
none				

Applicant's residence last five years. List present address first.

Street and Number	City	Province or State	Country	From Month	From Year	To Month	To Year
68 Watertown Blvd, #12	Erie	PA	U.S.	11	2010	Present Time	
42, Raiska Gradina Street	Sofia		Bulgaria	02	2003	11	2010

Applicant's last address outside the United States of more than 1 year.

Street and Number	City	Province or State	Country	From Month	From Year	To Month	To Year
42, Raiska Gradina Street	Sofia	Bulgaria		02	2003	11	2010

Applicant's employment last five years. (If none, so state.) List present employment first.

Full Name and Address of Employer	Occupation (Specify)	From Month	From Year	To Month	To Year
Berlitz Language Center, Penn Center, Ste. 800, Pittsburgh PA 15276	language teacher	12	2010	Present Time	
Chech Cultural Center, 123 Sveta Serdika Str., Sofia Bulgaria	language teacher	08	2004	10	2010

Last occupation abroad if not shown above. (Include all information requested above.)

This form is submitted in connection with an application for: ☐ Naturalization ☐ Other (Specify): ☒ Status as Permanent Resident	Signature of Applicant *Anda Michelski*	Date 3/7/2012

If your native alphabet is in other than Roman letters, write your name in your native alphabet below:

Анда Мичелски

Penalties: Severe penalties are provided by law for knowingly and willfully falsifying or concealing a material fact.

Applicant: Print your name and Alien Registration Number in the box outlined by heavy border below.

Complete This Box (Family Name)	(Given Name)	(Middle Name)	(Alien Registration Number)
MICHELSKI	Anda	Marina	A 12345677

Form G-325A (Rev. 08/08/11) Y

list it under Line 8. People tend to overlook this line, because it's so small—make sure you don't accidentally skip over it.

Line 19 (This form is submitted in connection with an application for): Your U.S. citizen spouse should check "Other," and write "in support of spouse's I-130." You should check "status as permanent resident."

Line 20 (If your native alphabet uses non-Roman letters): For example, if you're from Russia or China, fill this in using the native writing script.

Line 21 (The dark box): Self-explanatory.

3. Documents to Assemble for Visa Petition

The I-130 visa petition asks you to submit supporting documents and payment along with the form. You're not done with this form until you have gathered together the following:

- **Proof of the U.S. citizen status of your petitioning spouse.** Depending on how your spouse became a citizen, he or she should copy a birth certificate, passport, certificate of naturalization, or Form FS-20 (Report of Birth Abroad of a United States Citizen).

- **Proof that you're legally married.** This should include at a minimum a copy of your marriage certificate, most likely from a government source (see Chapter 4, Section C, for details). In addition, if either you or your spouse have been previously married, you must include proof that these marriages were terminated, such as a copy of a death, divorce, or annulment certificate.

- **Photos.** You must each submit a color, passport-style photo, 2 x 2 inches in size, taken within the past six months, showing your current appearance. Passport style means that the photo shows your full face from the front, with a plain white or off-white background—and your face must measure between one inch and 1⅜ inches from the bottom of your chin to the top of your head. For more information, see the State Department website at http://travel.state. gov (under "Visas for Foreign Citizens," click "more," then "A–Z Subject Index," then go to "Photo Requirements" under letter "P"). However, USCIS regulations permit you to submit a photo that doesn't completely follow the instructions if you live in a country where such photographs are unavailable or are cost prohibitive.

- **Fees.** The current fee for an I-130 visa petition is $420. However, these fees go up fairly regularly, so double-check this on the USCIS website at www.uscis.gov, or by calling USCIS at 800-375-5283.

4. Where to Send Form I-130 Visa Petition

Where you'll send your Form I-130 visa petition will depend on whether you'll be allowed to complete your green card (adjustment of status) application in the United States or will be leaving to apply through an overseas U.S. consulate.

a. If You Will Be Adjusting Your Status in the U.S.

If you will be adjusting your status in the United States (either because you entered legally or because you can use an earlier-filed visa petition as your entry ticket to adjusting status), you can file the Form I-130 at the same time you file your adjustment of status forms, so don't send it anywhere yet! Simply keep the completed visa petition until you have completed your green card application.

SKIP AHEAD

Applicants who will be adjusting status in the United States can now skip to Chapter 14.

Where to Send the Form I-130 Visa Petition			
If the U.S. petitioner lives in:			**Send Form I-130 to:**
Alaska American Samoa Arizona California Colorado Florida Guam Hawaii Idaho	Kansas Montana Nebraska Nevada New Mexico North Dakota Northern Mariana Islands Oklahoma	Oregon Puerto Rico South Dakota Texas Utah Virgin Islands Washington Wyoming	**USCIS Phoenix Lockbox** For U.S. Postal Service (USPS) deliveries: USCIS ATTN: I-130 P.O. Box 21700 Phoenix, AZ 85036 For Express Mail and courier deliveries: USCIS Attn: I-130 1820 E. Skyharbor Circle S Suite 100 Phoenix, AZ 85034
Alabama Arkansas Connecticut Delaware District of Columbia Georgia Illinois Indiana Iowa Kentucky Louisiana	Maine Maryland Massachusetts Michigan Minnesota Mississippi Missouri New Hampshire New Jersey New York	North Carolina Ohio Pennsylvania Rhode Island South Carolina Tennessee Vermont Virginia West Virginia Wisconsin	**USCIS Chicago Lockbox** For U.S. Postal Service: USCIS P.O. Box 804625 Chicago, IL 60680-4107 For Express Mail and courier deliveries: USCIS Attn: I-130 131 South Dearborn–3rd Floor Chicago, IL 60603-5517
If the U.S. petitioner prefers to send the I-130 by private courier (non-U.S. Postal Service), then regardless of where the petitioner lives, send Form I-130 to:			**USCIS Lockbox** Attn: SAI-130 131 South Dearborn–3rd Floor Chicago, IL 60603-5517

b. If You Will Be Completing the Process Overseas

If you will ultimately be leaving the United States to apply for your green card through a U.S. consulate, your spouse must send the Form I-130 and all its attachments to a USCIS office called a "lockbox" that serves the region where he or she lives. The lockbox office will then forward your visa petition to a USCIS Service Center, which will make the final decision approving or denying it.

The form can be sent in any time, before or after you leave the United States.

Your spouse should make a copy of everything being sent (including the checks and photographs). Certified mail with a return receipt is the safest way to send anything to USCIS. The lockbox address is below (and in Appendix B), or double-check this information on the USCIS website. Once USCIS has approved the I-130, it will transfer your file to the National Visa Center (NVC), which will link you up with an overseas U.S. consulate.

5. What Happens After You Mail in Form I-130 Visa Petition

Your spouse will get a receipt notice from USCIS a few weeks after the visa petition is mailed. The notice will tell you to check the USCIS website for information on how long the application is likely to remain in processing, which is currently about five months. Processing times can change, however, and you can check the USCIS website for the most up-to-date information by going to www.uscis.gov, clicking "Processing Times" in the bar on the left side of the page, selecting the Service Center with jurisdiction over your petition from the drop-down menu marked "Service Center" at the bottom of the next page, then clicking the "Service Center Processing Dates" button. Be sure to look in the column for I-130s submitted by a "U.S. citizen filing for a spouse, parent, or child under 21."

The result shown in the final column may be either a number of months or a date. If it's a date, that tells you that USCIS is currently working on visa petitions filed on that date, so you'll have to do the math to figure out how long it's taking.

As long as your petition is not beyond the "normal processing time," USCIS will ignore any inquiries from you or your spouse asking what is going on. USCIS lockbox offices and Service Centers seem like walled fortresses—you can't visit them, and it's impossible to talk with the person working on your case. If USCIS needs additional documentation to complete your application, it will send your spouse a letter asking for it. (See Chapter 15 for what to do if you don't get a timely answer from USCIS.)

Eventually your spouse will receive a denial or an approval of the visa petition.

a. If the Visa Petition Is Denied

If the visa petition is denied, USCIS will give a reason for the denial. The fastest thing to do is to fix the problem and try again.

For example, if the denial is because your petitioning spouse did not appear to be divorced from his or her previous spouse, your spouse will need to see a lawyer and obtain new and better documentation showing that there was a final divorce. Then your spouse can file a new visa petition.

b. If the Visa Petition Is Approved

Assuming your case is approved, your spouse will receive a notice from the USCIS Service Center. An example of a visa petition approval notice is shown below. As you can see, it's nothing fancy. But it is an important document. Make a few photocopies of it and store these and the original in safe places.

As you'll see when you get to the next step, you'll use a copy of the approval notice as part of your green card application.

6. Using the Checklist for Step One, Visa Petition

This checklist shows every form, document, and other item needed for the initial visa petition that your spouse, with your help, will assemble and submit to USCIS.

✓ **CHECKLIST**
A copy of this checklist is available in Appendix C.

Sample I-130 Receipt Notice

Department of Homeland Security
U.S. Citizenship and Immigration Services

I-797C, Notice of Action

THE UNITED STATES OF AMERICA

RECEIPT NUMBER		CASE TYPE	I130 IMMIGRANT PETITION FOR RELATIVE, FIANCE(E), OR ORPHAN
MSC-12-041-00000			
RECEIVED DATE April 21, 2010	**PRIORITY DATE**	**PETITIONER** MICHELA, GRUN	
NOTICE DATE April 23, 2012	**PAGE** 1 of 1	**BENEFICIARY** MICHELSKI, ANDA	

ILONA BRAY
RE: ANDA M. MICHELSKI
950 PARKER STREET
BERKELEY, CA 94710

Notice Type: Receipt Notice

Amount received: $ 420.00

Section: Husband or wife of U.S. citizen, 201(b)(2)(A)(i) INA

Receipt notice - If any of the above information is incorrect, call customer service immediately.

Processing time - Processing times vary by kind of case.
- You can check our current processing time for this kind of case on our website at **uscis.gov**.
- On our website you can also sign up to get free e-mail updates as we complete key processing steps on this case.
- Most of the time your case is pending the processing status will not change because we will be working on others filed earlier.
- We will notify you by mail when we make a decision on this case, or if we need something from you. If you move while this case is pending, call customer service when you move.
- Processing times can change. If you don't get a decision or update from us within our current processing time, check our website or call for an update.

If you have questions, check our website or call customer service. Please save this notice, and have it with you if you contact us about this case.

Notice to all customers with a pending I-130 petition - USCIS is now processing Form I-130, Petition for Alien Relative, as a visa number becomes available. Filing and approval of an I-130 relative petition is only the first step in helping a relative immigrate to the United States. Eligible family members must wait until there is a visa number available before they can apply for an immigrant visa or adjustment of status to a lawful permanent resident. This process will allow USCIS to concentrate resources first on cases where visas are actually available. This process should not delay the ability of one's relative to apply for an immigrant visa or adjustment of status. Refer to **www.state.gov/travel** **<http://www.state.gov/travel>** to determine current visa availability dates. For more information, please visit our website at www.uscis.gov or contact us at 1-800-375-5283.

Always remember to call customer service if you move while your case is pending. If you have a pending I-130 relative petition, also call customer service if you should decide to withdraw your petition or if you become a U.S. citizen.

Please see the additional information on the back. You will be notified separately about any other cases you filed.
U.S. CITIZENSHIP & IMMIGRATION SVC
CALIFORNIA SERVICE CENTER
P.O. BOX 30111
LAGUNA NIGUEL CA 92607-0111
Customer Service Telephone: (800) 375-5283

Form I-797C (Rev. 08/31/04) N

Sample I-130 Approval Notice

Department of Homeland Security U.S. Citizenship and Immigration Services	**I-797, Notice of Action**

THE UNITED STATES OF AMERICA

RECEIPT NUMBER		CASE TYPE	I130 IMMIGRANT PETITION FOR
MSC-12-047-00000			RELATIVE, FIANCE(E), OR ORPHAN

RECEIPT DATE	PRIORITY DATE	PETITIONER
April 21, 2012		MICHELA, GRUN

NOTICE DATE	PAGE	BENEFICIARY
October 11, 2012	1 of 1	MICHELSKI, ANDA

ILONA BRAY RE: TERESE MARIA MANCINI 950 PARKER STREET BERKELEY, CA 94710	**Notice Type:** Approval Notice Section: Husband or wife of U.S. citizen, 201(b)(2)(A)(i) INA

The above petition has been approved. We have sent the original visa petition to the **Department of State National Visa Center (NVC), 32 Rochester Avenue, Portsmouth, NH 03801-2909.** NVC processes all approved immigrant visa petitions that need consular action. It also determines which consular post is the appropriate consulate to complete visa processing. NVC will then forward the approved petition to that consulate.

The NVC will contact the person for whom you are petitioning(beneficiary) concerning further immigrant visa processing steps.

If you have any questions about visa issuance, please contact the NVC directly. However, please allow at least 90 days before calling the NVC if your beneficiary has not received correspondence from the NVC. The telephone number of the NVC is **(603) 334-0700**.

THIS FORM IS NOT A VISA NOR MAY IT BE USED IN PLACE OF A VISA.

Please see the additional information on the back. You will be notified separately about any other cases you filed.

U.S. CITIZENSHIP & IMMIGRATION SERVICES
P.O. BOX 68005
LEE'S SUMMIT, MO 68005
Customer Service Telephone: (800) 375-5283

Form I-797 (Rev. 01/31/05) N

Checklist for Visa Petition by U. S. Citizen

☐ Form I-130 (see line-by-line instructions in Section D1, above)

☐ Documents to accompany Form I-130 (photocopies only):

   ☐ Your marriage certificate (see Chapter 4, Section C, on obtaining vital documents)

   ☐ Proof of the U.S. citizenship status of your petitioning spouse, such as a birth certificate, passport, certificate of naturalization, or Form FS-20 (Report of Birth Abroad of a United States Citizen)

   ☐ Proof of termination of all previous marriages, such as certificates of death, divorce, or annulment (see Chapter 4, Section C, regarding how to obtain vital documents)

   ☐ One color photo of you; passport style

   ☐ One color photo of your spouse (passport style), and

   ☐ Fees: Currently $420 for an I-130, but double-check this at www.uscis.gov or call 800-375-5283

☐ Form G-325A, Biographic Information, filled out by you (see Section D2, above, for line-by-line instructions)

☐ Form G-325A, Biographic Information, filled out by your U. S. citizen spouse (see Section D2, above, for line-by-line instructions)

Next Step If You Entered The U.S. Legally

You will be applying for your green card in the United States:	See Chapter 14 on applying to adjust your status to permanent resident.
You will be applying for your green card overseas:	See Chapter 7, starting at Section B4, on consular processing procedures.

Next Step If You Entered The U.S. Ilegally

If you are grandfathered into being allowed to adjust status in the United States:	See Chapter 14 regarding adjustment of status application procedures.
If you leave the United States before six months are up:	See Chapter 7, starting at Section B4, on consular processing procedures.
If you plan to leave the United States after six months have passed and apply for a waiver:	See an attorney; Chapter 17 contains tips on finding a good one.

Spouses of Permanent Residents, in the U.S.

If you are in the United States—legally or illegally—and you are married to a U.S. lawful permanent resident, you are not immediately eligible to obtain permanent residence. Only foreign nationals married to U.S. citizens are immediately eligible for permanent residence.

As the spouse of a permanent resident, you are known as a preference relative. There are quotas on the number of preference relatives who are allowed green cards each year, which means there are long waiting lists. Your spouse can, and should, put you on the waiting list for a green card right away. But you'll probably be on the waiting list for three to five years. And no matter what your circumstances, it probably won't be legal for you to live in the United States while you wait (unless you happen to have a nonimmigrant visa that will last for all those years).

The key to how and where you'll get your green card is whether you entered the United States legally or illegally. If you entered illegally, you lose certain important rights. Start by reading Section A to see whether your entry is considered legal or illegal, then move on to the subsections that match your current situation.

A. Did You Enter Legally or Illegally?

If you entered the United States with permission of the U.S. authorities, you entered legally. Whether you got that permission in advance or were simply allowed in when you arrived, the important thing is that you were personally met and allowed to enter by an officer of the U.S. border control. This might have occurred at the border itself or some other port of entry, such as an airport, seaport, or bus station. The usual ways people enter legally are:

- with a visa (a tourist, student, or temporary worker visa, for example)
- with a border crossing card (a special pass allowing regular entries)
- under the Visa Waiver Program (whereby citizens of certain countries are allowed to enter the U.S. as tourists by showing only

their passport, without first obtaining an entry visa).

An illegal entry is, naturally, the opposite of a legal entry. People entering illegally have failed to obtain permission to enter. They may pay someone to sneak them across the U.S. border, wait until the dead of night and find an unguarded point on the U.S. border, or conceal themselves in the trunk of a car. USCIS says that they entered "without inspection," which means that they weren't personally met and approved for entry by a U.S. border control official. (USCIS refers to such people as "EWIs," pronounced "ee-wee," which stands for entry without inspection.) The immigration laws make getting a green card very difficult for people who entered the United States without inspection, or illegally.

 **SKIP AHEAD**
If you entered the United States by crossing the border illegally, skip ahead to Section C.

B. Spouses Who Entered Legally

This section explains the immigration choices for foreign nationals who entered the United States legally and still live here. It applies to those of you who have overstayed your visa as well as those who are still within the visa's time limit.

1. Options and Strategies

USCIS expects the application process for every spouse of a permanent resident—even those who happen to be in the United States already—to follow this sequence:

1. Your permanent resident spouse puts you on the waiting list for a green card by filing a visa petition on Form I-130.
2. You wait overseas for an average of three to five years until you reach the top of the waiting list.
3. You apply for an immigrant visa at a U.S consulate in your home country.

4. Only when you have your immigrant visa do you come to the United States to claim your green card.

Unfortunately, what USCIS expects and what immigrant applicants want are often two different things. We're guessing that since you are already in the United States, you would like to stay here with your spouse while you apply for your green card. Many couples have stayed illegally in the past, and for brief periods Congress allowed them to apply for their green cards here—but these laws are gone (although a few people can still take advantage of them; see Section 3, below). It will be difficult or impossible for the spouses of permanent residents living in the United States to remain in the United States while they apply for a green card. Nevertheless, the options outlined below will cover every possible way to get your green card in the United States and will tell you how and where to apply if you can't.

CAUTION

The six-month problem. If you've already stayed in the United States for six or more months beyond the expiration of your permitted stay, you have a very good reason to look for a way to get your green card without leaving the United States. If you leave the country and apply for permission to come back as a permanent resident, you can be prevented from entering the United States for three or ten years even if you are otherwise entitled to a green card through marriage (see Chapter 2, Section A, to review the time bar penalties for illegal stays).

The spouse of a U.S. lawful permanent resident has five options (though we don't recommend all of them, as you'll see in the subsequent discussion):

- stay in the United States legally (if your nonimmigrant visa lasts long enough to get you through the waiting period) and adjust your status to permanent resident in the United States; this option is covered in Section 2, below
- stay in the United States illegally, hoping for a way to adjust your status to green card holder

in the United States; this path is explained in Section 3
- leave the United States before you have overstayed your visa by six months or more, wait overseas, then apply for a green card at a U.S. consulate; this possibility is explained in Section 4
- leave the United States after you have overstayed your visa by more than six months but less than one year, wait out your waiting period at the same time that you serve your three-year penalty for overstaying, then apply for a green card at a U.S. consulate; this possibility is explained in Section 5, or
- leave the United States after you have overstayed your visa by more than six months or a year, wait overseas, then apply for your green card at a U.S. consulate, together with a request for a waiver (forgiveness) of your overstay; this option is described in Section 6.

2. Stay in the U.S. Legally

If you can make your current visa (the one you used to enter the United States) last for the full three to five years that you are likely to spend on the waiting list for a green card, you may be able to apply for your green card without leaving the United States. However, all of the following will need to be true when your waiting period is over and it's time for you to apply for your green card:

- you entered the United States legally
- you have never been out of lawful U.S. immigration status
- you have never worked illegally in the United States, and
- your visa waiting period is over and you are immediately eligible to apply for your green card.

CAUTION

If you are already out of lawful immigration status or have worked illegally, skip to Section 3, below. If you're uncertain, consult an attorney; see Chapter 17 for tips on finding a good lawyer.

If your current stay (as probably shown on your I-94) has not expired and you haven't worked illegally, your spouse should file an initial visa petition for you as soon as possible. This is the application that will put you on the waiting list for a green card. (See Section D below for how to prepare and submit this petition.) You should have no problem getting USCIS approval to put you on the waiting list. Then the important question is: Will your current visa status (student, temporary worker, or some other) really last long enough to get you through the waiting period?

If you are on a tourist visa, the answer is probably no. Your waiting period is likely to last three to five years or more—but your tourist visa is probably good for no more than six months, with the possibility of one six-month extension. If you are on some other visa, such as a student or temporary worker visa, you may have a chance. In fact, academic student visas can be extended by moving on to a more advanced program; and some temporary worker visas can be renewed. Just be sure not to work illegally, which would destroy your eligibility to adjust status.

CAUTION
Watch out if you're in the U.S. on a work-based visa. If you entered the U.S. on certain types of employment-based visas, applying for a green card through your U.S. citizen spouse puts you at risk of losing your visa status. See the discussion called, "Here on an Employment Visa? The Risks of Applying for a Green Card," in Chapter 2, Section A.

SEE AN EXPERT
A full discussion of which visas are renewable and how long you can make them last is outside the scope of this book. You may wish to consult with an attorney.

If your visa runs out and you are still on the waiting list, what should you do? You will need to make an educated guess at how much longer you will be on the waiting list (see Section E below for

help). If your wait is probably going to be another six months or more from the date your visa expires, you would be best advised to leave the United States within those six months to avoid facing a three- or ten-year bar on reentering (be sure to save proof of your departure date, such as a plane ticket). You could try returning to the United States with another temporary visa, but the U.S. consulate is unlikely to grant one, knowing that your true intention is to stay in the United States permanently (which the consulate would see as a misuse of the temporary visa).

Another option is to consider when your spouse will become a U.S. citizen. Once he or she becomes a citizen, you move off the waiting list and can apply for a green card right away, no matter how long you overstayed your visa. But you will be living in the United States illegally between the time your visa runs out and when you turn in your green card application. USCIS or DHS is unlikely to look for you, but if it happens to catch you, it will probably deport you. (See Section 3 below for a discussion of living in the United States illegally and for more on the benefits of your spouse becoming a citizen.)

If you do need to finish your wait in your home country, you will ultimately apply for your green card through a U.S. consulate. So long as you didn't stay unlawfully in the United States for more than six continuous months, this is not a risky procedure. Hopefully, you won't have to wait overseas for long.

SKIP AHEAD
If an option described in this section definitely fits your situation, go to Section D below for the next step.

3. Stay in the U.S. Illegally

It is illegal to stay in the United States past the expiration of any temporary visa while you are on the waiting list for a green card. However, a number of people take this risk. The people most likely to do so are those who know or believe that an exception to the law allows them access to a local USCIS office to apply for their green card (adjustment of status) at the end of their wait. For these few people, taking the risk of waiting illegally may have a big payoff at the end, because there will be no penalty for their illegal stay when they apply to adjust status. By contrast, any applicant abroad who goes to a U.S. consulate to apply for a green card is exposed to penalties for their illegal stay—a three- or ten-year bar on returning to the United States, depending on the length of their stay. Still, staying in the United States illegally is a gamble that we only describe, not recommend.

> **CAUTION**
> **People who attempt to stay in the United States illegally can be picked up and placed in removal proceedings at any time.** Your marriage to a permanent resident will not be enough by itself to protect you from deportation. For more on the risks, see Subsection 3c, below.

Some people choose to wait illegally in the United States knowing that they won't be permitted to adjust their status at the end of the waiting period. Their only hope is that the immigration laws will change in their favor. This is a huge gamble—recent changes in the immigration laws have made them harsher, not gentler on immigrants. But none of us has a crystal ball, and some immigrant families find it unthinkable to separate now, come what may later.

There are two categories of people who might be allowed to adjust their status to permanent resident at a USCIS office, even after their visa has run out and they have stayed illegally. These are people whose spouses become U.S. citizens during the waiting period, and people who fall into narrow exceptions within the immigration laws.

a. If Your Spouse Becomes a U.S. Citizen

If your permanent resident spouse becomes a U.S. citizen, your situation will dramatically improve.

For this reason, your spouse should be planning now for U.S. citizenship.

i. Move Off the Waiting List and Adjust Status

When your spouse becomes a U.S. citizen, you become eligible to adjust your status to permanent resident in the United States right away. This is true even if your spouse becomes a citizen after your visa runs out and you've stayed in the United States illegally, no matter how long your illegal stay. Regardless of your status, you would move off the green card waiting list and become what is known as an immediate relative.

You'll become eligible for a green card just as soon as you can get through the rest of the application procedures. And you won't have to leave the United States to apply for that green card. Because you entered the United States legally and your spouse is a U.S. citizen, you are eligible to file your green card application in the United States, using the adjustment of status procedure.

> **CAUTION**
> **Don't leave the United States until your green card is approved.** Having your spouse become a U.S. citizen doesn't solve everything. If you stayed illegally for more than six months in the United States after the expiration of your visa and before turning in your green card application, watch out. Leaving the United States before your green card is approved will subject you to bars on reentry of three or ten years.

ii. When Your Spouse Can Apply for Citizenship

A permanent resident can apply for U.S. citizenship five years after approval for residence (with some exceptions).

Unless your spouse faces some serious impediment to citizenship—such as not knowing English or having a criminal record—he or she should apply for citizenship as soon as possible. USCIS permits people to submit the application three months before the end of their waiting period—but no more than three months, or USCIS will reject the application.

RESOURCE

Want more information on the process and requirements of applying for U.S. citizenship? See the USCIS website at www.uscis.gov, or *Becoming a U.S. Citizen: A Guide to the Law, Exam & Interview,* by Ilona Bray (Nolo).

b. A Few People Can Adjust Status in the U.S.

A very few people living illegally in the United States might be lucky enough to fall into an exception to the immigration laws and be allowed to change their status to permanent resident at a local USCIS office. The key is whether an employer or a family member of yours, even if it wasn't your spouse, filed an immigrant visa petition on your behalf either:

- before January 14, 1998, or
- between January 14, 1998 and April 30, 2001, if you can also prove that you were physically present in the United States on December 21, 2000.

If that visa petition was approved, or if it was denied only because of a mistake by the INS (as USCIS was then called), then you will be "grandfathered in" under the old laws and allowed to change your status to permanent resident at a USCIS office. Immigrants who can take advantage of the time windows mentioned above are among the lucky few who won't have to travel to a U.S. consulate to apply for their green card. (For more details on the grandfathering clauses, see Chapter 2, Section A.)

This grandfathering exception only lets you submit and receive a decision on your green card application at a USCIS office as opposed to an overseas consulate. It doesn't mean that you can stay in the United States illegally while on the waiting list (for permission to submit the green card application). But many people take the risk of staying, in order to be with their spouse during the application process. (USCIS doesn't normally search these people out, but will deport them if it happens to find them.)

If you get to the end of the waiting period without any contact with USCIS, you'll be allowed to apply for your green card.

The opportunity to adjust status in the United States is especially valuable to people who have already stayed for more than six months past the expiration date of their visa. If they leave the United States, they can be kept out for three or ten years. (See Chapter 2, Section A.)

c. The Risks of Staying Illegally

If you decide to stay in the United States illegally, you will be taking some chances. USCIS so far has not made efforts to catch waiting spouses of permanent residents—they have other things on top of their enforcement priority list, such as going after criminal or terrorist aliens or people with no family members here. But this policy could change. In addition, you could be picked up in a raid, or after someone with a grudge has tipped off USCIS or DHS to your whereabouts.

If you are picked up, you will probably be removed (deported)—and hit with a ten-year bar on returning to the United States. Your marriage to a U.S. permanent resident won't help you if you are still on the waiting list for a visa. It could only help you if you were immediately eligible to apply for your green card, either because your waiting period was over or your spouse had become a U.S. citizen.

 SEE AN EXPERT

If you are discovered by USCIS or DHS, get a lawyer right away. The lawyer can fully evaluate your case and possibly defend you against deportation. Whatever you do, don't ignore the summons to go to court—that could destroy your chances of getting a green card later.

4. Leave Before You Have Overstayed by Six Months or Less

If you haven't stayed more than six months past the expiration date of your visa or other right to be here (such as having entered under the Visa Waiver Program), your safest bet is to leave the United States before that date rolls around. It is particularly important to think about when you are going to leave if you won't be allowed to submit your green card application to a USCIS office (because your situation does not fit into Subsection 3a or 3b, above). If you must leave, it's better to leave sooner rather than later. Remember, if you leave before you have overstayed your visa for six months, there are no penalties. But if you've overstayed a visa (or status) by 180 to 365 continuous days, you can be barred from returning to the United States for three years. If you overstay for more than a year, you can be barred for ten years.

> ! **CAUTION**
> **Make sure you can prove you overstayed by less than six months.** When the time comes to apply for your green card, the consulate will want proof of how long you stayed illegally in the United States. Collect and keep all evidence, such as your plane tickets, store receipts, medical records, credit card statements, and anything else relevant to show that you left the United States before six months was up.

After you are overseas and your waiting period is over or your spouse becomes a U.S. citizen, you can receive a green card through normal procedures at an overseas consulate. Obviously, this may also mean many years of separation from your spouse while you wait overseas to rise to the top of the waiting list. But five years of separation now might be better than ten years of separation (because of a time bar penalty) later.

5. Leave After You Have Overstayed by More Than Six Months but Less Than One Year

If you have stayed past the expiration date of your visa by more than six months but less than year, the law would only bar you from returning to the United States for a three-year period. If you

left the United States now, your three-year penalty would likely be over by the time you reach the top of the waiting list and you are allowed to apply for your immigrant visa and green card.

Leaving the United States before you overstay your visa by a year or more might be safer than staying around for the whole green card waiting period and risking being caught by the immigration authorities. You could be deported and prevented from reentering the United States for ten years.

> ! **CAUTION**
> **Make sure you can prove you overstayed by less than one year.** When the time comes to apply for your green card, the consulate will want to see proof of how long you stayed illegally in the United States. Collect and keep all evidence, such as your plane tickets, store receipts, medical records, credit card statements, and anything else relevant to show that you left before a year was up.

6. Leave After You Have Overstayed a Year or More and Apply for a Waiver

If you have stayed in the United States more than a year after your visa expired and cannot apply for a green card there, you face a long wait overseas. Overstaying by more than a year means you will be prevented from returning to the United States for ten years. (See Chapter 2, Section A.)

If you are outside the United States after an illegal stay of a year or more and your visa waiting period ends, you will have to finish out your ten-year penalty before applying for a green card to return. You will, however, keep your place on the waiting list. The only way to avoid the ten-year bar is to ask USCIS to forgive your illegal time in the United States. This is called asking for a waiver (which spouses of permanent residents can do only after leaving the U.S., at the time they submit the final portions of the green card application). This procedure is best handled by an experienced immigration attorney.

The attorney can give you a sense of how likely it is that your waiver will be approved. There are certainly no guarantees. To get a waiver request approved, you will have to show that your not receiving a visa will cause extreme hardship to your spouse in the United States and if you happen to have a U.S. citizen or permanent resident parent in the U.S., to him or her, too—and when the law says extreme, it means much more than the sadness they will feel at your being thousands of miles away. The classic case of extreme hardship is someone whose U.S. spouse or parent has severe medical or emotional problems that require the immigrating spouse's constant attention. Financial hardship will also be taken into account

With a waiver, you can return to the United States as soon as your waiting period is over and you get through the immigrant visa/green card application process, which usually takes about one year.

SEE AN EXPERT

These waivers are relatively new. Look for an attorney who has experience preparing and presenting them. See Chapter 17 for tips on finding a good attorney.

C. Spouses Who Entered Illegally

This section is for foreign nationals living in the United States after entering illegally. Unfortunately, your path to a green card is a difficult one, involving unattractive choices. Before explaining them in detail, we need to warn one group of readers to see an attorney if:

- you've entered the U.S. illegally two or more times and
- the total amount of illegal time in the U.S. is one year or more; or
- you've been deported.

These would-be immigrants may be permanently barred from immigrating to the United States. See Chapter 2, Section A, for further information about the permanent bar.

1. Options and Strategies

USCIS expects the application process for every spouse of a permanent resident—even those already living in the United States—to follow this sequence:

1. Your permanent resident spouse puts you on the waiting list for a green card by filing a visa petition on Form I-130.
2. You wait overseas (for an average of three to five years) until you reach the top of the waiting list.
3. You apply for an immigrant visa at a U.S consulate in your home country.
4. Only when you have your immigrant visa do you come to the United States to claim your green card.

But what USCIS expects and what immigrant applicants want are often two different things. We're guessing that since you are already in the United States, you would like to stay here with your spouse while you apply for your green card. Many couples have stayed illegally in the past, and for brief periods of time Congress allowed them to apply for their green cards here—but these laws are gone (although a few people can still take advantage of them. See Section 2, below). It will be difficult or impossible for the spouses of permanent residents now living in the United States to remain in the United States while they apply for a green card. It is particularly difficult for people who entered illegally, because unlike people who entered with a visa, you will not be allowed to submit your green card application in the United States even if your spouse becomes a U.S. citizen.

Nevertheless, the options outlined below will consider every possible way to get your green card in the United States and will tell you how and where to apply if you can't.

CAUTION

The six-month problem. If you've already stayed illegally in the United States for six months or more, you have a very good reason to look for a way to get your green card without leaving the United States. If you leave the country and apply for permission to come back as a legal permanent resident, you can be prevented from entering the United States for three or ten years even if you are otherwise entitled to a green card through marriage. (See Chapter 2, Section A, to review the time bar penalties for illegal stays.)

You have four options (though we don't recommend all of them, as you'll see in the subsequent discussion):

- stay in the United States illegally, hoping for a way to adjust your status to permanent residence through a local USCIS office; this option is covered in Section 2, below
- leave the United States before you have stayed illegally for six months or more, wait out your waiting period, and apply for your green card through a U.S. consulate overseas; this path is explained in Section 3
- leave the United States after you have stayed illegally for more than six months but less than a year, wait out your waiting period at the same time that you serve your three-year penalty for staying illegally, and apply for your green card through a U.S. consulate overseas; this possibility is explained in Section 4
- leave the United States after you have stayed illegally for more than a year, wait overseas, then apply for your green card along with a waiver of your illegal stay through a U.S. consulate overseas; this option is described in Section 5.

2. Stay in the U.S. Illegally

If you've entered the U.S. illegally, it's against the law to stay in the United States while you are on the waiting list for a green card. However, a number of people take this risk.

The people most likely to risk living in the United States illegally are those who know or believe that an exception to the law allows them access to a local USCIS office to apply for their green card

(adjustment of status) at the end of their wait. For these few people, taking the risk of waiting illegally may have a big payoff at the end, because there will be no penalty for their illegal stay when they apply to adjust status. By contrast, any applicant who goes to a U.S. consulate to apply for a green card is exposed to penalties for their illegal stay—a three- or ten-year bar on returning to the United States, depending on the length of their stay. Staying in the United States illegally is a gamble that we only describe, not recommend.

 CAUTION
People who attempt stay in the United States illegally can be picked up and placed in removal proceedings at any time. Your marriage to a permanent resident is not enough by itself to protect you. For more on the risks, see Subsection 2b, below.

There is another option, which we also don't recommend. You could wait in the United States illegally, hoping that the immigration laws will change in your favor and make you eligible to apply for a green card at a USCIS office. This is a huge gamble—recent changes in the immigration laws have made them harsher, not gentler on immigrants. But none of us has a crystal ball, and some immigrant families find it unthinkable to separate now, come what may later.

 TIP
Some immigrants may become legal some other way. It is possible, although rare, for someone to enter the United States illegally and later acquire the right to be there, temporarily or permanently. For example, someone might enter illegally but apply for political asylum and be given the right to live in the U.S. while the claim is being decided. These situations are outside the scope of this book. If you are proceeding on more than one immigration application at once, you should see an attorney for help. See Chapter 17 for tips on finding a good lawyer.

a. A Few Who Entered Illegally Can Adjust Their Status in the U.S.

Only certain categories of immigrants are now allowed to apply for their green card in the United States using the adjustment of status procedure. People who entered the United States illegally are normally not among them. However, a very few people might be lucky enough to fall into an exception to these laws, based on having started the application process before the laws changed. The key is whether a prospective employer or a close family member of yours, even if it wasn't your spouse, filed an immigrant labor certification or visa petition (Form I-130 for family members) on your behalf either:

- before January 14, 1998, or
- between January 14, 1998 and April 30, 2001, if you can also prove that you were physically present in the United States on December 21, 2000.

If that visa petition was approved, or if it was denied only because of a mistake by the INS (as USCIS was then called), you may be allowed to adjust your status to permanent resident at a USCIS office. People who may take advantage of one of these time windows are said to be "grandfathered in" under the old laws. (For more details on who is grandfathered in, see Chapter 2, Section A. Also check whether Congress has extended the deadlines for taking advantage of these grandfathering provisions; see the legal updates to this book on Nolo's website at www.nolo.com.) In short, if your labor certification or visa petition was on file as described above, you have a ticket to adjust your status in the United States, even though you entered the country illegally.

This exception only lets you use a USCIS office instead of an overseas consulate to submit and receive a decision on your green card application. It doesn't mean that you can stay in the United States while on the waiting list (before submitting the green card portion of your application). But many people take the risk of staying, in order to be with their spouse during the application process. (USCIS doesn't normally search these people out, but will deport them if it happens to find them.) If you get to the end of the waiting period without any contact with USCIS, you'll be allowed to walk right into a USCIS office and apply for your green card.

The opportunity to change status in the United States is especially valuable to people who have already stayed illegally for more than six months. If they leave the United States, they can be kept out for three or ten years. (See Chapter 2, Section A.)

b. The Risks If You Stay Illegally

If you decide to stay in the United States illegally, you will be taking some chances. USCIS has not made efforts to catch waiting spouses of permanent residents—they have other things on top of their enforcement priority list, such as going after criminal aliens or people with no family members here. But this policy could change. In addition, you could be picked up in a USCIS raid, or after someone with a grudge tips off USCIS to your whereabouts.

If you are picked up, you will probably be deported—and hit with a ten-year bar on returning to the United States. Your marriage to a U.S. permanent resident won't help you if you are still on the waiting list for a visa. It could only help you if you were immediately eligible to apply for your green card because your waiting period was over.

 SEE AN EXPERT

If you are discovered by USCIS or DHS, get a lawyer right away. The lawyer can fully evaluate your case and possibly defend you against deportation. Whatever you do, don't ignore the summons to go to court—that could destroy your chances of getting a green card later.

3. Leave Before You Have Stayed Illegally for Six Months

If you haven't stayed illegally in the United States for more than six months, your safest bet is to leave before that date rolls around. It is particularly important to think about when you are going to leave if you won't be allowed to submit your green card application to a USCIS office (because your situation does not fit into Subsection 2a, above). If you must leave, it's better to leave sooner rather than later. Remember, if you leave before you have stayed illegally for six months, there are no penalties. But if you've stayed illegally for 180 to 365 continuous days, you can be barred from returning to the United States for three years. If you stay illegally for more than a year, you can be barred for ten years.

> **CAUTION**
> **Make sure you can prove you stayed for less than six months.** When the time comes to apply for your green card, the consulate will want to see proof of how long you stayed illegally in the United States. Collect and keep all evidence, such as your plane tickets, store receipts, medical records, credit card statements, and anything else that shows where you were and when.

After you are overseas and your waiting period is over, you can receive a green card through normal procedures at an overseas consulate. Obviously, this may also mean many years of separation from your spouse while you wait overseas to rise to the top of the waiting list. But five years of separation now might be better than ten years of separation (because of a time bar penalty) later.

4. Leave After You Have Stayed Illegally for More Than Six Months but Less Than One Year

If you have stayed in the United States illegally for more than six months but less than one year, the law will bar you from returning to the United States for only a three-year period. If you leave the United States now, your three-year penalty period will likely be over by the time you reach the top of the waiting list and are allowed to apply for your immigrant visa and green card.

Leaving the United States before you have stayed illegally for a year or more might be safer than staying around for the whole green card waiting period and risking being caught by the immigration authorities. You could be deported and prevented from reentering the United States for ten years.

> **CAUTION**
> **Make sure you can prove you stayed illegally by less than one year.** When the time comes to apply for your green card, the consulate will want to see proof of how long you stayed illegally in the United States. Collect and keep all evidence, such as your plane tickets, store receipts, medical records, credit card statements, and anything else relevant to show where you were and when.

5. Leave After You Have Stayed Over One Year Illegally and Apply for a Waiver

If you have stayed illegally in the United States for more than a year and cannot apply for a green card there, you face a long wait overseas. Staying more than a year gets you a ten-year bar on returning to the United States. (See Chapter 2, Section A.)

If you are outside the United States after an illegal stay of a year or more and your visa waiting period ends, you will have to finish out your ten-year penalty before applying for a green card to return. You will, however, keep your place on the waiting list. The only way to avoid the ten-year bar is to ask USCIS to forgive your illegal time in the United States. This is called asking for a waiver (which you would do at the same time as you submitted the final portions of your green card application). This procedure is best handled by an experienced immigration attorney.

The attorney can give you a sense of how likely it is that your waiver will be approved. There are certainly no guarantees. To get a waiver request approved, you will have to show that your not receiving a visa will cause extreme hardship to your spouse and parents (if they happen to be U.S. citizens or permanent residents) in the United States—and when the law says extreme, it means much more than the sadness they will feel at your being thousands of miles away. The classic case of extreme hardship is someone whose U.S. spouse or parent has severe medical problems that require the immigrating spouse's constant attention. Financial hardship will also be taken into account.

With a waiver, you can return to the United States as soon as your waiting period is over and you get through the immigrant visa/green card application process, which usually takes about one year.

 SEE AN EXPERT
These waivers are relatively new. Look for an attorney who has actual experience with them. Even some experienced immigration attorneys may have requested only a few of these waivers. See Chapter 17 for tips on finding a good attorney.

D. Step One: I-130 Visa Petition

Regardless of whether you apply for and receive your green card overseas or in the United States, there is one thing that you should do right away. Have your spouse file a visa petition to get you onto the waiting list. Don't worry that this petition will alert USCIS or DHS that you are in the United States illegally (if you are)—the immigration authorities don't usually use this information to track people down to deport them. The sooner your spouse files the visa petition, the sooner your wait to receive your green card will be over.

The visa petition asks USCIS to acknowledge that you're married and let you go forward with green card processing. Approval of the visa petition does not mean you're guaranteed approval of your green card, however. This is only the first step in the process. Like every immigrant, you will eventually have to file your own, extensive portion of the green card application. At that time, the U.S. government will take a hard look at your financial situation and other factors that might make you inadmissible.

 CAUTION
If the U.S. petitioner has a criminal record, see an attorney. Under the Adam Walsh Child Protection and Safety Act of 2006, U.S. citizens and lawful permanent residents who have been convicted of any "specified offense against a minor" are prohibited from filing a family-based immigrant petition on behalf of any beneficiary (whether a child or not). USCIS will run security checks on all petitions and may call the petitioner in for fingerprinting. If the petitioner has a conviction for one of the specified offenses against a minor, then the petition will not be approved unless USCIS determines that the U.S. petitioner poses no risk to the beneficiary.

1. Line-by-Line Instructions for Visa Petition Forms

This section will give you precise instructions for filling in the forms that are listed on the visa petition checklist below. Before proceeding, see Chapter 4 for general instructions on filling in USCIS forms. Also, as you read these instructions, you should have a copy of the appropriate form in hand.

a. Form I-130

The first thing to notice about Form I-130 is that it runs in two columns (except for the tiny Part A near the top). The left column, or Part B, asks for information about the petitioner—that's your U.S. permanent resident spouse. Don't be thrown off by the fact that the form addresses your spouse as "you"—after all, it's your spouse who fills in and signs this form. The right column asks for information about you, referred to as the relative. Now for the questions.

WEB RESOURCE
Form I-130 is available on the USCIS website at www.uscis.gov. Below is a sample filled-in version of this form.

Sample Form I-130, Petition for Alien Relative—Page 1

Department of Homeland Security
U.S. Citizenship and Immigration Services

OMB No. 1615-0012; Expires 01/31/2012

I-130, Petition for Alien Relative

DO NOT WRITE IN THIS BLOCK - FOR USCIS OFFICE ONLY

A#

Section of Law/Visa Category
- [ ] 201(b) Spouse - IR-1/CR-1
- [ ] 201(b) Child - IR-2/CR-2
- [ ] 201(b) Parent - IR-5
- [ ] 203(a)(1) Unm. S or D - F1-1
- [ ] 203(a)(2)(A)Spouse - F2-1
- [ ] 203(a)(2)(A) Child - F2-2
- [ ] 203(a)(2)(B) Unm. S or D - F2-4
- [ ] 203(a)(3) Married S or D - F3-1
- [ ] 203(a)(4) Brother/Sister - F4-1

Action Stamp

Fee Stamp

Petition was filed on: _____ (priority date)
- [ ] Personal Interview
- [ ] Pet. [ ] Ben. " A" File Reviewed
- [ ] Field Investigation
- [ ] 203(a)(2)(A) Resolved
- [ ] Previously Forwarded
- [ ] I-485 Filed Simultaneously
- [ ] 204(g) Resolved
- [ ] 203(g) Resolved

Remarks:

A. Relationship   You are the petitioner.   Your relative is the beneficiary.

1. I am filing this petition for my:
[X] Husband/Wife   [ ] Parent   [ ] Brother/Sister   [ ] Child

2. Are you related by adoption?
[ ] Yes   [X] No

3. Did you gain permanent residence through adoption?
[ ] Yes   [X] No

B. Information about you

1. Name (Family name in CAPS)   (First)   (Middle)
NGUYEN   Teo   Thanh

2. Address (Number and Street)   (Apt. No.)
1640 Lincoln Park

(Town or City)   (State/Country)   (Zip/Postal Code)
Beaverton   Oregon   97006

3. Place of Birth (Town or City)   (State/Country)
Saigon   Vietnam

4. Date of Birth
4/12/1986

5. Gender
[X] Male
[ ] Female

6. Marital Status
[X] Married   [ ] Single
[ ] Widowed   [ ] Divorced

7. Other Names Used (including maiden name)
None

8. Date and Place of Present Marriage (if married)
May 22, 2012 – Salem, Oregon

9. U.S. Social Security Number (If any)
756-91-0637

10. Alien Registration Number
A22334455

11. Name(s) of Prior Husband(s)/Wive(s)
None

12. Date(s) Marriage(s) Ended

13. If you are a U.S. citizen, complete the following:

My citizenship was acquired through (check one):
- [ ] Birth in the U.S.
- [ ] Naturalization. Give certificate number and date and place of issuance.

- [ ] Parents. Have you obtained a certificate of citizenship in your own name?
   - [ ] Yes. Give certificate number, date and place of issuance.   [ ] No

14. If you are a lawful permanent resident alien, complete the following:

Date and place of admission for or adjustment to lawful permanent residence and class of admission.

1/12/1989, SFR, IR-2

14b. Did you gain permanent resident status through marriage to a U.S. citizen or lawful permanent resident?
[ ] Yes   [X] No

C. Information about your relative

1. Name (Family name in CAPS)   (First)   (Middle)
NGUYEN   Lea   Nadres

2. Address (Number and Street)   (Apt. No.)
1640 Lincoln Park

(Town or City)   (State/Country)   (Zip/Postal Code)
Beaverton   Oregon   97006

3. Place of Birth (Town or City)   (State/Country)
Quezon City   Philippines

4. Date of Birth
7/18/86

5. Gender
[ ] Male
[X] Female

6. Marital Status
[X] Married   [ ] Single
[ ] Widowed   [ ] Divorced

7. Other Names Used (including maiden name)
Pebet

8. Date and Place of Present Marriage (if married)
May 22, 2012 – Salem, Oregon

9. U.S. Social Security Number (If any)
989-99-9898

10. Alien Registration Number
A 23456789

11. Name(s) of Prior Husband(s)/Wive(s)
None

12. Date(s) Marriage(s) Ended

13. Has your relative ever been in the U.S.?   [X] Yes   [ ] No

14. If your relative is currently in the U.S., complete the following:
He or she arrived as a: Student
(visitor, student, stowaway, without inspection, etc.)

Arrival/Departure Record (I-94)   **Date arrived**
1 4 6 ▬ 0 7 7 1 2 2 1 0   12/23/2008

Date authorized stay expired, or will expire, as shown on Form I-94 or I-95
D/S

15. Name and address of present employer (if any)
None

Date this employment began

16. Has your relative ever been under immigration proceedings?
[X] No   [ ] Yes   Where _____   When _____
[ ] Removal   [ ] Exclusion/Deportation   [ ] Rescission   [ ] Judicial Proceedings

INITIAL RECEIPT   RESUBMITTED   RELOCATED: Rec'd ____   Sent ____   COMPLETED: Appv'd ____   Denied ____   Ret'd ____

Form I-130 (01/08/12) Y

Sample Form I-130, Petition for Alien Relative—Page 2

C. Information about your alien relative (continued)

17. List husband/wife and all children of your relative.

(Name)	(Relationship)	(Date of Birth)	(Country of Birth)
N/A			

18. Address in the United States where your relative intends to live.

(Street Address)	(Town or City)	(State)
1640 Lincoln Park	Beaverton	Oregon

19. Your relative's address abroad. (Include street, city, province and country) — Phone Number (if any)

1678 Trout Chautoco Roxas District, Q.C., Philippines

20. If your relative's native alphabet is other than Roman letters, write his or her name and foreign address in the native alphabet.

(Name) — Address (Include street, city, province and country):

N/A

21. If filing for your husband/wife, give last address at which you lived together. (Include street, city, province, if any, and country):

		From:	To:
11640 Lincoln Park	Beaverton, Oregon	5/09	Present

22. Complete the information below if your relative is in the United States and will apply for adjustment of status.

Your relative is in the United States and will apply for adjustment of status to that of a lawful permanent resident at the USCIS office in:

If your relative is not eligible for adjustment of status, he or she will apply for a visa abroad at the American consular post in:

Portland	Oregon	Manila	Philippines
(City)	(State)	(City)	(Country)

NOTE: Designation of a U.S. embassy or consulate outside the country of your relative's last residence does not guarantee acceptance for processing by that post. Acceptance is at the discretion of the designated embassy or consulate.

D. Other information

1. If separate petitions are also being submitted for other relatives, give names of each and relationship.

2. Have you ever before filed a petition for this or any other alien? ☐ Yes ☒ No

If "Yes," give name, place and date of filing and result.

WARNING: USCIS investigates claimed relationships and verifies the validity of documents. USCIS seeks criminal prosecutions when family relationships are falsified to obtain visas.

PENALTIES: By law, you may be imprisoned for not more than five years or fined $250,000, or both, for entering into a marriage contract for the purpose of evading any provision of the immigration laws. In addition, you may be fined up to $10,000 and imprisoned for up to five years, or both, for knowingly and willfully falsifying or concealing a material fact or using any false document in submitting this petition.

YOUR CERTIFICATION: I certify, under penalty of perjury under the laws of the United States of America, that the foregoing is true and correct. Furthermore, I authorize the release of any information from my records that U.S. Citizenship and Immigration Services needs to determine eligiblity for the benefit that I am seeking.

E. Signature of petitioner

Teo Thanh Nguyen Date June 11, 2012 Phone Number (503) 555-1493

F. Signature of person preparing this form, if other than the petitioner

I declare that I prepared this document at the request of the person above and that it is based on all information of which I have any knowledge.

Print Name ___ Signature ___ Date ___

Address ___ G-28 ID or VOLAG Number, if any. ___

Form I-130 (01/08/12) Y Page 2

Part A

Question 1: Check the first box, Husband/Wife.

Question 2: This question, about whether you're related by adoption, is meant for people who use this form to apply for an adopted child. We're assuming you can answer this question "No."

Question 3: If the petitioning spouse gained permanent residence through adoption, check **Yes.** But no matter which box you check, it won't affect the application, since this question is mainly directed at people immigrating through parent/child relationships—something not covered in this book.

Part B

Question 1: The petitioning spouse must enter his/her last name (surname) in capital letters, but the first and middle name in small letters. For example, Samuel Lawrence Cole would write COLE, Samuel Lawrence. Use your spouse's current married name if it was changed at the time of your marriage. See "What's Your Name?" in Chapter 4, Section B.

Questions 2-5: Self-explanatory.

Question 6: This refers only to the petitioning spouse's most recent marital status, so he or she should only check "Married," even if there was a previous divorce.

Question 7: See "What's Your Name?" in Chapter 4, Section B.

Question 8: Self-explanatory.

Question 9: Self-explanatory.

Question 10: Enter the eight- or nine-digit A-number on the U.S. permanent resident's green card.

Question 11: Self-explanatory.

Question 12: USCIS wants to know when your U.S. spouse's prior marriage ended so that it can determine whether your current marriage is valid. If your petitioning spouse's prior marriage(s) ended after your present marriage began, yours is not a lawful marriage. If your petitioning spouse has just discovered that the divorce wasn't final when your marriage took place, it may not be necessary to run to a lawyer. Assuming that the divorce has since become final, you can simply correct the problem by remarrying. (If there was fraud involved in your hasty marriage, consult a lawyer before proceeding.)

Question 13: Enter N/A, since your spouse is not yet a citizen.

Question 14a: Some of the information requested here is on your green card. (See the illustration below.) The date of admission shown on the older cards usually starts with the year, so that Dec. 3, 1998 would be 981203. The city is in code on the old cards: for example, SFR is San Francisco, BUF is Buffalo, and LIN is the Service Center in Lincoln, Nebraska. Why a Service Center? The applicant became a conditional resident first, then two years later received permanent residence from the Lincoln, Nebraska, Service Center. If you have a new card, you'll have to figure out where you entered the U.S. with your immigrant visa or were approved for a green card. Class of Admission asks for the type of visa or remedy through which the person got permanent residence, such as a Fourth Preference visa or political asylum.

New-Style Green Card (Front)

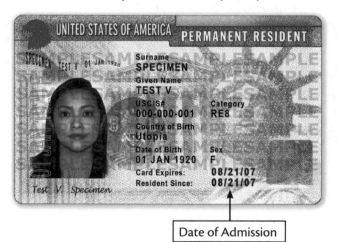

Date of Admission

Question 14b: If your petitioning spouse checks "yes" here, indicating that he or she received U.S. permanent residence through marriage, find out how long it has been since your spouse's approval for permanent residence. A petitioning spouse who immigrated through marriage cannot petition for a new spouse for five years, unless the first spouse died or your spouse can prove by "clear and convincing evidence" that the previous marriage was bona fide (real). USCIS is concerned that the first marriage was just a sham, with the long-term goal of getting both of you into the United States by piggybacking on a sham marriage.

To prove that the first marriage was bona fide, your spouse should enclose documentary evidence showing that he or she and the former spouse shared a life, such as shared rent receipts, club memberships, children's birth certificates, utility bills, and insurance agreements. As for what makes for "clear and convincing," this is one of those legal standards that is easy to state but hard to pin down. The bottom line is, your spouse has a lot of proving to do to persuade a suspicious government official that his or her previous marriage was bona fide.

Part C: (This section asks for information about you, the immigrant beneficiary)

Question 1: Your current name, with your last name (surname) in capital letters. If you have any doubt about what name to use, see "What's Your Name?" in Chapter 4, Section B.

Question 2: Self-explanatory.

Questions 3-5: Self-explanatory.

Question 6: Enter your current marital status only.

Question 7: See "What's Your Name?" in Chapter 4, Section B.

Question 8: Self-explanatory.

Question 9: If you don't have a Social Security number, just write N/A. You probably won't have a Social Security number unless you have had a work permit, a visa allowing you to work, or U.S. residence. If you have used a made-up or borrowed number in order to work while you were here illegally, consult an attorney.

Question 10: The Alien Registration Number is an eight- or nine-digit number following a letter A, which the former INS or USCIS will have assigned to you. You won't have one yet unless you've previously applied for immigration benefits, or been

in deportation/removal proceedings. (Of course, if your previous application was denied because you were inadmissible or you lied on that application, you should call a lawyer before going any further.)

Questions 11 and 12: See advice to Questions 11 and 12 in Part B, above.

Question 13: Put an X in the "Yes" box. Since you have chosen to read this chapter, you have apparently been (and may still be) in the United States.

Question 14: Enter information about your most recent entry to the United States, even if this was only after a brief trip and you moved to the United States long ago.

CAUTION
If you know that you must leave the United States to get your green card, be careful here. This question gives the government information on when you were living in the United States—perhaps unlawfully. It could lead to your being punished for your illegal stay with a three- or ten-year bar on reentry (see Chapter 2 for further discussion). It would be best to have already left the United States when your spouse sends this in, in which case he or she won't have to answer the question at all.

If you entered legally, state the type of visa you used to enter the United States, such as an F-1 student or Visa Waiver (if you came from a country from which you didn't have to get a formal U.S. visa). Your I-94 is the little white or green card that the border official gave you when you arrived; the number is on the card. The date your stay expires or expired should be on the I-94 card (or in your passport). Note that this date is different than the expiration date on your original visa.

If you entered illegally, write "without inspection."

Question 15: State your employer's name and address. To date, there are no reports of the government using this information to go after employers who hired people illegally. However, if you not only worked illegally but used false documents (such as a fake green card) to do it, you should consult with an attorney. (See Chapter 17 for information on finding a good lawyer.)

Question 16: If you've previously been placed in Immigration Court proceedings, see a lawyer, whether you won or lost, but particularly if you lost.

Question 17: This is the continuation of Part C, so all questions still refer to you, the immigrant beneficiary. Since your spouse is already covered in this application, just list your children, if any. This means all your children, including by previous relationships.

Question 18: Self-explanatory.

Question 19: Enter N/A if you're living in the United States. However, if you're here only temporarily and will be returning home to finish the green card application process, enter your overseas address.

Question 20: If your native language uses a non-Roman script (for example, Russian, Chinese, or Arabic), you'll need to write your name and address in that script.

Question 21: Self-explanatory. But if you're going to be leaving the United States after living here unlawfully, this is another time to be careful—the information about how long you and your spouse lived at the same address could be used against you.

Question 22:

If you entered legally: If you are going to take advantage of the option to stay in the United States to adjust your status, enter the closest city and state with a USCIS office. Add the name of the consulate from your last country of residence, as a backup— though you won't necessarily need to go there.

If you are choosing to return to your home country and apply through a U.S. consulate, you do not need to answer this question.

If you entered illegally: Unless you are grandfathered in to being allowed to stay in the United States to apply for your green card, you'll have to apply at a U.S. consulate closest to where you live in your home country and need not fill in this box.

Part D: Other Information.

Now we're back to questions to be answered by the petitioning U.S. spouse.

Question 1: This refers to other petitions being submitted simultaneously, (for example, for your children from this or other marriages), so that USCIS can process the petitions together. Enter the children's names here.

Question 2: As you can probably imagine, if your petitioning spouse has a history of short marriages to people whom he/she then helped get green cards, USCIS may initiate a marriage fraud investigation. You should see a lawyer (Chapter 17 has tips on finding a good one).

Signature Line: The petitioning spouse signs here.

Signature of person preparing this form, if other than the petitioner. If you are preparing your own application, leave this blank. A little typing assistance or advice from a friend doesn't matter —the only people who need to complete this line are lawyers or agencies who fill out these forms on others' behalf.

b. Form G-325A

The information you and your spouse supply on this form will allow the U.S. government to check your background. Most of the form is self-explanatory. If you really can't remember or are unable to find out an exact date, enter whatever you can remember, such as the year. Alternately, you can simply say "unknown," but if you overuse the "unknowns" USCIS may return your entire application for another try. Since the questions aren't numbered, we refer to them by the approximate line.

 WEB RESOURCE
Form G-325A is available on the USCIS website at www.uscis.gov. Below is a sample filled-in version of this form.

Lines 1 and 2 (Family Name, etc.): Self-explanatory.
Line 3 (Father/Mother): Self-explanatory.
Line 4 (Husband or Wife): Self-explanatory.
Line 5 (Former Husbands or Wives): Self-explanatory.

Sample Form G-325A, Biographic Information

Department of Homeland Security U.S. Citizenship and Immigration Services	OMB No. 1615-0008; Expires 08/31/2012 **G-325A, Biographic Information**

(Family Name) Nguyen	(First Name) Lea	(Middle Name) Nadres	☐ Male ☒ Female	Date of Birth (mm/dd/yyyy) 07-18-1986	Citizenship/Nationality Filipina	File Number A 23456789

All Other Names Used (include names by previous marriages) Pebet	City and Country of Birth Quezon City, Philippines	U.S. Social Security # (if any) 989 99 9898

	Family Name	First Name	Date of Birth (mm/dd/yyyy)	City, and Country of Birth (if known)	City and Country of Residence
Father	Pebet	Antero	11/23/1963	Manila, Philippines	Philippines, Manila,
Mother (Maiden Name)	Martino Philippines	Flores	05-02-1965	Quezon City,	Philippines, Manila,

Current Husband or Wife (If none, so state) Family Name (For wife, give maiden name) Nguyen	First Name Teo	Date of Birth (mm/dd/yyyy) 04-12-1986	City and Country of Birth Saigon Vietnam	Date of Marriage 05-22-2012	Place of Marriage Salem, OR

Former Husbands or Wives (If none, so state) Family Name (For wife, give maiden name) none	First Name	Date of Birth (mm/dd/yyyy)	Date and Place of Marriage	Date and Place of Termination of Marriage

Applicant's residence last five years. List present address first.

Street and Number	City	Province or State	Country	From Month	From Year	To Month	To Year
1640 Lincoln Park	Beaverton	OR	U.S.A.	05	2012	Present Time	
13 Dao Street, Valle Zende	Metro Manila		Philippines	06	2009	05	2012
918 E. Market Street	Boston	MA	U.S.A.	12	2007	06	2009
4031 Ignacia Ave	Quezon City		Philippines	07	1985	12	2007

Applicant's last address outside the United States of more than 1 year.

Street and Number	City	Province or State	Country	From Month	From Year	To Month	To Year
13 Dao Street, Valle Zende	Metro Manila		Philippines	06	2009	05	2012

Applicant's employment last five years. (If none, so state.) List present employment first.

Full Name and Address of Employer	Occupation (Specify)	From Month	From Year	To Month	To Year
Beaverton College, Beaverton, OR	student	05	2012	Present Time	
Boston College, 140 Commonwealth Ave, Chestnut Hill, MA 02467	student	12	2007	06	2009

Last occupation abroad if not shown above. (Include all information requested above.)

This form is submitted in connection with an application for: ☐ Naturalization ☐ Other (Specify): ☒ Status as Permanent Resident	Signature of Applicant *Lea Nadres Nguyen*	Date 6/27/2012

If your native alphabet is in other than Roman letters, write your name in your native alphabet below:

Penalties: Severe penalties are provided by law for knowingly and willfully falsifying or concealing a material fact.

Applicant: Print your name and Alien Registration Number in the box outlined by heavy border below.

Complete This Box (Family Name) NGUYEN	(Given Name) Lea	(Middle Name) Nadres	(Alien Registration Number) A 23456789

Form G-325A (Rev. 08/08/11) Y

Line 7 (Applicant's Residence Last Five Years): Be careful here. These need to be in reverse chronological order, starting with your most recent address and working your way down the last five years. For instance, if you now live in Detroit but lived in Ann Arbor before, your Detroit address goes on the top line. Practice making this list on another sheet of paper before you enter the information here.

Line 12 (Applicant's last address outside the United States of more than one year): This may overlap with one of the addresses in Line 6—that's okay.

Line 13 (Applicant's employment last five years): Again, be careful to put this in reverse chronological order. If you've been unemployed, self-employed, or were a housewife or house-husband, say so here—in other words, try to account for all five years.

Line 14 (Show below last occupation abroad if not listed above): This line asks you to list your last overseas employment if you didn't already mention it under Line 8. People tend to overlook this line, because it's so small—make sure you don't accidentally jump over it.

Line 19 (This form is submitted in connection with application for): On your spouse's form, he or she should check "Other" and write "in support of spouse's I-130." On your form, you should check "status as permanent resident."

Line 20 (If your native alphabet uses non-Roman letters): For example, if your native language is Russian or Chinese, fill this in using the native writing script.

Line 21 (The dark box): Self-explanatory.

2. Documents to Assemble for Visa Petition

The I-130 visa petition asks you to submit supporting documents and payment along with the form. You're not done with your petition until you have gathered together the following:

- **Proof of the U.S. permanent resident status of your petitioning spouse.** This can be either a copy of his or her green card (front and back) or of the stamp placed in his or her passport to indicate permanent resident status.

- **Proof that you're legally married.** This should include at a minimum a copy of your marriage certificate, most likely from a government source (see Chapter 4, Section C, for details). In addition, if either you or your spouse have been previously married, you must include proof that these marriages were terminated, such as a copy of a death, divorce, or annulment certificate.

- **Photos.** You must each submit one color passport-style photo, 2 x 2 inches in size, taken within the past six months, showing your current appearance. Passport style means that the photo shows your full face from the front, with a plain white or off-white background—and your face must measure between one inch and $1\frac{3}{8}$ inches from the bottom of your chin to the top of your head. For more information, see the State Department website at http://travel.state.gov (under "Visas for Foreign Citizens," click "more," then "A–Z Subject Index," then go to "Photo Requirements" under letter "P"). However, government regulations permit you to submit a photo that doesn't completely follow the instructions if you live in a country where such photographs are unavailable or are cost prohibitive.

- **Fees.** The current fee for an I-130 visa petition is $420. However, these fees go up fairly regularly, so double-check this on the USCIS website at www.uscis.gov, or by calling USCIS at 800-375-5283.

3. Where to Send the Visa Petition

After your spouse—with your help—has prepared and assembled all the forms and other items on the checklist below, he or she should make photocopies for your records. Your spouse must send the packet to the USCIS "lockbox" office serving the region where he or she lives. The lockbox office will, after some initial processing, forward the visa petition to a USCIS Service Center, which will make the decision approving or denying the petition. Certified mail with a return receipt is the safest way

Where to Send the Form I-130 Visa Petition			
If the U.S. petitioner lives in:			**Send Form I-130 to:**
Alaska American Samoa Arizona California Colorado Florida Guam Hawaii Idaho	Kansas Montana Nebraska Nevada New Mexico North Dakota Northern Mariana Islands Oklahoma	Oregon Puerto Rico South Dakota Texas Utah Virgin Islands Washington Wyoming	**USCIS Phoenix Lockbox** For U.S. Postal Service (USPS) deliveries: USCIS ATTN: I-130 P.O. Box 21700 Phoenix, AZ 85036 For Express Mail and courier deliveries: USCIS Attn: I-130 1820 E. Skyharbor Circle S Suite 100 Phoenix, AZ 85034
Alabama Arkansas Connecticut Delaware District of Columbia Georgia Illinois Indiana Iowa Kentucky Louisiana	Maine Maryland Massachusetts Michigan Minnesota Mississippi Missouri New Hampshire New Jersey New York	North Carolina Ohio Pennsylvania Rhode Island South Carolina Tennessee Vermont Virginia West Virginia Wisconsin	**USCIS Chicago Lockbox** For U.S. Postal Service: USCIS P.O. Box 804625 Chicago, IL 60680-4107 For Express Mail and courier deliveries: USCIS Attn: I-130 131 South Dearborn–3rd Floor Chicago, IL 60603-5517
If the U.S. petitioner prefers to send the I-130 by private courier (non-U.S. Postal Service), then regardless of where the petitioner lives, send Form I-130 to:			**USCIS Lockbox** Attn: SAI-130 131 South Dearborn–3rd Floor Chicago, IL 60603-5517

to send anything to USCIS. The address is found above (and in Appendix B). You can double-check this information on the USCIS website.

4. What Happens After Sending in the Form I-130 Visa Petition

A few weeks after your spouse sends in your visa petition, he or she should get a receipt notice from USCIS. The receipt notice will tell you to check the USCIS website for information on how long the application is likely to remain in processing. See the sample receipt notice below.

In fact, the processing times can change, however, so you might want to regularly check the USCIS website for the most up-to-date information. Go to www.uscis.gov, click "Processing Times" in the bar on the left side of the page, select the Service Center with jurisdiction over your petition from the drop-down menu marked "Service Center" at the bottom of the next page, then click the "Service Center Processing Dates" button. Be sure to look in the column for I-130s filed by "Permanent resident filing for a spouse or child under 21."

The result shown in the final column may be either a number of months or a date. If it's a date,

Sample I-130 Receipt Notice

Department of Homeland Security
U.S. Citizenship and Immigration Services

I-797C, Notice of Action

THE UNITED STATES OF AMERICA

RECEIPT NUMBER		CASE TYPE I130 IMMIGRANT PETITION FOR
MSC-12-054-00000		RELATIVE, FIANCE(E), OR ORPHAN

RECEIVED DATE	PRIORITY DATE	PETITIONER
JUNE 30, 2012	JUNE 30, 2012	NGUYEN, TEO

NOTICE DATE	PAGE	BENEFICIARY
July 1, 2012	1 of 1	NGUYEN, LEA

ILONA BRAY
RE: LEA NADRES NGUYEN
950 PARKER STREET
BERKELEY, CA 94710

Notice Type: Receipt Notice
Amount received: $ 420.00

Section: Husband or wife of permanent
resident, 203(a)(2)(A)INA

Receipt notice - If any of the above information is incorrect, call customer service immediately.

Processing time - Processing times vary by kind of case.
- You can check our current processing time for this kind of case on our website at **uscis.gov**.
- On our website you can also sign up to get free e-mail updates as we complete key processing steps on this case.
- Most of the time your case is pending the processing status will not change because we will be working on others filed earlier.
- We will notify you by mail when we make a decision on this case, or if we need something from you. If you move while this case is pending, call customer service when you move.
- Processing times can change. If you don't get a decision or update from us within our current processing time, check our website or call for an update.

If you have questions, check our website or call customer service. Please save this notice, and have it with you if you contact us about this case.

Notice to all customers with a pending I-130 petition - USCIS is now processing Form I-130, Petition for Alien Relative, as a visa number becomes available. Filing and approval of an I-130 relative petition is only the first step in helping a relative immigrate to the United States. Eligible family members must wait until there is a visa number available before they can apply for an immigrant visa or adjustment of status to a lawful permanent resident. This process will allow USCIS to concentrate resources first on cases where visas are actually available. This process should not delay the ability of one's relative to apply for an immigrant visa or adjustment of status. Refer to **www.state.gov/travel** <http://www.state.gov/travel> to determine current visa availability dates. For more information, please visit our website at www.uscis.gov or contact us at 1-800-375-5283.

Always remember to call customer service if you move while your case is pending. If you have a pending I-130 relative petition, also call customer service if you should decide to withdraw your petition or if you become a U.S. citizen.

Please see the additional information on the back. You will be notified separately about any other cases you filed.
U.S. CITIZENSHIP & IMMIGRATION SERVICES
P.O. BOX 68005
LEE'S SUMMIT, MO 68005
Customer Service Telephone: (800) 375-5283

Form I-797C (Rev. 08/31/04) N

Sample I-130 Approval Notice

Department of Homeland Security
U.S. Citizenship and Immigration Services

I-797, Notice of Action

THE UNITED STATES OF AMERICA

RECEIPT NUMBER		CASE TYPE	I130 IMMIGRANT PETITION FOR
MSC-12-054-00000			RELATIVE, FIANCE(E), OR ORPHAN
RECEIPT DATE	PRIORITY DATE	PETITIONER	
JUNE 30, 2012	JUNE 30, 2012		NGUYEN, TEO
NOTICE DATE	PAGE	BENEFICIARY	
November 11, 2012	1 of 1		NGUYEN, LEA

ILONA BRAY
RE: LEA NADRES NGUYEN
950 PARKER STREET
BERKELEY, CA 94710

Notice Type: Approval Notice

Section: Husband or wife of permanent
resident, 203(a)(2)(A)INA

The above petition has been approved. We have sent the original visa petition to the **Department of State National Visa Center (NVC), 32 Rochester Avenue, Portsmouth, NH 03801-2909**. NVC processes all approved immigrant visa petitions that need consular action. It also determines which consular post is the appropriate consulate to complete visa processing. NVC will then forward the approved petition to that consulate.

The NVC will contact the person for whom you are petitioning(beneficiary) concerning further immigrant visa processing steps.

If you have any questions about visa issuance, please contact the NVC directly. However, please allow at least 90 days before calling the NVC if your beneficiary has not received correspondence from the NVC. The telephone number of the NVC is **(603) 334-0700**.

THIS FORM IS NOT A VISA NOR MAY IT BE USED IN PLACE OF A VISA.

Please see the additional information on the back. You will be notified separately about any other cases you filed.

U.S. CITIZENSHIP & IMMIGRATION SERVICES
P.O. BOX 68005
LEE'S SUMMIT, MO 68005
Customer Service Telephone: (800) 375-5283

Form I-797 (Rev. 01/31/05) N

that tells you that USCIS is currently working on visa petitions filed on that date, so you'll have to do the math to figure out how long it's taking.

As long as your petition is not beyond the "normal processing time," USCIS will ignore any inquiries from you or your spouse asking what is going on. These lockboxes and Service Centers seem like walled fortresses—you can't visit them, and it's almost impossible to talk to a live person there. If USCIS needs additional documentation to complete your application, it will send your spouse a letter asking for it. (See Chapter 15 for what to do if you don't get a timely answer from USCIS.)

Eventually your spouse will either receive a denial or an approval of the visa petition.

a. If the Visa Petition Is Denied

If the visa petition is denied, USCIS will give you a reason for the denial. The fastest thing to do is to fix the problem and try again. For example, if the denial was because your petitioning spouse did not appear to be actually divorced from his or her previous spouse, your spouse would need to see a lawyer and obtain new and better documentation showing that there had been a final divorce. Then your spouse could file a new visa petition.

b. If the Visa Petition Is Approved

When your visa petition is approved, your spouse will receive a notice from the USCIS Service Center. An example of a visa petition approval notice is shown above. As you can see, it's nothing fancy. But it is an important document. Make a few photocopies of it and store these and the original in safe places. Note the "Priority Date" listed in the box of that name—that is the date USCIS received your visa petition and that date will become very important in determining your place on the waiting list, as discussed in Section E below.

At the same time that the USCIS Service Center notifies your spouse of the approval of your visa petition, it will forward your case to the National Visa Center (NVC) in New Hampshire. This office will take over and maintain your file through the waiting period.

5. How to Use the Checklist for Step One: Visa Petition

This checklist lists every form, document, and other item included in the initial visa petition that your spouse, with your help, will need to assemble and submit to USCIS. By checking off the boxes as items are completed or found, your spouse will be able to ensure that nothing gets forgotten.

Checklist for Visa Petition by Lawful Permanent Resident

☐ Form I-130 (see line-by-line instructions in Section D1a, above)

☐ Documents to accompany Form I-130:

  ☐ Proof of the U.S. permanent resident status of your petitioning spouse, such as a copy of his or her green card (front and back) or of the stamp placed in his or her passport to indicate permanent resident status

  ☐ Your marriage certificate (see Chapter 4, Section C, for how to obtain such documents)

  ☐ Proof of termination of all previous marriages, yours or your spouse's, such as certificates of death, divorce, or annulment

  ☐ One color photo of you (passport style)

  ☐ One color photo of your spouse (passport style)

  ☐ Fees: $420 currently, but double-check at www.uscis.gov

☐ Form G-325A, Biographic Information, filled out by you (see line-by-line instructions in Section D1b, above)

☐ Form G-325A, Biographic Information, filled out by your spouse (see line-by-line instructions in Section D1b, above).

CHECKLIST

A copy of this checklist is available as a tearout in Appendix C.

E. The Waiting Period

Visa waiting periods are not set periods of time. Some attorneys tell their clients, "It will probably be two years." When two years go by and their green card hasn't come through, the clients worry that something has gone wrong. The truth is that waiting periods are only partly predictable. They depend on supply and demand, combined with monthly decisions by the U.S. government. You won't know for sure how long you'll have to wait until your wait is almost over. This section will help you to understand the mechanics of this wait and how to deal with it.

1. Why You Are in Category 2A

USCIS ranks preference relatives, generally giving visas quicker to those at the top. Below, you'll see the complete list of preference relatives. As you'll see, you are in the second category down ("2A"). This means that the U.S. government has allotted a higher priority to your visa than to those of the people further down the list. That may be small comfort as the months and years go by, however.

- **First Preference:** The unmarried sons or daughters of a U.S. citizen who are over 21 and are therefore no longer considered children. (If they were still children, they could qualify as immediate relatives, who are immediately eligible for visas.)
- **Second Preference:** The second preference category, which is where you fit, is actually made up of two subcategories, each with different waiting periods. In subcategory 2A are spouses or unmarried sons or daughters under age 21 of a permanent resident (green card holder). In subcategory 2B are the unmarried sons and daughters over age 21 of a permanent resident (they usually wait longer than 2As).
- **Third Preference:** The married sons or daughters, any age, of a U.S. citizen.
- **Fourth Preference:** The brothers or sisters of a U.S. citizen who is age 21 or older.

2. How Visas Are Allotted Year by Year

Each year, the U.S. government allots a certain number of immigrant visas in each preference category. For purposes of visa allocation, the government follows its fiscal year, which starts and ends in October. This might affect you if the government runs out of visas for your category before October. You'll know at that point that you have no chance of advancing on the waiting list until the "new year" begins October 1.

Currently, the total worldwide numbers are:

- **First Preference:** 23,400, plus any visas not used for fourth preference
- **Second Preference:** 114,200, with 77% of these going to category 2A, 23% to category 2B
- **Third Preference:** 23,400, plus any not used for first and second preference
- **Fourth Preference:** 65,000 plus any not used for the first three preferences.

This may sound like a lot of visas, but far more people want immigrant visas than can get them every year. The government gives out visas month by month, making sure never to go over the annual limit.

There are also limits on the number of visas allowed for any one country. No more than 7% of the total visas each year can go to any one country, and often the percentage turns out to be less.

There are more complexities to the allocation and numbers of these visas, but a full understanding of these numbers won't help you speed up your waiting time. The important thing to know is how to chart your own place on the waiting list.

3. How to Chart Your Place on the Waiting List

It would be nice if you could just call the government and ask how long you have to wait for your green card. No such luck. Instead, the State Department publishes a monthly *Visa Bulletin*, the one source of information on visa waiting periods. The *Visa Bulletin* is accessible online at http://travel. state.gov (under "Visas for Foreign Citizens," click "more," then on the left side of the page click "*Visa Bulletin*," and then click the date next to "This month's *Visa Bulletin*"). The same information is available by phone at 202-663-1541, but you have to be quick with your pencil and paper, because they talk fast.

The *Visa Bulletin* comes out monthly, around the middle of the month, but not on any particular day. Below is a sample of what a family-based chart in the *Visa Bulletin* looks like.

Although it's confusing at first glance, you will be able to make your way through this chart. Here's how:

1. Locate your preference category (2A) in the first column.
2. Locate your country across the top. China, India, Mexico, and the Philippines often have their own columns because of the large number of applicants—and as a result, people from these countries wait longer than others. All other countries are included in the second column called All Chargeability Areas Except Those Listed.
3. Draw a line across from your preference category (2A) and down from your country of origin. Where the two lines cross is what is called the Visa Cutoff Date—the key date which you will compare with your own Priority Date to chart your progress.

Every prospective immigrant has his or her own Priority Date—the date the INS or USCIS first received their Form I-130 visa petition. Your Priority Date is on the I-130 approval notice you received. Prospective immigrants whose Priority Dates are at or earlier than the Cutoff Date listed in that month's bulletin will become eligible for visas or green cards.

The earlier your Priority Date, the better off you are, because it means you are in line ahead of other applicants. But as you can see, the current Cutoff Date doesn't tell you how long it will be before your own visa or green card is issued.

Look again at the sample I-130 Approval Notice in Section D4, above. The Priority Date is in a box on the second line, with the date of June 30, 2012.

The following examples should help you understand how to read the *Visa Bulletin* chart.

EXAMPLE 1: Toshiko is a citizen of Japan, married to a U.S. permanent resident.

Toshiko's husband submitted an I-130 for her several years ago and she received a Priority Date of September 12, 2009. What does Toshiko learn by looking at the *Visa Bulletin* chart? After locating the box for Japan (under All Chargeability Areas) in category 2A, she sees that the Priority Date that is now current is October 8, 2009.

That means that Toshiko is now eligible for a visa. If you're confused by the fact that Toshiko's Priority Date isn't an exact match with the *Visa Bulletin* Cutoff Date, look at it this way: Earlier is always better. Toshiko's husband actually submitted her I-130 a few

	Cutoff Dates for April 2012				
Family	All Chargeability Areas Except Those Listed	China— mainland born	India	Mexico	Philippines
F1	01APR05	01APR05	01APR05	08MAY93	22JUN97
F2A	08OCT09	08OCT09	08OCT09	01SEP09	08OCT09
F2B	15JAN04	15JAN04	15JAN04	01DEC92	08DEC01
F3	15FEB02	15FEB02	15FEB02	15JAN93	22JUL92
F4	08NOV00	08NOV00	08NOV00	01JUN96	08JAN89

weeks before some other people who also became current under this month's *Visa Bulletin*. If this process were like taking a number at the bakery counter, she would have become eligible for her visa (or get to choose her doughnut) a little before the people with October 8, 2009 Priority Dates. But the *Visa Bulletin* jumps by days and weeks worth of Priority Dates every month, so people get lumped into larger groups. Anyone with a Priority Date of October 8, 2009 or earlier is therefore considered to have become visa eligible, or "current."

EXAMPLE 2: Yumiko is also a citizen of Japan, who got married to a U.S. permanent resident more recently than Toshiko in the example above. Yumiko's husband submitted her I-130 on August 1, 2010, so that is now her Priority Date.

What does Yumiko learn by looking at the *Visa Bulletin* chart? She must look at the same box as Toshiko did, to see that the current Cutoff Date is October 8, 2009. But with Yumiko's Priority Date of August 1, 2010 she is certainly not current, and not yet eligible for a visa. It's safe to say there are a number of people in line ahead of her and thus a long wait ahead.

If you follow the *Visa Bulletin* chart month by month, you might notice a couple of odd things. Sometimes the government gets backed up with visa applications and the Cutoff Dates just don't change. In the example above, it could be that Toshiko's Priority Date actually became current a month or two earlier—but she forgot to check it then, and the number didn't change. Sometimes the Cutoff Dates get stuck for months at a time, while the government deals with a backlog of visa applications. If the government hits a huge logjam, you may even see the Cutoff Dates go backwards.

Another odd thing you might see is a box that contains the letter C or U, instead of a date. The letter C (for "current") means there are plenty of

visas in that category and no one has to wait. It's as if everyone's Priority Date suddenly were current. The letter U (for "unavailable") is the opposite, meaning that all the visas have been used up for that year. If, for example, this were February 2012, and Yumiko saw a U in her category 2A box, she'd know she could forget about getting closer to a visa until October 2012 (when the new year starts in the visa allocation process).

4. Figuring How Long You Will Wait

To roughly determine how long you will have to wait for a visa, you can subtract the Cutoff Date on the current month's *Visa Bulletin* chart from today's date. That will tell you the approximate length of time that other applicants are now waiting for a visa—though this method is complicated by the fact that they applied during a different time period than you, and demand may have risen or fallen during that time. There is no exact science to computing your probable wait.

5. How to Deal With the Long Wait

You will probably feel like nothing at all is happening during the years that you wait for your visa to become available. But in fact, the Priority Dates will be inching forward, and there are steps that you should be taking to make sure that you can claim your visa as soon as it becomes available.

a. Organizing Your Papers and Checking the *Visa Bulletin*

After your U.S. permanent resident spouse files a visa petition for you, you will get your own I-130 approval notice; looking much like the one shown in Section D4, above. The approval notice will show your Priority Date. Take careful note of the date and keep the notice in a safe place.

Look in the current *Visa Bulletin* to get an idea of how long your wait will be. (See Section 3, above for how to find and read the *Visa Bulletin*.) If your wait looks to be three years, for example, for the first year and a half you probably don't need to check the *Visa Bulletin* more than every six months. Then start checking the bulletin every three months after that. As your Priority Date gets close to being current, you should check it monthly, so you can find out as soon as you are current and can make sure that the U.S. government realizes that you are current and still alive and interested, as explained below.

TIP

You can ask to have the *Visa Bulletin* sent to you monthly, by email. This is a great way to make sure you don't forget to check how your Priority Date is advancing. Complete instructions for how to subscribe to this service can be found toward the bottom of any *Visa Bulletin*.

b. If You Change Addresses

Don't rely on the U.S. government to tell you when your Priority Date is current—the National Visa Center makes an effort, but some files will get buried in the shuffle. However, you're guaranteed not to hear from them if they don't know where to find you. Also, under rare circumstances, such as a major change in the U.S. immigration laws, the government may send out mass mailings that you also wouldn't want to miss.

If either you or your petitioning spouse change addresses, the place to contact is the National Visa Center (NVC), which keeps your case file until your Priority Date is close to being current. Advise the NVC of your new address by writing to them at The National Visa Center, 32 Rochester Avenue, Portsmouth, NH 03801-2909. You can also send them an email at NVCINQUIRY@state.gov. Be sure to include your case number from the INS or USCIS approval notice.

CAUTION

In addition, within ten days of moving, you (and every immigrating member of your family) must separately advise a central USCIS office of your move. The law requires this of all non-U.S. citizens over 14

years old who are remaining in the U.S. for more than 30 days—even if they're in the U.S. illegally. Failure to do so is a misdemeanor and can be punished with a jail term of up to 30 days, a fine of up to $200, or your removal from the United States. (See I.N.A. § 265; 8 U.S.C. § 1305.) The procedure is to file Form AR-11, which you can do online. Go to www.uscis.gov, and in the left-hand column, click "Online Change of Address." Follow the instructions. When you have finished filling out the form, you will be asked to click on "Signature," and the form will be e-filed. Print a copy for your records. It will show the date and time the form was filed, and will contain a USCIS confirmation number as proof of filing. There is no fee required for this form.

c. What to Do When Your Priority Date Is Current

One day, your Priority Date will be current—in other words, you'll finally see the exact date of your original application, or a later date, on the *Visa Bulletin* chart. Then you'll know that it's time for you to move forward in the process of getting your visa or green card.

When you see that your Priority Date is current, don't wait for the government to call you. If you don't hear from them within a few weeks, contact the National Visa Center (see Subsection b, above, for their contact information) and ask them to send you what's called the "Instruction Packet."

d. What Happens If No One Notices Your Current Priority Date

Some immigrants forget to check the *Visa Bulletin* and their Priority Date becomes current without their noticing. Sometimes, the NVC has tried to notify them, but has only an old address. Or, the NVC may have failed to keep track of the person's file. These problems can delay or destroy a person's hopes of immigrating.

You have one year after your Priority Date becomes current to pursue your visa or green card. If you do not, the government assumes you have abandoned it—and will give your visa to the next person in line. You may have an argument for getting the visa back if the government completely failed to contact you, but it's better to avoid such situations altogether. Keep track of your own Priority Date and follow the procedures in Subsection c, above, as soon as your date, or a later date, is listed in the *Visa Bulletin*.

6. How to Get Your Children Onto the Waiting List

Like other immigrants, you can bring certain family members along when you come to the United States. Your children who are unmarried and under age 21 qualify as what are called derivative beneficiaries by having been named on your Form I-130. See Chapter 2, Section B, to review who counts as a child. As a practical matter, this means that your children won't need a separate visa petition to start off the process. They will share your Priority Date and place on the waiting list. (Eventually, however, they will have to fill in some forms of their own.)

As you'll see in Section 7, below, children can lose their derivative beneficiary status. For example, if your spouse becomes a U.S. citizen, or if children turn 21 or get married, the children would no longer be considered derivative beneficiaries and would have to take further steps or find another way to immigrate. Section 7, below, will tell you which of these situations can be cured and how to cure them.

Be aware that if your derivative beneficiary children have children of their own, those children (your grandchildren) will not be considered your derivative beneficiaries. The law says that no one can be the derivative of someone who is already a derivative beneficiary. In this circumstance, the grandchildren would have to stay behind for at least a few years—a heartbreaking situation for some families. Unfortunately, there are no separate visas for grandchildren.

7. What Happens If Your Lawful Permanent Resident Petitioner Dies

Until recently, if you were the spouse of a permanent resident who died before you could immigrate, the visa petition was cancelled and you could no longer become a permanent resident. In October of 2009, however, Congress changed the law. Now, under certain conditions, the visa petition filed by your now-deceased spouse may still go forward.

If USCIS approves the petition, you (and your children) may be able to adjust status once your Priority Date becomes current, assuming you lived in the U.S. at the time of your spouse's death and continue to live in the United States. (This assumes that there are no other bars to your adjustment of status, such as your being out of status.)

There are also provisions for allowing a substitute Affidavit of Support, given that your spouse can no longer submit one. (Unlike the spouse of a U.S. citizen, however, this new law does not allow you to petition for yourself if your spouse never filed the petition.)

This is a new area of the law. USCIS has written some of the regulations needed in order to know how to process these cases (but how these cases will actually work in practice remained unclear, as of the time this book went to press). If you are in the unfortunate situation of dealing with the untimely death of the petitioner in your immigration case, consult an immigration attorney.

8. Changing Visa Preference Categories

Now that you know all about life as a 2A, you need to learn how to keep or improve on your visa category. It is possible for people to move into a different preference category, which will speed up or delay their waiting time. For example, you would get a visa quicker—by moving to immediate relative category—if your spouse became a U.S. citizen. Or, life changes can push people out of their visa category, and into a lower one or out of the race altogether. Here are the most typical situations affecting married couples and their children.

a. If a Permanent Resident Petitioner Becomes a Citizen

If your spouse becomes a citizen, it is good news for you. You go from category 2A straight to immediate relative. This means that you jump off the waiting list and immediately move forward with your visa processing.

If your permanent resident spouse qualifies for U.S. citizenship, he or she would be wise to apply as soon as possible. Most permanent residents can apply within five years of receiving their residence (with some exceptions). They must also be of good moral character, meet certain U.S. residency requirements, and be able to pass a test on the English language and U.S. history and government. (If you know that your spouse is going to become a U.S. citizen very soon, you should read Chapter 11, Spouses of U.S. Citizens, Living in the U.S.)

If your petitioning spouse becomes a citizen, advise the government and send them a copy of your spouse's citizenship certificate and your I-130 approval notice. The National Visa Center (NVC) will upgrade your status to immediate relative. The sample letter below shows how to explain this fortunate turn of events.

RESOURCE

For more on the eligibility and procedural requirements for obtaining U.S. citizenship: see the USCIS website at www.uscis.gov or *Becoming a U.S. Citizen: A Guide to the Law, Exam & Interview*, by Ilona Bray (Nolo).

SKIP AHEAD

If your spouse becomes a citizen, and you have children who will be immigrating with you, be sure to read Subsection h, below. For certain children, immigrating may now become more difficult.

Letter Requesting Upgrade to Immediate Relative

123 Salmon Way
Seattle, WA 98105
206-555-1212

April 20, 20xx

National Visa Center
32 Rochester Avenue
Portsmouth, NH 03801-2909

RE: Petitioner: Sam Washington
    Beneficiary: Marta Moscow
    Preference Category: 2A, Spouse of LPR
    Case Number: WAC-08-054-000

Dear Sir/Madam:

I am the petitioner in the above case. I recently became a U.S. citizen. A copy of my citizenship certificate is enclosed. Please upgrade my wife, Marta Moscow, from category 2A to immediate relative, and proceed with consular processing. Thank you.

Very truly yours,

Sam Washington

Sam Washington
Encl: U.S. citizenship certificate

b. If the Petitioner and Beneficiary Divorce

If you and your spouse get divorced before you apply for your immigrant visa or green card, you are out of luck. The visa petition is cancelled and you and your derivative beneficiaries lose your green card eligibility.

There is an exception for immigrants who are victims of emotional or physical abuse by their spouse. They can file a special self-petition (Form I-360) any time until the divorce becomes final, or for two years afterward, if they can show that the divorce was related to the domestic violence. (These self-petitions are not covered in this book. Talk to a local nonprofit organization or consult an attorney. See Chapter 17 for suggestions on locating help.)

c. If a Beneficiary Dies

If you were to die, your children would lose their opportunity for a visa as well—unless your spouse has filed or can file a separate petition for them in category 2A or 2B.

If your family is in this situation, the U.S. permanent resident petitioner should ask USCIS to "recapture" the deceased parent's Priority Date when the permanent resident submits the new visa petitions. If USCIS assigns the deceased parent's date to the children, the children won't have to start the waiting game all over.

d. If the Petitioner Who Has Become a U.S. Citizen Dies

It's possible that, in the years since your visa petition was filed, your spouse became a U.S. citizen, but died before you had a chance to complete your application for a green card. Under the new law passed in October of 2009, the surviving spouse of a U.S. citizen can petition for him or herself, regardless of the length of the marriage prior to the spouse's death. This changed the old law, which had required the couple to have been married for at least two years at the time the U.S. citizen died in order for the surviving spouse to self-petition.

If you need to self-petition, know that the petition must be filed within two years of your U.S. citizen spouse's death (unless your spouse died before the passage of this new law—October 28, 2009—in which case your petition must have been filed within two years of the new law, that is, by October 28, 2011). The form that you will use is the Form I-360 rather than the Form I-130. You are allowed to include your children who are under 21 years old on that petition. You will still have to show that you and your spouse had a bona fide marriage, and that you have not remarried.

As this is a new area of the law, USCIS is still in the process of implementing needed regulations for these self-petitions (as of the time this book went to print). We recommend that you consult with an immigration attorney if you find yourself dealing with the death of your petitioner.

e. If the Petitioner Loses His Permanent Resident Status

If the permanent resident petitioner loses the right to live in the United States, the immigrant applicants lose the right to live there also. In theory, permanent residence or a green card gives a person the right to live in the United States permanently—but this right can be taken away. If, for example a permanent resident spends many months overseas, USCIS may decide that he abandoned his U.S. residency and refuse to let him reclaim it. Or, if the petitioner commits certain crimes, her permanent residency could be taken away and she could be deported.

Even if a permanent resident has had a crime on record for a long time, he or she may not be safe. Recent laws have allowed USCIS to deport people for crimes that would not have made them deportable when the crime was committed. Since the goal of the law is to reunite families, it makes sense that the government would refuse to grant immigrant visas to the family members of former permanent residents.

f. What Happens When a Child Beneficiary Turns 21

If there is a chance that your child might turn 21 before his or her Priority Date becomes current, watch out! The minute a child hits age 21, he or she will automatically drop into a different visa category, from 2A to 2B. The child can, however, subtract from his or her age the amount of time it took USCIS to approve the initial visa petition. This is a protection created in 2002 by the Child Status Protection Act (CSPA). Basically, you have to wait until two events have occurred: your family's visa petition has been approved, and the child's Priority Date has become current. At that time, you add up the number of days that the visa petition was pending with USCIS, and subtract it from the child's actual age. If the result of the calculation is a number less than 21, the child may continue with the green card application. (Act quickly, however; the child has only a year after becoming eligible to submit the green card application.)

EXAMPLE 1: Nengah's mother marries a U.S. permanent resident named Frank when Nengah is 18 years old. Immediately after, Frank files a visa petition for the mother that includes Nengah as a derivative. USCIS takes five years to approve the petition, which happens right around the time their Priority Date becomes current. By now, Nengah is 23 years old—which, in theory, should drop her into category 2B. Fortunately, under the CSPA, she can subtract the five years that it took USCIS to approve the petition—which puts her age back at 18. As long as Nengah files for permanent residence within one year of becoming eligible, her case should be approved.

EXAMPLE 2: Kareem's father marries a U.S. permanent resident woman named Alyssa when Kareem is 17 years old. Immediately after, Alyssa files a visa petition for the father that includes Kareem as a derivative. It takes USCIS only one year to approve the visa petition. However, another five years pass before Kareem and his father's Priority Date becomes current. By this time, Kareem is 23 years old. Kareem can subtract only one year from his age of 23, which makes him legally 22 years old under the CSPA formula, and thus ineligible to adjust status under category 2A—he'll drop to category 2B and face a longer wait before immigrating.

If the CSPA doesn't help, and your child does drop into category 2B, he or she will face a wait of up to a few years before being eligible for a visa. This problem is known as "aging out." (However, if your child turns 21 after your spouse has become a U.S. citizen, the prospects may be brighter, as discussed below in Subsection h, and in Chapter 2, Section B.)

It can be very stressful when a child beneficiary is close to getting a visa or green card and is about to turn 21. But until your family's Priority Date has become current or your spouse becomes a U.S. citizen, there's nothing you can do.

g. What Happens When a Child Beneficiary Marries

In preference categories 2A (children of permanent residents, under age 21) and 2B (children of permanent residents, over age 21), the beneficiaries must be unmarried. If your children marry, their beneficiary status is revoked forever. Their only hope is for you or your spouse to become a U.S. citizen and file a new petition for them later.

If you plan to bring along your children in either the 2A or 2B categories, make sure to advise them not to marry until after they get their green card. (USCIS may not find out about the marriage now, but it often catches such cases when the immigrant applies for U.S. citizenship—and then it strips them of their green card.)

h. What Happens to Your Children When Your Spouse Becomes a U.S. Citizen

As you remember from Subsection a above, if your spouse becomes a U.S. citizen it will help you immigrate more quickly. The same is true for your children's immigration—but there's a twist. Children of U.S. citizens need to have their own visa petitions (Forms I-130) on file with the INS or USCIS in order to immigrate as the children of a U.S. citizen. They can't enjoy the benefits of that parent's new citizenship if they are merely named on their immigrating parent's petition.

When this whole process began, your spouse may have simply entered your children's names on the visa petition for you—which would have been enough for them to immigrate if your spouse had remained a permanent resident. To put this in more technical terms, your children were eligible to immigrate as your derivative beneficiaries when your spouse was a permanent resident, but once your spouse became a U.S. citizen, they lost their derivative beneficiary status. They now need to have visa petitions of their own.

Fortunately, it's not too late for your spouse to file separate visa petitions for your children even after having become a citizen. So long as the children are still unmarried, under age 21, and are your spouse's natural children or legal stepchildren (that is, the marriage took place before they turned 18), they qualify as immediate relatives just like you. As immediate relatives, they will be able to immigrate at the same time as you. It may take around five months for the new visa petitions to be approved, but for most children, it should all work out in the end. However, there are three groups of children who are, to varying degrees, still left out in the cold: those who have married, those who are not your spouse's legal stepchildren, and those who have turned 21.

Children who have married. Your children who have married could not have immigrated with you when your spouse was a permanent resident, so your spouse's citizenship doesn't actually make their situation worse. In fact, it could improve their situation if your spouse is the children's natural father or legal stepfather, because your spouse can file a visa petition for them in the third preference category.

Children who are not your spouse's legal step-children. As part of filing new visa petitions for your children, your spouse will have to prove that he or she has a direct relationship with each child, either as natural parent or legal stepparent. To be their legal stepparent, your spouse will have to show that your marriage took place before the child turned 18. If it didn't, then that child cannot immigrate until you yourself become a permanent resident and file a second preference visa petition for your child.

Children who have turned 21. If your child has turned 21 and no separate visa petition was filed for him or her, you're in for some extra work. As with your other children, your U.S. citizen spouse can file a new, separate visa petition if he or she is the child's natural parent or legal stepparent—but if you don't alert USCIS to the situation, your child won't become an immediate relative like you. Instead, the child will be put into the first

preference visa category, which is subject to annual quotas. The child will get a Priority Date, but it will be at the very end of the first preference waiting list.

EXAMPLE: Ricardo, a U.S. permanent resident, filed an I-130 visa petition for his Mexican wife Soledad and their four children on January 2, 2004. Soledad got an approval notice showing her January 2, 2004 Priority Date. Because the children were named on the I-130 visa petition and Ricardo was a permanent resident, USCIS knew that the children were derivative beneficiaries and shared Soledad's Priority Date. But on February 3, 2008 Ricardo was sworn in as a U.S. citizen. No more derivative beneficiaries for this family; Ricardo must file a separate I-130 for each child. He does so, on February 10, 2008. That works fine for three of his children, who are under age 21—as minor, unmarried children of a U.S. citizen, they are still immediate relatives and immediately eligible for a visa, just like their mother. But the fourth child, Jorge, has since turned 21. Jorge's Priority Date is now February 10, 2008. If you look on the *Visa Bulletin* chart in Section 3 above, you'll see that in his category, Mexico First Preference, the current Priority Date is July 8, 1992. Jorge is facing an approximate 16-year wait for a visa. If Ricardo had planned ahead and filed a separate I-130 for Jorge in 2004 when he filed for the rest of the family, he could have shaved many years off Jorge's wait.

But this isn't fair! True enough. Luckily, there is a remedy for children in this situation. When your U.S. citizen spouse files the new visa petition, he or she can ask USCIS not to put the child at the bottom of the waiting list, but to give the child the same Priority Date as the rest of the family, even in this new category. In other words, your spouse asks USCIS to pretend that a separate I-130 visa petition was submitted for the over-21-year-old at the same time that the visa petition for the whole family was submitted, perhaps years ago.

This is called "recapturing" a Priority Date. Below is a sample letter showing how to ask for a recapture. The petitioner also needs to include complete copies of the original I-130 visa petition, the original INS or USCIS approval notice showing the family's old Priority Date, and the petitioner's citizenship certificate.

Approval of recaptured dates is supposed to be automatic. Unfortunately, the USCIS Service Centers aren't used to this procedure and may pay no attention to your request—even if you write the most compelling letter and include complete documentation. You might get an approval notice showing a new Priority Date rather than your family's old one. Your only recourse would be to write many letters trying to get USCIS to correct the date (or to hire a lawyer).

> **TIP**
>
> **Plan ahead—submit separate I-130 visa petitions for any children who will soon turn 21.** If you are at the beginning of the immigration process, and have children who may turn 21 before the process ends, or you know that your spouse is likely to apply for U.S. citizenship, you can avoid the hassles involved in recapturing Priority Dates. Your spouse should simply file separate petitions for them from the outset.

9. Should You Wait Until Your Spouse Is a U.S. Citizen?

Applicants sometimes ask, "If I can avoid the Visa Preference System by waiting for my spouse to become a U.S. citizen, shouldn't I do so and avoid the quotas and waiting period?" The answer is no, you don't really gain anything by waiting, and you may actually lose time if your spouse's citizenship gets delayed.

You don't gain anything because your spouse will have to submit the visa petition sometime, even after becoming a U.S. citizen. The form is the same, no matter your spouse's status. Your approval notice will remain good even after your spouse becomes a citizen. Besides this, the longer you wait, the higher

Letter Requesting Recaptured Priority Date

111 Seaside Lane
Orlando, FL 32801

June 1, 20xx

USCIS Texas Service Center
P.O. Box 850919
Mesquite, TX 75185-0919
[See Appendix B for the address of the USCIS Service Center serving your geographic region.]

RE: Petitioner: Ricardo Torres
     Beneficiary: Jorge Torres
     I-130 Visa Petition with Priority Date Recapture Request

Dear Sir/Madam:

I am the Petitioner named above. Enclosed please find an I-130 visa petition for the above-named Beneficiary (my son) with supporting documents, including:

1. Copy of my son's birth certificate
2. Copy of his mother's and my marriage certificate
3. Copy of my citizenship certificate
4. Fee of $420 (money order).

In addition, please note that I am requesting a recapture of an earlier Priority Date for this application. My son was formerly a Derivative Beneficiary on an approved visa petition that I filed for his mother in 2004, with Priority Date January 2, 2004. I recently became a U.S. citizen, and so my son lost his derivative status. Please grant my son the earlier, January 2, 2004, Priority Date on the approval of this I-130 petition. In support of this request, I also enclose the following:

1. Copy of original I-130, showing my son's name
2. Copy of USCIS notice approving this I-130, with January 2, 2004, Priority Date.

Thank you for your attention to this matter.

Very truly yours,

Ricardo Torres

Ricardo Torres

the application fee is likely to go. There is also a risk of losing time because you don't really know when your spouse will become a U.S. citizen.

Let's take an imaginary permanent resident spouse named Kari. Kari is only one year away from being eligible to apply for citizenship. Her immigrating spouse, Sven, might think it's better to wait until Kari is a citizen before she files the I-130 on Sven's behalf. But after Kari turns in the citizenship application, she waits another year before her interview. Then the officer tells her, "I can't approve this until you show me proof of all your divorces, and you need to amend your last year's tax return and pay back the extra tax that you owe to show me that you have good moral character." This takes time to pull together, and Kari waits a few months more for the final approval.

You can see how things might drag on. Even after your spouse is approved for citizenship, it could be a few months more before he or she attends the ceremony to be sworn in as a U.S. citizen. By waiting for your spouse to attain U.S. citizenship, you could end up waiting even longer than you would have as a Preference Relative.

SKIP AHEAD

After examining and choosing one of the options described in this chapter, and getting your I-130 visa petition prepared and/or approved, see the charts below for where you'll go next.

Next Step If You Entered The U.S. Legally	
If you can stay in the United States legally through your waiting period:	When your waiting period is over and you are ready to adjust status, see Chapter 14 regarding adjustment of status application procedures.
If you plan on staying illegally, and can change status in the United States at the end of your waiting period (by being grandfathered in, or because your spouse becomes a U.S. citizen):	When your waiting period is over and you are ready to adjust status, see Chapter 14 regarding adjustment of status application procedures.
If you are interested in leaving the United States and applying for a marriage-based immigrant visa, and will not need a waiver of your visa overstay:	When your waiting period is over, see Chapter 8, Section A, regarding marriage visa application procedures for overseas spouses of U.S. lawful permanent residents (or Chapter 7, Section B, if your spouse becomes a U.S. citizen).
If you will have to leave the United States but will need a waiver to return:	See an attorney; Chapter 17 contains tips on finding a good one.

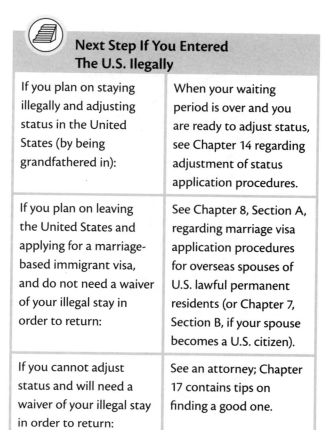

Next Step If You Entered The U.S. Ilegally

If you plan on staying illegally and adjusting status in the United States (by being grandfathered in):	When your waiting period is over and you are ready to adjust status, see Chapter 14 regarding adjustment of status application procedures.
If you plan on leaving the United States and applying for a marriage-based immigrant visa, and do not need a waiver of your illegal stay in order to return:	See Chapter 8, Section A, regarding marriage visa application procedures for overseas spouses of U.S. lawful permanent residents (or Chapter 7, Section B, if your spouse becomes a U.S. citizen).
If you cannot adjust status and will need a waiver of your illegal stay in order to return:	See an attorney; Chapter 17 contains tips on finding a good one.

Interviews With USCIS or Consular Officials

The final step in obtaining your visa or green card is to attend an interview with a U.S. consular or USCIS official. Until the date of your interview, it's quite possible that neither you nor your U.S. fiancé or spouse will have had any personal contact with any immigration official. For that reason, many applicants approach the interview with needless fear. Below, we guide you on what to expect and how to treat the interview as important—without suffering it as an ordeal.

With all the paperwork you've submitted by now, you might think the government should be able to approve your visa or green card without having to meet you face-to-face. However, the government views the interview as its opportunity to confirm the contents of your application after you've sworn to tell the truth (even though you represented that the answers on your application forms were true and correct when you signed them). The interview also allows the government to ask questions that will test whether your marriage is real or a sham.

Whether you're submitting your application overseas or in the United States, most of the advice in this chapter will apply to you. Overseas applicants should also read Section C regarding unique practices at U.S. consulates. U.S.-based applicants should read Section D covering practices at USCIS offices.

A. Who Must Attend an Interview?

Every hopeful immigrant can count on being required to attend an interview, whether they're applying for a fiancé visa, a marriage visa, or a green card. If you're applying for a green card at a USCIS office, your spouse will be required to attend the interview with you.

If you're applying for a fiancé or marriage visa from overseas, however, your U.S. fiancé or spouse is not required to attend the interview—but it's an excellent idea to do so. After all, one of the main topics of discussion will be a form your spouse filled out—the Affidavit of Support—

showing your spouse's financial situation. If your spouse can confirm the contents of the affidavit in person, so much the better. And your spouse's willingness to travel to be with you for this part of the immigration process is a pretty good way of showing that your marriage is not a sham.

A few applicants—or more likely their U.S. fiancés or spouses—may also be asked to attend a so-called fraud interview. This happens when USCIS or the consulate has suspicions that your marriage or intended marriage is not real. Preparing for fraud interviews is covered in Section E, below.

B. Preparing for Your Interview

The key to a smooth interview is preparation. If you haven't already done so, prepare all the appropriate forms and documents. For immigrants coming from overseas, these are the ones mentioned in the mailing that you got containing your consular appointment notice. For immigrants in the United States, these are the ones discussed in Chapter 14, Section F.

1. What to Review

In order to prepare for the oral part of the interview, your most important homework task is to review your paperwork. Look at the questions and answers on every form that you've submitted or that has been submitted for you, including the ones filled out by your U.S. citizen fiancé or spouse. Though they seem to contain only boring, dry bits of information, this information is loaded with meaning to a USCIS or consular official. The dates of your visits to different places, the financial figures, and your immigration history can all add up to a revealing picture in the official's eyes.

EXAMPLE: Leticia hates dealing with money issues, so she didn't read the Affidavit of Support that her husband filled out. And she didn't notice that her husband wrote on the form that he has "no dependents." At the interview, the officer observed, "It looks like your husband doesn't earn much. How will you be supported?" Leticia replied, "Oh, I'm sure we'll make do financially. After all, my husband's aging parents and orphan nephew all live with him and don't work and he seems to support them just fine." Leticia just created a huge problem. It's now apparent that her husband lied on his Affidavit of Support and has several dependents. He is clearly less capable of supporting Leticia than it originally appeared. As a result, the consular officer may find Leticia inadmissible as a potential public charge.

The example above shows why you and your fiancé or spouse should review all the paperwork and forms carefully to be sure both of you understand them completely. If there have been any changes or if you've noticed any errors since filling out the forms, be prepared to explain the changes and provide documents confirming the new information, if appropriate.

After you've reviewed your written work, spend some time with your fiancé or spouse reviewing the facts and circumstances surrounding your relationship, such as where you met, how your relationship developed, how you've corresponded or visited and when, and why you decided to get married.

If you're applying for a fiancé visa, be ready to explain your plans for your wedding and subsequent life together. If you're already married, recall what occurred at your wedding and how you settled into your marriage. The officer will ask you about these details in order to test whether you are truly establishing a life together, not just committing a fraud in order to obtain a green card.

> **CAUTION**
> **Your memory may let you down.** Even if you and your fiancé or spouse think you know and remember everything about one another, you each may remember things differently. Couples have been known to disagree to the tune of a hundred people regarding how many

attended their wedding ceremony. And plenty of people can't remember what they did for their spouse's last birthday. The more you know about your shared history, the better prepared you'll be for the interview. You can make a game of testing each other on domestic facts: What color are the curtains in your house, how often do you see your in-laws, what's the name of your child's best friend? To help you with this game, take a look at the list of questions in Section F, below.

2. What to Wear

The interviewing officer's decision rests almost entirely on whether he or she believes that you're telling the truth. You'll come across as more sincere if you're dressed neatly, professionally, and even conservatively. Avoid T-shirts or jewelry with slogans or symbols that might make the officer wonder about your lifestyle or morals. We suggest that you dress as if you were going to visit your grandmother. Think about what you'll wear to your interview earlier than the night before, so that you're not up late with your ironing board.

> **EXAMPLE:** Jon showed up at his interview wearing expensive leather shoes and, around his neck, a chain with a solid gold marijuana leaf dangling from it. The officer took one look at this and went right into questioning him as to whether he had ever tried, abused, or sold drugs. When Jon wouldn't admit to anything, she referred him for another medical exam. The doctor found evidence of drug use in Jon's bloodstream, and he was denied the visa.

3. What to Bring

You'll need to bring a number of documents to your interview, for purposes of proving your identity, the validity of your marriage, and more. You'll be given a list of the required documents when you receive your appointment notice.

Also check the chapter of this book that describes all of the applications and documents someone

Sample Interview Appointment Notice

AMERICAN CONSULATE GENERAL -	VISA SECTION
LOPEZ MATEOS 924 N.	P.O. BOX 10545
CD. JUAREZ, CHIH, MEX.	EL PASO, TX 79995

IMMIGRANT VISA INFORMATION NUMBERS:
FROM U.S.A. : **1-900-225-5520** (8:00AM-4:30PM, MOUNTAIN TIME)
CHARGED TO CALLER AT US$1.00 PER MINUTE
FROM MEXICO: **01-900-849-7474** (8:00AM-4:30PM, MOUNTAIN TIME)
CHARGED TO CALLER AT MEX$10.00 (PESOS) PER MINUTE

Date: 14 Dec 2010

ILONA BRAY
950 PARKER STREET
BERKELEY, CA 94610

Dear LOPEZ, EMMA RUIZ DE:

This office is ready to begin final processing of the immigrant visa applicant(s) named below in this case. We have scheduled an appointment for a visa interview in the Immigrant Visa section on the date printed below. This letter must be presented upon your arrival at this office on the appointment date.

Please see the enclosed information for further instruction about the medical examination required for all intending immigrants. Be sure to read all the enclosed information and follow the instructions very carefully. When communicating with this office either by telephone or letter, please provide your name and case number exactly as shown in this letter.

Sincerely,

Chief, Immigrant Visa Branch

Visa Appointment			Medical Appointment	
Date	Time		Date	Time
*********************			*********************	
29-Jan-2011	08:00			

Case Number: CDJ5555555555

Name (P) : LOPEZ, EMMA RUIZ DE
Traveling Applicants:

(P)	LOPEZ, EMMA RUIZ DE	15-SEP-1961
(S)	LOPEZ PEREZ, JAVIER	12-MAR-1947
(C)	LOPEZ RUIZ, LUIS FERNANDO	31-AUG-1986
(C)	LOPEZ RUIZ, DIANA	24-MAR-1989
(C)	LOPEZ RUIZ, DANIEL	08-JUL-1995

Preference Category: F4 - MEX

Encl: Packet 4

in your precise situation must prepare. This will give you more detail than the government's lists, particularly on the important topic of what documents to bring to prove that your marriage is the real thing.

4. Prepare for Security Screening

Most if not all U.S. consulates now have airport-style security checkpoints that screen visitors and visa applicants before they are allowed to enter. By organizing your documents in advance and making some simple preparations before going to the consulate, you can save yourself a lot of time, hassle, and unneeded stress before your interview.

- Leave any portable electronics and devices like your mobile phone, PDA, tablet, camera, music player, or similar items at home or somewhere safe.
- Don't bring any food or drink with you.
- Leave any cosmetics, perfumes or colognes, brushes and combs, and similar items at home.
- Don't bring any packages, parcels, or sealed envelopes that are unrelated to your visa application. Bring only the documents and papers you need for your visa interview.
- If possible, bring your documents and visa application materials in a clear plastic folder or envelope. This will allow consular security to easily screen your visa materials.

C. Procedures for Consular Interviews

If you're coming from overseas, as a fiancé or spouse, your interview notice will tell you where and when to go for your visa interview. The appointment notice will look much like the one above.

1. Getting There Safely and On Time

If you don't live in the same city as the consulate, you'll want to arrive at least a few days in advance.

You will need time to complete your medical exam (at a clinic designated by the consulate) and to get the test results back.

On the day of your interview, it's best to arrive early, in case there's a line. Don't be surprised if you have to wait beyond your scheduled appointment time—the consulates often schedule applicants in large groups, telling all the members of each group to show up at the same time.

CAUTION

Beware of crime around U.S. consulates. Criminals know where the U.S. consulates are and they know that many people going for interviews are carrying large sums of money for visa fees. Take whatever precautions are appropriate in your country. Watch out for con artists who hang around the consulate, trying to convince people that they won't get through the front door unless they hand over some money first.

2. What the Consular Officials Will Do and Say

Here's what will happen when you arrive at the consulate for your interview. First, a clerk will check the packet of forms and other items that you've brought, to make sure you've brought all that's needed.

After these preliminaries, a consular officer will meet with you, place you under oath, and review the contents of your entire application. Don't expect a cozy fireside chat in the official's office. Many consulates now conduct interviews through bulletproof glass windows that make you feel like you're in a bank or a prison.

The officer will probably start by reviewing your forms and documents. He or she may ask you questions that are identical to the ones on your forms. Since you will have reviewed these carefully, this shouldn't be a problem—but if you can't remember something, it's much better to say so than to guess at the answer.

Next, you'll have to answer questions designed to test whether your marriage or intended marriage is the real thing. The officer will probably start by asking general questions, such as how you and your U.S. citizen fiancé or spouse met, when you decided to get married, and other facts regarding your visits or correspondence. If you're already married, the official may ask how many people attended the ceremony and how you've visited or corresponded with one another in recent years.

If everything looks to be in order, the officer may ask only two or three questions—but he or she can ask more. If you have children in common, USCIS is much less likely to question whether your marriage is bona fide.

It's natural to feel embarrassed about sharing these personal details. It may be helpful to remember that the officers have heard it all by now. Their main interest is to see if you sound like a real fiancé or spouse. Again, it's advisable not to make guesses if you don't know the answer to a question. For example, if an officer asks you, "How many people attended your engagement party?" and you don't know or have forgotten, you could reply, "I don't remember the exact number." Even better would be to add a relevant detail that you do remember, such as, "But I can tell you that the guests drank 32 cases of champagne pretty quickly!"

If You're Pregnant at Your Fiancé Visa Interview

Don't worry if you're pregnant when you go for your fiancé visa interview—the consular officer will arrange to give the baby a separate visa if it's born before you depart for the United States. But believe it or not, before either of you are approved for the visa, the consulate will need to receive a written acknowledgment from your U.S. citizen fiancé that he is still willing to marry you. This appears to be based on the worry that your U.S. citizen fiancé may not be the father of the baby and may therefore change his mind about the engagement.

The interview can take as little as 20 minutes, in cases where the marriage is obviously real, all documents are in order, and the applicant doesn't fall into any of the grounds for inadmissibility. Don't panic if it lasts longer. If you find yourself getting nervous, remember to curb that understandable instinct to start babbling. People with real marriages have nevertheless gotten themselves into deep trouble by being unable to stop talking.

EXAMPLE: Arthur, a U.S. citizen, is attending a visa interview with his immigrating wife, Natalya. He's jet-lagged and anxious to have everything go well. He starts babbling to the officer, saying, "I'm so glad to finally be getting this over with. My family thought we'd never finish up. They keep teasing me about my 'mail order bride' and acting like I don't know what I'm doing. My little brother even asked me how much Natalya was paying me to marry her, can you believe it?" Unfortunately the consular officer is in the business of believing such rumors. Arthur's little speech means that he and Natalya have to endure a whole new and harsher round of questioning before her visa is finally approved.

At the end of the interview, don't expect an immediate decision. Even if everything looks good, the consulate will need to run some final security checks with the FBI and other law-enforcement agencies. This might take only a few days or it could take several months.

Different consulates notify you that your visa has been approved (or denied) in different ways. Some just post your case number online, and you have to check. Others call you by phone, or require that you give them a return mailer, and still others allow you to email the consulate and ask. You'll find out at your interview what to expect.

3. Delayed Decisions

Even if there's a problem in your case, officers rarely deny applications on the spot. If the problem can be corrected or if you are inadmissible but are eligible to apply for a waiver, they will normally ask you to provide additional materials.

Politely ask that the officer or official to put any requests for more materials in writing, stating exactly what is needed and why. If there are any questions about the validity of your marriage, the consular officer may send your file back to the United States for investigation.

> **EXAMPLE:** A U.S. consular officer in Guatemala told Estela that he couldn't approve her immigrant visa until she brought in her "sister's tax returns." What was the problem? No such tax returns existed, because the sister (who was helping sponsor Estela financially) hadn't even been working long enough to reach a tax deadline. Her lawyer in the United States wrote a letter explaining this, but the consulate continued to ask for these tax returns. Because Estela didn't have the consulate's original request in writing, this led to months of arguing back and forth, with the consular officials continually changing or forgetting what it was they were looking for.

Usually you have to return to the consulate a few days later to pick up your visa—which is actually a thick envelope stuffed full of all your supporting documents.

> ! CAUTION
> **Do not open the visa envelope!** You will give the envelope to the United States border officer when you arrive. The officer will examine the contents and do a last check for any problems. The border official, not the consulate, will place a stamp in your passport indicating that you are either a fiancé visa holder, a permanent resident, or a conditional resident.

D. Procedures for USCIS Interviews

About three to four months after you submit your adjustment of status packet to USCIS, USCIS will schedule your interview at one of its local offices, hopefully near where you live. This could be your biggest day since your wedding: If the interview goes well—your marriage is obviously the real deal, you don't fall into any of the grounds for inadmissibility, and your documents are in order— the interview can take as little as 20 minutes. If you have children in common, USCIS is much less likely to question whether your marriage is bona fide. You will be approved for permanent residence or conditional residence (if you've been married for less than two years or entered the United States on a fiancé visa).

The appointment notice will look much like the one below. Read the notice carefully—there's a chance that your local USCIS office has added requirements that were not covered in this book.

1. Arrange for an Interpreter

USCIS doesn't provide interpreters at interviews in the United States. A few of their officers speak Spanish or other languages, but you can't count on getting a bilingual officer, nor can you request one. If you're not comfortable in English, you'll need to bring a friend or hire an interpreter to help. Even if your spouse is capable of interpreting for you, the USCIS office probably won't allow it, because it reduces their ability to compare your answers and detect marriage frauds.

The interpreter must be over 18 and fluent in both your language and in English. Some officers also require that the interpreter be a legal resident or citizen of the United States (of course, if they're here illegally, they'd be foolish to walk into a USCIS office).

Sample Interview Notice

Department of Homeland Security
U.S. Citizenship and Immigration Services

I-797, Notice of Action

THE UNITED STATES OF AMERICA

REQUEST FOR APPLICANT TO APPEAR FOR INITIAL INTERVIEW		NOTICE DATE May 25, 2013
CASE TYPE FORM I-485, APPLICATION TO REGISTER PERMANENT RESIDENCE OR ADJUST STATUS		A# A 012 345 677
APPLICATION NUMBER NSC0612345678	RECEIVED DATE March 21, 2013	PRIORITY DATE March 21, 2013
		PAGE 1 of 1

ANDA MICHELSKI
c/o ILONA BRAY
950 PARKER ST
BERKELEY CA 94710

You are hereby notified to appear for the interview appointment, as scheduled below, for the completion of your Application to Register Permanent Residence or Adjust Status (Form I-485) and any supporting applications or petitions. *Failure to appear for this interview and/or failure to bring the below listed items will result in the denial of your application. (6 CFR 103.2(b)(13))*

Who should come with you?

☐ **If your eligibility is based on your marriage, your husband or wife must come with you to the interview.**
☐ **If you do not speak English fluently, you should bring an interpreter.**
☐ Your attorney or authorized representative may come with you to the interview.
☐ If your eligibility is based on a parent/child relationship and the child is a minor, the petitioning parent and the child must appear for the interview.

NOTE: Every adult (over 18 years of age) who comes to the interview must bring Government-issued photo identification, such as a driver's license or ID card, in order to enter the building and to verify his/her identity at the time of the interview. You do not need to bring your children unless otherwise instructed. Please be on time, but do not arrive more than 45 minutes early. We may record or videotape your interview.

YOU MUST BRING THE FOLLOWING ITEMS WITH YOU: (Please use as a checklist to prepare for your interview)

☐ This Interview Notice and your Government issued photo identification.
☐ A completed medical examination (Form I-693) and vaccination supplement in a sealed envelope (unless already submitted).
☐ A completed Affidavit(s) of Support (Form I-864) with all required evidence, including the following, for each of your sponsors (unless already submitted):
    ☐ Federal Income Tax returns and W-2's, or certified IRS printouts, for the past 3 years;
    ☐ Letters from each current employer, verifying current rate of pay and average weekly hours, and pay stubs for the past 2 months;
    ☐ Evidence of your sponsor's and/or co-sponsor's United States Citizenship or Lawful Permanent Resident status.
☐ All documentation establishing your eligibility for Lawful Permanent Resident status.
☐ Any immigration-related documentation ever issued to you, including any Employment Authorization Document (EAD) and any Authorization for Advance Parole (Form I-512).
☐ All travel documents used to enter the United States, including Passports, Advance Parole documents (I-512) and I-94s (Arrival/Departure Document).
☐ Your Birth Certificate.
☐ Your petitioner's Birth Certificate and your petitioner's evidence of United States Citizenship or Lawful Permanent Resident Status.
☐ If you have children, bring a Birth Certificate for each of your children.
☐ If your eligibility is based on your marriage, in addition to your spouse coming to the interview with you, bring:
    ☐ A certified copy of your Marriage Document issued by the appropriate civil authority.
    ☐ Your spouse's Birth Certificate and your spouse's evidence of United States Citizenship or Lawful Permanent Resident status;
    ☐ If either you or your spouse were ever married before, all divorce decrees/death certificates for each prior marriage/former spouse;
    ☐ Birth Certificates for all children of this marriage, and custody papers for your children and for your spouse's children not living with you;
☐ Supporting evidence of your relationship, such as copies of any documentation regarding joint assets or liabilities you and your spouse may have together. This may include: tax returns, bank statements, insurance documents (car, life, health), property documents (car, house, etc.), rental agreements, utility bills, credit cards, contracts, leases, photos, correspondence and/or any other documents you feel may substantiate your relationship.
☐ Original and copy of each supporting document that you submitted with your application. Otherwise, we may keep your originals for our records.
☐ If you have ever been arrested, bring the related Police Report and the original or certified Final Court Disposition for each arrest, even if the charges have been dismissed or expunged. If no court record is available, bring a letter from the court with jurisdiction indicating this.
☐ A certified English translation for each foreign language document. The translator must certify that s/he is fluent in both languages, and that the translation in its entirety is complete and accurate.

YOU MUST APPEAR FOR THIS INTERVIEW- If an emergency, such as your own illness or a close relative's hospitalization, prevents you from appearing, call the U.S. Citizenship and Immigration Services (USCIS) National Customer Service Center at 1-800-375-5283 as soon as possible. Please be advised that rescheduling will delay processing of application/petition, and may require some steps to be repeated. It may also affect your eligibility for other immigration benefits while this application is pending.

If you have questions, please call the USCIS National Customer Service Center at 1-800-375-5283 (hearing impaired TDD service is 1-800-767-1833).

PLEASE COME TO: U.S. Citizenship and Immigration Services 630 SANSOME ST 2ND FLOOR - ADJUSTMENT OF STATUS SAN FRANCISCO CA 94111	ON: Monday, July 17, 2013 AT: 12:45 PM
6	REPRESENTATIVE COPY

Form I-797 (Rev. 01/31/05) N

2. What the USCIS Officials Will Do and Say

In spite of the fact that hundreds of very different couples are interviewed each day across the United States, these interviews tend to follow a pattern. Here's what will probably happen at your adjustment interview, step by step.

1. After sitting in the waiting room with dozens of other couples for so long that you're sure they've forgotten you, you'll be summoned to the inner rooms of the USCIS adjustments unit.

2. You'll be brought to the USCIS officer's desk, where your identification will be checked. Just when you're seated comfortably, you, your spouse, and your interpreter (if you've brought one) will have to stand up again, raise your right hands, and take oaths to tell the truth. The officer will ask to see all of your passports and travel documents, your work permit (if you have one), your Social Security card (if you have one), and your driver's license (if you have one). The officer will also want to see documents from your spouse, such as a driver's license, Social Security card (if available), and proof of legal U.S. immigration status.

3. The officer will start by going through your written application, asking you about the facts and examining the medical and fingerprint reports for factors that might make you ineligible for a green card. As discussed earlier, this is one of the most important parts of the interview. You'll sign the application to confirm its correctness.

4. The officer will ask you and your spouse about your married life. At this stage, the questions will be polite ones, such as where you met, when and why you decided to get married, how many people attended your wedding, or what you did on your most recent birthday or night out. You'll back up your answers with documents that illustrate the genuine nature of your marriage, such

as rental agreements and joint utility bills. (Chapter 14, Section F, lists other persuasive documents you might use.)

5. If there's a problem in your application that you can correct by submitting additional materials, the officer will usually put your case on hold and send you home with a list of additional documents to provide by mail within a specified time. For example, if your spouse's earnings are insufficient, the officer may suggest you find another family member to sign an Affidavit of Support. Rarely does USCIS deny an application on the spot.

6. If the officer suspects that your marriage is fraudulent, however, a whole new step will be added to the process. You will meet the Fraud Unit. There, an officer will interview you and your spouse separately—and intensively. The officer will compare the results of your two interviews. For details on what to expect and how to prepare for a Fraud Interview, see Section E, below.

 CAUTION

Truly married couples get called in for fraud interviews too. If, as we hope, your marriage isn't fraudulent, you may be inclined to skip the section below that addresses fraud interviews. However, couples whose personal characteristics or living situations already raise red flags in the eyes of USCIS might need to do some extra planning. The USCIS officers are on the lookout for couples who, for example, do not seem to share a common language; have large differences in their age, religion, class, cultural, or educational background; or who don't live at the same address.

At the end of the interview, if you are approved, you will be given a letter stating that your case is approved. The letter is just for your records and cannot be used like a green card to travel in and out of the United States. Several weeks later, however, your actual green card will arrive by mail. If you receive conditional residence, you'll have to file an application about 21 months from your approval date in order to progress to permanent residency.

3. Presenting Marital Problems at the Adjustment Interview

The USCIS officer will be most likely to approve you for a green card if you're in a happy, traditional marriage. However, this doesn't mean that marital arguments or even living separately should lead the officer to deny your green card. If you have serious problems, be reasonably open about the cause and the detailed steps you're taking to deal with them (such as meeting with a marriage counselor or religious leader on a regular basis). Sometimes this is the strongest evidence of a real, bona fide marriage! If, however, the officer appears to wrongly believe that only happy marriages qualify you for a green card (which is not uncommon), ask to reschedule the interview so that you can bring a lawyer.

If you've actually received a legal separation (court ordered) or filed for divorce, however, your prospects for approval are dimmer. A legal separation or divorce filing will ultimately lead to a denial of your green card. There is an exception if your U.S. citizen or permanent resident spouse is subjecting you to abuse (physical or emotional cruelty). In that case, divorce will not destroy your green card eligibility if you file what's called a self-petition on Form I-360. You must do so before the divorce decree becomes final, or within two years of the final decree if you can show that the divorce was connected to the abuse.

The self-petition declares that since you're being abused, your spouse can't be counted on to help you through the green card application process. It allows you to start or continue the process on your own. Domestic violence situations and self-petitions are not addressed in this book. Talk to your local battered women's shelter or other nonprofit or charity organization; or see a lawyer if spousal violence is holding up your application. (See Chapter 17 for more on how to find a lawyer to represent you.)

E. The Fraud Interview

If USCIS has serious doubts about whether your marriage is a real one, it will summon you and/or your fiancé or spouse for a fraud interview. A fraud interview is similar to the initial interview, but includes questions that are far more probing and intense. Such interviews are usually held only in the United States. If you are overseas, your fiancé or spouse will have to attend the interview alone, and should read Section 3, below. If you are applying within the United States, however, USCIS will no doubt call both of you in for the fraud interview.

Being called for a fraud interview is definitely not a good sign. It means that your application has been singled out because it misses facts that would prove a real marriage, contains some inconsistencies, or presents grounds for suspicion. But if your marriage really is authentic, now's the time to show them.

1. Times When a Fraud Interview May Be Required

There are various times during the application process when USCIS may call for a fraud interview. These include after your spouse files the initial visa petition (Form I-129F for fiancés or Form I-130 for spouses) and after your USCIS or consular interview. If you haven't reached your second wedding anniversary by the time you're ready for residence approval, you'll get conditional residency, which lasts for two years—and a fraud interview can be scheduled during or at the expiration of that time, too.

 SEE AN EXPERT

Applicants often get advance notice of a fraud interview—this is a good time to hire a lawyer. Ask the lawyer to attend the interview. The lawyer doesn't really have much power over the questions that you are required to answer, but can be a calming influence on everyone. Also, if the lawyer attends the interview, he or she will be better prepared to deal with any follow-up matters.

2. What They'll Ask

In the classic fraud interview, a USCIS officer puts you and your spouse in separate rooms and asks each of you an identical set of questions. Later, the officer compares your answers to see if they match up. If you are applying in the United States, you can count on experiencing this type of interview.

If you are applying from overseas, the USCIS officer in the United States will probably not be able to interview you—and will have to settle for speaking to your fiancé or spouse alone. In that case, the officer will want to hear your fiancé or spouse give a realistic account of the development of your relationship. The officer will also try to spot any inconsistencies within your U.S. fiancé or spouse's story or between his or her story and the application forms and documents.

The person who attends the interview should be ready for any and all types of questions, from what you gave each other for your last birthdays to the form of birth control you use. The questions vary among different officers and different years. A list of possibilities is provided in Section F, below, but no official list exists (or if it does, it's well-guarded in the government's top secret files).

> **TIP**
>
> **Bring matching sets of house keys if you live in the United States.** USCIS officers have been known to ask husband and wife to produce their house keys. The officer then compares them to make sure that they fit the same locks.

One San Francisco officer is reputed to be obsessed with how technology fits into the couple's life, asking questions about how many TV remote controls are in the couple's shared house and who keeps the garage door opener in their car. Others might be more interested in food—asking about your favorites and who cooks what. If your fiancé or spouse lives with you, try going through your daily routine, noticing all the details, such as:

- how often and what time you call each other by phone

- how many people attended your wedding (if you're married)
- which holidays you celebrate together
- your activities the last time one of you visited the other, and
- which of your financial matters are shared, or who (if either) supports the other financially.

If you're not yet married, and applying for a fiancé visa, the questions might also cover things like:

- how your families feel about your plans
- whether the families have met you or your fiancé
- how much time you've spent together, and
- whether you had an engagement party or made a formal announcement of your engagement to family and friends.

There are no limits to the possible questions. Obviously, many of the questions in our sample list in Section F below are most suited to a couple who are already living together. For those of you who aren't yet living together, expect the officer to ask about times that the two of you have spent together.

3. How They'll Behave

Once you or your spouse gets to a fraud interview, you will have to meet with an officer whose main job is try to detect wrongdoers, not grant visas or green cards. The interviewer will not be trying to make you feel comfortable. His or her job is to push a person with questions until the person trips himself up, confesses to marriage fraud, or finally convinces the interviewer that the marriage is real.

Usually, straightforward, hard questioning is enough. Couples perpetrating a fraudulent marriage can do all the homework in the world, but when one of them forgets or doesn't know something very obvious—like where they went right after their wedding—it sticks out like a sore thumb. After that, the applicant often crumbles.

Occasionally, a hard-nosed USCIS officer will engage in harsher tactics, such as falsely telling someone that their spouse has already "confessed" that the marriage is bogus, in order to push the interviewee into confessing. Or, the officer may use flat-out intimidation, reminding the interviewee about the jail time and money fines a person faces if caught committing marriage fraud.

Sensing that the interviewee is feeling low, the officer may ask him to sign something withdrawing the visa petition or stating that the marriage is a fraud. If your marriage really is an honest one, don't agree to or sign anything. Ask to stop the interview and to reschedule with a lawyer present.

4. How Your Spouse Should Handle an Interview Without You

If you are overseas and are not asked to attend the fraud interview, your U.S. fiancé or spouse will have to handle it alone. He or she won't need to worry that the two of you share similar memories about your relationship—but will have to find other ways to demonstrate that your relationship is real.

A good way for your U.S. fiancé or spouse to prepare is to put him or herself in the USCIS officer's shoes. Assume that the officer will be thinking some pretty cynical thoughts about you and your reasons for wanting to come to the United States. Your fiancé or spouse should then think about what to tell and show the officer to shatter these negative assumptions.

> EXAMPLE: Kevin goes in for his marriage fraud interview. As he anticipated, the officer is wearing a look on his face that says, "This guy's 20 years older than the immigrant, they probably can't even speak each other's language, so they barely know each other and she'd never marry him if there weren't a green card in it for her." Kevin has planned for this, however. He tells the officer about his and his beloved's unusual shared interest in wild horse training and describes their romantic first meeting while watching horse races on the Mongolian steppes. Kevin has mentally reviewed all the details of the time that he and she spent together and can tell the officer details about their conversations, what she

wore, and the new foods that she introduced him to. And the kicker is when Kevin shows the officer his homework from the class he's taking to learn her native language. By the end of the interview, the officer's opinion has been completely turned around.

Your relationship probably didn't happen quite like Kevin's. But your fiancé can be as thorough as Kevin was in showing what makes his relationship special. With every couple, there are unusual facts and circumstances that you can use to show that the two of you are a real couple, not just a bad statistic.

F. Sample Interview Questions

These are sample questions to help you prepare for your interview, whether it's a consular, adjustment of status, or marriage fraud interview. Remember, there is no guarantee that the interviewer will ask you all or any of these questions (though many of them are drawn from actual interviews). But these should get you and your fiancé or spouse started on the process of testing each other's memory.

1. Development of Your Relationship

- Where did you meet?
- What did the two of you have in common?
- Where did you go for dates?
- When did your relationship turn romantic?
- How long was it before you decided to get married?
- Who proposed to whom?
- Why did you decide to have a [long, short] engagement?
- Did your parents approve of the match? Why or why not?

2. The Wedding

- How many people attended your wedding?
- Did each of your parents attend?
- Where was the wedding held?

- Was there music or other entertainment?
- What kind of cake (or other food) did you serve?
- Who were the bridesmaids/groomsmen?
- How late did the guests stay?
- Did the bride change clothes for the reception?
- Did you serve liquor? What kind?
- Did anyone get drunk or otherwise embarrass themselves at the reception? Who? Describe.
- What time did you and the [bride or groom] leave the reception?
- Did you go on a honeymoon? When did you leave? How did you get there? What airlines?

3. Regular Routines

- Who gets up first? At what time?
- How many alarm clocks do you set in the morning?
- Who makes breakfast?
- What do each of you eat for breakfast?
- Does your spouse drink coffee in the morning?
- What time do the working spouse or spouses arrive home?
- Who cleans the house?
- What day is your garbage picked up?
- Who takes care of paying the bills?
- Do you have a joint bank account? Where?
- Do you have a cat, dog, or other pet? Who feeds it? Who walks it (or cleans its kitty litter box, cage, etc.)?
- Do you and/or your spouse attend regular religious services? Where?
- Where do you keep the spare toilet paper?

4. The Kids

- Who picks up the children at school?
- Who packs lunches for the kids?
- What are their favorite toys/activities?
- What are their least favorite foods?
- Which children (if any) still use a car seat?

- What is your usual babysitter's name?

5. The Cooking

- How many times a week on average do you eat out?
- What is your favorite restaurant for special occasions? For weekly outings?
- Who does most of the cooking?
- Who does the grocery shopping? Where?
- Is there a particular food that you eat every week?
- What is your spouse's favorite/least favorite food?
- What color are the kitchen curtains?
- Do you have a barbecue grill? Do you use it?

6. Other Family Members

- Have you met each other's parents?
- How often do you see each other's parents?
- When was the last time you saw them? Where? For how long?
- On important holidays, do you buy individual gifts for your parents-in-law? Do they buy individual gifts for you?
- How do each of you get along with your parents-in-law?
- Which other members of your spouse's family do you see frequently? When was the last time you saw them? What did you do together?

7. Home Technology

- How many telephones are in your house? Where are they?
- Do you have an answering machine on your telephone? Who checks the messages?
- How many televisions are in the house? In which rooms? Do you watch shows together, or separately? Name one show that you always watch together.
- Do you record any television shows?
- Do you subscribe to a DVD rental service?

- Does your spouse listen to the radio? What station?
- How many cars do you have?
- Do you have a garage? Who parks in it? Do you use a garage door opener?
- Do you have a camera? Who uses it most often? Who takes pictures at important family occasions?

8. In the Bedroom

- What size is your bed (Twin, Queen, or King)?
- Do you have a regular mattress, futon, or waterbed?
- How many windows are there in your bedroom?
- What color are your spouse's pajamas?
- Who sleeps on each side of the bed?
- What form of contraception (birth control) do you use?
- When was your wife's last menstrual period?
- Where do you keep your toothbrushes? What kind of toothpaste, soap, and shampoo does each of you use?
- Do either of you read or watch television before going to sleep? Do you have lamps next to your bed?
- Have you ever had an argument that resulted in one of you sleeping in another room? Who, and which room?

9. The Rest of the House

- Do you live in a home or apartment? Who pays the mortgage or rent? How much is it?
- Is there a carpet in your front hallway? What color?
- Is your sofa a regular one or does it have a pull-out bed? Have you ever had houseguests sleep there?
- What type of curtains or window coverings are in your living room? What color?
- How many staircases are in your house?

- How many sinks, toilets, and showers are there in your house or apartment in total?
- Do you leave any lights on when you go to sleep at night?

10. Celebrations

- When is your spouse's birthday?
- What did you do for your spouse's last birthday?
- How did you celebrate your most recent wedding anniversary?
- What religious holidays do you celebrate together?
- What's the most important holiday of the year in your household? Where do you typically celebrate it?
- Have you and your spouse gone to see a movie or other form of entertainment lately? When, and what did you see?
- What did the two of you do last New Year's Eve? Fourth of July?

G. What to Do If an Interview Is Going Badly

Your chances of a smooth interview will be greatly increased by the advance preparation and organizing you're doing by using this book. Unfortunately, your efforts can't entirely guarantee a successful interview. A lot will hinge on the personality or mood of the government official.

It's important to have a balanced view of the USCIS and consular officers who will be interviewing you. They're human—and they know that part of their goal is to reunite families. Some of them can get downright sentimental as they look at your wedding photos.

Certain immigration officers have been known to go out of their way to help people—for example, spending hours searching for something in a room full of old files; or fitting a person's interview into their schedule even when the person arrived two hours late. On the other hand, some officers can get downright rude or hostile, perhaps due to their heavy caseload or the number of marriage frauds they've uncovered. Remember that they hold much of the power—getting angry will get you nowhere fast. Remain respectful and answer honestly if you don't know or remember something. Never guess or lie.

Some immigrant applicants have heard wild rumors about how to win over a U.S. government official. One showed up for his USCIS interview wearing a loud tie covered with American flags. He interjected comments about America's greatness and what a terrific member of society he would be. Not surprisingly, the officer rolled her eyes and got irritated. Most USCIS officers just want to see someone who won't waste their time, has an orderly, clean case, and is legally eligible for the green card or other benefit.

TIP

Try to get the officer's name. USCIS and consular officers often don't tell you their name, but it may be shown on their desk. The best thing to do is politely ask their name at the beginning of the interview (not when things have already started to go badly, when they may get defensive). Then write the name down. This tidbit of information may become important later. For example, if you need to file a complaint, discuss the matter with a supervisor, or consult with an attorney, you'll have an edge if you know whom you dealt with.

(An experienced attorney will know all the local USCIS officers by name and can better understand your description of what happened after learning who was involved.)

Some officers are irate no matter how the applicant behaves. You might encounter an officer who makes irrelevant accusations, acts in a discriminatory manner based on your race or gender, becomes uncontrollably angry, or persists with a line of questions or statements that is completely inappropriate. If any of these things happens, ask to see a supervisor.

If things are going badly, you don't have to let the situation go from bad to worse, ending with an on-the-spot rejection of your application. To avoid letting the officer make a final, negative decision, offer to supply any information that the officer asked for, so that your case will be postponed ("pended" in USCIS lingo). When you get home, write down as many details as you can remember of the interview, while it's fresh in your mind. Then, consider consulting an attorney about your experience to learn what you can do to improve USCIS's reaction to your application.

Even if you don't speak with a lawyer, write a letter to USCIS, asking that a supervisor consider the interviewer's conduct when making a final review of your case. Supervisors review all cases, but they will assume the officer acted appropriately unless you tell them otherwise.

Applying for a Green Card at a USCIS Office

If you are married and living in the United States, you're one step away from becoming a U.S. permanent resident. Now you need to apply to your local USCIS office for a green card. Of course, like most things involving the USCIS bureaucracy, it's not as simple as it sounds.

The process of getting a green card in the United States is called "adjustment of status." It involves paperwork and an interview. Most of your work will happen before you have any personal contact with USCIS. You'll prepare an adjustment of status packet, including various forms, documents, fees, a medical exam, and more. Some people go screaming to a lawyer as soon as they see the mountain of forms. Take heart—much of the requested information is routine and repetitive. You'll feel like an old pro by the time you're done.

After filing the adjustment of status packet, you'll wait about one month for fingerprinting and another two or more months for an interview with USCIS. At or soon after that interview, you should be approved for residency.

This chapter guides you through the application process, all the way from compiling your application forms to waiting for your interview, and ends with information on getting green cards for your children. It explains:

- the documents and materials, such as copies of tax returns and photos, that you will need in order to complete your adjustment of status packet (Section A)
- how to fill in the USCIS forms, line by line (Section B)
- how to turn in the forms (Section C)
- how to handle vacations or moves while you wait for your interview (Section D)
- your fingerprint appointment (Section E)
- how to start preparing for your adjustment of status interview (Section F), and
- how to obtain green cards for your children (Section G).

You'll also want to read Chapter 13, which discusses what will happen at the adjustment of status interview and what questions to prepare for.

Even though you are still months away from getting the green card, applying for it will give you some immediate rights. You can remain in the United States while USCIS works on your application, and you'll get a work permit, which will allow you to get a job during the adjustment of status process.

> **CAUTION**
>
> **Do not apply to adjust status until you are sure you are eligible to obtain a green card through this procedure.** If you are not eligible, filing the adjustment of status papers could trigger removal or deportation procedures. Make sure you have read and followed the instructions in Chapter 11 or 12, whichever is appropriate to your situation, before applying to adjust status in the United States.

A. Documents and Information to Have on Hand

Before you begin filling in the mound of forms required by USCIS, it will be helpful to first assemble the documents and materials that must accompany the forms when you turn them in. Some of this requested material, such as copies of forms you've already filed, needs no explanation here; but other documentation, such as proof of your sponsor's employment, isn't so obvious. This section covers the materials that are not self-explanatory. At the end, there's a helpful checklist that shows all the documents and forms you'll need.

1. Your Sponsor's Tax Returns

Your spouse or other sponsor must be able to prove to USCIS that the sponsor can support you if necessary—and is willing to promise to do so. To fulfill these requirements, the sponsor(s) fill in an Affidavit of Support on Form I-864 or I-864EZ. In order to measure your sponsor's financial situation, USCIS will ask for a copy of your sponsor's federal

Applying for Immigrant Visa in the United States (Married Applicants)

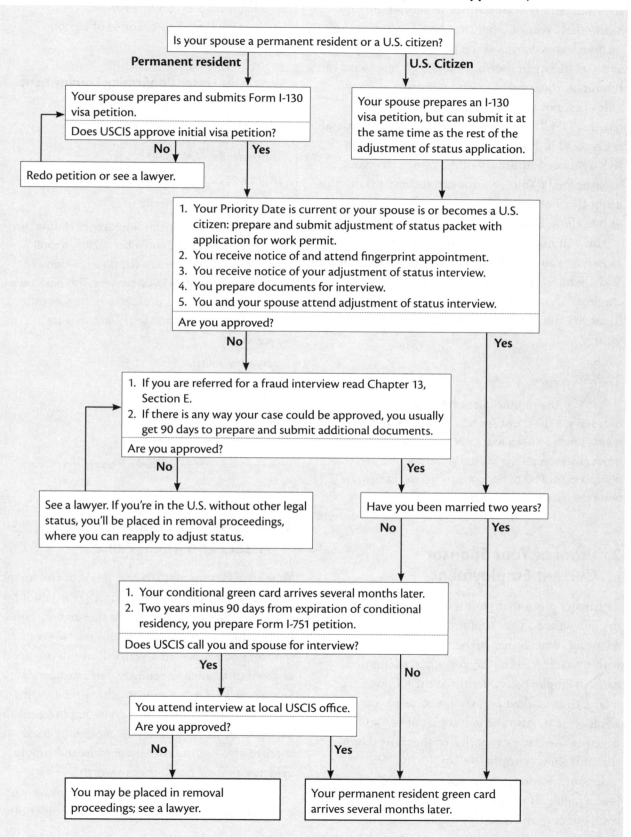

tax returns for the last year. Strictly speaking, the rules require your sponsor to submit only the most recent year's tax returns, but if your sponsor's income hovered around the poverty line last year and was higher in previous years, you may want to submit all three years' worth of returns anyway.

It's best not to simply photocopy the sets of returns. USCIS prefers to see your sponsor's federal tax returns in the form of an IRS transcript (an IRS-generated summary of the return that your sponsor filed). Your sponsor can request a transcript using IRS Form 4506T (available from www.irs.gov or by calling 800-829-1040).

You will not need to include state tax forms. However, you must include copies of your sponsor's W-2s, which are small print-outs from his or her employer showing total earnings over the last year (these are usually attached to the front of the tax return).

 TIP

Use photocopies of the tax returns if necessary. If the transcript hasn't come from the IRS by the time you need to submit the I-864 (the IRS often takes several weeks), use your sponsor's personal photocopies of his or her tax returns. You can always bring the transcripts to your interview.

2. Proof of Your Sponsor's Current Employment

As further proof that your sponsor will be able to contribute to your support, USCIS likes to see proof of his or her current employment. Start with a letter from the employer describing the dates of employment, nature of the job, wages or salary, time worked per week, and prospects for advancement. Also include copies of pay stubs covering the last six months, or the most recent stub if it shows cumulative pay.

If your sponsor is self-employed, a tax return is acceptable. If possible, add a business license, copies of current receipts, business cards, or other

documents that will show USCIS that your sponsor runs a legitimate, ongoing business.

Below, you'll find an example of a good employer's letter.

Sample Letter Confirming Employment

Hitting the Road Trucking
222 Plaza Place
Outthereville, MA 90000

May 22, 20xx

To Whom It May Concern:

Ron Goodley has been an employee of Hitting the Road Trucking since September 4, 20xx, a total of over five years. He has a full-time position as a driver. His salary is $45,000 per year. This position is permanent, and Ron's prospects for performance-based advancement and salary increases are excellent.

Very truly yours,

Bob Bossman

Bob Bossman
Personnel Manager
Hitting the Road Trucking

---

3. Proof of Your Sponsor's Assets and Their Value

Your sponsor's tax returns and proof of employment may be enough to convince USCIS that you'll be adequately taken care of. But if they're not, Form I-864 asks the sponsor to list any assets—your sponsor's or yours—that you will be relying upon as proof of financial adequacy. For example, if your spouse owns a home or other property, it will count toward meeting the income requirement. But listing these assets will not be enough by itself—the sponsor also has to prove ownership and supply evidence of how much they're worth.

- **Proof of ownership.** You or your sponsor can establish ownership by attaching copies of deeds or bills of sale. Skip ahead to pages 8 and 9 of Form I-864, "Use of Assets to Supplement Income," for a more detailed explanation of the types of documents USCIS will accept.

- **Value.** The value of an item must be the likely sale price today, not how much you or your sponsor paid for it. For real estate, use a current tax assessment to show the property's value. If you believe that the assessment is too low, or for property other than real estate, hire a professional appraiser to prepare an estimate and report. For cars, however, you can use the value listed in the *Kelley Blue Book*. You can find the *Blue Book* in your local library or bookstore, or online at www.kbb.com.

- **Remaining debt.** The asset-owner must also document the amount of any debt remaining on any listed asset. If no debt remains, submit proof of the final payment—most likely a receipt from a bank or lender.

- **Calculating assets' worth for immigration purposes.** Asset dollars are considered to be worth either one-fifth or one-third as much as income dollars, depending on whether the sponsor is a U.S. citizen or not. If your petitioner is a U.S. citizen, you'll need to divide each dollar of assets by three in order to arrive at its worth for purposes of sponsoring you. For all other sponsors, you'll need to divide each dollar of assets by five. To qualify based on the value of assets, the total value of the assets must equal at least five times the difference between the total household income and the current *Poverty Guidelines* amount (or at least three times the difference if the petitioner is a U.S. citizen).

EXAMPLE: Anna Marie, who is a U.S. citizen, petitions for her husband. For the Affidavit of Support, Anna Marie needs to show that her income is at least $18,212. Unfortunately, Anna Marie is earning only $15,000 at her current job. If she is going to use assets to make up the difference, it isn't enough for Anna Marie to show that she has $3,212 in assets. She will need to show that she has at least three times that amount in assets—that is, $9,636. (If she were a permanent resident, she would need to show that she has at least five times that amount in assets—$16,060.)

4. Eligibility of Your Sponsor's Household Joint Sponsor, If Applicable

If your spouse does not meet the financial requirements of USCIS, he or she may get help from a relative or dependent who lives in the same household. This person will be known as a household joint sponsor. If necessary, your sponsor can enlist the help of more than one. On Form I-864, you'll have to attach proof that:

- **The household joint sponsor(s) live with the primary sponsor.** You can use a copy of the rental agreement or lease showing the household member's name; or you can use copies of the household joint sponsor's documents that show the same address as the sponsor, such as a driver's license, school records, utility bills, or personal correspondence, and

- **The household joint sponsors are dependents of or related to the primary sponsor.** Joint sponsors who are dependents will be listed on the main sponsor's tax return, which will be enough proof by itself. For relatives who aren't listed as dependents, however, the best proof is a birth certificate. For example, if the sponsor and household joint sponsor are parent and child, the child's birth certificate will suffice. If they are brother and sister, the combination of both their birth certificates will work, since these certificates together show that they share the same parent or parents.

Keep in mind that for every household joint sponsor, you will need to provide federal tax returns, proof of employment, and proof of ownership and value of the joint sponsor's assets (if you list any on the form), just as you did for your spouse and/or primary sponsor.

5. Proof That You Are Eligible to Use the Adjustment of Status Procedure

USCIS will not accept your application at all unless you can satisfy them that you are among the few immigrants allowed to have their application processed by a USCIS office within the United States. There are four ways to meet this requirement.

- **You are married to a U.S. citizen and you entered legally.** To prove that you entered legally, include a copy of your passport, visa, and I-94 card. People who entered using Border Crossing Cards should photocopy both sides of the card. Proving your legal entry is extremely important. If you don't have such proof, and aren't otherwise eligible to apply from within the United States, don't risk deportation—see a lawyer before going further.

- **You didn't enter legally or your spouse is only a permanent resident, but you are grandfathered in.** For example, you might use the adjustment of status procedure if a visa petition was on file with the INS (as USCIS was then called) by one of the legal deadlines described in Chapters 2, 9, 11, and 12. To prove that you are grandfathered in, include a copy of the Form I-130 that was filed in time to grandfather you in, any proof of its mailing, and the subsequent INS approval notice. In addition, if you were grandfathered in based on an I-130 that was filed between January 14, 1998 and April 30, 2001, include proof that you were physically present in the United States on December 21, 2000. If you were in the U.S. on December 21, 2000, but don't have any documents showing your presence on that exact date, submit proof that you were in the U.S. both before and after that date. Such proof might include copies of immigration stamps in your passport, hotel or rent receipts, medical records, school records, utility bills, tax returns, car registrations, traffic tickets, employment payroll documents, and anything else you think appropriate.

- **You entered the U.S. with a K-1 fiancé visa and have since gotten married.** In that case, you'll need to attach copies of your Form I-129F approval notice and your marriage certificate.

- **You entered the U.S. with a K-3 visa.** Attach a copy of your Form I-129F approval notice and of your passport, visa, and I-94 card.

6. Fees

You'll need to submit the correct fee with your application. Because the fees go up frequently, check them on www.uscis.gov. (Go to the page for Form I-485, which will give you complete fee instructions.) In mid-2012 the fee for most adults was $1,070, ($985 plus a biometrics fee of $85). However, if you are 79 years of age or older, you don't have to pay the biometrics fee, so your fee total would be $985. And if you have children under age 14, they pay $635 so long as they're filing along with you. (If they're not, they pay $985.)

Also, if you're one of the few people who are adjusting status based on the old law Section 245(i), and submitting Form I-485A, you'll need to pay the added penalty fee of $1,000.

The application fee includes applying for a work permit (using Form I-765), so don't worry when you see instructions saying some people must pay a separate fee with this form.

You should write one check or money order to cover each person's application. Checks should be made payable to "U.S. Department of Homeland Security."

7. Using the Checklist for Adjustment of Status Packet

The checklist below lists every form, document, and other item that you and your spouse will need to gather and submit to USCIS as your adjustment of status (green card) application. As you get items ready, check off the appropriate box. That way you'll ensure that nothing gets forgotten.

Checklist for Adjustment of Status Packet

☐ One of the following:

☐ a copy of the INS or USCIS approval notice if you already submitted Form I-130, Petition for Alien Relative (most likely in cases where your spouse is a permanent resident), or

☐ a copy of your previously filed Form I-129F and USCIS approval notice (which you'll have if you entered the United States on a fiancé visa), or

☐ Form I-130 itself, with additional documents and forms (which you should have completed according to instructions in Chapter 11 or 12, whichever was applicable)

☐ Form(s) G-325A, filled out by you, the immigrant, and by your spouse if he or she hasn't already submitted one (see Section B1, below, for line-by-line instructions)

☐ Form I-485, Application to Register Permanent Residence or Adjust Status (see Section B2, below, for line-by-line instructions)

☐ Form I-485, Supplement A (see Section B3, below, for line-by-line instructions), for people who must pay a penalty fee in order to use adjustment of status as an application procedure

☐ Form I-693, Medical Exam (unless you entered as a fiancé, in which case your earlier medical exam is all you need, and USCIS will have it on file); see Section B4

☐ If you're exempt from the Affidavit of Support requirement, Form I-864W (to explain why you don't need to fill out Form I-864) (see Section B5, below)

☐ Form I-864 or I-864EZ, Affidavit of Support Under Section 213A of the Act (see Section B6 for line-by-line instructions)

☐ Documents to accompany Form I-864:

☐ A copy of your spouse or sponsor's federal income tax returns for the last year, with W-2

☐ Proof of your sponsor's current employment

☐ A list of assets (the sponsor's and/or the immigrant's), if they're being used to prove financial capacity

☐ Proof of location and ownership of any listed assets (including the sponsor's and the immigrant's)

☐ A list of the financial need-based public benefits programs and dates of receipt, if sponsor or sponsor's dependents have used such programs within the last three years

☐ Form I-864A, Contract Between Sponsor and Household Member, if needed because primary sponsor lacks financial capacity (see Section B7, below, for line-by-line instructions)

☐ Documents to accompany Form I-864A:

☐ Proof that the household joint sponsors live with the primary sponsor

☐ Proof that the household joint sponsors are related to the primary sponsor (if they're not already listed as dependents on the primary sponsor's tax return)

☐ Copies of the household joint sponsors' financial information (tax return for the last year, proof of employment, proof of the ownership, value, and location of assets, if any were listed, and a list of need-based public benefits programs and dates of receipt, if used in the last three years)

☐ I-765, Application for Employment Authorization (see Section B8, below, for line-by-line instructions)

☐ Proof that you are eligible to use the adjustment of status procedure (see Section A5, above)

☐ A copy of your birth certificate, with certified translation (see Chapter 4 on how to obtain vital records)

☐ Two photos of you (passport style)

☐ Application fees (currently $1,070 for most adults, but see USCIS website, www.uscis.gov)

✓ **CHECKLIST**
The checklist for adjustment of status is available as a tear-out in Appendix C of this book.

B. Line-by-Line Instructions for Adjustment of Status Forms

Here are instructions for filling out the forms and suggestions on how to answer many of the questions. If you don't need to use one of the forms covered below, such as Form I-864A, which is filled out by a household joint sponsor, just skip it.

1. Form G-325A, Biographic Information

The data you supply on this form will allow the U.S. government to check your background. Most of the form is self-explanatory. If you really can't remember or are unable to find out an exact date, enter whatever you can remember, such as the year. Alternately, you can simply say "unknown," but if you overuse the "unknowns," USCIS may return your entire application for another try. Since the questions aren't numbered, we refer to them by the approximate line.

If your spouse already submitted the I-130 visa petition to a USCIS Service Center, the two of you will have already filled in Forms G-325A. Nevertheless, you (but not your spouse) will need to fill in another Form G-325A as part of your adjustment of status application. But if you haven't yet submitted the I-130 visa petition because you are allowed to include it with your adjustment of status packet, you, the immigrant, need to fill in Form G-325A only once.

🖥 **WEB RESOURCE**
Form G-325A is available on the USCIS website at www.uscis.gov. Below is a filled-in sample of this form.

Lines 1 and 2 (Family Name, etc.): Self-explanatory.

Line 3 (Father/Mother): Self-explanatory.

Line 4 (Husband or Wife): Self-explanatory.

Line 5 (Former Husbands or Wives): Self-explanatory.

Line 7 (Applicant's residence last five years): Be careful here. List these addresses in reverse chronological order, starting with your most recent address and working your way down the last five years. For example, if you live in Detroit now but lived in Ann Arbor before, your Detroit address will go on the top line. Practice making this list on another sheet of paper before you enter the information here.

Line 12 (Applicant's last address outside the United States of more than one year): This may overlap with one of the addresses in Line 6—that's okay.

Line 13 (Applicant's employment last five years): As with Line 6, be careful to enter this information in reverse chronological order. If you've been unemployed, self-employed, or were a housewife or house-husband, say so here—in other words, try to account for all five years. If you're an immigrant who's been working illegally in the United States, identify your employers. To date, USCIS has not gone after the employers.

💼 **SEE AN EXPERT**
Showing false documents is a ground of inadmissibility. If you presented false documents to employers so that you could work illegally in the United States, such as showing a fake green card or Social Security card, see a lawyer. Simply using a fake Social Security number, however, without showing a fake Social Security card, is usually not considered a problem.

Line 14 (Show below last occupation abroad if not listed above): People tend to overlook this line, because it's so small—make sure you fill it in.

Line 19 (This form is submitted in connection with application for): Check "status as permanent resident."

Line 20 (If your native alphabet uses non-Roman letters): Self-explanatory.

Line 21 (The dark box): Self-explanatory.

Sample Form G-325A, Biographic Information

Department of Homeland Security
U.S. Citizenship and Immigration Services

OMB No. 1615-0008; Expires 08/31/2012

G-325A, Biographic Information

(Family Name)	(First Name)	(Middle Name)	☐ Male ☒ Female	Date of Birth (mm/dd/yyyy)	Citizenship/Nationality	File Number
Michelski	Anda	Marina		06-28-1984	Bulgarian	**A** 12345677

All Other Names Used (include names by previous marriages)	City and Country of Birth	U.S. Social Security # *(if any)*
none	Sofia Bulgaria	

	Family Name	First Name	Date of Birth (mm/dd/yyyy)	City, and Country of Birth (if known)	City and Country of Residence
Father	Michelski	Liski	12/24/64	Sofia, Bulgaria	Sofia, Bulgaria
Mother (Maiden Name)		Anastasia	3/10/65	Sofia, Bulgaria	Sofia, Bulgaria

Current Husband or Wife (If none, so state) Family Name (For wife, give maiden name)	First Name	Date of Birth (mm/dd/yyyy)	City and Country of Birth	Date of Marriage	Place of Marriage
Michela	Grun	03-17-1985	Hershey U.S.	12-17-2010	Hershey, PA

Former Husbands or Wives (If none, so state) Family Name (For wife, give maiden name)	First Name	Date of Birth (mm/dd/yyyy)	Date and Place of Marriage	Date and Place of Termination of Marriage
none				

Applicant's residence last five years. List present address first.

Street and Number	City	Province or State	Country	From Month	From Year	To Month	To Year
68 Watertown Boulevard, #12	Erie	PA	U.S.	11	2010	Present Time	
42, Raiska Gradina Street	Sofia		Bulgaria	2	2003	11	2010

Applicant's last address outside the United States of more than 1 year.

Street and Number	City	Province or State	Country	From Month	From Year	To Month	To Year
42, Raiska Gradina Street	Sofia	Bulgaria		02	2003	11	2010

Applicant's employment last five years. (If none, so state.) List present employment first.

Full Name and Address of Employer	Occupation (Specify)	From Month	From Year	To Month	To Year
Berlitz Language Center, Penn Center, Suite 800, Pittsburgh, PA 15276	language teacher	12	2010	Present Time	
Chech Cultural Center, 123 Sveta Serdika Street, Sofia Bulgaria	language teacher	8	2004	10	2010

Last occupation abroad if not shown above. (Include all information requested above.)

This form is submitted in connection with an application for:	Signature of Applicant	Date
☐ Naturalization ☐ Other (Specify): ☒ Status as Permanent Resident	*Anda Michelski*	4/20/2012

If your native alphabet is in other than Roman letters, write your name in your native alphabet below:

Penalties: Severe penalties are provided by law for knowingly and willfully falsifying or concealing a material fact.

Applicant: Print your name and Alien Registration Number in the box outlined by heavy border below.

Complete This Box (Family Name)	(Given Name)	(Middle Name)	(Alien Registration Number)
MICHELSKI	Anda	Marina	**A** 12345677

Form G-325A (Rev. 08/08/11) Y

2. Form I-485, Application to Register Permanent Residence or Adjust Status

Form I-485 is the primary application used for immigrants adjusting status in the United States. It collects basic information about your identity and admissibility. The information on this form all refers to you, the immigrating beneficiary.

WEB RESOURCE

Form I-485 is available on the USCIS website at www.uscis.gov. Below is a sample filled-in form.

Part 1

Family Name is your last name, or surname. Give your real address, not a mailing address. The **c/o** line is for people who have asked others to receive mail for them (unless you've asked someone to do so, leave this line blank). As with Form I-130, the questions regarding your arrival refer to your most recent entry to the United States. Your **Current USCIS Status** is the type of visa you're currently on, such as F-2 (student), "overstay" if the expiration date on your visa or permitted stay has passed, or "EWI" (entry without inspection) if you crossed the border illegally but somehow became eligible to use the adjustment of status procedure.

Part 2

Put an "X" in **box a** if you did not use a K-1 fiancé visa to enter the United States (in other words, if you are either an immediate relative or a preference relative with a current Priority Date and a right to use the adjustment of status procedure). Put an "X" in **box c** if you entered on a K-1 fiancé visa and are applying for your green card based on having married this fiancé in the United States.

Part 3

Once you've filled out Form I-130, Section "A" should be self-explanatory. In Section "B" you list information about your spouse and all of your children (including adult children and step-children).

Part of the purpose of **Question C** is to weed out terrorists. If you've been with an organization that has a violent wing or advocates violence, even if you were only in its nonviolent subgroup, consult a lawyer. Incidentally, you can improve the USCIS officer's opinion of you by listing organizations that you have volunteered with, such as religious organizations, to show that you are a moral person.

For the rest of the questions in "Part 3"—one through 18—hopefully your answers are all "no." If they aren't, don't lie—see a lawyer.

Part 4

If you need special accommodations for your interview because of a disability or impairment, explain what you need in this section.

Part 5

This is where you, the beneficiary, sign. There is also a place for an interpreter to sign, if you relied on an interpreter to answer the questions.

3. Form I-485, Supplement A

Not too many of you will need to complete this form. You'll complete it only if you are one of those few people who entered illegally, but are grandfathered in because you happen to possess an approved visa petition from a pre-January 14, 1998, or pre-April 30, 2001, filing (see Chapter 9, 11, or 12, whichever fits your current status, to review this issue).

> **EXAMPLE:** Danuta came to the United States by flying to Canada as a tourist, then sneaking across the Canadian border in the trunk of someone's car. She entered without inspection, or illegally. Danuta married Johan, who was then a U.S. permanent resident. Johan began the application process for Danuta by filing a visa petition (Form I-130) for Danuta before January 14, 1998, and the petition was approved.
>
> Luckily for Danuta, the date when Johan filed the visa petition is early enough that she

Sample Form I-485, Application to Register Permanent Residence or Adjust Status—Page 1

OMB No. 1615-0023

Department of Homeland Security
U.S. Citizenship and Immigration Services

Form I-485, Application to Register Permanent Residence or Adjust Status

START HERE - Type or Print (Use black ink)

Part 1. Information About You

Family Name (Last Name)	Given Name (First Name)	Middle Name
Michelski	Anda	M.

Address - Street Number and Name — Apt. #
Grun Michela

C/O (in care of)
68 Watertown Boulevard   12

City	State	Zip Code
Erie	Pennsylvania	19380

Date of Birth (mm/dd/yyyy)	Country of Birth
6/28/1984	

Country of Citizenship/Nationality	U.S. Social Security # (if any)	A # (if any)
Bulgaria	128-46-9255	A12345677

Date of Last Arrival (mm/dd/yyyy)	I-94 #
11/4/2011	123 123 123

Current USCIS Status	Expires on (mm/dd/yyyy)
H-1B	5/1/2012

For USCIS Use Only

Returned	Receipt
Resubmitted	
Reloc Sent	
Reloc Rec'd	
Applicant Interviewed	

Section of Law
- [ ] Sec. 209(a), INA
- [ ] Sec. 209(b), INA
- [ ] Sec. 13, Act of 9/11/57
- [ ] Sec. 245, INA
- [ ] Sec. 249, INA
- [ ] Sec. 1 Act of 11/2/66
- [ ] Sec. 2 Act of 11/2/66
- [ ] Other

Country Chargeable

Eligibility Under Sec. 245
- [ ] Approved Visa Petition
- [ ] Dependent of Principal Alien
- [ ] Special Immigrant
- [ ] Other

Preference

Action Block

Part 2. Application Type (Check one)

I am applying for an adjustment to permanent resident status because:

a. [X] An immigrant petition giving me an immediately available immigrant visa number that has been approved. (Attach a copy of the approval notice, or a relative, special immigrant juvenile, or special immigrant military visa petition filed with this application that will give you an immediately available visa number, if approved.)

b. [ ] My spouse or parent applied for adjustment of status or was granted lawful permanent residence in an immigrant visa category that allows derivative status for spouses and children.

c. [ ] I entered as a K-1 fiancé(e) of a U.S. citizen whom I married within 90 days of entry, or I am the K-2 child of such a fiancé(e). (Attach a copy of the fiancé(e) petition approval notice and the marriage certificate.)

d. [ ] I was granted asylum or derivative asylum status as the spouse or child of a person granted asylum and am eligible for adjustment.

e. [ ] I am a native or citizen of Cuba admitted or paroled into the United States after January 1, 1959, and thereafter have been physically present in the United States for at least 1 year.

f. [ ] I am the husband, wife, or minor unmarried child of a Cuban described above in **(e)**, and I am residing with that person, and was admitted or paroled into the United States after January 1, 1959, and thereafter have been physically present in the United States for at least 1 year.

g. [ ] I have continuously resided in the United States since before January 1, 1972.

h. [ ] Other basis of eligibility. Explain (for example, I was admitted as a refugee, my status has not been terminated, and I have been physically present in the United States for 1 year after admission). If additional space is needed, see **Page 2** of the instructions. _____

I am already a permanent resident and am applying to have the date I was granted permanent residence adjusted to the date I originally arrived in the United States as a nonimmigrant or parolee, or as of May 2, 1964, whichever date is later, and: (Check one)

i. [ ] I am a native or citizen of Cuba and meet the description in **(e)** above.

j. [ ] I am the husband, wife, or minor unmarried child of a Cuban and meet the description in **(f)** above.

To be Completed by
Attorney or Representative, **if any**
- [ ] Fill in box if Form G-28 is attached to represent the applicant.

VOLAG #

ATTY State License #

Form I-485 (Rev. 01/18/11) Y

Sample Form I-485, Application to Register Permanent Residence or Adjust Status—Page 2

Part 3. Processing Information

A. City/Town/Village of Birth
Sofia

Current Occupation
Language teacher

Your Mother's First Name
Anastasia

Your Father's First Name
Liski

Give your name exactly as it appears on your Form I-94, Arrival-Departure Record
Anda Michelski

Place of Last Entry Into the United States *(City/State)*
JFK Airport, New York

In what status did you last enter? *(Visitor, student, exchange visitor, crewman, temporary worker, without inspection, etc.)*
H-1B temporary worker

Were you inspected by a U.S. Immigration Officer?   Yes [X]   No [ ]

Nonimmigrant Visa Number
1062745139652

Consulate Where Visa Was Issued
Sofia

Date Visa Issued *(mm/dd/yyyy)*
7/2/2009

Gender
[ ] Male [X] Female

Marital Status
[X] Married [ ] Single [ ] Divorced [ ] Widowed

Have you ever applied for permanent resident status in the U.S.?   [X] Yes *(If "Yes" give date and place of filing and final disposition.)*   [ ] No

B. List your present spouse and all of your children (include adult sons and daughters). (If you have none, write "None." If additional space is needed, see **Page 2** of the instructions.)

Family Name *(Last Name)*	Given Name *(First Name)*	Middle Initial	Date of Birth *(mm/dd/yyyy)*
None			
Country of Birth	Relationship	A # *(if any)*	Applying with you? Yes [ ] No [ ]
Family Name *(Last Name)*	Given Name *(First Name)*	Middle Initial	Date of Birth *(mm/dd/yyyy)*
Country of Birth	Relationship	A # *(if any)*	Applying with you? Yes [ ] No [ ]
Family Name *(Last Name)*	Given Name *(First Name)*	Middle Initial	Date of Birth *(mm/dd/yyyy)*
Country of Birth	Relationship	A # *(if any)*	Applying with you? Yes [ ] No [ ]
Family Name *(Last Name)*	Given Name *(First Name)*	Middle Initial	Date of Birth *(mm/dd/yyyy)*
Country of Birth	Relationship	A # *(if any)*	Applying with you? Yes [ ] No [ ]
Family Name *(Last Name)*	Given Name *(First Name)*	Middle Initial	Date of Birth *(mm/dd/yyyy)*
Country of Birth	Relationship	A # *(if any)*	Applying with you? Yes [ ] No [ ]

Form I-485 (Rev. 01/18/11) Y Page 2

Sample Form I-485, Application to Register Permanent Residence or Adjust Status—Page 3

Part 3. Processing Information *(Continued)*

C. List your present and past membership in or affiliation with every organization, association, fund, foundation, party, club, society, or similar group in the United States or in other places since your 16th birthday. Include **any military service** in this part. If none, write "None." Include the name of each organization, location, nature, and dates of membership. If additional space is needed, attach a separate sheet of paper. Continuation pages must be submitted according to the guidelines provided on **Page 2** of the instructions under "What Are the General Filing Instructions?"

Name of Organization	Location and Nature	Date of Membership From	Date of Membership To

Answer the following questions. (If your answer is **"Yes"** to any question, explain on a separate piece of paper. Continuation pages must be submitted according to the guidelines provided on **Page 2** of the instructions under "What Are the General Filing Instructions?" Information about documentation that must be include with your application is also provide in this section.) Answering **"Yes"** does not necessarily mean that you are not entitled to adjust status or register for permanent residence.

1. Have you EVER, in or outside the United States:

   a. Knowingly committed any crime of moral turpitude or a drug-related offense for which you have not been arrested? Yes ☐ No ☒

   b. Been arrested, cited, charged, indicted, convicted, fined, or imprisoned for breaking or violating any law or ordinance, excluding traffic violations? Yes ☐ No ☒

   c. Been the beneficiary of a pardon, amnesty, rehabilitation decree, other act of clemency, or similar action? Yes ☐ No ☒

   d. Exercised diplomatic immunity to avoid prosecution for a criminal offense in the United States? Yes ☐ No ☒

2. Have you received public assistance in the United States from any source, including the U.S. Government or any State, county, city, or municipality (other than emergency medical treatment), or are you likely to receive public assistance in the future? Yes ☐ No ☒

3. Have you EVER:

   a. Within the past 10 years been a prostitute or procured anyone for prostitution, or intend to engage in such activities in the future? Yes ☐ No ☒

   b. Engaged in any unlawful commercialized vice, including, but not limited to, illegal gambling? Yes ☐ No ☒

   c. Knowingly encouraged, induced, assisted, abetted, or aided any alien to try to enter the United States illegally? Yes ☐ No ☒

   d. Illicitly trafficked in any controlled substance, or knowingly assisted, abetted, or colluded in the illicit trafficking of any controlled substance? Yes ☐ No ☒

4. Have you EVER engaged in, conspired to engage in, or do you intend to engage in, or have you ever solicited membership or funds for, or have you through any means ever assisted or provided any type of material support to any person or organization that has ever engaged or conspired to engage in sabotage, kidnapping, political assassination, hijacking, or any other form of terrorist activity? Yes ☐ No ☒

Sample Form I-485, Application to Register Permanent Residence or Adjust Status—Page 4

Part 3. Processing Information *(Continued)*

5. Do you intend to engage in the United States in:

   a. Espionage?   Yes ☐   No ☒

   b. Any activity a purpose of which is opposition to, or the control or overthrow of, the Government of the United States, by force, violence, or other unlawful means?   Yes ☐   No ☒

   c. Any activity to violate or evade any law prohibiting the export from the United States of goods, technology, or sensitive information?   Yes ☐   No ☒

6. Have you **EVER** been a member of, or in any way affiliated with, the Communist Party or any other totalitarian party?   Yes ☐   No ☒

7. Did you, during the period from March 23, 1933, to May 8, 1945, in association with either the Nazi Government of Germany or any organization or government associated or allied with the Nazi Government of Germany, ever order, incite, assist, or otherwise participate in the persecution of any person because of race, religion, national origin, or political opinion?   Yes ☐   No ☒

8. Have you **EVER** been deported from the United States, or removed from the United States at government expense, excluded within the past year, or are you now in exclusion, deportation, removal, or rescission proceedings?   Yes ☐   No ☒

9. Are you under a final order of civil penalty for violating section 274C of the Immigration and Nationality Act for use of fraudulent documents or have you, by fraud or willful misrepresentation of a material fact, ever sought to procure, or procured, a visa, other documentation, entry into the United States, or any immigration benefit?   Yes ☐   No ☒

10. Have you **EVER** left the United States to avoid being drafted into the U.S. Armed Forces?   Yes ☐   No ☒

11. Have you **EVER** been a J nonimmigrant exchange visitor who was subject to the 2-year foreign residence requirement and have not yet complied with that requirement or obtained a waiver?   Yes ☐   No ☒

12. Are you now withholding custody of a U.S. citizen child outside the United States from a person granted custody of the child?   Yes ☐   No ☒

13. Do you plan to practice polygamy in the United States?   Yes ☐   No ☒

14. Have you **EVER** ordered, incited, called for, committed, assisted, helped with, or otherwise participated in any of the following:

   a. Acts involving torture or genocide?   Yes ☐   No ☒

   b. Killing any person?   Yes ☐   No ☒

   c. Intentionally and severely injuring any person?   Yes ☐   No ☒

   d. Engaging in any kind of sexual contact or relations with any person who was being forced or threatened?   Yes ☐   No ☒

   e. Limiting or denying any person's ability to exercise religious beliefs?   Yes ☐   No ☒

15. Have you **EVER**:

   a. Served in, been a member of, assisted in, or participated in any military unit, paramilitary unit, police unit, self-defense unit, vigilante unit, rebel group, guerrilla group, militia, or insurgent organization?   Yes ☐   No ☒

   b. Served in any prison, jail, prison camp, detention facility, labor camp, or any other situation that involved detaining persons?   Yes ☐   No ☒

16. Have you **EVER** been a member of, assisted in, or participated in any group, unit, or organization of any kind in which you or other persons used any type of weapon against any person or threatened to do so?   Yes ☐   No ☒

Sample Form I-485, Application to Register Permanent Residence or Adjust Status—Page 5

Part 3. Processing Information *(Continued)*

17. Have you **EVER** assisted or participated in selling or providing weapons to any person who to your knowledge used them against another person, or in transporting weapons to any person who to your knowledge used them against another person? Yes ☐ No ☒

18. Have you **EVER** received any type of military, paramilitary, or weapons training? Yes ☐ No ☒

Part 4. Accommodations for Individuals With Disabilities and/or Impairments *(See **Page 10** of the instructions before completing this section.)*

Are you requesting an accommodation because of your disability(ies) and/or impairment(s)? Yes ☐ No ☒

If you answered "Yes," check any applicable box:

☐ **a.** I am deaf or hard of hearing and request the following accommodation(s) (if requesting a sign-language interpreter, indicate which language (e.g., American Sign Language)):

☐ **b.** I am blind or sight-impaired and request the following accommodation(s):

☐ **c.** I have another type of disability and/or impairment (describe the nature of your disability(ies) and/or impairment(s) and accommodation(s) you are requesting):

Part 5. Signature *(Read the information on penalties on **Page 10** of the instructions before completing this section. You must file this application while in the United States.)*

Your Registration With U.S. Citizenship and Immigration Services

"I understand and acknowledge that, under section 262 of the Immigration and Nationality Act (INA), as an alien who has been or will be in the United States for more than 30 days, I am required to register with U.S. Citizenship and Immigration Services (USCIS). I understand and acknowledge that, under section 265 of the INA, I am required to provide USCIS with my current address and written notice of any change of address within **10** days of the change. I understand and acknowledge that USCIS will use the most recent address that I provide to USCIS, on any form containing these acknowledgements, for all purposes, including the service of a Notice to Appear should it be necessary for USCIS to initiate removal proceedings against me. I understand and acknowledge that if I change my address without providing written notice to USCIS, I will be held responsible for any communications sent to me at the most recent address that I provided to USCIS. I further understand and acknowledge that, if removal proceedings are initiated against me and I fail to attend any hearing, including an initial hearing based on service of the Notice to Appear at the most recent address that I provided to USCIS or as otherwise provided by law, I may be ordered removed in my absence, arrested, and removed from the United States."

Selective Service Registration

The following applies to you if you are a male at least 18 years of age, but not yet 26 years of age, who is required to register with the Selective Service System: "I understand that my filing Form I-485 with U.S. Citizenship and Immigration Services (USCIS) authorizes USCIS to provide certain registration information to the Selective Service System in accordance with the Military Selective Service Act. Upon USCIS acceptance of my application, I authorize USCIS to transmit to the Selective Service System my name, current address, Social Security Number, date of birth, and the date I filed the application for the purpose of recording my Selective Service registration as of the filing date. If, however, USCIS does not accept my application, I further understand that, if so required, I am responsible for registering with the Selective Service by other means, provided I have not yet reached 26 years of age."

Sample Form I-485, Application to Register Permanent Residence or Adjust Status—Page 6

Part 5. Signature *(Continued)*

Applicant's Statement *(Check one)*

[X] I can read and understand English, and I have read and understand each and every question and instruction on this form, as well as my answer to each question.

[ ] Each and every question and instruction on this form, as well as my answer to each question, has been read to me in the _____ language, a language in which I am fluent, by the person named in **Interpreter's Statement and Signature**. I understand each and every question and instruction on this form, as well as my answer to each question.

I certify, under penalty of perjury under the laws of the United States of America, that the information provided with this application is all true and correct. I certify also that I have not withheld any information that would affect the outcome of this application.

I authorize the release of any information from my records that U.S. Citizenship and Immigration Services (USCIS) needs to determine eligibility for the benefit I am seeking.

Signature *(Applicant)*	Print Your Full Name	Date *(mm/dd/yyyy)*	Daytime Phone Number *(include area code)*
Anda Michelski	Anda Michelski	5/19/12	314 276-9440

NOTE: *If you do not completely fill out this form or fail to submit required documents listed in the instructions, you may not be found eligible for the requested benefit, and this application may be denied.*

Interpreter's Statement and Signature

I certify that I am fluent in English and the below-mentioned language.

Language Used *(language in which applicant is fluent)*

I further certify that I have read each and every question and instruction on this form, as well as the answer to each question, to this applicant in the above-mentioned language, and the applicant has understood each and every instruction and question on the form, as well as the answer to each question.

Signature *(Interpreter)*	Print Your Full Name	Date *(mm/dd/yyyy)*	Phone Number *(include area code)*

Part 6. Signature of Person Preparing Form, If Other Than Above

I declare that I prepared this application at the request of the above applicant, and it is based on all information of which I have knowledge.

Signature	Print Your Full Name	Date *(mm/dd/yyyy)*	Phone Number *(include area code)*

Firm Name and Address	E-Mail Address *(if any)*

Form I-485 (Rev. 01/18/11) Y Page 6

Sample Supplement A to Form I-485—Page 1

OMB No. 1615-0023

Department of Homeland Security
U.S. Citizenship Immigration and Service

Supplement A to Form I-485,
Adjustment of Status Under Section 245(i)

NOTE: Use this form only if you are applying to adjust status to that of a lawful permanent resident under section 245(i) of the Immigration and Nationality Act.

Part A. Information About You

	For USCIS Use Only
	Action Block

Last Name | First Name | Middle Name
SEBASTIAN | Danuta | Rasa

Address: In Care Of

Street Number and Name | Apt. Number
555 Front Street | 2

City | State | Zip Code
Chicago | IL | 60611

Alien Registration Number (A #) if any | Date of Birth *(mm/dd/yyyy)*
| 2/10/82

Country of Birth | Country of Citizenship/Nationality
Lithuania | Lithuania

Telephone Number | E-Mail Address, if any

Part B. Eligibility *(Check the correct response)*

1. I am filing Supplement A to Form I-485 because:

a. [X] I am the beneficiary of a visa petition filed on or before January 14, 1998.

b. [ ] I am the beneficiary of a visa petition filed on or after January 15, 1998, and on or before April 30, 2001.

c. [ ] I am the beneficiary of an application for a labor certification filed on or before January 14, 1998.

d. [ ] I am the beneficiary of an application for a labor certification filed on or after January 15, 1998, and on or before April 30, 2001.
If you checked box b or d in Question 1, you must submit evidence demonstrating that you were physically present in the United States on December 21, 2000.

2. And I fall into one or more of these categories: *(Check all that apply to you)*

a. [ ] I entered the United States as an alien crewman;

b. [ ] I have accepted employment without authorization;

c. [X] I am in unlawful immigration status because I entered the United States without inspection or I remained in the United States past the expiration of the period of my lawful admission;

d. [ ] I have failed (except through no fault of my own or for technical reasons) to maintain, continuously, lawful status;

e. [ ] I was admitted to the United States in transit without a visa;

f. [ ] I was admitted as a nonimmigrant visitor without a visa;

g. [ ] I was admitted to the United States as a nonimmigrant in the S classification; or

h. [ ] I am seeking employment-based adjustment of status and am not in lawful nonimmigrant status.

Part C. Additional Eligibility Information

1. Are you applying to adjust status based on any of the below reasons?

a. You were granted asylum in the United States;

b. You have continuously resided in the United States since January 1, 1972;

c. You entered as a K-1 fiancé(e) of a U.S. citizen;

d. You have an approved Form I-360, Petition for Amerasian, Widow(er), Battered or Abused Spouse or Child, or Special Immigrant, and are applying for adjustment as a special immigrant juvenile court dependent or a special immigrant who has served in the U.S. armed forces, or a battered or abused spouse or child;

Form I-485 Supplement A (Rev. 01/18/11)Y

Sample Supplement A to Form I-485—Page 2

Part C.   Additional Eligibility Information *(Continued)*

e.   You are a native or citizen of Cuba, or the spouse or child of such alien, who was not lawfully inspected or admitted to the United States;

f.   You are a special immigrant retired international organization employee or family member;

g.   You are a special immigrant physician;

h.   You are a public interest parolee, who was denied refugee status, and are from the former Soviet Union, Vietnam, Laos or Cambodia (a "Lautenberg Parolee" under Public Law 101-167); or

i.   You are eligible under the Immigration Nursing Relief Act.

☐ **No.**   I am not applying for adjustment of status for any of these reasons. *(Go to next question)*

☒ **Yes.**   I am applying for adjustment of status for any one of these reasons. **(If you answered "Yes," do not file this form.)**

2.   **Do any of the following conditions describe you?**

   a.   You are already a lawful permanent resident of the United States.

   b.   You have continuously maintained lawful immigration status in the United States since November 5, 1986.

   c.   You are applying to adjust status as the spouse or unmarried minor child of a U.S. citizen or the parent of a U.S. citizen child at least 21 years of age, and you were inspected and lawfully admitted to the United States.

   ☒ **No.**   None of these conditions describe me. *(Go to **Part D**. Signature)*

   ☐ **Yes.   If you answered "Yes," do not file this form.**

Part D.   Signature   *Read the information on penalties in the instructions before completing this section.*

I certify, under penalty of perjury under the laws of the United States of America, that this application and the evidence submitted with it is all true and correct. I authorize the release of any information from my records that the U.S. Citizenship and Immigration Services needs to determine eligibility for the benefit being sought.

Signature	Print Name	Date
Danuta Sebastian	Danuta Sebastian	3/14/2012

Part E.   Signature of Person Preparing Form, If Other Than Above
Read the information on penalties in the instructions before completing this section.

I certify, under penalty of perjury under the laws of the United States of America, that I prepared this form at the request of the above person and that to the best of my knowledge the contents of this application are all true and correct.

Signature	Print Name	Date

Firm Name and Address

Daytime Phone Number *(Area Code and Number)*

E-Mail Address, if any

Form I-485 Supplement A (Rev. 01/18/11)Y Page 2

is grandfathered into being eligible to use the adjustment of status procedure (apply for her green card in the United States). Now Danuta's Priority Date is current. Danuta must use Form I-485 Supplement A and pay an extra fee in order to do her green card processing in the United States. But Danuta is lucky—many people with later-filed applications must process in overseas consulates, where the consequence of their illegal entry and stay is that they may be prevented from returning for three or ten years.

 WEB RESOURCE
Form I-485A is available on the USCIS website at www.uscis.gov. Above is a sample filled-in version of this form.

Part A

Review our instructions for Forms I-130 and I-485.

Part B

Check only one box under Question 1, but as many as fit you in Question 2.

Part C

Questions 1 and 2: Your answer should be **No.** If in fact you did enter the United States as a K-1 fiancé of a U.S. citizen (as mentioned in 1c), and you married the U.S. citizen and are applying to adjust status on that basis, you're already eligible to adjust status and don't need to file this form.

Part D

Sign your name.

4. Form I-693, Medical Exam for Adjustment of Status Applicants

You'll need to have a medical exam unless you entered the United States on a K-1 fiancé visa. Applicants who entered the United States on K-1 fiancé visas and are now applying for a green card on the basis of their subsequent marriage can use

the results of their earlier medical exam (done to get the fiancé visa). The results of that exam should already be in the local USCIS office's files, because they were included in the sealed packet of paperwork that served as the fiancé's entry visa.

Your medical exam can only be conducted by a USCIS-approved doctor. A list of these doctors is available at www.uscis.gov; on the left-hand side of the page, click "Find a Medical Doctor (Civil Surgeon)." On the next page you can find an approved doctor in your area by entering your zip code. You can also get this information by calling the Customer Service Center at 800-375-5283. The fee varies among doctors, so you might want to call a few before choosing one.

It's best to wait to have your medical exam done until you're almost ready to turn in your adjustment of status packet, since USCIS considers the results to be good for only one year. This is not based on any law, it is just USCIS policy. But that policy could change, so it's best to play it safe.

For further description of the medical exam, see Chapter 2, Section A. Once all the results are in, the doctor will fill in the Form I-693 and return it to you in a sealed envelope. If you've given the doctor a version of the form that was photocopied or downloaded from the Internet, remind him or her to sign every page separately. Do not open the envelope—this will invalidate the results.

 WEB RESOURCE
Form I-693 is available on the USCIS website at www.uscis.gov. Below is a picture of the first page of this form.

5. Form I-864W, Intending Immigrant's Affidavit of Support Exemption

Only a few lucky people will be able to use this form, namely those who are exempt from the Affidavit of Support requirement because the immigrant has either:

Form I-693, Medical Exam for Adjustment of Status Applicants—Page 1

OMB No. 1615-0033; Expires 10/31/2012

Department of Homeland Security
U.S. Citizenship and Immigration Services

Form I-693, Report of Medical Examination and Vaccination Record

START HERE - Type or print in CAPITAL letters (*Use black ink*)

Part 1. Information About You (*To be completed by the person requesting a medical examination, not the civil surgeon*)

Family Name (Last Name)   Given Name (First Name)   Full Middle Name

Home Address: Street Number and Name   Apt. Number   Gender: ☐ Male   ☐ Female

City   State   Zip Code   Phone # (*Include Area Code*) *no dashes or ()*

Date of Birth (*mm/dd/yyyy*)   Place of Birth (*City/Town/Village*)   Country of Birth   A-Number (*if any*)   U.S. Social Security # (*if any*)

Applicant's Certification

I certify under penalty of perjury under United States law that I am the person who is identified in **Part 1** of this Form I-693, Report of Medical Examination and Vaccination Record, and that the information in **Part 1** of this form is true to the best of my knowledge. I understand the purpose of this medical exam, and I authorize the required tests and procedures to be completed. If it is determined that I willfully misrepresented a material fact or provided false/altered information or documents with regard to my medical exam, I understand that any immigration benefit I derived from this medical exam may be revoked, that I may be removed from the United States, and that I may be subject to civil or criminal penalties.

Signature - Do not sign or date this form until instructed to do so by the civil surgeon   **Date** (*mm/dd/yyyy*)

To be completed by civil surgeon: Form of applicant ID presented (*e.g., passport, driver's license*)   **ID Number** (*if any*)

Part 2. Summary of Medical Examination (*To be completed by the civil surgeon*)

Summary of Overall Findings:

☐ No Class A or Class B Condition

☐ Class A Conditions (*see Civil Surgeon Worksheet, sections 1-3*)
☐ Class B Conditions (*see Civil Surgeon Worksheet, sections 1-4*)

Date of First Examination (*mm/dd/yyyy*)   **Date(s) of Follow-up Examination(s) if Required:**

Date of Exam (*mm/dd/yyyy*)   **Date of Exam** (*mm/dd/yyyy*)   **Date of Exam** (*mm/dd/yyyy*)

Part 3. Civil Surgeon's Certification (*Do not sign form or have the applicant sign in Part 1 until all health follow-up requirements have been met*)

I certify under penalty of perjury under United States law that: I am a civil surgeon designated to examine applicants seeking certain immigration benefits in the U.S. OR a physician who qualifies under a blanket designation specified by policy or law; I have a currently valid and unrestricted license to practice medicine in the state where I am performing medical examinations unless otherwise exempted; I performed this examination of the person identified in Part 1 of this Form I-693, after having made every reasonable effort to verify that the person whom I examined is in fact the person identified in Part 1; that I performed the examination in accordance with the Centers for Disease Control and Prevention's *Technical Instructions*, and all supplemental information or updates; and that all information provided by me on this form is true and correct to the best of my knowledge, and belief.

Type or Print Full Name (*First, Middle, Last*)

Address (*Street Number and Name, City, State, and Zip Code*)

(For Health Departments Only:
Place official stamp or seal here)

Name of Medical Practice or Health Department

Signature

E-Mail/Daytime Phone # (*Include Area Code*)

Date (*mm/dd/yyyy*)

Form I-693 (10/11/11) N

- worked for 40 Social Security quarters in the U.S. (approximately ten years)
- been married while the U.S. spouse worked for 40 Social Security quarters, or
- a combination of the above.

The deal is that a financial sponsor's responsibility lasts until the immigrant has (among other possibilities) earned 40 work quarters credited toward Social Security. (A work quarter is approximately three months, but it depends partly on how much you earn.) So if you've already reached the 40 quarters on your own, through lawful employment—perhaps while in the U.S. as a student or H-1B worker—there's no point in the sponsor filling out an Affidavit of Support for you. And, in an interesting twist, the immigrant can be credited for work done by the U.S. spouse during their marriage.

You'll need to prove to USCIS how many quarters of work your spouse or you has done. Contact Social Security about getting a certified statement with this information.

Because Form I-864W is fairly easy to fill out, we won't include a sample here. The form is available at www.uscis.gov. In Part 2, you would check the first box.

6. Form I-864, Affidavit of Support Under Section 213A of the Act

This is the place for your spouse to assure USCIS that you will be adequately provided for once you become a permanent resident. If your spouse's income is insufficient and there are no household members who can contribute, a separate sponsor from outside the household can fill in an additional Affidavit of Support on your behalf, also using the instructions below.

The instructions and sample we give below are for the long version of Form I-864. However, if the petitioner is not self-employed, is relying on earned income without help from assets or other people, and is agreeing to sponsor only one person for each affidavit, you can use a shorter version, called I-864EZ, also available at www.uscis.gov.

 WEB RESOURCE

Form I-864 is available on the USCIS website at www.uscis.gov. Below is a sample filled-in version of this form. Our sample shows a sponsor whose income and assets are enough without getting help from others.

 TIP

Need to prepare Affidavits for several family members at once? If the sponsor is bringing in more than one person using the same Form I-130 visa petition, such as you and your children, he or she can make copies of Form I-864 (and its supporting documents) after signing it. This will be possible for only a few applicants, however, primarily those whose U.S. spouse is a permanent resident. If your spouse is a U.S. citizen, all your children will have needed their own Forms I-130, and will also need separately filled-out Forms I-864.

Parts 1-4

These sections are self-explanatory, with the following notes:

- **In Part 1,** spouses check box a; long-lost cousins, fairy godmothers, and other nice friends who agreed to fill in this form as joint sponsors check either box d or box e.
- **In Part 3,** note that there's a place to list children. You don't need to name children who were born in the United States, because the sponsor has no obligation to support them (at least not under the immigration laws, though they will be counted elsewhere within this form to test the sponsor's overall financial capacity). The form says "Do not include any relatives listed on a separate visa petition"— that's because, if the sponsor is a U.S. citizen, the children must have been mentioned on a separate I-130 visa petition and so, need their own separate Forms I-864 as well.
- **In Part 4,** note that the sponsor's place of residence must be in the United States in order to be eligible as a financial sponsor. If your sponsor lives outside the U.S., he or she can meet this requirement by showing the steps taken to return to the U.S. and make it

Sample Form I-864, Affidavit of Support Under Section 213A of the Act—Page 1

OMB No. 1615-0075; Expires 09/30/2012

Department of Homeland Security
U.S. Citizenship and Immigration Services

I-864, Affidavit of Support
Under Section 213A of the Act

Part 1.   Basis for filing Affidavit of Support.

	For Government Use Only

1. **I,** Grun Michela   ,
am the sponsor submitting this affidavit of support because (Check only one box):

This I-864 is from:

- [ ] the Petitioner
- [ ] a Joint Sponsor #

a. [X] **I am the petitioner. I filed or am filing for the immigration of my relative.**

b. [ ] **I filed an alien worker petition on behalf of the intending immigrant, who is related to me as my** _____

- [ ] the Substitute Sponsor
- [ ] 5% Owner

c. [ ] **I have an ownership interest of at least 5 percent in** _____ , **which filed an alien worker petition on behalf of the intending immigrant, who is related to me as my** _____

d. [ ] **I am the only joint sponsor.**

This I-864:

- [ ] does not meet the requirements of section 213A.
- [ ] meets the requirements of section 213A.

e. [ ] **I am the** [ ] **first** [ ] **second of two joint sponsors.** *(Check appropriate box.)*

f. [ ] **The original petitioner is deceased. I am the substitute sponsor. I am the intending immigrant's** _____ .

Part 2. Information on the principal immigrant.

2. Last Name   Michelski

First Name		Middle Name
Anda		Marina

Reviewer

Location

3. Mailing Address Street Number and Name *(Include Apartment Number)*
68 Watertown Boulevard, Apt. 12

Date *(mm/dd/yyyy)*

City	State/Province	Zip/Postal Code	Country
Erie	PA	19380	U.S.

Number of Affidavits of Support in file:

4. Country of Citizenship	5. Date of Birth *(mm/dd/yyyy)*
Bulgaria	06/28/1984

6. Alien Registration Number *(if any)*	7. U.S. Social Security Number *(if any)*
A- none	none

[ ] 1   [ ] 2

Part 3. Information on the immigrant(s) you are sponsoring.

8. [X] I am sponsoring the principal immigrant named in Part 2 above.

[X] Yes   [ ] No (Applicable only in cases with two joint sponsors)

9. [ ] I am sponsoring the following family members immigrating at the same time or within six months of the principal immigrant named in **Part 2** above. Do not include any relative listed on a separate visa petition.

Name	Relationship to Sponsored Immigrant	Date of Birth *(mm/dd/yyyy)*	A-Number *(if any)*	U.S.Social Security Number *(if any)*
a. none				
b.				
c.				
d.				
e.				

10. Enter the total number of immigrants you are sponsoring on this form from **Part 3**, Items **8** and **9**.   [1]

Form I-864 (09/19/11) Y

Sample Form I-864, Affidavit of Support Under Section 213A of the Act—Page 2

Part 4. Information on the Sponsor.

11. Name	Last Name		For Government Use Only
	Michela		
	First Name	Middle Name	
	Grun	Branimir	

12. Mailing Address	Street Number and Name *(Include Apartment Number)*	
	68 Watertown Boulevard, Apt. 12	
	City	State or Province
	Erie	PA
	Country	Zip/Postal Code
	U.S.	19380

13. Place of Residence *(if different from mailing address)*	Street Number and Name *(Include Apartment Number)*	
	City	State or Province
	Country	Zip/Postal Code

14. Telephone Number *(Include Area Code or Country and City Codes)*
314-276-9440

15. Country of Domicile
U.S.

16. Date of Birth *(mm/dd/yyyy)*
03/17/1984

17. Place of Birth *(City)*	State or Province	Country
Hershey	PA	U.S.

18. U.S. Social Security Number *(Required)*
123-45-6789

19. Citizenship/Residency

[X] I am a U.S. citizen.

[ ] I am a U.S. national (for joint sponsors only).

[ ] I am a lawful permanent resident. My alien registration number is A-_____

If you checked box (b), (c), (d), (e) or (f) in line 1 on Page 1, you must include proof of your citizen, national, or permanent resident status.

20. Military Service (To be completed by petitioner sponsors only.)

I am currently on active duty in the U.S. armed services.   [ ] Yes   [ ] No

Sample Form I-864, Affidavit of Support Under Section 213A of the Act—Page 3

Part 5. Sponsor's household size.

21. Your Household Size - <u>DO NOT COUNT ANYONE TWICE</u>

| | | For Government Use Only |

Persons you are sponsoring in this affidavit:

a. Enter the number you entered on line 10. [ ] [1]

Persons NOT sponsored in this affidavit:

b. Yourself. **[1]**

c. If you are currently married, enter "1" for your spouse. [ ]

d. If you have dependent children, enter the number here. [ ] [ ]

e. If you have any other dependents, enter the number here. [ ] [ ]

f. If you have sponsored any other persons on an I-864 or I-864 EZ who are now lawful permanent residents, enter the number here. [ ] [ ]

g. OPTIONAL: If you have <u>siblings, parents, or adult children</u> with the same principal residence who are combining their income with yours by submitting Form I-864A, enter the number here. [ ] [ ]

h. Add together lines and enter the number here. **Household Size:** [ ] [2]

Part 6. Sponsor's income and employment.

22. I am currently:

a. [X] Employed as a/an ___chef___ .

    Name of Employer #1 *(if applicable)* ___Erie Food Service___ .

    Name of Employer #2 *(if applicable)* _____ .

b. [ ] Self-employed as a/an _____ .

c. [ ] Retired from _____ since _____ .
            (Company Name)   *(Date)*

d. [ ] Unemployed since _____ .
              (Date)

23. My current individual annual income is: $ ___16,000.00___
                                   (See Step-by-Step Instructions)

Sample Form I-864, Affidavit of Support Under Section 213A of the Act—Page 4

24. My current annual household income:

    a. List your income from line 23 of this form. $ _16,000.00_

    b. Income you are using from any other person who was counted in your household size, including, in certain conditions, the intending immigrant. (See step-by-step instructions.) Please indicate name, relationship and income.

Name	Relationship	Current Income
_____	_____	$ _____
_____	_____	$ _____
_____	_____	$ _____
_____	_____	$ _16,000.00_

    c. Total Household Income: $ _____

    (Total all lines from 24a and 24b. Will be Compared to Poverty Guidelines -- See Form I-864P.)

    d. ☐ The persons listed above have completed Form I-864A. I am filing along with this form all necessary Forms I-864A completed by these persons.

    e. ☐ The person listed above, _____ does not need to
                                       (Name)
       complete Form I-864A because he/she is the intending immigrant and has no accompanying dependents.

25. Federal income tax return information.

    ☒ I have filed a Federal tax return for each of the three most recent tax years. I have attached the required photocopy or transcript of my Federal tax return for only the most recent tax year.

    My total income (adjusted gross income on IRS Form 1040EZ) as reported on my Federal tax returns for the most recent three years was:

Tax Year		Total Income
_2011_	*(most recent)*	$ _20,000.00_
_2010_	*(2nd most recent)*	$ _35,000.00_
_2009_	*(3rd most recent)*	$ _20,000.00_

    ☐ *(Optional)* I have attached photocopies or transcripts of my Federal tax returns for my second and third most recent tax years.

For Government Use Only

Household Size =

_____

Poverty line for year

_____ is:

$ _____

Sample Form I-864, Affidavit of Support Under Section 213A of the Act—Page 5

Part 7. Use of assets to supplement income. *(Optional)*	For Government Use Only
If your income, or the total income for you and your household, from line 24c exceeds the Federal Poverty Guidelines for your household size, YOU ARE NOT REQUIRED to complete this Part. Skip to Part 8.	**Household Size =** _____

26. Your assets *(Optional)*

    a. Enter the balance of all savings and checking accounts. $ __6,000__

    b. Enter the net cash value of real-estate holdings. (Net means current assessed value minus mortgage debt.) $ _____

    c. Enter the net cash value of all stocks, bonds, certificates of deposit, and any other assets not already included in lines 26 (a) or (b). $ __6,000__

    d. **Add together lines 26 a, b and c and enter the number here.**   **TOTAL:** $ _____

Poverty line for year _____ **is:**

$ _____

27. Your household member's assets from Form I-864A. *(Optional)*

Assets from Form I-864A, line 12d for

    $ _____

_____
(Name of Relative)

28. Assets of the principal sponsored immigrant. *(Optional)*

The principal sponsored immigrant is the person listed in line 2.

    a. Enter the balance of the sponsored immigrant's savings and checking accounts. $ _____

    b. Enter the net cash value of all the sponsored immigrant's real estate holdings. (Net means investment value minus mortgage debt.) $ _____

    c. Enter the current cash value of the sponsored immigrant's stocks, bonds, certificates of deposit, and other assets not included on line a or b. $ _____

    d. **Add together lines 28a, b, and c, and enter the number here.** $ __6,000__

The total value of all assests, line 29, must equal 5 times (3 times for spouses and children of USCs, or 1 time for orphans to be formally adopted in the U.S.) the difference between the poverty guidelines and the sponsor's household income, line 24c.

29. Total value of assets.

Add together lines 26d, 27 and 28d and enter the number here.   **TOTAL:** $ _____

Sample Form I-864, Affidavit of Support Under Section 213A of the Act—Page 6

Part 8. Sponsor's Contract.

Please note that, by signing this Form I-864, you agree to assume certain specific obligations under the Immigration and Nationality Act and other Federal laws. The following paragraphs describe those obligations. Please read the following information carefully before you sign the Form I-864. If you do not understand the obligations, you may wish to consult an attorney or accredited representative.

What is the Legal Effect of My Signing a Form I-864?

If you sign a Form I-864 on behalf of any person (called the "intending immigrant") who is applying for an immigrant visa or for adjustment of status to a permanent resident, and that intending immigrant submits the Form I-864 to the U.S. Government with his or her application for an immigrant visa or adjustment of status, under section 213A of the Immigration and Nationality Act these actions create a contract between you and the U. S. Government. The intending immigrant's becoming a permanent resident is the "consideration" for the contract.

Under this contract, you agree that, in deciding whether the intending immigrant can establish that he or she is not inadmissible to the United States as an alien likely to become a public charge, the U.S. Government can consider your income and assets to be available for the support of the intending immigrant.

What If I choose Not to Sign a Form I-864?

You cannot be made to sign a Form 1-864 if you do not want to do so. But if you do not sign the Form I-864, the intending immigrant may not be able to become a permanent resident in the United States.

What Does Signing the Form I-864 Require Me to do?

If an intending immigrant becomes a permanent resident in the United States based on a Form I-864 that you have signed, then, until your obligations under the Form I-864 terminate, you must:

-- Provide the intending immigrant any support necessary to maintain him or her at an income that is at least 125 percent of the Federal Poverty Guidelines for his or her household size (100 percent if you are the petitioning sponsor and are on active duty in the U.S. Armed Forces and the person is your husband, wife, unmarried child under 21 years old.)

-- Notify USCIS of any change in your address, within 30 days of the change, by filing Form I-865.

What Other Consequences Are There?

If an intending immigrant becomes a permanent resident in the United States based on a Form I-864 that you have signed, then until your obligations under the Form I-864 terminate, your income and assets may be considered ("deemed") to be available to that person, in determining whether he or she is eligible for certain Federal means-tested public benefits and also for State or local means-tested public benefits, if the State or local government's rules provide for consideration ("deeming") of your income and assets as available to the person.

This provision does **not** apply to public benefits specified in section 403(c) of the Welfare Reform Act such as, but not limited to, emergency Medicaid, short-term, non-cash emergency relief; services provided under the National School Lunch and Child Nutrition Acts; immunizations and testing and treatment for communicable diseases; and means-tested programs under the Elementary and Secondary Education Act.

Contract continued on following page.

Sample Form I-864, Affidavit of Support Under Section 213A of the Act—Page 7

What If I Do Not Fulfill My Obligations?

If you do not provide sufficient support to the person who becomes a permanent resident based on the Form I-864 that you signed, that person may sue you for this support.

If a Federal, State or local agency, or a private agency provides any covered means-tested public benefit to the person who becomes a permanent resident based on the Form I-864 that you signed, the agency may ask you to reimburse them for the amount of the benefits they provided. If you do not make the reimbursement, the agency may sue you for the amount that the agency believes you owe.

If you are sued, and the court enters a judgment against you, the person or agency that sued you may use any legally permitted procedures for enforcing or collecting the judgment. You may also be required to pay the costs of collection, including attorney fees.

If you do not file a properly completed Form I-865 within 30 days of any change of address, USCIS may impose a civil fine for your failing to do so.

When Will These Obligations End?

Your obligations under a Form I-864 will end if the person who becomes a permanent resident based on a Form I-864 that you signed:

- Becomes a U.S. citizen;
- Has worked, or can be credited with, 40 quarters of coverage under the Social Security Act;
- No longer has lawful permanent resident status, and has departed the United States;
- Becomes subject to removal, but applies for and obtains in removal proceedings a new grant of adjustment of status, based on a new affidavit of support, if one is required; or
- Dies.

Note that divorce **does not** terminate your obligations under this Form I-864.

Your obligations under a Form I-864 also end if you die. Therefore, if you die, your Estate will not be required to take responsibility for the person's support after your death. Your Estate may, however, be responsible for any support that you owed before you died.

30. I, _Grun Michela_____ ,

(Print Sponsor's Name)

certify under penalty of perjury under the laws of the United States that:

a. I know the contents of this affidavit of support that I signed.

b. All the factual statements in this affidavit of support are true and correct.

c. I have read and I understand each of the obligations described in Part 8, and I agree, freely and without any mental reservation or purpose of evasion, to accept each of those obligations in order to make it possible for the immigrants indicated in Part 3 to become permanent residents of the United States;

d. I agree to submit to the personal jurisdiction of any Federal or State court that has subject matter jurisdiction of a lawsuit against me to enforce my obligations under this Form I-864;

e. Each of the Federal income tax returns submitted in support of this affidavit are true copies, or are unaltered tax transcripts, of the tax returns I filed with the U.S. Internal Revenue Service; and

Sign on following page.

Sample Form I-864, Affidavit of Support Under Section 213A of the Act—Page 8

f. I authorize the Social Security Administration to release information about me in its records to the Department of State and U.S. Citizenship and Immigration Services.

g. Any and all other evidence submitted is true and correct.

31. _Grun Michela_ _____   _08/20/2012_ _____
(Sponsor's Signature)   (Date-- mm/dd/yyyy)

Part 9. Information on Preparer, if prepared by someone other than the sponsor.

I certify under penalty of perjury under the laws of the United States that I prepared this affidavit of support at the sponsor's request and that this affidavit of support is based on all information of which I have knowledge.

Signature: _____   **Date:** _____
                                                    (mm/dd/yyyy)

Printed Name: _____

Firm Name: _____

Address: _____

Telephone Number: _____

E-Mail Address : _____

Business State ID # *(if any)* _____

his or her residence as soon as you enter. Such steps might include finding U.S. employment, locating a place to live, and registering children in U.S. schools. The sponsor should also demonstrate having made arrangements to give up residence outside the United States.

Part 5, Sponsor's household size

This section is self-explanatory. Remember not to count anyone twice!

Part 6, Sponsor's income and employment

Question 22: The sponsor needs to fill in information about his or her employment here. Self-employment is fine. Be aware that if a self-employed sponsor has underreported income in the past, the earnings shown may not be sufficient to support you. In that case, the sponsor will need to file an amended tax return and pay a penalty before the newly reported income is accepted as meeting the guidelines for sponsorship.

Question 23: Here, the sponsor is supposed to enter the income shown on his or her most recent tax return. But what if the sponsor's income has risen since filing those taxes? In that case, the sponsor should enter the more recent income figure, but put an asterisk (an *) next to it. Then find some white space somewhere on the page and write "this figure reflects present earnings, not earnings shown on tax return; see supporting documentation." The documentation the sponsor is already providing, such as an employer's letter, should be enough to show current income.

Question 24: This question is important for sponsors whose income is not enough by itself, but who will be using the income of members of their household to help meet the *Poverty Guidelines* minimum requirements. First, every sponsor must state his or her own income. Then, if the sponsor wants other people's income counted, they must be mentioned in Question 24b. Unless anyone of these household members is the actual immigrant, they must plan to complete a separate agreement with the sponsor, using Form I-864A. The total income

from the sponsor and household members goes in Question 24c.

Question 25: Self-explanatory.

Part 7, Use of assets to supplement income

The sponsor needs to complete this section only if his or her income wasn't enough by itself to meet the *Poverty Guidelines* requirements. If the sponsor needs to add assets which may include such items as a house, car, or boat, remember to subtract debts, mortgages, and liens before writing down their value. And remember that the value of these assets will later be divided by three before being used to meet the *Poverty Guidelines* minimum if your spouse is a U.S. citizen, and will be divided by five if your spouse is a permanent resident. If some of the assets being used to meet the minimum belong to the immigrant, attach a separate page describing these (and of course attach documents to prove their ownership, location, and value).

If the combination of the sponsor's household available income and either one-third or one-fifth (as appropriate) of the sponsor's and/or the immigrant's assets don't yet meet the *Poverty Guidelines* minimum, you'll still need to hand in this Affidavit. But you'll definitely want to look for a joint sponsor.

Part 8, Sponsor's Contract

Unlike past versions of this form, the sponsor's signature does not need to be witnessed by a notary public.

7. Form I-864A

Not every sponsor needs to use this form. It is required only if, on the main Form I-864, the sponsor had to use the income of members of the sponsor's household to meet the *Poverty Guidelines*. In that case, the sponsor will have to ask these persons to fill in portions of Form I-864A. Then both the sponsor and the household member(s) will need to sign it. The sponsor will attach Form I-864A to the main Form I-864.

If the household member whose income is being counted is you, the immigrant spouse, you don't

Sample Form I-864A, Contract Between Sponsor and Household Member—Page 1

OMB No. 1615-0075; Expires 09/30/2012

Department of Homeland Security
U.S. Citizenship and Immigration Services

I-864A, Contract Between
Sponsor and Household Member

Part 1. Information on the Household Member. (You.)			For Government Use Only
1. Name	Last Name Michela		**This I-864A relates to a household member who:**
	First Name Marta	Middle Name Larita	☐ is the intending immigrant.
2. Mailing Address	Street Number and Name *(include apartment number)* 68 Watertown Boulevard, Apt. 12		
	City Erie PA	State or Province	☐ is not the intending immigrant.
	Country U.S. 19380	Zip/Postal Code	
3. Place of Residence *(if different from mailing address)*	Street Number and Name *(include apartment number)*		
	City	State or Province	Reviewer
	Country	Zip/Postal Code	Location
4. Telephone Number	*(Include area code or country and city codes)* 314-276-9440		
5. Date of Birth	*(mm/dd/yyyy)* 03/28/1959		Date *(mm/dd/yyyy)*
6. Place of Birth	City State/Province Country Sofia Bulgaria		
7. U.S. Social Security Number *(if any)*	123-45-6677		

8. Relationship to Sponsor (Check either a, b or c.)

a. ☐ I am the intending immigrant and also the sponsor's spouse.

b. ☐ I am the intending immigrant and also a member of the sponsor's household.

c. ☒ I am not the intending immigrant. I am the sponsor's household member. I am related to the sponsor as his/her.

    ☐ Spouse

    ☐ Son or daughter *(at least 18 years old)*

    ☒ Parent

    ☐ Brother or sister

    ☐ Other dependent (specify)

Form I-864A (09/19/11) Y

Sample Form I-864A, Contract Between Sponsor and Household Member—Page 2

9. I am currently:

a. [X] Employed as a/an _choir director_.
Name of Employer # 1 *(if applicable)* _Erie School_.
Name of Employer #2 *(if applicable)* _____.

b. ☐ Self-employed as a/an _____.

c. ☐ Retired from_____ since _____.
(Company Name) *(mm/dd/yyyy)*

d. ☐ Unemployed since _____.
(mm/dd/yyyy)

For Government Use Only

10. My current individual annual income is: $ _30,000_.

11. Federal income tax information.

[X] I have filed a Federal tax return for each of the three most recent tax years. I have attached the required photocopy or transcript of my Federal tax return for only the most recent tax year.

My total income (adjusted gross income on IRS Form 1040EZ) as reported on my Federal tax returns for the most recent three years was:

Tax Year		Total Income
2011	*(most recent)*	$ 30,000
2010	*(2nd most recent)*	$ 25,000
2009	*(3rd most recent)*	$ 20,000

☐ *(Optional)* I have attached photocopies or transcripts of my Federal tax returns for my second and third most recent tax years.

12. My assets (complete only if necessary).

a. Enter the balance of all cash, savings, and checking accounts. $_____.

b. Enter the net cash value of real-estate holdings. (Net means assessed value minus mortgage debt.) $_____.

c. Enter the cash value of all stocks, bonds, certificates of deposit, and other assets not listed on line a or b. $_____.

d. **Add together Lines a, b, and c and enter the number here.** $_____.

Form I-864A (09/19/11) Y Page 2

Sample Form I-864A, Contract Between Sponsor and Household Member—Page 3

	For Government Use Only

Part 2. Sponsor's Promise.

13. I, THE SPONSOR, _____Grun Michela_____
(Print Name)

in consideration of the household member's promise to support the following intending immigrant(s)

and to be jointly and severally liable for any obligations I incur under the affidavit of support, promise

to complete and file an affidavit of support on behalf of the following ____1____ named intending
(Indicate Number)

immigrant(s) (see Step-by-Step instructions).

Name	Date of Birth *(mm/dd/yyyy)*	A-number *(if any)*	U.S. Social Security Number *(if any)*
a. Anda Marina Michelski	06/28/1984		387-33-8877
b.			
c.			
d.			
e.			

14. _____Grun Michela_____   08/20/2012
     (Sponsor's Signature)   *(Date--mm/dd/yyyy)*

Part 3. Household Member's Promise.

15. I, THE HOUSEHOLD MEMBER, _____Marta Michela_____
(Print Name)

in consideration of the sponsor's promise to complete and file an affidavit of support on behalf of the

above ____1____ named intending immigrant(s):
(Number from line 13)

a. Promise to provide any and all financial support necessary to assist the sponsor in maintaining the sponsored immigrant(s) at or above the minimum income provided for in section 213A(a)(1)(A) of the Act (not less than 125 percent of the Federal Poverty Guidelines) during the period in which the affidavit of support is enforceable;

b. Agree to be jointly and severally liable for payment of any and all obligations owed by the sponsor under the affidavit of support to the sponsored immigrant(s), to any agency of the Federal Government, to any agency of a State or local government, or to any other private entity that provides means-tested public benefit;

c. Certify under penalty under the laws of the United States that all the information provided on this form is true and correct to the best of my knowledge and belief and that the Federal income tax returns submitted in support of the contract are true copies or unaltered tax transcripts filed with the Internal Revenue Service.

d. Consideration where the household member is also the sponsored immigrant: I understand that if I am the sponsored immigrant and a member of the sponsor's household that this promise relates only to my promise to be jointly and severally liable for any obligation owed by the sponsor under the affidavit of support to any of my dependents, to any agency of the Federal Government, to any agency of a State or local government, and to provide any and all financial support necessary to assist the sponsor in maintaining any of my dependents at or above the minimum income provided for in section 213A(s)(1)(A) of the Act (not less than 125 percent of the Federal poverty line) during the period which the affidavit of support is enforceable.

e. I authorize the Social Security Administration to release information about me in its records to the Department of State and U.S. Citizenship and Immigration Services.

16. _____Marta Michela_____   08/20/2012
     (Household Member's Signature)   *(Date--mm/dd/yyyy)*

need to sign Form I-864A unless you are agreeing to support your immigrating children as well.

WEB RESOURCE
Form I-864A is available on the USCIS website at www.uscis.gov. Above is a sample filled-in version of this form. The sample changes the fact pattern from the previous form and assumes the sponsor's mother lives with him.

Part 1: Self-explanatory; filled in by the household member.

Part 2: This part is filled in and signed by the sponsor. Self-explanatory.

Part 3: This is filled in and signed by the household member. Self-explanatory.

8. Form I-765, Application for Employment Authorization

Applying for employment authorization is optional, and there's no separate fee for it. But even if you're not planning to work, the employment authorization card, or work permit, is a helpful piece of photo identification. You can use it to get a Social Security card and a driver's license.

WEB RESOURCE
Form I-765 is available on the USCIS website at www.uscis.gov. Below is a sample filled-in version of this form.

If this is your first work permit, under **"I am applying for,"** check "Permission to accept employment." If you've applied for a previous work permit (for example, if you're applying now as part of your green card application but previously applied for and received a work permit as a fiancé), check the box for renewals.

Questions 1-14: Self-explanatory.

Question 15: You are an "Adjustment Applicant."

Question 16: Your eligibility category as an Adjustment of Status applicant is (c)(9).

Don't be confused by the various mailing addresses contained in the instructions to this form.

At the adjustment of status application stage, you simply mail Form I-765 to the same address as the rest of your adjustment of status application.

TIP
Think you'll travel outside the United States while awaiting your adjustment of status interview? If so, also include an application for Advance Parole with your adjustment of status packet. Complete instructions are in Section D2, below.

9. Form G-1145, E-Notification of Application/Petition Acceptance

Use this form only if you want USCIS to send you an email or text message to let you know that your application has been received and accepted. It does not take the place of the paper receipt that you will be sent a few weeks later, which is discussed in Section C1, below.

C. Submitting the Adjustment of Status Packet

Formerly, applicants could submit their adjustment of status packet to a local USCIS District Office. New procedures, however, require you to send it to an office in Chicago. (USCIS refers to this as a "lockbox," but in fact people work there.) USCIS made this change in hopes of speeding up the handling of applications. (Your interview, however, will be handled by your local USCIS district office.)

Make a complete copy of every form, document, photo, and check or money order in your packet, then send it to either:

- USCIS, P.O. Box 805887, Chicago, IL 60680-4120, if you're using the U.S. Postal Service, or
- USCIS Attn: FBAS, 131 South Dearborn, 3rd Floor, Chicago, IL 60603-5517, if you're using a private delivery service such as DHL or FedEx instead of the U.S. Postal Service.

Sample Form I-765, Application for Employment Authorization

OMB No. 1615-0040

I-765, Application For
Employment Authorization

Department of Homeland Security
U.S. Citizenship and Immigration Services

Do not write in this block.

Remarks	Action Block	Fee Stamp
A#		

Applicant is filing under §274a.12 _____

☐ Application Approved. Employment Authorized / Extended *(Circle One)*   until _____ (Date).

    Subject to the following conditions: _____ (Date).
    Application Denied.
      ☐ Failed to establish eligibility under 8 CFR 274a.12 (a) or (c).
      ☐ Failed to establish economic necessity as required in 8 CFR 274a.12(c)(14), (18) and 8 CFR 214.2(f)

I am applying for:
   ☒ Permission to accept employment.
   ☐ Replacement *(of lost employment authorization document)*.
   ☐ Renewal of my permission to accept employment *(attach previous employment authorization document)*.

1. Name (Family Name in CAPS) (First) (Middle)
MICHELSKI   Anda   Marina

2. Other Names Used (include Maiden Name)
none

3. Address in the United States (Street Number and Name) (Apt. Number)
68 Watertown Boulevard   12

(Town or City) (State/Country) (ZIP Code)
Erie   PA   19380

4. Country of Citizenship/Nationality
Bulgaria   H-1B worker

5. Place of Birth (Town or City) (State/Province) (Country)
Sofia

6. Date of Birth (mm/dd/yyyy)   **7. Gender**
06/28/1984   ☐ Male   ☒ Female

8. Marital Status   ☒ Married   ☐ Single   ☐ Widowed   ☐ Divorced

9. Social Security Number (include all numbers you have ever used) (if any)
387 33 8877

10. Alien Registration Number (A-Number) or I-94 Number (if any)
A 12345677

11. Have you ever before applied for employment authorization from USCIS?
☐ Yes (If "Yes," complete below)   ☒ No

Which USCIS Office?   Date(s)

Results (Granted or Denied - attach all documentation)

12. Date of Last Entry into the U.S. (mm/dd/yyyy)
11/04/2011

13. Place of Last Entry into the U.S.
JFK Airport, New York

14. Manner of Last Entry (Visitor, Student, etc.)

15. Current Immigration Status (Visitor, Student, etc.)
Adjustment applicant

16. Go to **Part 2** of the Instructions, Eligibility Categories. In the space below, place the letter and number of the category you selected from the instructions (For example, (a)(8), (c)(17)(iii), etc.).

Eligibility under 8 CFR 274a.12 (   ) (c) (9)

17. If you entered the Eligibility Category, (c)(3)(C), in item 16 above, list your degree, your employer's name as listed in E-Verify, and your employer's E-Verify Company Identification Number or a valid E-Verify Client Company Identification Number in the space below.

Degree:

Employer's Name as listed in E-Verify: _____

Employer's E-Verify Company Identification Number or a valid E-Verify Client Company Identification Number _____

Certification

Your Certification: I certify, under penalty of perjury under the laws of the United States of America, that the foregoing is true and correct. Furthermore, I authorize the release of any information that U.S. Citizenship and Immigration Services needs to determine eligibility for the benefit I am seeking. I have read the Instructions in **Part 2** and have identified the appropriate eligibility category in **Block 16**.

Signature	Telephone Number	Date
Anda Michelski	(314) 276-9440	5/19/12

Signature of Person Preparing Form, If Other Than Above: I declare that this document was prepared by me at the request of the applicant and is based on all information of which I have any knowledge.

Print Name	Address	Signature	Date

Remarks	Initial Receipt	Resubmitted	Relocated		Completed		
			Rec'd	Sent	Approved	Denied	Returned

Form I-765 (Rev. 01/19/11)Y

Sample Form G-1145, E-Notification of Application/Petition Acceptance

OMB No. 1615-0109

Form G-1145, E-Notification of Application/Petition Acceptance

Department of Homeland Security
U.S. Citizenship and Immigration Services

Who Can Receive E-Mails and/or Text Messages?

When you file an immigration form at one of the three U.S. Citizenship and Immigration Services (USCIS) Lockbox facilities, you will have the option to receive an e-mail and/or text message informing you that USCIS has accepted your application or petition. If you provide an e-mail address and a mobile phone number, you will receive both types of electronic notification (e-Notification) messages.

The three USCIS Lockbox facilities are located in Chicago, IL, Phoenix, AZ, and Lewisville, TX.

You should verify where to file by reviewing the filing instructions related to your immigration form(s). Please note that some immigration forms will continue to be filed with USCIS Service Centers or Field Offices. USCIS Service Centers or Field Offices will not provide e-mail and text message notifications at this time. USCIS will continue to expand its e-Notification messaging capabilities to include these filings.

When Will I Be Notified?

USCIS will notify you within 24 hours of accepting your immigration form(s).

What Will the E-Mail or Text Message Include?

The message will provide a receipt number as information but will not constitute official notice of acceptance. The e-mail notice will also provide a brief statement on how to get additional information about the status of your case.

USCIS will then send the official receipt notice, Form I-797C, Notice of Action, to the person seeking the benefit or the person's representative, as appropriate, via the U.S. Postal Service. There will be no e-Notification for acceptance of Form G-28, Notice of Entry of Appearance as Attorney or Accredited Representative. E-mail or text messages that cannot be delivered will not be retransmitted.

What If I Want to Submit Multiple Applications?

If you are submitting multiple immigration forms for one applicant, please clip this entire form with the e-mail address and/or mobile phone number (see below) to the front of the first immigration form of the package. You will receive a separate e-mail and/or text message for each accepted immigration form.

For representatives who file multiple unrelated immigration forms in one envelope, and who want their clients to receive e-Notification(s), this form, with the notification information

provided below, must be clipped to the front of each related package of immigration forms. The e-Notification message will provide a receipt number for each immigration form but will not include the applicant's name because the message cannot be sent over a secure network. One e-mail and/or text message will be sent per accepted immigration form; e-Notification will only be sent to the person requesting the benefit(s).

Does the E-Notification Grant Any Type of Status or Benefit?

No. The e-mail or text message does not grant any immigration status or benefit. You may not present a copy of the e-mail or text message as evidence that USCIS has granted you any immigration status or benefit. Receipt of the transmission cannot be used as supporting evidence for other benefits.

Will USCIS Cover My Costs to Receive E-Mails and Text Messages?

No. USCIS assumes no legal responsibility for your costs to receive e-mail and/or text messages. USCIS will not reimburse you for any costs related to e-Notification.

How Can I Request E-Mails or Text Messages?

If you submit your immigration form(s) to a USCIS lockbox facility and include your e-mail and/or mobile phone number in the appropriate box below, USCIS will use this information as permission to send an e-Notification to you. If you reside overseas and file Form G-1145, you will not be able to receive a text message notifying you that your application/petition has been accepted.

Paperwork Reduction Act

An agency may not conduct or sponsor an information collection and a person is not required to respond to a collection of information unless it displays a currently valid OMB control number. The public reporting burden for this collection of information is estimated at three minutes per response, including the time for reviewing instructions and completing and submitting the form. Send comments regarding this burden estimate or any other aspect of this collection of information, including suggestions for reducing this burden, to: U.S. Citizenship and Immigration Services, Regulatory Products Division, 111 Massachusetts Avenue, N.W., 3rd Floor, Suite 3008, Washington, DC 20529-2210. OMB No. 1615-0109. This form expires May, 31, 2012. **Do not mail your application to this address.**

Complete this form and clip it on top of the first page of your immigration form(s).

Applicant/Petitioner Full Last Name	Applicant/Petitioner Full First Name	Applicant/Petitioner Full Middle Name
Michela	Grun	Branimir

E-Mail Address	Mobile Phone Number (Text Message)
gmichela@email.com	

Form G-1145 (Rev. 05/25/11) Y

1. Your Filing Receipts

Once USCIS has received and accepted your adjustment of status packet for processing, they will put you on the waiting list for an interview. Regardless of whether or not USCIS has sent you an E-Notification about your application, it will send you paper receipt notices—one for your I-485, and one each for your I-130, I-765, and I-131, if you filed those applications at the same time. (See the sample receipt below.) The receipt is a very important document. Before you risk letting the dog eat it, make several photocopies and store them in secure places.

Among other things, the receipt will contain your A-number, which you'll need if you have to correspond with USCIS about your case. (Remember, USCIS is a big bureaucracy—your number will now become more important than your name.)

Soon after getting your receipt(s) you should receive an Application Support Center (ASC) Appointment Notice. The notice schedules you for an appointment to have your fingerprints, photo, and signature taken. The photo and signature are used to create your work permit and your Advance Parole travel document, if you requested those. Your fingerprints are taken for processing your application for adjustment of status.

When this book went to print, USCIS was taking approximately three months to issue the work permit and the Advance Parole document. The work permit is good for one year. Once your case is approved and you become a permanent resident, you no longer need a work permit. Your right to work is evidenced by your permanent resident card. In case your application is delayed for some reason, however, you can renew the work permit for one-year periods for as long as you are waiting for a decision on your adjustment of status application.

D. Moving or Traveling While Waiting for Your Interview

After you've submitted your adjustment of status packet you will wait for a few months before your interview is scheduled. Of course, your life continues on and you may want to move your residence or make travel plans. Read the material below before you do.

1. If You Change Addresses

You do not have to live in one place while waiting for your green card. However, your application will go most smoothly if you and your spouse settle yourselves at a stable address and stay there. This will help ensure that you receive notices of important USCIS appointments (first for fingerprints, then for the interview). If you do move, then within ten days of moving, you (and every immigrating member of your family) must advise a central USCIS office. The law requires this of all non-U.S. citizens over 14 years old and remaining in the U.S. for more than 30 days—failure to do so is a misdemeanor and can be punished with a jail term of up to 30 days, a fine of up to $200, or your removal from the United States. (See I.N.A. § 265; 8 U.S.C. § 1305.) The procedure for advising USCIS of your move is to use Form AR-11. To file the AR-11 online, go to www.uscis.gov and, from the right-hand column, click "Change Your Address Online." Follow the instructions. When finished, click "Signature" to e-file the form. Print a copy for your records. It will show the date and time the form was filed, and will contain a USCIS confirmation number. There is no fee for this form. One advantage to e-filing your AR-11 is that you will be asked whether you have applications pending, so that the office that will interview you will automatically be informed of your address change (a big improvement over the old system, in which you had to separately advise each office handling your application).

If you prefer to file your AR-11 by regular mail, print out the form from the USCIS website and mail it to the address shown on the form. It's best to file by certified mail and retain copies of the filed forms and proof of mailing. Realize, however, that if you mail your AR-11, you will still have to send an additional letter to the USCIS interviewing

Sample Adjustment of Status Application Receipt Notice

Department of Homeland Security
U.S. Citizenship and Immigration Services

I-797C, Notice of Action

THE UNITED STATES OF AMERICA

Receipt Number: MSC-12-006-000	Case Type: I-485 - Application to Register Permanent Residence or Adjust Status	
Received Date: October 05, 2012	Priority Date:	Applicant: A087
Notice Date: October 12, 2012	Page 1 OF 1	ASC Code: 3

ANDA MICHELSKI 68 WATERTOWN BLVD. APT. 12 ERIE, PA 19380	Notice Type: Receipt Notice Amount Received: $1,070.00

The above application has been received. **Please notify us immediately if any of the above information is incorrect.** If you find it necessary to contact this office in writing, you must include a copy of this receipt notice with your inquiry.

BIOMETRICS-

The next step is to have your biometrics taken, if required, at a US Citizenship and Immigration Services (USCIS) Application Support Center (ASC).

PLEASE NOTE-

USCIS WILL SCHEDULE YOUR BIOMETRICS APPOINTMENT. You will be receiving an appointment notice with a specific time, date and place where you will have your fingerprints and/or photos taken.

WHAT TO BRING TO Your appointment -
Please bring this letter and your photo identification to your appointment. Acceptable kinds of photo identification are:
- a passport or national photo identification issued by your country,
- a driver's license,
- a military photo identification, or
- a state-issued photo identification card.

If you do not bring this letter and photo identification, we cannot process you.
Please bring a copy of all receipt notices received from USCIS in relation to your current application for benefits.

CASE STATUS -
Information about your local office processing times may be obtained by calling the NCSC at 1-800-375-5283.

If you have Internet access, you can visit the United States Citizenship and Immigration Services website at www.USCIS.gov where you can find valuable information about forms, filing instructions, and immigration services and benefits.

U. S. Citizenship and Immigration Services
P.O. Box 648005
Lee's Summit, MO 64064
National Customer Service Center: 1-800-375-5283

5318005   0531800507

Form I-797C (Rev. 01/31/05) N

office to notify it of your address change. If you move to another city, your entire file may have to be sent to a different USCIS office. This always results in long delays. If you know before you file your adjustment of status application that you'll be moving to a different city, it's wise to wait until after your move to file your application.

How Long Will You Wait Until Your Interview?

The easiest way to find out how long you will likely have to wait for your interview is to go to the USCIS home page at www.uscis.gov. Click the link on the left side of the page entitled "Processing Times." On the next page scroll to the bottom of the page and, from the drop-down menu labeled "Field Office," choose the name of the district office where your file is pending. The resulting page will contain a list of different types of applications being processed at that office. The one you're interested in is an I-485.

The result you'll see can be a little confusing: It shows the date upon which the oldest application that USCIS has finally gotten around to dealing with was filed. If you filed yours earlier than that, there may be a problem, and you should visit or contact your local district office. If you filed yours later than that, you'll know you've still got some time to wait—but probably not much time if the two dates (that of your filing and the filings of people whose applications are now being decided upon) are coming close together.

---

2. Traveling While Waiting for Your Interview

While waiting for your adjustment of status interview, you may want or need to visit your home country, to visit family or continue arranging your move to the United States, for example. You can travel, but must use great care. If you simply get up and go without getting official permission, the law says you will have given up (or abandoned,

in USCIS terminology) your adjustment of status application. You will need to start all over.

There are a few narrow exceptions. If you arrived in the United States on a K-3 visa (a so-called "fiancé visa" designed especially for already married couples), you can use these to reenter the United States as many times as you like until a decision has been made on your green card application.

Similarly, if you entered the U.S. on an H-1B or L-1 visa (which are both types of employment-based visas), you can use your visa to reenter the U.S. as long as it is still valid and you are returning in order to resume the same employment.

To protect yourself (if you don't have a K-3 visa), ask USCIS for advance permission to leave (called "Advance Parole"). You can either file the Advance Parole application together with your adjustment of status application, or you can file it separately, along with proof that your adjustment of status application has already been filed. Once you've received Advance Parole, your adjustment of status application will be preserved, including its place in line. Your trip shouldn't delay the processing of your application. In fact, you may be granted a multiple entry Advance Parole document, meaning you can take many trips within a certain time period.

a. Qualifying for Advance Parole

Advance Parole used to be granted only for emergencies. Fortunately, USCIS has become far more lenient, recognizing the hardship caused by its own processing delays. Family visits or even a vacation with your spouse are usually considered an acceptable reason to leave the United States.

The form you'll complete will ask you to attach a page explaining how you qualify for Advance Parole and why your application deserves to be approved. This explanation doesn't need to be very long. You can simply write your name and A-number at the top of a page and then say something like this: "*I qualify for Advance Parole because I am the spouse of a U.S. citizen awaiting my adjustment of status interview. I would like to travel to my native country to visit my sister, whom I haven't seen in years and who has just had a baby."*

However, if you are traveling because of an emergency, it may help or speed up your application to explain and substantiate the crisis. For example, if it's a family medical emergency, provide a letter from your family member's doctor explaining your family member's condition and the need for your visit. (If the letter is in another language, be sure to have it translated; see Chapter 4, Section C, on how to translate documents for USCIS.)

b. Be Cautious About Leaving

The Advance Parole document is your ticket back into the United States, but it is not a guaranteed ticket. Its function is to keep your adjustment of status application alive while you're gone—but it won't necessarily protect you from being found inadmissible for any of the reasons on the list in Chapter 2, Section A—though it will, at least, protect you from the time bars, according to B.I.A. Interim Decision #3748. So if you have any doubts about your admissibility to the United States, don't leave at all.

Don't be alarmed, however, if upon returning to the United States, you are pulled into a separate line. This is called "secondary inspection," and it is the normal procedure for anyone returning with an Advance Parole document.

> **CAUTION**
> **Applicants who have spent time unlawfully in the United States should definitely not leave.** If you've spent more than 180 continuous days unlawfully in the United States, don't even think of leaving. If you do leave, you will be barred from returning (discussed in Chapter 2, Section A2, "Dealing With Unlawful Time in the United States"). Even getting permission in the form of an Advance Parole document won't overcome the problems discussed in that section. If your unlawful time in the United States was less than 180 days, it's still unwise to leave—the border control officer may not be able to count as well as you.

c. Using the Checklist for Applying for Advance Parole

The checklist below details what you'll need to apply for Advance Parole. Mark off the relevant items as you complete or obtain them to make sure that you haven't forgotten anything. USCIS prefers that you send in your application more than six weeks before you plan to travel.

Checklist for Applying for Advance Parole

- ☐ Form I-131
- ☐ A separate sheet of paper, in accordance with Part 7 of the application form, explaining how you qualify for Advance Parole and why your application deserves to be approved (no need to spend too much time on this—most requests are approved without question)
- ☐ If you are traveling because of an emergency, evidence to prove it
- ☐ Copy of the receipt notice you got when you filed your adjustment of status packet (if you are filing your I-131 after already having filed your I-485)
- ☐ Copy of a photo ID, such as a driver's license
- ☐ Two color photos of you, passport style
- ☐ Fee: there is no fee as long as your I-485 is pending

The form you'll use for Advance Parole is Form I-131, Application for Travel Document. This form is largely self-explanatory. However, it is also used by applicants applying for other immigration benefits, so there are some portions that don't apply to you. The only parts that you need to fill in are Parts 1, 2 (put an "X" in **box d**), 3, 4, 7, and 8.

When you're done, make a complete copy of your paperwork (for your records). If you are filing it at the same time as the I-485, just send the original with the I-485 to the lockbox that accepts filing of your I-485. If you are filing it after having

Sample Form I-131, Application for Travel Document—Page 1

Department of Homeland Security	OMB No. 1615-0013; Expires 03/31/2012
U. S. Citizenship and Immigration Services	**I-131, Application for Travel Document**

DO NOT WRITE IN THIS BLOCK		**FOR USCIS USE ONLY** (except G-28 block below)

Document Issued
- ☐ Reentry Permit
- ☐ Refugee Travel Document
- ☐ Single Advance Parole
- ☐ Multiple Advance Parole
  Valid to:

Action Block

Receipt

If Reentry Permit or Refugee Travel Document, mail to:
- ☐ Address in Part 1
- ☐ U.S. Embassy/consulate at:
- ☐ Overseas DHS office at:

☐ Document Hand Delivered
On _____ By _____

To be completed by Attorney/Representative, if any.
Attorney State License # _____
☐ Check box if G-28 is attached.

Part 1. **Information About You** *(Type or print in black ink)*

1. A Number	2. Date of Birth *(mm/dd/yyyy)*	3. Class of Admission	4. Gender
12345677	06/28/1984	H-1B	☐ Male ☒ Female

5. Name *(Family name in capital letters)*	*(First)*	*(Middle)*
MICHELSKI	Anda	Marina

6. Address *(Number and Street)*		Apt. Number
68 Watertown Boulevard		12

City	State or Province	Zip/Postal Code	Country
Erie	PA	19380	U.S.

7. Country of Birth	8. Country of Citizenship	9. Social Security # *(if any)*
Bulgaria	Bulgaria	none

Part 2. **Application Type** *(Check one)*

a. ☐ I am a permanent resident or conditional resident of the United States, and I am applying for a reentry permit.

b. ☐ I now hold U.S. refugee or asylee status, and I am applying for a Refugee Travel Document.

c. ☐ I am a permanent resident as a direct result of refugee or asylee status, and I am applying for a Refugee Travel Document.

d. ☒ I am applying for an advance parole document to allow me to return to the United States after temporary foreign travel.

e. ☐ I am outside the United States, and I am applying for an Advance Parole Document.

f. ☐ I am applying for an Advance Parole Document for a person who is outside the United States. *If you checked box "f," provide the following information about that person:*

1. Name *(Family name in capital letters)*	*(First)*	*(Middle)*

2. Date of Birth *(mm/dd/yyyy)*	3. Country of Birth	4. Country of Citizenship

5. Address *(Number and Street)*	Apt. #	Daytime Telephone # *(area/country code)*

City	State or Province	Zip/Postal Code	Country

Form I-131 (11/05/11) Y

Sample Form I-131, Application for Travel Document—Page 2

Part 3. Processing Information

1. Date of Intended Departure *(mm/dd/yyyy)*	2. Expected Length of Trip
7/3/13	3 weeks

3. Are you, or any person included in this application, now in exclusion, deportation, removal, or rescission proceedings? [X] Yes [ ] No *(Name of DHS office)*:

If you are applying for an Advance Parole Document, skip to Part 7.

4. Have you ever before been issued a reentry permit or Refugee Travel Document?
   [ ] No [ ] Yes *(If "Yes," give the following information for the last document issued to you)*:

Date Issued *(mm/dd/yyyy)*:   Disposition *(attached, lost, etc.)*:

5. Where do you want this travel document sent? *(Check one)*

a. [X] To the U.S. address shown in **Part 1** on the first page of this form.

b. [ ] To a U.S. Embassy or consulate at: City: Country:

c. [ ] To a DHS office overseas at: City: Country:

d. If you checked "b" or "c," where should the notice to pick up the travel document be sent?

[ ] To the address shown in **Part 2** on the first page of this form.

[ ] To the address shown below:

Address *(Number and Street)*	Apt. #	Daytime Telephone # *(area/country code)*

City	State or Province	Zip/Postal Code	Country

Part 4. Information About Your Proposed Travel

Purpose of trip. *(If you need more room, continue on a separate sheet of paper.)*	List the countries you intend to visit.
Attend cousin's wedding; take a vacation	Germany, New Zealand

Part 5. Complete Only If Applying for a Reentry Permit

Since becoming a permanent resident of the United States (or during the past five years, whichever is less) how much total time have you spent outside the United States?	[ ] less than six months [ ] two to three years [ ] six months to one year [ ] three to four years [ ] one to two years [ ] more than four years

Since you became a permanent resident of the United States, have you ever filed a Federal income tax return as a nonresident or failed to file a Federal income tax return because you considered yourself to be a nonresident? *(If "Yes," give details on a separate sheet of paper.)*	[ ] Yes [ ] No

Part 6. Complete Only If Applying for a Refugee Travel Document

1. Country from which you are a refugee or asylee:

If you answer "Yes" to any of the following questions, you must explain on a separate sheet of paper.

2. Do you plan to travel to the country named above?	[ ] Yes [ ] No

3. Since you were accorded refugee/asylee status, have you ever:
   a. Returned to the country named above? [ ] Yes [ ] No
   b. Applied for and/or obtained a national passport, passport renewal, or entry permit of that country? [ ] Yes [ ] No
   c. Applied for and/or received any benefit from such country (for example, health insurance benefits). [ ] Yes [ ] No

4. Since you were accorded refugee/asylee status, have you, by any legal procedure or voluntary act:
   a. Reacquired the nationality of the country named above? [ ] Yes [ ] No
   b. Acquired a new nationality? [ ] Yes [ ] No
   c. Been granted refugee or asylee status in any other country? [ ] Yes [ ] No

Form I-131 (11/05/11) Y Page 2

Sample Form I-131, Application for Travel Document—Page 3

Part 7. Complete Only If Applying for Advance Parole

On a separate sheet of paper, explain how you qualify for an Advance Parole Document, and what circumstances warrant issuance of advance parole. Include copies of any documents you wish considered. *(See instructions.)*

1. How many trips do you intend to use this document? ☐ One Trip ☒ More than one trip

2. If the person intended to receive an Advance Parole Document is outside the United States, provide the location (city and country) of the U.S. Embassy or consulate or the DHS overseas office that you want us to notify.

City

Country

3. If the travel document will be delivered to an overseas office, where should the notice to pick up the document be sent?:

☐ To the address shown in **Part 2** on the first page of this form.

☐ To the address shown below:

Address *(Number and Street)*

Apt. #

Daytime Telephone # *(area/country code)*

City

State or Province

Zip/Postal Code

Country

Part 8. Signature

Read the information on penalties in the instructions before completing this section. If you are filing for a reentry permit or Refugee Travel Document, you must be in the United States to file this application.

I certify, under penalty of perjury under the laws of the United States of America, that this application and the evidence submitted with it are all true and correct. I authorize the release of any information from my records that U.S. Citizenship and Immigration Services needs to determine eligibility for the benefit I am seeking.

Signature	Date *(mm/dd/yyyy)*	Daytime Telephone Number *(with area code)*
Anda Michelski	05/19/13	314-276-9440

Note: If you do not completely fill out this form or fail to submit required documents listed in the instructions, you may not be found eligible for the requested document and this application may be denied.

Part 9. Signature of Person Preparing Form, If Other Than the Applicant *(Sign below)*

I declare that I prepared this application at the request of the applicant, and it is based on all information of which I have knowledge.

Signature

Print or Type Your Name

Firm Name and Address

Daytime Telephone Number *(with area code)*

Fax Number *(if any)*

Date *(mm/dd/yyyy)*

filed your I-485, then where you send the original depends on the first three letters of the receipt number on your I-485 receipt notice. Check the Form I-131 instructions for the correct addresses.

If you are asking that your application be handled more speedily because of an emergency, it's best to use the courier address rather than the P.O. Box address.

Alternatively, you can submit the application form online through the USCIS website by going to the page for Form I-131 and clicking "Electronic Filing." If you choose this online, "E-Filing" option, however, you will still have to submit the remainder of your documents by mail, to an address that you'll get in your confirmation receipt.

WEB RESOURCE
Form I-131 is available on the USCIS website at www.uscis.gov.

E. Your Fingerprint Appointment

About one month after submitting your adjustment of status packet to USCIS, you'll get an appointment for fingerprinting (called "biometrics"). In most cases, USCIS will insist that you be fingerprinted at a USCIS-authorized site. In some nonurban areas of the United States, USCIS also offers mobile fingerprinting vans. If you can't make it at the scheduled time, you can ask to be rescheduled.

Your fingerprints will be reviewed by the U.S. Federal Bureau of Investigation (FBI), which will check them against records held by the police as well as by USCIS (which often takes the fingerprints of people caught crossing the border illegally). The FBI will send a report to USCIS to confirm your identity and to show whether you have committed any crimes or immigration violations that might make you inadmissible.

SEE AN EXPERT
If you think you might have a criminal record but aren't sure, consult a lawyer. You won't discover until you get to your adjustment of status interview what the FBI report says about you. The lawyer can help you request a separate fingerprint report from the FBI and deal with whatever it shows, to help you get your green card.

F. Advance Preparation for Your Adjustment of Status Interview

Although you will wait several months for your adjustment of status interview, when the appointment letter finally comes it will probably give you a date only two weeks away—or less. For this reason, it is important to prepare yourself and your documents well in advance.

TIP
Remember to read Chapter 13 for your final interview preparation. It will give you a complete picture of what will happen at the interview and describes how to make it a success.

1. Positioning Yourself for a Good Interview

Your adjustment of status interview is most likely to go smoothly if you and your spouse live together. Also, the two of you should combine as many practical aspects of your life as possible, including bank accounts, insurance policies, electric, plumbing, and other utility accounts, club memberships, and the ownership of cars, houses, and other major property. You can refer to all of these to prove that your marriage is real.

As you combine these parts of your life, pay attention to the paperwork that comes with them. Save those important contracts, receipts, and other forms of documentation. You'll want to take copies to your interview.

TIP

If you've had to live apart, think about how you'll prove that you are still a true couple. For example, if one of you has a job and the other is attending college ten hours away, living together won't be possible. While USCIS understands that such situations occur and won't automatically deny your green card on this basis, they will require additional proof that your marriage is real. You could show USCIS evidence that you spent holidays and vacations together and spent many hours conversing on the phone.

2. Assembling Documents for Your Interview

Preparation is the key to a smooth interview. You will want to arrive with a number of documents and other items in hand, as explained in the following subsections. Keep track of these items in the months leading to the interview and reread this section a few days before your interview. You'll also find a checklist below, to help you make sure you've assembled the right material.

a. Photo Identification and Passport

You and your spouse will each need to present photo identification. Your passport is best. If you don't have a passport, use a separate form of photo identification for the interview. The U.S. citizen or permanent resident spouse usually presents a driver's license.

b. Original Documents and All INS or USCIS Permits

Assemble the originals of the documents you used to enter the United States, and any other documents you've received from U.S. consulates or INS or USCIS offices (for example, an Advance Parole travel permit). Also, if you've mailed copies of documents to USCIS, such as your marriage and birth certificates, bring the originals.

Your spouse will need to bring the original proof of his or her U.S. citizenship status (a birth certificate, naturalization certificate, or passport) or permanent resident status (a green card or stamp in his or her passport).

The officer may not ask for all of these, but you'll be glad you brought them if he or she does ask.

c. Updates to Materials in the Application

Has anything important in your life changed since filing the adjustment of status paperwork? If, for example, you or your spouse have a new or different job, bring a letter from the new employer and copies of recent pay stubs. (Of course, your spouse's income still needs to be high enough to deal with the Affidavit of Support requirements. If it has gone down, you, the immigrant, may be able to help by bringing proof that you are now working in the United States.) If you and your spouse have reached the two-year anniversary of your marriage since filing the application, be ready to remind the officer of this, so you'll be approved for permanent, not conditional, residency. If a tax year has passed, bring a copy of your latest tax returns (or better yet, an IRS transcript of these returns).

And even if nothing has changed, prove that fact with a recent pay stub showing that the financial sponsor is still bringing in the income.

d. Proof That Your Marriage Is Real

The interview is often the first opportunity that the USCIS officer has to decide whether your marriage is "for real." The documents that you show are important factors in the decision. They should show that you and your spouse's lives are intertwined and that you trust each other with your financial and personal matters.

Below is a list of documents most immigrants present. However, this list isn't engraved in stone. Use your imagination and be ready to do some organized "show-and-tell." No need to flood the officer with paper—copies of six items from this list would be a reasonable amount.

- rental agreements, leases, or mortgages showing that you live together and/or have leased or bought property in both spouses' names

- your mutual child's birth certificate or a doctor's report saying that one of you is pregnant
- utility bills in both your names
- joint bank statements
- joint credit card statements
- evidence that one spouse has made the other a beneficiary on his/her life or health insurance or retirement account
- auto registrations showing joint ownership and/or addresses
- joint club memberships
- receipts from gifts that you purchased for one another (these should be typical gift purchases, such as jewelry, flowers, or candy)
- letters from friends and family to each or both of you mailed to your joint address
- photos of you and your spouse taken before and during your marriage, including photos from your wedding. (USCIS knows wedding pictures can be faked, but many officers enjoy seeing them anyway.) The photos should, if possible, include parents and other relatives from both families. Write the date taken and a brief description of what the photo shows on the back (or underneath, if you're photocopying them). Don't bother with videos of the wedding or other events—there won't be time or a space to view them.

3. Using the Checklist for Adjustment of Status Interview

The checklist below lists all of the documents and other items that you are normally required to bring to your adjustment of status interview. By checking off each item as you collect it, you'll be sure that nothing gets left at home on your interview day.

CHECKLIST

A copy of this checklist is available in Appendix C at the back of this book.

Checklist for Adjustment of Status Interview

☐ Photo identification/passport
☐ Original documents for review/comparison with copies
☐ Updates to material in the application
☐ Proof that your marriage is bona fide

TIP

Photocopy every document you intend to bring. If there are new items you want to show the officer, such as bank statements or utility bills, the officer probably won't consider them unless you're willing to leave the document behind. You won't want to turn over your original documents to a USCIS file. Bring a copy along with the original.

G. Green Cards for Your Children

This section contains an overview of the procedures for submitting adjustment of status applications for your children, but complete details (especially line-by-line instructions on filling out the forms for your children) are outside the scope of this book. But having filled out all the paperwork required for your own green card, you'll be well-positioned to complete these forms for your children. Of course, you might be more comfortable using a lawyer.

1. The Form I-130

If your spouse is a lawful permanent resident, then you have probably already dealt with Form I-130, and can skip to Section 2.

However, if your spouse is a U.S. citizen you will accordingly need to fill out a separate visa petition (Form I-130) for each child. The exception is if you entered on a K-1 fiancé visa, and your children are in K-2 status (and still unmarried and under age 21). Your child remains your derivative, and can file his or her adjustment of status application with no need for a Form I-130 visa petition. However, USCIS must approve the child's adjustment of status application before the child turns 21, or the child will "age out" (lose eligibility under this visa category). The Child Status Protection Act (CSPA) will not help your child in this situation, since CSPA does not apply to K-2 visas. You'll need to request that USCIS expedite (speed up) your case to avoid the age-out problem. Include a written request within your cover letter on top of your adjustment of status packet, and write in red letters "Request for expedite—age-out problem" on top of the letter.

No exception is made for children in K-4 status (if you were a K-3)—they need separate Forms I-130 filed for each of them, or a receipt notice proving that one has already been filed, to accompany their adjustment of status applications. (Remember that in Chapter 7, we recommended that your spouse submit the children's Forms I-130 at the same time as your I-130.)

Of course, before your spouse can file an I-130 on your children's behalf, they must legally qualify as your spouse's children—which is easy if they're your spouse's biological or adopted children, but not so easy if you're hoping to get them in as stepchildren. Regardless of the fact that your children qualify for a K-4 visa until they're 21, to qualify as stepchildren, they must have been under 18 when your marriage took place. If they can't even qualify as stepchildren, they'll probably have to leave the United States when their K-4 status expires (their I-94 runs out, they turn 21, or you become a permanent resident, whichever happens first) and wait for you to become a permanent resident and petition them in category 2A of the family preference system (which will involve a wait of many years).

Your child's application will be submitted to the same place as yours.

For the documents accompanying Form I-130, you'll be happy to hear that your children do not need to fill out Form G-325A, nor do they need to include their photos. Include copies of your and your spouse's marriage certificate, as well as copies of the children's birth certificates, to show the family relationships.

2. The Remainder of Your Children's Adjustment of Status Packet

Each unmarried child under 21 who wishes to get a green card along with you will have to submit a separate adjustment of status packet. (This includes some children who are actually over 21, but who remain legally under that age because of the Child Status Protection Act.) This packet will be nearly identical to yours.

Children who are derivatives on your visa petition (that is, didn't have a separate I-130 filed for them) won't need a separately signed and notarized Affidavit of Support (Form I-864). They can submit a photocopy of yours. Of course, you'll want to make sure that the children's names are listed in your Form I-864 and that your spouse or other sponsor has shown enough income and assets to cover all the children. And children who had their own I-130s need a separate I-864, too.

Children under 14 need not be fingerprinted. Pay close attention to the fees; while a separate set of fees needs to be paid for each immigrant, the rates are sometimes reduced for children.

As long as you submit your adjustment of status packet together with those of your children—that is, in the same envelope—you can expect to be interviewed at the same time. The children probably won't have to answer more than one or two questions at the interview.

3. If You Have Children Already Over 21 or Married

In some situations, your children may be unable to adjust status right away. For example, if your spouse is a permanent resident (not a citizen) and your child turns 21 before his or her Priority Date becomes current, then your child drops into a different visa category (2B) and must return to the waiting list before becoming eligible to adjust status.

Or, if your child entered on a K-2 visa and you were unable to both submit an adjustment of status application and get it approved before the child's 21st birthday, the child loses his or her eligibility to carry on with the process.

Even more complex, if your child entered on a K-4 visa and your U.S. citizen spouse didn't or couldn't file a Form I-130 on the child's behalf before the child turned 21 (thereby gaining the protection of the Child Status Protection Act) the child will lose his or her eligibility to immigrate on the same schedule as you. (If a K-4 child's I-130 is filed after the child's 21st birthday, the child will be placed in the family first preference category, which has a wait, but moves fairly quickly.)

Similarly, if your child has gotten married, he or she drops to a lower visa category if your spouse is a U.S. citizen, and becomes completely ineligible for a green card if your spouse is a permanent resident.

Do not even try to submit an adjustment of status packet for your children at the same time as yours under any of these circumstances. The children could be placed in deportation proceedings if they are not in the United States legally.

But don't give up on your child's immigration prospects. Hopefully your spouse has already submitted separate Forms I-130 to a USCIS Service Center for any children eligible to immigrate (see discussion of eligibility in Chapter 2), thereby placing them on a waiting list for a future green card.

Unfortunately, if your spouse is a U.S. citizen and is not the child's biological parent, then he or she can file Form I-130 only if he or she qualifies as a "stepparent"—and that will work only if your marriage occurred before the child's 18th birthday. But you do have the option of filing a visa petition for the child yourself, as soon as you are approved for permanent residence, placing the child in category 2A (if the child is under 21) or 2B (if the child is over 21) of the family preference system (meaning an approximate four- to ten-year wait before they are eligible for visas). Even when you're a permanent resident, however, you can't file visa petitions for your children who are already married—you'll need to wait until you're a U.S. citizen to do that.

CAUTION
Children on a K-2 or K-4 visa who can't or don't want to adjust status must leave the U.S. when their permitted stay expires. Regardless of the expiration date on the visa itself, their status runs out either when the date on their Form I-94 (a little white card in their passport) passes, they turn 21, or you become a permanent resident (which means the child is no longer your derivative). Failure to leave on time could result in the child spending illegal time in the United States, and thereby becoming subject to the time bars discussed in Chapter 2.

SEE AN EXPERT
A lawyer can help you evaluate the rights of your children over 21 to immigrate, and prepare the applications if necessary. Chapter 17 tells you how to find a good lawyer.

CAUTION
Your approval for U.S. residency is cause for celebration, but not necessarily the end of your dealings with USCIS. If you were given conditional, not permanent residency, you will need to apply for permanent residency in approximately 21 months (see Chapter 16 for instructions). Also read Chapter 16 on how to protect and enjoy your U.S. residency.

Dealing With Bureaucrats, Delays, and Denials

If you think your visa petition or green card application is taking too long, welcome to the crowd. You are one of thousands of people applying for immigration benefits, and all of you are simultaneously dealing with governmental agencies that are often slow and inefficient. And if you think your application has been unfairly denied, you're not alone in this, either.

Fortunately, there are steps you can take—before, during, and after the application process—that will minimize the chances for delay or denial. This chapter discusses

- how to anticipate and deal with problems during any part of the immigration process (Section A), and
- how to respond to negative decisions (Sections B and C).

A. Anticipating and Dealing With Delays

In view of the number of people applying for visas and green cards, it's almost guaranteed that your application will spend some time in processing limbo. As an example, in early 2002 the INS (now called USCIS) reported that around 122,000 people had been waiting three or more years for decisions on I-130 Visa Petitions. Although you can't prevent delays, you can anticipate them and be ready to deal with them when the time comes.

CAUTION

Don't even think of bribing a U.S. government official. Although there are countries where the only way to get anything from a government official is to offer cash or other gifts, the United States is not one of them. Personnel at USCIS and the consulates may sometimes be difficult, but it's generally not because they're expecting money. In fact, most of them are proud of the fact that the United States operates strictly according to the rule of law. Offering a bribe will most likely hurt your chances of getting a green card or visa.

Behind the Scenes

Reporters for *The Oregonian* newspaper visited the immigration service center in Burlington, Vermont, and found "crates of files teeter[ing] along the walkways between overstuffed cubicles. Even with new computers, the center relies on time-tested filing techniques. 'I don't know what we'd do without hand trucks and milk crates,' says Paul E. Novak, Jr., director of the Vermont Service Center."

The reporters also described a 1998 incident in which "officials stored 30,000 files in a storage room where workers later found asbestos. A crew had to seal off the room—but the INS didn't bother to notify the applicants." (See "INS Bureaucracy, Blundering Create 'Agency from Hell'," by Brent Walth and Kim Christensen, *The Oregonian*, Monday, December 11, 2000.)

Although the name has changed, USCIS has inherited most all of the INS's antiquated facilities and procedures.

---

1. Plan Ahead for Lost or Wayward Papers

Knowing the likelihood of problems in advance, you can minimize them by keeping a copy of everything you send and (in the United States) sending everything by certified mail with a return receipt. If you're mailing from your own country, use the safest method available, preferably with some form of tracking. No matter where you are, be aware that many USCIS addresses are Post Office boxes, where services like FedEx will not always deliver. (These delivery companies need an actual person at the destination to sign for the article.) For P.O. box addresses, you'll need to use regular mail. However, check the USCIS website—sometimes they offer alternate addresses for courier services.

By taking these steps, you'll have the evidence you need in case you must show immigration authorities that it was their fault that a file was delayed or mislaid.

2. When Should You Start Inquiring About Delays?

When it comes to delays, how long is too long? That is the million-dollar question. Processing times for USCIS and consular applications vary depending on the number of people applying.

a. How Long Should You Wait for Your Initial Receipt?

If you are waiting for an initial receipt, such as one for an I-129F or I-130 visa petition that your fiancé or spouse filed with USCIS, six weeks is the longest you should wait. After that, you should probably make an inquiry. First, check with you bank to see if the check you submitted with the application was cashed. If it was, try to read the receipt number on the back of the check. Then call USCIS Customer Service at 800-375-5283. Even without a receipt number (which USCIS usually likes to use to track a case), they may be able to track your application using your other identifying information, such as your A-number, date of birth, and address.

b. How Long Should You Wait for a Decision on Your Case From USCIS?

Before you submit your applications to USCIS, you will probably want to know how long you can expect to wait for a decision. You can usually get this information from the USCIS website.

Go to www.uscis.gov and, in the bar on the left-hand side of the page, click "Processing Times." What you choose on the next page depends on which application you want information about. If you want to know how long you will wait for an interview on your adjustment of status application, check the processing times at the office where you will be interviewed. Choose your local field office from the drop-down menu at the bottom of that page, and click "Field Office Processing Dates." In the table that appears, check the I-485 processing time frame.

If, however, you want information about an I-130 that was filed alone, then instead of clicking "Field Office Processing Dates," select the Service Center with jurisdiction over your petition from the drop-down menu marked "Service Center" at the bottom of the page, then click the "Service Center Processing Dates" button. Be sure to look at the column for I-130s filed by people in your category. There are several categories of I-130s and some are processed more quickly than others.

These charts tell you the receipt dates of the applications that USCIS is currently working on. If your application was filed later than the applications that are currently being worked on, USCIS considers your petition to be within its normal processing time, and will ignore any inquiries from you.

Keep in mind that processing times change. Although you may have checked the processing time several months earlier when you submitted your application, check it again before contacting USCIS. Once the USCIS office has gone beyond its normal processing time, it's time to contact them.

c. How Long Should You Wait to Be Scheduled for an Interview at the Consulate?

Some consulates post information about average wait times on their website. Go to the U.S. Department of State website at www.usembassy.gov, and select your consulate. If you don't find the processing times listed, you may need to call their public information number.

Many consulates now rely on the National Visa Center (NVC) to schedule appointments for them. If your case is at the NVC, you can email them at nvcinquiry@state.gov, or call 603-334-0700. The NVC does not provide general information about average wait times, but will respond to your specific questions about your case. Be ready to provide your NVC case number, which is on all correspondence from them.

3. Information Needed for an Inquiry

At some point, you will be sent a receipt notice with a processing number. You'll recognize it because it starts with a three-letter abbreviation. The main ones are WAC, LIN, EAC, TSC, and MSC. These refer to the Service Center that issued the receipt.

The receipt notice processing number is your single most important piece of information for tracking your application and making inquiries.

If you are processing your case at a consulate, once the National Visa Center gets your case, it assigns you a case number. The first three letters of that number refer to the consulate that will process your case. Once your case is at the NVC or the consulate, the case number is your single most important piece of information for tracking your application and making inquiries.

4. Emergency Attention

If there is some reason that your application really should be given immediate attention—that is, put ahead of all the other waiting applications—be sure to highlight this, most likely in a letter. It's better to attach this letter to your application than to send it later asking that your application be moved out of the normal processing category into expedited processing.

If you have to send such a letter later, be sure to include your application's receipt number. You can also make a note on the outside of your envelope, in large, bold letters, saying: "URGENT! PLEASE EXPEDITE!" That way, you'll alert the people in the mail room to the fact that you need your request to get to an adjudicating officer as quickly as possible. But limit your cries for help to true emergencies, such as:

- a family member is dying in your home country and you need permission to leave the country during your green card processing to visit them, or
- you have scheduled surgery on the same day as an important USCIS appointment.

If possible, include proof of any claimed emergency, such as a letter from a doctor.

5. How to Inquire About Delays

Once you've determined that USCIS or a consulate is taking longer than it should, the question is what you can do about it. Your best course of action depends on where your application is.

a. Delays at a USCIS Office

If any USCIS office has your application, and it has been there beyond the normal processing time, probably the most effective way to make an inquiry is to speak face-to-face with a USCIS Information Officer.

For most offices, you need to have an appointment to speak with someone, although sometimes they will talk to you even if you drop in. To make an INFOPASS appointment, go to www.uscis.gov and from the left-hand side click "INFOPASS Schedule a Free Appointment." Follow the instructions. You will need a current photo identification to get into the office. Of course, only people who have proof that they are in valid immigration status should do this.

It's possible that the INFOPASS information officer will be able to resolve your case problem while you wait. More likely, however, the officer will take information from you and begin the inquiry process, then let you know when to expect a response.

Another way to make an inquiry, which does not involve traveling to a USCIS office, is to call the USCIS Customer Service number at 800-375-5283. Although the person you speak with will most likely not be able to tell you anything useful during that call, he or she will start an inquiry and tell you when to expect a response.

The least useful course of action is to write a letter to USCIS. You are unlikely to get a response, except perhaps a boilerplate letter suggesting that you either call the Customer Service number or make an INFOPASS appointment. The one exception is if you were already interviewed and were told that you should expect to receive a decision by mail. In this situation, if you do not want to make an inquiry through INFOPASS or use the Customer Service number, you can write directly to the office where you were interviewed and ask for a decision on your case.

Sample I-129F Receipt Notice

Department of Homeland Security
U.S. Citizenship and Immigration Services

I-797C, Notice of Action

THE UNITED STATES OF AMERICA

RECEIPT NUMBER		CASE TYPE	
WAC-12-041-00000		I129F PETITION FOR FIANCE(E)	

RECEIVED DATE	PRIORITY DATE	PETITIONER
November 18, 2012		ANDERSON, CHRISTA

NOTICE DATE	PAGE	BENEFICIARY
December 1, 2012	1 of 1	CUEVAS, BERNARDO

ILONA BRAY
RE: BERNARDO CUEVAS
950 PARKER ST.
BERKELEY, CA 94710

Notice Type: Receipt Notice

Amount received: $340.00

Receipt notice - If any of the above information is incorrect, call customer service immediately.

Processing time - Processing times vary by kind of case.
- You can check our current processing time for this kind of case on our website at **uscis.gov**.
- On our website you can also sign up to get free e-mail updates as we complete key processing steps on this case.
- Most of the time your case is pending the processing status will not change because we will be working on others filed earlier.
- We will notify you by mail when we make a decision on this case, or if we need something from you. If you move while this case is pending, call customer service when you move.
- Processing times can change. If you don't get a decision or update from us within our current processing time, check our website or call for an update.

If you have questions, check our website or call customer service. Please save this notice, and have it with you if you contact us about this case.

Notice to all customers with a pending I-130 petition - USCIS is now processing Form I-130, Petition for Alien Relative, as a visa number becomes available. Filing and approval of an I-130 relative petition is only the first step in helping a relative immigrate to the United States. Eligible family members must wait until there is a visa number available before they can apply for an immigrant visa or adjustment of status to a lawful permanent resident. This process will allow USCIS to concentrate resources first on cases where visas are actually available. This process should not delay the ability of one's relative to apply for an immigrant visa or adjustment of status. Refer to **www.state.gov/travel** <http://www.state.gov/travel> to determine current visa availability dates. For more information, please visit our website at www.uscis.gov or contact us at 1-800-375-5283.

Always remember to call customer service if you move while your case is pending. If you have a pending I-130 relative petition, also call customer service if you should decide to withdraw your petition or if you become a U.S. citizen.

Please see the additional information on the back. You will be notified separately about any other cases you filed.
U.S. CITIZENSHIP & IMMIGRATION SERVICES
P.O. BOX 68005
LEE'S SUMMIT, MO 68005
Customer Service Telephone: (800) 375-5283

Form I-797C (Rev. 08/31/04) N

Although you may feel frustrated by delays in your case, remember to be polite. The officer you are speaking with is not the one who caused your delay; in fact, this officer is the one you are relying on to help you. You may be justifiably outraged by USCIS's action or inaction, but never insult or threaten the officer with whom you are speaking. At best, such behavior is never helpful; at worst, it could be interpreted as a threat, which could lead to criminal prosecution as well as a quick denial.

b. Delays at a Consulate

If the NVC delays in sending your case to the consulate, you can email a case-specific inquiry to nvcinquiry@state.gov, or call 603-334-0700. Be ready with your NVC case number, which you'll find on all correspondence from the NVC.

If your case is delayed at the consulate after the interview, you will need to find out how that particular consulate prefers to receive inquiries. The possibilities are: visiting, calling, or writing a letter. Be sure to provide your NVC case number.

6. Incomplete or Lost Portions of Your Application

If USCIS or the NVC needs something to complete your application, such as further evidence of your bona fide marriage, or a missing financial document, they will usually mail you a request. If you receive a request for more documentation, try to gather whatever was asked for and get it in the mail as soon as possible. Don't forget to include the notification form as a cover sheet—but make a copy for yourself first. A sample of the kind of notice the NVC might send is shown below.

What should you do if you're asked for something that you know you've already sent? This is a surprisingly common occurrence—in fact, an investigative report by *The Oregonian* newspaper found that, "With 25 million case files in storage, the INS [as it was then called] misplaces tens of thousands of files each year … and leaves immigrants to resubmit applications and pay fees all over again." (From "INS Bureaucracy, Blundering Create 'The Agency From

Hell,'" by Brent Walth and Kim Christensen, *The Oregonian*, Monday, December 11, 2000.) If the requested item is something inexpensive or easy to come by, don't even try arguing with USCIS or the NVC—even if you have photocopies proving that you already sent the item. Just assume it's been lost and send another one.

Lost checks or money orders are a different matter. Don't send USCIS another check or money order until you've found out what happened to the first draft. If you sent a check and haven't received information about it with your monthly bank statement, ask your bank to tell you whether your check has been cashed. If so, get the check and send USCIS a copy of both sides, so that USCIS officials can see their own stamp and processing number.

If you sent a money order and kept the receipt with the tracer number, call the company that issued the money order to find out whether it's been cashed. Ask for a copy of the cashed money order or other evidence that you can use to prove to USCIS that they were the ones who cashed it. If you can't get a copy of the cashed money order, send USCIS a copy of your receipt and an explanation. Hopefully, they will stop bugging you for the money.

B. What to Do If an Application Is Denied

First, a word of reassurance: Neither USCIS nor the NVC or consulates like to deny visas to eligible applicants. Unless you are clearly ineligible, they will usually give you many chances to supplement your application and make it worthy of approval. Maybe this is the good side of a slow-moving bureaucracy—every decision takes time, even a negative one. (But don't use this as an excuse to be sloppy in putting your application together the first time.)

 **SEE AN EXPERT**

If your visa or green card has been denied, it's time to think about getting a lawyer. This advice is particularly important if the denial was due to something

Sample NVC Request for Missing Documents—Page 1

National Visa Center
32 Rochester Avenue
Portsmouth, NH 03801-2909

February 20, 2012

|||||||||||||||||||||||||||||||| CHECKLIST

Dear

We have reviewed the documents which you submitted in support of an application for an immigrant visa. Please review the information listed under each applicant's name and provide any documents which are indicated as missing or need additional information. You must submit the required information. Failure to provide the requested information will delay your immigrant visa interview.

Please read the enclosed information to determine where to send all required copies of missing documents. If you have any questions regarding this letter, please call the National Visa Center at (603) 334-0700 between the hours of 7:30am and midnight ET.

Please include a copy of this letter with your correspondence and write your case number clearly (exactly as it appears below) on the upper right-hand corner of **all** documents.

If a period of one year passes without contacting the NVC (by e-mail, telephone, or mail), all submitted fees and documents will expire. Upon expiration, the fees and documents would need to be resubmitted in order to continue the immigration process.

Case Number: ISL
Beneficiary's Name:
Preference Category: -
Priority Date:

Sample NVC Request for Missing Documents—Page 2

YOU **MUST RETURN THIS PAGE** WITH YOUR DOCUMENTATION.
FAILURE TO DO THIS MAY RESULT IN A **DELAY** IN PROCESSING YOUR DOCUMENTS. PLEASE ATTACH THIS PAGE TO THE **FRONT** OF THE DOCUMENTS FOR <u>**THIS CASE ONLY**</u> AND MAIL IN AN ENVELOPE CONTAINING INFORMATION FOR <u>**THIS CASE ONLY**</u>
(putting multiple case information in the same envelope may delay the processing of your cases)
TO:

NATIONAL VISA CENTER
ATTN. DR
32 ROCHESTER AVENUE
PORTSMOUTH, NH 03801-2909

<u>**(Checklist Letter Response)**</u>

[JEI 02/20/2008] [ISL   ]Page 2 of 9

Sample NVC Request for Missing Documents—Page 3

MISSING DOCUMENT LIST FOR:
∧∧∧

_____PASSPORT:_____
Please submit a copy of the biographic data page of this person's passport, including the expiration date of the passport. The passport must be **valid**.

_____OF-230-II:_____
Please submit a completed copy of the form DS-230 Part II, Application for Immigrant Visa and Alien Registration - Sworn Statement, for this applicant. To download a form with complete instructions, please visit http://Travel.state.gov/visa/immigrants/info/info_1335.html. If you would only like the form, you can download it by visiting http://www.state.gov/documents/organization/81807.pdf.

Your visa application cannot be processed until this form is complete. We appreciate your assistance in this matter. Please DO NOT sign the DS-230 Part II; the consular officer will ask you to sign it during the visa interview.

_____BIRTH CERTIFICATE:_____
Please submit this person's original birth certificate or a certified copy of the original, obtained from the issuing government authority. The original birth certificate or the certified copy of the original must contain the person's place and date of birth and names of both parents. If the birth certificate is a certified copy of the original, it must come from the issuing government authority and it must contain annotation by the issuing government authority indicating that it is an extract from the official records.

If a birth was never officially recorded, or if it is impossible to obtain a birth certificate because records have been destroyed or the appropriate government authority will not issue one, you should obtain a certified statement from the appropriate government authority stating the reason your birth record is not available. Please submit this with secondary evidence of birth. The secondary evidence must be an original, or a certified copy of the original. For example, a baptismal certificate that contains the date and place of birth and both parent's names providing the baptism took place shortly after birth; an adoption decree for an adopted child; or an affidavit from a close relative, preferably the applicant's mother, stating the date and place of birth, both parent's names, and the mother's maiden name. An affidavit must be executed before an official authorized to take oaths or affirmations.

Information regarding the procedure for obtaining birth certificates is usually available from the embassy or consulate of the country concerned.

All documents not in English must be accompanied by a certified translation. Your translation must include a statement signed by the translator that states the following:
        *Translation is accurate, and
        *Translator is competent to translate.

[JEI 02/20/2008] [ISL

more serious than a bureaucratic mistake or a lack of documentation on your part. You'll definitely need a lawyer for the complicated procedures mentioned below, including removal proceedings and motions to reopen or reconsider. See Chapter 17 on finding a lawyer.

1. Denial of Initial Fiancé or Immigrant Visa Petition

If USCIS denies your initial I-129F fiancé visa petition or I-130 visa petition, the best thing for your fiancé or spouse to do is to start over and file a new one. This is true even if a lawyer is helping you. There is an appeal process, but hardly anyone ever uses it. You'll probably spend less time starting over, and the fee is about the same. Besides, no government agency likes to admit it was wrong, so there is a tactical advantage to getting a fresh start.

2. Denial of Visa or Green Card

If USCIS or the consulate denies an application further along in the process, your response will depend on where you are—in the U.S. or overseas.

a. Denial of Green Card After Adjustment of Status Application in the U.S.

If you are applying for adjustment of status in the United States, there is technically no appeal after a denial. If, as is likely, you have no other legal right to be in the United States when the application is denied (such as a pending political asylum application), you may be placed in removal proceedings in Immigration Court. There, you will have the opportunity to renew your marriage-based green card application before an immigration judge. In rare circumstances, you might need to file a motion to have your case reopened or reconsidered; or you may need to file a separate suit in federal court.

CAUTION
Never ignore a notice to appear in Immigration Court. Attorneys regularly receive questions from immigrants who were scheduled for a hearing in Immigration Court and either forgot, couldn't make it, or just hoped the problem would go away. Failing to appear for a court date is the worst thing you can do to your hopes of immigrating. It will earn you an automatic order of removal (deportation), which means that USCIS can pick you up and put you on a plane home anytime, with no more hearings. You'll also be hit with a ten-year prohibition on returning to the United States and further punishments if you return illegally. The fact that your spouse is a U.S. citizen or resident won't be worth much after an order of removal has been entered.

b. Denial of Fiancé Visa at U.S. Consulate

If you are applying for a fiancé visa through a consulate overseas, you have no appeal after a denial. The consulate is at least required to tell you the reason for the denial, and often the fastest thing is to fix the problem and reapply. If the issue was whether you truly intended to get married, it might be wise to marry in your home country and work on gathering evidence that your marriage is the real thing before you apply for an immigrant visa.

c. Denial of Marriage-Based Visa at U.S. Consulate

If you are applying for an immigrant (marriage-based) visa, the consulate will give you one year after the denial of your visa application to provide information aimed at reversing the denial. If you feel you are being treated unfairly, this is a good time to get the U.S. spouse's local Congressperson involved (see Section C, below). At the end of the year, your application will close and you must start all over again. There is no appeal from the denial or the closure.

CAUTION
Don't attempt multiple, inconsistent applications. The U.S. government keeps a record of all your applications. If you come back five years later with a new U.S. citizen fiancé or spouse and a new visa or green card application, USCIS or the consulate will be happy to remind you of any past fraud or other reasons

for inadmissibility. (Changing your name won't work—by the end of the application process, USCIS will have your fingerprints.)

C. When All Else Fails, Call Your U.S. Congressperson

If your case turns into a true bureaucratic nightmare or a genuine miscarriage of justice, your U.S. citizen or permanent resident spouse can ask a local Congressperson for help. Some of them have a staff person dedicated to helping constituents who have immigration problems. A simple inquiry by a Congressperson can end months of USCIS or consular stonewalling or inaction. In rare cases, the Congressperson's office might be willing to put some actual pressure on USCIS or the consular office.

> **EXAMPLE:** Rodrigo, a U.S. citizen, was trying to get permission for his wife Sandra to immigrate from Mexico. She attended her visa interview and was told to come back with more proof that she would be financially supported and not become a public charge. Although Rodrigo's income was already over the *Poverty Guidelines*, he found a joint sponsor, who submitted an additional Affidavit of Support for Sandra. The consulate still wasn't willing to grant the visa. Rodrigo consulted with an attorney, who wrote letters to the consulate—but got no reply. Finally his attorney wrote a letter to Rodrigo's Congressperson asking for help. They submitted copies of all the relevant documents, so that the Congressperson would fully understand the problem. The visa was granted—with no explanation—a week after the Congressperson's inquiry.

Your Congressperson probably won't be surprised to hear from you. Illinois Congresswoman Janice Schakowsky reported that eight out of ten calls from her constituents were complaints about the INS (as USCIS was then called). (See "Unchecked Power of the INS Shatters American Dream," by Kim Christensen, Richard Read, Julie Sullivan, and Brent Walth, *The Oregonian*, Sunday, December 20, 2000.)

After You Get Your Green Card

If you're reading this after becoming a permanent or conditional resident, congratulations! But don't stop reading. This chapter will give you some important tips on how to protect and enjoy your new status, and how to turn conditional residence into permanent residence.

It's Not Too Early to Plan for U.S. Citizenship

If your spouse was a U.S. citizen when you were approved for residency, you can apply for U.S. citizenship 90 days before your three-year anniversary of approval. Immigrants who were initially approved as conditional residents don't have to wait any longer. Your two years of conditional residence count toward the three years' wait for citizenship, as long as you did eventually become a permanent resident.

Take a look at your permanent resident card to identify your initial approval date. For example, if you were approved for residency on April 1, 2010, you can apply for citizenship anytime after January 1, 2013.

The time period changes to *five* years minus 90 days if you are married to a *permanent resident*, or if you were married to a U.S. *citizen* but you divorce or stop living together during the required three years.

To become a U.S. citizen, you'll need to learn English, prove that you've lived in the United States for much of your time as a permanent resident, prove that you're of good moral character, and pass a test in U.S. history and civics. For more information, see *Becoming a U.S. Citizen: A Guide to the Law, Exam & Interview*, by Ilona Bray (Nolo), and the USCIS website at www.uscis.gov.

A. How to Prove You're a U.S. Resident

Your best proof that you are either a conditional permanent resident (if you have been married for less than two years) or a permanent resident is your permanent resident card—known as the green card. Usually, you will receive it in the mail within a few weeks of your application being approved.

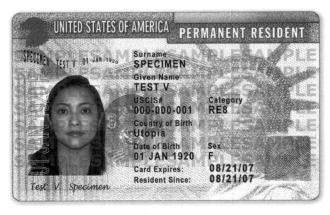

Sample Green Card

If you enter the U.S. after being approved at a consulate, you will also get a stamp in your passport when you enter. This stamp serves as temporary evidence of your permanent residence while you are waiting for your green card to be mailed to you. You can show this stamp to employers or use it to travel in and out of the United States.

If you get permanent residence by adjusting your status (within the U.S.), most USCIS officers are reluctant to put a stamp in your passport. If you know you will need proof of your permanent residence before you get your green card, however —for example if you need to leave the U.S.—they will usually give you the temporary stamp.

After your case is approved, but before you get the actual green card, you will receive an Approval Notice and a Welcome Notice. It's always a relief to see these notices, but don't try to use them as if they were your green card. If you leave the U.S., you cannot use them to get back in. If you're over the age of 18, the law requires you to carry your green card or other evidence of your status at all times. But keep a photocopy of it in a safe place, in case it's lost or stolen—this will make it much easier to get a replacement card from USCIS.

Sample Notice of Approval for Residency

Department of Homeland Security
U.S. Citizenship and Immigration Services

I-797, Notice of Action

THE UNITED STATES OF AMERICA

RECEIPT NUMBER		CASE TYPE I485 APPLICATION TO ADJUST TO PERMANENT
MSC-12-12345		RESIDENT STATUS

RECEIPT DATE	PRIORITY DATE	APPLICANT A012 345 677
March 24, 2012		ANDA MICHELSKI

NOTICE DATE	PAGE	
July 28, 2012	1 of 1	

ILONA BRAY
950 PARKER ST
BERKELEY CA 94710

Notice Type: Welcome Notice
Section: Adjustment as direct
beneficiary of immigrant
petition
COA: IR1

WELCOME TO THE UNITED STATES OF AMERICA

This is to notify you that your application for permanent residence has been approved. It is with great pleasure that we welcome you to permanent resident status in the United States.

At the top of this notice you will see a very important number. It is your INS A# (A-number). This is your permanent resident account and file number. This permanent account number is very important to you. You will need it whenever you contact us.

We will soon mail you a new *Permanent Resident Card.* You should receive it within the next 3 weeks. You can use it to show your new status. When you receive your card you must carry it with you at all times if you are 18 or older. It is the law.

Please call us at **(800) 375-5283** if any of the information about you shown above is incorrect, if you move before you receive your card, or if you don't receive your card within the next 3 weeks. If you call us, please have your A# and also the receipt number shown above available. The receipt number is a tracking number for your application.

Please read the notice that comes with your card. It will have important information about your card, about your status and responsibilities, and about permanent resident services available to you.

Your new card will expire in ten years. While card expiration will not directly affect your status, you will need to apply to renew your card several months before it expires. When the time comes and you need filing information, or an application, or if you ever have other questions about permanent resident services available to you, just call our *National Customer Service Center* at **1-800-375-5283** or visit the INS website at **www.bcis.gov**. (If you are hearing impared, the NCSC's TDD number is **1-800-767-1833**.) The best days to call the NCSC are Tuesday through Friday.

Once again, welcome to the United States and congratulations on your permanent resident status.

THIS FORM IS NOT A VISA NOR MAY IT BE USED IN PLACE OF A VISA..

Please see the additional information on the back. You will be notified separately about any other cases you filed.
NATIONAL BENEFITS CENTER
USCIS, DHS
P.O. BOX #648004
LEE'S SUMMIT MO 64064
Customer Service Telephone: (800) 375-5283

Form I-797 (Rev. 01/31/05) N

Applying for a Social Security Number

With your U.S. residency, you are eligible for a Social Security number. This is a number given to all people legally living and working in the United States, to identify them and allow them to pay into a system of retirement insurance. You may have already applied for a Social Security number if you received a work permit before getting your green card. If not, now is the time to apply. You'll need this number before you start work—your new employer will ask for it in order to file taxes on your behalf.

To apply for your number, visit your local Social Security office. You can find it in your phone book within the federal government pages (usually blue) or on the Social Security Administration's website at www.ssa.gov.

B. Traveling Abroad

There's no question about it—travel outside the United States is one of your rights as a conditional or permanent resident. But don't stay away too long. As the term "resident" suggests, you are expected to reside—that is, make your home—in the United States. If you make your home outside the United States, you could lose your green card.

Border officers are on the front lines of deciding whether returning green card holders are living outside the country. The officer will ask when you left the United States, what you were doing while you were away, and where you make your home. If you were outside the U.S. for more than one year, and did not get advance permission before leaving, the law presumes that you abandoned your permanent residence. To challenge that presumption, you will probably have to attend Immigration Court and convince an Immigration Judge that you did not intend to abandon your status.

Even if you stay out of the U.S. for less than a year on each particular trip, making many trips outside the U.S. creates a risk of being found to have abandoned your residency if, over the course of several years, you spend more time outside the U.S. than within it. Trips outside the U.S. for more than six months are treated more seriously than shorter trips, but even shorter trips can raise questions if you make so many that it looks like you are merely visiting the U.S. instead of living here.

If the border officer wonders whether you abandoned your permanent resident status, in addition to your length of time outside the U.S., the officer may consider whether you:

- pay U.S. taxes
- own a home or apartment or have a long-term lease in the United States
- were employed in the foreign country
- took your family to the foreign country
- are returning to the U.S. with a one-way ticket or a round-trip ticket back to the foreign country, and
- maintain other ties with the United States.

If you're coming back after a trip of several months, you can make your entry to the United States easier by bringing copies of documents that show that your home base is still in the United States. These documents could include your U.S. tax returns, home lease, evidence of employment, or other relevant documents.

In case you have a problem convincing a border official that you did not abandon your permanent residence, know that you do not have to accept the officer's decision as final. You have the right to present your case in Immigration Court. Only an Immigration Judge has the authority to make a final decision about whether you abandoned your status. For help with this, contact an attorney.

 TIP

Get permission before leaving. If you know in advance that you're going to have to spend more than a year outside the United States, apply for a reentry permit. Use Form I-131, Application for Travel Document, available at www.uscis.gov. You will want to check Box a in Part 2 for reentry permits. You will have to explain to USCIS the purpose of your trip and how much time you've already spent outside the United States. You don't need to wait for the permit to be approved before you leave the U.S., but you do need to get your biometrics taken for the permit before you leave (a process that is currently taking three to four weeks from the time you submit the I-131).

C. Your Immigrating Family Members' Rights

If children immigrated with you, their legal status will pretty much match yours. If you received conditional, rather than permanent residency, so did they—and they will also have to apply for permanent residency 90 days before the second anniversary of the date they won conditional residency (see Section G, below, regarding application procedures).

One difference between your children's status and yours may be the number of years that they must wait before they apply for U.S. citizenship. If your spouse was a permanent resident when you were approved, then you as well as your children must wait five years before applying for U.S. citizenship.

However, if your spouse was a U.S. citizen when you were approved, then it's possible that your children are on a fast track to U.S. citizenship. A U.S. citizen's biological and adopted children automatically become U.S. citizens upon entry to the U.S., on the condition that the children live within the U.S. and in the custody of their U.S. citizen parent. This right comes from the Child Citizenship Act of 2000, but it applies only to biological and adopted children, not to the stepchildren of U.S. citizens.

The children who benefit from this law will automatically receive a certificate of citizenship from USCIS by mail, within about six weeks of entering the United States. Children who would qualify for automatic citizenship except for the fact that they are over 18 when they become permanent residents will have to wait five years before applying for citizenship (despite the fact that you, their parent, need wait only three years).

RESOURCE
Want more information on how to obtain citizenship through family members? Talk to a lawyer or local nonprofit organization, or see Nolo's free online immigration articles at www.nolo.com.

D. Sponsoring Other Family Members

Once you are a permanent (not conditional) resident, you have limited rights to petition or sponsor other members of your family to immigrate. After you become a U.S. citizen, the law adds a few more family members to the list of those for whom you can petition.

The chart below, "Bringing the Family Over," shows the relatives whom you can help immigrate. (This chart does not discuss which relatives can immigrate immediately and which will have to wait until a visa is available.)

Bringing the Family Over
If you are a permanent resident, you can bring:
• Unmarried children
• Spouse.
If you are a U.S. citizen, you can bring:
• Parents
• Spouse
• Children (unmarried or married)
• Brothers and sisters.

The pathways represented in the chart above work only within your own family line—even if your spouse is a U.S. citizen he or she cannot bring in *your* parents, brothers, or sisters. Put another way, no one can petition for their in-laws.

Your children are another matter, however—as discussed in Chapter 2, Section B, your U.S. citizen spouse can petition not only for children who are his or her own biological offspring, but also for his or her legal stepchildren (if your marriage took place before they turned 18).

1. Your Unmarried Children

Your unmarried children under 21 probably immigrated with you. If they didn't, you have a few options. First, if you came directly from overseas, it may not be too late to use the application you filled out, which resulted in your permanent residency. Adding children to an existing application is called "following to join." Ask your consulate about the procedures for doing this.

Your second option is to look again at whether your spouse can file a visa petition for your children. If they are your spouse's biological children, this will be no problem. If your spouse is a U.S. citizen, the children under 21 are considered immediate relatives; if your spouse is a permanent resident, the children go in category 2A of the Preference System. Either way, your spouse can follow the same procedures in petitioning for them to immigrate as he or she did for you. If the children are not your spouse's biological children, he or she can petition for them only if they are his or her legal stepchildren. To be legal stepchildren, your marriage must have taken place before their 18th birthday.

Your third option is to file a visa petition for your children yourself. However, this won't get them a visa for at least a few years. As children of a permanent resident, they will be in the second preference category of the Visa Preference System, meaning that there are quotas on how many such people are given visas each year. They will have to be on a waiting list for an average of six years before becoming eligible to immigrate. (See Chapter 8, Section A2, for more details on the Visa Preference System.)

If you have unmarried children over 21, look again at whether your spouse can petition for them. If he or she is a U.S. citizen and the children's biological parent or legal stepparent, they will be placed in the first preference category of the Visa Preference System. That means they will have to be on a waiting list—but the first preference category usually moves quickly. You too could file a visa petition for your unmarried children over 21, but that would put them in category 2B of the Visa Preference System, and it will be a long wait for them (currently about eight or more years).

2. Your Married Children

If your children are married and neither you nor your spouse are U.S. citizens, you cannot apply for them to immigrate. When one of you becomes a citizen, that person can file a petition to place the children in the third preference category, which moves rather slowly—the current wait time is about eight or more years. If your spouse is going to file the petition, the children must be his or her biological children or legal stepchildren.

3. Parents, Brothers, and Sisters

You are not permitted to file a petition for your parents until you are a U.S. citizen. When you get your citizenship, they will be considered immediate relatives and won't face any waiting periods.

When you are a U.S. citizen, you will also be able to file petitions for your brothers and sisters, but they will have to wait in the Visa Preference System (as members of the fourth, and last, preference). Their wait will be longer than anyone's—averaging 11 years for most applicants and 23 years for applicants from the Philippines. To make matters worse, Congress keeps threatening to do away with the fourth preference category.

E. Losing Your Permanent Resident Status

You can lose your U.S. permanent resident status by violating the law (committing a crime) or violating the terms of your residency, such as by staying out of the United States and living abroad for too long, as explained above in Section B. If you are in the United States, a violation of the law could make you deportable, in which case USCIS might start Immigration Court proceedings against you and eventually send you away. If you attempt to return to the United States, you could be found inadmissible and kept out.

You Can Be Deported for Not Telling USCIS You've Changed Your Address

In 2002, the Immigration and Naturalization Service (INS, now called USCIS) shocked immigrants and their advocates by starting to enforce little-known provisions of the immigration law that make it a crime for immigrants not to submit immediate notifications whenever they change their address. The potential punishments include fines, imprisonment, or deportation. While the immigration authorities largely ignored these legal provisions in the past, their post-September 11th security focus changed this. Unfortunately, a number of innocents may be caught in the trap.

As a green card holder, you must take steps to protect yourself. Within ten days of your move, send USCIS a notice either online at www.uscis.gov or by mail using Form AR-11. Note that you can't just send one form per family—every member of your household needs to have a separate form submitted for him or her.

Form AR-11 itself is fairly self-explanatory. The question about your "last address" refers only to your last address in the United States, not overseas. The address you supply should be where you actually live, not a P.O. Box or work address. There is no fee for filing Form AR-11.

To file Form AR-11 online, go to www.uscis.gov, and from the right-hand column, click "Change Your Address Online." Follow the instructions. You will be asked whether you have any applications pending with USCIS. Be sure to check off all appropriate applications, so as to prompt USCIS into passing your new address to the right places. When you have finished, click on "Signature" to e-file the form.

Print a copy of the filed form for your records. It will show the date and time the form was filed, and will contain a USCIS confirmation number. There is no fee for this form.

If you prefer to file your AR-11 by regular mail, you can print out the form from the USCIS website and mail it to the address shown on the form. For proof of filing, it's best to file by certified mail and retain copies of the filed forms and proof of mailing. If you have any applications pending with USCIS and you file your AR-11 by mail, USCIS has no mechanism to send your change of address to all the appropriate offices, and you will have to inform them separately. Check with the office handling your application for its procedures—a letter may be enough.

If you have a case in Immigration Court or at the Board of Immigration Appeals, or if your case is at the National Visa Center or a consulate, these places are separate from USCIS, and Form AR-11 information is not shared with them. Be sure to contact these places separately to let them know about your change of address. Whenever you mail a change of address to any of the agencies, make copies of the notification, and mail everything by certified mail with return receipt. Put your copies and the return receipt in a safe place.

What if more than ten days have already passed and you've only just discovered your responsibility to file Form AR-11? Most attorneys advise that you fill out the form now, to show USCIS you made an attempt to comply and to assure that it has your current address. USCIS can forgive failures to notify it that weren't willful (intentional).

RESOURCE

For more on inadmissibility, see the discussion in Chapter 2 and I.N.A. § 101(a)(13)(C); 8 U.S.C. § 1101(a)(13)(c). The grounds of inadmissibility overlap with the grounds of removal or deportability, but they are set out separately in the immigration laws, and there are significant differences. See I.N.A. § 237(a), or 8 U.S.C. § 1227(a) for more on removal or deportability.

Men 18–26 Must Register for the Military Draft

Lawful U.S. resident males (green card holders) between the ages of 18 and 26 are required to register for military service, otherwise known as the Selective Service. USCIS won't deport you if you don't register, but it will hold up your eventual citizenship application. As of the year 2000, immigrants who apply to adjust status in the United States are supposed to be registered automatically, but don't count on this. It's easy to make sure you are registered. Go to the Selective Service website at www.sss.gov, click "Check a Registration," and enter the requested information. If you are not yet registered, you can do so on the same website. From the home page, click "Register Online." If you prefer to register by mail, pick up the Selective Service form at any U.S. Post Office.

A full discussion of inadmissibility and deportability is beyond the scope of this book. In brief, you become removable or deportable if you:

- are involved in document fraud or alien smuggling
- go on welfare (become a public charge) within the first five years of entry, unless you need public support because of something beyond your control, such as a disabling accident (see I.N.A. § 237(a)(5); 8 U.S.C. § 1227(a)(5))
- fail to comply with a condition of your green card (such as failing to follow a course of treatment to cure an illness you had when you were approved for residency)
- commit crimes, or

- violate the immigration laws (for example, participate in a sham marriage or immigrant smuggling).

You probably aren't planning on a crime spree as soon as you get your green card. But the message to take from these criminal grounds is that you have to be extra careful. Your U.S. citizen friends might not worry too much about engaging in certain illegal activities, such as shooting a gun at the sky on the Fourth of July or sharing a marijuana cigarette among friends. But if you are caught participating in these same activities, you could lose your green card and be deported.

F. How to Renew or Replace Your Green Card

This section is about the green card itself—the little laminated card that shows you're a resident. If something happens to the card—if it expires or gets lost—you don't ordinarily lose your status. (The only exception is that when the cards of conditional, not permanent residents expire, their status expires along with it, as discussed in Section G, below). However, the law requires you to have a valid green card in your possession, and it's not a bad thing to have on hand in case you travel, get a new job, or get picked up by an overeager USCIS officer who thinks you "look" illegal.

1. Renewing Expiring Green Cards

If you are a permanent resident (not a conditional resident), your status does not expire—but your green card *does* expire, every ten years. When the expiration date on your green card is six months away, you will need to apply to renew it. Use Form I-90, available at your local USCIS office, by mail from 800-870-3676, or on the USCIS website at www.uscis.gov. You can also submit this form electronically, or through the USCIS website—though you'll still have to mail in the supporting documentation. Instructions are not included in this book, but Form I-90 comes with a fairly complete set of instructions, and you can read more on the USCIS website.

Alternately, if you are ready and eligible to apply for U.S. citizenship, you can submit the citizenship application instead of renewing the green card. USCIS doesn't mind if you carry around an expired green card in this circumstance. If you need to change jobs or travel, however, you will probably want to renew the green card, to prove to the rest of the world that you are still a permanent resident.

2. Replacing Lost or Stolen Green Cards

If your green card is lost, stolen, accidentally dropped into a blender, or otherwise destroyed, you will need to apply for a new one. Like renewal, this is done using Form I-90 (see instructions in Section 1, above, on where to obtain the form).

TIP

Report all stolen green cards to the police. Green cards are a hot item, and there is always a possibility that yours will be stolen and sold. If this happens to you, be sure to file a police report. You may not get your card back, but when you apply for a replacement card, the report will help convince USCIS that you didn't sell your own card.

G. Converting From Conditional to Permanent Residence

If you were married for less than two years at the time of your approval for residency, or if you entered the United States as a K-1 fiancé, you will be given conditional residence. This means that your status will expire in two years. USCIS will take a second look at whether your marriage is indeed real (bona fide) before it allows you to stay permanently.

During your two years of conditional residency, you'll have all the day-to-day rights of a permanent resident. You'll be able to work, travel in and out of the United States, and even count your time toward the three or five years you'll need to accumulate

before applying for U.S. citizenship. But if, during this period, USCIS discovers that your marriage was not real in the first place, it can place you in removal proceedings and take away your green card and your immigration status.

CAUTION

You must ask for your residence to be made permanent, or you'll lose it. Read the rest of this section carefully. If you do not follow the procedures, you risk losing your conditional and permanent resident status and could face deportation.

1. When Will Your Conditional Residence Expire?

If you've just been approved for residency and you are not sure whether you're a conditional resident or when your residency will expire, take another look at the stamp in your passport. It should look much like the one below.

The notation CR-1 in this passport indicates that its holder received only conditional residency. The date on the top is when he entered: July 23, 1987. The date below the CR-1, July 22, 1989, shows when his two years of conditional residency will end. (When this person eventually got permanent residency, a separate stamp was placed on another page of his passport.)

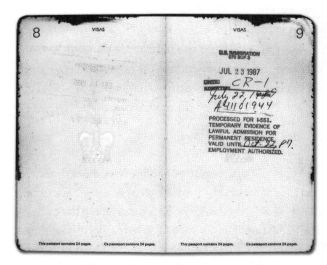

Sample Conditional Residence Stamp

Don't be confused by the other date you see on the sample, October 22, 1987. This is the date when the *stamp* in the passport expired, meaning that its holder should have received his separate green card by then. Every immigrant's passport stamp will have its own expiration date, even the immigrants who receive permanent, not conditional residency. If the passport holder from our sample hadn't received his green card by the October 1987 date, he could have gone to a USCIS office for a new passport stamp. Your initial green card will also show a two-year expiration date if you receive conditional residency.

2. The Application Procedures

To convert your conditional status to permanent status, you will need to submit a Petition to Remove the Conditions on Residence (Form I-751), complete with documents and fees, to a USCIS Service Center up to 90 days before the date your conditional residence status expires. Below, you'll find a checklist for this petition. If you send this petition too soon, that is, earlier than 90 days before your conditional residence expires, you'll get it right back. But if the petition is not filed by the expiration date, your card and your conditional residence status will both expire and you could be deported. So you see, you have a three-month window in which to complete and file your application.

Keep track of the deadline. USCIS will not always tell you when the petition is due. Put the due date on every calendar you own; tape it to your refrigerator, bedroom mirror, or forehead—do whatever you need to do to remember the date.

 SEE AN EXPERT

If you miss the deadline by a short time, don't just give up. If you're late by only a few weeks, mail the application with a cover letter, explaining the delay. The regulations allow you to file late for "good cause" (see 8 C.F.R. § 216.4(a)(6)). Good cause might mean a family or medical crisis, a move, or changes at your job—whatever

the issue, back up your explanations with documentary proof. If it's been longer, see a lawyer right away. You've probably got about three to six months before USCIS puts you into removal proceedings, at which point continuing with your application becomes much harder.

The information you need to have on hand is fairly straightforward, as you can see by looking at the checklist, below. One item merits mention, however—evidence of your marital relationship. This key portion of the application should be nothing new—remember the types of documents you had to provide for your adjustment of status or consular interview? These might include copies of rent receipts, joint bank or credit card statements, and children's birth certificates. Include only documents covering the last two years (don't resubmit items that USCIS has already seen).

3. What If Your U.S. Spouse Won't Sign the Joint Petition?

A lot of things can happen to a marriage in two years. People can get divorced or separated or the petitioning spouse might die. In some cases, the immigrant becomes the victim of domestic violence at the hands of a spouse who will no longer help with the immigration paperwork.

Any of these circumstances will make it impossible to submit the Petition to Remove Conditions on Residence in its standard and simplest form, as a joint petition signed by both spouses. But you're not necessarily out of luck. In fact, Form I-751 allows you to check boxes showing that you are divorced after a good faith marriage, widowed, the victim of being battered or extreme cruelty in a good faith marriage, or cannot file the petition jointly with your spouse for some other reason, but would suffer extreme hardship if you were denied permanent residency. If you check any of these boxes, you will still submit the form, but you won't have your spouse's signature.

Extreme hardship. This is the most general ground for a waiver—and you technically don't even need to prove a good faith marriage—but it's also considered the hardest to qualify for. You must show that political or economic changes have arisen in your country since the time you became a conditional resident that would cause you extreme hardship if you were to return. (See I.N.A. § 216(c)(4)(a); 8 U.S.C. § 1186a(c)(4)(a).) For example, if you've recently become an outspoken public critic of a repressive government's policies and might be persecuted upon your return, you'd have a good case.

Divorce. This ground is more clear-cut; except that the divorce must actually be final before you can file this waiver. And, depending on where you live, the courts may take many months to grant you a divorce. This means you may want to file the divorce papers yourself in order to get the process going, instead of waiting for your U.S. spouse. On the other hand, the longer you stay married, the better your chances of showing that the marriage was bona fide in the first place. If worst comes to worst, you could either file your waiver request without the divorce decree (in order to preserve your status) but with a promise to send it later; or file your waiver request late, arguing that the upheaval in your life caused by your marital troubles was good cause for your lateness.

Battery or extreme cruelty. You might qualify for this section of the waiver if you've been the victim of "any act or threatened act of violence [by your U.S. spouse], including any forceful detention, which results in physical or mental injury. Psychological or sexual abuse or exploitation, including rape, molestation, incest (if the victim is a minor), or forced prostitution shall be considered acts of violence." (See 8 C.F.R. § 216.5(e)(3)(i).) You don't have to be divorced or even separated from your spouse.

The main challenge here will be documenting the good faith marriage (particularly if you've had to quickly leave the home where you and your spouse lived), as well as documenting the abuse (with things like police and medical reports, photos, psychological evaluations, witness statements, letters from shelters, and more). And don't worry—USCIS will not advise the abusive spouse about the application.

You'll need substantial documentation of your eligibility for approval under the category you marked—including both documents showing that your marriage was entered into in good faith (similar to what you supplied when you got your conditional residence) and documents proving the divorce, spouse's death, abuse, or hardship. A complete explanation of this process is outside the scope of this book. Consult a lawyer, a local nonprofit that serves immigrants, or a battered women's shelter for help.

4. Line-by-Line Instructions for Form I-751

Use this form to convert your conditional residency to permanent residency.

 WEB RESOURCE

Form I-751 is available on the USCIS website at www.uscis.gov. For a sample filled-in form, see below.

Part 1, "Information about you": This time "you" means the immigrating spouse. The rest of this Part should be self-explanatory.

Part 2: If you are still married and your spouse is cooperating with the process of applying for your permanent residency, put an "X" in Box a.

Part 3: Mostly self-explanatory. You will probably know if you are in **"removal or deportation proceedings."** You'll be in this situation if you've done something—or the government thinks you've done something—that gets you into Immigration Court. Common examples include being convicted of a crime or giving USCIS reason to believe that your marriage is fraudulent. If you are in court proceedings, you should already have a lawyer. If you don't, see Chapter 17 on how to find a good one.

If you check "yes" to the question about whether a fee was **"paid to anyone other than an attorney in connection with this petition,"** you haven't done anything wrong, but that person needs to enter his or her name and other information.

Sample Form I-751, Petition to Remove the Conditions on Residence—Page 1

OMB No. 1615-0038; Expires 01/31/2013

Department of Homeland Security
U.S. Citizenship and Immigration Services

I-751, Petition to Remove Conditions on Residence

START HERE - Type or print in black ink.

For USCIS Use Only

Part 1. Information About You

Family Name (Last Name)	Given Name (First Name)	Full Middle Name
HOLLIS	Nigel	Ian

Address: (Street Number and Name): 114 Fulton Street Apt. # 6E

C/O: (In care of)

City	State/Province
New York	NY

Country	Zip/Postal Code
USA	10038

Mailing Address, if different than above (Street Number and Name): Apt. #

C/O: (In care of)

City / State/Province

Country / Zip/Postal Code

Date of Birth (mm/dd/yyyy)	Country of Birth	Country of Citizenship
8/18/1984	U.K.	U.K.

Alien Registration Number (A-Number)	Social Security # (if any)
A12345678	888-11-8888

Conditional Residence Expires on (mm/dd/yyyy)	Daytime Phone # (Area/Country Code)
08/07/2014	212-555-1212

For USCIS Use Only

Returned — Date / Date
Resubmitted — Date / Date
Reloc Sent — Date / Date
Reloc Rec'd — Date / Date
☐ Petitioner Interviewed on ___

Remarks

Part 2. Basis for Petition (Check one)

a. ☒ My conditional residence is based on my marriage to a U.S. citizen or permanent resident, and we are filing this petition together.

b. ☐ I am a child who entered as a conditional permanent resident, and I am unable to be included in a joint petition filed by my parent(s).

OR

My conditional residence is based on my marriage to a U.S. citizen or permanent resident, I am unable to file a joint petition, and I request a waiver because: **(Check one)**

c. ☐ My spouse is deceased.

d. ☐ I entered into the marriage in good faith, but the marriage was terminated through divorce or annulment.

e. ☐ I am a conditional resident spouse who entered a marriage in good faith, and during the marriage I was battered by or was the subject of extreme cruelty by my U.S. citizen or permanent resident spouse or parent.

f. ☐ I am a conditional resident child who was battered by or subjected to extreme cruelty by my U.S. citizen or conditional resident parent(s).

g. ☐ The termination of my status and removal from the United States would result in an extreme hardship.

Action Block

To Be Completed by Attorney or Representative, if any
☐ Fill in box if Form G-28 is attached to represent the applicant.

ATTY State License #

Form I-751 (Rev. 01/12/11) Y

Sample Form I-751, Petition to Remove the Conditions on Residence—Page 2

Part 3. Additional Information About You

1. Other Names Used *(including maiden name)*: None

2. Date of Marriage *(mm/dd/yyyy)*: 11/05/2012
3. Place of Marriage: New York, NY
4. If your spouse is deceased, give the date of death *(mm/dd/yyyy)*:

5. Are you in removal, deportation, or rescission proceedings? ☐ Yes ☒ No
6. Was a fee paid to anyone other than an attorney in connection with this petition? ☐ Yes ☒ No
7. Have you ever been arrested, detained, charged, indicted, fined, or imprisoned for breaking or violating any law or ordinance (excluding traffic regulations), or committed any crime which you were not arrested in the United States or abroad? ☐ Yes ☒ No
8. If you are married, is this a different marriage than the one through which conditional residence status was obtained? ☐ Yes ☒ No
9. Have you resided at any other address since you became a permanent resident? *(If "Yes," attach a list of all addresses and dates.)* ☐ Yes ☒ No
10. Is your spouse currently serving with or employed by the U.S. Government and serving outside the United States? ☐ Yes ☒ No

If you answered "Yes" to any of the above, provide a detailed explanation on a separate sheet of paper and refer to "What Initial Evidence Is Required?" to determine what criminal history documentation to include with your petition. Place your name and A-Number at the top of each sheet and give the number of the item that refers to your response.

Part 4. Information About the Spouse or Parent Through Whom You Gained Your Conditional Residence

Family Name	First Name	Middle Name
Beach	Sandra	Leah

Address: 114 Fulton Street #6E

Date of Birth *(mm/dd/yyyy)*	Social Security # *(if any)*	A-Number *(if any)*
12/20/1986	123-456789	None

Part 5. Information About Your Children-List All Your Children *(Attach other sheets if necessary)*

Name *(First/Middle/Last)*	Date of Birth *(mm/dd/yyyy)*	A-Number *(if any)*	If in U.S., give address/immigration status	Living with you?
Nadine Anne Hollis	12/02/2012	U.S. citizen		☒ Yes ☐ No
				☐ Yes ☐ No
				☐ Yes ☐ No
				☐ Yes ☐ No
				☐ Yes ☐ No

Part 6. Accommodations for Individuals With Disabilities and Impairments

(Read the information in the instructions before completing this section.)

I am requesting an accommodation:

1. Because of my disability(ies) and/or impairment(s). ☐ Yes ☒ No
2. For my spouse because of his or her disability(ies) and/or impairment(s). ☐ Yes ☒ No
3. For my included child(ren) because of his or her (their) disability(ies) and/or impairment(s). ☐ Yes ☒ No

If you answered "Yes," check any applicable box. Provide information on the disability(ies) and/or impairment(s) for each person:

☐ Deaf or hard of hearing and request the following accommodation(s) (if requesting a sign-language interpreter, indicate which language (e.g., American Sign Language)):

☐ Blind or sight-impaired and request the following accommodation(s):

☐ Other type of disability(ies) and/or impairment(s) (describe the nature of the disability(ies) and/or impairment(s) and accommodation(s) being requested):

Form I-751 (Rev. 01/12/11) Y Page 2

Sample Form I-751, Petition to Remove the Conditions on Residence—Page 3

Part 7. Signature *(Read the information on penalties on Page 5 of the instructions before completing this section. If you checked block "a" in Part 2, your spouse must also sign below).*

I certify, under penalty of perjury of the laws of the United States of America, that this petition and the evidence submitted with it is all true and correct. If conditional residence was based on a marriage, I further certify that the marriage was entered in accordance with the laws of the place where the marriage took place and was not for the purpose of procuring an immigration benefit. I also authorize the release of any information from my records that U.S. Citizenship and Immigration Services needs to determine eligibility for the benefit sought.

Signature	Print Name	Date *(mm/dd/yyyy)*
Nigel Hollis	Nigel Hollis	06/01/2014

Signature of Spouse	Print Name	Date *(mm/dd/yyyy)*
Sandra Beach	Sandra Beach	06/01/2014

NOTE: If you do not completely fill out this form or fail to submit any required documents listed in the instructions, you may not be found eligible for the requested benefit and this petition may be denied.

Part 8. Signature of Person Preparing Form, If Other than Above

I declare that I prepared this petition at the request of the above person, and it is based on all information of which I have knowledge.

Signature	Print Name	Date *(mm/dd/yyyy)*

Firm Name and Address

Daytime Phone Number
(Area/Country Code)

E-Mail Address
(if any)

Part 4: This Part refers to the petitioning spouse, not the immigrant. Self-explanatory.

Part 5: Self-explanatory.

Part 6: If you are requesting an accommodation at your interview because of a disability or impairment—such as having a sign-language interpreter—explain that here.

Part 7: It is very important that both of you remember to sign. Your two signatures are an indication of the ongoing validity of your marriage.

Checklist for Filing Joint Petition to Remove Conditions on Residence

Here's what you'll need to assemble for your joint petition to remove the conditions on your residency and become a permanent resident:

- ☐ Form I-751
- ☐ Required supporting documents, including:
- ☐ Application fee (currently $505, but fees change often so double-check this at www.uscis.gov, or by calling 800-375-5283); you can mail a check or money order
- ☐ Biometrics fee (for photos and fingerprints; currently $85)

---

5. Where to File the Joint Petition

When you and your spouse are finished preparing the joint petition, make a complete copy for your files. Then send the packet of forms and documents to a USCIS Service Center—the address is in Appendix B, and you can double-check it on the instructions that come with the form or by calling the USCIS information number at 800-375-5283.

As you may have learned by now, Service Centers are different than the local USCIS offices that you can actually visit. All contact with the Service Center will have to be by mail.

Certified mail with return receipt requested is highly recommended—these Service Centers receive a huge volume of mail. When you request a return receipt, you will prepare a little postcard that is attached to your envelope. It will be signed by the person at USCIS who physically receives your envelope. The postcard will be mailed to you, which will be your proof that USCIS received your petition. You can use this postcard to convince USCIS to look for the petition if it gets misplaced.

6. Your Receipt Notice

Once your application is received and the USCIS Service Center has reviewed it to see that you've included all the appropriate documents and fee, you'll get a receipt notice. It may be several weeks before you get this receipt notice. This notice is an important document. It extends your residency for a period of 12 months. It will be your only proof of your legal status at this time—it's a bit awkward to show to employers, border patrol officers, and others, but it really is an official document. You must, however, also carry your expired green card at the same time (since the card, unlike the receipt, has your photo on it).

During this time period, you will also be sent an appointment notice stating when and where you must appear for biometric processing. (It's usually at a USCIS Application Support Center.) Biometric processing includes taking your photograph, signature, and index fingerprint, for use in generating your new green card. If you're between ages 14 and 79, it also includes taking your fingerprints, in order to do another criminal background check.

Most people receive their permanent resident cards before the expiration of their one-year extension. If you fall into the group of people who do not get their cards in a timely manner, don't worry that this will affect your legal status in the United States—you will remain a conditional resident until USCIS makes a decision on your application. If, however, you need evidence of your legal status, visit your local USCIS office. (You'll need to make an appointment first, at www.uscis.gov; click "INFOPASS.") Bring an unexpired passport, your old green card, and your receipt notice. The USCIS officer will take your green card, and in return give you what's called an I-551 stamp in your passport. This stamp will serve as evidence of your status, and will not expire for another year.

> ⚠ CAUTION
>
> **Do not travel with an expired receipt notice!** If you don't get your permanent resident card by the time your receipt notice expires, make an INFOPASS appointment through the USCIS website and get a temporary stamp in your passport before you leave the United States—otherwise, you may not be let back in.

7. Approval by Mail

With any luck at all, the Service Center will approve your permanent residence by mail. If you don't receive an approval by the time your one-year extension expires, take your receipt notice and your passport and visit your local USCIS office (after making an appointment online). If no decision has been made, USCIS will stamp your passport, extending your conditional residence. If you request it, the information officer will also send an inquiry to the Service Center handling your case, pointing out that your case has gone beyond normal processing time.

8. Approval After Interview

You and your spouse may be called in for an interview regarding the joint petition. If so, it probably means USCIS has some doubts about your marriage being real (although they also seem to regularly choose a few couples at random). Try to figure out why you're being called for an interview. Are you and your spouse living in different places? Did issues arise at your earlier USCIS or consular interview (when you got your conditional residence)? If so, think about how you can overcome these issues.

For example, if you and your spouse are living separately because one of you is in school, bring school transcripts and copies of documents showing that you often phone or visit one another. Or, if you are temporarily separated, get a letter from your marriage counselor or religious advisor confirming that she or he sees you regularly and is helping you face problems in your relationship and work them through.

Don't be surprised if the Service Center informs you that you'll be interviewed but the local USCIS office takes many months before scheduling an appointment. This delay doesn't have anything to do with the merits of your application. It just means that the local offices have numerous other applicants to interview before you.

> 💼 SEE AN EXPERT
>
> **Being called in for an interview at this stage is somewhat unusual.** You might want to ask a lawyer to help you prepare and to attend the interview with you. See Chapter 17 for tips on finding a good lawyer. Also see Chapter 13 for practice questions.

9. After You Are Approved or Denied

If you are required to attend a USCIS interview, and your case is approved at or after the interview, you will receive your permanent resident card in the mail a few weeks later.

If your application is denied, you will be placed in removal proceedings, unless you are lucky enough to have an alternate legal status.

> 💼 SEE AN EXPERT
>
> **If you are placed in removal proceedings and you haven't already found a lawyer, do it now.** For tips on finding a good one, see Chapter 17. Whatever you do, don't skip a court date. Failure to appear results in an automatic order of deportation and could permanently ruin your chances of immigrating.

Legal Help Beyond This Book

You are not required to have a lawyer when applying for an immigrant visa or green card in the United States or overseas. In fact, if you are overseas, lawyers cannot attend consular interviews with you, though they are allowed to prepare the paperwork and have follow-up communications with the consulates.

However, there are many times when you may need or want a lawyer's help. Because immigration law is complicated, even a seemingly simple case can suddenly become nightmarish. If so, you'll need good legal help, fast. And you can avoid some problems by hiring a lawyer from the get-go. In this chapter, we'll explain:

- when applicants typically need to consult an attorney (Section A)
- how to find suitable counsel (Sections B, C, and D)
- hiring, paying, and (if necessary) firing your lawyer (Sections E, F, and G), and
- how to do some legal research on your own (Section H).

CAUTION

If you are or have ever been in deportation (removal) proceedings, you must see a lawyer. If the proceedings aren't yet over or are on appeal, your entire immigration situation is in the power of the courts—and you are not allowed to use the procedures described in this book. Even if the proceedings are over, you should ask a lawyer whether the outcome affects your current application. A past order of removal can make you inadmissible.

A. When Do You Need a Lawyer?

The most common legal problem encountered by would-be immigrants is the claim by USCIS or the consulate that they are inadmissible for one or more of the reasons listed in Chapter 2, such as having committed a crime or previously lied to the U.S.

government. If you know that any of these grounds apply to you, it makes sense to get legal help before you begin the application process.

Another circumstance that often drives people to lawyers is the failure of USCIS or the consulate to act on or approve the application, for reasons that have more to do with bureaucracy than law. For example, an applicant who moves from Los Angeles to San Francisco after filing the green card application might find that the application has disappeared into a bureaucratic black hole for several months. Delays at the USCIS Service Centers are also ridiculously common.

Lawyers don't have a lot of power in such circumstances. But at least the lawyer may have access to inside fax or email inquiry lines, where they (and only they) can ask about delayed or problematic cases. Unfortunately, even lawyers have trouble getting answers to such inquiries, but it's often worth a try. An experienced lawyer may have contacts inside USCIS or the consulate who can give information or locate a lost file. But these lawyers can't use this privilege on an everyday basis, and long delays are truly an everyday occurrence.

The bottom line is that a lawyer may be able to help, but has no magic words that will force the U.S. government into taking action.

CAUTION

Don't rely on advice by USCIS information officers. Would you want the receptionist in your doctor's office to tell you whether to get brain surgery? Asking USCIS information officers for advice about your case (beyond basic procedural advice such as where to file an application and what the fees are) is equally unsafe. The people who staff USCIS phone and information services are not experts. USCIS takes no responsibility if their advice is wrong—and won't treat your application with any more sympathy. Even following the advice of officials higher up in the agency may not be safe. Always get a second opinion.

B. Where to Get the Names of Good Immigration Lawyers

Finding a good lawyer can involve a fair amount of work. Immigration law is a specialized area—in fact it has many subspecialties within it—so you obviously don't want to consult the lawyer who wrote your best friend's will. And whatever you do, don't just open the telephone book and pick the immigration lawyer with the biggest advertisement. Even bar association referral panels (lawyer listing services run by groups of lawyers) tend not to be very helpful. Such services tend to assume that any one of their lawyer-members is qualified to handle your case, and they may simply refer you to the next lawyer on their list with no prescreening.

It is far better to ask a trusted person for a referral. You probably know someone in the United States who is sophisticated in practical affairs and has been through an immigration process. Perhaps this person can recommend his or her lawyer, or can ask that lawyer to recommend another.

Local nonprofit organizations serving immigrants can also be excellent sources for referrals. A nonprofit organization is a charity that seeks funding from foundations and individuals to help people in need. Since they exist to serve others rather than to make a profit, they charge less and are usually staffed by people whose hearts and minds are in the right places. In the immigrant services field, examples include the Northwest Immigrant Rights Project (Seattle), El Rescate Legal Services (Los Angeles), the International Institutes (nationwide), and Catholic Charities (nationwide).

USCIS offers a list of "free legal service providers" at its website, www.uscis.gov (click "Resources," then "Finding Legal Advice," then "Free Legal Service Providers.") This list includes both attorneys and nonprofits. But don't be surprised to find that they're not all really free. Many attorneys at least charge a nominal consultation fee, and many nonprofits must charge fees to cover their costs as well.

Yet another good resource is the American Immigration Lawyers Association (AILA), at 800-954-0254 or at www.aila.org. AILA offers a lawyer referral service. Their membership is limited to lawyers who have passed a screening process, which helps keep out the less scrupulous practitioners. But not all good immigration lawyers have joined AILA (membership is a bit pricey).

Also check out Nolo's Lawyer Directory at www.nolo.com (under "Find a Lawyer," enter "Immigration" and the city or zip code where you live, or the nearest large city). This allows you to view lawyers' photos, and personal profiles describing their areas of expertise and practice philosophy.

Try to get a list of a few lawyers whom you've heard do good work, then meet or talk to each and choose one. We'll talk more about lawyers' fees below.

C. How to Avoid Sleazy Lawyers

There are good and bad immigration lawyers out there. Some of the good ones are candidates for sainthood—they put in long hours dealing with a difficult bureaucracy on behalf of a clientele that typically can't pay high fees.

The bad ones are a nightmare—and there are more than a few of them. They typically try to do a high-volume business, churning out the same forms for every client regardless of their situation. Such lawyers can get clients into deep trouble by overlooking critical issues in their cases or failing to submit applications or court materials on time. But the one thing they never seem to forget is to send a huge bill for their supposed help. Some signs to watch for are:

- **The lawyer approaches you in a USCIS office or other public location and tries to solicit your business.** This is not only against the lawyers' rules of professional ethics, but no competent lawyer ever needs to find clients this way.
- **The lawyer makes big promises, such as "I guarantee I'll win your case," or "I've got a special contact that will put your application at the front**

of the line." The U.S. government is in ultimate control of your application, and any lawyer who implies they have special powers is either lying or may be involved in something you don't want to be a part of.

- **The lawyer has a very fancy office and wears a lot of flashy gold jewelry.** A fancy office or a $2,000 outfit aren't necessarily signs of a lawyer's success at winning cases. These trappings may instead be signs that the lawyer charges high fees and counts on impressing clients with clothing rather than results.
- **The lawyer encourages you to lie on your application.** This is a tricky area. On the one hand, a good lawyer can assist you in learning what information you don't want to needlessly offer up, and can help you present the truth in the best light possible. But a lawyer who coaches you to lie—for example, by telling you to pretend you lost your passport and visa when in fact you entered the United States illegally—isn't ethical. There's every chance that USCIS knows the lawyer's reputation and will scrutinize your application harder because of it.

You might think that the really bad lawyers would be out of business by now, but that isn't the case. Sad to say, neither the attorney bar associations nor the courts nor even the police take much interest in going after people who prey on immigrants. Occasionally, nonprofits devoted to immigrants' rights will attempt to get the enforcement community interested in taking action. Unfortunately, this threat of official scrutiny isn't much of a deterrent.

 TIP

If you are the victim of an unscrupulous lawyer, complain! Law enforcement won't go after lawyers who prey on immigrants until there is enough community pressure. If a lawyer, or someone pretending to be a lawyer, pulls something unethical on you, report it to the state and local bar association and the local District Attorney's office. Ask your local nonprofits if anyone else in your area is collecting such information.

D. How to Choose Among Lawyers

Once you've got your "short list" of lawyers, you'll want to speak to each one. How much a lawyer charges is bound to be a factor in whom you choose (see Section F, below). But it shouldn't be the only factor. Here are some other important considerations.

1. Familiarity With Cases Like Yours

As mentioned above, immigration law is a specialized area. And some immigration lawyers spend much of their time in subspecialties, such as helping people obtain political asylum or employment-based visas. To learn how much experience a lawyer has in fiancé or marriage-based visas, ask some very practical questions, such as:

- How long do you expect my case to take?
- What is the reputation of the officers at the USCIS or consular office who will handle my case?
- How many marriage-based cases did you handle this year?

An experienced lawyer should be able to provide detailed, insightful answers to your questions and should be handling at least 50 marriage-based cases annually.

2. Client Rapport

Your first instinct in hiring a lawyer may be to look for a shark—someone you wouldn't want to leave your child with, but who will be a tough fighter for your case. This isn't necessarily the best choice in the immigration context. Since you may need to share some highly confidential issues with your lawyer, you'll want to know that the person is discreet and thoughtful. Also, realize that a lawyer's politeness goes a long way in front of immigration officials—sharks often produce a bureaucratic backlash, whereas the lawyers with good working relations with USCIS may have doors opened to them.

3. Access to Your Lawyer

You'll want to know that you can reach your lawyer during the months that your application winds its way through the USCIS or consular bureaucracy. A lawyer's accessibility may be hard to judge at the beginning, but try listening to the lawyer's receptionist as you wait in his or her office for the first time. If you get the sense that the receptionist is rude and trying to push people off or give them flimsy excuses about why the lawyer hasn't returned their calls or won't talk to them, don't hire that lawyer.

Many immigration lawyers are sole practitioners and use an answering machine rather than a receptionist. In that case, you'll have to rely on how quickly they answer your initial calls. In your first meeting, simply ask the lawyer how quickly he or she will get back to you. If the lawyer regularly breaks promises, you'll have grounds on which to complain. Of course, you too have a responsibility not to harass your lawyer with frequent calls. The lawyer should be available for legitimate questions about your case, including inquiries about approaching deadlines.

4. Explaining Services and Costs

Take a good look at any printed materials the lawyer gives you on your first visit. Are they glitzy, glossy pieces that look more like advertising than anything useful? Or are they designed to acquaint you with the process you're getting into and the lawyer's role in it? Think about this issue again before you sign the lawyer's fee agreement, described in the section immediately below. Being a good salesperson doesn't necessarily make someone a good lawyer.

E. Signing Up Your Lawyer

Many good lawyers will ask you to sign an agreement covering their services and the fees you will pay them. This is a good idea for both

of you, and can help prevent misunderstandings. The contract should be written in a way you can understand; there's no law that says it has to be in confusing legal jargon. The lawyer should go over the contract with you carefully, not just push it under your nose, saying, "Sign here." Some normal contract clauses include:

- **Scope of work.** A description of exactly what the lawyer will do for you.
- **Fees.** Specification of the amount you'll pay, either as a flat fee (a lump sum you pay for a stated task, such as $1,000 for an adjustment of status application) or at an hourly rate, with a payment schedule. If you hire someone at an hourly rate, you can ask to be told as soon as the hours have hit a certain limit.

 TIP

Don't pay a big flat fee up front. Since the lawyer already has your money, he or she will have little incentive to please you. And if you don't like the lawyer later on, chances are you won't get any of your money back. Instead, pay for a few hours' service—then if you don't like the lawyer's work, end the relationship.

- **Responsibility for expenses.** Most lawyers will ask you to cover the incidental expenses associated with the work that they do, such as phone calls, postage, and photocopying. This is fair. After all, if your case requires a one-hour phone call to the consulate in Brunei, that call shouldn't eat up the lawyer's fee. But check carefully to be sure that the lawyer charges you the actual costs of these items. Some lawyers have been known to turn a tidy profit by charging, for example, 20 cents a page for a photocopy job that really costs only three cents a page.
- **Effect of nonpayment.** Many lawyers charge interest if you fail to pay on time. This is normal and probably not worth making a big fuss about. If you have trouble paying on time, call the lawyer and ask for more time—he or

she may be willing to forgo the interest if it's clear you're taking your obligation seriously.

- **Exclusion of guarantee.** The lawyer may warn you that there's no guarantee of winning your case. Though this may appear as if the lawyer is looking for an excuse to lose, it is actually a responsible way for the lawyer to protect against clients who assume they're guaranteed a win; or who later accuse the lawyer of having made such promises. After all, USCIS or the consulate is the ultimate decision maker on your case.

Watch Out for Nonlawyers Practicing Immigration Law

Because much of immigration law involves filling in forms, people assume it's easy. They're wrong. Be careful about whom you consult with or hand your case over to. Unless the person shows you certification that they are a lawyer or an "accredited representative," or a paralegal working under the direct supervision of a lawyer, they should be thought of as typists. (An accredited representative is a nonlawyer who has received training from a lawyer and been recognized by USCIS as qualified to prepare USCIS applications and represent clients in court.) And this is true even though they may go by fancy names such as "immigration consultant" or "notary public"—these people do not have a law degree. To check on whether someone is really a lawyer, ask for their Bar Number and call the state bar association.

Hiring a nonlawyer or nonaccredited representative is only appropriate if you want help with the form preparation, and no more. But as you know from reading the information on filling out forms in Chapter 4, even the address you enter can have legal consequences. Don't just turn your case over and let the consultant make the decisions.

If you feel you've been defrauded by an immigration consultant, you may want to sue in Small Claims Court; see *Everybody's Guide to Small Claims Court*, by Ralph Warner (Nolo).

- **Effect of changes in case.** Most lawyers will warn you that if there is something you didn't tell them about (for example, that you are still married to another spouse) or a significant life change affects your case (for instance, you get arrested), they will charge you additional fees to cover the added work these revelations will cause. This too is normal; but to protect yourself against abuse, make very sure that the contract specifies in detail all the work that is already included. For example, a contract for a lawyer to help you with a green card application within the United States might specify that the lawyer will be responsible for "preparation of visa petition and adjustment of status packet, filing all applications with USCIS, representation at interview, and reasonable follow-up with USCIS." If the lawyer agrees to include work on any special waivers or unusual documents, make sure these are mentioned in the contract (for example, a waiver or an extra Affidavit of Support from a joint sponsor).

F. Paying Your Lawyer

You may have to pay an initial consultation fee as well as a fee for the lawyer's services. The initial consultation fee is usually around $100. Some good lawyers provide free consultations. But many have found that they can't afford to spend a lot of their time this way, since many immigrants have no visa or remedy available to them, which means the lawyer gets no work after the initial consultation. Be ready to pay a reasonable fee for your initial consultation, but do not sign any contracts for further services until you're confident you've found the right lawyer. This usually means consulting with several lawyers first.

1. Flat Rates and Hourly Rates

Many lawyers charge flat rates for green card applications. That means you can compare prices.

The current range in the United States for a basic fiancé visa is between $700 and $2,000, and a marriage-based application runs anywhere from $800 to $3,000. If the lawyer quotes an hourly rate instead, expect to pay between $100 and $350 per hour.

A higher rate doesn't necessarily mean a better lawyer. Those who charge less may be keeping their overhead low, still making their name in the business, or philosophically opposed to charging high fees. But an extremely low fee may be a sign that the person isn't really a lawyer, as covered in "Watch Out for Nonlawyers Practicing Immigration Law," above.

2. If All the Rates Are Too High

If the prices you are being quoted are beyond your reach but you definitely need legal help, you have a couple of options. One is to ask the lawyer to split the work with you. With this arrangement, the lawyer consults with you solely about the issue causing you difficulty, reviews a document, or performs some other key task, at the hourly rate; while you do the follow-up work, such as filling out the application forms and translating or writing documents, statements, letters, or more.

Be forewarned, though, that while many lawyers will sell you advice on an hourly basis, most won't want to get into a mixed arrangement unless they are sure they won't end up cleaning up after anything you might do wrong. For example, a lawyer might not agree to represent you in a USCIS interview if the lawyer wasn't hired to review your forms and documents before you submitted them to USCIS.

Another option is to look for a nonprofit organization that helps people with family visa cases. A few provide free services, while most charge reduced rates. But don't get your hopes too high. The U.S. government does not fund organizations that provide services to immigrants (except for very limited types of services), which means that most nonprofits depend on private sources of income, and are chronically underfunded. The result is that many nonprofits will have long backlogs of cases and may not be able to take your case at all.

G. Firing Your Lawyer

You have the right to fire your lawyer at any time. But before you take this step, make sure that your disagreement is about something that is truly the lawyer's fault. Many people blame their lawyer for delays that are actually caused by USCIS or the consulates. You can always consult with another lawyer regarding whether your case has been mishandled. Ask your lawyer for a complete copy of your file first (to which you have a right at any time). If it appears that your case was mishandled, or if relations with your lawyer have deteriorated badly, firing the lawyer may be the healthiest thing for you and your immigration case.

You will have to pay the fired lawyer for any work that has already been done on your case. If you originally paid a flat fee, the lawyer is permitted to keep enough of the fee to cover the work already done, at the lawyer's hourly rate, limited by the total flat fee amount. Ask for a complete list of hours worked and how those hours were spent. Don't count on getting any money back, however—flat fees are often artificially low, and it's very easy for a lawyer to show that your fee got used up on the work that was done.

Firing your lawyer will not affect the progress of your applications with USCIS or the consulate. However, you should send a letter to the last USCIS or consular office you heard from, directing them to send all future correspondence directly to you (or to your new lawyer).

H. Do-It-Yourself Legal Research

With or without a lawyer, you may at some point wish to look at the immigration laws yourself. If so, we applaud your self-empowerment instinct—but need to give you a few warnings. A government spokesperson once called the immigration laws a "mystery, and a mastery of obfuscation" (spokeswoman Karen Kraushaar, quoted in *The Washington Post*, April 24, 2001). She couldn't have said it better. One is tempted to think that the members of the U.S. Congress who write and amend the immigration laws deliberately made them unreadable, perhaps to confuse the rest of the representatives so they wouldn't understand what they were voting on.

The result is that researching the immigration laws is something even the experts find difficult—which means you may be wading into treacherous waters if you try it on your own. Figuring out local USCIS office procedures and policies can be even more difficult. Lawyers learn a great deal through trial and error, or by attending meetings and reading articles written by other lawyers who tried something first or who learned important information from USCIS or State Department cables, memos, or other instructions. Unfortunately, you won't have ready access to these sources.

Does all this mean that you shouldn't ever look further than this book? Certainly not. And some research inquiries are quite safe—for instance, if we've cited a section of the law and you want to read the exact language or see whether that section has changed, there's no trick to looking up the law and reading it. But in general, be cautious when researching, and look at several sources to confirm your findings.

Immigration laws are federal, meaning they are written by the U.S. Congress and do not vary from one state to another (however, procedures and priorities for carrying out the laws may vary among USCIS offices in different cities or states, and federal courts in the various circuits may interpret the laws differently). Below we give you a rundown on the most accessible research tools—and not coincidentally, the ones that immigration lawyers most often use.

1. The Federal Code

The federal immigration law is found in Title 8 of the United States Code. Any law library (such as the one at your local courthouse or law school) should have a complete set of the U.S. Code (traditionally abbreviated as U.S.C.). The library may also have a separate volume containing exactly the same material, but called the Immigration and Nationality Act, or I.N.A.

Unfortunately, the two sets of laws are numbered a bit differently, and not all volumes of the I.N.A. cross-reference back to the U.S. Code, and vice versa. For this reason, when code citations are mentioned in this book, we include both the U.S.C. and I.N.A. numbers.

The easiest way to access the INA is at www.uscis.gov. (Click "Laws," then Immigration and Nationality Act.)

2. USCIS and State Department Regulations and Guidance

Another important source of immigration law is the Code of Federal Regulations, or C.F.R. Federal regulations are written by the agencies responsible for carrying out federal law. The regulations are meant to explain in greater detail just how the federal agency is going to carry out the law. You'll find the USCIS regulations at Title 8 of the C.F.R., and the Department of State regulations (relevant to anyone whose application is being decided at a U.S. consulate) at Title 22 of the C.F.R. The USCIS and Department of State regulations are helpful, but certainly don't have all the answers. Again, your local law library will have the C.F.R.s, as does the USCIS website.

If you are applying from overseas, you may also wish to look at the State Department's *Foreign Affairs Manual*. This is primarily meant to be an internal government document, containing instructions to the consulates on handling immigrant and nonimmigrant visa cases. However, it is available for public researching as well; your local law library may be able to find you a copy, or see the State Department's website, at http://travel.state.gov (under "Visas," click "Laws, Regulations, and Policy" and choose "Foreign Affairs Manual" from the dropdown menu).

3. Information on the Internet

If you have Internet access, you will want to familiarize yourself with the USCIS and State Department websites. The addresses are www.uscis.gov and http://travel.state.gov. The USCIS website offers advice on various immigration benefits and applications, downloads of most immigration forms, and current fees.

On the State Department website, most of the useful information is found under "Visas," including the monthly *Visa Bulletin,* links to U.S. embassies and consulates overseas, and downloads of a few consular forms.

The Internet is full of sites put up by immigration lawyers as well as immigrants. Because the quality of these sites varies widely, we don't even attempt to review them here. Many of the lawyers' sites are blatant attempts to give out only enough information to bring in business. The sites by other immigrants are well-meaning and can be good for finding out about people's experiences; but they're not reliable when it comes to hard legal or procedural facts.

That said, a couple of lawyer sites that contain useful information include www.shusterman.com (with regular news updates); www.visalaw.com (run by the firm of Siskind, Susser, Haas, & Devine, and including regular updates on immigration law matters); and www.ilw.com (the "Immigration Daily" website, which includes news and blogs from various attorneys).

4. Court Decisions

Immigrants who have been denied visas or green cards often appeal these decisions to the federal courts. The courts' decisions in these cases are supposed to govern the future behavior of USCIS and the consulates. However, your marriage-based visa case should never get to the point where you're discussing court decisions with a USCIS or State Department official, arguing that your case should (or should not) fit within a particular court decision. For one thing, the officials are not likely to listen until they get a specific directive from their superiors or the court decision is incorporated into their agency's regulations (the C.F.R.). For another thing, such discussions probably mean that your case has become complicated enough to need a lawyer. We do not attempt to teach you how to research federal court decisions here.

5. Legal Publications

Some high-quality and popular resources used by immigration lawyers include *Interpreter Releases,* a weekly update published by Thomson Reuters Westlaw; *Immigration Law and Procedure,* a multivolume, continually updated looseleaf set published by LexisNexis, and *Kurzban's Immigration Law Sourcebook,* published by AILA. Again, you should be able to find both at your local law library. Both are very well indexed. They are written for lawyers, so you'll have to wade through some technical terminology.

Internet Resources

This list summarizes the useful Internet sites that have been mentioned in this book.
- U.S. Citizenship and Immigration Services (USCIS): www.uscis.gov
- The U.S. Department of State: http://travel.state.gov
- U.S. consulates and embassies abroad: www.usembassy.gov
- Attorney Carl Shusterman: www.shusterman.com
- Siskind, Susser, Haas & Devine: www.visalaw.com
- "Immigration Daily" website: www.ilw.com.

Words You Will Need to Know

A-Number. An eight- or nine-digit number following the letter A (for Alien) that USCIS assigns to you when you apply for your green card. People who apply for certain other immigration benefits, or who are placed in removal proceedings, also receive an A-number. Once you are assigned this number, USCIS uses it to track your file. You should include it on any correspondence with USCIS.

Adjustment interview. Normally the final step in applying for adjustment of status or a green card within the United States. At the interview, a USCIS officer personally reviews the application, speaks with the applicant, and approves or denies the application.

Adjustment of status. The procedure for becoming a lawful permanent resident without having to leave the United States. Adjustment of status is available only to immigrants who fit certain eligibility criteria. Many immigrants will have to use the traditional method of gaining permanent residence, even if they already live in the United States, which involves applying for an immigrant visa at a U.S. consulate or embassy abroad (consular processing).

Alien. USCIS uses this term to refer to "a foreign-born person who is not a citizen or national of the United States." I.N.A. Section 101(a)(3); 8 U.S.C. Section 1101(a)(3). In other words, the word covers everyone from illegal aliens to green card holders. We don't use the term very much in this book, but you'll need to get used to the word if you do additional research.

Beneficiary. A person intending to immigrate to the United States, for whom a family member in the United States has filed a visa petition in order to sponsor the would-be immigrant.

Border Patrol. The informal name for an agency called Customs and Border Protection (CBP), which, like USCIS, is part of the Department of Homeland Security (DHS). Its primary functions include keeping the borders secure from illegal crossers, and meeting legal entrants at airports and border posts to check their passports and visas and decide whether they should be allowed into the United States.

Citizen (U.S.). A person who owes allegiance to the U.S. government, is entitled to its protection, and enjoys the highest level of rights due to members of U.S. society. People become U.S. citizens through their birth in the United States or its territories, through their parents, or through naturalization (applying for citizenship and passing the citizenship exam). Citizens cannot have their status taken away except for certain extraordinary reasons. See Nolo's website at www.nolo.com for more information.

Citizenship exam. The test that a lawful permanent resident must pass before he or she can become a U.S. citizen, covering the English language as well as U.S. civics, history, and government.

Conditional resident. A person whose status is almost identical to that of a lawful permanent resident, except that the status expires after a set period of time. Immigrants whose marriages to U.S. citizens haven't reached their second anniversary by the time they're approved for residency or enter the U.S. on their immigrant visa become conditional residents. Their residency will expire after another two years. USCIS may then approve the person for permanent residency. On rare occasions where it becomes apparent even before the two-year expiration date that the marriage was a sham, USCIS can terminate a conditional resident's status immediately (see I.N.A. Section 216(b)(1); 8 U.S.C. Section 1186a(b)(1)).

Consular interview. Normally the final major step in the process of applying for a green card from overseas. At the interview, a U.S. consular officer personally reviews the application, speaks with the applicant, and approves or denies an immigrant entry visa. (The U.S. border officer has the final say, however, in whether the entry visa can be exchanged for the green card or lawful permanent resident status.)

Consular processing. The green card application process for immigrants whose final interview and visa decision will happen at an overseas U.S. embassy or consulate.

Consulate. An office of the U.S. Department of State located overseas and affiliated with a U.S. embassy in that country's capital city. The consulate's responsibilities usually include processing visa applications.

Customs and Border Protection (CBP). See Border Patrol, above.

Department of Homeland Security (DHS). A government agency created in 2003 to handle immigration and other security-related issues. DHS became the umbrella agency encompassing USCIS, ICE, and CBP.

Department of Justice. An agency of the U.S. federal government that oversees the Immigration Courts.

Department of State. An agency of the United States federal government that oversees U.S. embassies and consulates.

Deport/Deportation. See Removal, below.

Deportable. An immigrant who falls into one of the grounds listed at I.N.A. Section 237; 8 U.S.C. Section 1227, is said to be deportable, and can be removed from the United States after a hearing in Immigration Court. Even a permanent resident can be deported.

Direct consular filing. A service provided at some U.S. consulates overseas, by which a person can submit all of the paperwork for a marriage-based visa directly to the consulate. This service saves the time that applicants must normally spend waiting for certain portions of their application to be approved by or transferred from USCIS offices in the United States.

EAD. See Employment Authorization Document, below.

Embassy. The chief U.S. consulate within a given country, usually located in the capital city. This is where the U.S. ambassador lives. Most of the embassies handle applications for visas to the United States.

Employment Authorization Document (EAD). More commonly called a work permit, this is a card with one's photo on it that indicates that the card holder has the right to work in the United States. Green card holders no longer need to have an EAD.

Executive Office for Immigration Review. See Immigration Court, below.

Expedited removal. This refers to the all-too-short and not-so-sweet procedures by which Customs and Border Patrol officers at U.S. borders and ports of entry may decide that a person cannot enter the United States. See I.N.A. Section 235(b); 8 U.S.C. Section 1225(b). The officers can refuse entry when they believe the person has used fraud or is carrying improper documents. People removed this way are barred from reentering the United States for five years.

Family Unity. A special program for spouses and children of people who received residency through Amnesty or Cuban/Haitian Adjustment in the late 1980s (Amnesty was a one-time program, benefiting people who had been living or doing farm work illegally in the United States). Through the Family Unity program, these family members receive a temporary right to live and work in the United States while waiting to become eligible for permanent residence through a family visa petition.

Field Office. One of 33 USCIS offices in the United States that serves the public in a specified geographical area. Field Offices are where most USCIS field staff are located. These offices usually have an information desk, provide USCIS forms, and accept and make decisions on some—but not all—applications for immigration benefits. For a list of locations, see the USCIS website at www.uscis.gov.

Fraud interview. A specialized USCIS interview in which one or both members of an engaged or married couple are examined separately to see whether their marriage is real, or just a sham to get the foreign-born person a green card. If both are interviewed, they will separately be asked the same set of questions, and their answers compared.

Green card. This slang term refers to the green identification card carried by lawful permanent residents of the United States. In this book, we also use it to refer to the card received by conditional residents. The USCIS name for the green card is an "I-551" or "Alien Registration Receipt Card." Don't confuse it with the other card often carried by noncitizens, the work permit or Employment Authorization Document.

Green card holder. This is the common slang term, used widely in this book, for an immigrant or a lawful resident, whether permanent or conditional.

I-94. A small green or white card that is placed in all nonimmigrants' passports when they enter the United States. The I-94 shows the date when the person's authorized stay expires. Many people wrongly believe that they can stay until the expiration date in their original visa. Unfortunately, it's the date in the I-94 that controls (although if the visa remains valid, the person may reenter the United States).

Illegal alien. Illegal alien is more of a slang term than a legal term, usually referring to people who have no permission to live in the United States. The preferred legal term is "undocumented person."

Immediate relative. An immediate relative is the spouse, parent, or unmarried child under age 21 of a U.S. citizen. Immediate relatives can apply for green cards without worrying about quotas or waiting periods. "Spouses" include widows and widowers who apply for the green card within two years of the U.S. citizen spouse's death. Parents must wait until their U.S. citizen child is age 21 to apply. Children can include stepchildren and adopted children (subject to further requirements).

Immigrant. Though the general public usually calls any foreign-born newcomer to the United States an immigrant, USCIS prefers to think of immigrants as including only those persons who have attained "permanent residency" or a green card. Everyone else is called a nonimmigrant, even though they're rightfully in the United States.

Immigration Court. Also known as the "Executive Office for Immigration Review" or "EOIR." This is the first court that will hear your case if you are placed in removal proceedings. Cases are heard by an "Immigration Judge," who doesn't hear any other type of case. USCIS has its own crew of trial attorneys who represent the agency in court.

Immigration and Customs Enforcement (ICE). This agency of the Department of Homeland Security handles enforcement of the immigration laws within the U.S. borders.

Immigration and Nationality Act (I.N.A.). A portion of the federal code containing all the immigration laws. The I.N.A. is also contained in the United States Code (U.S.C.) at Title 8. You can find the I.N.A. at www.uscis.gov.

Immigration and Naturalization Service (INS). Formerly, a branch of the United States Department of Justice, responsible for controlling the United States borders, enforcing the immigration laws, and processing and judging the cases of immigrants living in the United States. However, in 2003, the INS was absorbed into the Department of Homeland Security, and its functions divided between U.S. Citizenship and Immigration Services (USCIS), Customs and Border Protection (CBP), and Immigration and Customs Enforcement (ICE).

Inadmissible. A person to whom the U.S. government will deny a visa, green card, or admission to the United States because he or she falls into one of the categories listed at I.N.A. Section 212; 8 U.S.C. Section 1182. Broadly speaking, these categories of inadmissibility cover people who might be a burden on or risk to the U.S. government or public for health, security, or financial reasons. Replaces the formerly used term "excludable." Green card holders who leave the United States for 180 days or more can also be found inadmissible upon attempting to return.

K-1 visa. The State Department's name for a fiancé visa.

K-2 visa. The State Department's name for the visa given to unmarried children under age 21 who accompany someone on a K-1 fiancé visa.

K-3 visa. The State Department's name for the new visa (added by Congress in December 2000) for already-married persons who would prefer to use a so-called fiancé visa as a faster mode of entering the United States. They often apply to adjust status.

K-4 visa. Given to children of K-3 visa holders.

Lawful permanent resident. See Permanent resident, below.

National Visa Center (NVC). An intermediary office responsible for receiving the files of approved visa petition applicants from the various USCIS Service Centers, sending the applicants instructions and requests for forms and fees, and ultimately transferring the cases to overseas U.S. consulates. In some cases, the NVC may hold onto an applicant's files for years, while the immigrant is on the waiting list for a visa.

Naturalization. When an immigrant succeeds in attaining U.S. citizenship through submitting an application and passing the citizenship exam, he or she is said to have "naturalized."

Nonimmigrant. A broad term meant to cover everyone who comes to the United States temporarily. Most nonimmigrants have a specific expiration date attached to their stay. Some others may stay for the "duration of status," or "D/S," such as students, who can stay until they complete their education.

NVC. See National Visa Center, above.

Permanent residence. The status of being a permanent resident; see below.

Permanent resident. A "green card holder." Also called a "lawful permanent resident." This is a person who has been approved to live in the United States for an unlimited amount of time. However, the status can be taken away for certain reasons, such as having committed a crime or made one's home outside the United States. Though the green card itself needs to be renewed every ten years, the actual status doesn't expire. After a certain number of years (usually five), a permanent resident can apply for U.S. citizenship. But many people remain in the United States for decades without applying for citizenship. Although they cannot vote, permanent residents enjoy many other rights, such as the right to work and travel freely.

Petitioner. Someone who has filed a visa petition in order to sponsor a family member to immigrate to the United States.

Public charge. The immigration law term for an immigrant who has insufficient financial support and goes on welfare or other need-based government assistance. Likelihood of becoming a public charge is a ground of inadmissibility.

Removal. A new immigration law term combining the former terms "exclusion" and "deportation." Removal means the process of sending an alien back to his or her home country because he or she is (or has become) inadmissible or deportable. (Before the laws changed a few years ago, "exclusion" meant sending a person back before they'd entered the United States, and "deportation" meant sending someone away who was already in the United States.)

Resident. Someone who is residing legally in the United States, whether temporarily, permanently, or conditionally.

Service Center. A USCIS office responsible for accepting and making decisions on particular applications from people in specified geographical areas. Unlike USCIS Field Offices, Service

Centers are not open to the public; all communication must be by letter, with limited telephone access. Though inconvenient to work with, you often have no choice—an application that must be decided by a Service Center will not be accepted or decided by a Field Office. For information on Service Center locations, see Appendix B, call the USCIS information line at 800-375-5283, or see the USCIS website at www.uscis.gov.

Sponsor (noun). The traditional but nonlegal term for a Petitioner. In this book, we use "sponsor" more narrowly to refer to someone who is sponsoring an immigrant financially (by signing an Affidavit of Support on the immigrant's behalf).

Sponsor (verb). To "sponsor" an immigrant is the traditional term for "petitioning" the person to come to the United States—that is, initiating a process allowing the immigrant to apply for legal admission and/or status by virtue of a family relation to the sponsor.

Status. In the USCIS's vocabulary, to have "status" means to have a legal right (temporary or permanent) to remain in the United States. For example, green card holders have "permanent resident" status; people on student visas are in student status.

Summary exclusion. See Expedited removal.

Time bars. The common name for the three or ten years that a person may have to spend outside the United States as a penalty for having previously been present there unlawfully for six months or more. See Chapter 2, Section A, for details.

United States Code. See Immigration and Nationality Act, above.

Unlawful time. "Unlawful" is a legal term referring to time spent in the United States without documents, an unexpired visa, or any other legal right to be here. How much time a person has spent in the United States unlawfully has become extremely significant within immigration law, for reasons explained in Chapter 2, Section A.

Visa. A right to enter the United States. Physically, the visa usually appears as a stamp in the applicant's passport, given by a United States consulate overseas. In some cases, the visa is used only to enter the United States, at which time the visa is immediately exchanged for a "status" (such as that of permanent resident); in other cases a person's entire stay in the United States is covered by a visa (such as a tourist or student visa). Sometimes, however, you'll hear the terms "visa" and "status" used as if they were interchangeable—in part reflecting the fact that immigrants switching to a new status within the United States are technically granted a visa, or at least a visa number, although they may never see it. Different types of visas have different names, usually with letter codes. For example, a "B" visa is a visitor visa; an "F" visa is a student visa.

Visa petition. In the context of this book, the first application filed by a U.S. citizen or lawful permanent resident petitioner, which starts the process of bringing their family member to the United States as an immigrant. This application is sometimes referred to by its form number, I-130.

Visa Waiver Program. A program that allows citizens of certain countries to enter the United States without a visa and stay for up to 90 days. For details and a list of countries, see http://travel.state.gov, or talk to your local U.S. consulate.

Waiver. An application that a hopeful immigrant files with USCIS, usually on Form I-601, asking them to overlook, or forgive, something that would normally make that person inadmissible, ineligible for an immigration benefit or for entry to the United States. Only certain problems can be waived.

Work permit. See Employment Authorization Document (EAD), above.

Table of Visas and Immigration Benefits

Immigrant Visas (for Permanent Resident Status)

Type of Visa or Benefit	Basis for Eligibility
Family Based	
Immediate Relative	Minor unmarried children or spouses of a U.S. citizen; parent of an over-21-year-old U.S. citizen.
First Preference	Unmarried adult child of a U.S. citizen.
Second Preference: 2A	Spouses and unmarried sons and daughters of lawful permanent residents.
Second Preference: 2B	Unmarried sons and daughters, over the age of 21, of lawful permanent residents.
Third Preference	Married sons and daughters of U.S. citizens.
Fourth Preference	Brothers and sisters of U.S. citizens.
Employment Based	
First Preference	Priority workers who have "extraordinary ability" or are "outstanding professors and researchers" in their field. Also certain multinational executives and managers.
Second Preference	"Members of the professions holding advanced degrees" or "aliens of exceptional ability" in their field.
Third Preference	Skilled workers (2 years' training or experience), professionals, and "other workers" (capable of performing unskilled, but not temporary or seasonal labor).
Fourth Preference	Special immigrants including ministers, religious workers, former U.S. government employees, and others.
Fifth Preference	Investors in job-creating enterprises in the U.S. ($500,000 to $1 million).
Other Benefits or Remedies	
Refugees and Asylees	People who fear persecution in their home country based on their race, religion, nationality, political opinion, or membership in a particular social group. Refugees are processed overseas, asylees within the United States.
"NACARA" for Nicaraguans and Cubans	An amnesty-like program for Nicaraguans and Cubans who entered the United States before December 1, 1995.
"NACARA" Suspension of Deportation	For Salvadorans, Guatemalans, and nationals of several former Soviet and Eastern European countries who entered the United States before 1990 (exact date varies by country) and who applied for asylum, "ABC," or Temporary Protected Status by certain dates; they can apply for "suspension of deportation," described below.
Suspension of Deportation	A remedy normally only available to persons placed in deportation proceedings before April 1, 1997. If the person can prove that he or she has lived in the United States for seven continuous years, has had good moral character, and that the person's deportation would cause extreme hardship to his or her self or his or her spouse, parent, or children who are U.S. citizens or permanent residents, a judge can grant the person permanent residency.

Immigrant Visas (for Permanent Resident Status) (continued)	
Type of Visa or Benefit	**Basis for Eligibility**
Other Benefits or Remedies (continued)	
Cancellation of Removal	A remedy only available to persons in removal proceedings. If the person can prove that he or she has lived in the United States for ten continuous years, has good moral character, hasn't been convicted of certain crimes, and that his or her deportation would cause exceptional and extreme hardship to his or her lawful permanent resident or U.S. citizen spouse, child, or parent, then a judge may approve the person for permanent residency.
"VAWA" Cancellation of Removal	For spouses and children of U.S. citizens and permanent residents who have been battered or been victims of extreme cruelty. If such persons can prove that they not only fall into this category but have lived continuously in the United States for three years, have been of good moral character and not committed certain crimes, and that their removal would cause extreme hardship to them, their child, or (if the applicant is a child), their parent, a judge may approve them for permanent residency.
Registry	People who have lived in the United States continuously since January 1, 1972 can apply to adjust status to permanent residence.
Temporary Protected Status	People from certain Congressionally designated countries experiencing war or civil strife; they may apply for a temporary right to stay in the United States until conditions in their home country have improved.

Nonimmigrant Visas (Summary List)	
Type of Visa or Benefit	**Basis for Eligibility**
A-1	Diplomatic employees
A-2	Officials or employees of foreign governments
B-1	Business visitors
B-2	Tourists or visitors for medical treatment
C-1 "Transit visa"	For passing through at a U.S. airport or seaport
D-1 "Crewmember"	For people serving on a ship or plane, landing or docking temporarily
E-1	Treaty Traders
E-2	Treaty Investors
F-1, F-2	Students (academic), including at colleges, universities, seminaries, conservatories, academic high schools, other academic institutions, and in language training; and their spouses and children
F-2	Spouses and children of F-1 visa holders
F-3	Citizens or residents of Mexico or Canada commuting to the U.S. to attend an academic school
G-1	Employees of international organizations who are representing foreign governments; and their spouses and children
H-1B	Temporary professionals (for specialty occupations such as doctors, engineers, physical therapists, computer professionals; must have at least a bachelor's degree)
H-1C	Nurses who will work for up to three years in areas of the U.S. where health professionals are recognized as being in short supply
H-2A	Temporary agricultural workers coming to the U.S. to fill positions for which a temporary shortage of American workers has been recognized by the U.S. Department of Agriculture
H-2B	Temporary agricultural workers
H-3	Trainees coming for temporary job training
I-1	Representatives of international media
J-1, J-2	Exchange visitors; and their spouses and children
K-1, K-2	Fiancées and fiancés of U.S. citizens and their children
K-3, K-4	Spouses of U.S. citizens awaiting approval of their marriage-based visa petition and a green card, and their children
L-1, L-2	Intracompany transferees working as executives, managers, or persons with specialized knowledge; and their spouses and children
M-1, M-2	Vocational students; and their spouses and children
M-3	Citizens or residents of Mexico or Canada commuting to the U.S. to attend vocational school
N-8	Parents of certain special immigrants

Nonimmigrant Visas (continued)	
Type of Visa or Benefit	**Basis for Eligibility**
N-9	Children of certain special immigrants
NATO-1, NATO-2, NATO-3, NATO-4, and NATO-5	Associates coming to the U.S. under applicable provisions of the NATO Treaty; and their spouses and children
NATO-6	Civilians accompanying military forces on missions authorized under the NATO Treaty
NATO-7	Attendants, servants, or personal employees of NATO-1 through NATO-6 visa holders
O-1, O-2	People with extraordinary ability in sciences, arts, business, athletics, or education, and their support staff
P-1	Internationally recognized entertainers, performers, and athletes, and their support staff
P-2	Cultural exchange entertainers
P-3	Artists and entertainers in groups presenting culturally unique programs
P-4	Spouses and children of P-1, P-2, and P-3 visa holders
Q-1	Exchange visitors in cultural exchange programs
Q-2	Participants in the Irish Peace Process Cultural and Training Program (Walsh visas)
Q-3	Spouses and children of Q-1 visa holders
R-1, R-2	Religious leaders and workers; and their spouses and children
S-5	Witnesses in a criminal investigation
S-6	People coming to the U.S. to provide information about a terrorist organization
T-1, T-2, T-3	Women and children who are in the United States because they are victims of human trafficking, cooperating with law enforcement; and their spouses and children
U-1, U-2, U-3	Victims of criminal abuse in the United States who are assisting law enforcement authorities; and their spouses and children
V	Spouses and unmarried sons and daughters (2A) of U.S. lawful permanent residents who have already waited three years for approval of their visa petition or the availability of a green card, and whose visa petition was on file by December 21, 2000

USCIS Application Processing Addresses

The following is a list of the USCIS addresses to which you may need to send certain USCIS forms, including Forms I-129F (for a K-1 visa), I-130, I-765, and I-751.

Most of the Service Centers designate different Post Office boxes for receipt of the different forms, so always check this list before sending a new form. (In the future, if you need to submit forms not covered by this book, you'll need to see the USCIS website at www.uscis.gov for the appropriate address. If you do not have Internet access, call the USCIS information line at 800-375-5283.)

An I-129F for a K-1 visa or I-130 visa petition should be sent to the USCIS Service Center or lockbox office that covers the region where the U.S. petitioner lives. An I-751 petition should be sent to the Service Center that covers the region where the immigrant spouse lives (hopefully at the same address as the petitioning spouse).

Note: For K-3 visa petitions on Form I-129F, follow the instructions provided in Chapter 7 of this book.

Where to Send the Form I-129F Visa Petition (no matter where you live)	
For U.S. Postal Service (USPS) deliveries:	For private couriers (non-USPS) deliveries:
USCIS P.O. Box 660151 Dallas, TX 75266	USCIS Attn: I-129F 2501 South State Highway 121 Business Suite 400 Lewisville, TX 75067

Form I-130 Visa Petition (when submitted alone, not concurrently with I-485 application for adjustment of status)

If the U.S. petitioner lives in:	Send Form I-130 to:
Alaska, American Samoa, Arizona, California, Colorado, Florida, Guam, Hawaii, Idaho, Kansas, Montana, Nebraska, Nevada, New Mexico, North Dakota, Northern Mariana Islands, Oklahoma, Oregon, Puerto Rico, South Dakota, Texas, Utah, Virgin Islands, Washington, Wyoming	**USCIS Phoenix Lockbox** For U.S. Postal Service (USPS) deliveries: USCIS ATTN: I-130 P.O. Box 21700 Phoenix, AZ 85036 For Express Mail and courier deliveries: USCIS Attn: I-130 1820 E. Skyharbor Circle S Suite 100 Phoenix, AZ 85034
Alabama, Arkansas, Connecticut, Delaware, District of Columbia, Georgia, Illinois, Indiana, Iowa, Kentucky, Louisiana, Maine, Maryland, Massachusetts, Michigan, Minnesota, Mississippi, Missouri, New Hampshire, New Jersey, New York, North Carolina, Ohio, Pennsylvania, Rhode Island, South Carolina, Tennessee, Vermont, Virginia, West Virginia, Wisconsin	**USCIS Chicago Lockbox** For U.S. Postal Service: USCIS P.O. Box 804625 Chicago, IL 60680-4107 For Express Mail and courier deliveries: USCIS Attn: I-130 131 South Dearborn–3rd Floor Chicago, IL 60603-5517
A country outside the United States	**USCIS Chicago Lockbox** For U.S. Postal Service: USCIS P.O. Box 804625 Chicago, IL 60680-4107 For Express Mail and courier deliveries: USCIS Attn: I-130 131 South Dearborn–3rd Floor Chicago, IL 60603-5517

Form I-751			
If the U.S. petitioner lives in:			**Send Form I-751 to:**
Alabama	Maryland	Puerto Rico	USCIS Vermont Service Center
Arkansas	Massachusetts	Rhode Island	75 Lower Welden Street
Connecticut	Mississippi	South Carolina	P.O. Box 200
Delaware	New Hampshire	Tennessee	Saint Albans, VT 05479-0001
District of Columbia	New Jersey	Texas	
Florida	New Mexico	Vermont	
Georgia	New York	Virginia	
Kentucky	North Carolina	U.S. Virgin Islands	
Louisiana	Oklahoma	West Virginia	
Maine	Pennsylvania		
Alaska	Indiana	North Dakota	USCIS California Service Center
American Samoa	Iowa	Ohio	P.O. Box 10751
Arizona	Kansas	Oregon	Laguna Niguel, CA 92607-1075
California	Michigan	South Dakota	
Colorado	Minnesota	Utah	
Guam	Missouri	Washington	
Hawaii	Montana	Wisconsin	
Idaho	Nebraska	Wyoming	
Illinois	Nevada		

Form I-765 (for K-1 fiancé visa applicants)

If you live in:			Send Form I-765 to:
Alaska	Kansas	Ohio	For U.S. Postal Service (USPS) deliveries:
Arizona	Michigan	Oregon	USCIS
California	Minnesota	South Dakota	P.O. Box 21281
Colorado	Missouri	Utah	Phoenix, AZ 85036
Hawaii	Montana	Washington	For Express Mail and courier deliveries:
Idaho	Nebraska	Wisconsin	USCIS
Illinois	Nevada	Wyoming	Attn: AOS
Indiana	North Dakota	Guam	1820 E. Skyharbor Circle S
Iowa	Northern Mariana Islands		Suite 100
			Phoenix, AZ 85034
Alabama	Maryland	Rhode Island	For U.S. Postal Service (USPS) deliveries:
Arkansas	Massachusetts	South Carolina	USCIS
Connecticut	Mississippi	Oklahoma	P.O. Box 660867
Delaware	New Hampshire	Tennessee	Dallas, TX 75266
District of Columbia	New Jersey	Texas	For Express Mail and courier deliveries:
Florida	New Mexico	Vermont	USCIS
Georgia	New York	Virginia	Attn: AOS
Kentucky	North Carolina	U.S. Virgin Islands	2501 S. State Hwy. 121 Business
Louisiana	Pennsylvania	West Virginia	Suite 400
Maine	Puerto Rico		Lewisville, TX 75067

Form I-485 (no matter where you live)	
For U.S. Postal Service (USPS) deliveries:	**For private couriers (non-USPS) deliveries**
USCIS P.O. Box 805887 Chicago, IL 60680-4120	USCIS Attn: FBAS 131 South Dearborn, 3rd Floor Chicago, IL 60603-5157

Tear-Out Checklists

Checklists for Chapter 5, Overseas Fiancés of U.S. Citizens:

Checklist for K-1 Fiancé Visa Petition

Checklist for Fiancé Mailing to Consulate

Checklist for Fiancé Appointment Package

Checklists for Chapter 7, Overseas Spouses of U.S. Citizens:

Checklist for Marriage-Based Immigrant Visa Petition

Checklist for Immigrant Visa Forms and Documents

Checklist for K-3 Visa Petition

Checklist of Forms K-3 Applicant Mails In

Checklist for K-3 Appointment Package

Checklists for Chapter 8, Overseas Spouses of Lawful Permanent Residents:

Checklist for Visa Petition by Lawful Permanent Resident

Checklist for Immigrant Visa Forms and Documents

Checklist for Chapter 11, Spouses of U.S. Citizens, Living in the U.S.:

Checklist for Visa Petition by U.S. Citizen

Checklist for Chapter 12, Spouses of Permanent Residents, In the U.S.:

Checklist for Visa Petition by Lawful Permanent Resident

Checklists for Chapter 14, Applying for a Green Card at a USCIS Office:

Checklist for Adjustment of Status Packet

Checklist for Applying for Advance Parole

Checklist for Adjustment of Status Interview

Checklist for Chapter 16, After You Get Your Green Card:

Checklist for Filing Joint Petition to Remove Conditions on Residence

Checklist for K-1 Fiancé Visa Petition

☐ Form I-129F

☐ Form G-325A (one filled out by you and one by your fiancé)

☐ A color photo of you (passport style)

☐ A color photo of your fiancé (passport style)

☐ Fee (currently $340; double-check at www.uscis.gov)

☐ Proof of the U.S. citizenship of your petitioner: a birth certificate, passport, naturalization certificate, or Report of Birth Abroad of a United States Citizen

☐ Proof that the two of you are legally able to marry

☐ A statement written by your U.S. citizen petitioner describing how you met

☐ Proof that the two of you have met within the last two years, or that you qualify for an exception to this requirement

☐ Additional proof that the two of you truly intend to marry, whether or not you have met in person

☐ If the U.S. citizen petitioner has ever been convicted of certain crimes, certified copies of police and court records showing the outcome (get a lawyer's help)

☐ If the U.S. citizen has filed two or more K-1 visa petitions for other immigrants in the past (no matter how long ago), or had a K-1 visa petition approved for another immigrant within the two years before filing your petition, a letter requesting a waiver (get a lawyer's help)

Checklist for Fiancé Mailing to Consulate	
☐ Form DS-156 (prepared in duplicate) ☐ Form DS-156K (filled in but unsigned)	☐ Form DS-230, Part I

Checklist for Fiancé Appointment Package

- ☐ Original USCIS Notice of Action approving your K-1, or fiancé, visa petition

- ☐ A complete copy of your Fiancé Visa Petition (the items in the checklist in Chapter 5, Section F2) in case USCIS did not forward it to the consulate

- ☐ Originals of documents submitted in connection with the visa petition, such as your fiancé's U.S. birth certificate and proof that any previous marriages were legally ended

- ☐ Form DS-230, Part II

- ☐ Form I-134, Affidavit of Support, if the consulate requested it

  - ☐ Documents to accompany Form I-134, including:

  - ☐ Proof of U.S. citizen's employment

  - ☐ Copy of U.S. citizen's most recent federal tax return(s)

- ☐ Letter from U.S. citizen's bank(s) confirming the account(s)

- ☐ Form DS-1858, Sponsor's Financial Responsibility Under the Social Security Act (if the consulate requests it)

- ☐ A valid passport from your home country, good for at least six months

- ☐ Your original birth certificate

- ☐ An original police clearance certificate, if this is available in your country (the instructions from the consulate will tell you)

- ☐ Three additional photographs of you, the immigrating fiancé (according to the consulate's photo instructions)

- ☐ Fingerprints (you'll receive instructions from the consulate)

- ☐ Results of your medical examination, in an unopened envelope, unless the doctor sent the results directly to the consulate

- ☐ Additional documents proving your relationship (to cover the time period since submitting the fiancé visa petition), such as copies of:

  - ☐ phone bills showing calls to one another

  - ☐ correspondence between you

  - ☐ photos taken together while one fiancé visited the other

- ☐ Any other items or forms requested by the consulate

- ☐ Visa Application fee (currently $240). In some countries, you may also be charged an issuance fee if your visa is approved

Checklist for Marriage-Based Immigrant Visa Petition

This checklist shows every form, document, and other item needed for the initial visa petition that your spouse, with your help, will assemble and submit to USCIS.

- ☐ Form I-130
- ☐ Documents to accompany Form I-130:
  - ☐ Your marriage certificate
  - ☐ Proof of the U.S. citizen status of your petitioning spouse
  - ☐ Proof of termination of all previous marriages, such as a copy of a death, divorce, or annulment certificate
- ☐ One color photo of you
- ☐ One color photo of your spouse
- ☐ Fee: currently $420 but double-check this at www.uscis.gov
- ☐ Form G-325A, Biographic Information, filled out by you
- ☐ Form G-325A, Biographic Information, filled out by your spouse

Checklist for Immigrant Visa Forms and Documents

This checklist lists the forms, documents, and other items that your spouse, with your help, will need to assemble.

☐ Form DS 230, Parts I and II

☐ Form I-864, Affidavit of Support

☐ Documents to accompany Form I-864:

　☐ A copy of your spouse/sponsor's federal income tax returns for the last one to three years, with W-2s

　☐ Proof of your sponsor's current employment

　☐ A list of assets, (the sponsor's and/or the immigrant's) if they must be used to meet the *Poverty Guidelines'* minimum

　☐ Proof of ownership of assets (the sponsor's and/or the immigrant's), if any were listed

　☐ If sponsor or sponsor's dependents have used financial need-based public benefits in the last three years, a list of the programs and dates of receipt

☐ Form I-864A, Contract Between Sponsor and Household Member (only needed if sponsor's income is insufficient)

☐ Documents to accompany Form I-864A:

　☐ Proof that the household joint sponsors live with the primary sponsor

　☐ Proof that the household joint sponsors are related to the primary sponsor (if they're not already listed as dependents on the sponsor's tax return)

　☐ Copies of the household joint sponsors' tax returns for the last one to three years

☐ Proof of the household joint sponsors' employment

☐ Proof of ownership of household joint sponsors' assets, if any were listed

☐ If the household joint sponsors or their dependents have used financial need-based public benefits in the last three years, a list of the benefits programs and dates of receipt

☐ If you're exempt from the Affidavit of Support requirement, Form I-864W, together with a certified statement of your Social Security earnings history

☐ Other documents:

　☐ Original and one photocopy of your birth certificate

　☐ Original and one photocopy of your marriage certificate

　☐ If applicable, original and one photocopy of proof of termination of all previous marriages, such as a death, divorce, or annulment certificate

　☐ Original INS or USCIS notice of approved I-130 (Form I-797)

　☐ Two color photographs of you (passport style)

　☐ Police Certificate, if available in your country

　☐ Military records, if applicable

　☐ Court and prison records, if applicable

☐ Fees (currently $230, plus a $74 security surcharge)

Checklist for K-3 Visa Petition

☐ Form I-129F

☐ Form G-325A (one filled out by you and one by your spouse, identical to the G-325As you already filled out to accompany the Form I-130 visa petition)

☐ Proof that U.S. citizen already filed Form I-130 Visa Petition with USCIS (a copy of I-797 receipt notice is best)

☐ A color photo of you (passport style)

☐ A color photo of your spouse (passport style)

☐ Proof of U.S. citizenship of U.S. citizen spouse

Checklist of Forms K-3 Applicant Mails In

☐ Form DS-156 Part I	☐ Form DS-156K

Checklist for K-3 Appointment Package

- ☐ Original INS or USCIS Notice of Action approving your I-129F visa petition

- ☐ A complete copy of your I-129F visa petition (the items in the checklist earlier) in case USCIS did not forward it to the consulate

- ☐ Originals of documents submitted in connection with the I-129F visa petition, such as your spouse's U.S. birth certificate and proof that any previous marriages were legally ended, and photocopies of each original

- ☐ Two copies of Form DS-156, nonimmigrant visa application

- ☐ One copy of Form DS-156K, nonimmigrant fiancé visa application form

- ☐ Form I-134, Affidavit of Support, if the consulate requested it

- ☐ Documents to accompany Form I-134, including:
  - ☐ Proof of U.S. citizen's employment
  - ☐ Copy of U.S. citizen's federal tax return(s)
  - ☐ Letter from U.S. citizen's bank confirming the account

- ☐ A valid passport from your home country, good for at least six months after the interview

- ☐ Your original birth certificate plus a copy, and birth certificates for any children who will be accompanying you

- ☐ An original police clearance certificate, if this is available in your country (the instructions from the consulate will tell you)

- ☐ Your original marriage certificate

- ☐ Two color photos of you, the immigrating fiancé, passport style

- ☐ Your medical examination, in an unopened envelope

- ☐ Fingerprints (you will receive instructions from the consulate)

- ☐ Proof that your marriage is the real thing

- ☐ Any other items or forms requested by the consulate

- ☐ Nonimmigrant visa application fee (currently $240)

Checklist for Visa Petition by Lawful Permanent Resident

- ☐ Form I-130

- ☐ Documents to accompany Form I-130:

  - ☐ Proof of the U.S. permanent resident status of your petitioning spouse

  - ☐ Your marriage certificate

  - ☐ Proof of termination of all previous marriages, yours or your spouse's, such as certificates of death, divorce, or annulment

- ☐ One color photo of you (passport style)

- ☐ One color photo of your spouse (passport style)

- ☐ Fee: currently $420

- ☐ Form G-325A, Biographic Information, filled out by you

- ☐ Form G-325A, Biographic Information, filled out by your spouse

Checklist for Immigrant Visa Forms and Documents

- ☐ Form DS 230 Parts I and II

- ☐ Form I-864, Affidavit of Support

- ☐ Documents to accompany Form I-864:

  - ☐ A copy of your spouse/sponsor's federal income tax returns for the last one to three years, with W-2s

  - ☐ Proof of your sponsor's current employment

  - ☐ A list of assets, (the sponsor's and/or the immigrant's) if they're being used to meet the *Poverty Guidelines*' minimum

  - ☐ Proof of ownership of assets (the sponsor's and/or the immigrant's), if any were listed

  - ☐ If sponsor or sponsor's dependents have used financial need-based public benefits in the last three years, a list of the programs and dates of receipt

- ☐ Form I-864A, Contract Between Sponsor and Household Member (only needed if sponsor's income is insufficient)

- ☐ Documents to accompany Form I-864A:

  - ☐ Proof that the household joint sponsors live with the primary sponsor

  - ☐ Proof that the household joint sponsors are related to the primary sponsor (if they're not already listed as dependents on the sponsor's tax return)

  - ☐ Copies of the household joint sponsors' tax returns for the last one to three years

- ☐ Proof of the household joint sponsors' employment

- ☐ Proof of ownership of household joint sponsors' assets, if any were listed

- ☐ If the household joint sponsor or their dependents have used financial need-based public benefits in the last three years, a list of the benefits programs and dates of receipt

- ☐ If you're exempt from the Affidavit of Support requirement, Form I-864W, together with a certified statement of your Social Security earnings history

- ☐ Additional documents to accompany forms:

  - ☐ Original and one photocopy of your birth certificate

  - ☐ Original and one photocopy of your marriage certificate

  - ☐ If applicable, original and one photocopy of proof of termination of all previous marriages

  - ☐ Original INS or USCIS notice of approved I-130 (Form I-797)

  - ☐ Two color photographs of you (passport style)

  - ☐ Police Certificate, if available in your country

  - ☐ Military records, if applicable

  - ☐ Court and prison records, if applicable

  - ☐ Fees (currently $230 plus a $74 security surcharge)

Checklist for Visa Petition by U. S. Citizen

☐ Form I-130

☐ Documents to accompany Form I-130 (photocopies only):

  ☐ Your marriage certificate

  ☐ Proof of the U.S. citizenship status of your petitioning spouse, such as a birth certificate, passport, certificate of naturalization, or Form FS-20 (Report of Birth Abroad of a United States Citizen)

  ☐ Proof of termination of all previous marriages, such as certificates of death, divorce, or annulment

☐ One color photo of you; passport style

☐ One color photo of your spouse (passport style), and

☐ Fees: Currently $420 for an I-130, but double-check this at www.uscis.gov or call 800-375-5283

☐ Form G-325A, Biographic Information, filled out by you

☐ Form G-325A, Biographic Information, filled out by your U. S. citizen spouse

Checklist for Visa Petition by Lawful Permanent Resident

☐ Form I-130

☐ Documents to accompany Form I-130:

    ☐ Proof of the U.S. permanent resident status of your petitioning spouse, such as a copy of his or her green card (front and back) or of the stamp placed in his or her passport to indicate permanent resident status

    ☐ Your marriage certificate

    ☐ Proof of termination of all previous marriages, yours or your spouse's, such as certificates of death, divorce, or annulment

☐ One color photo of you (passport style)

☐ One color photo of your spouse (passport style)

☐ Fees: $420 currently, but double-check at www.uscis.gov

☐ Form G-325A, Biographic Information, filled out by you

☐ Form G-325A, Biographic Information, filled out by your spouse

Checklist for Adjustment of Status Packet

- ☐ One of the following:

  - ☐ a copy of the INS or USCIS approval notice if you already submitted Form I-130, Petition for Alien Relative (most likely in cases where your spouse is a permanent resident), or

  - ☐ a copy of your previously filed Form I-129F and USCIS approval notice (which you'll have if you entered the United States on a fiancé visa), or

  - ☐ Form I-130 itself, with additional documents and forms (which you should have completed according to instructions in Chapter 11 or 12, whichever was applicable)

  - ☐ Form(s) G-325A, filled out by you, the immigrant, and by your spouse if he or she hasn't already submitted one

  - ☐ Form I-485, Application to Register Permanent Residence or Adjust Status

  - ☐ Form I-485, Supplement A, for people who must pay a penalty fee in order to use adjustment of status as an application procedure

  - ☐ Form I-693, Medical Exam (unless you entered as a fiancé, in which case your earlier medical exam is all you need, and USCIS will have it on file)

  - ☐ If you're exempt from the Affidavit of Support requirement, Form I-864W (to explain why you don't need to fill out Form I-864)

  - ☐ Form I-864 or I-864EZ, Affidavit of Support Under Section 213A of the Act

- ☐ Documents to accompany Form I-864:

  - ☐ A copy of your spouse or sponsor's federal income tax returns for the last year, with W-2

  - ☐ Proof of your sponsor's current employment

  - ☐ A list of assets (the sponsor's and/or the immigrant's), if they're being used to prove financial capacity

  - ☐ Proof of location and ownership of any listed assets (including the sponsor's and the immigrant's)

  - ☐ A list of the financial need-based public benefits programs and dates of receipt, if sponsor or sponsor's dependents have used such programs within the last three years

  - ☐ Form I-864A, Contract Between Sponsor and Household Member, if needed because primary sponsor lacks financial capacity

- ☐ Documents to accompany Form I-864A:

  - ☐ Proof that the household joint sponsors live with the primary sponsor

  - ☐ Proof that the household joint sponsors are related to the primary sponsor (if they're not already listed as dependents on the primary sponsor's tax return)

  - ☐ Copies of the household joint sponsors' financial information (tax return for the last year, proof of employment, proof of the ownership, value, and location of assets, if any were listed, and a list of need-based public benefits programs and dates of receipt, if used in the last three years)

  - ☐ I-765, Application for Employment Authorization

  - ☐ Proof that you are eligible to use the adjustment of status procedure

  - ☐ A copy of your birth certificate, with certified translation

- ☐ Two photos of you (passport style)

- ☐ Application fees (currently $1,070 for most adults, but see USCIS website, www.uscis.gov)

Checklist for Applying for Advance Parole

☐ Form I-131

☐ A separate sheet of paper, in accordance with Part 7 of the application form, explaining how you qualify for Advance Parole and why your application deserves to be approved (no need to spend too much time on this—most requests are approved without question)

☐ If you are traveling because of an emergency, evidence to prove it

☐ Copy of the receipt notice you got when you filed your adjustment of status packet (if you are filing your I-131 after already having filed your I-485)

☐ Copy of a photo ID, such as a driver's license

☐ Two color photos of you, passport style

☐ Fee: there is no fee as long as your I-485 is pending

Checklist for Adjustment of Status Interview

- ☐ Photo identification/passport
- ☐ Original documents for review/comparison with copies
- ☐ Updates to material in the application
- ☐ Proof that your marriage is bona fide

Checklist for Filing Joint Petition to Remove Conditions on Residence

Here's what you'll need to assemble for your joint petition to remove the conditions on your residency and become a permanent resident:

- ☐ Form I-751
- ☐ Required supporting documents, including:

- ☐ Application fee (currently $505, but fees change often so double-check this at www.uscis.gov, or by calling 800-375-5283); you can mail a check or money order
- ☐ Biometrics fee (for photos and fingerprints; currently $85)

Index

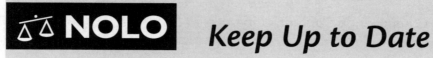
NOLO   *Keep Up to Date*

1 Go to Nolo.com/newsletters to sign up for free newsletters and discounts on Nolo products.

- **Nolo's Special Offer.** A monthly newsletter with the biggest Nolo discounts around.

- **Landlord's Quarterly.** Deals and free tips for landlords and property managers.

2 Don't forget to check for updates. Find this book at **Nolo.com** and click "Legal Updates."

Let Us Hear From You

3 Register your Nolo product and give us your feedback at Nolo.com/customer-support/productregistration.

- Once you've registered, you qualify for technical support if you have any trouble with a download (though most folks don't).

- We'll send you a coupon for 15% off your next Nolo.com order!

IMAR7

⚖ NOLO and USA TODAY

Cutting-Edge Content, Unparalleled Expertise

The Busy Family's Guide to Money
by Sandra Block, Kathy Chu & John Waggoner • $19.99

The Work From Home Handbook
Flex Your Time, Improve Your Life
by Diana Fitzpatrick & Stephen Fishman • $19.99

Retire Happy
What You Can Do NOW to Guarantee a Great Retirement
by Richard Stim & Ralph Warner • $19.99

The Essential Guide for First-Time Homeowners
Maximize Your Investment & Enjoy Your New Home
by Ilona Bray & Alayna Schroeder • $19.99

Easy Ways to Lower Your Taxes
Simple Strategies Every Taxpayer Should Know
by Sandra Block & Stephen Fishman • $19.99

First-Time Landlord
Your Guide to Renting Out a Single-Family Home
by Attorney Janet Portman, Marcia Stewart & Michael Molinski • $19.99

Stopping Identity Theft
10 Easy Steps to Security
by Scott Mitic, CEO, TrustedID, Inc. • $19.99

The Mom's Guide to Wills & Estate Planning
by Attorney Liza Hanks • $21.99

Running a Side Business
How to Create a Second Income
by Attorneys Richard Stim & Lisa Guerin • $21.99

Nannies and Au Pairs
Hiring In-Home Child Care
by Ilona Bray, J.D. • $19.99

The Judge Who Hated Red Nail Polish
& Other Crazy But True Stories of Law and Lawyers
by Ilona Bray, Richard Stim & the Editors of Nolo • $19.99

Prices subject to change.

ORDER DIRECTLY FROM NOLO.COM AND SAVE!

 **NOLO**

Online Legal Forms

Nolo offers a large library of legal solutions and forms, created by Nolo's in-house legal staff. These reliable documents can be prepared in minutes.

Create a Document

- **Incorporation.** Incorporate your business in any state.
- **LLC Formations.** Gain asset protection and pass-through tax status in any state.
- **Wills.** Nolo has helped people make over 2 million wills. Is it time to make or revise yours?
- **Living Trust (avoid probate).** Plan now to save your family the cost, delays, and hassle of probate.
- **Trademark.** Protect the name of your business or product.
- **Provisional Patent.** Preserve your rights under patent law and claim "patent pending" status.

Download a Legal Form

Nolo.com has hundreds of top quality legal forms available for download—bills of sale, promissory notes, nondisclosure agreements, LLC operating agreements, corporate minutes, commercial lease and sublease, motor vehicle bill of sale, consignment agreements and many, many more.

Review Your Documents

Many lawyers in Nolo's consumer-friendly lawyer directory will review Nolo documents for a very reasonable fee. Check their detailed profiles at **Nolo.com/lawyers**.

Nolo's Bestselling Books

U.S. Immigration Made Easy
$44.99

Becoming a U.S. Citizen
A Guide to the Law, Exam & Interview
$34.99

How to Get a Green Card
$39.99

Legal Research
How to Find & Understand the Law
$49.99

Nolo's Plain-English Law Dictionary
$29.99

Every Nolo title is available in print and for download at Nolo.com.

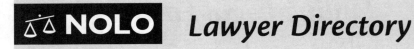

NOLO *Lawyer Directory*

Find an Attorney

Qualified lawyers • In-depth profiles

When you want help with a serious legal problem, you don't want just any lawyer—you want an expert in the field who can give you and your family up-to-the-minute advice. You need a lawyer who has the experience and knowledge to answer your questions about personal injury, wills, family law, child custody, drafting a patent application or any other specialized legal area you are concerned with.

Nolo's Lawyer Directory is unique because it provides an extensive profile of every lawyer. You'll learn about not only each lawyer's education, professional history, legal specialties, credentials and fees, but also about their philosophy of practicing law and how they like to work with clients.

www.nolo.com

The photos above are illustrative only. Any resemblance to an actual attorney is purely coincidental.